INTRODUCTORY

READINGS

ON LANGUAGE

INTRODUCTORY READINGS ON LANGUAGE

revised edition

WALLACE L. ANDERSON
& NORMAN C. STAGEBERG

STATE COLLEGE OF IOWA

Holt, Rinehart and Winston
NEW YORK   CHICAGO   SAN FRANCISCO   TORONTO   LONDON

Copyright © 1962, 1966 by Holt, Rinehart and Winston, Inc.
All rights reserved
Library of Congress Catalog Card Number: 66–12911
20409–0316
Printed in the United States of America

TO THE INSTRUCTOR

This book is designed primarily as a text for freshman English, though it should also prove useful in the increasing number of undergraduate English courses devoted to the study of language. It has three major purposes:

(1) To present basic information about language as a subject interesting and important in its own right. The intent is to make the students aware of the nature of language and some of its multifarious aspects.
(2) To make students more perceptive of the artistic uses of language in literature.
(3) To arouse the students' intellectual curiosity about language to the point where they want to know more about it.
(4) To influence the students' own use of language and to enable them to cope more successfully with the welter of words, both spoken and written, that surrounds us all.

It is our conviction that the major concern of freshman English should be language. Most freshman English courses are planned to help students to write with clarity, if not with grace, and to read with understanding and discrimination. Usually, composition is taught in conjunction with a book of readings containing examples of good writing in a variety of styles and on a variety of topics. This variety of topics can prove troublesome. Oftentimes discussion tends to center in the content of the essays, so that the instructor finds himself of necessity taking on the role of sociologist, historian, scientist, and philosopher. The topics dealt with are important ones, to be sure, but they are probably better treated elsewhere by specialists in those fields. To the extent that this shift in roles occurs, the course becomes blurred; it loses its focus. Moreover, it inhibits the instructor's dealing with one of the subjects in which he is at home, namely, language. And this is one thing students need to know more about.

College freshmen are, for the most part, linguistically unsophisticated. Their attitudes toward language are often naïve; indeed, they have many misconceptions about language—misconceptions which they share with the general populace. One function of the English instructor is to rid college students of these misconceptions, to replace false beliefs with a more enlightened view of language in general, and of their own language in particular. For many college students, the freshman course is the sole course in English that they will take. Freshman English is the only place where these students will have the opportunity to gain real insight into the workings of language. They should not come to us naïve and leave older but still naïve in a matter of such vital import. Hence this book of readings on language.

We realize that other kinds of content may be justifiably defended in a freshman English course, but we also believe that the rationale offered here has a cogency that cannot be lightly dismissed.

These essays constitute an introductory course in language. Although they deal with various linguistic topics, they are not a course in linguistics. They are intended to be complementary to a composition text or handbook; hence matters of rhetoric and mechanics have for the most part been excluded. The readings have been selected on the basis of three criteria: (1) that they be soundly informative, (2) that they be in line with current linguistic thought, and (3) that they be within the intellectual reach of the average freshman. We have been particularly mindful that these readings are for beginning college students. The topics chosen are basic to an understanding of the nature of language; yet they do not presuppose previous technical knowledge. In the main the selections themselves are nontechnical. The single exception is the essay on the classification of English vowels and consonants, pp. 291–309; here of necessity phonetic terminology and symbols are used. (This essay should precede the others in the section.) The few technical terms that do occur are clearly defined in the text or in footnotes of definition and illustration which we have provided.

In addition to the explanatory footnotes, we have included three kinds of editorial assistance: headnotes, suggested assignments, and lists of further readings. These are an integral part of the book. The headnotes prepare the students for the reading to follow by providing background material and by raising questions. Their purpose is to arouse interest, to stimulate thought, and to direct attention to the particular issues involved. The "assignments" are in a sense extensions of the readings themselves. Their purpose is to make the readings more meaningful by giving the students an opportunity to come to grips with specific issues by means of a variety of oral and written assignments. Many of the assignments are adaptable to either discussion or written work. The readings are included as a source of information for research papers; they may also serve to open more doors for those students desirous of gaining further insight into the nature of language.

The arrangement of topics is one that makes sense to us. However, it is not inflexible. The most appropriate order will depend, as it should, on the ingenuity of the instructor and his view of the course.

W.L.A.
N.C.S.

Cedar Falls, Iowa
November 1965

TO THE STUDENT

To use language is the mark of a man; to understand language, in the deepest sense, is the mark of an educated man. From about the age of six, you have been using language with really a high degree of efficiency. And so have 300 million other speakers of English. But your understanding of your native tongue is probably fragmentary and riddled with misconceptions. In the course of twelve years of schooling, if you are like many college freshmen, you have gathered into your intellectual granary sundry notions about language, varying in worth from known truths to halftruths down to palpable nontruths. An illustration will make this clear. With which of the following propositions would you agree?

(1) The languages of primitive peoples are simpler than those of more advanced nations.

(2) An excellent way to find the correct pronunciation of a word is to look it up in the dictionary.

(3) If you pronounce *pursuing* to rime with *ruin*, you are dropping the *g*.

(4) The word *humor* should be pronounced with an *h* because it is spelled with an *h*.

(5) Since the real meaning of *awful* is "full of awe," this word should not be used as a general term of condemnation.

(6) Many words have a specific and universal connotation.

(7) In the question "Who is it for?" one should say *whom* because it is the object of the preposition *for*.

If you agree with any of these, you are in error, for each states or implies a concept that is to some degree untrue. These errors, however, are no cause for alarm, since each of us entertains misconceptions in areas of knowledge with which he is unfamiliar. But the situation is one that demands correction because, as you go through college, you will gain much of your education through the medium of language. You will listen to classroom lectures where you will have to catch and interpret words on the fly. You will have heavy reading assignments where you will have to read closely, with sharp attention to nuances of meaning and validity of reasoning. You will have compositions to write where you must use language with scrupulous precision. You will have to do serious thinking, which can be done only through language. All of these activities you should be able to perform more capably when you understand the language matters presented in this book—such matters, for example, as the symbolic nature of language, the basis of good usage, the uses of metaphor, the ever-present hazards of ambiguity, the pitfalls of analogy, the uniqueness of meanings, and the fallacies of causal reasoning.

Language study, in addition to being a practical pursuit, is also a cultural subject. It is a social science, concerned with an aspect of man's behavior that sets him apart from the lower animals—his use of an intricate system of speech sounds to communicate with his peers and his use of written symbols to transmit the accumulated knowledge of the race to his descendants. You will get an inkling of the scientific side of language study when you read the selections on linguistic geography, usage, and structural grammar. You will discover fragments of history embedded in words when you dig into etymology. You will touch upon philosophy when you inquire into the symbolic nature of words. And you will deepen your understanding of literature when you examine the means by which the richness and complexity of imaginative writing are achieved.

Of the whole fascinating drama of language behavior, you will receive a series of quick, revealing glances as scholars draw the curtain aside on various scenes. And you will emerge, it is hoped, with a deepened comprehension of the foundation stone of man's humanity—language.

CONTENTS

2   LANGUAGE HISTORY

3   WORDS: FORMS AND MEANINGS

4   SEMANTICS

6   THE SOUNDS OF LANGUAGE

7   USAGE

8   LINGUISTIC GEOGRAPHY

9   STRUCTURAL AND
       TRANSFORMATIONAL GRAMMAR

10   CLEAR THINKING

INTRODUCTORY

READINGS

ON LANGUAGE

1

THE NATURE
OF LANGUAGE

Language Defined

EDWARD SAPIR

Language is so much a part of us that we tend to regard it as
both natural and simple. Moreover, because education in our
culture is carried on primarily by means of books, many of
us think of language primarily in its written form—black
marks imprinted on paper, or wiggly lines made with pen or
pencil. But in many parts of the world it is impossible for
people to communicate in that way. They have no written
language; they communicate solely by means of the spoken
word—sound waves in the air. Are we to conclude, then, that
writing is not language? Or are there two kinds of language?
What is the relationship between speech and writing? And
how, in either case, does communication take place? How do
these sound waves or wiggly lines mean anything? These are
some of the basic questions that Edward Sapir deals with.
One of the pioneers of modern linguistic science, Sapir was
an authority on American-Indian languages; he was also one
of the first to study the relationships between linguistics and
anthropology.

Speech is so familiar a feature of daily life that we rarely pause to define
it. It seems as natural to man as walking, and only less so than breathing. Yet it needs but a moment's reflection to convince us that this

From *Language: An Introduction to the Study of Speech* by Edward Sapir, copyright 1921,
by Harcourt, Brace & World, Inc.; renewed, 1949, by Jean V. Sapir. Reprinted by
permission of the publishers.

1

naturalness of speech is but an illusory feeling. The process of acquiring speech is, in sober fact, an utterly different sort of thing from the process of learning to walk. In the case of the latter function, culture, in other words, the traditional body of social usage, is not seriously brought into play. The child is individually equipped, by the complex set of factors that we term biological heredity, to make all the needed muscular and nervous adjustments that result in walking. Indeed, the very conformation of these muscles and of the appropriate parts of the nervous system may be said to be primarily adapted to the movements made in walking and in similar activities. In a very real sense the normal human being is predestined to walk, not because his elders will assist him to learn the art, but because his organism is prepared from birth, or even from the moment of conception, to take on all those expenditures of nervous energy and all those muscular adaptations that result in walking. To put it concisely, walking is an inherent, biological function of man.

Not so language. It is of course true that in a certain sense the individual is predestined to talk, but that is due entirely to the circumstance that he is born not merely in nature, but in the lap of a society that is certain, reasonably certain, to lead him to its traditions. Eliminate society and there is every reason to believe that he will learn to walk, if, indeed, he survives at all. But it is just as certain that he will never learn to talk, that is, to communicate ideas according to the traditional system of a particular society. Or, again, remove the newborn individual from the social environment into which he has come and transplant him to an utterly alien one. He will develop the art of walking in his new environment very much as he would have developed it in the old. But his speech will be completely at variance with the speech of his native environment. Walking, then, is a general human activity that varies only within circumscribed limits as we pass from individual to individual. Its variability is involuntary and purposeless. Speech is a human activity that varies without assignable limit as we pass from social group to social group, because it is a purely historical heritage of the group, the product of long-continued social usage. It varies as all creative effort varies — not as consciously, perhaps, but none the less as truly as do the religions, the beliefs, the customs, and the arts of different peoples. Walking is an organic, an instinctive, function (not, of course, itself an instinct); speech is a non-instinctive, acquired, "cultural" function.

There is one fact that has frequently tended to prevent the recognition of language as a merely conventional system of sound symbols, that has seduced the popular mind into attributing to it an instinctive basis that it does not really possess. This is the well-known observation that under the stress of emotion, say of a sudden twinge of pain or of unbridled joy, we do involuntarily give utterance to sounds that the hearer interprets as indicative of the emotion itself. But there is all the difference in the world between such involuntary expression of feeling and the normal type of communication of ideas that is speech. The former kind of utterance is indeed instinctive, but it is non-symbolic; in other words, the sound of pain or the sound of joy does not, as such, indicate the emotion, it does not stand aloof, as it were, and announce that such and such an emotion is being felt. What it does is to serve as a more or less automatic overflow of the emotional energy; in a sense, it is part and parcel of the emotion itself. Moreover, such instinctive cries hardly constitute communication in any strict sense. They are not addressed to any one, they are merely overheard, if heard at all, as the bark of a dog, the sound of approaching footsteps, or the rustling of the wind is heard. If they convey certain ideas to the hearer, it is only in the very general sense in which any and every sound or even any phenomenon in our environment may be said to convey an idea to the perceiving mind. If the involuntary cry of pain which is conventionally represented by "Oh!" be looked upon as a true speech symbol equivalent to some such idea as "I am in great pain," it is just as allowable to interpret the appearance of clouds as an equivalent symbol that carries the definite message "It is likely to rain." A definition of language, however, that is so extended as to cover every type of inference becomes utterly meaningless.

The mistake must not be made of identifying our conventional interjections (our "oh!" and "ah!" and "sh!") with the instinctive cries themselves. These interjections are merely conventional fixations of the natural sounds. They therefore differ widely in various languages in accordance with the specific phonetic genius of each of these. As such they may be considered an integral portion of speech, in the properly cultural sense of the term, being no more identical with the instinctive cries themselves than such words as "cuckoo" and "killdeer" are identical with the cries of the birds they denote or than Rossini's treatment of a storm in the overture to "William Tell" is in fact a storm. In other words, the interjections and sound-imitative words of normal speech are related to their natural prototypes as is art, a purely social or cultural thing, to nature. It may be objected that, though the interjections differ somewhat as we pass from language to language, they do nevertheless offer striking family resemblances and may therefore be looked upon as having grown up out of a common instinctive base. But their case is nowise different from that, say, of the varying national modes of pictorial representation. A Japanese picture of a hill both differs from and resembles a typical modern European painting of the same kind of hill. Both are suggested by and both "imitate" the same natural feature. Neither the one nor the other is the same thing as, or, in any intelligible sense, a direct outgrowth of, this natural feature. The two modes of representation are not identical because they proceed from differing historical traditions, are executed with differing pictorial techniques. The interjections of Japanese and English are, just so, suggested by a common natural prototype, the instinctive cries, and are thus unavoidably suggestive of each other. They differ now greatly, now but little, because they are builded out of historically diverse materials or techniques, the respective linguistic traditions, phonetic systems, speech habits of the two peoples. Yet the instinctive cries as such are practically identical for all humanity, just as the human skeleton or nervous system is to all intents and purposes a "fixed," that is, an only slightly and "accidentally" variable, feature of man's organism.

Interjections are among the least important of speech elements. Their discussion is valuable mainly because it can be shown that even they, avowedly the nearest of all language sounds to instinctive utterance, are only superficially of an instinctive nature. Were it therefore possible to demonstrate that the whole of language is traceable, in its ultimate historical and psychological foundations, to the interjections, it would still not follow that language is an instinctive activity. But, as a matter of fact, all attempts so to explain the origin of speech have been fruitless. There is no tangible evidence, historical or otherwise, tending to show that the mass of speech elements and speech processes has evolved out of the interjections. These are a very small and functionally insignificant proportion of the vocabulary of language; at no time and in no linguistic province that we have record of do we see a noticeable tendency towards their elaboration into the primary warp and woof of language. They are never more, at best, than a decorative edging to the ample, complex fabric.

What applies to the interjections applies with even greater force to the sound-imitative words. Such words as "whippoorwill," "to mew," "to caw" are in no sense natural sounds that man has instinctively or automatically reproduced. They are just as truly creations of the human mind, flights of the human fancy, as anything else in language. They do not directly grow out of nature, they are suggested by it and play with it. Hence the onomatopoetic theory of the origin of speech, the theory that would explain all speech as a gradual evolution from sounds of an imitative character, really brings us no nearer to the instinctive level than is language as we know it today. As to the theory itself, it is scarcely more credible than its interjectional counterpart. It is true that a number of words which we do not now feel to have a sound-imitative value can be shown to have once had a phonetic form that strongly suggests their origin as imitations of natural sounds. Such is the English word "to laugh." For all that, it is quite impossible to show, nor does it seem intrinsically reasonable to suppose, that more than a negligible proportion of the elements of speech or anything at all of its formal apparatus is derivable from an onomatopoetic source. However much we may be disposed on general principles to assign a fundamental importance in the languages of primitive peoples to the imitation of natural sounds, the actual fact of the matter is that these languages show no particular preference for imitative words. Among the most primitive peoples of aboriginal America, the Athabaskan tribes of the Mackenzie River speak languages in which such words seem to be nearly or entirely absent, while they are used freely enough in languages as sophisticated as English and German. Such an instance shows how little the essential nature of speech is concerned with the mere imitation of things.

The way is now cleared for a serviceable definition of language. Language is a purely human and non-instinctive method of communicating ideas, emotions, and desires by means of a system of voluntarily produced symbols. These symbols are, in the first instance, auditory and they are produced by the so-called "organs of speech." There is no discernible instinctive basis in human speech as such, however much instinctive expressions and the natural environment may serve as a stimulus for the development of certain elements of speech, however much instinctive tendencies, motor and other, may give a predetermined range or mold to linguistic expression. Such human or animal communication, if "communication" it may be called, as is brought about by involuntary, instinctive cries is not, in our sense, language at all.

I have just referred to the "organs of speech," and it would seem at first blush that this is tantamount to an admission that speech itself is an instinctive, biologically predetermined activity. We must not be misled by the mere term. There are, properly speaking, no organs of speech; there are only organs that are incidentally useful in the production of speech sounds.[1] The lungs, the larynx, the palate, the nose, the tongue, the teeth, and the lips, are all so utilized, but they are no more to be thought of as primary organs of speech than are the fingers to be considered as essentially organs of piano-playing or the knees as organs of prayer. Speech is not a simple activity that is carried on by one or more organs biologically adapted to the purpose. It is an extremely complex and ever-shifting network of adjustments — in the brain, in the nervous system, and in the articulating and auditory organs — tending towards the desired end of communication. The lungs developed, roughly speaking, in connection with the necessary biological function known as breathing; the nose, as an organ of smell; the teeth, as organs useful in breaking up food before it was ready for digestion. If, then, these and other organs are being constantly utilized in speech, it is only because any organ, once existent and in so far as it is subject to voluntary control, can be utilized by man for secondary purposes. Physiologically, speech is an overlaid function, or, to be more precise, a group of overlaid functions. It gets what service it can out of organs and functions, nervous and muscular, that have come into being and are maintained for very different ends than its own.

It is true that physiological psychologists speak of the localization of speech in the brain. This can only mean that the sounds of speech are localized in the auditory tract of the brain, or in some circumscribed portion of it, precisely as other classes of sounds are localized; and that the motor processes involved in speech (such as the movements of the glottal cords in the larynx, the movements of the tongue required to pronounce the vowels, lip movements required to articulate certain consonants, and numerous others) are localized in the motor tract precisely as are all other impulses to special motor activities. In the same way control is lodged in the visual tract of the brain over all those processes of visual recognition involved in reading. Naturally the particular points or clusters of points of localization in the several tracts that refer to any element of language are connected in the brain by paths of association, so that the outward, or psycho-physical, aspect of language, is of a vast network of associated localizations in the brain and lower nervous tracts, the auditory localizations being without doubt

[1] For a diagram of the speech organs, and a further discussion of the production of speech sounds, see pp. 291–309. [eds.]

the most fundamental of all for speech. However, a speech-sound localized in the brain, even when associated with the particular movements of the "speech organs" that are required to produce it, is very far from being an element of language. It must be further associated with some element or group of elements of experience, say a visual image or a class of visual images or a feeling of relation, before it has even rudimentary linguistic significance. This "element" of experience is the content or "meaning" of the linguistic unit; the associated auditory, motor, and other cerebral processes that lie immediately back of the act of speaking and the act of hearing speech are merely a complicated symbol of or signal for these "meanings." . . . We see therefore at once that language as such is not and cannot be definitely localized, for it consists of a peculiar symbolic relation — physiologically an arbitrary one — between all possible elements of consciousness on the one hand and certain selected elements localized in the auditory, motor, and other cerebral and nervous tracts on the other. If language can be said to be definitely "localized" in the brain, it is only in that general and rather useless sense in which all aspects of consciousness, all human interest and activity, may be said to be "in the brain." Hence, we have no recourse but to accept language as a fully formed functional system within man's psychic or "spiritual" constitution. We cannot define it as an entity in psycho-physical terms alone, however much the psycho-physical basis is essential to its functioning in the individual.

From the physiologist's or psychologist's point of view we may seem to be making an unwarrantable abstraction in desiring to handle the subject of speech without constant and explicit reference to that basis. However, such an abstraction is justifiable. We can profitably discuss the intention, the form, and the history of speech, precisely as we discuss the nature of any other phase of human culture — say art or religion — as an institutional or cultural entity, leaving the organic and psychological mechanisms back of it as something to be taken for granted. . . .

I have already pointed out that the essence of language consists in the assigning of conventional, voluntarily articulated, sounds, or of their equivalents, to the diverse elements of experience. The word "house" is not a linguistic fact if by it is meant merely the acoustic effect produced on the ear by its constituent consonants and vowels, pronounced in a certain order; nor the motor processes and tactile feelings which make up the articulation of the word; nor the visual perception on the part of the hearer of this articulation; nor the visual perception of the word "house" on the written or printed page; nor the motor processes and tactile feelings which enter into the writing of the word; nor the memory of any or all of these experiences. It is only when these, and possibly still other, associated experiences are automatically associated with the image of a house that they begin to take on the nature of a symbol, a word, an element of language. But the mere fact of such an association is not enough. One might have heard a particular word spoken in an individual house under such impressive circumstances that neither the word nor the image of the house ever recur in consciousness without the other becoming present at the same time. This type of association does not constitute speech. The association must be a purely symbolic one; in other words, the word must denote, tag off, the image, must have no other significance than to serve as a counter to refer to it whenever it is necessary or convenient to do so. Such an association, voluntary and, in a sense, arbitrary as it is, demands a considerable exercise of self-conscious attention. At least to begin with, for habit soon makes the association nearly as automatic as any and more rapid than most.

But we have traveled a little too fast. Were the symbol "house"— whether an auditory, motor, or visual experience or image — attached but to the single image of a particular house once seen, it might perhaps, by an indulgent criticism, be termed an element of speech, yet it is obvious at the outset that speech so constituted would have little or no value for purposes of communication. The world of our experiences must be enormously simplified and generalized before it is possible to make a symbolic inventory of all our experiences of things and relations; and this inventory is imperative before we can convey ideas. The elements of language, the symbols that ticket off experience, must therefore be associated with whole groups, delimited classes, of experience rather than with the single experiences themselves. Only so is communication possible, for the single experience lodges in an individual consciousness and is, strictly speaking, incommunicable. To be communicated it needs to be referred to a class which is tacitly accepted by the community as an identity. Thus, the single impression which I have had of a particular house must be identified with all my other impressions of it. Further, my generalized memory or my "notion" of this house must be merged with the notions that all other individuals who have seen the house have formed of it. The particular experience that we started with has now been widened so as to embrace all possible impressions or images that sentient beings have formed or may form of the house in question.[2] This first simplification of experience is at the bottom of a large number of elements of speech, the so-called proper nouns or names of single individuals or objects. It is, essentially, the type of simplification which underlies, or forms the crude subject of, history and art. But we cannot be content with this measure of reduction of the infinity of experience. We must cut to the bone of things, we must more or less arbitrarily throw whole masses of experience together as similar enough to warrant their being looked upon — mistakenly, but conveniently — as identical. This house and that house and thousands of other phenomena of like character are thought of as having enough in common, in spite of great and obvious differences of detail, to be classed under the same heading. In other words, the speech element "house" is the symbol, first and foremost, not of a single perception, nor even of the notion of a particular object, but of a "concept," in other words, of a convenient capsule of thought that embraces thousands of distinct experiences and that is ready to take in thousands more. If the single significant elements of speech are the symbols of concepts, the actual flow of speech may be interpreted as a record of the setting of these concepts into mutual relations. . . .

Language is primarily an auditory system of symbols. In so far as it is articulated it is also a motor system, but the motor aspect of speech is clearly secondary to the auditory. In normal individuals the impulse to speech first takes effect in the sphere of auditory imagery and is then transmitted to the motor nerves that control the organs of speech. The motor processes and the accompanying motor feelings are not, however, the end, the final resting point. They are merely a means and a control leading to auditory perception in both speaker and hearer. Communication, which is the very object of speech, is successfully effected only when the hearer's auditory perceptions are translated into the appropriate and intended flow of imagery or thought or both combined. Hence the cycle of speech, in so far as we may look upon it as a purely external instrument, begins and ends in the realm of sounds. The concordance between the initial auditory imagery and the final auditory perceptions is the social seal or warrant of the successful issue of the process. As we have already seen, the typical course of this process may undergo endless modifications or transfers into equivalent systems without thereby losing its essential formal characteristics.

The most important of these modifications is the abbreviation of

[2] Sapir is here discussing the processes of abstraction and classification. For a more complete discussion of this topic, see pp. 150–167. [eds.]

the speech process involved in thinking. This has doubtless many forms, according to the structural or functional peculiarities of the individual mind. The least modified form is that known as "talking to one's self" or "thinking aloud." Here the speaker and the hearer are identified in a single person, who may be said to communicate with himself. More significant is the still further abbreviated form in which the sounds of speech are not articulated at all. To this belong all the varieties of silent speech and of normal thinking. The auditory centers alone may be excited; or the impulse to linguistic expression may be communicated as well to the motor nerves that communicate with the organs of speech but be inhibited either in the muscles of these organs or at some point in the motor nerves themselves; or, possibly, the auditory centers may be only slightly, if at all, affected, the speech process manifesting itself directly in the motor sphere. There must be still other types of abbreviation. How common is the excitation of the motor nerves in silent speech, in which no audible or visible articulations result, is shown by the frequent experience of fatigue in the speech organs, particularly in the larynx, after unusually stimulating reading or intensive thinking.

All the modifications so far considered are directly patterned on the typical process of normal speech. Of very great interest and importance is the possibility of transferring the whole system of speech symbolism into other terms than those that are involved in the typical process. This process, as we have seen, is a matter of sounds and of movements intended to produce these sounds. The sense of vision is not brought into play. But let us suppose that one not only hears the articulated sounds but sees the articulations themselves as they are being executed by the speaker. Clearly, if one can only gain a sufficiently high degree of adroitness in perceiving these movements of the speech organs, the way is opened for a new type of speech symbolism — that in which the sound is replaced by the visual image of the articulations that correspond to the sound. This sort of system has no great value for most of us because we are already possessed of the auditory-motor system of which it is at best but an imperfect translation, not all the articulations being visible to the eye. However, it is well known what excellent use deaf-mutes can make of "reading from the lips" as a subsidiary method of apprehending speech. The most important of all visual speech symbolisms is, of course, that of the written or printed word, to which, on the motor side, corresponds the system of delicately adjusted movements which result in the writing or typewriting or other graphic method of recording speech. The significant feature for our recognition in these new types of symbolism, apart from the fact that they are no longer a by-product of normal speech itself, is that each element (letter or written word) in the system corresponds to a specific element (sound or sound-group or spoken word) in the primary system. Written language is thus a point-to-point equivalence, to borrow a mathematical phrase, to its spoken counterpart. The written forms are secondary symbols of the spoken ones — symbols of symbols — yet so close is the correspondence that they may, not only in theory but in the actual practice of certain eye-readers and, possibly, in certain types of thinking, be entirely substituted for the spoken ones. Yet the auditory-motor associations are probably always latent at the least, that is, they are unconsciously brought into play. Even those who read and think without the slightest use of sound imagery are, at last analysis, dependent on it. They are merely handling the circulating medium, the money, of visual symbols as a convenient substitute for the economic goods and services of the fundamental auditory symbols.

The possibilities of linguistic transfer are practically unlimited. A familiar example is the Morse telegraph code, in which the letters of written speech are represented by a conventionally fixed sequence of longer or shorter ticks. Here the transfer takes place from the written word rather than directly from the sounds of spoken speech. The letter of the telegraph code is thus a symbol of a symbol of a symbol. It does not, of course, in the least follow that the skilled operator, in order to arrive at an understanding of a telegraphic message, needs to transpose the individual sequence of ticks into a visual image of the word before he experiences its normal auditory image. The precise method of reading off speech from the telegraphic communication undoubtedly varies widely with the individual. It is even conceivable, if not exactly likely, that certain operators may have learned to think directly, so far as the purely conscious part of the process of thought is concerned, in terms of the tick-auditory symbolism or, if they happen to have a strong natural bent toward motor symbolism, in terms of the correlated tactile-motor symbolism developed in the sending of telegraphic messages.

Still another interesting group of transfers are the different gesture languages, developed for the use of deaf-mutes, of Trappist monks vowed to perpetual silence, or of communicating parties that are within seeing distance of each other but are out of earshot. Some of these systems are one-to-one equivalences of the normal system of speech; others, like military gesture-symbolism or the gesture language of the

Plains Indians of North America (understood by tribes of mutually unintelligible forms of speech) are imperfect transfers, limiting themselves to the rendering of such grosser speech elements as are an imperative minimum under difficult circumstances. In these latter systems, as in such still more imperfect symbolisms as those used at sea or in the woods, it may be contended that language no longer properly plays a part but that the ideas are directly conveyed by an utterly symbolic process or by a quasi-instinctive imitativeness. Such an interpretation would be erroneous. The intelligibility of these vaguer symbolisms can hardly be due to anything but their automatic and silent translation into the terms of a fuller flow of speech.

We shall no doubt conclude that all voluntary communication of ideas, aside from normal speech, is either a transfer, direct or indirect, from the typical symbolism of language as spoken and heard or, at the least, involves the intermediary of truly linguistic symbolism. This is a fact of the highest importance. Auditory imagery and the correlated motor imagery leading to articulation are, by whatever devious ways we follow the process, the historic fountain-head of all speech and of all thinking. One other point is of still greater importance. The ease with which speech symbolism can be transferred from one sense to another, from technique to technique, itself indicates that the mere sounds of speech are not the essential fact of language, which lies rather in the classification, in the formal patterning, and in the relating of concepts. Once more, language, as a structure, is on its inner face the mold of thought. . . .

There is no more striking general fact about language than its universality. One may argue as to whether a particular tribe engages in activities that are worthy of the name of religion or of art, but we know of no people that is not possessed of a fully developed language. The lowliest South African Bushman speaks in the forms of a rich symbolic system that is in essence perfectly comparable to the speech of the cultivated Frenchman. It goes without saying that the more abstract concepts are not nearly so plentifully represented in the language of the savage, nor is there the rich terminology and the finer definition of nuances that reflect the higher culture. Yet the sort of linguistic development that parallels the historic growth of culture and which, in its later stages, we associate with literature is, at best, but a superficial thing. The fundamental groundwork of language — the development of a clear-cut phonetic system, the specific association of speech elements with concepts, and the delicate provision for the formal expression of all manner of relations — all this meets us rigidly perfected and systematized in every language known to us. Many primitive languages have a formal richness, a latent luxuriance of expression, that eclipses anything known to the languages of modern civilization. Even in the mere matter of the inventory of speech the layman must be prepared for strange surprises. Popular statements as to the extreme poverty of expression to which primitive languages are doomed are simply myths. Scarcely less impressive than the universality of speech is its almost incredible diversity. Those of us that have studied French or German, or, better yet, Latin or Greek, know in what varied forms a thought may run. The formal divergences between the English plan and the Latin plan, however, are comparatively slight in the perspective of what we know of more exotic linguistic patterns. The universality and the diversity of speech lead to a significant inference. We are forced to believe that language is an immensely ancient heritage of the human race, whether or not all forms of speech are the historical outgrowth of a single pristine form. It is doubtful if any other cultural asset of man, be it the art of drilling for fire or of chipping stone, may lay claim to a greater age. I am inclined to believe that it antedated even the lowliest developments of material culture, that these developments, in fact, were not strictly possible until language, the tool of significant expression, had itself taken shape.

SUGGESTED ASSIGNMENTS

1. Montaigne, a famous sixteenth-century French writer, learned to speak Latin before his native tongue. "I was above six years of age," he wrote, "before I understood either French or Perigordin, any more than Arabic." Yet he was born of French parents, brought up in France, and lived in a house with many servants, one of whom was German by birth. What circumstances must have been present to account for the writer's learning to speak Latin first? For the facts of the case, read Montaigne's essay "Of the Education of Children."

2. Human beings are not the only creatures that communicate with each other. Some animals have elaborate signalling systems. Bees, for example, have a systematic dance routine to indicate the source of food; jackdaws have a group of calls that apparently are meaningful. Look up one of the following references and make a report to the class: On bees, see Karl von Frisch, *Bees, Their Vision, Chemical Senses, and Language;* on jackdaws, see

Konrad Lorenz, *King Solomon's Ring*. Both of these studies are summarized and discussed in Roger Brown's *Words and Things*, Chapter 5.

3. Commenting on the interjectional and onomatopoetic elements in language, Sapir remarked that "all attempts so to explain the origin of speech have been fruitless." Although evidence about the origin of speech will always remain theoretical and inconclusive, nonetheless the various theories are of interest because they reveal something of the complexity of the problem and because they show us some of the approaches linguists have taken in their attempts to solve the problem. See, for example, Otto Jespersen, *Language, Its Nature, Development, and Origin*, Chapter 21; Edgar H. Sturtevant, *Linguistic Science*, Chapter 5; and Roger Brown, *Words and Things*, pp. 131–136.

4. At first glance the following statement will not make much sense to you:

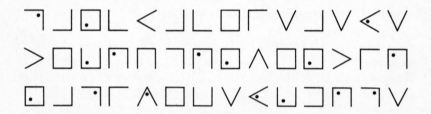

The reason is that you do not know what the symbols represent. Once you know the code, however, you can easily decipher the message. Use the following code to discover it:

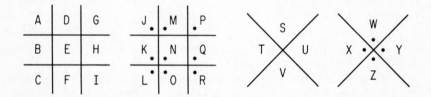

How many steps is the coded statement removed from the speech act itself?

5. Study these three definitions of language:
   a. Language is the expression of thought by means of speech sounds.
   b. Language is the instrument for the expression and communication of human thought.
   c. Language is nothing but a set of human habits, the purpose of which is to give expression to thoughts and feelings, and especially to impart them to others.

Choose one and write a theme explaining its deficiencies.

6. Write a single-paragraph definition of *pond*, *gymnasium*, or *cottage*. In class the paragraphs will be compared in an effort to discover which characteristics the group attributes to this class of objects, and which characteristics are merely personal.

7. Write a theme telling which language skills, both general and specific, you think will be most valuable to you in your college work. At the end of the first semester, if you re-read this theme, you may be surprised at how you misjudged your needs.

Language, Logic, and Grammar

L. M. MYERS

Language, we have seen, is a system of conventionalized symbols by which we communicate with each other. One would think that, since we use the same symbols, we would always understand one another. Yet we do not always say what we mean, nor do we always understand what other people mean. If we do not know the meaning of a particular word, we are told, we can always consult the dictionary. But what do we find in the dictionary? Other words! In one sense these other words are the meaning of the first word. But aren't we only saying that both mean the same thing? What is this other meaning? Is meaning only verbal? This whole question of the meaning of meaning is of fundamental importance in the study of language. In the following essay, L. M. Myers, Professor of English at Arizona State University, identifies three kinds of meaning.

A language may be defined roughly as consisting of a set of words and some habitual ways of putting them together. Dictionaries deal primarily with the individual words; grammars with characteristic forms and with ways of arranging words in coherent communications. There is inevitably some overlapping between the two.

From *American English, a Twentieth-Century Grammar* by L. M. Myers. Reprinted by permission of the author, copyright 1952. Published by Prentice-Hall, Inc.

Word-form and word-order

In some languages the connections between words are shown largely by changes in form. Thus in Latin, "Marcus vidit Quintum" and "Marcum vidit Quintus" mean quite different things, although the same three words are used in the same order. The first means that Marcus saw Quintus; the second, that Quintus saw Marcus. The endings in -*us* and -*um* show which is the subject and which is the object of the action, regardless of the order.

In some other languages, like Chinese, words never change their form. The meaning of a group of words therefore depends on the choice of words and the order in which they are arranged.

Originally, English was very much like Latin in this respect. Most words were *inflected;* that is, they had a number of forms that showed variations in their basic meanings, and indicated their relations to each other. Now most of these inflections have been lost, and the structure of the language has become more like that of Chinese. Even the endings that remain have lost most of their power to show distinctions. Look at the following sentences:

He and I saw it yesterday.
Him and me seen it yesterday.

There are good reasons . . . for avoiding the second. But we understand it as readily as the first, and take it to mean the same thing. Our usual way of showing differences in meaning is by varying the *order* of words, as in the following sentences.

John hit Tom.
Tom hit John.

On the other hand, there are times when changes in the forms of words make a considerable difference in the meaning:

The man helps the boys.
The men helped the boy.

A study of English grammar therefore involves both the forms and the order of words.

The problem of meaning

If we want to keep our feet on the ground while we are making such a study, we had better begin by trying to understand something about how words came to "mean" anything at all. If we simply take it for granted that they do and go on from there, we will never have any real understanding of the language, no matter how many grammatical rules we memorize.

Let us suppose that on an uninhabited island a freak rock-formation has resulted in the white streaks on a cliff forming the letters P A I N. This would mean absolutely nothing to the animals, the trees, or the rocks themselves. It would still mean nothing if an illiterate savage landed on the island and looked at it. But if an American landed, the letters would look to him like a familiar word, and would call up reactions connected with earlier acquaintance with that word. For the first time the letters would suggest a meaning — "pain." This meaning would occur in the man's mind. The cliffs and the letters would be no more intelligent than before.

If a Frenchman landed on the island and noticed the same letters, an entirely different meaning would be suggested, since it happens that in French the letters P A I N also form a word — but the word means "bread," and not an uncomfortable sensation.

Most of us probably have a feeling that the letters must somehow mean something all by themselves, even if there is nobody there to appreciate them; but it is hard to see how they could mean two such different things as "pain" and "bread." If we think the matter over, we are forced to agree that meaning is the product of human nervous systems, and does not reside in the letters on the cliff.

The next question that comes up is, would the letters on the cliff have a meaning of their own if they had been deliberately written to form a word? Suppose the American had written down the sentence, "I have a *pain* in my back," and had then torn up the paper so that one piece contained just the word "pain." If the Frenchman happened to pick that piece up, it would suggest to him the idea "bread." Would the word "really" mean what the American intended to convey, or what it happened to suggest to the Frenchman?

Three kinds of meaning

We could argue this point forever without getting anywhere, for the fact is that we use the words *mean* and *meaning* in a number of different ways; and if we don't keep at least three of these carefully separated in our minds, we can become badly confused.

Meaning (1) What the speaker intends to indicate.

Meaning (2) What is suggested to a particular listener.

Meaning (3) A more or less general habit of using a given word to indicate a given thing.

A good many writers on the language neglect the first two of these and treat the third far too rigidly, as if the connection between the word and the thing were absolute, instead of a never-quite-uniform habit. You have probably heard such statements as: "*Buffalo* does not mean the American bison, but an entirely different animal"; or: "*Penny* really means an English coin — the American coin is a *cent*." This is putting the cart before the horse. We can discover meaning (3) — often referred to as the "real" meaning — only by observing the occurrences of meanings (1) and (2). To deny that these meanings are real is as unreasonable as it would be to deny the reality of a family of two or eleven on the grounds that the "average" family consists of five. It is quite true that the English used the word *penny* for one kind of a coin before we used it for another. But it is equally true that the newer meaning is very common in America; and it is *not* true (in spite of what some dictionaries say) that this meaning is merely "colloquial." Even our most formal writers might say, "He had a dime, two nickels, and three *pennies*," though they probably express the total by saying "twenty-three *cents*."

Of course we could not communicate at all without some sort of agreement that certain words are to be used to stand for certain things. Therefore meaning (3) — "a more or less general habit of using a given word to indicate a given thing"— is also perfectly legitimate. But we should not pretend that this more or less general habit is absolutely uniform, or that any number of books or teachers can ever make it so.

We can only guess how the habit started, and a number of very different guesses have been made. A linguist can trace the connection between English *father* and Latin *pater*, or between English *fish* and Latin *piscis;* but he cannot give a satisfactory reason why one of these pairs of words should be applied to male parents and the other to animals that live in the water. They would work exactly as well if their meanings were reversed. This last point is important. The "agreement" to use certain words for certain things is basically arbitrary. It is also, in the main, informal, habitual, and unenforceable.

Why communication is never perfect

We cannot understand each other unless we approximate the habits of those with whom we communicate; but we can only approximate. Until we find two people with identical physical equipment, nervous systems, and backgrounds of past experience, we cannot expect to find even two people who use a language in exactly the same way. Schools and other forces tend to keep our language habits somewhat similar, but perfect uniformity is not even theoretically possible. This is true of both individual words and of ways of putting them together. Moreover, it is true of the ways we react to language as well as of the ways we express it.

Let us look at a single short sentence:

John hurt Mary.

Most of us would say offhand that we understand this perfectly. Yet it conveys, by itself, very little definite information, as we can see by trying to answer the following questions: Are John and Mary people, pigs, or one of each? Are they real or imaginary? Was the hurting mental, physical, or what?

Suppose that as I wrote the sentence I was thinking of one pig biting another; that Jim Smith, as he reads it, gets the impression of one child scratching and kicking another; and that Sally Jones builds up the picture of a love affair marked by deep spiritual suffering. Each of these "meanings" is perfectly legitimate; but unless we can somehow get closer together, our communication will not be very successful. From the *words themselves* we get only the following information:

(1) *John* is presumably male and animate, and there is some probability that he is human. He may be either real or imaginary.

(2) *Mary* is presumably female. Her other possibilities are parallel to John's.

(3) *Hurt* indicates some sort of action with an unpleasant effect that has already occurred.

(4) The position of the words indicates that the direction of the action was from John to Mary.

Thus each word, by itself, *limits the possibilities* a good deal; and the relative position of the words limits them still further. The question is, can we limit them enough to communicate our ideas accurately and effectively?

We can make some progress in this direction by using additional words. Suppose I expand the sentence to read: "My little black pig, John, hurt my little white pig, Mary, by biting her in the left ear." This answers two of the questions listed above — John and Mary are pigs rather than people, and the hurting was physical. The reader may even accept the fact that the pigs are real rather than imaginary, although this cannot be proved by words alone. But other questions remain — how big is *little*, how much it hurt, and so forth. No matter how many words we use, or how carefully we arrange them, we can never directly transfer an idea from one mind to another. We can only hope to stimulate in the second mind an idea *similar* to that in the first. The words pass through our minds. The pigs, we hope, stay in their pens. And the exact nature of the connection between the words, the minds, and the pigs is not the easiest thing in the world to explain. At the very least we have to consider:

(1) The relation between the words and the minds of the people who use them.

(2) The relations between the words and the things and activities they stand for.

(3) The relations of the words to each other.[1]

Words and the human nervous system

The human brain operates something like an electronic computing machine. It contains millions of short nerve-lengths comparable to wires, and millions of nerve-connections comparable to switches. The workings of this complex system are not fully understood, but we do know that electrical impulses pass through it at a very regular speed of about four hundred feet per second. It is the passage of these impulses that constitutes our thinking.

Even the simplest thought requires the passage of a current over a complicated circuit containing innumerable switches. When an impulse starts, it might follow any one of an enormous number of routes, depending on how the switches click. But once a route has been selected, there is some tendency for the switches to set, so that a second impulse starting from the same point as the first can more easily dupli-

[1] Myers' discussion of this topic is not included here, since it is dealt with in the section on structural grammar. [eds.]

cate the route than pick out a new one of its own. It is by this setting of the switches that memory and habits develop. It may take a number of repetitions to have a significant effect.

A switch may be set so firmly that a possible connection is blocked out temporarily, or even permanently. For instance, most of us have had the experience of doing a complicated problem of arithmetic, in the midst of which we have made a very obvious mistake, such as multiplying two by two and getting two as the result. We have then checked it over several times without finding the error — two times two still seems to give us two. One of our switches has temporarily been jammed in the wrong position. Forunately, not every passage of a nerve impulse jams a switch; it merely makes it easier for it to turn one way than another.

There are always a number of impulses passing through different circuits, and these affect each other. The way we think at a given time is therefore determined largely by our previous experiences — not only the things we have encountered, but the particular paths that our nerve impulses have followed as a result of encountering them. No two of us started out with exactly the same wiring system, and the original differences have been increased by later activity.

The explanation just given is greatly oversimplified, but perhaps it will help us to understand something about the way we use words. Early in life we learn to associate words with people, things, events, and relations. Words as such are not permanently stored in the brain like cards in a filing cabinet. When a man hears or sees a word he receives an impulse which must pass along some circuit, determined by his previous experience with both words and things. When he hears it again, the new impulse tends to follow the same circuit, unless some intervening experience modifies it. On the other hand, when some other stimulus sends an impulse along part of the same circuit, he "remembers" the word. Meanwhile it, as a word, has completely disappeared from his mind. But the effect it has had on his nervous system, by operating some of the switches, persists. Consequently, if he has associated the word with a given situation, the recurrence of some aspect of that situation, either in physical fact or in mental review, is likely to reactivate the circuit, and he is again conscious of the word.

For instance, I look into a pen and see one animal bite another, and hear the second one squeal. I would not say anything, even to myself, unless I was to some extent interested in the activity. But if I was interested enough to notice it, part of the reaction of noticing would probably be the passing of words through my mind. The particular words that passed would be determined by my previous experiences. If I had seen similar animals before, I might say "One pig bit the other," or "One pig hurt the other," depending on whether I was more impressed by the action or its effect. If they were my own animals, I would probably think of them as individuals rather than simply as pigs, and might therefore say, "John hurt Mary."

Simple as this sentence is, I could not possibly have said it without having had a number of past experiences — enough to guess at the probable effect of John's teeth on Mary's ear and nervous system, and the significance of her squeal. Not being, myself, a small female pig, I must base my guess on a whole chain of assumptions; but I can be reasonably confident of its accuracy.

Certain events in the outside world have made impressions on my nervous system. I have associated words with these *impressions*, and not directly with the events themselves. If I attempt to communicate by the use of words, I must try to arouse *similar impressions in the nervous system* of the man I am talking to. Similar, not identical. His own past experiences, which cannot possibly be exactly the same as mine, are bound to affect his reactions. Even if he realizes that I am talking about my two pigs, his internal response may be quite surprising. I am expecting him to feel something like "Isn't that too bad?" but his actual sentiments may be "So what?" or even "Three cheers for John!"

We may be tempted to say: "Oh, he understands, all right. He just reacts differently." But what we call his understanding is merely a part of his total reaction, and cannot be separated, except verbally, from the rest of it. If you don't believe this, try telling a mother some time: "Oh, your boy is all right; he just broke a leg and a couple of ribs." The only thing she will understand from the word *just* is that you are an inhuman brute. As for the rest of the sentence, you have sent out a message saying "The damage to your son is temporary, so there is nothing to worry about." She has received one saying: "My darling is suffering, and there is no justice, and how do I know that one of his ribs hasn't punctured a lung?" And if you try to tell her that that is not a reasonable interpretation of your words, she will simply say (if she is still bothering to speak to you), "You have never been a mother." Her past experiences and her set of values are different from yours, especially where her son is concerned. Even if you had been more tactful in your report, your words could not possibly "mean" to her what they "mean" to you.

Words and things

The second relation — between words and the things they stand for — also needs some attention. We have already seen that the connection between a word and a thing is neither necessary nor direct. It is also important to realize that it is never quite the same twice, because the thing itself is always changing. If you buy a quart of milk, drink half of it, leave the rest in a warm kitchen for a couple of days, and then drink *that*, are you drinking the *same* milk?

The question cannot be answered intelligently without realizing that two quite different ideas are indicated by the word *same*. In the sense of continuity, it *is* the same milk you left there. In the sense of identity of structure, it is *not*. Important changes have taken place, and your tongue recognizes the effect of some of these changes at the first sip. Moreover, these changes have been taking place every instant that the milk has been there, and other changes have been taking place in the bottle. Such changes are not always perceptible, and we can often afford to disregard them, but they are inevitably taking place *all the time;* and the fact that we don't notice them does not prevent them from being real. It does no good to say that for "all practical purposes" a thing remains the same, unless we are quite sure that we can predict in advance what "all practical purposes" will be. If the bottle crystallizes and breaks at a tiny jar, or the milk picks up and multiplies germs that kill us, we cannot dispose of the unfortunate results by insisting that the "same" things were perfectly all right a while ago.

To go one step further into the matter, we may bring up the question of whether anything is the same, even at a given instant, to two different observers. Again the answer seems to be no. Since our senses, nervous systems, and backgrounds of past experience vary, no two people can get identical impressions of the "same" thing. The actual thing (unless it is something like a bullet or an axe) does not get into our heads. What does get in — what we are conscious of and what we talk about — is merely the impression made on our nervous system. Therefore when two people look at a Pekingese dog, and she says, "Oh, the cute little darling!" while he says "What a disgusting little slug," they are not applying different words to the *same* thing. Each of them is describing, not the physical dog, but the impression created in his own mind by a combination of his present sense-perceptions and his past experiences. Even if they agree verbally that it is a Pekingese, the meeting of their minds is not complete; because the word Pekingese still "means" something different to each of them.

It follows that "using the same words for the same things" is not even theoretically possible, because there simply aren't any "same things." The best we can hope for is a reasonable approximation. Our remote ancestors, when they developed the language, did not know this. A few of them had imaginative glimpses of the truth, but on the whole they believed very firmly that many things were identical, permanent, and alike to all observers; and the structure of the language, like the structure of their physical theories, reflected this belief. Until the development of modern physics and neurology there was no definite proof that they were wrong.

A good many men, for a good many centuries, have been trying to devise and encourage the use of a language suitable for perfect communication — a language in which every word has a fixed meaning, which any properly trained person can recognize; and in which the arrangement of words is completely systematic and "logical."[2] We can now see that such a language would be possible only if words operated in a vacuum, or at least in a perfectly uniform medium, of which each human skull somehow contained a part. We must therefore lower our sights.

Of course an approximate agreement as to the significance of words and word-arrangements is possible, or we could not communicate at all; and among people of similar backgrounds and training, communication over a limited range of subjects may reach a high degree of reliability. Dictionaries and grammars, if they are well made and sensibly used, may increase the uniformity of our language habits and thus improve the quality of our communication. But they may do us more harm than good if we let them blind us to the fact that language is not, and never can be, an independent, objective structure governed by its own laws. At its theoretical best, language can only stimulate similar (never identical) reactions in necessarily different nervous systems. Aside from its effect on these nervous systems, it has no importance at all.

The man who goes through life complaining that his friends (a)

[2] A large number of artificial languages for international use have been invented, fifty-three between 1880 and 1907. Volapük and Esperanto are the two most notable. Recently the International Auxiliary Association of New York proposed a new one, Interlingua, made up of components common to the languages most widely used today. [eds.]

don't say what they mean, and (*b*) don't understand him when he speaks plain English, deserves pity rather than blame. He suffers from a delusion that makes it hard for him to look through the words and find out what the man behind them means; and equally hard for him to select and arrange his own words with some attention to the response that they probably will arouse, rather than the one they "should" arouse. If his delusion makes him haughty and ill-tempered, it is probably because of continual frustration rather than natural viciousness.

SUGGESTED ASSIGNMENTS

1. According to Myers, the same word means different things to different people, depending on their experience. To a metallurgist, *gold* means a heavy, yellowish, metallic chemical element (Au), with a high degree of ductility and malleability, and an atomic weight of 197.2. What differences in meaning would you assume the term *gold* to have for a jeweler, a guard at Fort Knox, the Secretary of the U.S. Treasury, a woman who has just received some in the form of a wedding ring, a worker in a gold mine, and an Eskimo untouched by civilization?

2. $E = mc^2$ was rather meaningless to most people until a few years ago. What does it mean to an atomic physicist? To you? To a Bantu warrior? To a victim of Hiroshima? To what do you attribute these differences in meaning?

3. Both *dog* and *cur* refer to the same quadruped known to zoologists as *Canis familiaris*. Do they mean the same thing? If not, explain the difference. Similarly, explain the differences between the words in each of the following pairs: *horse, nag; stingy, thrifty; cocky, confident*.

4. Compare the different meanings of the word *dog* in each of the following contexts:

    a. A dog is man's best friend.
    b. He leads a dog's life.
    c. You are a dirty dog!
    d. He is always putting on the dog.
    e. Let sleeping dogs lie.

5. Construct five sentences in which you use the same word in five different contexts.

6. Write a brief theme in which you describe a personal experience of a

misunderstanding caused by the speaker and the listener understanding a word in different senses.

7. A Greek philosopher once said, "You cannot walk through the same river twice." Write a theme interpreting this saying in relation to words.

The Uses of Language

IRVING M. COPI

Language is often referred to as a tool. The implication is that, like a hammer, drill, or saw, it can be used to perform certain jobs. Most tools, however, have a single function; each job requires a special tool. We use a hammer to drive nails, a drill to bore holes, and a saw to cut wood. If language is a tool, it is the most remarkable invention we have; it will beat any combination knife, can opener, screwdriver, bottlecap remover, or other gadget on the market. What jobs does language perform? To reply "speech and writing" misses the point; it merely says that language has two ways of doing its various jobs. To reply "poetry and prose" comes closer, but it is still an oversimplification. If we classify all that is not poetry as prose, does that mean that the language of prose has a single function? Think of the language of science, newspaper reporting, advertising, political oratory, the language of the church—prayers and the litany. Depending on the job at hand, we use language differently, and we respond differently to the various uses of language. What these uses are and how they differ one from another are discussed by Irving M. Copi in his essay. Copi, a logician, is Professor of Philosophy at the University of Michigan.

I. Three basic functions of language

Language is so subtle and complicated an instrument that the multiplicity of its uses is often lost sight of. Here, as in many other situations, there is danger in our tendency to oversimplify things.

A not uncommon complaint of those who take too narrow a view

From *Introduction to Logic* by Irving M. Copi. Copyright 1953 by The Macmillan Company and used with their permission.

of the legitimate uses of language concerns the way in which words are "wasted" at social functions. "So much talk, and so little said!"sums up this kind of criticism. And more than one person has been heard to remark, "So and so asked me how I felt. What a hypocrite! He doesn't care in the least how I feel!" Such remarks reveal a failure to understand the complex purposes for which language is used. It is shown also in the deplorable conduct of the bore, who, when asked how he feels, actually proceeds to tell about the state of his health — usually at great length and in much detail. But people do not usually talk at parties to instruct each other. And ordinarily the question "How are you?" is a friendly greeting, not a request for a medical report.

One very important use of language is to communicate information. Ordinarily this is accomplished by formulating and affirming (or denying) propositions. Language used to affirm or deny propositions, or to present arguments, is said to be serving the *informative function*. In this context we use the word "information" to include misinformation: false as well as true propositions, incorrect as well as correct arguments. Informative discourse is used to *describe* the world, and to reason about it. Whether the alleged facts that are being described are important or unimportant, general or particular, does not matter; in any case the language used to describe or report them is being used informatively.

We may distinguish two basic uses or functions of language in addition to the informative, and refer to them as the *expressive* and the *directive*. Just as science provides us with the clearest examples of informative discourse, so poetry furnishes us the best examples of language serving an *expressive* function. The following lines of Burns:

> O my Luve's like a red, red rose
> That's newly sprung in June:
> O my Luve's like the melodie
> That's sweetly play'd in tune!

are definitely not intended to inform us of any facts or theories concerning the world. The poet's purpose is to communicate not knowledge but feelings and attitudes. The passage was not written to report any information but to *express* certain emotions that the poet felt very keenly and to evoke feelings of a similar kind in the reader. Language serves the *expressive* function whenever it is used to vent or communicate feelings or emotions.

Not all expressive language is poetry, however. We express sorrow by saying "That's too bad," or "Oh my," and enthusiasm by shouting

"Wow!" or "Oh boy!" The lover expresses his delicate passion by murmuring "Darling!" or "Oh baby!" The poet expresses his complex and concentrated emotions in a sonnet or some other verse form. A worshipper may express his feeling of wonder and awe at the vastness and mystery of the universe by reciting the Lord's Prayer or the twenty-third Psalm of David. All these are uses of language not to communicate information but to express emotions, feelings, or attitudes. Expressive discourse *as expressive* is neither true nor false. For a person to apply only the criteria of truth or falsehood, correctness or incorrectness, to expressive discourse like a poem is to miss its point and to lose much of its value. The student whose enjoyment of Keats' sonnet *On first looking into Chapman's Homer* is marred by his historical knowledge that Balboa rather than Cortez discovered the Pacific Ocean is a "poor reader" of poetry. The purpose of the poem is not to teach history, but something else entirely. This is not to say that poetry can have no literal significance. Some poems *do* have an informative content which may be an important ingredient in their total effect. Some poetry may well be "criticism of life," in the words of a great poet. But such poems are more than merely expressive, as we are using the term here. Such poetry may be said to have a "mixed usage," or to serve a multiple function. This notion will be explained further in the following section.

Expression may be analyzed into two components. When a man curses to himself when he is alone, or a poet writes poems which he shows to no one, or a man prays in solitude, his language functions to express or evince his own attitude but does not serve to evoke a similar attitude in anyone else. On the other hand, when an orator seeks to inspire his audience — not to action, but to share enthusiasm; when a lover courts his beloved in poetic language; when the crowd cheers its athletic team; the language used not only evinces the attitudes of the speakers but also is intended to evoke the same attitudes in the hearers. Expressive discourse, then, is used either to *evince* the speaker's feelings or to *evoke* certain feelings on the part of the auditor. Of course it may do both.

Language serves the *directive* function when it is used for the purpose of causing (or preventing) overt action. The clearest examples of directive discourse are commands and requests. When a mother tells her little boy to wash his hands before supper, she does not intend to communicate any information to him or to evince or evoke any particular emotion. Her language is intended to get results, to cause action of the indicated kind. When the same mother asks the grocer to deliver certain goods to her house, she is again using language directively, to motivate or effect *action*. To ask a question is ordinarily to request an answer, and is also to be classified as directive discourse. The difference between a command and a request is a rather subtle one, for almost any command can be translated into a request by adding the word "please," or by suitable changes in tone of voice or in facial expression.

In its nakedly imperative form, directive discourse is neither true nor false. A command such as "Close the window" cannot be either true or false in any literal sense. Whether the command is obeyed or disobeyed does not affect or determine its truth-value, for it has none. We may disagree about whether a command has been obeyed or not; we may disagree about whether a command should be obeyed or not; but we never disagree about whether a command is true or false, for it cannot be either. However, the reasonableness or propriety, the unreasonableness or impropriety of commands are properties somewhat analogous to the truth or falsehood of informative discourse. And questions of the propriety of given commands can be raised and resolved in ways that are strictly within the scope of logic.

II. Discourse serving multiple functions

In the preceding section the examples presented were chemically pure specimens, so to speak, of the three basic kinds of communication. The threefold division proposed is illuminating and valuable, but it cannot be applied mechanically, because almost any ordinary communication will probably exemplify, to a greater or less extent, all three uses of language. Thus a poem, which is primarily expressive discourse, may have a moral and be in effect a command to the reader (or hearer) to lead a certain kind of life, and may also convey a certain amount of information. On the other hand, although a sermon is predominantly directive, seeking to cause certain appropriate action by members of the congregation (whether to abandon their evil ways, or to contribute money to the church, or what not), it may evince and evoke sentiments, thus serving the expressive function, and may also include some information, communicating some factual material. And a scientific treatise, essentially informative, may evince something of the writer's own enthusiasm, thus serving an expressive function, and may also, at least implicitly, serve some directive function or other, perhaps bidding the reader to verify independently the author's conclusion. Most ordinary uses of language are mixed.

It is not always the result of any confusion on the part of the speaker when his language serves mixed or multiple functions. It is rather the case that *effective* communication demands certain combinations of function. Few of us stand to each other in the relation of parent to child or employer to employee. And outside the context of such formal relationships as these, one cannot simply issue an order with any expectation of having it obeyed. Consequently a certain indirection must be employed: a bald command would arouse antagonism or resentment and be self-defeating. One cannot cause action by merely voicing an imperative; it is necessary to use a more subtle method of stimulating the desired action.

Action may be said to have very complex causes. Motivation is more properly to be discussed by a psychologist than a logician, but it is common knowledge that actions are usually caused by both desires and beliefs. A man who *desires* to eat food will not touch what is on his plate unless he *believes* it to be food; and even though he *believes* it to be food he will not touch it unless he *desires* to eat. This fact is relevant to our present discussion because desires are a special type of what we have been calling "attitudes."

Consequently actions may be caused by evoking appropriate attitudes *and* communicating relevant information. Assuming your listeners to be benevolent, you may cause them to contribute to a given charity by informing them of its effectiveness in accomplishing benevolent results. In such a case your use of language is ultimately directive, since its purpose is to cause action. But a naked command would be far less effective in this situation than the informative discourse used. Suppose, on the other hand, that your listeners are already persuaded that the charity in question does accomplish benevolent results. Here again you cannot simply command with any great hope of being obeyed, but you may succeed in causing them to act in the desired fashion by somehow arousing a sufficiently benevolent feeling or emotion in them. The discourse you use to realize your end is expressive discourse; you must make a "moving appeal." Thus your language will have a mixed use, functioning both expressively and directively. Or finally, let us suppose that you are seeking a donation from people who have *neither* a benevolent attitude *nor* a belief that the charity serves a benevolent purpose. Here you must use *both* informative and expressive language. In such a case the language used serves all three functions, being directive, informative, and expressive all at once, not accidentally as a mere mixture that just happens to occur, but essentially, as necessary to successful communication.

Some writers on language have suggested that discourse serves more than these three distinct functions. It is possible, however, to understand any other function as a mixture or combination of two or possibly all three of the basic uses that have been distinguished here. The most important of these others has frequently been called the "ceremonial" use of language. Included within this category are many different kinds of phrases, ranging from relatively trivial words of greeting to the more portentous discourse of the marriage ceremony, phrasings of state documents, and the verbal rituals performed on holy days in houses of worship. But these can all be regarded as mixtures of expressive and directive discourse, rather than some altogether different and unique kind. For example, the usual ceremonial greetings and chit-chat at social gatherings serve the purpose of evincing and evoking goodwill and sociability. Perhaps for some speakers they are intended also to serve the directive purpose of causing their hearers to act in certain definite ways, to patronize the speaker's business, to offer him employment, or to invite him to dinner. At the other extreme, the impressive language of the marriage ceremony is intended to emphasize the solemnity of the occasion (its expressive function), and also to cause the bride and groom to perform in their new roles with heightened appreciation of the seriousness of the marriage contract (its directive function).

SUGGESTED ASSIGNMENTS

1. Classify the following selections in terms of function, i.e., informative, expressive, directive. Substantiate your judgments. Remember that language may serve multiple functions.

   a. In the beginning God created the heaven and the earth.
   And the earth was without form, and void; and darkness was upon the face of the deep. And the spirit of God moved upon the face of the waters.
   And God said, Let there be light: and there was light.
   And God saw the light, that it was good: and God divided the light from the darkness.
   And God called the light Day, and the darkness he called Night. And the evening and the morning were the first day.
   And God said, Let there be a firmament in the midst of the waters, and let it divide the waters from the waters.

   Genesis 1:1–6

b.   Save me, O God; for the waters are come in unto my soul.
  I sink in deep mire, where there is no standing: I am come into deep
  waters, where the floods overflow me.
  I am weary of my crying: my throat is dried: mine eyes fail while I wait
  for my God.
  They that hate me without a cause are more than the hairs of mine head:
  they that would destroy me, being mine enemies wrongfully, are mighty:
  then I restored that which I took not away.

Psalm 69:1–4

c.   A BIRTHDAY

         My heart is like a singing bird
           Whose nest is in a watered shoot:
         My heart is like an apple-tree
           Whose boughs are bent with thickset fruit;
         My heart is like a rainbow shell   5
           That paddles in a halcyon sea;
         My heart is gladder than all these
           Because my love is come to me.

         Raise me a dais of silk and down;
           Hang it with vair and purple dyes;   10
         Carve it in doves and pomegranates,
           And peacocks with a hundred eyes;
         Work it in gold and silver grapes,
           In leaves and silver fleurs-de-lys;
         Because the birthday of my life   15
           Is come, my love is come to me.

Christina Rossetti

d.   Sea King Sailing Surf Board. Wonderful for summer sailing—you don't
  have to be an expert. Easy to handle aluminum boom. Non-sinkable balsa
  wood flotation. Special non-skid deck for safety; removable centerboard,
  kick-up rudder for shallow water. 14-ft. Fiberglass covered hull. With
  3-ft. beam. Maximum 10 in. deep 14-ft. gunwale length; transom 18 in.
  wide by 4 in. deep.

(A mail-order catalog)

e.   Every Price Cut $1. Famous Pinehurst at Low Prices. It's like walking on
  air. Heel-to-toe foam rubber shock absorbing cushion for greater foot
  ease. Fashioned of extra fine leathers. Finest Goodyear welt construction.
  Supertex lining resists athlete's foot. $11.99.

(A mail-order catalog)

f.   I dug my cellar in the side of a hill sloping to the south, where a woodchuck had formerly dug his burrow, down through sumach and black-
  berry roots, and the lowest stain of vegetation, six feet square by seven
  deep, to a fine sand where potatoes would not freeze in any winter. The
  sides were left shelving, and not stoned; but the sun having never shone

on them, the sand still keeps its place. It was but two hours' work. I took particular pleasure in this breaking of ground, for in almost all latitudes men dig into the earth for an equable temperature. Under the most splendid house in the city is still to be found the cellar where they store their roots as of old, and long after the superstructure has disappeared posterity remark its dent in the earth. The house is still but a sort of porch at the entrance of a burrow.

(*Thoreau's Walden*)

g. None of them knew the color of the sky. Their eyes glanced level, and were fastened upon the waves that swept toward them. These waves were of the hue of slate, save for the tops, which were of foaming white, and all of the men knew the colors of the sea. The horizon narrowed and widened, and dipped and rose, and at all times its edge was jagged with waves that seemed thrust up in points like rocks. Many a man ought to have a bath-tub larger than the boat which here rode upon the sea. These waves were most wrongfully and barbarously abrupt and tall, and each froth-top was a problem in small-boat navigation.

(*Stephen Crane's "The Open Boat"*)

h. These are the times that try men's souls. The summer soldier and the sunshine patriot will, in this crisis, shrink from the service of their country; but he that stands it *now*, deserves the love and thanks of man and woman. Tyranny, like hell, is not easily conquered; yet we have this consolation with us, that the harder the conflict, the more glorious the triumph. What we obtain too cheap, we esteem too lightly; it is dearness only that gives every thing its value. Heaven knows how to put a proper price upon its goods; and it would be strange indeed if so celestial an article as FREEDOM should not be highly rated.

(*Thomas Paine's "The Crisis"*)

2. Choose two of the above passages which differ in function and write a paper explaining in some detail exactly how they differ.

3. Assume that you are the representative of a business firm that has sent you to investigate Community X as a possibility for future expansion of the business—a branch office, a new factory, or something of the sort. Write a theme in the form of a report to the company, making either a positive or negative recommendation. Your intent is to be informative. As a contrastive exercise, assume that you are the Secretary of the Chamber of Commerce of Community X. Write a theme in the form of a letter to the same company. Your purpose is to induce the company to establish its business in Community X. Make an analysis of how the two themes differ in their use of language.

4. Assume that you are Chairman of the Board of Student Governors at your college. You are disturbed at the apathy of some student organizations for failing to send representatives to the monthly meeting of the Board.

Write a letter, directive in intent, to the presidents of the sluggard organizations, announcing the next meeting. You want their representatives to attend the meeting. Keep in mind as you write that you want to gain their support, not to lose it completely

The Gift of Tongues

CLYDE KLUCKHOHN

It is often assumed that what can be expressed in one language can be expressed in another; all one has to do is to substitute the words of one language for equivalents in the other. The matter is not so simple. What if there are no equivalents? Cultures differ not only in dress and behavior, in political, economic, and social institutions, but also in language, which is a form of social behavior. Each language is a product of a particular culture, and it reflects the culture of the people and their view of the world. This *Weltanschauung* is built into the very structure of a language. Whether language determines the way a person thinks is a moot question, but it is believed by many that it does affect his perception of the world about him. It is not, as Harry Hoijer has pointed out, "that linguistic patterns limit sensory patterns but that they direct perception and thinking into certain habitual channels." The fascinating topic of the relationship between language and culture is discussed by the late Clyde Kluckhohn, eminent Professor of Anthropology at Harvard.

Our misapprehension of the nature of language has occasioned a greater waste of time, and effort, and genius, than all the other mistakes and delusions with which humanity has been afflicted. It has retarded immeasurably our physical knowledge of every kind, and vitiated what it could not retard.

—*A. B. Johnson,*
Treatise on Language[1]

With permission of the publishers from *Mirror for Man* by Clyde Kluckhohn. Copyright, 1949, by the McGraw-Hill Book Company.

[1] Alexander Bryan Johnson, *A Treatise on Language*, David Rynin, ed. (Berkeley, University of California Press, 1947).

It's a pity that so few of us have lived down our childhood struggles with grammar. We have been made to suffer so much from memorizing rules by rote and from approaching language in a mechanical, unimaginative way that we tend to think of grammar as the most inhuman of studies. Probably Americans, who dramatize themselves and their independence, have a kind of unconscious resentment against all patterns that are so set as to constitute a gratuitous insult to the principle of free will. For whatever reasons, Americans have been characteristically inept at foreign languages. Like the British, we have expected everybody else to learn English.

Yet nothing is more human than the speech of an individual or of a folk. Human speech, unlike the cry of an animal, does not occur as a mere element in a larger response. Only the human animal can communicate abstract ideas and converse about conditions that are contrary to fact. Indeed the purely conventional element in speech is so large that language can be regarded as pure culture. A Burmese weaver, moved to Mexico, would know at once what a fellow craftsman in Mexico was doing, but would not understand one word of the Nahuatl tongue. No clues are so helpful as those of language in pointing to ultimate, unconscious psychological attitudes. Moreover, much of the friction between groups and between nations arises because in both the literal and the slangy senses they don't speak the same language.

We live in an environment which is largely verbal in the sense that we spend the most of our waking hours uttering words or responding actively or passively to the words of others. We talk to ourselves. We talk to our families and friends — partly to communicate to them and to persuade them, partly just to express ourselves. We read newspapers, magazines, books, and other written matter. We listen to the radio, to sermons, lectures, and movies. As Edward Sapir says:

Language completely interpenetrates direct experience. For most persons every experience, real or potential, is saturated with verbalism. This perhaps explains why so many nature lovers do not feel that they are truly in touch with nature until they have mastered the names of a great many flowers and trees, as though the primary world of reality were a verbal one, and as though one could not get close to nature unless one first mastered the terminology that somehow magically expresses it. It is this constant interplay between language and experience which removes language from the cold status of such purely and simply symbolic systems as mathematical symbolism or flag signalling.[2]

[2] From "Language," by Edward Sapir, *Encyclopedia of the Social Sciences*, vol. ix. Copyright 1933 by The Macmillan Company and used with their permission.

The dictionaries still say that "language is a device for communicating ideas." The semanticists and the anthropologists agree that this is a tiny, specialized function of speech. Mainly, language is an instrument for action. The meaning of a word or phrase is not its dictionary equivalent but the difference its utterance brings about in a situation. We use words to comfort and cajole ourselves in fantasy and daydream, to let off steam, to goad ourselves into one type of activity and to deny ourselves another. We use words to promote our own purposes in dealing with others. We build up verbal pictures of ourselves and our motives. We coax, wheedle, protest, invite, and threaten. Even the most intellectual of intellectuals employs only a minute fraction of his total utterance in symbolizing and communicating ideas that are divorced from emotion and action. The primary social value of speech lies in getting individuals to work more effectively together and in easing social tensions. Very often what is said matters much less than that something is said.

To the manipulation of this verbal environment, the anthropological linguist has made some immediately practical contributions. Forced by the absence of written materials and by other circumstances attendant upon work with primitives, he has become an expert on "the direct method." He knows how to learn a language by using it. Though sensitive to the broader implications of the subtler, rarer forms of a language, he is skilled in the socially practical. He knows how to dodge the subjunctive when the immediate objective is to get a conversation going. The training of the conventional teacher of languages tempts him to his besetting sin of preoccupation with the niceties. He loves complicated rules and even more the exceptions to those rules. This is one of the principal reasons that after eight years of instruction in French an American can read a French novel with pleasure but is terrified to ask street directions in Paris. The anthropologist can't look up the rules in the book. He is hardened to making small and large mistakes. His tradition is to break through, to concentrate on the essential, to get on with the talk at all costs.

Since many odd languages were of military significance during World War II, the anthropological linguist had a chance to introduce his method of working directly with the native informant. He prepared educational materials that highlighted anthropological short cuts in learning how to speak languages. The results have influenced the traditional methods of language instruction in the United States. The anthropological linguist has also worked out ways of teaching adults who have no written language and ways of teaching illiterates to write and read their own tongue.

Because anthropological linguists have usually been trained as ethnologists and have often done general field work, they have tended less than other students of language to isolate speech from the total life of the people. To the anthropologist, language is just one kind of cultural behavior with many interesting connections to other aspects of action and thought. Analysis of a vocabulary shows the principal emphases of a culture and reflects culture history. In Arabic, for example, there are more than six thousand different words for camel, its parts, and equipment. The crudity and the special local words of the vocabulary of Spanish-speaking villages in New Mexico reflect the long isolation of these groups from the main stream of Latin culture. The particular archaisms used show that the break with the main continuity of the Spanish language occurred during the eighteenth century. The fact that the Boorabbee Indians of Panama use words like *gadsoot* (gadzooks), *forsoo'* (forsooth), *chee-ah* (cheer), and *mai-api* (mayhap) suggests a possible connection with Elizabethan buccaneers.

A great deal is now known about the history of languages, especially those languages that have been the great carriers of culture: Greek, Latin, Sanskrit, Arabic, Chinese, and English. Certain regularities have been discovered. In contrast to the general course of cultural evolution, languages move from the complex to the simple. Chinese and English have today lost almost all inflections. The uniformities of phonetic change are most encouraging to those who believe that there is a discoverable order in human events. As Bloomfield has said:

These correspondences are a matter of historical detail, but their significance was overwhelming, since they showed that human action, in the mass, is not altogether haphazard, but may proceed with regularity even in so unimportant a matter as the manner of pronouncing the individual sounds within the flow of speech.[3]

The phonetic side of language beautifully illustrates both the selective nature of culture and the omnipresence of patterning. The sound of the p in pin is uttered with a slight puff of breath that is lacking when we sound the p in spin. Yet the speakers of English have entered into an unconscious agreement to treat them as the same signals, though

[3] Leonard Bloomfield, *Language*, (New York, Holt, Rinehart & Winston, Inc., 1933).

they are not acoustically identical. It is like the motorist trained to stop at a light that is any shade of red. If I am investigating an unknown language and discover two sounds that are somewhat similar to those represented by English "b" and "d" but differ in being softly whispered, I can immediately predict that sounds in the new language of "g" type will conform to the same pattern.

Language is as consistently nonrational as any aspect of culture. We cling stubbornly to functionless capital letters. One may also instance our absurd English spelling. "Ghiti" ought to spell fish — gh as in laugh, ti as in ambition. In hiccough, gh has a p sound. "Ghoughteighteau" could be read as potato — figure it out yourself. We say "five houses" when "five house" would be simpler and convey the meaning equally well.

Small peculiarities of linguistic usage are very revealing. It is no accident that French Catholics address the deity with the familiar form of the personal pronoun (*tu*) and Protestants with the formal (*vous*). In all sectors of French society save the old aristocracy spouses use *tu* to each other. But in the *Faubourg St. Germain* the duke calls his duchess *vous* — it being well understood between them that he reserves *tu* for his mistress.

A whole monograph could well be written on differences in the social structure of European nations as exposed by linguistic habits relating to the second personal pronoun. In France one comes to *tutoyer* few people after adolescence. This familiarity is restricted to immediate relatives and to a few intimate friends of childhood. In the German-speaking world, however, a student who did not soon come to use the familiar *Du* with those whom he saw frequently would be regarded as stuffy. In the army of imperial Austria all officers in the same regiment called each other *Du* regardless of rank. Failure to use the familiar form was equivalent to a challenge to the duel. In Austria and in other European countries the initiation of the familiar usage between adults is formalized in a ceremony. There is an embrace and a drink from each other's glasses. In Spain and Italy the introduction of the *tu* relationship in later life is considerably easier than in France but less frequent than in southern Germany and Austria. In Italy there is the further complication of a special form of respectful address (*Lei*). Choice of *Lei* or the more common formal pronoun became a political issue. The Fascist Party forbade the use of *Lei*. In Sweden also, passions have been aroused over the pronoun *ni* which is used toward those of lower social status — and, in accord with the familiar principle of inverted snobbery,[4] toward royal personages. Clubs were formed to abolish this word. Individuals wore buttons saying, "I don't use *ni* and I hope you don't either." Persons were brought into court for using *ni* toward people who considered themselves the equals or superiors of those who derogated them by using *ni* in address. "You are *ni* to me; I am not *ni* to you."

There are also instances of the intensely emotional symbolism of language. During the course of the development of nationalism and the romantic movement, every tongue was seized upon as the tangible manifestation of each culture's uniqueness. In the earlier part of the nineteenth century Magyar nobles spoke Latin in the Hungarian Parliament because they could not speak Magyar and would not speak German. Magyar, Irish, Lithuanian, and other tongues have been revived within the last hundred years from the category of practically dead languages. This tendency is about as old as written history. In the Bible we learn that the Gileadites slew everyone at the passages of Jordan who said *sibboleth* instead of *shibboleth*.

Groups within a culture emphasize their unity by a special language. Criminals have their own argot. So, indeed, do all the professions. One school in England (Winchester) has a language, compounded of medieval Latin and the accretions of the slang of many generations, that is utterly unintelligible to the uninitiated. "The linguistic community" is no meaningless phrase. The use of speech forms in common implies other things in common. The hunting or "county" set in England affects the dropping of final g's as a badge of their being set apart. Understatement is the mark of unshakable psychological security. If a member of the English upper classes is a member of the Davis Cup team he says "Yes, I play a little tennis." Individuals of many countries pronounce words in certain ways in order to associate themselves with particular social classes. The extent to which an elderly or middle-aged Englishman is still identifiable as Harrow or Rugby — and not as a Yorkshireman nor even as an Oxonian nor as an army man — proves the identification of distinctive language with social status. You can

---

[4] Another illustration of the "principle of inverted snobbery": In an American college that is small or struggling for prestige, faculty members who are members of Phi Beta Kappa would as soon appear on the campus without their pants as without their keys. In old, well-established universities, ΦBK keys are worn only by a few older professors.

pretty well place an Englishman by his tie and his accent. Idiomatic turns of speech identify to society at large the special positions and roles of its various members. Cliques and classes unconsciously use this device to prevent absorption into the larger group. "He talks like one of us" is a declaration of acceptance. Euphemisms, special terms of endearment, and slang are class labels.

The essential aroma of each culture or subculture may be caught as a fragrance of language. In the Berlin of 1930, when one met an acquaintance on the street one bowed and stiffly said, "Good day." In Vienna one called out, "I have the honor," to a superior; "May God greet thee (you)," to an intimate; or "Your servant," to a fellow student or fellow aristocrat. That *gewisse Liebenswürdigkeit* (a certain graciousness) which was the hallmark of Viennese culture came out most clearly and immediately in certain phrases that were not unknown in northern and Protestant Germany but were much less frequent in the stuff of daily conversation: "Live well," "the lady mother," "I kiss the hand, noble lady," and many others. In Austria when the delivery boy brought the groceries to the kitchen he said, "May God greet thee," if the maid received them; "Kiss the hand, noble lady," if the mistress were there.

Although one could press this point of view too far, there is *something* significant in the lists of words from each European language that have become widely current in other languages. From English: gentleman, fair play, week end, sport. From French: *liaison, maitresse, cuisine.* From Italian: *diva, bravo, bel canto.* From German: *Weltschmerz, Sehnsucht, Weltanschauung, Gemutlichkeit.* In *Englishmen, Frenchmen and Spaniards*, de Madariaga has suggested that the words, fair play, *le droit*, and *el honor* are the keys to the respective cultures. Here is a sample of his discussion of English:

There is deep satisfaction in the thought that English—the language of the man of action—is a monosyllabic language. For the man of action, as we know, lives in the present, and the present is an instant with room for no more than one syllable. Words of more than one syllable are sometimes called in English "dictionary" words, *i.e.*, words for the intellectual, for the bookworm, for the crank, almost for the un-English. They are marvellous, those English monosyllables, particularly, of course, those which represent acts. Their fidelity to the act which they represent is so perfect that one is tempted to think English words are the right and proper names which those acts are meant to have, and all other words but pitiable failures. How could one improve on splash, smash, ooze, shriek, slush, glide, speak, coo? Who could find anything better than hum or buzz or howl or whir? Who could think of anything more sloppy than slop? Is not the word sweet a kiss in itself and what could suggest a more peremptory obstacle than stop?[5]

Certainly the recurrent turns of phrase, the bromides, of each culture and of different time periods in the same culture are illuminating. They embody in capsule form the central strains and stresses of the society, major cultural interests, the characteristic definitions of the situation, the prime motivations. You can't swear effectively in British to an American audience and vice versa. The Navaho greeting is "All is well"; the Japanese, "There is respectful earliness"; the American, "How do you do?" "How are you getting on?" Each epoch has its stock phrases. As Carl Becker has written:

If we would discover the little backstairs door that for any age serves as the secret entranceway to knowledge, we will do well to look for certain unobtrusive words with uncertain meanings that are permitted to slip off the tongue or pen without fear and without research; words which, having from constant repetition lost their metaphorical significance, are unconsciously mistaken for objective realities. . . . In each age these magic words have their entrances and their exits.[6]

In a way there is nothing very new about semantics. The Roman grammarian, Varro, pointed out in a learned treatise that he had discovered 228 distinct meanings for the word "good." His basic point was the same as Aldous Huxley's: "There ought to be some way of dry-cleaning and disinfecting words. Love, purity, goodness, spirit — a pile of dirty linen waiting for the laundress." We are always bringing together by words things that are different and separating verbally things that are, in fact, the same. A Christian Scientist refused to take vitamin tablets on the ground that they were "medicine"; he willingly accepted them when it was explained that they were "food." An insurance company discovered that behavior toward "gasoline drums" was ordinarily circumspect, that toward "empty gasoline drums" habitually careless. Actually, the "empty" drums are the more dangerous because they contain explosive vapor.

The semantic problem is almost insoluble because, as John Locke said, "So difficult is it to show the various meaning and imperfections

[5] S. de Madariaga, *Englishmen, Frenchmen, and Spaniards* (Oxford University Press), 1929.

[6] Carl Becker, *Heavenly City of the Eighteenth Century Philosophers* (New Haven, Yale University Press, 1935).

of words when we have nothing else but words to do it by." This is one of the reasons that a cross-cultural approach is imperative. Anyone who has struggled with translation is made to realize that there is more to a language than its dictionary. The Italian proverb *"traduttore, tradittore"* (the translator is a betrayer) is all too correct. I asked a Japanese with a fair knowledge of English to translate back from the Japanese that phrase in the new Japanese constitution that represents our "life, liberty, and the pursuit of happiness." He rendered, "license to commit lustful pleasure." English to Russian and Russian back to English transmuted a cablegram "Genevieve suspended for prank" into "Genevieve hanged for juvenile delinquency."

These are obvious crudities. But look at translations into half-a-dozen languages of the same passage in the Old Testament. The sheer difference in length will show that translation is not just a matter of finding a word in the second language that exactly matches a word in the original. Renderings of poetry are especially misleading. The best metrical translation of Homer is probably the fragment done by Hawtrey. The ,final two lines of the famous "Helen on the wall" passage of the third book in the *Iliad* goes as follows:

> So said she; but they long since in earth's soft arms were reposing
> There in their own dear land, their fatherland, Lacedaemon.

Hawtrey has caught the musical effect of Greek hexameter about as well as it is possible to do in English. But the Greek says literally, "but them, on the other hand, the life-giving earth held fast." The original is realistic — Helen's brothers were dead and that was that. The English is sentimental.

Once in Paris I saw a play called "The Weak Sex." I found it charmingly risqué. A year later in Vienna I took a girl to see a German translation of the same play. Though she was no prude, I was embarrassed because the play was vulgar if not obscene in German.

I think I got my first genuine insight into the nature of language when my tutor at Oxford asked me to translate into Greek a few pages from an eighteenth-century British rhetorician which contained the following phrase, "she heaped the utmost virulence of her invective upon him." I struggled with this and finally committed the unforgivable sin of looking up each word in an English-Greek dictionary. My tutor glanced at the resultant monstrosity and looked up at me with mingled disgust, pity, and amazement. "My dear boy," he said, "don't you know that the only possible way you can render that is *deinos aedeitai*, she blamed very strongly?"

Really, there are three kinds of translation. There is the literal or word-for-word variety which is always distorted except perhaps between languages that are very similar in structure and vocabulary. Second, there is the official type where certain conventions as to idiomatic equivalents are respected. The third, or psychological type of translation, where the words produce approximately the same effects in the speakers of the second language as they did in those of the original, is next to impossible. At best, the rendering must be extremely free, with elaborate circumlocutions and explanations. I once heard Einstein make a slip of the tongue that stated the deeper truth. He said, "I shall speak in English this evening, but if I get excited during the discussion I shall break into German and Professor Lindeman will traduce me."

If words referred only to things, translation would be relatively simple. But they refer also to relations between things and the subjective as well as the objective aspects of these relationships. In different tongues relationships are variously conceived. The Balinese word *tis* means not to be cold when it is cold. The Balinese word *paling* designates the state of a trance or drunkenness or a condition of not knowing where you are, what day it is, where the center of the island is, the caste of the person to whom you are talking. The subjective aspects arise from the fact that we use words not only to express things and relationships but to express ourselves; words refer not only to events but to the attitudes of the speakers toward those events.

The words prostitute and whore have exactly the same denotation. The connotation, however, is very different. And a word's connotation is at least as important as the denotation in rousing feeling and producing action. Examine carefully the richest field of modern verbal magic — advertisements.

The same words often don't mean the same thing to different generations within the same culture. Margaret Mead writes:

Take the word *job*. To the parents a job was something you got when you finished school—the next step, a little grim, a little exciting, the end of carefree school days. A job was something you were going to get, bound to get, something that waited for you at the end of school, just as certainly as autumn follows summer. But job—to those born in 1914, 1915? Something that you might never get, something to be longed for and prayed for, to starve for and steal for, almost—a job. There weren't any. When these two generations talk together and the word *job* is used, how will they understand each other? Suppose the issue is the draft—"A shame a fellow has to give up his job." To the elders this is arrant unpatriotic selfishness. To the young it is obvious sense. They find it strange that older people can see the sacrifice involved when married men with children must leave their families to go away in the defense service. Yet these same people don't see that any one should mind leaving a job. "Don't they know what a *job* means now, in the thinking of those born in 1915, 1916, 1917? Don't they know that just as among the ancients one was not a man until one had begotten a male child, so today one can't think of one's self as a full human being, without a job? We didn't say a guy wouldn't go because he had a job. We just said it was tough on him. We weren't saying anything they wouldn't say themselves about a man with kids. But gee—how they blew up!"[7]

The British and the Americans are still under the delusion that they speak the same language. With some qualifications this is true as far as denotations are concerned, though there are concepts like "sissy" in American for which there are no precise English equivalents. Connotations, however, are often importantly different, and this makes for the more misunderstanding because both languages are still called "English" (treating alike by words things that are different). An excellent illustration is again supplied by Margaret Mead:

. . . in Britain, the word "compromise" is a good word, and one may speak approvingly of any arrangement which has been a compromise, including, very often, one in which the other side has gained more than fifty per cent of the points at issue. On the other hand, in the United States, the minority position is still the position from which everyone speaks; the President *versus* Congress, Congress *versus* the President, the State government *versus* the metropolis and the metropolis *versus* the State government. This is congruent with the American doctrine of checks and balances, but it does not permit the word "compromise" to gain the same ethical halo which it has in Britain. Where, in Britain, to compromise means to work out a good solution, in America it usually means to work out a bad one, a solution in which all the points of importance (to both sides) are lost. Thus, in negotiations between the United States and Britain, all of which had, in the nature of the case, to be compromises, as two sovereignties were involved, the British could always speak approvingly and proudly of the result, while the Americans had to emphasize their losses.[8]

The words, then, that pass so readily from mouth to mouth are not entirely trustworthy substitutes for the facts of the physical world. The smooth-worn standard coins are slippery steppingstones from mind to mind. Nor is thinking simply a matter of choosing words to express thoughts. The selected words always mirror social situation as well as

[7] Margaret Mead, "When Were You Born," *Child Study* (Spring, 1941).
[8] *Ibid.*

objective fact. Two men go into a bar in New York and are overcharged for bad liquor: "This is a gyp joint." The same thing happens in Paris: "The French are a bunch of chiselers."

Perhaps the most important contribution of anthropological linguistics has come from the difficulties the anthropologist goes through in trying to express the meanings contained in speech structures completely foreign to the pattern of all European tongues. This study and this experience has forced upon the anthropologist a rather startling discovery which is fraught with meaning for a world where peoples speaking many different idioms are trying to communicate without distortion. Every language is something more than a vehicle for exchanging ideas and information — more even than a tool for self-expression and for letting off emotional steam or for getting other people to do what we want.

Every language is also a special way of looking at the world and interpreting experience. Concealed in the structure of each different language are a whole set of unconscious assumptions about the world and life in it. The anthropological linguist has come to realize that the general ideas one has about what happens in the world outside oneself are not altogether "given" by external events. Rather, up to a point, one sees and hears what the grammatical system of one's language has made one sensitive to, has trained one to look for in experience. This bias is the more insidious because everyone is so unconscious of his native language as a system. To one brought up to speak a certain language it is part of the very nature of things, remaining always in the class of background phenomena. It is as natural that experience should be organized and interpreted in these language-defined classes as it is that the seasons change. In fact the naïve view is that anyone who thinks in any other way is unnatural or stupid, or even vicious — and most certainly illogical.

In point of fact, traditional or Aristotelian logic has been mainly the analysis of consistencies in the structures of languages like Greek and Latin. The subject-predicate form of speech has implied a changeless world of fixed relations between "substances" and their "qualities." This view, as Korzybski[9] has insisted, is quite inadequate to modern

---

[9] Alfred Korzybski, foremost proponent of General Semantics, wrote *Science and Sanity: An Introduction to Non-Aristotelian Systems and General Semantics*, a difficult but significant book on language and human behavior. Korzybski's views have been popularized by S. I. Hayakawa, Stuart Chase, and others. [eds.]

physical knowledge which shows that the properties of an atom alter from instant to instant in accord with the shifting relationships of its component elements. The little word "is" has brought us much confusion because sometimes it signifies that the subject exists, sometimes that it is a member of a designated class, sometimes that subject and predicate are identical. Aristotelian logic teaches us that something is or isn't. Such a statement is often false to reality, for both-and is more often true than either-or. "Evil" ranges all the way from black through an infinite number of shades of gray. Actual experience does not present clear-cut entities like "good" and "bad," "mind" and "body"; the sharp split remains verbal. Modern physics has shown that even in the inanimate world there are many questions that cannot be answered by an unrestricted "yes" or an unqualified "no."

From the anthropological point of view there are as many different worlds upon the earth as there are languages. Each language is an instrument which guides people in observing, in reacting, in expressing themselves in a special way. The pie of experience can be sliced in many different ways, and language is the principal directive force in the background. You can't say in Chinese, "answer me yes or no," for there aren't words for yes and no. Chinese gives priority to "how?" and nonexclusive categories; European languages to "what?" and exclusive categories. In English we have both real plurals and imaginary plurals, "ten men" and "ten days"; in Hopi plurals and cardinal numbers may be used only for things that can be seen together as an objective group. The fundamental categories of the French verb are before and after (tense) and potentiality vs. actuality (mood); the fundamental categories of one American Indian language (Wintu) are subjectivity vs. objectivity, knowledge vs. belief, freedom vs. actual necessity.

In the Haida language of British Columbia there are more than twenty verbal prefixes that indicate whether an action was performed by carrying, shooting, hammering, pushing, pulling, floating, stamping, picking, chopping, or the like. Some languages have different verbs, adjectives, and pronouns for animate and inanimate things. In Melanesia there are as many as four variant forms for each possessive pronoun. One may be used for the speaker's body and mind, another for illegitimate relatives and his loincloth, a third his possessions and gifts. The underlying conceptual images of each language tend to constitute a coherent though unconscious philosophy.

Where in English one word, "rough," may equally well be used to describe a road, a rock, or the business surface of a file, the Navaho language finds a need for three different words which may not be used interchangeably. While the general tendency is for Navaho to make finer and more concrete distinctions, this is not inevitably the case. The same stem is used for rip, light beam, and echo, ideas which seem diverse to speakers of European languages. One word is used to designate a medicine bundle with all its contents, the skin quiver in which the contents are wrapped, the contents as a whole, and some of the distinct items. Sometimes the point is not that the images of Navahos are less fluid and more delimited but rather just that the external world is dissected along different lines. For example, the same Navaho word is used to describe both a pimply face and a nodule-covered rock. In English a complexion might be termed "rough" or "coarse," but a rock would never, except facetiously, be described as pimply. Navaho differentiates two types of rouch rock: the kind which is rough in the manner in which a file is rough and the kind which is nodule-encrusted. In these cases the differences between the Navaho and the English ways of seeing the world cannot be disposed of merely by saying that the Navaho language is more precise. The variations rest in the features which the two languages see as essential. Cases can indeed be given where the Navaho is notably less precise. Navaho gets along with a single word for flint, metal, knife, and certain other objects of metal. This, to be sure, is due to the historical accident that, after European contact, metal in general and knives in particular took the place of flint.

Navahos are perfectly satisfied with what seem to Europeans rather imprecise discriminations in the realm of time sequences. On the other hand, they are the fussiest people in the world about always making explicit in the forms of the language many distinctions which English makes only occasionally and vaguely. In English one says, "I eat," meaning, "I eat something." The Navaho point of view is different. If the object thought of is actually indefinite, then "something" must be tacked on to the verb.

The nature of their language forces the Navaho to notice and report many other distinctions in physical events which the nature of the English language allows speakers to neglect in most cases, even though their senses are just as capable as those of the Navaho to register the smaller details of what goes on in the external world. For example, suppose a Navaho range rider and a white supervisor see that a wire fence needs repair. The supervisor will probably write in his notebook, "Fence at such and such a place must be fixed." If the Navaho reports the break, he must choose between forms that indicate whether the damage was caused by some person or by a nonhuman agency, whether the fence was of one or several strands of wire.

In general, the difference between Navaho thought and English thought — both as manifested in the language and as forced by the very nature of the linguistic forms into such patterns — is that Navaho thought is ordinarily much more specific. The ideas expressed by the English verb "to go" provide a nice example. When a Navaho says that he went somewhere he never fails to specify whether it was afoot, astride, by wagon, auto, train, airplane, or boat. If it be a boat, it must be specified whether the boat floats off with the current, is propelled by the speaker, or is made to move by an indefinite or unstated agency. The speed of a horse (walk, trot, gallop, run) is expressed by the verb form chosen. He differentiates between starting to go, going along, arriving at, returning from a point. It is not, of course, that these distinctions *cannot* be made in English, but that they *are not* made consistently. They seem of importance to English speakers only under special circumstances.

A cross-cultural view of the category of time is highly instructive. Beginners in the study of classical Greek are often troubled by the fact that the word *opiso* sometimes means "behind," sometimes "in the future." Speakers of English find this baffling because they are accustomed to think of themselves as moving through time. The Greeks, however, conceived of themselves as stationary, of time as coming up behind them, overtaking them, and then, still moving on, becoming the "past" that lay before their eyes.

Present European languages emphasize time distinctions. The tense systems are usually thought of as the most basic of verbal inflections. However, this was not always so. Streitberg says that in primitive Indo-European a special indicator for the present was usually lacking. In many languages, certainly, time distinctions are only irregularly present or are of distinctly secondary importance. In Hopi the first question answered by the verb form is that of the type of information conveyed by the assertion. Is a situation reported as actuality, as anticipated, or as a general truth? In the anticipatory form there is no necessary distinction between past, present, and future. The English translation must choose from context between "was about to run," "is about to run," and "will run." The Wintu language of California carries this stress upon implications of validity much farther. The sentence "Harry is chopping wood" must be translated in five different ways, depending upon whether the speaker knows this by hearsay, by direct observation, or by inference of three degrees of plausibility.

In no language are the whole of a sense experience and all possible interpretations of it expressed. What people think and feel and how they report what they think and feel are determined, to be sure, by their personal history, and by what actually happens in the outside world. But they are also determined by a factor which is often over-looked; namely, the pattern of linguistic habits which people acquire as members of a particular society. It makes a difference whether or not a language is rich in metaphors and conventional imagery.

Our imaginations are restricted in some directions, free in others. The linguistic particularization of detail along one line will mean the neglect of other aspects of the situation. Our thoughts are directed in one way if we speak a language where all objects are classified according to sex, in another if the classification is by social position or the form of the object. Grammars are devices for expressing relations. It makes a difference what is treated as object, as attribute, as state, as act. In Hopi, ideas referring to the seasons are not grouped with what we call nouns but rather with what we call adverbs. Because of our grammar it is easy to personify summer, to think of it as a thing or a state.

Even as between closely related tongues, the conceptual picture may be different. Let us take one final example from Margaret Mead:

Americans tend to arrange objects on a single scale of value, from best to worst, biggest to smallest, cheapest to most expensive, etc., and are able to express a preference among very complex objects on such a single scale. The question, "What is your favorite color?" so intelligible to an American, is meaningless in Britain, and such a question is countered by: "Favorite color for what? A flower? A necktie?" Each object is thought of as having a most complex set of qualities, and color is merely a quality of an object, not some-thing from a color chart on which one can make a choice which is transferable to a large number of different sorts of objects. The American reduction of complexities to single scales is entirely comprehensible in terms of the great diversity of value systems which different immigrant groups brought to the American scene. Some common denominator among the incommensurables was very much needed, and over-simplification was almost inevitable. But, as a result, Americans think in terms of qualities which have uni-dimensional scales, while the British, when they think of a complex object or event, even if they reduce it to parts, think of each part as retaining all of the complexities of the whole. Americans subdivide the scale; the British subdivide the object.[10]

Language and its changes cannot be understood unless linguistic

[10] Margaret Mead, "The Application of Anthropological Techniques to Cross-National Communication," *Transactions of the New York Academy of Sciences* (February, 1947).

behavior is related to other behavioral facts. Conversely, one can gain many subtle insights into those national habits and thought ways of which one is ordinarily unconscious by looking closely at special idioms and turns of speech in one's own and other languages. What a Russian says to an American doesn't really get across just from shuffling words — much is twisted or blunted or lost unless the American knows something about Russia and Russian life, a good deal more than the sheer linguistic skill needed for a formally correct translation. The American must indeed have gained some entrance to that foreign world of values and significances which are pointed up by the emphases of the Russian vocabulary, crystalized in the forms of Russian grammar, implicit in the little distinctions of meaning in the Russian language.

Any language is more than an instrument for conveying ideas, more even than an instrument for working upon the feelings of others and for self-expression. Every language is also a means of categorizing experience. The events of the "real" world are never felt or reported as a machine would do it. There is a selection process and an interpretation in the very act of response. Some features of the external situation are highlighted; others are ignored or not fully discriminated.

Every people has its own characteristic classes in which individuals pigeonhole their experiences. These classes are established primarily by the language through the types of objects, processes, or qualities which receive special emphasis in the vocabulary and equally, though more subtly, through the types of differentiation or activity which are distinguished in grammatical forms. The language says, as it were, "notice this," "always consider this separate from that," "such and such things belong together." Since persons are trained from infancy to respond in these ways, they take such discriminations for granted as part of the inescapable stuff of life. When we see two peoples with different social traditions respond in different ways to what appear to the outsider to be identical stimulus situations, we realize that experience is much less an objective absolute than we thought. Every language has an effect upon what the people who use it see, what they feel, how they think, what they can talk about.

"Common sense" holds that different languages are parallel methods for expressing the same "thoughts." "Common sense," however, itself implies talking so as to be readily understood by one's fellows — in the same culture. Anglo-American "common sense" is actually very sophisticated, deriving from Aristotle and the speculations of scholastic and modern philosophers. The fact that all sorts of basic philosophic questions are begged in the most cavalier fashion is obscured by the conspiracy of silent acceptance which always attends the system of conventional understandings that we call culture.

The lack of true equivalences between any two languages is merely the outward expression of inward differences between two peoples in premises, in basic categories, in the training of fundamental sensitivities, and in general view of the world. The way the Russians put their thoughts together shows the impress of linguistic habits, of characteristic ways of organizing experience, for

Human beings do not live in the objective world alone, nor alone in the world of social activity as ordinarily understood, but are very much at the mercy of the particular language which has become the medium of expression for their society. It is quite an illusion to imagine that one adjusts to reality essentially without the use of language and that language is merely an incidental means of solving specific problems of communication or reflection. The fact of the matter is that the 'real world' is to a large extent unconsciously built up on the language habits of the group. . . . We see and hear and otherwise experience very largely as we do because the language habits of our community predispose certain choices of interpretation.[11]

—Edward Sapir

A language is, in a sense, a philosophy.

SUGGESTED ASSIGNMENTS

1. Kluckhohn informs us that different languages divide the perceptual world in different ways. The way "you," the person spoken to, is handled is a convenient example. In English we have one word *you* which serves as singular and plural and as subject and object. But in some other languages, e.g., French, Italian, Spanish, Dutch, German, Russian, there are three, four and more forms to express "you," and these forms can express subtle shades of meaning and attitude. If you are acquainted with such a language, write a comparative description of the use of "you" in that language and in English. Include in your paper an evaluation of the two systems.
2. English once had four forms for "you" where we now have only one word in ordinary English. Look this matter up in *The Development of Modern English* by Stuart Robertson and Frederic Cassidy, pp. 125–126. Then find examples of all four forms in the King James version of the *Bible*.

[11] Edward Sapir, "Language," *Encyclopedia of the Social Sciences*, vol. ix (New York, The Macmillan Company, 1933).

Write a short theme in which you explain and illustrate the Elizabethan uses of "you." If you wish to go a little further with this subject, turn to *A Shakespearean Grammar* by E. A. Abbott, p. 153 ff., to discover some of the shades of meaning expressed by these pronouns. For an extended paper using a primary source, you might read a play by Shakespeare, say *Romeo and Juliet*, and discuss Shakespeare's use and confusion of the pronouns, correlating the choice of *thou-thee* and *ye-you* with the attitudes of the characters.

3. Under what circumstances are *thou* and *thee* still used in present-day English?

4. How do you account for the development of such forms as "you-all" and "yous"?

5. In English we have the forms *whither, where,* and *whence* to express the meanings "to where," "where," and "from where," but only *where* is in common use. In some languages, notably German, separate words are regularly used for these meanings. Can you think of cases in which English is less precise for having abandoned *whither* and *whence?* What would you say about the parallel cases of *hither, here, hence* and *thither, there, thence?*

6. Languages divide the world of family relatives in various ways. For example, French has separate masculine and feminine words, *le cousin* and *la cousin,* for our single *cousin;* and for our *uncle* Latin has two separate words, *avunculus* for a mother's brother and *patruus* for a father's brother. Do you think we are handicapped in expression by not having the distinctions of French and Latin?

7. When white light is passed through a prism or other diffracting medium it produces a spectrum, a series of colors shading from red to violet. Undoubtedly all people of normal vision are able to perceive variations of color produced in this way, but they do not necessarily make their divisions at the same places in the scale. In English the color names most frequently used are *red, orange, yellow, green, blue, purple, pink,* and *brown.* Look up the following references and write a short paper on how colors are categorized in other languages: Harry Hoijer, "The Relation of Language to Culture," in *Anthropology Today,* edited by A. L. Kroeber, pp. 558–559; Willis D. Wallis, *An Introduction to Anthropology,* pp. 420–421; and Lucien Lévy-Bruhl, *How Natives Think,* p. 171.

8. The vocabulary of a language is an index of items culturally important to the people speaking that language. Snow and ice play an important part in the lives of the Eskimos and the Lapps; consequently there are many specific words for snow and ice in various forms in the languages of these people. The Eskimos have separate words for snow on the ground, falling snow, drifting snow, melting snow, and so on. Lévy-Bruhl reports that the Lapps have 20 words for ice, 11 for cold, 41 for snow, and 26 verbs to express freezing and thawing. To most of us snow, no matter what its con-

dition, is *snow*. We have at least one group, however, to whom snow is important enough to warrant specialized terminology. Interview a skier, or consult a book on skiing, and make a list of words referring to different snow conditions.

FURTHER READINGS

Abbott, E. A. *A Shakespearean Grammar*. London: Macmillan and Co., 1878.

Bloomfield, Leonard. *Language*. New York: Holt, Rinehart and Winston, Inc., 1933. On meaning, see Chapters 2 and 9.

Brown, Roger. *Words and Things*. New York: The Free Press of Glencoe, Inc., 1958. On the origin of speech, see pp. 131–136; on animal "languages," pp. 155–172; on the *Weltanschauung* theory, pp. 229–263.

Carroll, John B. *The Study of Language*. Cambridge: Harvard University Press, 1953. For a definition of language and a discussion of the work of linguistic scientists, see pp. 7–15; on the *Weltanschauung* theory, see pp. 43–48.

Gleason, H. A., Jr. *An Introduction to Descriptive Linguistics*. New York: Holt, Rinehart and Winston, Inc., 1955, 1961. On language, see Chapter 1.

Gode, Alexander, and Hugh E. Blair. *Interlingua: A Grammar of the International Language*. New York: Storm Publishers, 1951.

Guérard, Albert Léon. *A Short History of the International Language Movement*. New York: Liveright Publishing Corp., 1922.

Hayakawa, S. I. *Language in Thought and Action*. New York: Harcourt, Brace & World, Inc., 1949. On the uses of language, see Chapters 5–7.

Hoijer, Harry. "The Relation of Language to Culture," in *Anthropology Today*, edited by A. L. Kroeber. Chicago: University of Chicago Press, 1953.

Jespersen, Otto. *Language, Its Nature, Development and Origin*. New York: The Macmillan Company, 1922. On the origin of speech, see Chapter 21.

Lee, Irving J. *Language Habits in Human Affairs*. New York: Harper & Row, Publishers, 1941. On meaning, see pp. 29–51.

Lévy-Bruhl, Lucien. *How Natives Think*. New York: Alfred A. Knopf, Inc., 1925.

Lorenz, Konrad. *King Solomon's Ring*. New York: Thomas Y. Crowell Company, 1952.

Robertson, Stuart, and Frederic G. Cassidy. *The Development of Modern English*, 2d ed. Englewood Cliffs, New Jersey: Prentice-Hall, Inc., 1954.

Sturtevant, Edgar H. *Linguistic Science*. New Haven: Yale University Press, 1947. On the origin of speech, see Chapter 5.

Von Frisch, Karl. *Bees, Their Vision, Chemical Senses, and Language*. Ithaca, New York: Cornell University Press, 1950.

Wallis, Willis D. *An Introduction to Anthropology*. New York: Harper & Row, Publishers, 1926.

Whatmough, Joshua. *Language, A Modern Synthesis*. New York: St. Martin's Press, Inc., 1956. On the uses of language, see Chapter 6.

2

LANGUAGE HISTORY

English: Its Origin and Relation to Other Languages

HENRY ALEXANDER

Languages, like people, have relatives, close and distant. Dutch, for example, is a close relative to English while Danish is more distant, and Greek still more distant. The position of English in its own family of languages, Indo-European, and its development in England are the subjects of the simple sketch which follows. Dr. Henry Alexander is an outstanding Canadian linguist and was, before his retirement, a professor of English at Queen's University, Kingston, Ontario.

In tracing the history of English it is convenient to distinguish three different periods. First, there is the earliest age, from the arrival of the English in Britain down to about 1100. This is usually called the Old English (O.E.) or Anglo-Saxon period. From 1100 to about 1500 we have Middle English (M.E.). Finally there is Modern English (Mod. E.) from 1500 to the present day. Although the migration of the English people from the Continent of Europe took place mainly in the fifth and sixth centuries, we have very few records of anything written in English before about the year 700, after which we find an unbroken sequence of documents from which the nature of the language can be seen. If we take 700 as our starting-point, and 1900, which is close

From *The Story of Our Language* by Henry Alexander. Reprinted by permission of the author, publisher, copyright 1940. Published by Thomas Nelson & Sons, Ltd.

enough to the present day, as our final date, we get a convenient division into three periods of 400 years each.

O.E.   700–1100
M.E.   1100–1500
Mod. E.   1500–1900

The outstanding literary work of the O.E. period is the epic poem *Beowulf*, written about 700; the most important M.E. work is the poetry of Chaucer, who died in 1400; while in Mod. E., starting with Spenser and Shakespeare in the sixteenth century, there is a continuous series of great writers down to our own day.

We must not imagine the change from one of these periods to the next as abrupt and sudden, that on a certain day or week people stopped speaking Old English and started to speak Middle English. The process was rather like passing from one county to another when traveling; there is little at any one moment to show the change, but after a time one finds oneself in a new region. The evolution of the language was always gradual and just as imperceptible as it is at the present day; in any age there must have been considerable overlapping between old and new, the older generation, more conservative, retaining the earlier forms of speech, the younger adopting innovations. Even in the work of an individual writer we can often find a mixture of old and new forms. It must also be borne in mind that these changes were largely unconscious; they were not due to any deliberate effort on the part of the speaker.

English is not the original language of England but, like the English people themselves, came over from the continent of Europe. We cannot say what was the first language in England; that lies far back in the mists of prehistory. But we do know that, before the arrival of the English people and their language, there had existed for several centuries a tongue belonging to quite a different family of languages, the Celtic group. This was spoken by the ancient Britons. During the Roman occupation of Britain (43–410) Latin must also have been widely used. Both these earlier languages have left some traces on Old English. It was not until the middle of the fifth century, when the invading Teutonic tribes from the continent began to conquer the Britons and to impose on the country their own speech and social organization, that the history of the English language in England began. It had of course a long previous history on the continent, but to consider this would take us too far afield.

These continental tribes came from different parts of Northern Europe. Their exact origin is still an unsolved problem. With regard to two branches — the Angles and the Saxons — the historians are fairly well agreed; they came from a region around what is now Northern Germany. But in addition there was a third tribe, whose original home is less certain. These were the Jutes, who, according to the traditional view, migrated from Jutland, the northern part of Denmark; many modern historians, however, do not accept this explanation, which is based largely on the resemblance of the two names, Jutes and Jutland. The Angles settled mainly in the north and central portions of England and gave their name both to the country and its language; the Saxons settled mainly in the south; the Jutes in Kent, the south-eastern corner of England, and in the Isle of Wight. Mingled with these three main races there may well have been representatives of several other tribes, such as the Frisians, who inhabited what is now part of Holland, and even possibly the Franks. Because of this mixed strain in the English people the term Anglo-Saxon is not quite accurate. To use Anglo-Saxon-Jute . . . etc. would be awkward; so the modern practice is to employ Old English to indicate this early stage of our language. This also has the advantage of being parallel to Middle English and Modern English and to the terminology applied to other languages, e.g. Old, Middle and Modern French. It also suggests the continuity of our language from its earliest stages. The Old English writers themselves used the term *englisc* or *engliscgereord*, "the English language." The use of "Anglo-Saxon" to indicate the English people and their language prior to the Norman Conquest arose at a relatively late period, in the 16th century.

We will now indicate how English is related to other languages. One of the far-reaching discoveries of the 19th century was that many languages show important resemblances in their structure, and that these features are to be explained, not by a process of borrowing but by descent from a common ancestor. Languages are like plants or animals, which may differ considerably today but may still exhibit certain characteristics pointing to a common origin or parent stock. By grouping together those which show these similarities we are able to draw up various genera, families and classes. Languages, too, may be divided into families. To indicate a common descent for a group of languages or a group of words we use the term *cognate*. Some idea of the evidence on which these relationships are based may be obtained from the following facts.

Let us make a list of some common terms in several European languages and compare their appearance. We may take the first four numbers and the closest family relationships; many striking resemblances will emerge, which cannot be accidental.

English	German	Dutch	Swedish	Danish
one	ein	een	en	een
two	zwei	twee	två	to
	(German *z* = *ts*)			
three	drei	drie	tre	tre
four	vier	vier	fyra	fire
	(German *v* = *f*)			
father	vater (*v* = *f*)	vader	fader	fader
mother	mutter	moeder	moder	moder
brother	bruder	broeder	broder	broder
sister	schwester	zuster	syster	søster

Notice also the pattern of the verbs:

	English	German	Dutch	Swedish	Danish
Infinitive	sing	singen	zingen	sjunga	synge
Past Tense	sang	sang	zong	sjöng	sang
Past Participle	sung	gesungen	gezongen	sjungit	sungen
	(O.E. gesungen)				
	fish	fischen	visschen	fiska	fiske
	fished (*-ed* pron. *t*)	fischte	vischte	fiskade	fiskede
	fished ” ” ”	gefischt	gevischt	fiskat	fisket

These and other similarities of an equally fundamental nature point to a common ancestry for this group of languages. They are called the Teutonic or Germanic group and are usually divided into three sub-groups, North Teutonic, East Teutonic and West Teutonic. All these are descended from one parent language, which is called Primitive Teutonic. The relationship can best be shown by the following table, which includes only the more important languages.

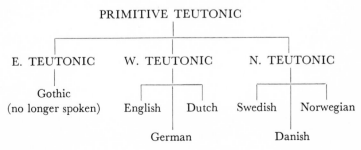

PRIMITIVE TEUTONIC

E. TEUTONIC   W. TEUTONIC   N. TEUTONIC

Gothic
(no longer spoken)   English   Dutch   Swedish   Norwegian

German   Danish

This, however, is not the whole story. If we go a stage further and compare this Teutonic group with non-Teutonic languages, we discover equally remarkable resemblances. Taking some of the words used before, let us compare their forms in English, representing a Teutonic language, with those found in Latin or Greek, which belong to two different branches, the Italic and the Hellenic respectively. We might also include French, which is a modern development from Latin, just as Modern English is from Old English.

English	Latin	French	Greek
one	unus	un	cf. oinos
			one (on dice)
two	duo	deux	duo
three	tres	trois	treis
father	pater	père	pater
mother	mater	mère	meter
brother	frater	frère	phrater

The resemblances are not so close as before, but they are too great to be merely accidental. A similar comparison with other languages, such as the Celtic group, would reveal more features in common. As a result of this evidence we can now draw up a more complete table to show the relationship between these larger linguistic units, the Teutonic, Italic, Hellenic, Celtic and other groups. There are altogether nine of these,[1] and they include most of the European and some of the Indian languages. For this reason they are often called the Indo-European family of languages. Another term is the Aryan family. Aryan is thus not a racial but a linguistic label. The people who speak the Aryan or Indo-European languages are not a racial unit; they include, and no doubt always included, many varied stocks. It is difficult to say when or where the parent language from which these groups are descended — primitive Aryan or Indo-European — was originally spoken, except that it was some time before 2000 B.C., possibly 3000 or 4000 B.C. Scholars formerly thought that the original home of this ancestral tongue was somewhere in Asia, but the modern view is that it was more probably in Northern or Central Europe.

The accompanying diagram shows the relationship of English to the Indo-European family. Again, only the more important languages and groups have been included — the table is considerably reduced and simplified; only six of the nine (or eleven) branches are shown.

[1] Or eleven, if we include the results of recent discoveries.

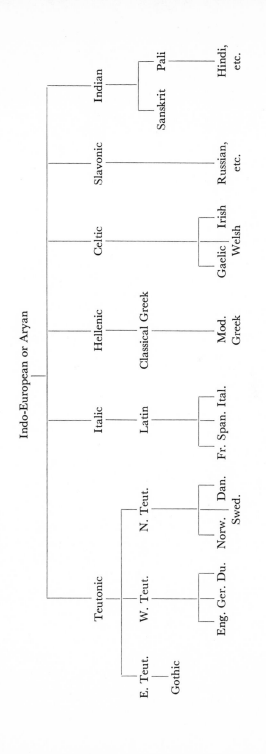

A glance at this genealogical table will show that the nearest relatives of English are German and Dutch; the Scandinavian languages are also very close, in some respects actually closer. Rather more distant are Greek and Latin (with its modern descendants French, Spanish and Italian) and the Celtic languages, including the language of the ancient Britons, and modern Celtic forms of speech, such as the Gaelic still spoken in the Highlands of Scotland and in parts of Canada, especially Nova Scotia, the recently revived Irish language of Eire, and the Cymric of Wales.

Outside the Indo-European family and, as far as we know, quite unrelated to it, are many other groups of languages, for instance, the Semitic group to which Hebrew and Arabic belong, another group which includes Chinese, and several besides these. Although they have attained a dominating position because of the political power and prestige of the nations who use them, the Indo-European languages thus constitute only a fraction of the world's total linguistic resources. They may not always maintain that supremacy.

Before leaving this part of the subject it should perhaps be explained that, even if we succeed in tracing languages back to the Indo-European parent-tongue and in reconstructing this primitive form of speech, we are nowhere near the stage at which language actually originated. Primitive Indo-European was a highly developed and complex instrument; for long ages before its appearance man or sub-man must have been articulate. The development of speech is perhaps the most important advance in the history of mankind. There has been much speculation as to how this means of communication was evolved. It is a mystery that may never be solved, as we have so little evidence to guide us. But several theories have been proposed, generally referred to rather disrespectfully by various nicknames. First, there is the "bow-wow" theory, which, as its name suggests, supposes that words were first made from the noises associated with natural objects: the bark of a dog, the noise of the wind, and similar sounds actually became the names of the dog and the wind. This theory has obvious weaknesses; it would at best account for only a limited number of words, as many objects do not make characteristic noises. Then there is the "ding-dong" theory, according to which man reacted to the presence of various external phenomena by making specific noises, just as a bell makes its "ding-dong" under the impact of an outside force. A somewhat similar explanation has been labelled the "pooh-pooh" theory; this attempts to explain words as originally spontaneous exclamations like our modern *Oh!*, *Ouch!*, etc. A more systematic attempt to explain the origin of language has been made by Jespersen, who comes to the conclusion, based on three different lines of enquiry, that language originated in the emotional, song-like outpourings of primitive man, which were gradually canalized into speech. This may be called the "hey nonny nonny!" theory. A later theory has been suggested by Paget. According to this, speech started not as sound but as gestures made by the hands. Then, after a considerable time, when man, in the course of his evolution, had to work so continuously with his hands that they could no longer be used for gesticulating, he carried out the same movements with his tongue inside his mouth; this series of tongue positions, acting on the air which is being inhaled and exhaled, would naturally give rise to definite sounds, which would then replace the original gesture and convey the same meaning. This theory is interesting but not quite convincing. It is obvious that all these explanations are highly speculative; possibly there is no need to assume any *one* way in which language originated; it may have been due to a combination of some of these processes, and perhaps others that have not yet been considered.

SUGGESTED ASSIGNMENTS

1. The three versions below of the first thirteen verses from the seventh chapter of *The Gospel According to St. Matthew* are examples of our language as it appeared in the Old English, Middle English, and Early Modern English periods. The O.E. text (ca. A.D. 995) shows how our language looked a millenium ago. Although you will recognize a few words, this is essentially a foreign language to the reader of today. The M.E. text (ca. 1389) is from Wycliffe's *New Testament*. Here the language is beginning to look familiar, and you can read it without much trouble. The third example represents Early Mod. English. It is from Tyndale's translation of the *New Testament*, printed in 1525 or 1526, which influenced greatly the King James Version of 1611. This is our own modern English, save for occasional differences in grammar, spelling, sound, and meaning.

Old English:

† CHAP VII. 1 Nellen ge déman, dæt ge ne sýn fordémede;

2 Wítodlíce đam ylcan dóme đe ge démaþ, eow biþ gedémed, and on đam ylcan gemete đe ge metaþ, eow byþ gemeten.

3 To hwí gesihst đú đæt mot on đínes bróđor égan, and đú ne gesyhst đone beam on đínum ágenum eagan?

4   Oðđe húmeta cwyst ðú to ðínum bréðer, Bróđur, þafa ðæt ic út-ádó ðæt mot of ðínum eagan, đonne se beam biþ on ðínum ágenum eagan?

5   Lá ðú líccetere, ádó ǽrest út đone beam of ðínum ágenum eagan, and beháwa đonne ðæt ðú út-ádó ðæt mot of ðínes bróđur eagan.

6   Nellen ge syllan ðæt hálige húndum, ne ge ne wurpen eowre mere-grotu tofóran eowrum swýnon, đe-læs hig mid hyra fótum hig fortredon, and hig đonne ongean gewende eow toslýton.†

7   Biddaþ, and eow biþ geseald; séceaþ, and ge hit fíndaþ; enuciaþ, and eow biþ ontýned.

8   Wítodlíce ǽlc ðæra đe bit, he onfehþ; and se đe séeþ, he hyt fínt; and đam cnuciendum biþ ontýned.

9   Hwylc man is of eow, gyf his sunu hyne bit hláfes, sylst ðú him stán?

10   Oðđe gyf he bytt fisces, sylst ðú him næddran?

11   Eornustlíce nú ge, đe yfele synt, cunnun góde sylena eowrum bearnum syllan, mycle má eower fæder đe on heofenum ys syleþ gód đam đe hyne biddaþ?

12   Eornustlíce ealle đa þing, đe ge wyllen ðæt men eow dón, dóþ ge him ðæt sylfe, ðæt ys sóþlíce ǽ and wítegena bebod.

13   Gangaþ inn þurh ðæt nearwe geat; forðon đe ðæt geat is swýđe wíd, and se weg is swíđe rúm đe to forspillednesse gelǽt, and swýđe manega synt đe þurh đone weg faraþ.

Wycliffe:

CHAP. VII.   1   Nyle ȝe deme, that ȝe be nat demyd;

2   For in what dome ȝe demen, ȝe shulen ben demyd, and in what mesure ȝe meten, it shal be meten to ȝou.

3   But what seest thou a festu in the eiȝe of thi brother, and thou seest nat a beme in thin owne eiȝe?

4   Or what maner saist thou to thi brother, Brother, suffre that I caste out a festu fro thin eiȝe, and loo! a beme is in thin owne eiȝe?

5   Ypocrite, cast out first a beme of thin eiȝe, and than thou shalt see for to cast out a festu of the eiȝe of thi brother.

6   Nyl ȝe ȝeue holy thing to houndis, nether sende ȝe ȝour margaritis before swyne, lest perauenture thei defoulen hem with theire feet, and lest *houndis* turned to gidre al to-breke ȝou.

7   Axe ȝe, and it shal be ȝouen to ȝou; seke ȝe, and ȝe shulen fynde; knocke ȝe, and it shal be opnyd to ȝou.

8   For eche that axith, takith; and he that sechith, fyndith; and it shal be opnyde to a man knokynge.

9   Other who ofȝou is a man, whom ȝif his sone axe breed, wher he shal dresse to hym a stoon?

10   Other ʒif he shal axe a fishe, wher he shal dresse to hym a serpent?

11   Therfore ʒif ʒe, when ʒe ben yuel men, han knowen for to ʒeue good thingus ʒouen to ʒoure sonys, hou myche more ʒoure fadir that is in heuenes shal ʒeue good thingis to men axinge hym?

12   Therfore alle thingis, what euer thingis ʒee wolen that men don to ʒou, and ʒe do to hem, forsothe these thingis *ben* the lawe and prophetis.

13   Entre ʒe bi the streyt ʒate; for the gate that ledith to perdicioun is brode, and the weye large, and ther ben many that entren bi it.

Tyndale:

CHAP. VII.   1 Iudge not, lest ye be iudged;

2   For as ye iudge, so shall ye be iudged, and with what mesur ye mete, with the same shall it be mesurd to you agayne.

3   Why seist thou a moote in thy brothers eye, and percevest not the beame that ys in thyne awne eye?

4   Or why sayest thou to thy brother, Suffre me to plucke oute a moote oute off thyne eye, and behold! a beame is in thyne awne eye?

5   Ypocryte, first cast oute the beame oute of thyne awne eye, and then shalte thou se clearly to plucke oute the moote oute off thy brothers eye.

6   Geve not that which is holy to dogges, nether cast ye youre pearles before swyne, lest they treade them vnder their fete, and the other tourne agayne and all to rent you.

7   Axe, and it shalbe geven you; seke, and ye shall fynd; knocke, and it shalbe opened vnto you.

8   For whosoever axeth, receaveth; and he that seketh, fyndeth; and to hym that knocketh it shalbe opened.

9   Ys there eny man among you, which wolde proffer his sonne a stone, if he axed him breed?

10   Or if he axed fysshe, wolde he proffer hyme a serpent?

11   Yff ye then, whiche are evyll, cann geve to youre chyldren good gyftes, howe moche moore shall youre father which ys in heven geve good thynges to them that axe off hym?

12   Therfore, whatsoever ye wolde that men shulde do to you, even so do ye to them, this ys the lawe and the prophettes.

13   Enter in at the strayte gate; ffor wyde is the gate; and broade ys the waye thatt leadeth to destruccion, and many there be which goo yn there att.

Now we shall examine these passages to note how a few particulars of grammar and meaning in the language of former days differ from those of today.

a. What was the M.E. plural form of *shall* (Wycliffe, verses 2 and 7)? Did this form survive into Early Modern (Cf. Tyndale)? What was the M.E. plural form of *will* (Wycliffe, verse 12)? The M.E. singular form was both *wil* and *wol*. How do you explain the vowel in "I won't"?

b. In what respect was the use of *thy* and *thine* like that of *a* and *an* today (Wycliffe, verse 3)? Had this usage changed by Tyndale's time?

c. In Wycliffe, verse 6, identify the objective form of *they*. No, this is not a misprint. This form has since been regularized to make it fit into the paradigm of they, their, ———. All three are not from O.E. but were borrowed from Old Norse, whereas *hem* in this passage is a surviving O.E. form.

d. *Ye* and *you* are plural forms. Each is restricted to its own grammatical situations in the sentence. Using both Wycliffe and Tyndale as your data, formulate a statement of the uses of these two pronouns. If *you* was a plural, objective form in the sixteenth and early seventeenth centuries, how can we justify its use today as a singular, nominative form?

e. Today the plural of *is* is *are*. What was it in Wycliffe and Tyndale (verse 13)?

f. Today we use the inflectional ending *-s* for the third-person present singular of the verb, as in "He asks." What was Tyndale's ending in this situation (verse 8)? By Shakespeare's time, the *-s* ending had come into London English, and we find both in the plays of the Bard, as in

> Who want*eth* food and will not say he want*s* it?
>
> *Pericles*

What advantage was the presence of these two forms to a poet who wrote in meter?

g. What did *deem* and *doom* mean in Wycliffe, verse 2? Which one has undergone a change of meaning since that time?

h. In Wycliffe, verse 6, the word *houndis* is used to express the general meaning of *dogs*. Today the meaning of *hounds* has been narrowed to denote particular breeds of dogs. What does Simeon Potter in "Etymology and Meaning" call this kind of meaning change? This kind of change is active in contemporary English, as in "They say he *drinks*" and "He told a *suggestive* story." Show how *smell, operate,* and *colored person* illustrate this change.

The questions in the first six subdivisions above illustrate the concept that grammar is a description of usage and that as usage changes, grammar must change.

2. Here is a descriptive writing assignment. Choose one act of a Shakespearean play you have studied. Then write a report of the grammatical forms you

find there that are no longer used. Do not present merely a list of forms; organize your findings into a coherent theme. Or, write a similar theme on the vocabulary. Here you might organize your theme around categories like these: obsolete words; words whose meaning has changed; words for things that no longer exist; neologisms that Shakespeare was one of the first to use (consult the Oxford English Dictionary for these); puns.

Early American Speech: Adoptions from Foreign Tongues

THOMAS PYLES

The English language is one of the great word-borrowers in history. About one-half of our word stock has been borrowed into English from Latin and its Romance descendants, and in the Renaissance alone words were adopted into English from more than fifty languages. This process did not stop when the English language was brought to our shores, and in the selection below Thomas Pyles describes how our early settlers took over the words they needed from the tongues with which they came in contact. Mr. Pyles is Professor of English at the University of Florida and is the author of *The Origin and Development of the English Language*.

Before there was any permanent settlement of English-speaking folk in this land, a number of Indian words had made their way into the language of England by way of Spanish or Portuguese — words from Nahuatl, the tongue of the Aztecs, who were the most highly advanced of the Indians that the Spanish found in Mexico, as well as from various Indian dialects spoken in Central and South America and the West Indies. Some of these words came in time to be current in all the languages of Europe.

The English language in those exuberant days of Elizabeth, of

From *Words and Ways of American English*, by Thomas Pyles. Copyright 1952 by Random House, Inc. Reprinted by permission.

Raleigh, Drake, Hawkins, Bacon, Marlowe, Jonson, and Shakespeare, had been particularly receptive to augmentations of its already rich word stock from foreign sources — the so-called "inkhorn" terms from the classical languages, along with words from French, Spanish, Italian, and Portuguese. Words from the New World must have had all the charm of lush exoticisms in a period when the language was being enriched from so many nearby Continental sources, though they seem for the most part commonplace enough today — words like *potato*, *tomato*, *chocolate*, *cocoa*, *canoe*, *cannibal*, *barbecue*, *maize*, and *savannah*, which must have been known to the first Englishmen to come to these shores with any intention of staying. One of them, *maize*, was by a strange perversity of linguistic fate to be replaced by *corn* in the English of America. The British use *corn* in the sense "wheat," while retaining the older meaning of "grain," as in the "Corn Laws." Another of them, *cannibal*, a modification of *Caribal* "Caribbean native," was used in slightly different form by Shakespeare in his play about the "vexed Bermoothes," for *Caliban*, if not simply a metathesized[1] form of *can(n)ibal*, is a variant of *Cariban*, itself a variant of *Caribal*. *Barbecue*, while appearing first in British English, is nevertheless much more familiar in America, and its use to designate an outdoor social or political meeting at which animals are roasted whole is exclusively American. But these words, while native to the New World, must be distinguished from those which entered the language of Englishmen who chose or were forced to transplant themselves permanently in this strange and savage land.

The colonizers of this country were confronted with a land whose topography, meteorological phenomena, trees, plants, birds, and animals were frequently quite different from what they had known in England. Inasmuch as an understanding of the principles of semantics is not congenital, people generally are wont to ask when they see some new object, "What is it?" and expect in answer to be told its name, supposing then that they have learned something really significant about it. This procedure, or something very similar to it, must have been gone through a great many times in the early days of the colonization of America when Indians were friendly enough to be asked and bright enough to divine what was being asked of them. Sometimes, too, these first white Americans made up their own names for what they saw, if there was no one to tell them the "true" names or if the "true" names were too difficult for them to pronounce. . . . They frequently

---

[1] Metathesis is a transposition of sounds (or letters), as in *aksed* for *asked*. [eds.]

combined or modified English words, as in *bullfrog* and *jimson weed* (originally *Jamestown weed*); sometimes they made use of sound alone, as in *bobolink*.

The situation with regard to the American Indian languages, with many tribes speaking apparently unrelated languages which are in turn subdivided into dialects, is extremely complex. Fortunately it need not concern us here, for to American English only one stock, the Algonquian, is important. This huge group of tribes, comprising among others the Arapaho, Blackfoot, Cheyenne, Cree, Delaware, Fox, Micmac, Ojibwa (Chippewa), and Penobscot, formerly occupied a larger area than any other North American Indian stock. It was they whom the first English settlers in Virginia and Massachusetts came in contact with.

As early as 1608 Captain John Smith in his *True Relation of . . . Virginia Since the First Planting of That Collony* recorded *raccoon*, though he did not spell it that way. He wrote it in various ways — for instance, *raugroughcun* and later, in his *General Historie of Virginia, New-England and the Summer Isles* of 1624, *rarowcun* — in his effort to reduce to symbols, which were, incidentally, ill-adapted to that purpose, what he heard or thought he heard from the Indians. It is highly unlikely, as a matter of fact, that a single English word of Indian origin would be immediately intelligible to an Indian today, for words have been clipped, like *squash* (the vegetable), which was originally *askutasquash*, folk-etymologized[2] like *whiskey-John* "blue jay" from *wisketjan*, or in one way or another made to conform to English speechways.

Early Indian loan words naming creatures neglected by Adam are *opossum*, *moose*, *skunk*, *menhaden*, *terrapin*, *woodchuck*, and *caribou*. *Opossum* usually occurs in speech and often in writing in an aphetic form as *possum*, as does *raccoon* as *coon*. *Woodchuck* is a folk-etymologizing of Cree or Ojibwa *otchek* or *odjik*. Noah Webster was quite proud, by the way, of deriving *woodchuck* from an Avestan word meaning "pig" and made frequent reference to this acute etymological discovery in lectures and prefaces. *Caribou*, as the spelling of its final syllable indicates, comes to us by way of Canadian French; an Englishman would have been more likely to write *cariboo*. These words, all of Algonquian origin, designate creatures indigenous to North America. Ojibwa

---

[2] Folk etymology is a change in the form of a word that is new or strange to a speaker to make it conform to a familiar word. For example, *Welsh rabbit* (melted cheese over toast), was a humorous expression like *Cape Cod turkey* for codfish or *prairie oysters* for eggs. Because it seemed a strange word for its referent, the more reasonable *Welsh rarebit* was substituted. [eds.]

chipmunk would seem to belong to this group, though it was first recorded considerably later, in Cooper's *Deerslayer* (1841); it was certainly in use much earlier.

A good many native plants, vegetables, trees and shrubs bear names of Indian origin: *hickory, pecan, poke(weed), chinquapin, squash, persimmon,* and *catalpa,* all but one of which are Algonquian. That one, *catalpa,* is of Muskhogean origin. A good many Southern place names are of this linguistic stock, which includes Creek, Chickasaw, and Choctaw, but *catalpa* (with its variant *catawba*) and the topographical *bayou* (from Choctaw *bayuk* "stream," coming to us by way of Louisiana French) are the only widely known words other than place names taken from the languages of these Indians, who formerly occupied an area of our country including most of Georgia, Alabama, and Mississippi and parts of Tennessee, Kentucky, Louisiana, and Florida.

Other early borrowings from the Indians include words denoting foods, customs, relationships, or artifacts peculiar to the Indians at the time of borrowing: *hominy, succotash, johnnycake, pone, pemmican, moccasin, tomahawk, totem, wigwam, toboggan, powwow, mackinaw, caucus* (perhaps), *wampum, sachem, papoose,* and *squaw. Toboggan* and *mackinaw* are first recorded later than the others in this group, though their earliest use in English certainly goes back considerably beyond their first recording. Both entered English by way of Canadian French; the latter word has a half-French spelling, *Mackinac,* when used as a name for the strait, the island, and the town in Michigan. The first element of *johnnycake* is probably from *jonakin* or *jonikin,* apparently of Indian origin and meaning a thin griddle cake made of corn meal. *Johnnycake* was folk-etymologized to *journey cake,* which Noah Webster thought the original form; he assumed that it meant cake to eat when one went on a journey. It has also been suggested that the word is a corruption of *Shawnee cake,* a kind of cake supposed to have been eaten by the Shawnee Indians — an explanation which Mr. Mencken in *The American Language, Supplement One* (New York, 1945) considers "much more plausible" than any other. *Jonikin* (usually spelled *johnnikin*) is still used for a corn griddle cake in the eastern part of the Carolinas and on the Eastern Shore of Maryland. . . .

All the other words in this last group save *johnnycake* have made the Atlantic crossing, and most of them are now about as familiar to the English as they are to us. In fact, all of them except *mackinaw* are listed in Wyld's *Universal Dictionary;* only *succotash* and *johnnycake* are labeled "U.S.A." The usual British pronunciation of *wigwam* rimes with *big dam*, a pronunciation never heard in this country. *Pemmican*, the Indian name for dried meat pounded into paste, mixed with fat and dried fruits, and then compressed into cakes, has even acquired the figurative meaning in British English of "condensed statement." On the continent of Europe also, most of these words are quite well known as a result of literary transmission, for generations of European children have thrilled to the novels of James Fenimore Cooper, as well as of his European imitators.

Tammany as a political designation is a well-known Americanism of Indian origin. Tammany was a Delaware chief who flourished in the latter part of the seventeenth century and who was jocularly canonized as an American saint in 1771. His name was later used to designate a political club which ultimately grew into the present powerful Democratic organization in New York City. References to *Tammany* as the name of the club, which was founded in 1789, occur from 1790 onwards. The organization uses *the Wigwam* as a designation for Tammany Hall, *sachem* for a high official of the society, and *brave* (not of Indian origin, but long used to mean an Indian warrior) for a rank-and-file member.

A good many other words of Indian origin are included in the *Dictionary of American English*, but most of them are not in wide current use: *tuckahoe* "edible part of a fungus found on roots of trees," which is also used to designate a poor white in Virginia and West Virginia, *carcajou* "wolverine," *manito* or *manitou* "a god," *quahog* or *quahaug* "hard clam," *sagamore* "chief," *samp* "corn porridge," *tamarack* "the American larch," *mugwump* "great man," and others considerably less familiar. *Mugwump*, though known much earlier, came into real prominence in the presidential campaign of 1884, when it was applied to those independent Republicans who, affecting an attitude of superiority, refused to support James G. Blaine as their party nominee. Nowadays the word is chiefly notable for the oft-recorded definition by a Congressional wag (would there were more of his kidney!) to the effect that a mugwump was one who always had his *mug* on one side of the fence and his *wump* on the other.

Some early Americanisms were translations or supposed translations of Indian words or phrases, for example, *paleface* (first used by James Fenimore Cooper), *war paint, warpath, firewater, pipe of peace, medicine man, Great Spirit, big chief, to scalp*, and *to bury the hatchet*. Frequently *Indian* was used in conjunction with another word, as in *Indian meal, Indian file, Indian summer*, and *Indian gift*, originally a gift for which one expected something of more value in return, but later a gift which the giver took back. *Indian giver* is first recorded, as far as we know, in Bartlett's *Glossary* of 1848, with the notation that "this term is applied by children to a child who, after having given away a thing, wishes it back again," though *Indian gift* occurs much earlier. The *Dictionary of American English* lists almost a hundred such combinations, though not all are early, for instance, *honest Injun*, which is not recorded until 1875. . . .

Before passing on to other non-English influences it is interesting to note that British English borrowed *Mohawk*, which it usually spelled *mohock*, early in the eighteenth century to designate, according to the *Oxford English Dictionary*, "one of a class of aristocratic ruffians who infested the streets of London at night," but the term has only a historical interest today. It has never had any currency in American English save among professors of eighteenth-century English literature. The *Apache* of *Apache dance*, a rowdy, sexy dance performed by a pair of dancers attired as a Parisian gangster and his "moll," did not come to us directly from the well-known American aborigines of that name. It came instead by way of French, which in the early twentieth century borrowed the name of the Indian tribe, Gallicized its pronunciation, and used it to designate a Parisian street bully.

It is perhaps not surprising, considering the ultimate reduction of the American Indians to the status of a conquered people, that the Indian element in American English is no larger than it is. As a matter of fact, if we leave out of consideration place names, of which there are an overwhelming number — more than half of our states bear Indian names, and a large portion of our rivers, lakes, mountains, towns, and cities as well — the Indian influence on our vocabulary must be characterized as slight.

The Indian languages were not, however, the only non-European influence upon the English of America in colonial days. More than a year before the Pilgrims landed on Plymouth Rock in search of religious freedom, a group of people were against their will brought here from the west coast of Africa — principally from Senegal, Gambia, Sierra Leone, Liberia, the Gold Coast, Togo, Dahomey, Nigeria, and Angola — and forthwith sold into slavery. The traffic in Negro slaves continued until shortly before the Civil War, though slackening somewhat after 1808, when the Slave Trade Act went into effect. A great majority of these Negroes were brought direct from Africa; some, however, had previously lived in the British West Indies, where they had picked up a bare working knowledge of English.

Most of the descendants of these transplanted Africans living in the South now speak conventional American English. Because of lack of social contacts with whites and lack of schooling, relics of older standard speech may occasionally be heard from them, such as the pronunciation *deef* for *deaf* and *obleege* for *oblige*. When a colored char-woman with some embarrassment informed me that her small daughter had suffered an injury in her *grine*, she was not using an un-English, "darky" pronunciation, but merely saying *groin* in a manner which went out of fashion in more sophisticated usage years ago. There is, of course, no connection whatever between race and the ability to articulate given speech sounds, though it is popularly believed that the Southern Negro speaks as he does because of a peculiar conforma-tion of speech organs, aided and abetted by indolence and stupidity. I was once gravely informed by a professor of government that the Negro does not have an *r* sound (my informant was of course referring only to *r* before a consonant sound and in final position) because the "letter *r*" did not exist in African languages — not one of which he had any acquaintance with, incidentally. When I presumed to disagree with his explanation, a corollary of which was that the speech of white Southerners was *r*-less because of the linguistic influence of Negro "mammies," and to point out that an Ohio-bred Negro has no diffi-culty whatsoever pronouncing *r* in all positions, he was grievously offended with me. The fact is that uneducated Negroes in the South by and large differ little in their speech from the uneducated whites. As for the presence of archaisms, they may also be heard from whites who have lived for a long time in cultural isolation, for instance, the Southern mountain folk.

There are, however, communities of Negro Americans engaged largely in the cultivation of rice, cotton, and indigo along the coastal region of South Carolina and Georgia, both on the Sea Islands and on the mainland, who have lived in cultural and geographical isolation for many generations. Most of them have had little contact with whites; some, indeed, have seldom seen white people. These Negroes, number-ing about a quarter of a million, speak a type of English which has been so heavily influenced by the African languages native to their remote ancestors that it is not readily intelligible to people, white or colored, from other parts of the country. Their language, Gullah or Geechee, retains a good many African characteristics in its system of sounds, its syntax, its morphology, its vocabulary, its methods of form-ing words, and, most striking of all to one hearing it for the first time, its intonation. The word *Gullah* is probably either from *Gola*, the name of a Liberian tribe and its language, or from *Angola*. *Geechee*, also used in the upcountry of South Carolina as a derisive nickname for a low-country white, particularly one living in the Charleston area, is probably derived from the name of another Liberian tribe and language.

It was very unlikely that Africans from the same tribe or language area would find themselves thrown together on a single plantation in sufficient numbers to enable them to maintain their native languages. The chances were all that they would be considerably dispersed upon their arrival at the various southern ports. Consequently, it became necessary for them to learn English as well as they could. It is not likely that anyone helped them to do so, unless there were prototypes of Mrs. Stowe's Little Eva gliding or floating about the plantations (for Little Eva seldom merely walked) in the seventeenth and eighteenth centuries. The only English many of them ever heard from native speakers was that of the illiterate or semiliterate white indentured servants with whom they worked in the fields or who were set over them as overseers. It was for them not simply a matter of translating word for word their native idioms into English. This cannot be done successfully even with related languages, where it may result in something intelligible if un-English, like *the bread is all*, a Pennsylvania Germanism (though heard in other parts of the country) from German *das Brot ist alle*. It was for these Negroes a matter of acquiring a quite different linguistic psychology, a new attitude towards the phenomena of life as expressed by language. It is not surprising that their accomplishment fell considerably short of perfect. Their English was a sort of jargon or pidgin, which passed into use by their descendants as a native language. This type of so called creolized language has been preserved largely in the speech of the Gullahs, Negroes who "stayed put" in a region in which they have always been far more numerous than whites and in which they have developed the only distinctive Negro speech in this country.

The principal importance of Gullah, aside from its intrinsic interest as a remarkable linguistic development, is that recent studies of it have been the means of identifying beyond a doubt the African source of a number of words in Southern American English, a few of which have passed into other types of American English and one of which, *banjo*, if it is indeed of African origin, is part of the English language wherever it is spoken. Until Lorenzo Dow Turner began his investigations about twenty years ago, Gullah was traditionally regarded as "a quaint linguistic mongrel," to quote from one serious commentator; it was thought to be characterized by "intellectual indolence," "slovenly and careless," a debased form of the "peasant English" of poor whites, a sort of baby talk. One writer even went so far as to attribute its phonological characteristics to the "clumsy tongues," "flat noses," and "thick lips" of the Negroes who speak it.

Professor Turner's studies of Gullah, culminating in his *Africanisms in the Gullah Dialect* (Chicago, 1949), identify thousands of words in Gullah which have or may have African sources. Unlike earlier commentators, who assumed that many words which seemed strange to them were either nonsense words or mispronunciations of English words, Turner, himself of African descent, took the trouble to acquire a good working knowledge of West African languages. His studies and conclusions have made short shrift of some of the theories of previous writers, who assumed, for instance, that a Gullah word for "tooth" which sounded to them something like *bong* was merely a childish, clumsy-tongued, flat-nosed, thick-lipped mispronunciation of English *bone*, and that the Gullah word *det* or the expression *det rain* "a long, hard rain" was really *death rain*, which involved the further assumption that to the Gullahs a long, hard rain is an omen of death to come — as it were, folklore made to order. The fact that in the Wolof language, spoken in Senegal and Gambia, the word for "tooth" is very like *bong* (it is impossible to indicate the exact pronunciation of the un-English final sound of this word, a palatal nasal, without using phonetic symbols) and that in the same language the word for "long, hard rain" is *det* ought to dispose of the "baby talk" explanation for good and all — though of course it will not, for most people prefer "quaint" explanations of linguistic phenomena to the true ones.

From many Gullah informants, some of them bearing names which are a delight to contemplate — among them Saki Sweetwine, Prince Smith, Samuel Polite, Sanko Singleton, Balaam Walker, Scotia Washington, Shad Hall, and Paris Capers — Dr. Turner collected more than five thousand African words in the Gullah region. About four-fifths of these are now used only as personal names, but most of the remainder are everyday words in the speech of the Gullahs. Some of these words, doubtless the common possession of Negroes in all the slaveholding states, passed into the vocabulary of whites at what must have been a very early date.

How did words from the language of humble slaves get into the speech of their white masters? M. M. Mathews, who devotes the final chapter of his *Some Sources of Southernisms* (University, Ala., 1948) to Africanisms in the word stock of Southern American English, speculates with some reason that such words were transmitted by white children, who would not have resisted the influences of what their elders considered an inferior culture. Dr. Mathews cites his aged aunt's aversion to the "Negro word" *cooter* "turtle" and her regret that her brother, Mathews' father, had sullied the "purity" of his speech by ever using the word.

Actually, the African contribution is rather meager. The remarkable thing is, considering the social and economic relationship of black to white, that there should have been any contribution. Many a white Southerner has imbedded in his vocabulary words whose African origin he probably never suspects. *Banjo* and *cooter* have already been cited. The first word has usually been considered as originating in a Negro mispronunciation of *bandore*, an English word of Spanish transmission denoting a musical instrument whose similarity to the banjo consisted mainly in the fact that it had strings to be plucked. According to Turner, the most probable source is Kimbundu, a language spoken in Angola, in which the word *mbanza* refers to an instrument very similar to the banjo. *Cooter* is very likely from *kuta*, a word appearing in two French West African languages, Bambara and Malinke, in which it has the same meaning as in the language of the Gullahs and in the English of many white Southerners.

Goober "peanut" is a modification of Kimbundu *nguba*, with similar forms occurring in Imbundu (also spoken in Angola) and Kongo (Belgian Congo and Angola). *Pinder*, with the same meaning, is from Kongo *mpinda*. Both these words are freely used on a colloquial level in the South; the first has probably gained a limited national currency.

A number of gustatory and culinary terms of African origin testify to the skill of Negro cooks. Many of these, however, are local terms, like *cush* "corn meal stuffing" and *cala* "sweetened rice" — the latter term confined to the New Orleans area. *Gumbo* is confined to no locality or region, nor is *yam*, which is found also in British English and which is of Portuguese transmission; in Scotland it is used for the common white potato. If the word *yam* was brought to these shores by our early settlers, as it may have been, it is of course not to be regarded as belonging with the group of words under discussion; but there is no reason to insist that, because it occurs also in British English, we could not have got it independently. The same people from whom the Portuguese got the word were right here, and the word might well have entered the American vocabulary, as Dr. Mathews points out, from the language of the slaves. At the least, its use in American English would have been reinforced by their use of it. The word survives as an Africanism in the Gullah dialect (in the form *yambi*) to mean a red sweet potato, which is its usual meaning in Southern American English.

Buckra "white man" is also of African origin, appearing as *mbakara* in Efik and Ibibio, spoken in Southern Nigeria. Loss of the initial nasal sound in the word probably occurred in Negro speech before the word was transmitted to whites and is due to the influence of English on the speech of the Negroes. Simplification of the initial consonant combinations *mb-, mp-, nd-, nt-,* and *ng-,* which do not occur in this position in English, is frequent in the Gullah pronunciation of African words.

The great blue heron is frequently called *poor Joe* (or *po' Joe*) in those regions of the South in which the bird is found. There can be no doubt that this is the same word as Vai (Liberia and Sierra Leone) *pojo* "heron." It is likely that *chigger* and its variant *jigger* — the dictionaries give a spelling *chigoe* which suggests a pronunciation seldom if ever heard — are of African transmission as far as their use in American English is concerned, and perhaps of African origin as well. At any rate, *jiga* "flea" is found in a number of African languages spoken in Senegal, Gambia, Togo, Dahomey, and Northern and Southern Nigeria. The word got into British English probably by way of the British West Indies and has been thought to be of Carib origin. It is likely, however, that its use in American English is due independently to Negro transmission, regardless of its ultimate origin.

Pickaninny, which is probably used nowadays by white more frequently than by Negroes, is of African transmission, but its source is Portuguese *pequenino* "very little." It is not impossible that the last part of the Portuguese word may have been identified by the Negroes with the Mende (Sierra Leone) word *nini* "female breast," *pequenino* being folk-etymologized into *pickaninny* after these Negroes acquired their English. The word is not exclusively American (the same is true of *buckra, jigger,* and others), though it is probably more commonly used here than elsewhere. It is, nevertheless, recorded in British English almost a century and a half earlier than in American English.

Hoodoo and its New Orleans variant *voodoo* are Africanisms. Both forms are in use by the Gullahs. They have, however, become somewhat differentiated in meaning, the latter usually referring to the cult which flourished in the West Indies and was later introduced into this country. *Hoodoo* is applied to a person or object that is thought to bring bad luck, *to hoodoo* consequently meaning "to bring bad luck to someone." Voodoo worship was introduced into Louisiana very early by slaves from the French colonies of Martinique, Guadeloupe, and Santo Domingo, where the cult — probably of African origin, as its name would indicate — raged furiously. It would seem to have grown rather slowly at first, but was a source of worry among the whites by 1782, when the Spanish governor of Louisiana prohibited further importation of Negroes from Martinique because slaves from there were thought to be "too much given to voudouism and make the lives of the citizens unsafe." Later, and partly for the same reason, a similar prohibition was extended to Negroes from Santo Domingo. After the American occupation, however, there were no such restrictions, and with the sudden influx of Negroes into Louisiana by way of New Orleans between 1806 and 1810, voodoo began to exert a strong influence upon the Louisiana Negroes. For a long time thereafter — until well after the Civil War, in fact — voodoo "queens" and "doctors" were persons of tremendous power and prestige among the Negroes, and even to some extent among the lower-class whites.

The most famous of the queens, who were the priestesses of the cult and much more influential than the doctors who shared with them their powers of sorcery, was the remarkable Marie Laveau, a free mulatto of striking beauty in her younger years, who was by profession a hairdresser and by avocation a procuress for white gentlemen. For more than forty years absolute ruler of the cult, she has remained a legend to this day. The visitor to New Orleans, if he is lucky, may still hear old Oscar "Papa" Celestin, a Robert Frost in ebony, sing *Marie Laveau*, an original composition which recounts some of the miracles performed by this celebrated "cunjer-lady."

Transmission into general use of African *zombi*, a word intimately associated with voodooism, is probably rather recent, though it must have been known to whites in certain areas of the South at an early date. Its present familiarity may well be credited to the cycle of "horror" films some years ago. The word originally designated the snake god which was the object of adoration in the voodoo cult. It later came to mean a supernatural force thought to restore corpses to life, and ultimately a corpse brought to life by means of this force. Recently it has been used, with an obvious appropriateness, to designate a mixed drink of (usually) rum and brandy.

Juke, which has come into general use among whites comparatively recently, mainly in the compounds *juke box* and *juke joint*, has been a part of the vocabulary of the Gullahs for a long time in the sense "disorderly," particularly in the combination *juke house*. Turner shows that the word is of African origin. In standard colloquial use its meaning has been considerably toned down, as has been that of *jazz*, which, though of unknown origin, is said to have been long used by Negroes, particularly in the New Orleans region. *Jazz* is very likely of African origin, though no African etymon has been found. These two words are included here because they have probably appeared in the English or creolized English speech of Negroes since pre-Revolutionary days, even though they may have been late in reaching the standard language. Their very nature would of course sufficiently explain the fact that they were not earlier transmitted to whites. *Jazz* as a verb is, as a matter of fact, sometimes used by whites, though only on a rather low social level, in the sexual sense which it seems originally to have had among the Negroes.

It would be pleasant to be able to record that Professor Turner's researches in Gullah have cleared up the origin of *to tote*, long an etymological puzzle, but there are circumstances in respect to it which indicate that final judgment had better be reserved. It is true that no satisfactory English etymon has been found. *Tote* is one of that sizable number of words of which the dictionaries can say only "orig. uncert.," "unknown origin," or something to that effect. Professor Turner found possible African sources in Kongo and Kikongo *tota* "to pick up," with related words in other West African languages mean "to carry." The fact that *tote* is used in Gullah does not rule out the possibility of an unknown English source, for very many English words are used by the Gullahs. It is likely, however, that if the word is not of African origin, its use has been reinforced, at least in the South and particularly among the Gullahs, by the African words. Though it is usually thought of as a Southernism, *tote* was first recorded in New England in the seventeenth century; it has also been found in upstate New York, northern Michigan, and northern Minnesota, occurring alone and in the combinations *tote road*, *tote wagon*, *tote team*, and *tote sled*. The fact that the word crops up in parts of the country where Negro influence is highly unlikely suggests that there may after all be an English source for the word which has been lost to us. If so, the fact that words of similar sound and meaning occur in West African languages would have to be due to sheer coincidence, like the similarity in American Indian *Potomac* and Greek *potamos* "river."

Contacts with other colonizing peoples have also contributed to the American vocabulary. Relations between the English and the New Amsterdam Dutch were, it is true, never very friendly; nevertheless from the language of these Dutch settlers American English gained *coleslaw, cooky, cruller, boss, dope, hay barrack, spook, stoop* "porch," *poppycock* (from *pappekak* "soft dung"), *patroon* (which the Dutch had in turn taken from Latin *patronus*), *sleigh, scow, to snoop, bowery* "a farm" (but now more famous as the street name), *pit* "fruit stone," *boodle, Santa Claus, waffle,* and probably *Yankee*. In addition American English incorporated a number of geographical terms used in the region of the Hudson: *kill* "creek, stream, river," *dorp* "village," and *clove* "valley," which also appear in place names. Many of these Dutch words were not used by writers until well into the nineteenth century, but we may be fairly sure that they occurred in English contexts much earlier; and we may be equally sure that many more Dutch words than are recorded were once in use. *Hay barrack* represents what English-speaking people did to Dutch *hooi-berg*. *Coleslaw* is from Dutch *koolsla* "cabbage salad"; folk etymology frequently converts it to *cold slaw*. *Dope* has acquired a good many slang uses, as in *to dope out, to get the dope on,* and *he's a dope* (i.e., a dolt). It seems to have begun its career in American English meaning a drug, later adding the connotation "narcotic." *Boss,* from *baas* "master," was a very useful word, for it allowed the American working man to enjoy the satisfying if purely verbal illusion that he had no master; only slaves had masters in early American democracy. *Father Christmas,* not *Santa Claus,* visits good English children on Christmas Eve. Our name for the jolly saint is from *Sante Klaas,* a Dutch dialect form of *Sant Nikolaas,* that is, "St. Nicholas"; it seems to have taken a long time catching on, and was probably not very common until the nineteenth century. In my childhood *Santa* was always pronounced *Santy* even by the most highly cultured; people nowadays have become much more conscious of spelling and may use a pronunciation which the spelling *Santa* seems to indicate to them.

The source of *Yankee* is uncertain, but the word is most probably from *Jan Kees* (a variant of *Jan Kaas,* which has been in Germany and Flanders a nickname of long standing for a Hollander), used by the English to designate a Dutch pirate, a sense in which it apparently came also to be used in New York as an expression of the contempt in which the English held the Dutch. Because of the final -*s*, the name seems to have been misunderstood to be a plural; the form *Yankee* is thus what is known to linguists as a back formation, like *shay* from *chaise.*[3] It should also be noted that *j* in Dutch has the sound of English *y;* hence the initial sound of the English form of the word. It is a little difficult to understand why the word was transferred from Dutchmen to people of English descent. Perhaps the shift in application was the result of the same type of humor involved in nicknaming the fattest boy in school "Skinny" — the *lucus a non lucendo* principle. . . .

The meaning of *Yankee* has been anything but static. By the mid-eighteenth century its use in this country to designate a New Englander seems to have been well established. During the Civil War Southerners were employing the term, usually derogatorily, for any Northerner, and it was not long before it acquired what was in the usage of many Southerners the inseparable prefix *dam,* as in *damyankee.*

Since the Revolutionary War the British have used the word to designate any American, with connotations no more derogatory than those of the word *American* itself as it is used by them. It is difficult to imagine any experience more painful to most deep Southerners than to be called *Yankees;* yet there is only sporadic evidence that G.I.'s of Southern origin stationed in England during either World War ever objected very vigorously to the appellation. *Yank* is about as common in British colloquial usage as the unabbreviated form; the clipped form has never been very frequent in American use, though it was the title of a magazine distributed to American soldiers and occurs in a line of the World War I song *Over There* ("The Yanks are coming").

Despite the large number of Germans in this country long before the outbreak of the Revolution, few German words entered the American vocabulary until about the middle of the nineteenth century, when many new immigrants from Germany arrived. The first large groups of Germans came from the Palatinate; they arrived on Delaware Bay in the early years of the eighteenth century, and, finding that the good lands around Philadelphia were already taken by descendants of Penn's colonists, proceeded to settle the back country. Those who subsequently moved on to other parts with the Scotch-Irish soon abandoned their native language. Those who stayed on in Pennsylvania kept pretty much to themselves — on farms and in villages where they continued speaking their dialect of German, which was in time considerably influenced by English but which had no appreciable effect upon English outside the areas in which they were settled. *Sauerkraut* appears in British English as early as 1617, though neither the word nor the food it designates ever really caught on in England.

[3] For back-formation, see page 97. [eds.]

It is most likely that it was borrowed independently in this country. Similarly, *noodle* is recorded in England before its first known appearance in America, but was probably reborrowed here. It is not improbable that other words which entered American English through Pennsylvania German were known outside the immediate German settlement area before the nineteenth century, but most of them are of such a nature that we should not expect to find them recorded as early as the eighteenth century. Some of them, like *ponhaus* "scrapple," are not listed in modern abridged dictionaries, probably because lexicographers do not consider them "standard," despite the fact that they are known and used by many speakers of standard American English at the present day. *Rainworm* "earthworm" is used in settlements of German origin and is probably a translation of *Regenwurm*. It occurs in the Pennsylvania German area and in the German settlements on the Yadkin in North Carolina, as well as in Nobleboro, Maine, which was settled from the Palatinate. Old English *regenwyrm* is doubtless the ancestor of the term as it occurs elsewhere, for instance, on Buzzards Bay in Massachusetts. *Sawbuck* is now widely disseminated but it originated in German and Dutch settlements from, respectively, *Sagebock* and *zaagbock*. The fact that each end of the rack on which wood is sawed is shaped like the letter X — the Roman symbol for ten — has given rise to the slang use of the term for a ten-dollar bill. *Woodbuck* is also heard over the entire German settlement area, obviously a partial translation of German *Holzbock*. *Hex* "a witch or the spell cast by a witch" and *to hex* "to cast a spell on" are fairly well known all over the country nowadays. *Ponhaus* (also occurring as *ponhoss*, *ponhorse*, *ponehoss*, and *pondhorse*) corresponds to standard German *Pfannhase;* it is current from the Pennsylvania German area proper westward to Ohio and is also well known in northwestern Maryland and northeastern West Virginia. Other gastronomical and culinary terms of Pennsylvania German origin are *sots* "yeast"; *snits* (also *schnitz*) "dried apples, pieces of fruit cut for drying" (also used as a verb "to cut into pieces"); *fat-cakes* "doughnuts" (*fettkuche*), *fossnocks* (*fasnachskuche* "Shrovetide cakes"); *thick-milk* "curdled milk" (*dickemilich*); *smearcase* "cottage cheese" (*schmierkäs*); and possibly, but by no means certainly, *applebutter*. *Clook* "setting hen," with its less frequent variant *cluck*, is from Pennsylvania German *kluck* (standard German *Klucke*). According to Hans Kurath's *Word Geography of the Eastern United States* (Ann Arbor, 1949), "the derogatory phrase *dumb cluck* obviously contains this word." *Belsnickel* (or *Belschnickel*) was, and still is, the southern Pennsylvania equivalent of *Santa Claus;* the last part of the name is an affectionate diminutive form of German *Nikolaus.* Another name of long standing for the unhappily commercialized saint who rewards good children at Christmas is *Kriss Kingle* (or *Kriss Kringle*); it is a modification of *Christkindl* "Christ child." *To dunk* "to dip (dough-nuts usually) into coffee or milk" is from Pennsylvania German *dunken* "to dip," corresponding to standard German *tunken.* It has not really been widely current for more than about twenty years, although it spread very rapidly once it caught on. There is no usage label for the word in the *American College Dictionary,* so that it is apparently considered standard American English nowadays. *Dunker* (or *Dunkard*) is the popular name of a member of the German Baptist Brethren, a pietistic sect which practices baptism by immersion, that is, by dunking.

From French explorers and colonizers American English acquired, usually by way of the Canadian border, such words as *prairie, bateau, voyageur, chowder, buccaneer, carryall* (vehicle), *levee, calumet,* and perhaps *gopher. Chowder* is a modification of *chaudière* "caldron." Although it is recorded first in England, *buccaneer* should probably be regarded as an Americanism by virtue of its many American historical associations; it is ultimately a Carib word, but comes to English by way of French *boucanier. Carryall* is a folk-etymologizing of *cariole. Gopher* is most likely from *gaufre* "honeycomb," in reference to the animal's burrowing habits. *Prairie* is of frequent occurrence in American English, alone and in a number of compounds such as *prairie dog, prairie wolf* "coyote," and *prairie schooner* "small covered wagon." The word is now perfectly familiar in British English also. *Levee* is a derivative of French *lever* "to raise." Its use to designate an embankment for preventing the overflow of a river is largely confined to the South, as is also its later sense "landing place for vessels." *Calumet,* ultimately a derivative of Latin *calamus* "reed," was the word used by the French explorers for the ceremonial tobacco pipe of the Indians.

A number of Spanish words, such as *mosquito* "little fly," *negro* "black" (an adjective which was soon converted into a noun), *pecadillo* "little sin," *armada* "armed (naval) forces" (originally a past participle), and *alligator* (from *el lagarto* "the lizard"), along with Nahuatl words adopted by the Spanish, such as those cited at the beginning of this chapter, entered the English language as early as the sixteenth century. These words, though some of them are more frequently used in this country than in England, should be distinguished from words taken from Spanish by English-speaking people settled on this continent.

Such words are very numerous at a later date but very rare before the nineteenth century. *Calaboose* "jail" is a modification of Spanish *calabozo*, used chiefly in the southern states; it is recorded first in the latter years of the eighteenth century. *Cockroach* (as *cacarootch*) first appears in the *General Historie* of Captain John Smith, who refers to it in a somewhat ambiguous passage as "a certaine India Bug, called by the Spaniards a *Cacarootch*, the which creeping into Chests they [that is, the "caca-rootches"] eat and defile with their ill-sented dung." The word used by Smith is a modification of Spanish *cucaracha* "wood louse," or possibly a variant form of it. It was later folk-etymologized to *cockroach* (just as Latin *asparagus* is converted by some speakers into *sparrow grass*) and subsequently clipped to *roach* in this country, American verbal prudery perhaps playing some part in the elimination of the first element of what deceptively appeared to be a compound of *cock* and *roach*. *Key* "reef or low island" from Spanish *cayo* was in English use before it was recorded in America, but its use is now mainly confined to this country, particularly to Florida. *Key West* is a modification of *Cayo Hueso* "bone key." The form *cay*, riming with *day*, is now more usual in British English than *key*. *Stevedore*, from Spanish *estivador*, occurs first in the form *stowadore* by association with English *to stow*.

SUGGESTED ASSIGNMENTS

1. Using a detailed map and, if necessary, the aid of a foreign-language student for data, write a composition on one of these subjects:
    a. Spanish place names in the Southwest
    b. French place names in the Mississippi Valley
    c. French place names in Louisiana
    d. Dutch place names in the Hudson Valley
    e. German place names in Pennsylvania
2. If you live in a town that retains some Old World flavor derived from its early foreign settlers, write a theme about the words of foreign origin that are generally known to the community. You might consider such questions as these: Have their pronunciations changed? Have their referents changed? What areas of life do they represent? Why are they used instead of American words? Have they become naturalized, e.g., do they take *-s* plurals or verb endings in *-ed* and *-ing*?
3. Using library sources, write a composition on the influence of one language upon either American English or British English.
4. If you have studied Latin, write a composition on Latin words and phrases

in English. Consider such matters as these: How have the meanings changed? Is the pronunciation Latin, English, or a combination of the two? Do the words fulfill a useful purpose? Among useful references for this assignment are these: Edwin Lee Johnson, *Latin Words of Common English;* E. E. Burriss and Lionel Casson, *Latin and Greek in Common Use;* and Jerome C. Hixson and I. Colodny, *Word Ways.*

5. Two historical dictionaries devoted to American English are *A Dictionary of American English,* edited by Sir W. A. Craigie and J. R. Hulbert, and *Dictionary of Americanisms,* edited by Mitford Mathews. Use these dictionaries to look up the following words to see when they are first recorded in American English and where they came from: *raccoon, skunk, moccasin, prairie, bureau, gopher, waffle, cockroach, mosquito.*

6. The following words are said to be examples of folk etymology: *country-dance, primrose, woodchuck, cockroach, tweed, lark* (spree). Find their originals, using your desk dictionary and larger dictionaries if needed.

FURTHER READINGS

Brook, G. L. *A History of the English Language.* New York: W. W. Norton & Company, Inc., 1958. (Paperbound in the Norton Library, 1964.) On the development of English, see pp. 28–58.

Chadwick, John. *On the Decipherment of Linear B.* New York: Random House, Inc., 1958.

Hughes, John P. *The Science of Language.* New York: Random House, Inc., 1962. On the languages of Europe, see pp. 73–93.

Pyles, Thomas. *The Origins and Development of the English Language.* New York: Harcourt, Brace & World, Inc., 1964. On recent British and American English, see pp. 217–261.

3

WORDS: FORMS AND MEANINGS

Word-Making in English

HENRY BRADLEY

As language continues to grow, its word stock is constantly changing. While some words sink into disuse and disappear, others are being added to meet new needs. Your grandfather, for instance, could have driven a *runabout* or *touring-car*, whereas now, two generations later, you are likely to be behind the wheel of a *hardtop* or a *station wagon*. The additions to our word stock are of two kinds. One consists of borrowings from other languages. In English this borrowing has gone on without stop ever since our language first appeared in England 1,500 years ago. It is illustrated in the selection by Thomas Pyles on page 65. The second kind of addition consists of new words formed from existing materials. That is to say, words and word-parts are re-formed into new combinations, and sometimes entirely new words are created from the repertory of English speech sounds. It is this second group that Mr. Bradley discusses here as he describes the three major processes by which new words come into being. Henry Bradley was one of the distinguished editors of that monumental lexicon, the *Oxford English Dictionary*.

The English language has augmented its resources not only by the adoption of words from other tongues, but also by the making of new words. There are three possible ways in which a new word can be made: (1) by *Composition*, which means the joining together of two existing

From *The Making of English* by Henry Bradley. Reprinted by permission of Collier-Macmillan, Ltd., and St. Martin's Press, Inc., copyright 1904.

words to form a compound; (2) by *Derivation*, which means the making
of a new word out of an old one, usually by the addition of some prefix
or suffix which is not itself a word, but is significant in combination;
and (3) by *Root-creation*, which is the invention of an entirely new word,
usually either imitative of some inarticulate noise, or suggested by some
instinctive feeling of expressiveness.

I. Composition

A compound word is a word formed by joining two or more words
to express a meaning that could be rendered by a phrase of which the
simple words form part. Some languages have no compound words at
all; and those which have them do not all form them after the same
manner. The principles of English word-compounding are, to a great
extent, inherited from the primitive Indo-Germanic language. In those
kinds of compounds that most frequently occur, the last element expresses a general meaning, which the prefixed element renders less
general. Thus an *apple-tree* is a tree, but only a particular kind of tree.
In the original Indo-Germanic language the prefixed element in a
compound of this sort was not, properly speaking, a *word*, but a word-
stem: that is to say, a word deprived of those grammatical characters
— case, number, gender, mood, tense, person, etc., which it would
possess if it occurred separately in a sentence.[1] It still has this character,
so far as meaning is concerned, in those English compounds that are
formed on the inherited pattern. Thus *apple-* in *apple-tree* is neither
singular nor plural, neither nominative, accusative, nor genitive. Hence
the phrase for which such a compound is the condensed expression
admits of great variety of form; the former of the two words may occur
in it in any case or in either number; and the meaning of the compound
varies accordingly. A *tree-frog* is a frog that lives in trees; a *tree-fern* is a
fern that is a tree; a *tree-fruit* is the fruit produced by a tree. As a general
rule, our knowledge of the things denoted by the simple words guides
us at once to a correct understanding of the meaning of the compound.
This, however, is not always the case. A *house-boat* might very well mean
a sort of boat usually kept in a boat-house, or a boat that belongs to a

[1] This comes out clearly in such a language as Greek, which has preserved the
primitive Indo-Germanic system of inflexions. Thus *oikodespotēs* is Greek for 'master
of a house'; but while *despotēs* 'master,' is a real word, *oiko-*, 'house,' is only a stem.
To make it into a word, capable of being used in a sentence, we must add the endings that mark case and number, as in *oikos*, nom. sing., *oikon*, acc. sing., *oikou*,
gen. sing., *oikoi*, nom. pl., *oikous*, acc. plural.

house, or that supplies the needs of houses. It is only custom that has decided that the compound word shall mean a boat that serves as a house. The general meaning of this class of compounds might be expressed by saying that the noun which is formed of the two nouns A and B means "a B which has some sort of relation to an A or to A's in general."

The compounds formed by prefixing one noun to another, however, constitute only one out of the many classes of compounds which exist in English. There are compounds of adjective and noun, as *blackbird, hotbed;* of adverb and noun, as *downfall;* of noun and adjective, as *grass-green, purse-proud, penny-wise;* of adjective or adverb and adjective, as *dark-blue, ever-young;* and of noun or adjective and verb, as *wiredraw, whitewash;* and the very many compounds of adverb and verb, such as *overcome, inlay, outlive, upturn.* In all these cases the literal meaning of the compound is that of the last element, only limited or specialised. . . . From the fifteenth century onwards many compound nouns and adjectives have been formed in imitation of French, in which the first element is a verb-stem (in the original examples it was the imperative of a verb) and the second element is a noun denoting the object of the action, as in *breakfast, breakneck, kill-joy, makeshift, save-all, scapegrace, scarecrow, spendthrift, tosspot, turnkey.* We have also many nouns and adjectives compounded with a verb-stem and an adverb, as *break-up, come-down, knock-out, run-away.*

. . . As any page of an "Anglo-Saxon" dictionary will show, compound words were abundant in Old English; and in every succeeding age of the language a multitude of new compounds have come into existence. And yet, if we take a page of modern German and place beside it a good translation into English, we shall not fail to perceive that the compound words are very much more numerous in the German original than in the English rendering. Another noteworthy fact is that a great number of compounds, once generally used, are now obsolete, although the simple words composing them are still universally familiar. It may be worth while to inquire why this has happened.

Although word-composition, in those languages which freely admit it, is one of the readiest means of supplying the need for new words, compounds are often somewhat awkward in actual use. A compound word is a description, often an imperfect description; and when an object of perception or thought is familiar to us, we desire that its name shall suggest the thing to our minds directly, and not through the intervention of irrelevant ideas. Accordingly, a compound word for a simple notion gives a certain sense of inconvenience, unless we are able to forget its literal meaning. It is true that we frequently succeed in doing this: we use multitudes of compound words without mentally analysing them at all. In such cases the compound often undergoes processes of phonetic change which a distinct consciousness of its etymological meaning would not have allowed to take place. Thus the Old English *gōdspel*, literally "good tidings" (which early became *gŏdspel*, through misreading the first element as "God" instead of "good"), is now *gospel;* the late Old English *hūsbonda*, a compound of *hūs* house and *bonda* dweller, cultivator, is now not *housebond* but *husband;* the poetical designation *day's eye* is now *daisy*, a word which we never think of as containing two elements; *holy day* has become *holiday; Christ's mass* is now *Christmas*, with an altered pronunciation which quite disguises the first word. This process is especially observable in place-names, where, even more than in ordinary compound words, the original descriptive meaning is a palpable irrelevance. Very few names of English places are now intelligible to persons unlearned in etymology, even when the separate words of which they are composed are still familiar in everyday speech. The Old English *stān* survives as "stone," and *tūn* as "town"; but the place-name *Stāntūn* is now not "Stonetown" but "Stanton." *Pedridan-tūn*, the "town" or farm enclosure on the river Pedride, is now Petherton, though the name of the river has come to be pronounced "Parret."

A consideration of these and similar examples will show that compound words have often the disadvantage that their etymological meaning has to be forgotten before they can become quite satisfactory instruments of expression. It would appear that the English are, from whatever cause, more conscious of this inconvenience than are the speakers of some other languages. At any rate, although many new compounds have been formed in every period of the language, a large proportion of them have been short-lived or of very limited currency: the general tendency has been to replace them by other words. In the Middle English period this tendency was fostered by the circumstance that the two fashionable languages, French and Latin, make very little use of composition; and the common practice of adopting words from these languages made it easy to find substitutes for the native compounds. The Old English names for arts and sciences — such as *lǣcecrǣft* (leechcraft) for medicine, *scopcrǣft* for poetry, *tungolcrǣft* for astronomy, *rīmcrǣft* for arithmetic — disappeared early from the language, their places being taken by words adopted through French from Latin, or through French and Latin from Greek. The fourteenth century monk who wrote *ayenbite* (*of inwyt*) for "remorse (of conscience)" did not succeed in inducing any other writer to use his new word: the Latin-French synonym was felt to be better for its purpose. Even now, a well-established compound is often partly superseded by a simple word or a derivative: for example, we use the word *steamer* more frequently than *steamboat* or *steamship*.

The habit of freely adopting foreign words, which has been produced by the conditions under which the English language has been developed, has had the good effect of relieving us from the necessity of having recourse to composition in cases where a compound, as such, is less suitable for our purpose than a simple word. But, on the other hand, our language has lost something of its capacity for forming compounds even where they would be useful. When Carlyle, imitating the German *Schadenfreude*, speaks of "a mischief-joy, which is often a justice-joy," we somehow feel that these formations are alien to the genius of the language, though if it were not for this the words would have been welcome additions to our vocabulary. It would seem un-English to say that a person was *rank-proud*, though the apparently analogous *purse-proud* has long been a recognised word; and *country-love* or *virtue-love* for "love of country," "love of virtue," would be equally inadmissible. And yet not only does modern English possess an enormous number of compounds, but new ones are continually introduced; and, what is still more remarkable, many of these additions to our language, when we first hear them, do not seem in the slightest degree novel. Probably nobody has ever used or ever will use the word *purple-eared;* but if the meaning ever needs to be expressed no one will say that the word is not English. It is not easy to say definitely what kinds of compounds are rejected by the instinct of the language and what kinds are freely admitted. In general, the new compounds that find ready acceptance are those which belong to some particular type or pattern which is exemplified in a large number of common words. One such type is that of the so-called "parasynthetic" formation, like *blue-eyed*, *long-haired*, *swallow-tailed*. English idiom leaves us almost as free to invent new compounds of the type of *blue-eyed* as to invent new phrases of the type of *with blue eyes*. When one or both the elements happen to be very commonly used in combinations of this kind, the compound adjective, whether we have met with it before or not, is quite as natural a mode of expression as the equivalent phrase. . . .

There are several other types of compositions which are so familiar to us from the multitude of existing specimens that we can employ them almost without restriction to form new words. For instance, we seldom hesitate to make, whenever we feel the need of it, a new compound on the pattern of *coach-house*, *hair-brush*, *water-jug*, where the first element indicates the particular use to which the object designated is adapted. It may be remarked that the composition of long polysyllables is generally avoided as ungraceful: and, further, that most of the words derived from French and Latin appear somewhat unfrequently in compounds, probably because in the periods when word-composition was most frequent they were still felt to be more or less exotic.

With reference to the formation of compound verbs, modern English is somewhat peculiar in its usages. Perhaps the reader may be familiar with the practice of modern German in dealing with what are called separable prefixes. In the German dictionaries we find a verb *aufgeben*, compounded of the adverb *auf* "up" and the verb *geben* "to give." In the infinitive this is written as one word, the adverbial part coming first. So it is, under certain conditions, in the indicative and subjunctive; but "I give it up" is ordinarily rendered in German by *ich gebe es auf*, where the two elements are treated as separate words, the adverb coming last, with the object-pronoun between it and the verb. Now combinations of this sort may, from one point of view, be regarded as phrases rather than as compounds; the adverb and the verb are really separate words. The idiom of the language requires that under some conditions the adverb shall precede the verb and that under other conditions it shall follow it; and in the former case custom has ordered that the two words shall be written as one. In Old English the position of the adverb was similarly variable (though the rules for its position were not so strict as in German); but in modern English prose we must always put the adverb last. In poetry, indeed, there are exceptions. Browning writes:

"Then a beam of fun *outbroke*
On the bearded mouth that spoke."

But *outbroke* is merely poetical: in plain prose we must say "broke out." We can, if we please, call *give up*, *break out*, *set up*, *put through*, and such like, "compound verbs"; and in a certain sense the appellation is quite justifiable. If we adopt this nomenclature the number of compound verbs in English is beyond all calculation, and in fact we are continually inventing new ones. In its power of expressing fine distinctions of meaning by this method English vies with Greek and German, and has a great advantage over the Romanic languages, which have hardly any compound verbs at all.

But alongside these "virtual compounds," English has a considerable number of verbs formed with prefixed adverbs, such as *overtake*, *upset, understand*. In most cases their meaning is not obvious from their composition, and it is usually quite different from that of the combination of the verb with the following adverb. "To overtake a person" does not mean the same as "to take a person over"; "to upset a thing" happens to have a meaning quite opposite to that of "to set a thing up." Compounds of this class originated in an older stage of the language; the principle of composition which they represent has almost died out, so that as a rule we cannot form any new words on the same pattern. We can, it is true, with some degree of freedom, prefix *over*, and *under*, with the sense "too much," "too little," to verbs; but in general the modern feeling of the language resists the introduction of compounds of this kind, and very few of them have come in since the sixteenth century.

It is equally foreign to the spirit of the modern language to add to the number of those compound nouns or adjectives which are formed by prefixing an adverb to a verb-stem, a verbal noun, or a participle, such as *outbreak, outfit, income, downfall, downsitting, uprising, onlooker, outfit, forthcoming, downtrodden*. The method of formation of these words is a relic of the time when in a verbal phrase the adverb could precede the verb — when, for instance, it was as natural to say "to out break" as "to break out"; but new compounds of the kind could be easily formed down to the seventeenth century. They are fairly abundant, and admirably expressive; but we have almost[2] entirely ceased to form new words on the same pattern. Although we perhaps more frequently say "to fit up" than "to fit out," it would seem very eccentric to speak of an *upfit*, or an *upfitter;* and we should not think of using *downbroken* as a parallel to *downtrodden*. Cyclists talk of "lighting-up time," not of "uplighting time," which would be quite un-idiomatic. Indeed many such compounds that were once current are now gone out of general use. The translators of our Bible could write "My downsitting and mine uprising"; but in natural modern English the equivalent expression would be "my sitting down and my rising up." Not long ago a

---

[2] A word of this formation which has recently gained some currency in journalistic use is *upkeep*, meaning "(cost of) keeping-up." It appears to have been imported from the Scottish dialect, in which this mode of composition has been more generally used than in standard English. From the same source we have obtained *outcome* (brought into literary English by Carlyle) and *uptake*.

very able foreign scholar, writing a grammatical treatise in English, puzzled his readers by using the word *down-toners* as a name for the class of adverbs which (like *rather, somewhat*) "tone down" the force of the words to which they are prefixed. No doubt, if the phrase "to tone down" had existed in the sixteenth century, a writer of that period could have spoken of a "down-toner" without any risk of not being understood. But in this respect the language has undergone a change, which may be a change for the worse, but which it would be vain to try to resist.

The composition of an agent-noun with a *following* adverb, which was foreign to English in its earliest stages, has been fairly common from the fourteenth century onwards. Chaucer has "*holdere up* of Troye"; Lydgate speaks of Nimrod as "*fynder up* of false religions"; Shakespeare has "the *finder-out* of this secret"; the Bible of 1611 has "a *setter-forth* of strange gods"; later examples of this mode of formation are *cutter-out, hanger-on, filler-in, fitter-up.* . . .

2. Derivation

Old English was considerably less rich than modern English in methods of making new words by derivation. It is true that a large portion of the Old English vocabulary consists of words derived from other words that existed in the language. But very many of these derivatives had been already formed before the English came over from the continent, and the processes by which they were made had become obsolete before the date of the earliest Old English literature. Perhaps this statement may need a little illustration to make it clear to readers unacquainted with philology. Everybody can see that the word *laughter* is derived from the verb *laugh;* and yet we should never think of forming a new substantive by the same process from any other verb. One of Mr. F. R. Stockton's personages, indeed, speaks of a dog "bursting into *barkter*," but nobody would seriously propose to coin a new word of this kind. The ending *-ter* is no longer "a living suffix," and, in fact, it had ceased to be such before Old English existed as a separate language. Many other suffixes which appear in Old English derivatives were, in like manner, never used in the formation of new words.

There is in English a large class of derivative verbs which, if there were no other evidence but that afforded by Old English itself, we should have to regard as formed from other Old English words, either nouns, adjectives, or verbs, by altering their vowel. Thus we find a noun *talu*, tale (in both senses, "number" and "story") and a verb *tellan*, to tell (again in both senses, "to count" and "to narrate"); a noun *salu*, sale, and a verb *sellan*, to sell. *Tȳnan*, to enclose, is derived from *tūn*, enclosure; *blēdan*, to bleed, from *blōd*, blood; *blǣcan*, to bleach, from *blāc*, white or pale; *fiellan*, to fell, cause to fall, from *feallan*, to fall. A comparison of these words with their equivalents in the other Germanic languages teaches us that the true account of their origin is as follows: By the addition of a suffix -*jo* (pronounced *yo*) to the stem of the substantive adjective or verb, a new verb-stem was formed, to which the endings of mood, tense, and person were appended. The earlier forms of the verbs above mentioned were *taljan*, *saljan*, *tūnjan*, *blōdjan*, *blaikjan*, *falljan*. In prehistoric Old English the *j* in this position always produced an alteration in the vowel of the preceding syllable (unless that vowel was *i*), and caused the preceding consonant to be lengthened or doubled if the vowel before it was short. Hence *taljan* became first *telljan* and then *tellan*, *blōdjan* became *blēdan;* and so with the rest. But all this had already taken place before Old English became a written language; and when it had taken place there was an end to the possibility of forming any new "verbs of making or causing" by the process which had previously been so easy. All the verbs apparently formed by vowel change that existed in Old English were inherited from prehistoric times. Perhaps we might have expected that new derivatives would have been formed by vowel-change, in imitation of those which already existed (for instance, a verb *gēdan*, to make good, might have been formed from *gōd*, imitating the relation between *cōl* cool and *cēlan* to cool); but, so far as we know, nothing of the sort ever happened. The Old English language, at the earliest period at which it is known to us, had already lost one of the most useful of the means for word-making which it originally possessed.

Almost all those modes of derivation which were actually current in Old English have continued in constant use down to the present time. Only a few of the most important of them need be mentioned here. In Old English, a verb could be formed from a noun by attaching the conjugational endings to the stem of the noun: thus, from *wilcuma*, a welcome guest, was formed the verb *wilcumian* to welcome (*ic wilcumige* I welcome, *ic wilcumode* I welcomed). In later English, through the dropping away of final syllables, the infinitive, the imperative, and the plural and the first person singular of the present indicative of the derived verb have the same form as the primary noun, so that what takes place seems to be not the making of a new word but the using of a noun as a verb. Hence the operation has become, in modern English, so easy that we perform it almost unconsciously. In colloquial language, we can make new verbs with extraordinary freedom, not only from nouns, but even from phrases. "He *my-dear-fellow*-ed me all the day," for instance, is quite permissible conversational English. Conversely, in modern English, we have an almost unlimited number of nouns which are merely verbs used substantively to denote an act. We can speak of "a wash," "a shave," "a think," "a tumble down," "a dig in the ribs." Occasionally it happens that a noun in this way gives rise to a verb, which in its turn gives rise to another noun, all three words being exactly alike in sound and spelling. Thus, in the following examples: (1) "The *smoke* of a pipe," (2) "To *smoke* a pipe," (3) "To have a *smoke*," the noun of (1) is not, strictly speaking, the same word as the noun of (3). . . .

The following words of modern origin may serve to illustrate the freedom with which we can still form new derivatives by means of suffixes inherited from Old English: clever*ness*, clever*ly*, gentleman*ly*, rogu*ish*, think*er*, nois*y*, horseman*ship*. The English reader will be able at once to recollect many other words formed with each of these suffixes, and will perceive also that he might, without seeming at all eccentric in so doing, venture to use any one of them to form quite new words. Similarly, we can prefix the Old English negative particle *un-* to almost any descriptive adjective. There is another prefix *un-* (of different origin) which we can prefix quite freely to verbs to express a reversal of the action, as in *unfasten, uncover;* and the list of verbs formed with *be-* (like *befog, bemuddle*) is almost interminable.

There are one or two Old English suffixes for which the later language has discovered new uses. The ending *-isc* (now *-ish*) was in Old English chiefly used to form adjectives from names of places or peoples, as in *Englisc* English, *Lundenisc* Londonish. It was also appended in a few instances to common nouns to form adjectives of quality, as in *folcisc* popular (from *folc*, "folk," people), *cildisc* childish. The suffix *-ish* is still a living formative in both these uses. But about 1400 it began to be attached to names of colour, to form adjectives denoting a colour approaching that expressed by the simple word, as in *bluish, blackish*. On the analogy of the adjectives thus formed it afterwards became common to add *-ish* to any sort of descriptive adjective, in order to express a slight degree of the quality which they indicate. It was thenceforth possible, instead of saying "somewhat good" or "somewhat bad," to express the idea by the single word *goodish* or *baddish*. To the characteristic English love of brevity this innovation was welcome; and in modern English we can append the suffix to any adjective denoting a quality that admits of degrees.

The ending *-ly*, representing the Old English *-līce*, forming adverbs of manner from adjectives, became in Middle English much more common, because the final *-e*, which in Old English was the ordinary adverbial suffix, ceased to be pronounced, so that the adjective and its related adverb became identical in form.[3] Early in the sixteenth century, the need was felt for adverbs to indicate position in a numbered series; that is to say, for single words with such meanings as "in the first, second, or third place." The need was supplied by the addition of the adverbial ending *-ly* to the ordinal numeral, as in *firstly, secondly, thirdly, fourthly*, which were unknown to the older language.

Since the close of the Old English period, the vocabulary of our language has been enriched by a multitude of new derivatives formed with the prefixes and suffixes that already existed in Old English; and there can be no doubt that the formation of new words by this means will continue in the future. But the native machinery of derivation, though very little of it has become obsolete, has not been found sufficient for the necessities of the language, and has been largely supplemented by additions obtained from other languages. The adoption of foreign formative machinery has been rendered possible by the fact that many Latin and French primitive words have been taken into the English language along with their derivatives, formed with French or Latin suffixes. When such pairs of words as *derive* and *derivation, esteem* and *estimation, laud* and *laudation, condemn* and *condemnation*, had found their way into the English vocabulary, it was natural that the suffix *-ation* should be recognised by English speakers as an allowable means of making "nouns of action" out of verbs. This particular suffix supplied a real want, because the only native means of forming nouns of

---

[3] For example, in Old English the adjective form was *hlūd* and the adverb *hlūde*, pronounced with two syllables. When the adverbial ending *-e* was no longer sounded in Middle English, the two forms became indistinguishable. But the other Middle English adverbial form in *-ly*, like *sweetly*, could be used to distinguish the adverb from the adjective *sweet*.

Another adverb of manner has been recently revived, that using the suffix *-wise* in expressions like *student-wise*. The Old English *wīse* meant manner. Later it was combined with nouns in the sense of "in the manner of," as in "Let us try once more to argue Cardinalwise," i.e., in the manner of a Cardinal. For further details consult the *Oxford English Dictionary*. [eds.]

action was the suffix -*ing*, which was not quite definite enough in meaning. It is true that this foreign suffix has not been very extensively attached to native words; as a rule, it has been felt to be more in accordance with fitness to adopt French or Latin nouns of action ready made. Still, such words as *botheration, starvation, fairation, flirtation, backwardation*, show that -*ation* has to some extent been regarded as an English formative. Another foreign suffix, -*ative*, though very common in words of Latin derivation, has been appended to a native verb only in one instance, viz. *talkative*. Such formations as *unwalkative* have been employed jocularly, but have never taken root in the language.

In some instances the attempt to naturalise a foreign suffix has failed because there was no real need to be supplied. Wycliff's *everlastingtee* (suggested by *eternitee* from *eterne*) did not find acceptance; the suffix -*tee* (now -*ty*) is confined to words either taken from French or Latin, or at least formed from French or Latin words. The native -*ness* answered all purposes, and the introduction of a foreign synonym was not required.

It was otherwise with many other French suffixes, such as -*age*, -*al* (as used in *withdrawal, upheaval, betrothal*), -*ment*, -*able*, which had nothing corresponding to them in English, and which have been used to form great numbers of words that the language could badly afford to do without. The endings -*ise*, -*ist*, -*ism*, -*ite*, originally Greek, have been very extensively used in the formation of English derivatives.

Old English, in comparison with most other Indo-Germanic languages, was remarkably poor in diminutive endings, and those which did exist were sparingly used. One of them was -*incel*, as in *tūnincel* a little "town" or homestead; but this did not survive into Middle English. The ending -*ling* can hardly be said to have had a diminutive force in Old English, but it was frequently so used in Old Norse, as in *gǣslingr*, which was adopted into English as *gosling* (dialectally *gesling*). The Norse suffix has in modern English become quite common as a means of forming diminutive nouns. We have *kingling, princeling, squireling*, and many similar words. In the fourteenth century the Dutch or Flemish diminutive ending -*kin* (identical with the German -*chen*) came into English use, chiefly from nicknames like *Willekin*, little William, *Jankin*, little John. The fashion of forming such nicknames from Christian names became exceedingly popular, and has left abundant traces in modern surnames like Jenkins, Atkins, Dawkins, Wilkins. In imitation of these proper names, the suffix was afterwards attached to ordinary substantives, and in modern English we can, at least in jocular speech, add -*kin* to almost any noun to form a diminutive. Even more common than -*kin*, and more dignified in use, is -*let*, which we have adopted from French, and have appended to many native words, as in *cloudlet, streamlet, brooklet, leaflet, ringlet, booklet.*

There are two or three foreign prefixes that have been so completely taken into English that we use them almost or quite as freely as we do those of native origin. The most useful of these is the Latin *re-*, again. No dictionary will ever contain all the words formed with this prefix that have been used by English writers; the compounds of *re-* with verbs and nouns of action are as innumerable as those of *un-* with adjectives. In Middle English *again-* was often used as a prefix, but the words so formed have become obsolete: the English love of brevity has caused the native prefix to be supplanted by the foreigner. The Latin and French *dis-* comes next in frequency of use. Although Lydgate, writing about 1430, uses the word *distrust*, it was not until a hundred years later that it became a common practice to attach this prefix to native words. In 1659 a grammarian writes that *dis-* like *un-* and *re-*, "may be prefixed at pleasure." Perhaps this statement was even at that time somewhat exaggerated, and it would certainly be far from correct now. Of the multitude of words beginning with this prefix coined in the sixteenth and seventeenth centuries the greater part are obsolete (though many are still current, amongst them being such familiar words as *dislike, distaste, dispraise*), and since 1700 very few new ones have come into use. The prefix, however, is still felt to be quite English: no one would find any difficulty in understanding such a word as *dislove*, though it has perhaps never been used for centuries. Writers of the nineteenth century have used the verbs *disgod, dishero*, and the nouns *dishealth, discharity;* but formations of this kind have now an appearance of being affected. The French *en-* or *em-* has been used to form several English derivatives, as *endear, embody, embog, enliven, ensare, entangle*. In recent times the Greek *anti-*, against, has become thoroughly naturalised. Words like *anti-slavery, anti-vaccinator, anti-income-tax, anti-corn-law, anti-radical*, are intelligible to every one, and their number is constantly increasing. Perhaps these formations should be placed rather under the head of combination than under that of derivation, though as the preposition *anti* has no separate existence in English this is a debatable question. There are other foreign elements which have in the same manner come into use as prefixes in the formation of English words, such as the Latin *pro* in *pro-Russian, pro-Boer;*

post in *post-Norman, post-date;* *ante* in *antedate, anteroom* (imitating *ante-chamber,* which is French); *præ* in *pre-Roman, pre-Conquest; co-* in *co-mate; sub* in *sub-let; ex* in *ex-king; inter* in *interlock, interleave; non* in *non-conductor, nonconformist, non-existence, non-natural.*

From these examples, to which many more might be added, it will be seen that the English language has not only very greatly enriched its vocabulary by direct borrowing from other tongues, but has also largely availed itself of foreign aid to increase its power of forming new words. There is very little in the borrowed machinery of suffixes and prefixes that can fairly be called superfluous. Almost without exception, it has been adopted, not out of foolish affection, but because it supplied the means of expressing necessary meanings with a degree either of precision or of brevity to which the native resources of the language were inadequate.

According to the definition which we gave of Derivation, "the making of a new word out of an old one," it includes two processes which have not hitherto been mentioned, but which have had a considerable share in the formation of the English vocabulary. These are *Back-formation* and *Shortening.*

BACK-FORMATION

There are many words in English which have a fallacious appearance of containing some well-known derivative suffix. It has not unfrequently happened that a word of this kind has been popularly supposed to imply the existence of a primary word from which it has been derived in the usual way. The result of this supposition is the unconscious creation of a new word, which is made out of the old one by depriving it of what is thought to be its suffix, or sometimes by the substitution of a different suffix. According to some eminent scholars, the verb *to beg* has been in this way formed from *beggar,* which is thought to be adopted from the old French *begar,* a member of the religious order called Beghards, who supported themselves, like the friars, by begging. This etymology is disputed; but there are many other instances of the process which are not open to question. The noun *butcher* is really from the French *boucher,* and the ending is not etymologically identical with the common English suffix of agent-nouns;[4] but in many dialects people have come to use the verb *to butch,* and to speak of "the

---

[4] The English agent-noun suffix is *-er,* as in *writer, singer.* It indicates one who performs the action named by the stem of the word. [eds.]

butching business." Other dialectal back-formations are *buttle*, to pour out liquor, from *butler*, and *cuttle*, to make knives, from *cutler*. The noun *pedlar* is older than the verb *to peddle* or the adjective *peddling*, and *broker* than the verb *to broke* (now obsolete) and the verbal noun *broking*. *Grovelling* was originally an adverb, meaning "face downwards"; it was formed out of the old phrase *on grufe* (which had the same meaning) by adding the suffix *-ling*, which occurs in many other adverbs, now mostly obsolete, such as *backling*, backwards, *headling*, head-first. But *grovelling* was misunderstood as a present participle, and the verb *grovel* was formed from it. Similarly the verbs *sidle* and *darkle* have been formed out of the old adverbs *sideling* and *darkling*. Probably the modern verb *nestle* is not, as is commonly said, the same as the Old English *nestlian* to build a nest, but has been evolved from *nestling*, an inhabitant of a nest, used adjectively as in "nestling brood." Many of the words that have been formed by this process are so happily expressive that the misunderstanding that has given rise to them must be accounted a fortunate accident. . . .

An excellent illustration of the working of this process is seen in the origin of the verb *edit*. The Latin *ēditor*, literally "one who gives out," from the verb *ēdere* to give out, was after the invention of printing often employed in a special sense as denoting the person who "gives to the world" a book or other literary work of which he is not the author. In this sense it has passed into English and other modern languages. But under modern conditions there are two different classes of persons concerned in the production of a book, to either of whom the word might be applied in its literal meaning with equal propriety. The "giver-out" of a book—for instance, of a classical text which has never before been printed—may mean what we now call the "publisher," the man who bears the expense of printing it and makes the arrangements for its circulation among the public, or it may mean the scholar who puts the text into order for publication and provides it with such illustrative matter as it is deemed to require. In early times these two functions were often united in the same person, but they are now ordinarily divided. Now while in French *éditeur* ("editor") has come to mean "publisher," in English it has become restricted to the other of its possible applications. When we use it we no longer think of its literal sense: the prominent function of an "editor" is not that of issuing a literary work to the public, but that of bringing it into the form in which it is to appear. Although *editor* is not a word of English formation, it has an ending which coincides in form with that of English agent-nouns, so that it has naturally suggested the coinage of a verb "to edit," meaning "to prepare for publication as an editor does," *i.e.*, to put into such a form as is thought suitable for the public to read. . . .

SHORTENING

The substitution, in hurried, careless, jocular or vulgar speech, of a part of a word for the whole, is common in most languages, and is especially congenial to the English fondness for brevity of utterance. It does not, by itself, constitute a mode of word-formation: the vulgar *taters* and *bacca*, for *potatoes* and *tobacco*, cannot be called new words, any more than any other mispronunciations can be so called. But when, as very often happens, the original word and its shortened form come both to be generally used by the same speakers with different meanings, or even only with a difference in the implied tone of feeling, a real addition has been made to the vocabulary of the language, and the lexicographer is bound to recognise the shortened form as a distinct word. Shortening, in such cases, is in the strictest sense a kind of derivation; and it is a process which has contributed not a little to increase the English store of words.

Even when the abbreviated form expresses precisely the same meaning as the original form, the two must often be reckoned as separate words, because the longer form is reserved for more dignified or more serious use. *Omnibus* and *bus* are synonymous in the sense that they denote the same objects; but they are not absolute synonyms, because the one is more familiar in tone than the other; the two are used on different occasions. The same thing may be said of *photograph* and *photo*, or *bicycle* and *bike*, though here the abbreviated forms are not universally accepted by educated people as legitimate. Sometimes what was at first only a jocular abbreviation has ousted the longer form from general use, as in the case of *wig* for *periwig*, which was originally an altered pronunciation of *peruke*.

But very frequently a word which has been formed by shortening undergoes a sense-development of its own, in which the original word does not share. Even if anybody is pedantic enough to deny that *bus* is a distinct word from *omnibus*, he cannot refuse to admit that *cab* is a real word, though it was originally a shortened pronunciation of *cabriolet*. A cab and a cabriolet are not the same kind of vehicle at all. So, too, *Miss*, the title given to an unmarried woman, and *Mrs.* (pronounced *Missis*) are now quite different in meaning from each other, and from *mistress*, from which both are derived by shortening. There was a time when *gent* was used by educated people as a familiar abbreviation for *gentleman*, without any depreciatory implication. But in this use it was gradually discarded from the speech of the upper classes, and came to be a contemptuous designation for the vulgar pretenders to gentility in whose vocabulary it still survived. . . .

Some words that originated as playful abbreviations of other words are now used without any consciousness of their origin. *Extra*, in such phases as "an extra allowance," is not the Latin word, but an abbreviation of *extraordinary*. An *extra*, meaning an edition of a newspaper out of the usual course, was at one time called "an *extraordinary*." . . . And only students of etymology know that *chap* is a shortening of *chapman*, properly meaning "trader."

In the Middle English and early Modern English periods it was very common, in the hurry of pronunciation, to drop an initial vowel which immediately preceded the stressed syllable of a word. In this way many words beginning with a vowel came to have an alternative form from which the first syllable was omitted; and almost in every case in which both forms have survived a difference of meaning has been developed. *Assize* and *size* are so different in sense that no one could think of them as the same word, and yet the one is only a shortened pronunciation of the other. The standard magnitude of an article of commerce was settled by an "assize" or sitting of some constituted authority. Hence the standard or authorised magnitude of anything was called its *assize* or *size*, and afterwards the latter form came to mean magnitude in general. *Tend*, as in the phrase "to tend the sick," was originally the same word as *attend;* but the two verbs are no longer synonymous. *Alone*, which stands for an earlier *all one*, was in the Elizabethan period shortened into *lone* when used as an adjective. The Middle English phrase *on live*, equivalent to "in life," was commonly pronounced *alive*, and this, by shortening, afterwards yielded the adjective *live*. *Mend* was originally the same word as *amend*. The shorter form, as usual, serves for the trivial occasions of ordinary life, while the longer form is of more dignified application. We speak of *mending* a stocking, but of *amending* an Act of Parliament. Sometimes other prefixes than those consisting only of a vowel were dropped in the same way. The verb to *vie* is shortened from *envie*—not the same word as the modern *envy*, but adopted from the French *envier*, which comes from the Latin *invitare* to challenge; so that *vie* and *invite* are in ultimate etymology the same. *Fence* is *defence* without its preffix; and *fend*, from which *fender* is derived, is short for *defend*. Several words that originally began with *dis-* or *des-* now begin with *s*. *Stain* is a shorter form of *distain*, which is the Old French *desteindre*, to take out the dye of anything, from the prefix, *des-*, *dis-*, and *teindre* to dye. *Despite*, from the Old French *despit*, the Latin *despectus*, a looking down, despising, has become *spite*. No word now sounds more thoroughly English than *sport*, which has, indeed, been adopted from English into foreign languages; yet it is a shortening of *disport*, which is a word of French origin. To "disport oneself" is, literally interpreted, "to carry oneself in a different direction" from that of one's ordinary business; and hence *disport* and *sport* came to mean amusement or pastime.

Besides the new words that owe their origin to shortening in pronunciation, there are others which have arisen out of abbreviations used in writing. Sometimes the mere initials of a phrase come to be treated as a word, the written letters being represented in pronunciations by their names. Thus we speak of "a question of £ s.d. (*el ess dee*)"; or, again of "an M.P. (*em pee*)," or "a D. C. L. (*dee cee el*)," meaning a person who is entitled to write those initials after his name. Sometimes, again, a word or phrase as abbreviated in writing happens to yield a pronounceable sequence of letters, and takes its place in the language as a word.[5] This occurs most frequently with Latin phrases. Many of the shortened forms are vulgar[6] or jocular, as *infra dig*, *incog*, *nem. con.*, "the *pros and cons*." But *per cent*, *cent per cent*, from the Latin (*centum*) *per centum*, are part of the ordinary English vocabulary. The most curious instance of the formation of a word by this process is *culprit*. Its origin is to be found in the strange corrupt Norman French once used in our courts of justice. When a prisoner had pleaded "not guilty," the reply made on behalf of the Crown was "culpable; prest." This meant "(he is) guilty, (and we are) ready (to prove it)." In the reports of criminal cases the phrase was commonly abbreviated *cul. prest*, and afterwards corruptly *cul. prit*. Then in some way, not very clearly understood, it seems to have come about that the clerks of the Crown, modelling their procedure on the pattern set in the written reports, fell into the practice of using the syllables *cul prit* as an oral formula; and as this formula was followed by the question, "How will you be tried?" addressed to the prisoner, it was popularly apprehended to mean "guilty man." The custom survived in the courts down to the

---

[5] Such a word is now called an acronym. Examples: AWOL, NATO, RADAR. Many acronyms appeared during and after World War II. [eds.]

[6] By *vulgar* Bradley does not mean "indecent." He is using the word in the linguists' sense of "belonging to the common people." [eds.]

eighteenth century; but when *culprit* became a current word with a new sense, it was probably felt that there was an injustice in addressing a prisoner by a term which presumed his guilt, and the use of the formula was discontinued.

3. Root-creation

Perhaps few, even among professed students of language, are aware how large a portion of the English vocabulary has, in the ordinary sense of the word, no etymology at all. We do not mean merely that there are many words the origin of which is and will always remain unknown because of the imperfection of our means of discovery. This is no doubt quite true. But there are also many words which were neither inherited from Old English, nor adopted from any foreign language, nor formed out of any older English or foreign words by any process of composition or derivation. It is to instances of this kind that the name of "root-creation" may be fitly applied.

One of the principal forms of root-creation is that which is known by the name of Onomatopoeia. The word is Greek, and literally means "name-making." It was used by the Greeks to express the fact (common in their own as in other languages) that a noise, or the object producing it, sometimes *makes its own name:* that is to say, is denoted by a word formed in imitation of the sound.

The number of "echoic" words (as they have been called by Dr. Murray) which have arisen in Middle and Modern English is very considerable. We may mention as examples *bang, boo, toom, cackle, cheep, fizz, gibber, giggle, hiss, hum, mumble, pop, quack, rumble, simmer, sizzle, titter, twitter, whirr, whiz, whip-poor-will,* and the reduplicated words *bow-wow, ding-dong, flip-flop, hee-haw, ping-pong, pom-pom, rub-a-dub, tick-tack.*

It is possible that some of the words in the first part of this list may go back to Old English; words of this kind are much more common in speech than in literature, and we are certainly far from knowing the whole of the Old English vocabulary. However, even if they are much older than they can be proved to be, there is no doubt that they are imitative in origin.

The imitation of inarticulate by articulate sounds can never be accurate. Perhaps one or two birds *do* really "make their names"; though even in the case of the cuckoo it is not quite certain that we actually hear the two consonants. But the cries of birds and animals produced by organs having more or less similarity to our own, may be regarded as in some measure articulate. In general the rendering of noises into the sounds of human speech involves some play of fancy, like that which is exercised when we see faces in the fire, or landscapes in the clouds. The resemblance which an imitative word is felt to bear to the inarticulate noise which it names consists not so much in similarity of impression on the ear as in similarity of mental suggestion. For instance, it is not at all literally true that a gun, or a heavy body impinging on a door, says *"bang."* But the sequence of three sounds of which the word consists is of such a nature that it can easily be uttered with force, so as to suggest the startling effect of a sudden violent noise, while the final consonant admits of being prolonged to express the notion of a continued resonance. In this instance and in many others, the so-called "imitative" word represents an inarticulate noise not so much by way of an echo as *symbolically.* That is to say, the elements composing the sound of the word combine to produce a mental effect which we recognise as analogous to that produced by the noise.

In much the same way, the sound of a word may suggest "symbolically" a particular kind of movement or a particular shape of an object. We often feel that a word has a peculiar natural fitness for expressing its meaning, though it is not always possible to tell why we have this feeling, and the reasons, when we can trace them, are different in different cases. Sometimes the notion of natural fitness is an illusion, due to the fact that the word obscurely reminds us of the sound of several other words which happen to have meanings somewhat similar to that which it expresses. But quite often the sound of a word has a real intrinsic significance. For instance, a word with long vowels, which we naturally utter slowly, suggests the idea of slow movement.[7] A repetition of the same consonant suggests a repetition of movement, slow if the vowels be long, and rapid if the vowels be short.[8] The vowels that are produced by the passage of the breath through a narrow opening, such as *ee* or *ĭ*, are suited to convey the notion of something slender or slight, while a full vowel such as *oo* suggests a massive object.[9] A syllable ending in a stopped consonant, especially an unvoiced one like *p, t, k,* preceded by a short vowel, affords a natural expression for the idea of some quick and abrupt action.[10] Sequences of consonants

---

[7] E.g., water *seeps.* [eds.]
[8] E.g., *cock-a-doodle-doo, titter.* [eds.]
[9] E.g., for smallness: *little, slim, bit, teeny, wee.* [eds.]
[10] E.g., *clap, flap, pat, crack, strike, knock, flick.* [eds.]

which are harsh to the ear, or involve difficult muscular effort in utterance, are felt to be appropriate in words descriptive of harsh or
violent movement.[11] It would be possible to say a great deal more
about the inherent symbolism of sounds; but it is not necessary here
to pursue the subject in further detail. The point that needs to be remarked is that this phonetic symbolism (which probably had a large
share in the primary origin of human language) has led to a very large
amount of root-creation in Middle and Modern English. It is worthy
of note that many of the words that have in this way been invented as
instinctive descriptions of action or form occur in groups of two or
three, in which the consonants are alike, while the vowel is varied to
express differences of mental effect. Thus we have *bleb, blob, blub-cheeked,*
all denoting something inflated. The ·initial *bl* was prehaps suggested
by the verb *blow;* the pronunciation of the syllables involves an inflation
of the cheeks which is symbolical of the notion common to the three
words, and the different degrees of fulness in the vowels are obviously
significant of differences of size in the object denoted. Other instances
in which the notion expressed by the consonantal skeleton is modified
by difference in the vowel are *jiggle, joggle; flip, flap, flop; chip, chap,
chop; fimble, famble, fumble; flash, flush.*

Among the many words that owe their origin to a sense of the intrinsic expressiveness of particular combinations of sounds are *bob,
brob, bunch, dab, dodder, fiddle-faddle, fidge, fidget, flabbergast, fudge, hug,
hugger-mugger, hump, jog, see-saw, squander, squelch, throb, thump, thwack,
twiddle, wobble.* Some of these, it is true, may in a certain sense be said
to have an etymology; but their actual meaning is not due to the word,
native or foreign, that may have suggested their formation in the first
instance, but to the impression which is made by their mere
sound.[12]

Many excellent examples of intentional root-creation may be
found among the invented words (not intended to be permanent additions to the language) in Lewis Carroll's *Alice in Wonderland, Through
the Looking-Glass,* and *The Hunting of the Snark.* These clever coinages
derive their effect partly from their suggestion of obscure reminiscences
of existing words, and partly from real phonetic expressiveness. Two
of them, *galumphing* and a verb *to chortle,* have come into pretty general
use, and have found their way into our dictionaries.

[11] E.g., "When Ajax strives some rock's vast weight to throw." Pope [eds.]
[12] For an application of the ideas above to literature, see "Sound Symbolism in
Poetry," pp. 246–257. [eds.]

SUGGESTED ASSIGNMENTS

1. One important kind of compound word is exemplified by *bláckbird*. The first part is given the stronger stress, and this part modifies the second part. This type of compound is sometimes printed as two words, e.g., *hót dog*, but it is nevertheless considered a single compound word if it meets the two qualifications mentioned. Thus both *sídewalk* and *drúg store* are compounds. Some compounds like these have a counterpart in a two-word combination of modifier plus noun. In these the stronger stress is on the second part, as in *black bírd* (any bird that is black in color) and *hot dóg* (a dog that is hot). The left-hand list below is composed of compounds and the right-hand list of their two-word counterparts. Explain the difference in meaning.

bláckberry	black bérry
Whíte House	white hóuse
géntleman	gentle mán
gáme fish	game físh
blúe book	blue boók
hígh chair	high cháir
súrplus store	surplus stóre
dáncing girl	dancing gírl
móving van	moving ván

2. In the light of the exercise above, explain the ambiguity in these sentences:
   a. The lawyer lost a brief case.
   b. I am an outdoor lover.
   c. Our school has two French teachers.
   d. The firemen burst into the smoking room.
   e. In the old creek bed he found a mammoth tooth.

3. Several uses of the suffix *-ish* are mentioned by Professor Bradley. In addition, it is used today to form pejoratives, that is, words with a derogatory meaning. For example, *womanish* is uncomplimentary while *womanly* is complimentary. You might say, "Now don't be teacherish," or "Now don't be baby brotherish," even though no one had ever before used these terms, and they would be accepted and understood. Write ten sentences in which you use the *-ish* suffix to make pejoratives.

4. Look up the following words in the *New English Dictionary* or the *Oxford English Dictionary* to find out their first recorded use: *typewrite, typewriter; donate, donation; subedit, subeditor; burgle, burglar.* Which of them seem to be back-formations?

5. What do you think is the source of the following back-formations: *to advance register, to henpeck, to laze, to bottleg, to coronate, to orate, to reminisce?*

6. What full words do these shortened forms represent: *lab, exam, co-ed, prom deb, varsity, bus, cab, still, flu, taxi, gin?*

7. Shortened forms like those above are often called clipped words or clippings. What clippings are a part of your everyday campus jargon?
8. What do these acronyms mean: WAC, SHAPE, ALCOA? What others do you know?
9. The language of the military services is filled with acronyms. Interview a veteran of World War II or of the Korean War and get a list of acronyms that he used in the service.
10. What onomatopoetic words do you find in these quotations?
   a. And the silken, sad, uncertain rustling of each purple curtain. (*Poe*)
   b. And murmuring of innumerable bees. (*Tennyson*)
   c. I hear lake water lapping with low sounds by the shore.[13] (*Yeats*)
   d. And the plashing of waterdrops
      In the marble fountain.[14] (*Amy Lowell*)
   e. With lisp of leaves and ripple of rain. (*Swinburne*)
11. Are any of these words not onomatopoetic: *thunder, tinkle, clink, boom, bubble, tick, whisper, wheeze, chug, coo, pop?*
12. Write a short paragraph describing something that is heard, using onomatopoeia to make vivid your description. You might use such topics as a train departing from a station, fast-running water in a stream, bird sounds in a wood, a child playing with metal toys, or starting a car engine on a cold winter morning.
13. What words were used to form the following blends: *brunch, smog, splatter, escalator, blurt, electrocute?*
14. Our English word stock is filled with inconsistencies and gaps. Among the reflexive pronouns we find *himself* not **hisself* but *myself* not **meself*. *Impossible* is the negative of *possible*, but *impassive* is the same as *passive*. One who professes *heterodoxy* is a *heretic*, but one steeped in *orthodoxy* is not an **orthetic*. We have many negative adjectives, like *inane, incessant, uncouth, insipid,* which do not have their logically positive forms of **ane, *cessant, *couth,* and **sipid*. This nonrational characteristic of English makes possible the kind of verbal play which we find in the poems that follow.[15] Explain each nonword.

SENSICAL SITUATION

Men often pursue in suitable style
The imical girl with the scrutable smile.

[13] From William Butler Yeats, *Collected Poems of William Butler Yeats*. New York: Macmillan Company, copyright 1928. Copyright renewed 1956 by Georgie Yeats.

[14] From Amy Lowell, *Complete Poetical Works*. Boston: Houghton Mifflin Company, copyright 1955.

[15] These poems are from Felicia Lamport's *Scrap Irony*. Reprinted by permission of the publisher, Houghton Mifflin Company, copyright 1961. Permission also granted by Victor Gollancz, Ltd.

HMM . . .
Nothing gives rise to such wild surmise
As the peachable widow with consolate eyes.

FINE OLD PROFESSOR
The students who had gnored him
Universally adored him
And he died beknownst and famous
A gnonimious gnoramus.

UTTERABLE WISDOM
The wife of a brilliant, becilic professor
Should never show anity too.
Unless she admits that her brain is the lesser
Their marriage will never stay skew.

Analogical Change

EUGENE NIDA

New word forms in language are created by a simple but important linguistic process called analogy or analogical change. You will understand analogy when you know why a child says *goed* for *went* or *deers* for *deer,* or why you sometimes make a slip of the tongue with a form like *teached.* You will hear examples of analogy nearly every day if you listen attentively to the language around you. Eugene Nida explains this process by means of a dialogue between a professor and four students. Dr. Nida—a specialist in New Testament Greek and in Mexican-Indian and African languages—is the author of two valuable books on linguistics: *A Synopsis of English Syntax* and *Morphology: A Descriptive Analysis of Words.*

Ann Ferrell: What do you mean by analogies and analogical changes?

Dr. Thompson: Your question is a good one. But let us turn to mathematics for a moment. It will be easier for us to understand.

From *Linguistic Interludes* by Eugene Nida, published by the Summer Institute of Linguistics, Glendale, California. Reprinted by permission of the author, copyright 1947.

Note the following proportion:

$$2 : 4 = 3 : 6 = 4 : x$$

You do not have to hesitate a moment before answering that x equals 8. The relationships between 2 and 4 and between 3 and 6 establish a pattern, so that x is equal to 8. In mathematics this is an analogical proportion. We have similar situations in languages.

Ann Ferrell: I only wish that languages were as simple.

Dr. Thompson: In some ways they are. A linguistic analogy is only the statement of a proportion or pattern in language. Let us suppose that one has heard the word *radio* for the first time and has never heard the plural of this word. He probably will not hesitate long in forming a plural for the word, for he has a pattern or proportion to guide him. For example,

banjo : banjos = billow : billows = radio : x

With practically no hesitation the speaker will say *radios*.

Bill Downing: But why specifically wouldn't he relate this word to a pattern with *-en*, as in *oxen?*

Dr. Thompson: In the first place, the *-en* occurs regularly with only one word, namely, *oxen*. It constitutes a very limited pattern, even when one includes the words *children* and *brethren*. But there is another feature. The speaker has no doubt had occasion before to note that if he formed a new word on the *s* plural pattern, his choice was correct. He has discovered then that the *s* plural pattern is the productive pattern and that the *-en* pattern is fixed and limited.

Richard North: Then, if one makes up a word such as *educationalize*, does he do so simply by following analogies?

Dr. Thompson: Right. I do not know if I have ever before heard the word *educationalize*, but it makes some "sense," because it is built up on the analogy of other words. There is a pattern and a very extensive one which permits the addition of *-al* to almost any noun ending in *-ion*. In turn, the pattern, or analogical proportion, is very extensive for adding the "factitive" suffix *-ize* to any adjective ending in this suffix *-al*.[1]

Bill Downing: Then the person who wishes to translate from one language into another, especially if he has to construct new words in the language into which he is translating, must by all means know the patterns of formation.

[1] Here the factitive suffix *-ize* has the meaning of make. Examples of this pattern are *legalize, rationalize, civilize*. [eds.]

Dr. Thompson: That is absolutely imperative, but few translators are fully aware of the importance of it.

Jack Sheridan: You mentioned, Dr. Thompson, that analogy affects all parts of a language. How does this involve the syntax?

Dr. Thompson: Every language is filled with such examples. One, however, which becomes involved in so much discussion is the matter of *like* employed as a conjunction.

Ann Ferrell: Dr. Zilch is especially opposed to such "corruption," as he calls it.

Dr. Thompson: Instead of corruption it is purely a matter of the pattern and the pressure of the pattern toward conformity. We have a word *than* which introduces a clause or a phrase. *Like* is employed generally in phrases and is analogically extended to introduce clauses. This conforms the function of *than* and *like*.

I work more than John : I work more than John works =
I work more like John : I work more like John works.

The fact that the word *more* is employed somewhat differently on the two sides of the equation does not alter the value of this analogical pattern. . . .

Bill Downing: Why is it that a language does not reach the static point where no further analogic change will take place?

Dr. Thompson: For one thing, phonetic change takes place continually. This means that items which would otherwise be in analogical conformity are thrown out of line. Moreover, languages cannot live to themselves; they borrow from other languages or dialects, and this necessitates the assimilation and adaptation of material. Furthermore, analogy must have free operation. If if were not for analogy in languages, there would be no such thing as speech; no one would be able to say anything which he had not heard before. Complex communications are only possible because languages are systems of patterns into which we can fit various lexical items in different arrangements from those we have heard before. The only way to prevent change is to stop life. Analogical change ceases only in a "dead"language.

Richard North: I remember that in the King James Version of the Bible *cow* is employed for singular and *kine* for plural. Does the fact that we no longer use *kine* for the plural of *cow* indicate the working of analogy?

Dr. Thompson: It does. An analogical pattern for *cow* : *cows* may have existed in *sow* : *sows*. Moreover, the *s* type of plural was at the time of this change growing in popularity. The *s* plural had become the productive pattern. We are not leveling plural formations now, except perhaps in a class of words such as *rooves* [ˈruwvz] versus *roofs* [ˈrufs] and *laths* [ˈlæðz], versus *laths* [ˈlæθs]. The operation of analogical leveling or pressure toward conformity will occur in one area of the language for a time and then in another.

Bill Downing: Can we tell in advance which part of the language is going to be subject to such leveling influence of analogical change?

Dr. Thompson: We cannot know. We only know that analogy operates in those parts of the language which are out of equilibrium with the general structure as a whole. At present in English considerable leveling appears to be operating in the matter of the so-called perfect participles. Note the fluctuation in the word *proved* versus *proven*. In a high percentage of words in English the form of the perfect participle and the past tense are identical.[2] This situation constitutes a pattern for leveling. At present many speakers employ *proven* in adjectival usage and *proved* in the verb phrase, as in *the proven fact* and *I have proved it*. Compare this with *a shaven face* and *I have shaved*.

Ann Ferrell: Why is it, if analogy attacks the parts of the language that are out of line, that it does not level such items as the irregular parts of the verb *to be?* It would seem that *am, are, is, was, were,* and *be* would be good objects for this analogical change.

Dr. Thompson: Your reaction is a good one, but it so happens that the more frequently employed words of a language resist analogical leveling the most. In many languages one finds that irregular forms appear chiefly among the commonest words and phrases of the language. The reason for this is not difficult to find. Let us presume that one has heard both *proved* and *proven*, but he has not heard them sufficiently often and in enough contexts so as to be sure precisely which one is to be used in a particular situation. He is more likely to choose the form *proved*, which fits the predominant pattern of formation. If the hearer reacts to the situation at all, his reaction will probably be more or less the same as the speaker's, for these forms *proven* and *proved* are probably not too common in his speech and hence the analogical pattern of conformity of past tense and "perfect passive participle" forms has more opportunity to operate. The speaker is easily understood and meets with no derision as to his choice of forms. Each time he uses *proved* in place of *proven* he meets with a similar experience, so continues to use the form representing the more common pattern. But if on the

[2] E.g., *moved, have moved; loved, have loved; seemed, have seemed; made, have made.* [eds.]

other hand the speaker should say *I is trying*, having chosen a less frequently employed form, but one which he may have heard from some speakers of sub-standard English, he may be somewhat misunderstood, and certainly he will not make the most favorable impression upon a speaker of standard English. The forms of the verb *to be* are too common to be objects of doubt. One who says *I is trying* may suffer derision or loss of prestige by such an expression. In many circumstances of life it is important that a speaker make a favorable impression upon those who speak standard English, for these standard-English speakers are those who more or less carry on the affairs of the English-speaking world. They are the ones of social and economic prestige and power. Hence conformity to such a standard will add to the prestige of the speaker and at the same time be a means of obtaining social and economic advantages.

Bill Downing: Does analogy account for the development of some new morphological element, such as *-ly*, which I understand came from *like?*

Dr. Thompson: You are right. The *-like* in such compounds as *manlike* and *woman-like* was changed phonetically to the present *-ly*, and it has become a productive affix which we may add to many nouns to form adjectives and to many adjectives to form adverbs.

Richard North: But if the *-like* in *man-like* changed to *-ly*, how is it that we still have the compound *man-like?* It doesn't seem to make sense to say that something changes, when it remains the same.

Dr. Thompson: The fact that we have *man-like* along with *manly* indicates that a new compound has been formed with the constituents *man* and *like*. The phonemic modification of elements of a compound and then the re-formation of a compound like the first is not uncommon. The compound [ǀhu · s-wi · f] "house-wife" has become modern *hussy*. However, another compound with the same constituents has been made so that we have both *house-wife* and *hussy*.

Ann Ferrell: I should imagine that people might get their analogies twisted at times, even as they do in popular etymologies.

Dr. Thompson: That is so, if you mean that the analogical formations are contrary to the historical pattern of derivation.

Jack Sheridan: You couldn't expect the common run of people to know the history of the language. Even the so-called scholars are caught making mistakes in etymology.

Dr. Thompson: We cannot expect people to follow historical principles, but we can expect them to follow analogical principles, and they do. People are always re-making a language to fit the patterns which they imagine should exist. As an example of this, one may cite the English forms *cherry* and *cherries*. These forms come from Old French *cherise*, borrowed as Middle English *cheris*. But this *s* ending evidently seemed to be a plural, for the speakers formed a new singular on the analogy of the *s* plural type, so that we have now *cherry* singular and *cherries* plural. This is called a back-formation. Note a similar situation in the verb *burgle* derived from the noun *burglar*.

Bill Downing: But do the speakers of a language actually reason out these types of analogies, or is it all quite accidental?

Dr. Thompson: We must never suppose that people apply any strict logistic methodology to their linguistic decisions. Most analogical formations are made quite unconsciously. People "slip" into a pattern without realizing just why they have said what they have. For a moment a speaker may have forgotten which form he has heard in a particular construction. But in normal speech one does not hesitate long, and so a form is produced which is in keeping with what seems to fit the general pattern. Perhaps a speaker wishes to use a past tense form of *dive*. He may have the impression that the vowel changes somewhat, but he doesn't remember exactly what form it is. He shifts then to the regular pattern and says *dived*.[3] Using this form he will probably meet with an understanding response and little if any unfavorable reaction from the hearers.

Jack Sheridan: But what is the relationship between analogy and fluctuations? Let us say that the speaker has heard both forms *dove* and *dived*. What is the factor which would induce him to say *dived* rather than *dove?*

Dr. Thompson: It is convenient to recognize as analogical formation the first occurrence of such an analogical form. From then on, if one has heard both forms, the choice of one or the other is a matter of fluctuation between forms.

Bill Downing: But doesn't analogy play an important role in the fluctuation of forms and the ultimate discarding of one or the other?

Dr. Thompson: It does. If the speaker has heard both *dove* and *dived*, he is very likely to choose *dived* because of the predominance of the regular pattern. In the fluctuation between forms we have to recognize the pressure of the pattern which influences the choice in accordance with the analogical conformity.

[3] The speaker might be moved to say *dove* by analogy with the pattern *ride, rode; drive, drove; write, wrote;* etc. [eds.]

SUGGESTED ASSIGNMENTS

1. The better desk dictionaries of the 1950's indicate that after *babysitter* had entered English, the back-formation *babysit* followed. To form the past tense, which analogical pattern would you expect users of English to follow—*pit, pitted* or *sit, sat?* Why?
2. The word *spatial* is sometimes misspelled *spacial*. What analogy might account for this misspelling?
3. If you wished to use the past tense of *ding*, a verb employed by Robert Burns, what two forms would first come to your mind? What is the analogical basis of each one?
4. What analogical patterns might bring about the use of the following non-standard forms: *knowed* for *knew; brang* for *brought; hisn* for *his?*
5. Collect any unusual word-forms or slips of the tongue that you notice in speech. Some of these probably have their source in analogy. Write a paragraph that will account for the forms that you consider analogical.
6. In the second-year English class of a Dutch high school, the students were heard to use the forms *oneth, twoth,* and *threeth* instead of *first, second,* and *third*. What was the source of these forms?

Etymology and Meaning

SIMEON POTTER

In the first two essays of this section we saw how changes in words and word forms are brought about. In this selection we shall see how word meanings are also altered. Meanings, as subjective phenomena, are especially unstable and elusive, and have not yet been subjected to the scientific analysis that other aspects of language have undergone. However, as we look back into linguistic history and observe successive changes in word meanings, we can discern specific directions in which words change. These directions, or "semantic categories," as Professor Potter calls them, are the subject of the essay which follows. Professor Simeon Potter, who was educated at the University of London and Oxford University, has taught in European universities and is now Professor of English at the University of Liverpool.

From *Our Language* by Simeon Potter. Reprinted by permission of the publisher, Penguin Books Ltd., copyright 1950.

Few words have fixed significations like the pure numbers of mathematics or the technical formulas of chemistry. The mathematical sign π denotes a constant, namely, the ratio of the circumference of a circle to its diameter, or 3.14159 . . . The chemical formula NaCl denotes a substance, sodium chloride, or salt, and it always means that substance and nothing else. These symbols π and NaCl cannot vary with time or circumstance, nor do they ever change with their contexts. Few expressions in daily use have such simple and direct denotations as these. Even words like *mother* and *father*, *sun* and *horse*, denoting primary human relationships or natural objects and creatures, are not quite so definite. All four words occur in Old English and their meanings have not changed in twelve centuries. But in such sayings as "Westminster is the mother of Parliaments," "The child is father of the man," "He seeks a place in the sun," and "He rides the high horse," the primary meanings of these words are manifestly transcended.

What is the *sun*? According to *The Oxford English Dictionary* it is "the brightest (as seen from the earth) of the heavenly bodies, the luminary or orb of day; the central body of the solar system, around which the earth and other planets revolve, being kept in their orbits by its attraction and supplied with light and heat by its radiation." And what is the *horse*? It is "a solid-hoofed perissodactyl quadruped (*Equus caballus*), having a flowing mane and tail, whose voice is a neigh." Now are these so-called "dictionary definitions" really definitions, or are they not descriptions? As long ago as 1891, when he was writing his magistral *Essai de Sémantique*, Michel Bréal demonstrated that the cause of shifting meaning in so many words lay in the impossibility of complete definition and in the varying complexity of the word-thing relationship. "Language," he wrote, "designates things in an incomplete and inaccurate manner: *incomplete*, since we have not exhausted all that can be said of the sun when we have declared it to be shining, or of the horse when we say that it trots; *inaccurate*, since we cannot say of the sun that it shines when it has set, or of the horse that it trots when it is at rest, or when it is wounded or dead."

Could the word or symbol *sun* ever alter its reference and come to mean "moon," or "star," or something else? That, surely, is inconceivable. *Sun* is an ancient word, indicating the same "heavenly body" as its ancestral equivalent in Indo-European five thousand and more years ago. Day by day during those five thousand years, man has observed it "coming forth as a bridegroom out of his chamber, and rejoicing as a giant to run his course." Nevertheless, it has happened that üλ, the etymological equivalent of *sun* in Albanian, has come to mean "star"; and *haul* and *súil*, its equivalents in Welsh and Erse respectively, have come to mean "eye." At some period in the history of each of these three languages that apparently simple and rigid relationship between word and thing, between *symbol* and *referent*, has been deflected and distorted. The meaning, we say, has been changed. The seemingly impossible has occurred and any notions that we may have entertained concerning the indissolubility of the links connecting *etymology* and *meaning* have been rudely dispelled. The shock is, to say the least, disconcerting. We should so much prefer to regard a "speech-form as a relatively permanent object to which the meaning is attached as a kind of changeable satellite" (Leonard Bloomfield, *Language*, p. 426). The study of language would be so much easier for us if we could be assured that the etymology of a word is not only something *real* and *true* (as, indeed, the Greek *etymon* implies) but also that it is something permanent; and that the basic form or *root* of a word has some inherent connexion with the thing, quality or action denoted. Primitive peoples still believe that word has power over thing, that somehow the word participates of the nature of the thing. The word, in fact, is the symbol and it has no direct or immediate relation with the referent except through the image in the mind of the speaker. As Henri Delacroix once said (in *Le Langage et la Pensée*), "All thought is symbolic. Thought first constructs symbols which it substitutes for things." The symbol *sun* has no connexion with the celestial luminary other than through the thoughts or images in the mind of the speaker and the hearer. Unless these two images are identical, there can be no complete understanding.

Latin grammarians sometimes taught wrong etymologies long ago and more recent writers, who should have known better, have occasionally had recourse to fictitious etymologies in order to buttress a theory or to point a moral. Carlyle liked to define *king* as "he who can," associating the word with German *können* "to be capable, to know how to"; and Ruskin found pleasure in reminding the married women in his audience that since *wife* meant "she who weaves," their place was in the home. On the other hand, a speaker may knowingly or unwittingly ignore an etymology. He may refer to a "dilapidated wooden shed," although *dilapidated* is strictly applicable only to a building of stone (Latin *lapis, lapidis*). He may say that "the battalion was well equipped," although *to equip* (French *équiper*, from Old Norse *skipa*) means historically "to fit out a ship." he may say that "the life-boat was manned by Wrens,"[1] "the ocean liner sailed," and "the cattle were shepherded into their stables." A rediscovered etymology may be highly informative and may give pleasure. Those two attractive birds, the nuthatch and the redstart, have most interesting names. The nuthatch is that little creeping bird that breaks or *hacks* the nuts in order to feed on the kernel. For the alternation between final plosive and affricative in *hack* and *hatch*,[2] you may like to compare *bake* and *batch, dike* and *ditch, lyke*wake and *lich*gate, *mickle* and *much, wake* and *watch*. The redstart is still called the fire-tail in some dialects and *start* "tail" survives in *Start* Point "tail-shaped promontory" and *stark*-naked, older *start*-naked. It is interesting to recall that a *governor* is etymologically a "steersman," a *marshal* a "horse-servant," and a *constable* a "companion of the stable." A *companion* is "one who eats bread" with another, a *fellow* is "one who lays down money," a *comrade* a "chamber-fellow," and a *friend* "one who loves."

If the meanings of words are not fixed, if they are liable to flux and change, is there any way of predicting in which direction they are most likely to change? Do changes in meaning admit of empirical generalizations? It is the aim of students of *semantics* or *semasiology* to find the answers to these questions. So far there has been little coordination of semantic research and investigators have fallen into two groups according to their preoccupation with mental processes (Bronislaw Malinowski, C. K. Ogden, and I. A. Richards) or with mathematical symbols (Ludwig Wittgenstein, A. N. Whitehead, Bertrand Russell, and Rudolf Carnap). At present these two groups—the linguistic psychologists and the mathematical logicians—seem to be moving on different planes. The student of language sees many parallels, and he is able to distinguish certain semantic categories, but he inclines to the view that generalizations are dangerous and unprofitable.

The most obvious semantic category is that involving specialization or narrowing. When a speech-form is applied to a group of objects or ideas which resemble one another in some respect, it may naturally become restricted to just one object or idea, and if this particular restriction gains currency in a speech community, a specialized meaning prevails. *Meat*, as in *sweetmeat* and as in the archaic phrase "meat

[1] A Wren is a member of a British World War II organization, the Women's Royal Naval Service. [eds.]

[2] Here the plosive, also called a stop, is the *k* sound; the affricative, or affricate, is the *ch* sound, as in *church*. [eds.]

and drink," meant any kind of food. It now means "edible flesh," a sense formerly expressed by *flesh* and *flesh meat*. *Deer*, like Dutch *dier* and German *Tier*, used to mean "animal" in general, as in Shakespeare's "mice and rats and such small deer." Latin *animal* and French *beast* have taken its place as the general words and *deer* now means "wild ruminant of a particular (antlered) species." *Fowl*, like Dutch and German *Vogel*, denoted "bird" in general as in Chaucer's "Parlement of Foules" and Biblical "fowls of the air" and as in modern names of larger kinds of birds used with a qualifying adjective, such as *sea fowl*, *water fowl*, and *wild fowl*. Otherwise, of course, *fowl* normally means a domestic cock or hen, especially when full grown. *Hound* formerly meant a dog of any breed and not, as now, a hunting-dog in particular. *Disease* was still conceived in Chaucer's day as being dis-ease "absence of ease." It might point to any kind of temporary discomfort and not, as now, to "a morbid physical condition." To *starve*, like Dutch *sterven* and German *sterben*, meant "to die," not necessarily from lack of food. In modern Yorkshire dialect a body can still "starve of cold." A *wed* was a pledge of any kind. In conjunction with the suffix *-lock* forming nouns of action, it has come to be restricted to "the marriage vow or obligation." To the Elizabethans an *affection* was a feeling of any kind and both *lectures* and *lessons* were "readings" of any kind. *Doctrine* was still teaching in general and *science* was still knowledge in general.

Sometimes a word has become restricted in use because a qualifier has been omitted. *Undertaker*, like French *entrepreneur* and German *Unternehmer*, used to mean "contractor, one who *undertakes* to do a particular piece of work." It is now used exclusively in the sense of *funeral undertaker*, although *mortician* has already superseded it in the cities and towns of America. In daily conversation *doctor* "teacher" means "medical doctor" and normally refers to a "general practitioner." Many words have both wider and narrower senses in the living language and many others have varying senses according to the persons addressed. *Pipe*, for example, evokes different images in the mind of the smoker, the plumber, the civil engineer, the geologist, the organist, and the boatswain. The *line* means a clothesline to the laundrywoman, a fishing line to the fisherman, the equator to the seaman (as in Joseph Conrad's *Crossing the Line*), a communication wire to the telephonist, a succession of descent to the genealogist, and a particular kind of article to the man of business. To the geographer *cataract* means a cascade or waterfall, to the engineer a hydraulic controller, but a disease of the crystalline lens to the oculist.

The processes of specialization and extension of meaning may take place in a language side by side. For instance, as we have just seen, *hound* has been restricted in the course of a thousand years from a dog in general to a hunting-dog in particular; contrariwise, *dog* . . . has been extended from "a dog of ancient breed" to include any sort of dog, ranging from a formidable Alsatian to a puny and insignificant lap-dog. *Bird* meant "young birdling," just as *pigeon* meant "young dove" and *pig* "young swine." *Place* has had a remarkable history in English, where it has largely superseded the older words *stead* and *stow*. It derives from the feminine form of the Greek adjective meaning "broad," as in *plateîa hodós* "broad way." In one of its senses it still means "a group of houses in a town or city, now or formerly possessing some of the characters (positive or negative) of a square," like its well-known cognate in French, as in *Place de la Concorde*, or like Italian *piazza*, Spanish *plaza*, and German *Platz*. Now, however, it is also used in a hundred ways. . . .

If we assume that the central meaning of *place* is still "square" and that these other diverse uses *radiate* from the centre, we might equally well put it into our third semantic category: radiation, polysemia, or multiplication. Another excellent example is the word *paper*. It is the same as *papyrus*, the paper-reed of the Nile from the thin strips of which writing-sheets were first made as a substitute for parchment. The name was naturally transferred to paper made of cotton and thence to paper of linen and other fibres. To-day a paper may mean a document of any kind, for instance, a Government White Paper; an essay, dissertation or article on some particular topic, especially a communication read or sent to a learned society; a set of questions in an examination; a journal or a daily newspaper. *Power* "ability to do, state of being able" may hold radiating meanings as diverse as "capacity for mental or bodily action" (power of intellect, power of movement); "mechanical or natural energy" (horse-power, candle-power, electric power-station); "political or national strength" (the balance of power); "possession of control or command over others, dominion, sway" (the power of the Cabinet); "a political state" (the four great powers); and "a mathematical conception" (5^4 or five to the fourth power). Because the *head* is that part of the human body containing the brain, it may be the top of anything, literally or metaphorically, whether it resembles the head in shape (the head of a nail, screw, pin, hammer, walking-stick, flower, or cabbage) or in position (the head of the page, the list, the bed, the table or the stairs); or it may signify the person who is the chief or leader (the head of the school, the business, the family, the house, the State, the Church). It may denote the head of a coin (that side of a coin bearing the sovereign's head); a headland or promontory (St. Bees Head, Great Ormes Head, or Beachy Head, from tautologous Beau Chef Head); a single person or beast (lunch at five shillings a head, fifty head of cattle); or one of the main points or logical divisions of a subject or discourse (dealing with a theme under several heads). These and other senses do not derive from one another. They radiate from a common centre and are therefore mutually independent. Some of these senses will be translated by German *Kopf*, by French *tête*, by Spanish *cabeza* or by the ordinary word for *head* in other languages, but many senses will not permit of such direct translation. Each sense must be considered separately and in the process of translating our linguistic knowledge may be severely put to the test. It is surprising that in ordinary conversation in English there is so little ambiguity.

It is surprising, too, that every day we use words in both literal and metaphorical senses and that there is little danger of being misapprehended. We may speak as we will of "bright sunshine" or "a bright boy"; "a sharp knife," "a sharp frost" or "a sharp rebuke"; "a cold morning" or "the cold war"; "the Black Country" or "the black market." A person who is slow-witted may be described metaphorically as "dull," "obtuse," or "dim," the latter term being associated with the German *dumm* meaning "stupid," although cognate with our *dumb*. "Dumb" in German is now *stumm*, which is related etymologically to our *stammer*. Many words are themselves old metaphors: *dependent* "hanging from" (Latin *dē-pendens*); *egregious* "selected from the herd" (Latin *ē* for *ex + grex, gregis* "herd"); *precocious* "too early ripe" (Latin *praecox* from *prae* "before" + *coquere* "to cook, ripen").

Our next category of semantic changes may be labelled concretization. The naming of abstract qualities, such as *whiteness*, *beauty*, and *justice*, comes late in the evolution of a language because it results from conscious or unconscious comparison in the mind of man. Does *beauty* really exist apart from beautiful things? On this question the medieval schoolmen argued for centuries. No sooner are abstract nouns formed than men tend to think of each appearance of a quality or action in the abstract as a separate entity and so, by concretization, they make abstractions tangible and visible once more. *Youth*, "youngness" in the abstract, becomes a "young man." In the form *geogoþ* this word occurs eleven times in *Beowulf*, five times with the abstract meaning "youth," but six times with the concrete and collective meaning "young men." In much the same way Latin *multitūdo* "maniness, the quality of being many" came to signify "a crowd" and *congregātio* "flocking together" came to mean "a body of people assembled." Barristers appointed counsel to the Crown are named *King's Counsel.* A judge is addressed as *Your Honour* and an archbishop as *Your Grace. Health* is the quality of being *hale* or *whole*, soundness of body and mind. Modern man seeks diligently to maintain physical, mental, and social health. It is Greek *hugíeia* (from the adjectival form of which comes our *hygiene*), Latin *salūs*, French *la santé*, and German *die Gesundheit.* Clearly these are all highly abstract forms. Nevertheless, even *health* becomes concrete in the sense of a toast drunk—"Here's a health unto His Majesty!" *Wealth* was primarily "weal," "welfare," or "well-being," the state of being "well." In the old assonantal formula "health and wealth" the two abstract substantives were practically synonymous. But side by side with this meaning of *wealth* the concretized sense of "worldly goods, riches, affluence" also developed. The expression *wealth of nations*, denoting "the collective riches of a people or country," was certainly current before it was adopted by Adam Smith in 1776 as the title of his epoch-making book. "Money," wrote John Stuart Mill in 1848, "being the instrument of an important public and private purpose, is rightly regarded as wealth." "Let us substitute welfare for wealth as our governing purpose," said Edward Hallett Carr in 1948, exhorting us, in fact, to restore to the word *wealth* its older meaning. *Kindness, mercy, opportunity,* and *propriety* are historically abstractions, but to-day we speak of *kindnesses* in the plural in the sense of "deeds of kindness," *mercies* as "instances or manifestations of mercy," *opportunities* as "favourable chances or occasions," and *proprieties* as "proper forms of conduct." Similarly *provision* "foreseeing, foresight" has come to be applied in the plural to "stores of food."

Sometimes words, like men, "fall away from their better selves" and show deterioration or catachresis. *Silly* once meant "happy, blissful, holy," as in the "sely child" of Chaucer's *Prioress's Tale.* Later it signified "helpless, defenceless," becoming a conventional epithet in the "silly sheep" of Milton, Cowper, and Matthew Arnold. Then it descended yet lower and came to imply "foolish, feeble-minded, imbecile." *Crafty* "strong" and *cunning* "knowing" were once attributes of unmingled praise. A crafty workman was one skilled in a handicraft; a cunning workman was one who knew his trade. *To counterfeit* meant simply "to copy, reproduce," conveying no suggestion of fraud. "What finde I here?" asked Bassanio, as he opened the leaden casket, "Faire Portias counterfeit." (*The Merchant of Venice*, III, ii, 115.) It was, in fact, no counterfeit in the modern sense, but a true and lifelike delineation that came "so near creation." A *villain* once meant "a slave serving in a country-house or *villa*," a man occupying a lowly station in life. Chaucer's *vileynye* already showed depreciation, for it connoted the opposite of *courteisye*, that comprehensive term for a noble and chivalrous way of life, implying high courtly elegance and politeness of manners. A *knave*, like German *ein Knabe*, was just "a boy"; later, as in "the kokes knave, thet wassheth the disshes" of the *Ancrene Riwle*, "a boy or lad employed as a servant"; later still, "a base and crafty rogue." Like *rogue* and *rascal*, *knave* may still be used jocularly without seriously implying bad qualities. *Varlet*, a variant of *valet*, has shown an almost identical catachresis. *Nice* has become just a pleasant verbal counter: anything or everything may be nice. But *nescius*, its Latin antecedent, had the precise meaning "ignorant, unaware," a meaning maintained in Chaucer side by side with that of "foolish." From "foolish" it developed the sense "foolishly particular about small things," and so "fastidious, precise," as in "nice in one's dress." Later it was made to refer to actions or qualities, as in "a nice discrimination" and "a nice sense of honour." Since then, as H. W. Fowler has sagaciously observed in *A Dictionary of Modern English Usage*, "it has been too great a favourite with the ladies, who have charmed out of it all its individuality and converted it into a mere diffuser of vague and mild agreeableness." It is a pleasant, lazy word which careful speakers are bound to avoid using in serious contexts. *Propaganda*, which now implies an organized and vicious distortion of facts for a particular purpose, has suffered sad depreciation in recent years. In 1622 Pope Gregory XV founded a special Committee or Congregation of Cardinals for the Propagation of the Faith, in Latin *Congregātio dē propāgandā fide*. That marked the beginning of the history of this word, which, you see, is the ablative singular feminine form of the gerundive of *propāgāre* "to fasten or peg down slips of plants for growth, to multiply plants by layering." Most appropriately the Latin metaphor is agricultural and botanical. *Propaganda* should mean, in its extended sense, the dissemination of news of any kind. Unfortunately, since the year 1880 the meaning of the word has been poisoned.[3] Propaganda and trustworthy news are

[3] Professor Potter explains as follows: "When I wrote that this semantic 'poisoning' has gone on 'since the year 1880' I was thinking more especially of British political life and of that bitterly contested General Election in that year which brought Benjamin Disraeli's glorious Ministry to an end. Since then the word has been in frequent political circulation as a smear-word, far removed from its first modern use by the Roman Catholic Church in 1622." [Letter to Joseph C. Bohme, Jr.] [eds.]

dissociated in our minds. We even hear of propaganda and counter-propaganda!

Now all these semantic categories—specialization, extension, radiation, metaphor, concretization, and deterioration—are very interesting. Others too might be added to show in yet greater detail how inconstant are the relationships between symbol, image, and referent (word, thought, and thing). Men have sometimes associated speech-forms wrongly and the meanings of words have thus been modified capriciously and unpredictably. Let us admit that there have been losses and gains. When we blunder and are forced to offer abject apologies, we talk of eating *humble pie* and not *umble pie*, one made of umbles or entrails. Vaguely and hazily we may associate the epithet with *humble bee*, which is the old *hummle bee*, the bee that continuously hums. Hazily and lazily we may associate an *insurance policy* with the Government's *foreign policy*, not pausing to recollect that these two *policies* are etymologically quite different words. We associate *touchy* with *to touch*, forgetting that *touchy*, *techy*, or *tetchy* derives from *tetch* "a fit of petulance or anger, a tantrum." We say *restive* "refusing to move or budge" when we are half thinking of *restless*. Pardonably, perhaps, we connect *uproar* with *roar* and *outrage* with *rage*.

Certain expressions, like *comity* and *fruition*, are frequently "used loosely," and, since they are correspondingly in danger of being "understood loosely" too, careful speakers are almost compelled to refrain from using them. *Comity* means "courtesy, urbanity," not "company, assembly." The *comity of nations* is "the obligation recognized by civilized nations to respect one another's laws and customs." *Fruition* signifies "enjoyment," not "bearing of fruit." "If we live by hope," said Bishop Hugh Latimer, "let us desire the end and fruition of our hope." Like Archbishop Thomas Cranmer in the Epiphany Collect, Latimer was here using the word correctly. To-day we frequently hear of plans and projects "coming, or being brought, to fruition." *Definitive* "having the quality or character of finality" should not be used as a more imposing form of *definite* "clear, precise, unmistakable." Our conception of the Middle Ages may be given a rosy tinge by an over-optimistic misinterpretation of the phrase "merry England," echoed by Sir Walter Scott in the opening sentence of *Ivanhoe*. King Charles II was "the merry monarch" and fun-fairs have their "merry-go-rounds," but "merry England" implied a pleasant and delightful countryside rather than a gay and carefree people. It was in the Northern *Cursor Mundi* that this epithet was first applied specifically to England. Later medieval poets repeated it and Spenser gave it wide currency in the First Book of *The Fairie Queene* (Canto X, Stanza 61) when he identified the Red Cross Knight with "Saint George of mery England." But Spenser's "mery England" in the sixteenth century meant much the same as Blake's "England's green and pleasant land" in the early nineteenth.

When Francis Bacon referred to various people in the course of his *Essays* as *indifferent, obnoxious,* and *officious,* he was describing them as "impartial," "submissive," and "ready to serve." When King James II observed that the new St. Paul's Cathedral was *amusing, awful,* and *artificial,* he implied that Sir Christopher Wren's recent creation was "pleasing, awe-inspiring, and skillfully achieved." When Dr. Johnson averred that Milton's *Lycidas* was "*easy, vulgar* and therefore *disgusting,*" he intended to say that it was "effortless, popular, and therefore not in good taste."

Men frequently find themselves at cross-purposes with one another because they persist in using words in different senses. Their long arguments emit more heat than light because their conceptions of the point at issue, whether Marxism, democracy, capitalism, the good life, western civilization, culture, art, internationalism, freedom of the individual, equality of opportunity, redistribution of wealth, social security, progress, or what not, are by no means identical. From heedlessness, sloth, or sheer lack of intelligence men do not trouble to clarify their conceptions. Symbols or counters remain unchanged, but as the argument proceeds images and referents (thoughts and things) vary without end. By the way, what do *you* mean by *progress?* To define your terms at every step may seem an intolerable burden, but it is a sobering and salutary discipline. It is, indeed, the only effective way to sharpen up a blunted word and to restore its cutting edge.

SUGGESTED ASSIGNMENTS

1. Write a theme on radiation, or polysemia, in relation to one of these words: *heart, root, run.* Use an unabridged dictionary to help you.
2. In the foregoing pages Professor Potter discusses degeneration in words but does not mention the opposite process, elevation, whereby word-meanings change in a more favorable direction. Using a large dictionary, find out how these words are examples of elevation: *knight, fond, steward, marshall, pastor, pluck, guts.*

3. Look up the derivation of the following words and indicate which process each exemplifies, specialization or extension: *dunce, minister, butcher, pocket, box, campus, colossal, poison, liquor, bootleg*.

4. Which semantic category is illustrated in these everyday expressions? He told a *suggestive* story. They say he *drinks*. Your examination *smells*.

5. Spend an hour poking around in your desk dictionary and collecting interesting etymologies. In some cases you may wish to refer to an unabridged dictionary for further information. Then write a theme on what you found, using some such title as "An Etymological Excursion through a Dictionary," or "Glimpses of the Past in a Dictionary."

6. When a word deteriorates, that is, takes on a worsened meaning, a substitute often comes into use to replace it in a neutral or favorable sense. This substitute is called a euphemism. A euphemism may be described as a softened, indirect expression used instead of one that seems too harsh or direct or unfavorable. For example, *he passed away* and *he is gone* are euphemisms for *he died*. Circumlocutions like these may arise from the desire to avoid giving pain and in such cases must be accounted useful terms. At times, however, euphemisms are employed merely through hypersensitivity or excess of delicacy. The Victorian use of *white meat* to avoid saying *breast*, and the Ozark woman's use of *lay down* to avoid the indelicate suggestiveness of *go to bed* seem to us cases of overconcern hinting of prudery. There is still a third reason for the use of euphemistic terms: to enhance prestige. The job of a garbage collector, for example, seems more prestigious if he is called a *sanitary engineer*.

    a. In everyday discourse the terms *insane, lunatic,* and *insane asylum* have given way to various euphemistic substitutes. List as many as you can for each term.

    b. Euphemisms are frequently employed in our daily lives; e.g., *perspiration* for *sweat*, *dentures* for *false teeth*, *underprivileged* for *stupid*, *custodian* for *janitor*. Write a theme on "Euphemisms in Common Use."

    c. Delineate a human situation in which you would find it advisable to use euphemisms and explain how you would handle the situation.

Words with Blurred Edges

STEPHEN ULLMANN

Words are not the specific and precise counters of meaning that we sometimes imagine. Rather, their meanings tend to be general and imprecise. What, for example, is a cat? A wild animal? A tractor? A spiteful woman? A domestic pet? Or, where is the dividing line between a hill and a valley,

between here and there, between red and pink? In this essay
Stephen Ullmann treats of vagueness in words—its sources,
uses, and disadvantages. Professor Ullmann has explored
problems of meaning in The Principles of Semantics and in
Words and Their Use.

Throughout the centuries, writers and thinkers have been critical of
the shortcomings of language. Some of their complaints were kept in
general terms; others singled out the word as the chief offender. In his
Seventh Epistle, Plato made some extravagant statements on the subject:
"No intelligent man will ever be so bold as to put in language those
things which his reason has contemplated; . . . if he should be betrayed
into so doing, then surely not the gods but mortals have utterly blasted
his wits." . . .

More specific criticisms of the word center mostly on its lack of
precision. Goethe's Faust sums up the position in a terse and forceful
image when he explains why he has no name for God: "Names are
sound and smoke, befogging a heavenly glow." Voltaire is more explicit about the vagueness of words: "Il n'est aucune langue complète,
aucune qui puisse exprimer toutes nos idées et toutes nos sensations;
leurs nuances sont trop imperceptibles et trop nombreuses . . . On est
obligé, par exemple, de désigner sous le nom général d'*amour* et de
haine, mille amours et mille haines toutes différentes; il en est de même
de nos douleurs et de nos plaisirs."[1] Byron too complains about the
ineffectiveness of our words:

> Oh that my words were colours! but their tints
> May serve perhaps as outlines or slight hints.
> *Don Juan, Canto VI, stanza cix.*

In our own day, Wittgenstein has spoken of concepts with "blurred
edges" and has compared them to indistinct photographs, adding: "Is
it even always an advantage to replace an indistinct picture by a sharp
one? Isn't the indistinct one often exactly what we need?" Some modern
schools of poetry would wholeheartedly agree with Wittgenstein, and
would value the suggestive and evocative power of words far higher

From *Semantics: An Introduction to the Science of Meaning* by Stephen Ullmann. Reprinted by permission of the publisher, Basil Blackwell, copyright 1962.

[1] "There is no complete language, none which could express all our ideas and
all our sensations; their shades are too imperceptible and too numerous . . . One is
forced, for example, to denote by the general terms *love* and *hatred* a thousand entirely different loves and hatreds; and the same happens with our pains and our
pleasures." (quoted by Nyrop, *Sémantique*, p. 444).

than any logical precision. This was a basic principle of the Symbolist movement and was developed in Verlaine's famous poem, *Art poétique:*

> Il faut aussi que tu n'ailles point
> Choisir tes mots sans quelque méprise:
> Rien de plus cher que la chanson grise
> Où l'Indécis au Précis se joint.[2]

Mallarmé put the same point more briefly and ironically in his poem *Toute l'âme résumée:*

> Le sens trop précis rature
> Ta vague littérature.[3]

. . . It would seem, then, that the vagueness of our words is a handicap in some situations and an advantage in others. If one looks more closely at this vagueness one soon discovers that the term is itself rather vague and ambiguous: the condition it refers to is not a uniform feature but has many aspects and may result from a variety of causes. Some of these are inherent in the very nature of language, whereas others come into play only in special circumstances.

(1) One of the principal sources of vagueness is the *generic* character of our words. Except for proper names and a small number of common nouns referring to unique objects, words denote, not single items but classes of things or events bound together by some common element. As Bloomfield very clearly put it . . . we must discriminate between "non-distinctive features," such as the size, shape or color of any particular apple, and the "distinctive features" which are common to all the objects of which we use the word *apple*. In the case of more complex terms, the process of generalization works somewhat differently. Wittgenstein has examined, for example, the nature of the concept of *game*. By comparing various types of games—board-games, card-games, ball-games, Olympic games, etc.—he found a "complicated network of similarities overlapping and criss-crossing," with common features appearing and disappearing as we consider more and more games: some are amusing, others are not; some are competitive, others solitary; some involve skill, others mere chance, and so on. Wittgenstein concludes that these similarities are rather like "family resemblances": "the various resemblances between members of a family: build, features, color of eyes, gait, temperament, etc., etc., overlap and criss-

---

[2] "It is also necessary that you should not always choose the right word: there is nothing more precious than the grey song where Vagueness and Precision meet."

[3] "Too precise a meaning will erase your vague literature."

cross in the same way." In this sense one could say that the various phenomena known as *games* form a family.

Except in the case of rigorously defined scientific or technical terms, this process of generalization will inevitably involve an element of vagueness. This has led some philosophers to describe the word as crude and banal, robbing our experiences of their personal content and finer nuances, and interposing a screen between us and the non-linguistic world. Bergson speaks of "le mot brutal, qui emmagasine ce qu'il y a de stable, de commun et par conséquent d'impersonnel dans les impressions de l'humanité, écrase ou tout au moins recouvre les impressions délicates et fugitives de notre conscience intellectuelle."[4] Elsewhere the same philosopher writes: "Le mot, qui ne note de la chose que sa fonction la plus commune et son aspect banal, s'insinue entre elle et nous . . . Nous ne saisissons de nos sentiments que leur aspect impersonnel, celui que le langage a pu noter une fois pour toutes parce qu'il est à peu près le même, dans les mêmes conditions, pour tous les hommes."[5] This is perfectly true and in some ways regrettable, but it is the price we have to pay for having a means of social communication flexible enough to cope with the infinite variety of our experiences.

The generic nature of our words has often been described as an element of *"abstractness"* in language. There is some danger of ambiguity here since the usual opposition between abstract and concrete does not correspond to that between generic and particular. A word may be extremely general in meaning and yet remain on the concrete plane; thus, the terms *animal* and *plant* are the widest in range in the whole system of zoological and botanical classification, and yet they are concrete in the sense that specific animals and plants are tangible, material things as opposed to pure abstractions such as *liberty* or *immortality*. In a wider sense, however, generic terms can be regarded as "abstract," i.e. more schematic, poorer in distinguishing marks than particular terms; as the logician would say, they have greater extension and lesser intension: they apply to a wider range of items but tell us less about them.

[4] "The crude word, which stores up that which is stable, common and therefore impersonal in the experiences of mankind, and crushes or at least overlays the delicate and fleeting impressions of our intellectual consciousness" (quoted from *La Conscience* in Nyrop, *Sémantique*, p. 448).

[5] "The word, which notes only the commonest function and the banal aspect of the object, interposes itself between the object and ourselves . . . We can grasp only the impersonal aspect of our feelings, that which language has noted once and for all because it is approximately the same for all men under the same conditions" (*Le Rire*, 15th ed., Paris, 1916, pp. 156 f.; cf. Nyrop, *Sémantique*, p. 447).

The word *tree*, for example, is more general and therefore more "abstract" than *beech;* in the same way, *plant* is more abstract than *tree*—in fact, it is such a wide and general concept that it did not exist in Classical Latin and only emerged in the course of the Middle Ages: the Latin word *planta* meant "sprout, slip, cutting," not "plant."[6]

Practically all our words are generic to a greater or lesser extent, yet there is a great deal of variation between different languages: some seem to favor particular terms while others lean towards the abstract and general type. For a long time it was customary for linguists, psychologists and anthropologists to regard the languages of primitive races as rich in specific terms and poor in generic ones. This was commonly interpreted as a sign of "pre-logical mentality," of undeveloped powers of generalization. These races, it was thought, literally could not see the wood for the trees: they were immersed in particular experiences and unable to rise above them, to analyze and classify them. The Zulus, for instance, were reported to have no word for "cow," only specific expressions for "red cow," "white cow," etc.; the Tasmanian aborigines had no single term for "tree" but possessed names for each variety of gum-tree and wattle-tree; in the Bakaïri language of Central Brazil each parrot has its special name but there is no word for "parrot" in general.[7] There are so many reports of this kind, and they sound so plausible, that there may well be some truth in the theory. Unfortunately, however, the evidence is suspect; it is sometimes based on faulty observations by early missionaries, which were uncritically accepted by successive generations of linguists quoting one another. In this way, the myth that there is no term for "washing" in the language of the Cherokee Indians was perpetuated until it was exploded a few years ago by an American specialist.[8] American linguists, who have done much valuable field-work on Indian tongues, are, as a matter of principle, opposed to the notion of "primitive languages"; as a philosopher pointed out during a recent symposium on language and culture, everyone was "quite willing to talk about the primitiveness of a culture," but most people were "quite unwilling to talk about the primitiveness of language."[9] Until all the evidence has been carefully

[6] Quoted, from an article by Wartburg, in Baldinger, *Cahiers de l'Association Internationale des Etudes Françaises*, xi, p. 259.

[7] Jespersen, *Language*, p. 429; cf. also Kronasser, *Handbuch der Semasiologie* (Heidelberg, 1952), ch. 11.

[8] A. A. Hill, "A Note on Primitive Languages," *International Journal of American Linguistics*, xviii (1952), pp. 172–7.

[9] H. Hoijer (ed.), *Language in Culture. Conference on the Interrelations of Language and other Aspects of Culture* (Chicago, 1954), p. 219.

sifted by modern scientific methods it is better to withhold judgment on this issue.[10]

It should also be noted that richness in particular terms is not necessarily a symptom of inability to generalize; it may be due to the influence of environment and living conditions. Thus it is not altogether surprising to learn that the Eskimos and the Lapps have a multiplicity of terms for different kinds of snow, whereas the Aztecs use the same word stem for "cold," "snow" and "ice."[11] Each environment creates its own particular needs and problems; for the inhabitants of the arctic region snow is a factor of such overriding importance that every state and aspect of it has to be carefully specified. Similarly the Paiute Indians, who live in a desert area, "speak a language which permits the most detailed description of topographical features, a necessity in a country where complex directions may be required for the location of water holes."[12] Language is, in the words of Sapir, "a complex inventory of all the ideas, interests, and occupations that take up the attention of the community."[13] . . .

Even between languages based on the same civilization there can be marked differences in the use of general and specific terms. French is usually regarded as a pre-eminently "abstract" language, whereas German and even English are "concrete" in comparison. There are various symptoms of this abstract streak in French. In some cases, a single, generic term in French—supplemented, if need be, by the context—will correspond to three or four particular expressions in German. The latter language will specify, for example, the various forms of locomotion which are all lumped together in French in the generic term *aller* "to go": *gehen* "to go, to walk," *reiten* "to ride on horseback," *fahren* "to drive, to travel by train or car, etc." It is of course possible to indicate the means of locomotion in French by adding a supplementary phrase to the verb (*aller à pied* "on foot," *à cheval* "on horseback," etc.), but this will be done only when necessary, whereas the more differentiated German terms will automatically convey this extra information. . . .

(2) Our words are never completely homogeneous: even the

[10] On the evidence of child language on this point, cf. W. Kaper, *Kindersprache mit Hilfe des Kindes* (Groningen, 1959), p. 11.

[11] See Segerstedt, *Die Macht des Wortes* (Zurich, 1947), pp. 56 ff., and Henle, *Language, Thought, and Culture* (Ann Arbor, 1958), p. 5.

[12] Ibid.

[13] Ibid. (Quoted from *Selected Writings by Edward Sapir*, D. Mandelbaum, ed. Berkeley, 1949, pp. 90 f.)

simplest and the most monolithic have a number of different facets depending on the context and situation in which they are used, and also on the personality of the speaker using them. This *multiplicity of aspects* is another important source of vagueness. . . . If we take an ordinary common noun with a concrete meaning, such as *book*, its significance will vary according to its users: it will mean rather different things to an author, a publisher, a printer, a bookseller, a book-collector, a librarian, a specialist reader, a non-specialist reader, a bibliographer and others. With abstract words, such differences in application are even more marked. Take, for instance, the following three examples of the adjective *mortal* in *Paradise Lost:*

> chase
> Anguish and doubt and fear and sorrow and pain
> From *mortal* and immortal minds.
>
> *Book I, ll. 557–9.*

> the fruit
> Of that forbidden tree whose *mortal* taste
> Brought death into the World.
>
> *Book I, ll. 2–3.*

> to redeem
> Man's *mortal* crime.
>
> *Book III, ll. 214–15.*

Clearly, the adjective has three different shades of meaning in the three passages: in the first one it means "subject to death, destined to die," in the second "causing death," and in the third "deadly," as opposed to "venial," sin. In fact, Milton obtains a very striking effect by playing on the diversity of these overlapping meanings. A fuller version of the last extract reads:

> Which of ye will be *mortal*, to redeem
> Man's *mortal* crime, and just, the unjust to save?

In some words, the process of diversification can go to remarkable lengths without destroying the fundamental unity of their meaning. The term *style* is an example in point. It comes from the Latin *stilus*, the name of the writing-rod, and was originally applicable to writing alone, but in the course of the centuries it has vastly extended its range. In the words of Sir Walter Raleigh:

. . . the fact that we use the word *style* in speaking of architecture and sculpture, painting and music, dancing, play-acting, and cricket, that we can apply it to the careful achievements of the housebreaker and the poisoner and to the spontaneous animal movements of the limbs of man or beast, is the noblest of unconscious tributes to the faculty of letters.[14]

As can be seen from these examples, such shifts in application can easily lead to multiple meaning. . . .

(3) A further factor making for vagueness is the *lack of clear-cut boundaries* in the non-linguistic world. Here again it is necessary to distinguish between concrete and abstract experiences. Even in our physical environment we are often faced with phenomena which merge into one another and which we have to divide up, as best we can, into discrete units. The spectrum of colors is, for example, a continuous band; it is we who introduce into it a certain number of more or less arbitrary distinctions which may vary from one language to another, and sometimes even from one period to another within the same idiom. . . . Another concrete sphere where sharp lines of demarcation are often lacking is the human body. This explains certain shifts in meaning where the name of one part of the body has come to denote a neighbouring region. Thus, the Latin word for "hip," *coxa*, has given *cuisse* in French, which means "thigh," not "hip." . . . It could not have occurred if there were a definite boundary between the two areas in our anatomy. There have been similar shifts of meaning between various parts of the facial region. Most of the Romance words for "mouth" which have replaced the Latin *os, oris:* French *bouche*, Italian *bocca*, Spanish *boca*, derive from Latin *bucca* "puffed up cheek;" the Rumanian *bucă* still means "cheek." A more intricate interchange can be seen in the history of English *chin* and cognate terms. The German *Kinn* and the Dutch *kin* have the same meaning as the English word, but Swedish *kind* means "cheek" and so does the Latin *gena* from the same family, whereas another related form, Sanskrit *hanuh*, signifies "jaw," and the Greek γένυς can mean either "jaw" or "cheek."[15]

When we turn to abstract phenomena, this lack of boundaries is even more conspicuous since the distinctions are largely man-made: they have no real existence without the linguistic forms in which they are clothed. Delimiting such concepts is often a difficult and delicate operation. The classic example is of course the frontier between *talent* and *genius*. Owen Meredith once wrote: "Genius does what it must, and Talent does what it can," but whether one accepts this formula or

[14] *Style*, 2nd ed., 1897, pp. 1–2.
[15] Cf. Bloomfield, *Language*, pp. 425 ff.

any other, there will always be border-line cases lying astride the boundary wherever one may trace it.[16]

For the specialist it is of the utmost importance to define his terms clearly and to distinguish them sharply from one another. Hence the endless and often acrimonious discussions in philosophical works, in the law courts and at diplomatic conferences, on the precise definition and delimitation of abstract words. A lawyer will carefully avoid any confusion between *felony* and *misdemeanor*, a theologian between *venial* and *deadly* (*mortal*) sins, a psychiatrist between *neurosis* and *psychosis*, a linguist between *phonemes* and *allophones*. The abstract terms of ordinary language are, however, far less precise, and it is left to the dictionary to introduce some semblance of order into their overlapping uses. . . .

(4) Yet another source of vagueness in words is *lack of familiarity* with the things they stand for. This is of course a highly variable factor, dependent on the general knowledge and the special interests of each individual. Many townspeople will have extremely hazy notions about the meaning of animal and plant names or agricultural terms which will be perfectly clear to any gardener or farmer. How many readers, for example, will be able to visualize some of the plants mentioned by Ophelia: "There's *fennel* for you, and *columbines*. There's *rue* for you; and here's some for me" (Act IV, scene 5)? On quite a different plane, how many people would be able to give a reasonably clear account of what is meant by *existentialism, logical positivism, surrealism, relativity, enzyme, electron,* or *cybernetics*? Yet these words, and many others like them, are key-terms in twentieth-century civilization, and some at least are apt to be used, in non-technical writings and even in the press or over the wireless, without any explanation.

Quite apart from these specialized terms, there are countless others which English has taken over from foreign languages, living or dead, and whose meaning is obscure for many speakers. The language bar . . . is a potent factor making for vagueness in English. . . . Jespersen tells the amusing but revealing story of a ploughman who, when asked by a parson what the word *felicity* meant for him, replied: "Summut in the inside of a pig, but I can't say altogether what" (*Growth and Structure,* p. 91). This happened nearly a century ago, and since then the situation has improved beyond recognition; nevertheless, this form of vagueness continues to represent a serious social and educational problem.

[16] See on this problem L. P. Smith, "Four Words: Romantic, Original, Creative, Genius," *Society for Pure English Tracts,* xvii (1924), reprinted in his book *Words and Idioms.*

SUGGESTED ASSIGNMENTS

1. Because many of the words we use are vague, we employ various methods
to make them more precise. One is to quantify. For example, *hot water* can
be made precise by saying *water of 190 degrees Fahrenheit.* Another is to
embed the vague word in a specifying context. Thus instead of "He is a
boor" we could say "He is a garrulous boor whose favorite subject is himself." A third method is to explain exactly what we mean by the vague
word.

    Write a paragraph in which you use a vague word in the opening
sentence and then define or describe what you mean by that word. Here
are some possible openers:

    a. Chloe's crowning quality is *grace.*
    b. Balthasar Gracian once wrote that women are *realists* and men are
        romanticists.
    c. Monsieur Thibault is a *gourmet* in many aspects of life.
    d. Too many college students have no *social consciousness.*
    e. Our university should provide as well for the *creative* student as for
        the mere learner from books.

2. Write a theme in which you explain what you understand by one of the
following words or terms: *justice, civil liberty, love, the middle class, an educated
man, a liberal education, genius.*

Dictionaries
and the English Language

ALBERT H. MARCKWARDT

The appearance of Webster's *Third New International Dictionary* in 1961 engendered a tornado of controversy. The
linguistically illiterate, including some newspaper editors
and litterateurs of note, were outraged, apparently because
it did not confirm their own verbal prejudices. Linguists in
general accepted it as a competent piece of lexicography.
In this account, Albert H. Marckwardt presents a coldly
serious and factual report on this latest scion of a long line
of distinguished dictionaries. Mr. Marckwardt is Professor
of English at Princeton University and author of *Introduction
to the English Language* and *American English.*

From *The English Journal* 52:326–345 (1963). Reprinted with the permission of the
National Council of Teachers of English and Professor Albert H. Marckwardt.

Now that much of the tumult and the shouting have subsided, and the controversy over *Webster's Third New International Dictionary* has attained the dignity of a casebook, it should be possible to consider both the dictionary and the varied reactions to it with a degree of detachment. Bergen Evans was quite correct in characterizing the storm of abuse provoked by the appearance of the new edition as a curious phenomenon. But how can it be explained? And more important still, what is there to be learned from it?

We must recognize, first of all, that a complete revision of our largest commercially produced dictionary of the English language has become a regularly recurring event in American life. Upon occasion the time table has varied a bit, but the following listing reveals an astonishing degree of regularity over the past century.

An American Dictionary of the English Language (Royal Quarto Edition, Unabridged)	1864
Webster's International Dictionary	1890
Webster's New International Dictionary	1909
Webster's New International Dictionary (Second edition)	1934
Webster's Third New International Dictionary	1961

Of the five Webster editions listed above, probably none has called forth such extremes of critical comment upon its appearance as the recent Webster Third. It was characterized as "a very great calamity." Its general tone was described as "a dismaying assortment of the questionable, the perverse, the unworthy, the downright outrageous." At the same time, other reviewers spoke of the work as "an intellectual achievement of the very highest order," and "a reference work which worthily carries on a tradition of great reference works."

These extremes of praise and blame are reminiscent of the reception of the 1828 edition of *An American Dictionary of the English Language*, compiled by Webster himself and the real parent of the long line of dictionaries which bear his name. At that time a reviewer in *The Southern Literary Messenger* denounced the treatment of pronunciation as horrible and the orthography as abominable. The English *Quarterly Review* judged it "a decided failure, conducted on perverse and erroneous principles," and in much the same vein as some of the critics of the Webster Third, complained that "we do not recollect ever to have witnessed in the same compass a greater number of crudities and errors, or more pains taken to so little purpose," But Webster's 1828 work had its admirers as well, particularly among the Germans, who praised the profound learning that it reflected.

The disparate comments on Webster's early work are of interest today only as a historical phenomenon, but those which have been applied to the Webster Third still give rise to considerable confusion. It is scarcely possible for both the critics and the admirers to be right in all that they say, and one may reasonably ask what a more dispassionate evaluation might be.

Two traditions

In approaching such an appraisal, we must understand first of all that the American lexicographer in his concern with current English faces something of a dilemma. He is the inheritor of two traditions clearly in conflict, both of which have their roots in England.

The earlier tradition is that of Samuel Johnson, the compiler of the 1755 *Dictionary of the English Language*, who lent the first touch of sheer genius to English lexicography. In the preface of this great work, he pointed out that "every language has its improprieties and absurdities, which it is the duty of the lexicographer to correct or proscribe." According to him, the function of a dictionary was one, "by which the pronunciation of our language may be fixed and its attainment facilitated; by which its purity may be preserved, its use ascertained, and its duration lengthened." That Johnson was expressing the spirit of his age is shown by comments such as that of Lord Chesterfield, who wrote, "We must have a resource to the old Roman expedient in times of confusion and choose a Dictator. Upon this principle I give my vote for Mr. Johnson to fill that great and arduous post."

This concept of the lexicographer as a linguistic legislator or arbiter, if not absolute dictator, is still strong in the United States. It is frequently reflected, and indeed encouraged, by the slogans which dictionary publishers—not the editors, let me hasten to say—choose to advertise their wares. The very phrase "Supreme Authority," which the G. and C. Merriam Company used to employ, supported this view of the dictionary; whether intentionally or not is open to conjecture.

The slightly later and opposed tradition is that of the lexicographer as the objective recorder of the language. For the English-speaking nations this concept was first realized on a substantial scale in what is now known as *The Oxford English Dictionary* but originally entitled *A New English Dictionary on Historical Principles*. Here the purpose is stated as follows:

The aim of this dictionary is to present in alphabetical series the words which have formed the English vocabulary from the time of the earliest records down to the present day, with all the relevant facts concerning their form, sense-history, pronunciation, and etymology. It embraces not only the standard language of literature and conversation, whether current at the moment or obsolete, or archaic, but also the main technical vocabulary, and a large measure of dialectal usage and slang.

Note that this statement contains not one word about fixing the language, about proscription or prescription of any kind. Operating on this basis, the lexicographer contents himself with setting down the record, leaving its interpretation to the reader. Needless to say, the prestige of the *Oxford English Dictionary* is enormous; it is generally conceded to be superior to the corresponding major dictionaries for the other western European languages. The principles on which it is based were formulated as early as 1859.

The conflict of principle which has been pointed out need not necessarily be troublesome. If the language involved is confined as to number of speakers and is the vehicle of a static and stabilized society, there is virtually no problem. An accurate description of the language as it is actually used, kept simple by the relative absence of variants, accurately designating social and regional status, will in itself serve prescriptive purposes. But this is not the case with English, which is spoken natively by some two hundred and seventy millions, spread over five continents of the globe. Under such circumstances, uniformity becomes a remote possibility. In the United States, at least, the language is that of a highly mobile society, both geographically and up and down the social scale. As a consequence the lines between class and regional dialects and the standard language inevitably tend to become blurred. Under such circumstances, the linguistic reporter and the legislator are more likely to seem to be working at cross purposes.

Nevertheless, it is clearly evident that as the various editions of Webster march down the century, the statements of principle which are to be found in them move steadily away from the Johnsonian or prescriptive concept toward the descriptive position of the Oxford editors. Even as early as 1864, Chauncey A. Goodrich, the chief editor of the first major revision after Webster's death, asserted that "The chief value of a dictionary consists in its Definitions; in giving a clear, full, and accurate exhibition, of all the various shades of meaning which belong, *by established usage*, to the words of a language."

Nor was the reportorial concept limited to the Webster series of dictionaries in this country. One of the principal competitors during the early years of the present century, Dr. Isaac K. Funk, wrote in the preface of the 1913 *Standard Dictionary of the English Language*, "The chief function of a dictionary is to record usage." It is true that this forthright statement of the descriptive function was followed by a somewhat unsuccessful attempt to reconcile it with the authoritarian concept, but nevertheless the principle had been stated.

1934 Edition

The immediate predecessor of the new Webster Third was the 1934 edition. The following excerpt from its front matter (p. xvi) refers specifically to pronunciation, but it is a fair representation of the attitude of its editors toward all language matters:

The function of a pronouncing dictionary is to record as far as possible the pronunciations prevailing in the best present usage, rather than to attempt to dictate what that usage should be. In so far as a dictionary may be known and acknowledged as a faithful recorder and interpreter of such usage, so far and no farther may it be appealed to as an authority.
In the case of diverse usages of extensive prevalence, the dictionary must recognize each of them.

A somewhat broader treatment of the editorial function is to be found in the Introduction (p. xi) to the 1934 Webster:

Both Samuel Johnson and Noah Webster conceived it to be a duty of the dictionary editor to maintain the purity of the standard language. However, with the growth in literacy of the past century, and the increase in fiction and drama, in radio and motion pictures, of the use of dialect, slang, and colloquial speech, it has become necessary for a general dictionary to record and interpret the vocabularies of geographical and occupational dialects, and of the livelier levels of the speech of the educated.

It would be difficult to imagine a more cogent or forthright exposition of the descriptive function of the dictionary than these two statements of editorial policy. The first of them apparently satisfied the the editors of the Webster Third, for they repeat it in their Introduction (p. 6a) with only one minor expansion: "best present usage" of the earlier edition now reads, "General cultivated conversational usage, both formal and informal." This offers additional support for the conclusion that with respect to the conflict between opposing lexicographical concepts, the descriptive had been wholly accepted, the prescriptive completely rejected in 1934. Whatever differences there may be between the 1934 and 1961 editions, they are not matters of policy or principle. They are instead differences in the way in which a principle common to both dictionaries has been realized.

Lexicographical policy is not ordinarily a matter of absorbing interest, but it has been necessary to deal with it at some length because the Webster Third has been criticized on occasion for repudiating, even sabotaging the principles of the second edition. Such charges serve only to reveal a total lack of awareness on the part of the critic as to what these principles were, how they have developed in this country, and how they reflect a steadily changing concept of the function of the dictionary. Actually, the furor over the Webster Third is a sad commentary on how inadequately the dictionary has been presented in the English classrooms of the nation and how insufficiently English teachers are informed about one of the principal tools of their profession.

Practical editorial decisions

The extremes of public reaction to the new Webster must also be considered in terms of editorial decisions on a practical rather than a theoretical level. Such an understanding may best be attained by considering certain of the practical questions which confronted the editors, what the decisions on them were, and what the reasons for them may have been.

At the very outset of their preparations, the editors apparently felt an obligation to increase considerably the amount of evidence upon which the new dictionary was to be based. Dictionary evidence normally exists in the form of citation slips, the products of an extensive reading program. The citations are filed under their appropriate headwords, and in the editing process they constitute the raw material for the definitions and in fact for most of the word treatment.

At the time of the compilation of the second edition, the files in the Springfield offices held some 1,615,000 citation slips. In the years intervening between the two editions, as the result of what must have been a tremendous effort, this figure was nearly quadrupled. Just under 4,500,000 citations were added, resulting in a total of 6,000,000, a number approximately equalling the collection for the *Oxford English Dictionary*, but far more heavily concentrated on the language of the present day. In addition, the *Dictionary of American English* and the *Dictionary of Americanisms* had both been completed in the years 1944 and 1951 respectively, constituting a further increase in the size of the corpus available to the editors of the Webster Third. As a result, they found themselves with approximately 50,000 new words (words not entered in the Webster Second) and 50,000 new meanings for words already entered.

At this point physical and financial factors enter into consideration. For a number of reasons, undoubtedly based upon a century of business experience, the publishers are firmly committed to a single-volume dictionary. They had made the Webster Second as large, that is to say thick, as any one volume could possibly get and still assure a back that might withstand the rigors of long and constant use, particularly in schools and libraries. Thus it was manifestly impossible to increase the number of pages by the ten or fifteen percent necessary to accommodate the new entries. If these were to be included, something had to come out. The kind of material that was removed forms the basis of some of the criticisms of the present edition.

The first excision consisted of the materials which, in earlier editions, had been placed below the horizontal line running across the page. These included archaisms, dialect forms, variant spellings, and proper names. To quote the editors, "Many obsolete and comparatively useless or obscure words have been omitted. These include, in general, words that had become obsolete before 1755 unless found in well-known major works of a few major writers." Incidentally, the significance of the date 1755 can scarcely escape one's attention. In the first place it was the publication year of Dr. Johnson's dictionary. Moreover, as a deadline for obsolescence, it marks an advance of two centuries and a half over the corresponding date of 1500 for the Webster Second. Thus, in word selections as well as in other matters, the emphasis is clearly placed upon the current state of the language.

Getting rid of the obsolete and the obscure did not in itself solve the space problem. Still other things had to go, and these taken together constitute the parts essential to a peripheral function of the dictionary long cherished by Americans—the encyclopedic function.

In the process of elimination, the editors removed among other things:

(1)   The gazetteer section.
(2)   The biographical section.
(3)   Titles of written works and works of art.
(4)   Names of characters in fiction, folklore, and mythology.
(5)   Names of battles, wars, organizations, cities, and states.
(6)   Mottoes and other familiar sayings.

There have been further excisions as well. Color plates and illustrations are reduced in a proportion somewhere between one-fourth and one-third. Even the number of pages has gone down from 3210 to 2720.

Elimination of material

This elimination of encyclopedic material has caused anguish. "Think, if you can," complains Wilson Follett, "of an unabridged dictionary from which you cannot learn who Mark Twain was, or what were the names of the apostles, or that the Virgin was Mary, the mother of Jesus of Nazareth, or what and where the District of Columbia is." Actually, this is not at all difficult. The great Oxford comes immediately to mind, as does Henry Cecil Wyld's *Universal Dictionary of the English Language*, or any of the great academy dictionaries of such languages as French or Spanish.

Nevertheless, Follett's reaction will be shared by many Americans. In the past, dictionaries published in this country have cheerfully served an encyclopedic as well as a lexicographic function, and ironically enough it was Noah Webster himself who was primarily responsible. His first dictionary, published in 1806 included tables of the moneys of most of the commercial nations in the world, tables of weights and measures, ancient and modern, the divisions of time among the Jews, Greeks, and Romans, and an official list of the post-offices in the United States, to mention only a few of the extra features. Although the editors of the current volume have broken with their progenitor in cutting out these impedimenta, they have not at all departed from the essential principles of lexicography in so doing.

Undoubtedly they felt that the considerable increase in the number of illustrative citations would readily compensate for the loss of the peripheral material. Such citations do constitute the core of the reportorial dictionary. For instance, there were no citations for the adjective *oratorical* in the second edition; the Third has three. The second edition gave three identified citations for *chase*, verb. In the Third, there are four identified and seven unidentified citations.

According to the Preface of the current edition, "More than 14,000 different authors are quoted for their use of words or for the structural pattern of their words. . ." Many of these are contemporary. The reader is also informed that the verbal illustrations (citations apparently unidentified as to author) are "mostly from the twentieth century."

This innovation has met with something less than universal approval, a reaction not so much attributable to the editorial policy itself as to some of the advertising antics of the business office. The original brochure, announcing this edition as "one of the most remarkable literary achievements of all time," included among the list of authors cited such names as Billy Rose, Fulton Lewis, Jr., Art Linkletter, Dinah Shore, Ted Williams, and Ethel Merman. In addition there were Harry Truman, Dwight D. Eisenhower, John F. Kennedy, and Richard Nixon, whose names were undoubtedly signed to reams of material which they did not compose. To the sympathetic this signalled a conscious attempt to include a wide range of current authors. To the critical it betokened a lack of discrimination and responsibility. Actually, the citations from such sources are few in number and small in proportion.

A point which must be taken into account here is that which was made at the very outset of this essay, namely that the life of a Webster edition is roughly calculated at twenty-five years. Thus, the overriding concern of the dictionary is quite appropriately the language in its current state. It is on these grounds that the editors may logically justify the preponderance of citations from current authors, irrespective of lasting literary merit. It may be assumed that in the 1986 edition many of them will be discarded, to be replaced by others from the 1970's and early 1980's. In this respect the Webster practice will differ sharply from that of the *Oxford English Dictionary*, for which no new edition was contemplated, although certainly only a small proportion of the authors cited in that work are literary giants of lasting reputation.

Status labels

Another departure in the Webster Third from the practice of earlier editions, which has given rise to considerable criticism, is the treatment of what are called *status labels*. Here again some of the disapproval has its source in misunderstanding. Basically, the editors have developed a terminology which is at once semantically neutral and more precise than that which has been employed in the past. The label *illiterate* has been discontinued. It has become a term of censure rather than a dispassionate indication of the inability to read and write. The current replacements, *substandard* and *nonstandard* are matter-of-fact rather than pejorative and permit a gradation of acceptability, the latter indicating a wider range of occurrence than the former, although it is applied to a smaller number of words and expressions. American dialect ascriptions represent a great advance in precision over those of the second edition in that they reflect an adaptation of the terminology for the various dialect areas developed by Professor Hans Kurath, editor of the Linguistic Atlas and the most eminent linguistic geographer in the country. It was unfortunate, however, that the editors chose not to indicate those words current in all regions of the United States but not in England or other parts of the English-speaking world.

Another innovation in the Webster Third is the elimination of the label *colloquial*. There are two conceivable reasons for this: In the first place the term is ambivalent, signifying informality on the one hand and the spoken rather than the written medium on the other. It is customary now among students of the language to be somewhat more precise, recognizing not only colloquial but *casual* and *intimate* as further gradations of the spoken variety of the language, any of which not only may be but are regularly employed by speakers of unquestioned cultivation.

An even greater objection to the label *colloquial* is the persistence with which an unfavorable connotation has adhered to it. Dictionary users never interpreted the term in the way in which dictionary editors intended. It was not meant as a condemnation either in the Webster Second or in the various abridged dictionaries based upon it. The editors took great pains to say so, both in the prefatory material and in the definition of the word itself, but this went unheeded. So for the present edition the staff was faced with the alternative of finding an acceptable substitute less liable to misinterpretation, or of eliminating the label altogether. It chose the latter, partly perhaps because of the unsatisfactory experience of other dictionaries which had experimented with a substitute.

In general the changes in the choice and ascription of labels reflect an endeavor to achieve greater precision and objectivity. The attempt at precision undoubtedly finds some adherents, although there will be disagreements over the application of the labels in specific instances. The attempt at objectivity has, understandably enough, resulted in the disappearance of the censorious tone which, for many seemed to be part of the proper function of the labels *colloquial* and *illiterate*. To such persons, the lack of censure has been understood as a lowering of standards.

Pronunciation

In dealing with pronunciation, the editors of the Webster Third had to contend with two factors which had not faced their predecessors. One was a new electronic development, namely voice amplification. The other was a new concept in the analysis of language, that of the phoneme or meaningful unit of sound.

Voice amplification affected the kind of pronunciation which the dictionary undertook to record. In pre-loud-speaker days, the second edition of Webster recorded what it called "formal platform speech," the speech of cultivated users of English, speaking formally with a view to being completely understood by their hearers. That there were other types of pronunciation wholly appropriate to less formal situations was readily conceded by the editors, but they evidently felt that their editorial responsibility could be discharged with the greatest amount of effectiveness and least confusion by indicating just the one.

The microphone has changed all this. Certain devices of articulation necessary for clarity when the speaker was forced to depend on lung power to make himself audible to the last row of a large auditorium are no longer necessary. Nor are they often employed today.

This change led the Webster editors into a complete revision of the manner in which evidence on pronunciation was collected. Where Webster Second had attempted a sampling, by means of written questionnaires, of the pronunciation of persons who did a considerable amount of public speaking, the Webster Third staff turned its attention directly to the language itself rather than to opinion about it. They listened to radio, television, and recordings; to speech in all parts of the country and in all types of situations. Again, as with the citations for word occurrences, forms, and meanings, the body of evidence was tremendously increased in range and scope, but certainly less skewed toward a single type of pronunciation.

In any English dictionary, and particularly one designed for use in the United States, a decision upon the particular system, or respelling, to indicate pronunciation always poses a problem. For a number of reasons, the American public has been unwilling to accept the International Phonetic Alphabet; nor is this a particularly economical device when a number of variants must be shown. The Webster Second continued with few changes the system of its predecessors, which was cumbersome in that a single sound was indicated by more than one transcription, and confusing in that a single character sometimes covered far more latitude than the user was likely to realize.

The editors of the current edition have attempted to take advantage of the phonemic concept, basic to present-day linguistic science. The general result has been the disappearance of a rash of diacritics which made the earlier dictionaries difficult to read and to interpret. Some useful characters have been taken over from the phonetic alphabet, notably the elongated *n* to indicate the usual sound of *ng*, and most important, the inverted *e* or schwa for the neutral vowel used in weakly stressed syllables. The latter, it must be confessed, is an innovation in which Webster followed some of its competitors. At all events, the public will no longer be misled into believing that the final vowel of *caucus* is somehow different from that of *fracas*.

Unfortunately the necessity of economizing on space has led to the excision of the authoritative treatments of the individual sounds of English which lent scholarly distinction to the second edition though perhaps read by only a few. Also, certain innovations of the Webster Third will cause annoyance until the public becomes accustomed to them. One of these may well be the indication of stress by a mark preceding rather than following the syllable. The removal of the pronunciation key from the bottom of the page is another. The use of a modified *d* character to indicate what the editors call, "the usual American pronunciation of *latter*," will seem to the critical like countenancing the slipshod, and it is possible that a *t* with a diacritic might have served quite as well without outraging quite so many sensibilities.

With pronunciation as with countless other features of the dictionary, the editors have attempted to present the facts of the language as they saw them. It is an honest presentation, maintaining the principles and the concept of the dictionary characteristic of previous editions, but carrying them out with greater consistency and basing them upon far more evidence. There have been errors of judgment, more often perhaps with respect to manner of presentation than in the interpretation of the facts which are reported, but this is inevitable in an undertaking of such magnitude.

My comments so far should have suggested, to a degree at least, the reasons for some of the changes which are to be found in the Webster Third. They have not yet given an answer to the question which was initially posed: why the extremes of praise and blame. The encomiums are easy to account for. They represent the approval of those who accept the descriptive principle and find in the current product a generally conscientious and more thorough implementation of it than is otherwise available.

Controversy

The chorus of protest is somewhat more complex in origin. It is in part the expression of a desire for linguistic authoritarianism, an attitude sincerely held by many which can be explained only in terms of a number of complex and interrelated factors in American cultural history. Added to this is the mistaken notion that the Webster Third represents a change in lexicographical principle, an error which is fostered by the more complete coverage and greater accuracy of the edition. The excision of certain kinds of nonessential material represented a sudden departure from a time-honored practice. Moreover, there is, as always, a tendency toward careless reading and inept comparison; upon occasion a judgment objected to in the third edition was already present in the second. This reflects a not uncommon situation. Even those who are willing to concede that language standards must ultimately rest upon usage are not infrequently distressed when they encounter a detailed and factual inventory of that usage. At such a point the normal reaction is to question the accuracy of the inventory and the soundness of the method upon which it is based.

An excellent illustration of this is to be found in the treatment of the very word that has given rise to so many headlines and caused so much acid comment—*ain't*. The statement which gave rise to the excitement, namely that *ain't* is used orally in most parts of the United States by many cultivated speakers, is merely a condensation of what has already been noted in Bagby Atwood's *A Survey of Verb Forms in the Eastern United States*, a study based upon the materials of the Linguistic Atlas of the United States and Canada. "Cultivated, our foot," comments the editor of the Chicago *Daily News;* yet the cultivated informants for the various regional atlases were selected on the basis of as rigorous a set of standards in terms of family background, education, and occupation as could be established.

The presumed role of structural linguistics in the Webster Third reflects a most unfortunate confusion, and ironically it is the editor of the dictionary who is in part responsible for it. In an article in *Word Study* prior to the publication of the dictionary, Dr. Gove unintentionally left careless and uninformed readers with the mistaken impression that Leonard Bloomfield in 1926 first stated the postulate that correctness rests upon usage. Despite the fact that Dr. Gove then went on to mention any number of areas in lexicography where linguistics had had no appreciable influence, the first part of his article appears to have left many readers with the mental image of a fifth column of structuralists burrowing their way through the Merriam-Webster files in Springfield.

This notion is wrong on two counts. First, the importance of usage in the establishment of a linguistic standard had been maintained by a host of scholars from the turn of the century on. They included Thomas Lounsbury, George P. Krapp, Louise Pound, Charles C. Fries, and Sterling A. Leonard, to mention only a few of the more distinguished. The structuralists accept this as a matter of course, but they did not invent the idea. Second, except for the treatment of pronunciation, structural concepts do not appear with any great frequency in the dictionary. Words are traditionally classified as nouns, adjectives, verbs, and so on. There was no attempt to substitute a scheme consistently based either upon form or function. This is a dictionary of words rather than of morphemes. I find it difficult to detect even a hint of structuralism in the handling of the definitions. Yet Dwight Macdonald speaks of the "direct application" of structural linguistics "to making dictionaries," and the idea has been echoed by others.

It is the English-teaching profession which should be seriously disturbed by the dictionary controversy. If the Webster war has proved little or nothing about dictionaries, it has demonstrated our ineptitude, if not absolute failure, in teaching our students what a dictionary is for, how it is made, and the proper way to use it. Much of the misunderstanding of principle, of the confusion of principle and practice, of the failure to read and interpret accurately can, with considerable justice, be laid at our door. After all, the embattled critics were once our students; had our teaching of the dictionary been soundly based, this comedy of errors should have been at least somewhat less comic.

To return to the dictionary itself, however, one can only say that by a more literal acceptance of its declared function, and by running counter more obviously to what people want or think they want in a dictionary and to what they think they have been getting, the Webster Third represents a calculated risk. Depending on one's point of view, it is either a courageous or a foolhardy venture into the latter half of the twentieth century. For the staff, who in the face of the public clamor must wonder if it has been at all worthwhile, there is only the dubious comfort in Macaulay's words, "The best lexicographer may well be content if his productions are received by the world in cold esteem."

SUGGESTED ASSIGNMENTS

1. There is no such thing as THE dictionary. There are many English dictionaries, and these differ widely in their accuracy and reliability as a record of English words and usages. Even among the good ones there are differences in the treatment of individual entries. Write a theme comparing your desk dictionary with a different one owned by another student. Note especially the differences in pronunciation, status labels, and the inclusion or noninclusion of new words that you know. A good way to begin this assignment is to spend an hour studying the explanatory material at the front of the dictionaries and browsing at random from A to Z. As an alternate assignment, you might compare your desk dictionary, presumably a new one, with an older edition, for example the *Webster's Seventh New Collegiate Dictionary* with the Fifth Edition.

2. Make a thorough examination of the kinds of information that your dictionary contains. Then write an expository theme telling an incoming college freshman how to use his dictionary intelligently.

3. Find out what your dictionary records about usage for the following items:
    a. That was *real* nice of you.
    b. You'd better go *slow*.
    c. *Who* did you see? (Instead of *whom*.)
    d. He looked *like* he was frightened. (*Like* as a conjunction.)
    e. Jane was *disinterested* in sports cars. (For *uninterested*.)
    f. She *sung* beautifully.
    g. Have you *drank* your medicine yet? (For *drunk* as past participle.) Does your dictionary agree with the *Linguistic Atlas* findings reported by Professor Allen on pages 406 ff.?
    h. Anyone can join, *irregardless* of race.

4. Review the pronunciation given in your dictionary for the following words: *vase, aunt, exquisite, advertisement, marry, merry, envelope, derby, nephew, weltschmerz, lingerie, chic.*

5. Check the position of your dictionary on the spelling of these words: *alright, judgement, enrolment, roommate, wooly, transferable, skilful, phoney, esthetic.*

6. Record what your dictionary states about these new words: *cosmonaut, heliport, helilift, audiophile, telegenic, escalate, discotheque, scuba, laser, levi, shunpike, re-entry* (into earth's atmosphere), *lunarnaut, computerize.*

FURTHER READINGS

Bradley, Henry. *The Making of English.* New York: The Macmillan Company, 1904. On meaning changes, see Chapter 5.

Brook, G. L. *A History of the English Language.* New York: Oxford University Press, Inc., 1958. On meaning and meaning changes, see Chapter 8.

Bryant, Margaret M. *Modern English and its Heritage,* 2d ed. New York: The Macmillan Company, 1962. On meaning changes, see Chapters 28, 29, 30.

Burriss, Eli E. and Lionel Casson. *Latin and Greek in Current Use.* Englewood Cliffs, New Jersey: Prentice-Hall, Inc., 1939.

Estrich, Robert M. and Hans Sperber. *Three Keys to Language.* New York: Holt, Rinehart and Winston, Inc., 1952. On meaning and meaning changes, see Chapters 9, 10, 11, 12.

Gray, Jack C. *Word, Words, and Words About Dictionaries.* San Francisco: Chandler Publishing Co., 1963.

Greenough, James B. and George L. Kittredge. *Words and Their Ways in English Speech.* New York: The Macmillan Company, 1901. (Paperbound by Beacon Press.) Although more than a half-century old, this book, which is both scholarly and popular, is still a valuable source of information about English words. For slang, see Chapter 6. For meaning changes, see Chapters 17, 18, 19, 20.

Grose, Francis. *A Classical Dictionary of the Vulgar Tongue,* edited by Eric Partridge. London: Routledge and Kegan Paul, Ltd., 1963. Accounts of the lower levels of the eighteenth century vocabulary.

Hixson, Jerome C. and I. Colodny. *Word Ways.* New York: American Book Company, 1946. On meaning changes, see Chapters 12, 13. On slang, see Chapter 16.

Johnson, Edwin L. *Latin Words in Common Use.* Boston: D. C. Heath & Company, 1931.

Marchand, Hans. *Categories and Types of Present-Day English Word-Formation.* Wiesbaden: Otto Harrassowitz, 1960. On back-formation, see Chapter 6. On clipping, see Chapter 9. On blends, see Chapter 10.

Potter, Simeon. *Language in the Modern World.* Baltimore: Penguin Books, Inc., 1960. On the making of words, see Chapter 5.

Potter, Simeon. *Modern Linguistics.* London: Andre Deutsch, 1957. On word making, see Chapter 4. This discussion is more detailed and technical than that in the preceding book.

Serjeantson, Mary S. *History of Foreign Words in English.* New York: E. P. Dutton Co., Inc., 1936.

Sledd, James and Wilma R. Ebbitt, eds. *Dictionaries and That Dictionary.* Chicago: Scott, Foresman & Company, 1962.

Wilson, Kenneth, R. H. Hendrickson, and Peter A. Taylor. *Harbrace Guide to Dictionaries.* New York: Harcourt, Brace, & World, Inc., 1963.

4

SEMANTICS

Categories

JEROME S. BRUNER,
JACQUELINE J. GOODNOW,
and GEORGE A. AUSTIN

Nouns are the names of categories, or classes, and it is
by means of categories that we package our countless and
varied minute-by-minute experiences verbally into neatly
labeled bundles. Without categories we would live in a be-
wildering and overwhelming world of unrelated particulars.
With categories these particulars are sorted and grouped
according to useful relations. This grouping helps us to
identify, to remember, to profit from past experiences, and
thus to cope with our environment. In this selection Jerome
S. Bruner and his colleagues explain categorization and
discuss five of its values. Mr. Bruner is Professor of Psychology at Harvard University and author of *The Process of
Education.*

We begin with what seems a paradox. The world of experience of any
normal man is composed of a tremendous array of discriminably
different objects, events, people, impressions. There are estimated to
be more than 7 million discriminable colors alone, and in the course of
a week or two we come in contact with a fair proportion of them. No
two people we see have an identical appearance and even objects
that we judge to be the same object over a period of time change
appearance from moment to moment with alterations in light or in the
position of the viewer. All of these differences we are capable of seeing,
for human beings have an exquisite capacity for making distinctions.

From *A Study of Thinking* by Jerome S. Bruner, Jacqueline J. Goodnow, and George
A. Austin. Reprinted by permission of the publisher, John Wiley & Sons, Inc.,
copyright 1956.

But were we to utilize fully our capacity for registering the differences in things and to respond to each event encountered as unique, we would soon be overwhelmed by the complexity of our environment. Consider only the linguistic task of acquiring a vocabulary fully adequate to cope with the world of color differences! The resolution of this seeming paradox—the existence of discrimination capacities which, if fully used, would make us slaves to the particular—is achieved by man's capacity to categorize. To categorize is to render discriminably different things equivalent, to group the objects and events and people around us into classes, and to respond to them in terms of their class membership rather than their uniqueness. Our refined discriminative activity is reserved only for those segments of the environment with which we are specially concerned. For the rest, we respond by rather crude forms of categorial placement. In place of a color lexicon of 7 million items, people in our society get along with a dozen or so commonly used color names. It suffices to note that the book on the desk has a "blue" cover. If the task calls for finer discrimination, we may narrow the category and note that it is in the class of things called "medium blue." It is rare indeed that we are ever called upon to place the book in a category of colors comprising *only* the unique hue-brightness-stauration combination it presents.

The process of categorizing involves, if you will, an act of invention. This hodgepodge of objects is comprised in the category "chairs," that assortment of diverse numbers is all grouped together as "powers of 2," these structures are "houses" but thôse others are "garages." What is unique about categories of this kind is that once they are mastered they can be used without further learning. We need not learn *de novo* that the stimulus configuration before us is another house. If we have learned the class "house" as a concept, new exemplars can readily be recognized. The category becomes a tool for further use. The learning and utilization of categories represents one of the most elementary and general forms of cognition by which man adjusts to his environment. . . .

Identity and equivalence categories

The full moon, the moon in quarter, and the crescent moon all evoke the same nominative response, "moon." From a common response made by a person to an array of objects we infer that he "has" an equivalence or identity category. The similar responses from which we draw such an inference need not be verbal. An air-raid siren, a dislodged piton while climbing, and a severe dressing-down by a superior may all produce a common autonomic response in a man and by this fact we infer that they are all grouped as "danger situations." Indeed, the person involved may not be able to verbalize the category. While this is in itself interesting, it is not crucial to our point, which is simply that an equivalence range is inferred from the presence of a common response to an array of discriminably different events. . . .

Two broad types of categorizing responses are obviously of interest. One of them is the identity response, the other the equivalence response, and each points to a different kind of category.

Without belaboring the obvious, identity categorization may be defined as classing a variety of stimuli as *forms of the same thing*. What lies behind the identity response is not clear, save that it is obviously a response that is affected by learning. It does not do to say simply that an object is seen as the identical object on a later encounter if it has not "changed its characteristics too much." The moon in its phases varies from a sliver to a circle, in color from luminous white to the bronzed hunter's moon. Sheldon collected a series of photographs of the same individual over a period of 15 years, the person standing in the same position against a uniform background. The photographs span the period from early boyhood to full manhood. As one riffles through the stack, there is a strong and dramatic impression of the identical person in the process of growth. Yet the pictures go through a drastic metamorphosis. Because such identity responses are ubiquitous and because they are learned very early in life, we tend to regard them somehow as a different process from other forms of categorizing— the recognition of two different people as both being people. Yet both depend upon . . . the presence of a *cachet spécifique* or essential quality. They are both forms of categorizing. What differs is the nature of the inference: in the one case we infer "identity" from the presence of the *cachet*, in the other case "equivalence."

How one comes to learn to categorize in terms of identity categories is, as we have said, little understood. . . . It suffices to note that its development depends notably upon learning.

That there is confusion remaining in the adult world about what constitutes an identity class is testified to by such diverse proverbs as *plus ça change, plus la même chose*[1] and the Heraclitan dictum that we never enter the same river twice. Indeed, in severe psychotic turmoil

---

[1] "The more it changes, the more it is the same thing." [eds.]

one sometimes notes an uncertainty about the identity category that is the "self" in states of depersonalization, and a rather poignant reminder that the identity of self is even equivocal in normal states is provided by the sign behind a bar in the Southwest:

> I ain't what I've been.
> I ain't what I'm going to be.
> I am what I am.

We speak of an equivalence class when an individual responds to a set of discriminably different things as the *same kind of thing* or as *amounting to the same thing*. Again we depend for our knowledge of the existence of a category upon the presence of a common response. While there is a striking phenomenological difference between identity and equivalence, both depend upon the acceptance of certain properties of objects as being criterial or relevant—again the *cachet spécifique*— and others as being irrelevant. One may distinguish three broad classes of equivalence categories, each distinguished by the kind of defining response involved. They may be called *affective*, *functional*, and *formal* categories.

Certain forms of grouping appear to depend very heavily upon whether or not the things placed in the same class evoke a common affective response. A group of people, books, weather of a certain kind, and certain states of mind are all grouped together as "alike," the "same kind of thing." Further inquiry may reveal that all of them were experienced during a particularly poignant summer of childhood. What holds them together and what leads one to say that some new experience "reminds one of such and such weather, people, and states" is the evocation of a defining affective response.

Characteristically, categories marked by an affective defining response are not amenable to ready description in terms of the properties of the objects comprising them. The difficulty appears to lie in the lack of correspondence between affective and linguistic categories. . . . Categories bound together by a common affective response frequently go back to early childhood and may resist conscious verbal insight by virtue of having been established before the full development of language. For categorizing activity at the preverbal stage appears to be predominantly nonrepresentational, depending not so much on the common external properties of objects as on the relation of things encountered to internal needs, or . . . on idiosyncratic and highly personalized impressions. Dollard and Miller argue persuasively that much of psychotherapy consists of the verbal labelling and re-sorting of such preverbal categories, so that they may become more accessible to the forms of symbolic or linguistic manipulation characteristic of adult problem-solving. . . .

The problems of specifying the properties of objects that mediate a common categorizing response become less arduous when the category is a functional or utilitarian one. Rather than an internal state rendering a group of things equivalent, now equivalence is based on an external function. The objects of a functional category fulfill a concrete and specific task requirement—"things large enough and strong enough to plug this hole in the dike." Such forms of defining response almost always have . . . a specific interpolative function ("gap filling") or a specific extrapolative function ("how to take the next step"). . . .

Formal categories are constructed by the act of specifying the intrinsic attribute properties required by the members of a class. Such categories have the characteristic that one can state reliably the diacritica of a class of objects or events short of describing their use. The formal properties of science are a case in point. Oftentimes the careful specification of defining properties even requires the constructions of special "artificial" languages to indicate that common-sense functional categories are not being used. The concept "force" in physics and the word standing for the functional class of events called "force" in common sense do not have the same kind of definition. What is accomplished in effect by formal categories is that one is able to devise classes whose defining properties are not determined by the suitability of objects to a specific task. The emphasis of definition is placed more and more on the attribute properties of class members and less and less on "utilitanda properties." . . . The development of formalization is gradual. From "things I can drive this tent stake with" we move to the concept "hammer" and from there to "mechanical force," each step being freer of definition by specific use than the former.

The development of formal categories is, of course, tantamount to science-making and we need not pause here to discuss this rather impenetrable problem. It suffices to note that formal categories and formal category systems appear to develop concurrently with methods for representing and manipulating them symbolically. What impels one to formalization we cannot say. That the urge is strong is unquestionable. Indeed, it is characteristic of highly elaborated cultures that symbolic representations of formal categories and formal category systems are eventually developed without reference to the classes of environmental events that the formal categories "stand for." Geometry provides a case in point, and while it is true that its original development was contingent upon the utilitarian triangulation systems used for redividing plots after floods in the Nile Valley, it is now the case that geometers proceed without regard for the fit of their formal categories to specific empirical problems.

It is obvious that there are close relationships between affective, functional, and formal categories and that they are often convertible one into the other. . . .

Language, culture, and categorizing

The categories in terms of which man sorts out and responds to the world around him reflect deeply the culture into which he is born. The language, the way of life, the religion and science of a people: all of these mold the way in which a man experiences the events out of which his own history is fashioned. In this sense, his personal history comes to reflect the traditions and thought-ways of his culture, for the events that make it up are filtered through the categorial systems he has learned. The typologies into which kinds of people are sorted, as, for example, witches and nonwitches among the Navaho; the manner in which kin are categorized in societies with and without primogeniture rules; the classification of women into "sisters" and "eligibles"; . . . the categorization of certain acts as friendly and others as hostile: all of these are projections of deep cultural trends into the experience of individuals. The principal defining attribute of an "intelligent man" for the Navaho is, according to one informant, a man who has seen a great many different things and travelled much. The word *yaigeh* which denotes this type of intelligent man does not include a man who, say, is noted for his domestic wisdom. It is difficult to determine whether there is a unitary category for "general intelligence" in Navaho. The first category used by our informant in specifying intelligence is especially interesting. The Navahos were historically a nomadic people who, though geographically no longer mobile, continue to show a great interest in distant things and events. . . .

The achievements of categorizing

What does the act of rendering things equivalent achieve for the organism? . . . A first achievement of categorizing has already been discussed. By categorizing as equivalent discriminably different events, the organism *reduces the complexity of its environment.* It is reasonably clear "how" this is accomplished. It involves the abstraction and use of defining properties in terms of which groupings can be made and much will be said of these things later.

A second achievement has also been mentioned: categorizing is the *means by which the objects of the world about us are identified.* The act of identifying some thing or some event is an act of "placing" it in a class. Identification implies that we are able to say either "There is thingum-bob again" or "There is another thingumbob." While these identifi-cations may vary in the richness of their elaboration, they are never absent. A certain sound may be heard simply as "that sound which comes from outdoors late at night." Or it may be heard as "those porcupines chewing on that old tree stump." When an event cannot be thus categorized and identified, we experience terror in the face of the uncanny. And indeed, "the uncanny" is itself a category, even if only a residual one.

A third achievement, a consequence of the first, is that the estab-lishment of a category based on a set of defining attributes *reduces the necessity of constant learning.* For the abstraction of defining properties makes possible future acts of categorizing without benefit of further learning. We do not have to be taught *de novo* at each encounter that the object before us is or is not a tree. If it exhibits the appropriate defining properties, it "is" a tree. It is in this crucial aspect, as we mentioned earlier, that categorizing differs from the learning of fiat classes. Learning by rote that a miscellany of objects all go by the nonsense name BLIX has no extrapolative value to new members of the class.

A fourth achievement inherent in the act of categorizing is the *direction it provides for instrumental activity.* To know by virtue of dis-criminable defining attributes and without need for further direct test that a man is "honest" or that a substance is "poison" is to know *in advance* about appropriate and inappropriate actions to be taken. Such direction is even provided when we come up against an object or event which we cannot place with finality. To the degree the new object has discriminable properties and these properties have been found in the past to be relevant to certain categories, we can make a start on the problem by a procedure of "categorial bracketing." The object appears to be animate; what does it do if it is poked? It stands on two legs like a man; does it speak? Much of problem-solving involves such repeated regrouping of an object until a pragmatically appropriate grouping has been found. In short, such successive categorizing is a principal form of instrumental activity.

A fifth achievement of categorizing is the opportunity it permits for *ordering and relating classes of events*. For we operate, as noted before, with category *systems*—classes of events that are related to each other in various kinds of superordinate systems. We map and give meaning to our world by relating classes of events rather than by relating individual events. "Matches," the child learns, will "cause" a set of events called "fires." The meaning of each class of things placed in quotation marks— matches, causes, and fires—is given by the imbeddedness of each class in such relationship maps. The moment an object is placed in a category we have opened up a whole vista of possibilities for "going beyond" the category by virtue of the superordinate and causal relationships linking this category to others. . . .

Classification

S. I. HAYAKAWA

Whenever you open your mouth you are likely to make classifications. If you should say, "Today I saw President Johnson," you would of course be referring to a single, unique individual; this would not be a classification. But think of all the other words you can use to refer to him; *humanitarian, rancher, dog lover, Christian, reformer, millionaire, national leader, ex-schoolteacher, politician, Texan.* In using any of these words to refer to Mr. Johnson, you are classifying him, that is, you are putting him into a class or group, the members of which possess certain common characistics. All such nouns are class-words. The class-word we choose to label any specific person or object depends on our purpose. Some such words express and evoke approval; others, disapproval. And the consequences of such classifications can be far-reaching, as you will soon see. Thus it is an important subject that S. I. Hayakawa deals with in this selection from his well-known book. Dr. Hayakawa is the editor of *ETC.: A Review of General Semantics.*

From *Language in Thought and Action* by S. I. Hayakawa, copyright, 1939, 1940, by S. I. Hayakawa, copyright, 1941, 1949, by Harcourt, Brace & World, Inc., and Allen & Unwin, Ltd.

Giving things names

The figure below shows eight objects, let us say animals, four large and four small, a different four with round heads and another four with square heads, and still another four with curly tails and another four with straight tails. These animals, let us say, are scampering about your village, but since at first they are of no importance to you, you ignore them. You do not even give them a name.

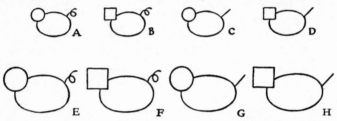

One day, however, you discover that the little ones eat up your grain, while the big ones do not. A differentiation sets itself up, and abstracting the common characteristics of A, B, C, and D, you decide to call these *gogo*; E, F, G, and H you decide to call *gigi*. You chase away the *gogo*, but leave the *gigi* alone. Your neighbor, however, has had a different experience; he finds that those with square heads bite, while those with round heads do not. Abstracting the common characteristics of B, D, F, and H, he calls them *daba*, and A, C, E, and G he calls *dobo*. Still another neighbor discovers, on the other hand, that those with curly tails kill snakes, while those with straight tails do not. He differentiates them, abstracting still another set of common characteristics: A, B, E, and F are *busa*, while C, D, G, and H are *busana*.

Now imagine that the three of you are together when E runs by. You say, "There goes the *gigi*"; your first neighbor says, "There goes the *dobo*"; your other neighbor says, "There goes the *busa*." Here immediately a great controversy arises. What is it really, a *gigi*, a *dobo*, or a *busa*? What is its *right name*? You are quarreling violently when along comes a fourth person from another village who calls it a *muglock*, an edible animal, as opposed to *uglock*, an inedible animal —which doesn't help matters a bit.

Of course the question, "What is it *really*? What is its *right name*?" is a nonsense question. By a nonsense question is meant one that is not capable of being answered. Things can have "right names" only if there is a necessary connection between symbols and things symbolized. . . . That is to say, in the light of your interest in protecting your grain, it may be necessary for you to distinguish the animal E as a *gigi;* your neighbor, who doesn't like to be bitten, finds it practical to distinguish it as a *dobo;* your other neighbor, who likes to see snakes killed, distinguishes it as a *busa.* What we call things and where we draw the line between one class of things and another depend upon the interests we have and the purposes of the classification. For example animals are classified in one way by the meat industry, in a different way by the leather industry, in another different way by the fur industry and in a still different way by the biologist. None of these classifications is any more final than any of the others; each of them is useful for its purpose.

This holds, of course, regarding everything we perceive. A table "is" a table to us, because we can understand its relationship to our conduct and interests; we eat at it, work on it, lay things on it. But to a person living in a culture where no tables are used, it may be a very big stool, a small platform, or a meaningless structure. If our culture and upbringing were different, that is to say, our world would not even look the same to us.

Many of us, for example, cannot distinguish between pickerel, pike, salmon, smelts, perch, crappies, halibut, and mackerel; we say that they are "just fish, and I don't like fish." To a seafood connoisseur, however, these distinctions are real, since they mean the difference to him between one kind of good meal, a very different kind of good meal, or a poor meal. To a zoologist, even finer distinctions become of great importance, since he has other and more general ends in view. When we hear the statement, then, "This fish is a specimen of the pompano, *Trachinotus carolinus,*" we accept this as being "true," even if we don't care, not because that is its "right name," but because that is how it is *classified* in the most complete and most general system of classification which people most deeply interested in fish have evolved.

When we name something, then, we are classifying. *The individual object or event we are naming, of course, has no name and belongs to no class until we put it in one.* To illustrate again, suppose that we were to give the *extensional* meaning of the word "Korean."[1] We would have to

---

[1] By the extensional meaning of a word Mr. Hayakawa means "that which it points to . . . in the extensional world," i.e., in the world outside your skin. For example, the extensional meaning of "my dog" is the little creature himself that leaps and barks and wags his tail. It is the *thing* referred to in the world you observe. [eds.]

point to all "Koreans" living at a particular moment and say, "The word 'Korean' denotes at the present moment these persons: A_1, A_2, A_3 . . . A_n." Now, let us say, a child, whom we shall designate as Z, is born among these "Koreans." *The extensional meaning of the word "Korean," determined prior to the existence of Z, does not include Z.* Z is a new individual belonging to no classification, since all classifications were made without taking Z into account. Why, then, is Z also a "Korean"? *Because we say so.* And, saying so—fixing the classification—we have determined to a considerable extent future attitudes toward Z. For example, Z will always have certain rights in Korea; he will always be regarded in other nations as an "alien" and will be subject to laws applicable to "aliens."

In matters of "race" and "nationality," the way in which classifications work is especially apparent. For example, the present writer is by "race" a "Japanese," by "nationality" a "Canadian," but, his friends say, "essentially" an "American," since he thinks, talks, behaves, and dresses much like other Americans. Because he is "Japanese," he is excluded by law from becoming a citizen of the United States; because he is "Canadian," he has certain rights in all parts of the British Commonwealth; because he is "American," he gets along with his friends and teaches in an American institution of higher learning without any noticeable special difficulties. Are these classifications "real"? Of course they are, and *the effect that each of them has upon what he may and may not do constitutes their "reality."*

There was, again, the story some years ago of the immigrant baby whose parents were "Czechs" and eligible to enter the United States by quota. The child, however, because it was born on what happened to be a "British" ship, was a "British subject." The quota for Britishers was full for that year, with the result that the newborn infant was regarded by immigration authorities as "not admissible to the United States." How they straightened out this matter, the writer does not know. The reader can multiply instances of this kind at will. When, to take another example, is a person a "Negro"? By the definition accepted in the United States, any person with even a small amount of "Negro blood"—that is, whose parents or ancestors were classified as "Negroes"—is a "Negro." *It would be exactly as justifiable to say that any person with even a small amount of "white blood" is "white."* Why do they say one rather than the other? Because the former system of classification *suits the convenience of those making the classification.*

There are few complexities about classifications at the level of dogs and cats, knives and forks, cigarettes and candy, but when it comes to classifications at high levels of abstraction,[2] for example, those describing conduct, social institutions, philosophical and moral problems, serious difficulties occur. When one person kills another, is it an act of murder, an act of temporary insanity, an act of homicide, an accident, or an act of heroism? As soon as the process of classification is completed, our attitudes and our conduct are to a considerable degree determined. We hang the murderer, we lock up the insane man, we free the victim of circumstances, we pin a medal on the hero.

The blocked mind

Unfortunately, people are not always aware of the way in which they arrive at their classifications. Unaware of the characteristics of the extensional Mr. Miller not covered by classifying him as "a Jew" and attributing to Mr. Miller all the characteristic *suggested* by the affective connotations of the term with which he has been classified, they pass final judgment on Mr. Miller by saying, "Well, a Jew's a Jew.[3] There's no getting around that!"

We need not concern ourselves here with the injustices done to "Jews," "Roman Catholics," "Republicans," "red-heads," "chorus girls," "sailors," "brass-hats," "Southerners," "Yankees," "school teachers," "government regulations," "socialistic proposals," and so on, by such hasty judgments or, as it is better to call them, fixed reactions. "Hasty judgments" suggests that such errors can be avoided by thinking more slowly; this, of course, is not the case, for some people think very slowly with no better results. What we are concerned

[2] The level of abstraction refers to the degree of generality of a word. For example, your dog, Duke, might be classified as a *bull terrier*, a *terrier*, a *dog*, an *animal*, a *pet*, or a *creature*. Here each successive term is more general than the preceding one; that is to say, each is on a higher level of abstraction than the one before it. Classifications at high levels of abstraction are extremely general words like *liberty*, *justice*, *democracy*, *officialdom*, *the American way*. Such words are hard to communicate with because they can mean so many different things. What, for example, does *the American way* mean? To a Russian, fed upon anti-American propaganda, it might mean all the objectionable things that he believes Americans do; it would include lynchings, acts of government corruption, illegal price fixing by large corporations, lavish living, gangster activities, oppression of the working man, denial of civil rights to Negroes, and many others. But to an American it might mean all of the good things we do: voting at the polls in secret, giving free education to all, allowing private citizens to speak their minds in public, giving voluntarily to charitable organizations, aiding underprivileged nations, and so on. Because the term can include so many thousands of specific acts, it is extremely vague. It is meaningless because it is so meaningful. [eds.]

[3] The affective connotations of a word are the feelings that it arouses. [eds.]

with is the way in which we block the development of our own minds by such automatic reactions.

To continue with our example of the people who say, "A Jew's a Jew. There's no getting around that!"—they are, as we have seen, confusing the denoted, extensional Jew with the fictitious "Jew" inside their heads. Such persons, the reader will have observed, can usually be made to admit, on being reminded of certain "Jews" whom they admire—perhaps Albert Einstein, perhaps Hank Greenberg, perhaps Jascha Heifetz, perhaps Benny Goodman—that "there are exceptions, of course." They have been compelled by experience, that is to say, to take cognizance of at least a few of the multitude of "Jews" who do not fit their preconceptions. At this point, however, they continue triumphantly, "But exceptions only prove the rule!"[4]—which is another way of saying, "Facts don't count." In extremely serious cases of people who "think" in this way, it can sometimes be observed that the best friends they have may be Isaac Cohens, Isidor Ginsbergs, and Abe Sinaikos; nevertheless, in explaining this, they will say, "I don't think of them as Jews at all. They're just friends." In other words, the fictitious "Jew" inside their heads remains unchanged *in spite of their experience.*

People like this *cannot learn from experience.* They continue to vote "Republican" or "Democratic," no matter what the Republicans or Democrats do. They continue to object to "socialists," no matter what the socialists propose. They continue to regard "mothers" as sacred, no matter which mother. A woman who had been given up both by physicians and psychiatrists as hopelessly insane was being considered by a committee whose task it was to decide whether or not she should be committed to an asylum. One member of the committee doggedly refused to vote for commitment. "Gentlemen," he said in tones of deepest reverence, "you must remember that this woman is, after all, a mother." Similarly such people continue to hate "Protestants," no matter which Protestant. Unaware of characteristics left out in the process of classification, they overlook, when the term "Republican" is applied to both the party of Abraham Lincoln and the party of Warren Harding, the rather important differences between them: "If the Republican party was good enough for Abe Lincoln, it's good enough for me!"

---

[4] This extraordinarily fatuous saying originally meant, "The exception *tests* the rule"—*Exceptio probat regulam.* This older meaning of the word "prove" survives in such an expression as "automobile proving ground."

Cow₁ is not cow₂

How do we prevent ouselves from getting into such intellectual blind alleys, or finding we are in one, how do we get out again? One way is to remember that practically all statements in ordinary conversation, debate, and public controversy taking the form, "Republicans are Republicans," "Business is business," "Boys will be boys," "Women drivers are women drivers," and so on, are *not true*. Let us put one of these back into a context in life.

"I don't think we should go through with this deal, Bill. Is it altogether fair to the railroad company?"

"Aw, forget it! *Business is business*, after all."[5]

Such an assertion, although it looks like a "simple statement of fact," is not simple and is not a statement of fact. The first "business" *denotes* transaction under discussion; the second "business" invokes the *connotations* of the word. The sentence is a *directive*, saying, "Let us treat this transaction with complete disregard for considerations other than profit, as the word 'business' suggests." Similarly, when a father tries to excuse the mischief done by his sons, he says, "Boys will be boys";[6] in other words, "Let us regard the actions of my sons with that indulgent amusement customarily extended toward those whom we call 'boys' " though the angry neighbor will say, of course, "Boys, my eye! They're little hoodlums; that's what they are!" These too are not informative statements but *directives, directing us to classify the object or event under discussion in given ways, in order that we may feel or act in the ways suggested by the terms of the classification.*

There is a simple technique for preventing such directives from having their harmful effect on our thinking. It is the suggestion made by Korzybski that we add "index numbers" to our terms, thus: Englishman ₁, Englishman ₂, . . . ; cow ₁, cow ₂, cow ₃, . . . ; Frenchman ₁, Frenchman ₂, Frenchman ₃, . . . ; communist ₁, communist ₂, communist ₃, . . . The terms of the classification tell us what the individuals in that class have in common; THE INDEX NUMBERS REMIND US OF THE CHARACTERISTICS LEFT OUT. *A rule can then be formulated as a general guide in all our thinking and reading: Cow ₁ is* NOT *Cow ₂, Jew ₁ is* NOT *Jew ₂; politician ₁ is* NOT *politician ₂, and so on. This rule, if remembered, prevents us from confusing levels of abstraction and forces us to*

[5] In "Business is business" the word *business* shifts its meaning. This expression may be translated "Commercial transactions are matters concerned with profits, not ethics." [eds.]

[6] The word *boy* shifts meaning here, as a translation will show: "Young males of the human species will be mischievous creatures." [eds.]

consider the facts on those occasions when we might otherwise find ourselves leaping to conclusions which we may later have cause to regret.

"Truth"

Most intellectual problems are, ultimately, problems of classification and nomenclature. Some years ago there was a dispute between the American Medical Association and the Antitrust Division of the Department of Justice as to whether the practice of medicine was a "profession" or "trade." The American Medical Association *wanted* immunity from laws prohibiting "restraint of trade"; therefore, it insisted that medicine *is* a "profession." The Antitrust Division *wanted* to stop certain economic practices connected with medicine, and therefore it insisted that medicine *is* a "trade." Partisans of either side accused the other of perverting the meanings of words and of not being able to understand plain English.

Can farmers operate oil wells and still be "farmers"? In 1947 the attorney general of the state of Kansas sued to dissolve a large agricultural co-operative, Consumers Co-operative Association, charging that the corporation, in owning oil wells, refineries, and pipe-lines, was exceeding the statutory privileges of purchasing co-operatives under the Co-operative Marketing Act, which permits such organizations to "engage in any activity in connection with manufacturing, selling, or supplying to its members machinery, equipment or supplies." The attorney general held that the co-operative, under the Act, could not handle, let alone process and manufacture, general farm supplies, but only those supplies used in the marketing operation. The Kansas Supreme Court decided unanimously in favor of the defendent (CCA). In so deciding, the court held that gasoline and oil *are* "farm supplies," and producing crude oil *is* "part of the business of farming."

"This court," said the decision, "will take judicial notice of the fact that in the present state of the art of farming, gasoline . . . is one of the costliest items in the production of agricultural commodities. . . . Anyway, gasoline and tractors are here, and this court is not going to say that motor fuel is not a supply necessary to carrying on of farm operations. . . . Indeed it is about as well put as can be on Page 18 of the state's Exhibit C where the defendant (CCA) says: '*Producing crude oil, operating pipelines and refineries, are also part of the business of farming. It is merely producing synthetic hay for iron horses. It is "off-the-farm farming" which the farmer, in concert with his neighbors, is carrying on. . . .*

Production of power farming equipment, then, is logically an extension of the farmers' own farming operations.' " (Italics supplied.)

Is a harmonica player a "musician"? Until 1948, the American Federation of Musicians had ruled that the harmonica was a "toy." Professional harmonica players usually belonged, therefore, to the American Guild of Variety Artists. Even as distinguished a musician as Larry Adler, who has often played the harmonica as a solo instrument with symphony orchestras, was by the union's definition "not a musician." In 1948, however, the AFM, finding that harmonica players were getting popular and competing with members of the union, decided that they were "musicians" after all—a decision that did not sit well with the president of AGVA, who promptly declared jurisdictional war on the AFM.

Is aspirin a "drug" or not? In some states, it is legally classified as a "drug", and therefore can be sold only by licensed pharmacists. If people want to be able to buy aspirin in groceries, lunchrooms, and pool halls (as they can in other states), they must have it reclassified as "not a drug."

Is medicine a "profession" or a "trade"? Is the production of crude oil "a part of farming"? Is a harmonica player a "musician"? Is aspirin a "drug"? The way in which such questions are commonly settled is by appeals to dictionaries to discover the "real meanings" of the words involved. It is also common practice to consult past legal decisions and all kinds of learned treatises bearing on the subject. The decision finally rests, however, not upon appeals to past authority, but upon *what people want*. If they want the AMA to be immune from antitrust action, they will go to the Supreme Court if necessary to get medicine "defined" as a "profession." If they want the AMA prosecuted, they will get a decision that it is a "trade." (They got, in this case, a decision from the Court that it did not matter whether the practice of medicine was a "trade" or not; what mattered was that the AMA had, as charged, *restrained* the trade of Group Health Association, Inc., a co-operative to *procure* medical services for its members. The antitrust action was upheld.)

If people want agricultural co-operatives to operate oil wells, they will get the courts to define the activity in such a way as to make it possible. If the public at large doesn't care, the decision whether a harmonica player is or is not a "musician" will be made by the stronger trade union. The question whether aspirin is or is not a "drug" will be decided neither by finding the dictionary definition of "drug" nor by staring long and hard at an aspirin tablet. It will be decided on the basis of where and under what conditions people want to buy their aspirins.

In any case, society as a whole ultimately gets, on all issues of wide public importance, the classifications it wants, even if it has to wait until all the members of the Supreme Court are dead and an entirely new court is appointed. When the desired decision is handed down, people say, "Truth has triumphed." *In short, society regards as "true" those systems of classification that produce the desired results.*

The scientific test of "truth," like the social test, is strictly practical, except for the fact that the "desired results" are more serevely limited. The results desired by society may be irrational, superstitious, selfish or humane, but the results desired by scientists are only that our systems of classification produce predictable results. Classifications, as amply indicated already, determine our attitudes and behavior toward the object or event classified. When lightning was classified as "evidence of divine wrath," no courses of action other than prayer were suggested to prevent one's being struck by lightning. As soon, however, as it was classified as "electricity," Benjamin Franklin achieved a measure of control over it by his invention of the lightning rod. Certain physical disorders were formerly classified as "demonic possession," and this suggested that we "drive the demons out" by whatever spells or incantations we could think of. The results were uncertain. But when those disorders were classified as "bacillus infections," courses of action were suggested that led to more predictable results. Science seeks only the *most generally useful* systems of classification; these it regards for the time being, until more useful classifications are invented, as "true."

SUGGESTED ASSIGNMENTS

1. A class-word, or classification, is sometimes accompanied in our minds by a mental picture, which is known as a stereotype. The following experiment will illustrate. Picture in your mind for a moment your idea of a little boy going fishing. Now answer these questions.
   a. Does he wear shoes or is he barefoot?
   b. If he has a hat, what is it made of?
   c. What is he carrying over his shoulder?
   d. What is it made of?
   e. Is his nose freckled or not?

f.   What is walking at his side?

g.   Are his clothes tidy or ragged?

Here are the answers: a. barefoot b. straw c. a fishing pole d. of cane or of a branch e. freckled f. a dog g. ragged. If you passed the test you have in mind the usual little-boy-going-fishing stereotype. What do you think is the source of this stereotype?

2.   Write a short description of a common stereotype, such as a grandmother, a traffic policeman, an old-maid school teacher, an army sergeant, a truck driver, a college professor. Now, write a second description of a real person you know who belongs in the same classification but who does not fit the stereotype.

3.   Write a short theme describing a situation you are acquainted with in which a classification makes a real difference. You might consider such classifications as these: resident-nonresident, amateur-professional, junior-senior, drunk-sober, speeding-reckless driving, weed-flower, sane-insane, war-police action, borrowing-stealing.

4.   A newspaper actually reported the following incident. An Oxford University student had a bass viol that was too large for taxis and too heavy to be carried. He solved the problem of moving it from place to place by providing it with a wheel on which he rolled it. But the police stepped in and classified it as a vehicle. The result was that he could wheel it only in the street, had to keep it off the sidewalk, and had to put head lights and a tail light on it. Whether he had to buy a license was not mentioned. What was the viol REALLY?

5.   The following letter appeared in a popular syndicated newspaper column:

Dear ———: Please settle an argument. Where I work there is this woman who has silver-gray hair but a young face and a good figure. She must be about 50 but looks younger. She has 12 grandchildren, but she goes swimming with them, rides a bicycle with them, and she belongs to three bowling leagues. She says she never baby-sits with her grandchildren unless there is an emergency. Everyone says I am all wet with my ideas but I think a grandmother should ACT like a grandmother and should be proud of her grandchildren and not of her bowling score.

What do you think is the cause of the writer's attitude?

Prejudice:
Linguistic Factors

GORDON W. ALLPORT

The first essay in this section dealt with the importance, indeed the necessity, of categorization in helping us to organize our experience in an efficient and meaningful way. The second essay both complemented and extended the first by clarifying the process of abstraction and by pointing out some of the dangers of classification. The following essay takes us further into the same topic, focusing attention on the ways in which classifiers (verbal group labels) oper- ate in the expression and dissemination of prejudice. Preju- dice rests on deep-seated and largely unconscious attitudes. An understanding of the extent to which these attitudes are embodied in language that colors our thinking and feelings may make us more sensitive to the inflammatory · nature of prejudicial language. It also may enable us to discriminate between informative statements and prejudicial statements.

Without words we should scarcely be able to form categories at all. A dog perhaps forms rudimentary generalizations, such as small-boys-are-to-be-avoided—but this concept runs its course on the conditioned reflex level, and does not become the object of thought as such. In order to hold a generalization in mind for reflection and recall, for identification and for action, we need to fix it in words. Without words our world would be, as William James said, an "empirical sand-heap."

Nouns that cut slices

In the empirical world of human beings there are some two and a half billion grains of sand corresponding to our category "the human race." We cannot possibly deal with so many separate entities in our thought, nor can we individualize even among the hundreds whom we encounter in our daily round. We must group them, form clusters. We welcome, therefore, the names that help us to perform the clustering.

The most important property of a noun is that it brings many grains of sand into a single pail, disregarding the fact that the same grains might have fitted just as appropriately into another pail. To

From *The Nature of Prejudice* by Gordon W. Allport. Reprinted by permission of Addison-Wesley Publishing Company, copyright 1954.

state the matter technically, a noun *abstracts* from a concrete reality some one feature and assembles different concrete realities only with respect to this one feature. The very act of classifying forces us to overlook all other features, many of which might offer a sounder basis than the rubric we select. Irving Lee gives the following example:

I knew a man who had lost the use of both eyes. He was called a "blind man." He could also be called an expert typist, a conscientious worker, a good student, a careful listener, a man who wanted a job. But he couldn't get a job in the department store order room where employees sat and typed orders which came over the telephone. The personnel man was impatient to get the interview over. "But you're a blind man," he kept saying, and one could almost feel his silent assumption that somehow the incapacity in one aspect made the man incapable in every other. So blinded by the label was the interviewer that he could not be persuaded to look beyond it.[1]

Some labels, such as "blind man," are exceedingly salient and powerful. They tend to prevent alternative classification, or even cross-classification. Ethnic labels are often of this type, particularly if they refer to some highly visible feature, e.g., Negro, Oriental. They resemble the labels that point to some outstanding incapacity— *feeble-minded, cripple, blind man*. Let us call such symbols "labels of primary potency." These symbols act like shrieking sirens, deafening us to all finer discriminations that we might otherwise perceive. Even though the blindness of one man and the darkness of pigmentation of another may be defining attributes for some purposes, they are irrelevant and "noisy" for others.

Most people are unaware of this basic law of language—that every label applied to a given person refers properly only to one aspect of his nature. You may correctly say that a certain man is *human*, a *philanthropist*, a *Chinese*, a *physician*, an *athelete*. A given person may be all of these; but the chances are that *Chinese* stands out in your mind as the symbol of primary potency. Yet neither this nor any other classificatory label can refer to the whole of a man's nature. (Only his proper name can do so.)

Thus each label we use, especially those of primary potency, distracts our attention from concrete reality. The living, breathing, complex individual—the ultimate unit of human nature—is lost to sight. As in the figure following, the label magnifies one attribute out of all proportion to its true significance, and masks other important attributes of the individual.

[1] I. J. Lee, *How Do You Talk about People?*, Freedom Pamphlet (New York, Anti-Defamation League, 1950), p. 15.

LABELS OF PRIMARY POTENCY

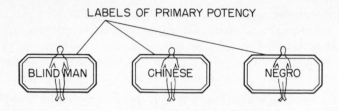

BLIND MAN   CHINESE   NEGRO

. . . a category, once formed with the aid of a symbol of primary potency, tends to attract more attributes than it should. The category labeled *Chinese* comes to signify not only ethnic membership but also reticence, impassivity, poverty, treachery. To be sure, . . . there may be genuine ethnic-linked traits making for a certain *probability* that the member of an ethnic stock may have these attributes. But our cognitive process is not cautious. The labeled category, . . . includes indiscriminately the defining attribute, probable attributes, and wholly fanciful, nonexistent attributes.

Even proper names—which ought to invite us to look at the individual person—may act like symbols of primary potency, especially if they arouse ethnic associations. Mr. Greenberg is a person, but since his name is Jewish, it activates in the hearer his entire category of Jews-as-a-whole.

The anthropologist, Margaret Mead, has suggested that labels of primary potency lose some of their force when they are changed from nouns into adjectives. To speak of a Negro soldier, a Catholic teacher, or a Jewish artist calls attention to the fact that some other group classifications are just as legitimate as the racial or religious. If George Johnson is spoken of not only as a Negro but also as a *soldier*, we have at least two attributes to know him by, and two are more accurate than one. To depict him truly as an individual, of course, we should have to name many more attributes. It is a useful suggestion that we designate ethnic and religious membership where possible with *adjectives* rather than with *nouns*.

Emotionally toned labels

Many categories have two kinds of labels—one less emotional and one more emotional. Ask yourself how you feel, and what thoughts you have, when you read the words *school teacher*, and then *school marm*. Certainly the second phrase calls up something more strict, more ridiculous, more disagreeable than the former. Here are four innocent letters: m-a-r-m. But they make us shudder a bit, laugh a bit, and scorn a bit. They call up an image of a spare, humorless, irritable old maid. They do not tell us that she is an individual human being with sorrows and troubles of her own. They force her instantly into a rejective category.

In the ethnic sphere even plain labels such as Negro, Italian, Jew, Catholic, Irish-American, French-Canadian may have emotional tone for a reason that we shall soon explain. But they all have their higher key equivalents: nigger, wop, kike, papist, harp, cannuck. When these labels are employed we can be almost certain that the speaker *intends* not only to characterize the person's membership, but also to disparage and reject him.

Quite apart from the insulting intent that lies behind the use of certain labels, there is also an inherent ("physiognomic") handicap in many terms designating ethnic membership. For example, the proper names characteristic of certain ethnic memberships strike us as absurd. (We compare them, of course, with what is familiar and therefore "right.") Chinese names are short and silly; Polish names intrinsically difficult and outlandish. Unfamiliar dialects strike us as ludicrous. Foreign dress (which, of course, is a visual ethnic symbol) seems unnecessarily queer.

But of all these "physiognomic" handicaps the reference to color, clearly implied in certain symbols, is the greatest. The word Negro comes from the Latin *niger*, meaning black. In point of fact, no Negro has a black complexion, but by comparison with other blonder stocks, he has come to be known as a "black man." Unfortunately *black* in the English language is a word having a preponderance of sinister connotations: the outlook is black, blackball, blackguard, blackhearted, black death, blacklist, blackmail, Black Hand. . . .

There is thus an implied value-judgment in the very concept of *white race* and *black race*. One might also study the numerous unpleasant connotations of *yellow*, and their possible bearing on our conception of the people of the Orient.

Such reasoning should not be carried too far, since there are undoubtedly, in various contexts, pleasant associations with both black and yellow. Black velvet is agreeable, so too are chocolate and coffee. Yellow tulips are well liked; the sun and moon are radiantly yellow. Yet it is true that "color" words are used with chauvinistic overtones more than most people realize. There is certainly condescension indicated in many familiar phrases: dark as a nigger's pocket, darktown strutters, white hope (a term originated when a white contender was sought against the Negro heavyweight champion, Jack Johnson), the white man's burden, the yellow peril, black boy. Scores of everyday phrases are stamped with the flavor of prejudice, whether the user knows it or not.[2]

Members of minority groups are often understandably sensitive to names given them. Not only do they object to deliberately insulting epithets, but sometimes see evil intent where none exists. Often the word Negro is spelled with a small *n*, occasionally as a studied insult, more often from ignorance. (The term is not cognate with white, which is not capitalized, but rather with Caucasian, which is.) Terms like "mulatto" or "octoroon" cause hard feeling because of the condescension with which they have often been used in the past. Sex differentiations are objectionable, since they seem doubly to emphasize ethnic difference: why speak of Jewess and not of Protestantess, or of Negress and not of whitess? Similar overemphasis is implied in terms like Chinaman or Scotchman; why not American man? Grounds for misunderstanding lie in the fact that minority group members are sensitive to such shadings, while majority members may employ them unthinkingly.

The communist label

Until we label an out-group it does not clearly exist in our minds. Take the curiously vague situation that we often meet when a person wishes to locate responsibility on the shoulders of some out-group whose nature he cannot specify. In such a case he usually employs the pronoun "they" without an antecedent. "Why don't they make these sidewalks wider?" "I hear they are going to build a factory in this town and hire a lot of foreigners." "I won't pay this tax bill; they can just whistle for their money." If asked "who"? the speaker is likely to grow confused and embarrassed. The common use of the orphaned pronoun *they* teaches us that people often want and need to designate out-groups (usually for the purpose of venting hostility) even when they have no clear conception of the out-group in question. And so long as the target of wrath remains vague and ill-defined specific prejudice cannot crystallize around it. To have enemies we need labels.

Until relatively recently—strange as it may seem—there was no agreed-upon symbol for *communist*. The word, of course, existed but it had no special emotional connotation, and did not designate a public

---

[2] L. L. Brown, "Words and White Chauvinism," *Masses and Mainstream* (1950), 3, pp. 3–11. See also *Prejudice Won't Hide! A Guide for Developing a Language of Equality* (San Francisco, California Federation for Civic Unity, 1950).

enemy. Even when, after World War I, there was a growing feeling of economic and social menace in this country, there was no agreement as to the actual source of the menace.

A content analysis of the *Boston Herald* for the year 1920 turned up the following list of labels. Each was used in a context implying some threat. Hysteria had overspread the country, as it did after World War II. Someone must be responsible for the postwar malaise, rising prices, uncertainty. There must be a villain. But in 1920 the villain was impartially designated by reporters and editorial writers with the following symbols:

alien, agitator, anarchist, apostle of bomb and torch, Bolshevik, communist, communist laborite, conspirator, emissary of false promise, extremist, foreigner, hyphenated-American, incendiary, IWW, parlor anarchist, parlor pink, parlor socialist, plotter, radical, red, revolutionary, Russian agitator, socialist, Soviet, syndicalist, traitor, undesirable.

From this excited array we note that the *need* for an enemy (someone to serve as a focus for discontent and jitters) was considerably more apparent than the precise *identity* of the enemy. At any rate, there was no clearly agreed-upon label. Perhaps partly for this reason the hysteria abated. Since no clear category of "communism" existed there was no true focus for the hostility.

But following World War II this collection of vaguely interchangeable labels became fewer in number and more commonly agreed upon. The out-group menace came to be designated almost always as *communist* or *red*. In 1920 the threat, lacking a clear label, was vague; after 1945 both symbol and thing became more definite. Not that people knew precisely what they meant when they said "communist," but with the aid of the term they were at least able to point consistently to *something* that inspired fear. The term developed the power of signifying menace and led to various repressive measures against anyone to whom the label was rightly or wrongly attached.

Logically, the label should apply to specifiable defining attributes, such as members of the Communist Party, or people whose allegiance is with the Russian system, or followers, historically, of Karl Marx. But the label came in for far more extensive use.

What seems to have happened is approximately as follows. Having suffered through a period of war and being acutely aware of devastating revolutions abroad, it is natural that most people should be upset, dreading to lose their possessions, annoyed by high taxes, seeing customary moral and religious values threatened, and dreading worse disasters to come. Seeking an explanation for this unrest, a single identifiable enemy is wanted. It is not enough to designate "Russia" or some other distant land. Nor is it satisfactory to fix blame on "changing social conditions." What is needed is a human agent near at hand: someone in Washington, someone in our schools, in our factories, in our neighborhood. If we *feel* an immediate threat, we reason, there must be a near-lying danger. It is, we conclude, communism, not only in Russia but also in America, at our doorstep, in our government, in our churches, in our colleges, in our neighborhood.

Are we saying that hostility toward communism is prejudice? Not necessarily. There are certainly phases of the dispute wherein realistic social conflict is involved. American values (e.g., respect for the person) and totalitarian values as represented in Soviet practice are intrinsically at odds. A realistic opposition in some form will occur. Prejudice enters only when the defining attributes of "communist" grow imprecise, when anyone who favors any form of social change is called a communist. People who fear social change are the ones most likely to affix the label to any persons or practices that seem to them threatening.

For them the category is undifferentiated, It includes books, movies, preachers, teachers who utter what for them are uncongenial thoughts. If evil befalls—perhaps forest fires or a rocket explosion— it is due to communist saboteurs. The category becomes monopolistic, covering almost anything that is uncongenial. On the floor of the House of Representatives in 1946, Representative Rankin called James Roosevelt a communist. Congressman Outland replied with psychological acumen, "Apparently everyone who disagrees with Mr. Rankin is a communist."

When differentiated thinking is at a low ebb— at it is in times of social crisis—there is a magnification of two-valued logic. Things are perceived as either inside or outside a moral order. What is outside is likely to be called "communist." Correspondingly—and here is where damage is done—whatever is called communist (however erroneously) is immediately cast outside the moral order.

This associative mechanism places enormous power in the hands of a demagogue. For several years Senator McCarthy managed to discredit many citizens who thought differently from himself by the simple device of calling them communists. Few people were able to see through this trick and many reputations were ruined. But the famous senator had no monopoly on the device. . . .

Verbal realism and symbol phobia

Most individuals rebel at being labeled, especially if the label is uncomplimentary. Very few are willing to be called *fascistic, socialistic,* or *anti-Semitic.* Unsavory labels may apply to others; but not to us.

An illustration of the craving that people have to attach favorable symbols to themselves is seen in the community where white people banded together to force out a Negro family that had moved in. They called themselves "Neighborly Endeavor" and chose as their motto the Golden Rule. One of the first acts of this symbol-sanctified band was to sue the man who sold property to Negroes. They then flooded the house which another Negro couple planned to occupy. Such were the acts performed under the banner of the Golden Rule.

When symbols provoke strong emotions they are sometimes regarded no longer as symbols, but as actual things. The expressions "son of a bitch" and "liar" are in our culture frequently regarded as "fighting words." Softer and more subtle expressions of contempt may be accepted. But in these particular cases, the epithet itself must be "taken back." We certainly do not change our opponent's attitude by making him take back a word, but it seems somehow important that the word itself be eradicated.

Such verbal realism may reach extreme lengths.

The City Council of Cambridge, Massachusetts, unanimously passed a resolution (December, 1939) making it illegal "to possess, harbor, sequester, introduce or transport, within the city limits, any book, map, magazine, newspaper, pamphlet, handbill or circular containing the words Lenin or Leningrad.[3]

Such naïveté in confusing language with reality is hard to comprehend unless we recall that word-magic plays an appreciable part in human thinking.

[3] S. I. Hayakawa, *Language in Action* (New York, Harcourt, Brace & World, Inc., 1941), p. 29.

Bias Words

F. A. PHILBRICK

A bias is literally a slant, from the French *biais*. In English
we use the word metaphorically to mean a slant in one's
judgment. Bias words, then, are those which show a slanted
judgment, either in favor of or against, in varying degrees
of intensity. For example, you may be *thrifty*, but a person
with the same characteristic whom you dislike is *stingy*.
Bias words tend to creep into our speech and writing when
we feel strongly about a subject. Though they have their
place in certain kinds of discourse—eulogy, invective, satire,
poetry—they are to be avoided in writing that purports to
be objective and considered. Several methods of indicating
bias are considered below by F. A. Philbrick. Mr. Philbrick,
a graduate of Balliol College, Oxford, where he took a "first"
in science, taught English at the University of Chicago and
at top-flight preparatory schools in England and the United
States. He was a keen observer of language and wrote about
it clearly and intelligibly.

There are three classes into which all the women past seventy that ever
I knew were to be divided: 1. That dear old soul; 2. That old woman;
3. That old witch.

Samuel Taylor Coleridge

NEUTRAL, FAVORABLE, AND UNFAVORABLE WORDS.   Languages differ in
the extent to which they allow a writer a choice of different words with
the same referent. In Spanish this variation often can be achieved by
different endings, such as *-ico, -ito, -uelo, -on, -ezo,* or *-acho*. For example,
the Spanish words for "dog" include *perro, perrazo, perillo, perrito,
perrezno,* and *perrico,* each with a differerent reference. The first is the
plain neutral word; the second implies large size and grotesqueness
("ugly" or "hulking"); the third, small size and pity ("poor little
wretch"); the fourth, small size and fondness ("darling little"); the
fifth, immaturity ("puppy"); and the sixth, what the dictionary, with
rare candor, calls "sprightly humor impossible to characterize." The
twist given by these endings to a neutral word, such as *perro,* is different

From *Understanding English* by F. A. Philbrick. Copyright 1942 by The Macmillan
Company and used with their permission.

for each word and is so subtle that all the manuals on the Spanish language advise the foreigner to be cautious in using such terminations or even not to use them at all. If he neglects this advice, a foreigner is apt to make awkward mistakes, and when wishing to compliment a Spanish lady on her "dear little baby", he may inadvertently suggest that the infant is undersized, contemptible, and of a disagreeable shape.

In English the possibilities are more limited, and the writer often has to choose from such a set as *dog, cur,* and *hound.* With fewer words available, each has to cover a wider range, so that while *cur* is always derogatory, *hound* sometimes implies grandeur ("majestic hound," "The Hound of the Baskervilles," "The Hound of Heaven") but sometimes the opposite ("mean hound," "wretched hound"). This variability does not make the word less effective, and "The Dog of the Baskervilles" or "The Dog of Heaven" are plainly less satisfactory than the actual titles. It is true that *hound,* like *perrazo,* implies large size, but even "The Large Dog of the Baskervilles" fails to come quite up to the original.

Words such as *cur* and *hound,* which have the same referent, but different references expressing different attitudes on the part of the user, will here be called *bias words.* Matthew Arnold called them words "touched by emotion," and Coleridge, calling them "watch-words," warned his readers against them, recommending "the beneficial after-effects of verbal precision in the preclusion of fanaticism, which masters the feelings more especially by indistinct watch-words."[1]

SOME BIAS WORDS EXAMINED.   While it must never be forgotten that a word owes much of its meaning to its setting, yet it is still possible to estimate the kind of bias that certain words have acquired. The writer's attitude can also be expressed by phrases. "John did not come" and "John failed to come" refer to the same fact, but the second phrase suggests, without clearly saying so, that John was at fault. Writers use such phrases because of the possibility of hinting at a meaning without committing themselves.

As a first example of a pair of bias words *liberty* and *license* may be considered in the phrase "liberty not license," In the referents of the two words there is no difference; each word suggests the absence of restrictions on the doing of something, but *license* implies the liberty to do something of which the writer does not approve. Thus, writers wishing to restrict someone else's liberty often refer to that liberty

[1] *Biographia Literaria,* Ch. 22.

as *license*, and sometimes draw attention to their own use of bias words as a substitute for reasoning by quoting the phrase itself. To call liberty *license* is not to advance an argument against it, but simply to say that we do not like it, and it tells the reader nothing about the thing referred to except that it is unwelcome to the writer. Again, the word *fad* may refer to any belief or practice that the writer disapproves of, with the implications that the person adhering to it (called the *faddist*) attaches too much importance to it, and that few others share his opinions. *Crank* is similar to *faddist*, with perhaps a deeper tinge of dislike and contempt.

Politics, as one of the great fields of controversy, is an abundant source of bias words. *Statesman* and *statesmanlike* are favorable words, *politician* and *political* often unfavorable. Here are two extracts from a recent account of the political situation in Washington:

Last week he was a great President, or a potentially great President, working in his study on great affairs of state. But all around him in the White House could be heard the ratlike sounds of politics, the scurrying and whispers . . .

Some of the truth about the incredibly tangled situation leaked out from Washington last week in little whiffs of rumor, in planted "true stories" circulated by each interested faction.[2]

The force of these sentences is chiefly derived from the bias words used in them. . . . *affairs of state* and *politics* are favorable and unfavorable words respectively, though with similar referents. *Faction* is also a bias word (compare the stronger word *pressure group*) and has no favorable word with the same referent; *party* is more nearly neutral, but in some settings is unfavorable, as in "And to party gave up what was meant for mankind." The quotation marks around *true stories* are to suggest that the stories were not true. *Whiff* is one of several words in the *odor* group; it has an unfavorable bias. Still more unfavorable words in the same group are the words *stink* and *stench*; *odor* and *smell* have a wide range of bias according to setting, but the middle of this range is perhaps almost neutral; *savor*, *aroma*, *perfume*, and *bouquet* (of wines) are all favorable. (Thus, an advertisement for cigars will refer to the *aroma* of the smoke, not to its *odor* or *smell*, still less to its *stench* or *stink*.) Finally, to revert to the quoted passages from *Time*, *scurrying* is an unfavorable word, and so are *rat* and *rat-like*. Zoological metaphors, as applied to people, are deservedly popular as being obvious and usually insulting. *Brute*, *animal*, and *creature* are unfavorable. *Lion*, *eagle*, and sometimes *tiger*

---

[2] *Time* (March 10, 1941).

are usually favorable; whereas unfavorable attitudes are suggested by *pig, donkey, mule, jackass, rat, monkey, ape, vulture, cat, bitch, fox, vixen, jackal, hyena, snake, reptile, worm, toad, skunk,* and *polecat.*

Metaphors and bias words drawn from family life are all favorable. To speak of *Mother Nature* is to emphasize the pleasanter features of our environment; consider too *alma mater* or *the father of his people.* To call a man *a son of Texas* (or South Dakota or any other place) is always to refer favorably to him—"one of Missouri's most loyal sons." Machine metaphors as applied to a person are also usually favorable as in *dynamo, steam engine,* or *steam roller,* but *machine politics* and *sausage machine* are unfavorable.

Our study of the language of persuasion may now be continued in tabular form, though a complete list would fill a small dictionary. Political words will be found near the beginning.

FAVORABLE	NEUTRAL	UNFAVORABLE
leader of the people	party leader	demagogue
tribune of the people		ringmaster
		rabble-rouser
		political boss
strong man (*e.g.,*	absolute ruler	dictator
"the strong man		
of Ruritania")		
community	people	mob[3]
		the many-headed
patriot[4]	nationalist	jingo
		chauvinist
rights[5]		privileges
	socialist	red
	communist	
	liberal	pink
social reformer		revolutionary
	conservative (adj.)	reactionary
		backward

[3] "Democracy dissolves communities into individuals and collects them again into mobs." Dean Inge, *Outspoken Essays, First Series* (London, Longmans, Green & Co., Ltd.).

[4] "The controversy quickly got into the newspapers, and was carried on for months, with American patriots on one side and Englishmen and Anglomaniacs on the other." H. L. Mencken, *The American Language* (New York, Alfred A. Knopf, Inc.).

[5] We are apt to contrast our own rights with people's privileges.

With reference to the Spanish War:

FAVORABLE	NEUTRAL	UNFAVORABLE
loyalist	supporter of the Spanish Republic	red
anti-red	supporter of General Franco	rebel
to develop the re- sources of		to exploit the re- sources of
a go-getter salesman	an energetic salesman	a high-pressure salesman
time-tested	old (has wide range)	out-of-date
old-established		outmoded
well-tried		obsolete
		antiquated
		old-fashioned (has wide range)
up-to-date	new	newfangled
progressive	modern (has wide range)	cranky
advanced		crackpot
thinking men	those who agree with me	
right-minded		wrong-headed
devout		bigoted
freethinker	atheist	infidel
esprit fort	unbeliever	pagan
		heathen
	to compel	to dragoon
A modern theory would suggest that	I think	
confidence		complacency
self-confidence		conceit
		arrogance

Many of the words in this list, and other words like them, are a valuable part of the English language, but a writer who uses them, or a reader who encounters them in the writing of others, should understand what is being done. Instead of giving information about the referent, these words give information about the writer; they express his attitudes and feelings and are chosen by him to convey, if possible, these attitudes and feelings to the reader. Such words are dangerous if they lead the writer or the reader to confuse the exposure of an attitude with the statement of an argument.

OTHER METHODS OF INDICATING BIAS. Direct statements of opinion, the selection of material, and the use of bias words by no means exhaust the means available to the writer who wishes to communicate his prejudices. The exploitation of words with multiple meaning is not a very common device, because it requires more skill than plain lying or calling names, but it is dangerous because less easily detected. *Progressive* is a word with multiple meaning, and as applied to a school it may mean either of two things—namely, that the school is devoted to certain theories of education, most concisely described as those of Dewey, Froebel, and Montessori, or alternatively, that the school makes progress along the scale from bad to good. Everybody must approve of progress of this second kind, because each person can put his own interpretation on *good* and *bad*, but it is not everyone who thinks that schools of the "progressive school" type are the best. Since many people are by no means well informed about multiple meaning, and believe, in a muddled kind of way, that things with the same name must be the same thing, it is possible for a dishonest writer (and easy for a speaker) to use the word *progressive* in two senses in the same passage, thereby convincing the thoughtless that a school "progressive" in one way must be "progressive" in the other.

The suggestion of inferences is a favorable method of persuasion, because readers are likely to hold more tenaciously to opinions supposedly their own than to those handed them ready-made by the author.[6] Rhetorical questions—"Should the American people entrust its destiny to unscrupulous politicians?"—are crude exploitations of the same theory, for it is supposed that the mental effort of discovering the answer will make the reader familiar with the line of reasoning employed, thereby convincing him that the conclusion must be true. But to achieve more lasting impressions the writer must use a less direct approach. "The scandal of Bishop X's connection with the Organ Fund," we read, "is now a thing of the past." The incautious

[6] An inference is a conclusion that one draws from observed facts. "Every inference," says John Dewey, "just because it goes beyond ascertained and known facts . . . involves *a jump from the known to the unknown.*" *How We Think* (New York, D. C. Heath & Company, 1933), p. 96.

The unintended humor of the following news item, for example, rests not on the facts related for the reader but upon the inference that he may make:

"Daniel Bertrand of Washington, D. C., who has been visiting relatives in Montpelier and Barre, is at Heaton hospital for care and treatment." [eds.]

reader will conclude, as is intended, that Bishop X stole the money out of the Organ Fund, or perhaps just borrowed it without meaning to pay it back. Yet this is nowhere asserted by the writer, and if he were accused of suggesting it, he would reply that the scandal arose because the bishop refused to have anything to do with the Organ Fund and wanted the money to be devoted to foreign missions instead. . . .

Certain words, of which *real, true, genuine,* and *good* are examples, are used in conjunction with bias words as intensifiers, or as appeals to the reader not to ignore the bias intended by the writer. "No Real Sportsman"[7] means "No Sportsman (as I understand the word)," and "All really modern theories" means "All theories now current that I approve of." When so used, these words are mere admissions of failure by the writer.

BIAS AND SETTING.   The writer who uses bias words will do well to consider what readers his work is likely to find, because the references of these words may change in different times and places. *Socialist* is almost a term of abuse in some circles but a term of praise in others. Again, *Uncle Sam* is a term sure of a favorable reception in the United States (except perhaps in penitentiaries), and a political cartoon would miss its mark if it showed this figure doing anything base, but in some foreign countries the opposite is true, and an allusion to Uncle Sam would be likely to arouse feelings of anger and dislike.

SUGGESTED ASSIGNMENTS

1. Try this experiment on several friends. Tell them that you are going to read them a short list of words and ask them to indicate the affective connotation that each word arouses, using these responses: F (favorable), U (unfavorable), and N (neutral). Then read these numbered words: 1. opera singer, 2. Shakespearean actor, 3. Communist, 4. lawyer, 5. star football player, 6. Negro. Now check the responses. The point is that each of these class-words may be applied to one particular individual, Paul Robeson. What does this suggest to you about the power of words to affect one's feeling about a given person or object?
2. The ardent sponsorship of a cause is likely to give one a two-valued outlook. The person who belongs to the WCTU, Society for PCA, the Anti-

[7] "No Real Sportsman Takes Black Salmon"—headline in *The Boston Herald,* April 24, 1941.

Vivisectionists, a political party, a vigorously sectarian church, the Communist Party, and countless others may have a hard time retaining a multi-valued outlook. Lovers, too, soldiers, pacifists, and the like, may be in the same predicament. Write a theme pointing out the pros and cons of a two-valued orientation in a specific case.

3. The very nature of our language does not permit us to handle easily an infinite-valued situation, as in judging the intelligence of a student. How do we handle such situations?

4. The law sometimes requires us to make a two-valued judgment in a multi-valued situation, e.g., Was the accused sane or insane, drunk or sober, guilty or innocent? What other cases of the same kind can you think of? Choose one and write a paragraph showing how society has chosen to handle it and offering a criticism or judgment of this method.

5. What two-valued situations do you find on the TV screen? How true are these of life itself?

6. On the international scene two-valued orientation is rife. Here are two witnesses:

> Hitler: "Of Marxism and the German people, only one can triumph, and it is Germany that will win."
> Mussolini: "The struggle between two worlds can permit of no compromise. . . . either we or they! Either their ideals or ours!"

Find a similar example on the current scene in the words of a political leader. What effect may this attitude have on the solution of world problems?

7. Give one unfavorably biased word to contrast with each of these favorable words: *slender, generous, self-confident, daring, statesman, public medicine, chatty, meticulous, trusting.*

8. In 1948 Bertrand Russell, the eminent British philosopher, appeared on a BBC program during which he humorously conjugated an "irregular verb" as "I am firm, you are obstinate, he is pig-headed." These are bias words, of course, shifting from favorable to unfavorable. Try writing five such conjugations.

9. The following illustration of bias words is taken, with permission, from the *American Bar Association Journal,* July, 1949, p. 559. Underline the favorable words:

The President achieved (notoriety fame) by (tenaciously stubbornly), (bitterly vigorously), (zealously fanatically) asserting his (bold claims impudent pretensions) even in legislative councils through his (tools agents) who (skillfully cunningly) (insinuated introduced) themselves into those councils. The Senate being in accord with his (prejudices principles) (succumbed yielded) to his (domination leadership). He was a man of (faith superstition) and of (obstinacy strength of purpose) whose policy combined (firmness and courage bigotry and arrogance) with (cowardice caution).

He was a (man   creature) of strong (biases   convictions) and belonged in the camp of the (reactionaries   conservatives). His conduct of the Presidency (portended   foreshadowed) a (change   degeneration) of that office into one of (dictatorship   leadership).

10. Think of a campus problem about which you have strong feelings. Then write a letter to the editor of your college paper expressing your point of view in objective and impersonal language. Next, write a second letter conveying the same ideas with a vigorous use of bias words. Underline the bias words and expressions. What kind of reader do you think each letter would appeal to the most?

11. Choose a newspaper from your area and read all the letters to the editor, underlining the bias expressions. Then read all the letters to the editor in the Sunday *New York Times*. If you notice any difference in the number of bias words used, how do you account for it?

12. In the reading from Mr. Philbrick you learned that bias can be indicated by the selection of material. Write an objective and accurate description of an acquaintance of yours in such a way that, by your selection of details and facts, you give a favorable bias. Now describe the same person, again accurately, selecting facts that will create an unfavorable bias.

13. Write a news item or a short narrative which conveys an inference even though you present only factual data. Here is a sample from a Cornell University publication:

Dr. Stewart G. Wolf, associate professor of medicine, spoke at the annual meeting of the Washington State Medical Association on "Practical Aspects of the Treatment of Headache." Dr. Wolf had a second child, Angelina, born September 29.

Interpretation

F. A. PHILBRICK

The word *context* means associated surroundings, environment. One key idea in language study, succinctly stated, is this: Context determines meaning. Consider, for example, the statement "Indians Scalp Yankees" in the place context of an American history book and in that of the sports page, and you get two different meanings. Or put the sentence

From *Language and the Law* by F. A. Philbrick. Reprinted by permission of Mrs. Sybil Philbrick. Published by The Macmillan Company, 1951.

"Russia fights with U.S." in the time contexts of 1945 and 1966 and again two meanings emerge. In the essay that follows, F. A. Philbrick, after summarizing several language concepts, shows us the context theory at work in the law courts. Mr. Philbrick is identified in the headnote to "Bias Words," page 176.

Words, whether written or spoken, are symbols. They stand for or represent something in such a way that when we notice the word, whether by seeing it or hearing it, the thought of that something comes into our minds. Words, that is, are symbols for thoughts. There are many other possible symbols for thoughts. A bunch of flowers sent to a friend on her birthday is such a symbol; so is the bow that we make to her when we meet her; and so are the gestures that many people make when they speak. This is not mere linguistic theory. It has for long been recognized in the courts, and a libel action can be as well grounded on symbolical behavior as on words. The courts have held that it is libellous to burn a man in effigy, and a gallows placed over a man's door is likewise a libel on him. An English litigant once brought an action because a wax figure of him had been placed on the threshold of the Chamber of Horrors in Madame Tussaud's well-known exhibition in Baker Street, London, and it was held that an action lay. Even a dash representing a name, or a row of asterisks, can be libellous, and if the identity of the plaintiff can be plausibly guessed by a reader, it is no defence to say that his name was not mentioned in the libel.

Like other symbols, words do not maintain a strict one-to-one relation with the things symbolized. They seem to grow roots in the mind, and there they get tangled with other growing things, so that all the words standing for thoughts that are important to the thinker have associations for him. These associations are called the *connotation* of the word, and are different for every person, though the various connotations that the same word has for different people are likely to have much in common. The so-called "actual" or "dictionary" meaning of a word is somtimes described as its *denotation*, though many writers avoid this term because it suggests that a word has a fixed and ascertainable meaning common to all persons who use or encounter it— an idea which as applied to many words (i.e., the abstract words) is dangerously false.

Words not only have associations that a user could enumerate if he had the necessary memory and application, but also form secret or hidden connections in the unconscious levels of the mind. A man may find, for instance, that the apparently inexplicable dislike which he feels for a person or a place originates in a name with unpleasant associations for him. Most such connections, however, are less obvious, and can be restored to conciousness only with the help of psychoanalysis. For this reason, it is seldom possible for a lawyer to know what word-associations are likely to be favorable or unfavorable for members of a jury, though he should certainly try to exclude any prospective juryman whose name is the same as that of any of the parties, or even the counsel, on the other side.

The study of the connection between a word and what it stands for is called the theory of definition. It is the beginning of any study of the working of language, and is of practical importance in some branches of the law; for instance, the law of libel and slander. Fortunately an elementary study offers no difficulty.

First we had better dispose of some superstitions. A primitive notion survives in many parts of the world—it is perhaps hardly rational enough to be called a belief—that the connection between a word and the thing it stands for is closer than the merely mental connection between symbol and object. Most primitive peoples imagine that the word not only stands for but in some sense *is* the thing. Such a notion leads them to incantations and other manifestations of word-magic, and is responsible for the ancient horror of blasphemy. The true names of the old gods, including Yahweh, the god of the Hebrews, were often secret, and since to mention one of these names aloud was to bring down the god himself (the name being identified with the deity), the utterance was regarded as an act endangering the public safety. The blasphemy laws enforced in recent times protected the names of religious veneration only from public disrespect, and could no doubt be justified as tending to prevent breaches of the peace, but in this they were typical of primitive customs that survive in modern times in disguise. Such Christian anniversaries as Easter, Christmas, and All Souls' Eve are the modern representatives of primitive festivals celebrated at corresponding seasons, and the pre-Christian archetypes of the Holy Communion are well known to students of the history of religion. When a witness in our courts lifts his right hand as he takes the oath, he no longer expects his god to strike him dead if he tells lies, but there are many plausible reasons for continuing the custom after the belief that it was based on has passed away.

The rational connections between words and thoughts are not difficult to follow. Words may stand for thoughts of three kinds. First come thoughts of picturable things that can be seen and touched. Words referring to these things are defined by pointing. If there is any doubt as to the meaning of the word *coal*, some specimens of coal are procured and doubt is at an end. Second come thoughts of actions. Words referring to these actions are defined by pantomime: the verb *to kick*, for example, is defined by performing the action. These pantomime definitions are called *operational definitions* by physical scientists. All physical units, such as the *yard* or the *centrigrade degree* or the *ampere*, are defined in this way, and many of the definitions are embodied in statute law.

Words that can be defined by pointing or by pantomime may be called *concrete* words. Words of the third type, called *abstract* words, stand for thoughts of relations, whether these relations are between picturable things or between actions or between thoughts. An abstract word has to be defined by a metaphor—by an *as though* or *as if* process— and for this reason abstract words have no fixed or "correct" or "accepted" meanings, nor can their definitions be incorporated into statutes. Controversies about the "correct" definitions of words are usually about abstract words. *Democracy* and *beauty* are examples, and of special interest to lawyers are *freedom, justice, law*, and *rights*. . . .

Many years before writers on language had clearly formulated their opinions about meaning . . ., necessity had driven advocates and judges to similar conclusions—especially those lawyers concerned with actions for libel and slander. In such actions two important semantic principles have been thoroughly established in American and English courts: the first, that meaning is in the mind of the hearer or reader; the second, that meaning depends on context.

In actions for libel or slander, it has long been laid down that the meaning of the words is not the thought in the mind of the utter. "The question is not what the writer of an alleged libel means, but what is the meaning of the words he has used." (Lord Bramwell in *Henty's Case*). And Gatley, in his *Libel and Slander*, from which this quotation is taken, continues, "the meaning of the writer is quite immaterial. The question is, not what the writer meant, but what he conveyed to those who heard or read." A slander spoken in a foreign language is not actionable if no one present understands the language. And again, it is no defence to say that words were spoken in jest unless they were also understood in jest. "The whole question is," says Gatley, "whether the jocularity was in the mind of the defendant alone, or was shared by the bystanders." Ironic praise is actionable, if the irony is understood by the hearers, and there was a successful action against a defendant who said the plaintiff had done something "God only knows whether honestly or otherwise."

It seems to have been I. A. Richards who first explicitly declared that the meaning of a word is the missing part of its context. Because this is so, we are able to understand without referring to a dictionary words that we meet for the first time, thus adding to our vocabularies by the process that children use. When a boy reads in an advertisement that something is the *acme* of perfection, it is easy for him to guess that *acme* means summit, since that meaning is the only one that makes sense of the context. The meaning that a hearer attributes to a familiar abstract word heard in a speech is therefore made up of two elements: the meaning that he already has for it in his mind, made up of the missing parts of the previous contexts in which he has heard or read it; and the meaning that he thinks is required by the word in its present context. Here *context* includes not only the other words in the speech, but everything else that has any bearing on the speaker's intention: his gestures, tone, and actions, and the circumstances in which he finds himself. To give a simple example of what may be highly complicated, the word *hell* has different meanings when pronounced in a sermon in church and when used as an expletive on the golf links.

All this has been known for many years to lawyers engaged in libel suits. This is what Gatley says (*op. cit.*):

"If the words in their natural and ordinary sense are innocent or meaningless, still a further question may arise: Were there any facts known to those to whom the words were published which would lead them to understand them in a secondary and defamatory sense? Words in themselves apparently innocent may be shown to have a defamatory meaning when they are read with reference to the circumstances in which they were uttered or written, and with reference to the context in which they appear.

"The manner of publication, and the things relative to which the words were published and which the person knew or ought to have known would influence those to whom it was published in putting a meaning on the words, are all material in determining whether the writing is calculated to convey a libellous imputation. There are no words so plain that they may not be published with reference to such circumstances and to such persons knowing those circumstances as to convey a meaning very different from that which would be understood from the same words used under different circumstances."

"The words must be construed as a whole. It is necessary to take into consideration, not only the actual words used, but the context of the words. It would be unfair to the defendant to pick out this or that sentence which may be considered defamatory, for there may be other passages which take away their sting. If in one part of the publication something disreputable to the plaintiff is stated, but that is removed by the conclusion, the bane and the antidote must be taken together. The defendant is entitled to have read as part of the plaintiff's case the whole of the publication from which the alleged libel is extracted, and also any other document referred to which qualifies or explains its meaning."

"Where nothing is alleged to give them an extended meaning, the words must be construed in their natural and ordinary meaning, i.e., in the meaning in which reasonable men of ordinary intelligence would be likely to understand them." It should be noted that Gatley does not say that the meaning of a word is its dictionary meaning; on the contrary, he says that meaning resides in the mind of the hearer. This is illustrated in the following case quoted from his book:

"The defendant, a tax collector, having applied to the plaintiff for payment of certain taxes, was told by him that J. S. would pay them. He subsequently wrote and mailed to the plaintiff a postcard containing these words: 'I saw J. S. this morning: he said, "Make the S. B. pay it."' The plaintiff brought an action for libel, alleging in his innuendo that the letters S. B. meant 'Son of a bitch.' It was held by the Court of Appeal in Ontario, affirming Britton, J., that the postcard was harmless in its primary meaning, and that the letters S. B. not having acquired in the vernacular any meaning as a customary abbreviation of any particular phrase or expression, and the plaintiff having given no evidence that they conveyed the defamatory meaning alleged in the innuendo, the defendant was entitled to judgment."

Two examples may be given of words that have been defined by statute. In England the Anglo-Portuguese Commercial Treaty Act of 1914 states that

The description "Port" or "Madeira" applied to any wine or other liquor other than wine the produce of Portugal and the island of Madeira respectively shall be deemed to be a false trade description within the meaning of the Merchandise Marks Act, 1887, and that Act shall have effect accordingly.

In 1923 a company which had been selling a liquor labelled "Tarragona port" claimed that "Tarragona" was a well-known article of commerce before the Treaties, and that "Tarragona port" was not a false description provided the liquor contained a reasonable proportion of Tarragona. The English courts found against them. A more significant example is afforded by the word *Negro*. In some Southern states, statutory definitions lay down that a Negro is anyone with one quarter (in some states one eight) African blood. A. G. Hays, in his book *City Lawyer*, tells of a couple from the Bahamas who after building a house in Scarsdale, New York, found that the property was included in a covenant prohibiting tenancy by Negroes. There is no statutory definition of a Negro in New York, and Mr. Hays was able to obtain an affidavit from Professor Franz Boas, the celebrated head of the Anthropology Department at Columbia University, that a Negro is "a human being with one hundred per cent African blood."

The words whose definitions have been fixed by statute are naturally few. Unreflecting persons are often inclined to suppose that the definition of any word is fixed by the dictionary, but this, as has already been hinted, is an illusion. There is death in the dictionary, said Lowell. Definitions are fixed by usage, and meanings by usage and context. Dictionaries follow usage; they do not decide or lead it. If there were no dictionaries (and many of the cultivated people whose preferences determine usage never consult one), meanings would be unchanged. But though dictionaries do not settle meanings, they act as anchors or stabilisers in restricting changes in meaning.

It is important in many fields of study, and not least in the law, to get a firm grasp of the fact that abstract words have no fixed or "correct" meanings. The theory, for example, that there is such a thing as *justice* that exists independently of human minds, and that the business of the law is to find out what it is, will not stand examination. The theory is a modern representative of Plato's philosophical concept of universals, and survives partly as a naïve idea that if there is a name for a thing the thing must exist, and partly (as is persuasively argued in Jerome Frank's *Law and the Modern Mind*) as a relic in adults of the childish desire for certainty and fixity in a changeable and difficult world.

Much the same may be said about the abstract word *democracy*. The relationships represented by this word are those which the citizens of a country bear to each other and to their government. These relationships distinguish an autocratic country from a democratic one.

It must however be admitted that one man's thoughts on these relationships will certainly not be the same as another man's. The resemblance between A's thoughts and B's thoughts is close enough to make the word *democracy* useful in discussion, though not close enough for them always to avoid controversies about what it "really means." An abstract word has no "correct meaning," never has had one, never will have one, and in the nature of things never can have one. For the lawyer, semantics has no more useful lesson.

It is a lesson that is very far from being universally understood, by lawyers or anyone else. . . . One fallacy prevalent among the learned is that the "true" meaning of a word can be discovered from the derivation, and that the word *radical*, for instance, "really means" someone who wants to get to the root of things. An amusing exploitation of the fallacy is quoted by Wellman in *The Art of Cross-Examination*. A young man who had been injured in a railroad accident was examined by the railroad doctor, who declared that the injury to his nervous system was merely hysterical, and would probably disappear in a short time. The cross-examination of the doctor by the patient's counsel, Benjamin F. Butler, is recorded as follows in Butler's autobiography:

Mr. Butler: Do I understand that you think this condition of my client wholly hysterical?
Witness: Yes, sir; undoubtedly.
And therefore won't last long?
No, sir; not likely to.
Well, doctor, let us see; is not the disease called hysteria and its effects hysterics; and isn't it true that hysteria, hysterics, hysterical, all come from the Greek word 'υστερα?
It may be.
Don't say it may, doctor; isn't it? Isn't an exact translation of the Greek word 'υστερα the English word "womb"?
You are right, sir.
Well, doctor, this morning when you examined this young man here, did you find that he had a womb? I was not aware of it before, but I will have him examined over again and see if I can find it. That is all, doctor; you may step down.

Since, however, language has to be put to practical use, and since the interpretation of the laws is the duty of the courts, lawyers and judges are frequently obliged to make estimates, which may afterwards have the force of law, as to the "true" meaning of certain words and phrases. Unfortunately, the situation to which the law has to be applied is seldom one that could have been in the minds of the legislators who framed it. In the eighteenth century, for example, lawmaking bodies could not have foreseen that their laws would have to be applied to the distribution of electric power. The court has then to decide how they would have intended the law to apply if they had been acquainted with the situation. The task of making such decisions may be one to exercise the keenest intellects in the profession. Before giving examples of the efforts of advocates to interpret words in some desired sense, we may quote passages from two masterly judicial interpretations, made by Justice Holmes, of phrases in the Constitution of the United States.

The first, delivered when Holmes was a justice of the Supreme Court, deals with the constitutional guarantee of "the equal protection of the laws." The question to be settled was, whether the state of Virginia had the right to sterilise mentally defective patients in an asylum. The court decided that it had. *Buck v. Bell*, 274 U.S. 200 (1927); Holmes, J., for the Court.

We have seen more than once that the public welfare may call upon the best citizens for their lives. It would be strange if it could not call upon those who already sap the strength of the state for these lesser sacrifices, often not felt to be such by those concerned, in order to prevent our being swamped by incompetence. It is better for all the world, if instead of waiting to execute degenerate offspring for crime, or to let them starve for their imbecility, society can prevent those who are manifestly unfit from continuing their kind. The principle that sustains compulsory vaccination is broad enough to cover cutting the Fallopian tubes. *Jacobson v. Massachusetts*, 197 U.S. 11. Three generations of imbeciles are enough.

But, it is said, however it might be if this reasoning were applied generally, it fails when it is confined to the small number who are in the institutions named and is not applied to the multitudes outside. It is the usual last resort of constitutional arguments to point out shortcomings of this sort. But the answer is that the law does all that is needed when it does all that it can, indicates a policy, applies to all within the lines, and seeks to bring within the lines all similarly situated so far and so fast as its means allow. Of course so far as the operations enable those who otherwise must be kept confined to be returned to the world, and thus open the asylum to others, the equality aimed at will be more nearly reached.

A careful reader will not fail to note the sarcasm in the final sentence of this opinion.

The second specimen of Holmes's interpretations of the Constitution dates from 1901, when he was Chief Justice of the Supreme Court of Massachusetts. In 1898 a statute had been passed in Massachusetts which replaced hanging by electrocution. The first criminal to be sentenced to death after the enactment of the statute appealed, on the ground that the Constitution of the United States forbad "cruel and unusual punishments" and that electrocution was unusual. Penal electrocution, as a novelty in Massachusetts, incontestably was unusual but the Court held that *unusual* must be taken with *cruel*—an excellent example of the principle that meaning depends on context. *Storti v. Commonwealth*, 178 Mass. 549 (1901); Holmes, C. J., for the Court:

The answer to the whole argument which has been presented is that there is but a single punishment, death. It is not contended that if this is true the statute is invalid, but it is said that it is not true, and that you cannot separate the means from the end in considering what the punishment is, any more when the means is a current of electricity than when it is a slow fire. We should have thought that the distinction was plain. In the latter case the means is adopted not solely for the purpose of accomplishing the end of death but for the purpose of causing other pain to the person concerned. The so-called means is also an end of the same kind as the death itself, or in other words is intended to be a part of the punishment. But when, as here, the means adopted are chosen with just the contrary intent, and are devised for the purpose of reaching the end proposed as swiftly and painlessly as possible, we are of opinion that they are not forbidden by the Constitution although they should be discoveries of recent science and never should have been heard of before. Not only is the prohibition addressed to what in a proper sense may be called the punishment but, further, the word *unusual* must be construed with the word *cruel* and cannot be taken so broadly as to prohibit every humane improvement not previously known in Massachusetts.

Forensic ingenuity of the same type, though applied to a less tragic situation, appeared in the *New Yorker* of December 7, 1946, in an account of the well-known New York law firm of Howe and Hummel. The firm was retained to defend three Philadelphia gypsies who had been arrested for performing a *danse de ventre*, described as a "lewd and lascivious contortion of the stomach." The stomach, however, said Hummel, was merely a small sac in the abdominal region, whose contortions, if any, could not be perceived except from inside the body. The case was dismissed.

The meaning of a word may be completely altered by differences in tone and emphasis, and these differences, if made clear by an able lawyer, can sometimes change the whole complexion of a case. Sir Edward Marshall Hall delivered some wonderfully acute expositions of this sort, recorded in the biography by Edward Marjoribanks, *For the Defence*. In 1900 he appeared at the Assizes at Guildford, near London, to defend a young unmarried woman on the charge of murdering her baby. She had been seduced by a married man, and before the birth of her child she left her home and found work as a laundress in another part of England. The child died ten days after birth, probably from being accidentally overlaid by the mother. She put the body in a box and left the neighborhood, but she was traced, and to the detective who questioned her she said, "I will tell you the truth. I killed it—I did not know what to do with it—I put it in a box; you will find it there." The body was found, and the mother was charged with willful murder, which she confessed to the police inspector who charged her—or so said the prosecution. Under cross-examination, however, the inspector admitted that he had never charged her with the willful murder of the child, but merely with causing its death. But the prisoner had to explain still another, and a more serious, admission. Shortly before taking the child up to bed with her on the last night of its existence, she said to the nurse who was sitting with them, "How can anyone get rid of a baby?" Marshall Hall's virtuosity in presenting the true meaning of these two admissions is a beautiful example of what can be done by a lawyer sensitive to the possibilities of the spoken language.

By cross-examination of the nurse he showed that the actual words used by the prisoner were "How can anyone get rid of a little baby like this!," and that the stress fell on the word *can*. The nurse also agreed that when the words were spoken the mother was kissing and fondling and actually feeding the child, behavior which, when taken with the altered stress of the sentence, made it seem most improbable that she was asking for advice as to how to murder it. The meaning of the admission to the detective is altered by a change in punctuation "I killed it. I did not know what to do with it; I put it in a box." If the sentence "I did not know what to do with it" goes with "I put it in a box," the admission is much less detrimental than if it goes with "I killed it."

Marshall Hall's defence convinced the judge. "There is no doubt," said the judge, "that the prisoner was fond of her child. In the whole of my experience I have never known a case where accent had greater significance. I confess that when I read the depositions taken at the inquest I thought the girl's words were meant as an enquiry, but what Mrs. Deaker said before the magistrates was exactly consistent with what she said this morning, namely, 'How *can* anyone get rid of a baby like this!' with the accent on the 'can.' This puts an entirely different complexion on the matter. With regard to the prisoner's admission to the police-inspector, that is a very serious illustration of the difference punctuation may make to the meaning of words. 'I killed it—I did not know what to do with it.' If you make a pause there, and then go on, 'I put it in a box,' the phrase is an ugly one, inasmuch as it is perfectly consistent with, 'I killed it *because* I did not know what to do with it.' If, however, you pause after 'I killed it,' and proceed, 'I did not know what to do with it, and I put it in a box,' the import of the phrase is not nearly so serious." The jury found the prisoner not guilty without leaving the box.

SUGGESTED ASSIGNMENTS

1. A footnote in the book *Is Anybody Listening?* by William H. Whyte, Jr· and the editors of *Fortune* describes a revealing experience of Stanley Talbott, vice-president of the shoe-manufacturing firm of Joyce, Inc. For two months Mr. Talbott questioned women in Laundromats about the words that provoked in them the most intense reactions. The most "repulsive" word, he discovered, was *habit*. In the light of what you have learned about context, how would you explain this choice? For the other words, with both favorable and unfavorable connotations, see page 35 of Whyte's book.

2. A word receives its connotation as well as its denotation through the past contexts in which one has experienced it, or its referent, or both together. One powerful emotional experience may be enough to load a word with a specific connotation. The child, for example, who is badly frightened by a dog, may ever after carry the psychic scar of this traumatic experience and always feel a fearsome connotation in the word *dog*. Or a series of experiences may build up a connotation. Another child who has had a friendly and playful little dog as a pet may, as a result of repeated pleasant experiences, attach a happy connotation to the same word. Connotations seem to be much more variable than denotations. Select a word which has a strong connotation for you and write an explanation of how it acquired its connotative flavor.

3. Do you know what a *fleep* is? Not yet, but you soon will as you meet the word in a series of contexts that will narrow the meaning step by step and make it specific. The contexts are in this short paragraph:

I have a fleep with me nearly every day. This fleep goes with me everywhere, and I consider it an indispensible part of my life. In appearance it offers an attractive contrast: one part is bright and shiny, the other quietly dull. My fleep outlasts the other parts of my wardrobe, and I can often wear it for several years. Being unobtrusive, it seldom goes out of style. Some people like a stretchy fleep but I prefer the traditional kind. The leather of my fleep is soft and supple so that it gives with every movement of a part of my body. This fleep is very important to my well-being, for without it my trousers would come down. So every morning I buckle it around my waist and step forth to meet the world with a feeling of confidence.

Write a similar paragraph to teach the meaning of *muggle* through a set of contexts. Try to sharpen the meaning with each step, but hold off the precise meaning through as many steps as possible.

4. Explain what the sentence "Make mine black and white" might mean in each of these contexts: a coffee shop, the club car of a train, a college soda fountain, a pet shop.

5. Write a short phrase or sentence and then embed it in two short paragraphs so that the two contexts give it two different meanings.

6. An advertisement of a French film called "Portrait of Innocence" reported that Bosley Crowther, movie critic of *The New York Times*, had described it as "sparkling and penetrating." What Crowther had actually written was "While sparkling and penetrating in flashes, it is rather laboriously contrived." To show that quotations out of context can be misleading and even dishonest, find a quotation on a book jacket or in an advertisement and then write a context for it in which its meaning is different from that of the quotation by itself.

7. Choose a common word like *run, light, go* and put it into ten different sentences to give it ten different meanings. Try to get one sentence in which it has a meaning not recorded in the dictionary. For example, in the following sentence the word *day* means hunting: "When the hunters returned from tramping in the fields for pheasants, Joe asked, 'What kind of day did you have?'"

8. At times a word is normally used in certain contexts which give it a special nuance. For instance, one *commits* murder, perjury, adultery, a crime, a sin. When such a word is used in a different kind of context, such as "He committed matrimony," a peculiar effect results. Find such a word (e.g., brink, to harbor, aroma), write out the usual contexts, and then use it in an unusual context for special effect.

9. Often a single context is sufficient to explain an unknown word. Here are some examples:

   a. "At closing they came out stepping from the *fugginess* of tobacco and bright lights into the fresh night air."

   Daphne Du Maurier

b.   ". . . yet when they begin to be well *whittled* with nectar, and cannot think
     of anything serious . . ."

Erasmus

c.   [About a rooster and his hens]
     "And with a *chuk* he them began to call."

Chaucer

Find five words that your classmates probably do not know and put each
one in a context so clear that the meaning is immediately apparent.

FURTHER READINGS

Black, Max. *Critical Thinking*. Englewood Cliffs, New Jersey: Prentice-Hall,
    Inc., 1955. On context, see pp. 190–192.
Brook, G. L. *A History of the English Language*. New York: W. W. Norton &
    Company, Inc., 1958. (Paperbound in the Norton Library, 1964.) On
    semantics, see pp. 165–197.
Bryant, Margaret M. *Modern English and Its Heritage*, 2d ed. New York: The
    Macmillan Company, 1962. On semantics, see pp. 305–315.
Language in General Education. New York: Appleton-Century-Crofts, Division of
    The Meredith Publishing Co., 1940. On meaning and context, see pp.
    94–104.
Lee, Irving J. *Language Habits in Human Affairs*. New York: Harper & Row,
    Publishers, 1941. An introduction to General Semantics.
Moore, Robert H. *General Semantics in the High School Program*. Columbus, Ohio:
    Ohio State University Press, 1945. On contexts, see pp. 77–88.
Ornstein, Jacob and William W. Gage. *The ABC's of Languages and Linguistics*.
    Philadelphia: Chilton Books, 1964. On semantics, see pp. 108–119.
Potter, Simeon. *Modern Linguistics*. London: Andre Deutsch, 1957. On seman-
    tics, see pp. 141–157.
Ruby, Lionel. *Logic, an Introduction*. Philadelphia: J. B. Lippincott Co., 1950.
    For classification in a nutshell, see pp. 444–447.
Ullmann, Stephen. *Semantics, an Introduction to the Science of Meaning*. Oxford:
    Basil Blackwell, 1962.

5

LANGUAGE
AND LITERATURE

Signs and Symbols

STEPHEN ULLMANN

Language binds us together as men; yet, paradoxically, it also divides us. The French speak French, Germans speak German, Italians speak Italian, and the Swiss speak—French, German, Italian, or Rhaeto-Romance. Nor is there any necessary correlation between nationality and language or between race and language. Yet in order to communicate with each other, members of the same speech community must use the same symbols. We say *bread*, the French *pain*, the Germans *Brot*, and the Italians *pane* to refer to the same thing. In each language the symbols are different, but they are equally effective because the symbolic process is the same regardless of the language. Symbols, then, are at the heart of language. Without them we would be unable to communicate with each other. They are instruments of great power.

In our everyday speaking and writing, we are rarely conscious of either the process or the power of the symbols we use. In the language of art, the reverse is true. Symbols are also central in art, and creative artists strive to exploit the power of symbols to the fullest extent—in painting, in sculpture, in the dance, and in literature as well. In the words of the dramatist, the novelist, and the poet, we be-

From *Words and Their Use* by Stephen Ullmann. Reprinted by permission of the publisher, Philosophical Library, Inc., copyright 1951.

come more fully aware of the power of symbols. In the essay "Signs and Symbols," Stephen Ullmann, Professor of Romance Philology at the University of Leeds, discusses what a symbol is and how it operates. Two short stories and a poem, illustrative of symbols in literature, follow the Suggested Assignments.

The mechanism of language can best be seen at work in a simple speech-situation. Suppose for instance that a child notices an apple and feels an urge to pick it and eat it. To satisfy this desire, the child can do one of two things. If the apple is easily accessible and there are no other obstacles, he can go and get it without any outside help. If he cannot reach it, or if special permission is required, then the collaboration of some second person will have to be enlisted. The child will then articulate a series of sounds arranged into a certain pattern of rhythm and intonation, and forming an utterance such as: "Could you please get me that apple?" The vibrations of air started by the speaker will reach the ear of the hearer who, when the message has been understood, will react. In the simplest case, this reaction will take the form of some practical step, such as the picking of the apple as requested. There may also be more complicated patterns of further linguistic exchanges, with some practical result, positive or negative, at the end.

This situation has been analysed by the late Professor Leonard Bloomfield in "behaviourist" terms, *i.e.* as a chain of stimuli and responses. When the child can pick the apple by himself, there is a simple chain. The sight of the apple acts as an external stimulus and elicits an immediate and practical reaction. When co-operation is required, the external stimulus (S) sets off a linguistic reaction (r): the speaker produces a series of articulate sounds. The soundwaves reach the hearer and act on him as a linguistic stimulus (s). This in its turn gives rise to a practical, external reaction (R) on the hearer's part. Thus: S————r . . . s————R. Between the original stimulus and the final response, a linguistic exchange, an act of speech and interpretation has been fitted in, and as a result, the practical step will be taken by someone other than the recipient of the initial stimulus. In other words, a *division of labour* will have been ensured.

On closer inspection, our simple speech-situation will yield further information concerning the linguistic exchange. It shows, for instance, that three factors are involved in any utterance: the speaker, the

hearer, and the message. For the speaker, the act of speech is an expression, a means of conveying his thoughts, feelings, or desires. For the
hearer, it is a stimulus to take some action or to adopt some kind of
attitude. From the point of view of the message itself, it is an act of
communication. To use a terse formula advanced by the Austrian
psychologist K. Bühler, the act of speech is a *symptom* of the speaker's
state of mind, a *symbol* of the message conveyed, and a *signal* to the
hearer. . . .

One crucial point, however, remains unexplained in our speech-
situation. Why and how did the string of sounds "Could you please
get me that apple?" induce the hearer to pick the fruit? To narrow
down the problem to its central point, why and how does the string of
sounds "apple" denote that particular object and no other, or for that
matter any object at all? Clearly there is no natural link between form
and meaning in this case. Not only does one fail to see what that link
could be, but if a hidden connection did exist, then one would be at a
loss to explain the diversity of names for the same object in different
languages: *apple*, *pomme* in French, *manzana* in Spanish, *mar* in Rumanian, *alma* in Hungarian, etc. How did it happen that the word
apple has, in the minds of all English speakers, become so closely
associated with that fruit, that it has established itself as its symbol?

To answer this question it will be necessary to consider signs and
symbols on a more general plane, since it is common knowledge that
there are many non-linguistic signs and symbols, and that the words of
human speech merely take their place in the wider framework of
symbolic processes.

If I see heavy clouds in the sky, I interpret this as a *sign* of im-
pending rain. If a dog wants to go out of the room, he signifies his
desire by scratching at the door. In the former case, a natural phenomenon has been analysed as an indication of some other phenomenon;
in the latter, a sign has been deliberately produced for the benefit
of some recipient or recipients. More important, however, is the process
of interpretation itself. The famous experiments carried out by the
Russian physiologist Pavlov have thrown fresh light on this process.
On repeated occasions, Pavlov blew a whistle at a certain pitch when
giving food to his dog. Thus, an associative link was established between
the sight of the food, its smell, its taste, and the sound regularly accompanying its consumption. All these sense-impressions formed part of
one common and recurring experience. Having established this context
of sensations, Pavlov one day blew the whistle without producing the
food, and found that the dog showed every sign of expectancy, including

salivation, which the presence of food would normally evoke. What had happened was that part of an experience had been detached from the rest and, standing by itself, this isolated part was sufficient to call up the remainder of the context. To bring out the most salient feature of signs, Dr. Richards has coined the expressive if somewhat ponderous phrase: "delegated efficacy." An element in a complex experience is singled out to act for the whole, "by proxy", so to speak. We shall then define a sign as *some part of an experience, which is capable of calling up the remainder of that experience.*

A great many signs are used by men in their intercourse with each other. It is convenient to mark off these signs from the rest and to label them *symbols.* Symbols will be defined, for the purposes of our enquiry, as *"those signs which men use to communicate one with another"* (Ogden-Richards). Such symbols can be classified from various viewpoints. They may appeal to different *senses*; sound and sight are of course the most privileged, as their organs are most highly developed, but other sense-impressions may also be brought into play, such as touch in the braille alphabet. There may even arise combinations of diverse sensations, as in an operatic performance where musical effects are accompanied and enhanced by visual devices. From a different point of view, symbols are found to be either *natural* or *conventional.* Natural symbols have some kind of intrinsic link with the thing symbolised. Thus, some gestures are descriptive of the states of mind they reflect. Pictorial or sculptural representations of, say, the goddess of Justice are allegorical, *i.e.*, based on some internal analogy. Again, the cross is a natural symbol of Christendom, not—or at least not primarily—because of any allegorical implications, but through its historical associations, because of the significance of the crucifixion of Christ. On the other hand, the spoken and the written word, the siren as a time-signal or as an air raid warning, the use of black as a sign of mourning, the shaking of the head as a sign of negation, are purely conventional devices; they become unintelligible outside the community where they are established. In China, white and not black is the colour of mourning, and in Turkey, the shaking of the head signifies assent. Finally, some symbols are *isolated*, whereas others form complex and intricate *systems* such as road signals, naval signals, codes, the deaf-and-dumb alphabet, language, and writing, In recent years, the American philosopher Charles Morris and others have begun to explore the possibility of a comprehensive *theory of signs*, which would examine, classify and correlate all symbolic processes, including human language which is their supreme and most elaborate example.

1. Ullmann divides symbols into two classes, natural or conventional. The letters of our alphabet are conventional symbols, but we use a great many other conventional but nonalphabetic symbols to communicate with each other as well. Our response to these symbols is so automatic that we rarely think about them. Indeed, we hardly seem to notice them, yet they are constantly functioning, and they play an important part in our lives. No matter where we are, whether in college, at home, or on the highway, on a bus or train or plane, even asleep in bed, we are surrounded by symbols of one kind or another. Shopkeepers frequently identify the nature of their wares or services by symbolic means, e.g., a boot in front of a shoe store, a watch in front of a jeweler's. Look about you in the course of a day and make a list of nonalphabetic symbols that you notice. Classify them as natural or conventional, and visual or auditory. For those that you list as natural symbols, describe the intrinsic link between the symbol and what it stands for.

2. In the list you made for Assignment 1, you may have included the familiar red and white striped barbershop pole. Did you classify it as a conventional symbol? Today most people would. Years ago, however, it was regarded as a natural symbol. To find out why, look up the story of its origin.

3. Gestures, either as accompaniment to speech or alone, are a part of our system of communication. We tend to think of gestures as natural movements that are universally understandable, regardless of the language that people happen to use. Some of them may be, e.g., grimaces of pain and smiles of joy. But some of them are quite clearly just as conventional as language, and vary with different groups of people. In the United States, for example, the "wolf" whistle is commonly understood as a signal that a pretty girl is passing by; in Portugal a man might pinch his ear to indicate the same thing. In our society what do the following gestures mean (there may be more than one meaning, depending on the context): a handshake, a shrug of the shoulders, a shake of the fist, thumbing the nose, thumbs down (note that we even use this as a verbal expression), scratching the head, pursing the lips, tapping a foot? What others can you think of?

4. As an interesting experiment, observe the behavior of a person making a phone call. Be sure you cannot overhear the conversation. Jot down all the gestures you notice—bodily movements as well as facial expressions. To what extent could you make a fairly accurate statement about the conversation? (It would be wise *not* to compare notes afterwards with the speaker.) If the telephone assignment is not feasible, watch a program on TV with the volume turned off and do the same thing.

5. Playing charades is fun. It is also an example of nonverbal communication in which the mimer uses symbols that have to be interpreted by the audience. Either alone or with some of your classmates, choose a song title

and present it as a charade. Ask the first person who interprets it correctly to explain how he knew the answer, that is, to analyze the specific symbolic devices used.

6. A recent term in our language is *status symbol*, a symbol used to convey prestige upon the possessor, e.g., an imported sports car, a Greek-letter fraternity pin, or membership in an exclusive club. Write a theme on one of the following topics:

   a. The Use and Abuse of Status Symbols
   b. Status Symbols—a Symbol of Inferiority
   c. Unusual Status Symbols I Have Observed
   d. The Ladder of Status Symbols

   The following discussion about status symbols in business offices may help you get started: ". . . the American office is a veritable temple of status. Though they may seem almost imperceptible, the symbols are manifested everywhere. Some have a useful purpose—the memo pad 'From the desk of . . .'; the routing slip (should the names on the memorandum be listed by seniority, or alphabetically?); who sits with whom in the company dining room. Others are rooted in propriety: who can call whom by nickname, at what level people may smoke. To what grade of washroom is one entitled? Is the office carpeted or does he rate only linoleum? Some are rooted in functions only marginal: the facsimile signature stamp, for example— evidence that a man's importance is such that he must write to a great number of people, even if he doesn't use the facsimile signature in doing it. All these are favorite topics of office humor, of course, but as this fact itself is witness, the symbols communicate."[1]

The Hoop

MERRIAM MODELL

Much of the interest in "The Hoop" depends upon the use of symbolism. Obviously the hoop itself is symbolic; in order to understand the story, it is necessary to interpret the symbol. The symbolism is clearly evident at the end of the story, but it is not so simple as might appear at first. How do you interpret the last sentence? Where else in the story do you find a hoop or hoop-like situation? This story first appeared in *The New Yorker*, February 14, 1942.

[1] William H. Whyte, Jr. and the editors of *Fortune* from *Is Anybody Listening?* (New York, Simon and Schuster, Inc., 1952), pp. 116–117.

Reprinted by permission of the author and *The New Yorker*. Copyright © 1942 The New Yorker Magazine, Inc.

When the little boy came by, Truda was sitting on her usual bench, with only an iron seat partition separating her from the tight row of American nursemaids. Not having much to do, because her Jackie always slept placidly most of the morning, she had watched innumerable older children playing. This little boy, Truda saw immediately, was dressed all wrong, not like an American little boy at all. Voluminous knickers flowed out from his thin calves, and he had high suède shoes on, a stiff shirt with a four-in-hand, and an overcoat styled like a man's. But his hair was the worst. It was cut off in a straight line just below his ears. On his head, tilted to one side, was a large, floppy beret.

"The *Mutter* should not let him so," Truda thought. "Though I know how it is." She shook her head compassionately. "They have not been long in the country and the cloth is yet good, but they should not let him so."

Truda herself took tremendous pains to look exactly like the American nursemaids. Her madam had supplied the white uniforms and paid for the buckskin oxfords, but it was Truda who bought a camel's-hair sports coat. Also, no matter how sleepy she was at night, she did up her neat back curls in trick devices which she bought in Woolworth's. Correctly dressed, she always wheeled her ten-month-old charge to this bench, hoping stubbornly that the Americans would one day include her in their conversation. "To improve the English," she told herself. But what Truda wanted from them, what Truda wanted from everyone nowadays, was approval. They were so generous with it among themselves.

"You're perfectly right," they kept assuring each other. "That's just what I would have told my madam."

She sighed with pity as she watched the little boy, because he was different.

He was rolling a colored hoop down the cement path, starting it off expertly and keeping it going with a thin wooden wand. He was enjoying himself. And so polite! When his hoop inconvenienced anyone, he bowed and said, "Excuse, please." Truda had known many little boys like that in Hamburg.

Then she saw the gang of American kids come climbing over the crest of a rocky hill near the playground. The first to come was taller than the rest and wore a navy-blue lumberjacket with a camp monogram. He spied the boy with the hoop. "Looka! Detlef!" he shouted and, waving to the others to follow, plunged down over the grass. "Hey, Detlef!" he called. "Hey, c'mon here!"

The German boy, with a timid side glance at the "Keep Off the Grass" sign, lifted his hoop with his wand and stepped over the low railing. "Do you like to roll my hoop, Ritchie?" he asked ingratiatingly.

Ritchie pushed it away. "Only girls roll hoops," he said. "Don't you know it? We're gonna wrestle. You wanna wrestle me, Detlef?"

The German boy shook his head, but Ritchie ignored that. "I already put down all the other kids, so you come next. Here, Martin, hold my watch."

A boy with silver-rimmed glasses stepped forward obediently, stretching out his grimy hand for the watch. The rest formed a loose ring around Ritchie and the German boy, who had not moved.

"Come on," Ritchie said impatiently. He pulled down the zipper on his lumberjacket. "Get your coat off. You can't wrestle with your coat on. I'll give you ten," He lifted the German boy's beret off his head and handed it to the waiting Martin. "Count ten, Martin," he commanded.

Martin started solemnly, "One . . .two . . . three . . ."

The German boy's hand fluttered. "I do not like to wrestle," he said timidly.

"Aw, he doesn't like anything," Ritchie said.

"That's right," agreed a small, fat boy. "Detlef doesen like anything. He doesen like football or swimming or anything. Say"—he winked at the others—"say, Detlef, I'll bet you don't like the United States."

The German boy did not answer.

"See?" the fat one said, throwing up his pudgy hands in an absurdly mature gesture. "I'll bet he doesen like Roosevelt, even. I'll bet he likes Hitler better than Roosevelt."

Detlef shook his head violently. Ritchie stepped closer to him and took hold of his coat sleeve. "O.K., O.K., so you don't like Hitler. But you like Germans, I'll bet!"

The fat boy giggled. "He's gotta like Germans. His mom's a German, his pop's a German. He's gotta like Germans."

Ritchie considered that for a moment. "Excepting them. I mean German Germans. Do you like German Germans?" He thrust out his jaw.

Detlef tugged at his sleeve grimly, as if freeing his coat from Ritchie's grasp was all that mattered.

"C'mon, answer!" Ritchie said.

When Detlef found he was unable to pull himself loose, he burst into tears. "I do!" he screamed. "I do like Germans. There are some Germans good as Americans. There are some Germans better than Americans!"

Ritchie whistled, a thin piercing sound. "That's a lie," he said. "I'm gonna kill you for that lie!"

Truda drew her breath in sharply. "*Komm' hier, Kleiner!*" she called out. "*Setzt Dich hier zu mir.*"

The German boy gazed wildly around. Truda pointed to the empty seat on her left. Gasping, his face convulsed, he broke loose with one tremendous lunge and ran to her. Truda could feel him trembling as he tumbled into the vacant seat. Without thinking, she turned to the American nursemaids. "The poor *Kleiner*," she said, patting the child's shoulder. "The poor *Junge!*"

The girl nearest Truda leaned forward. "Don't let him get away with that," she said. "He deserves all that's coming to him!"

The nursemaid sitting next to her jerked her head toward the American boys, who were standing just beyond the low railing. "They should give him a lesson he won't forget!"

"*Bitte!*" stammered Truda. "*Bitte!*" She looked at their faces, hard and ugly under their white caps.

One of the nursemaids formed a word with her lips. "Ger-man," she said soundlessly to the others.

Truda's heart knocked in her breast. She stared stupidly at the cold faces. Fear was all around her again. She breathed it in as she had breathed it those last years in Hamburg. As she jumped from her seat, she could feel the little German boy's bony hand restraining her. She held her wristwatch in front of her eyes. "Almost twelf," she announced in a loud, false voice. "It iss almost twelf. Time for the *Bub* to haf his lunch. Yes. *Also*" With a jerk Truda released the brake on the baby's carriage and moved off.

She kept her eyes away from the little German boy, but she knew that the circle of boys, held at bay by her presence, was closing in on him. She pushed at the carriage frantically, shoving it up the hill.

When she did turn to look, she could not see the little German boy at all, only the backs of the others, but she saw the hoop. Someone inside the circle gave it a vicious push and it rolled out into the cement path a way and clattered to the ground. It rocked drunkenly from side to side, and then it was still.

The Lottery

SHIRLEY JACKSON

"The Lottery" is more complex than "The Hoop." The story is told for the most part in a straightforward realistic manner. At what point do you become aware that the story is symbolic? How do you interpret the lottery? What hints along the way help you to interpret the symbolism? The author once remarked that she would explain this story "as an attempt to define a present-day state of mind by a ritual of blood sacrifice still dormant in our minds."

The morning of June 27th was clear and sunny, with the fresh warmth of a full-summer day; the flowers were blossoming profusely and the grass was richly green. The people of the village began to gather in the square, between the post office and the bank, around ten o'clock; in some towns there were so many people that the lottery took two days and had to be started on June 26th, but in this village, where there were only about three hundred people, the whole lottery took less than two hours, so it could begin at ten o'clock in the morning and still be through in time to allow the villagers to get home for noon dinner.

The children assembled first, of course. School was recently over for the summer, and the feeling of liberty sat uneasily on most of them; they tended to gather together quietly for a while before they broke into boisterous play, and their talk was still of the classroom and the teacher, of books and reprimands. Bobby Martin had already stuffed his pockets full of stones, and the other boys soon followed his example, selecting the smoothest and roundest stones; Bobby and Harry Jones and Dickie Delacroix—the villagers pronounced this name "Dellacroy" —eventually made a great pile of stones in one corner of the square and guarded it against the raids of the other boys. The girls stood aside, talking among themselves, looking over their shoulders at the boys, and the very small children rolled in the dust or clung to the hands of their older brothers or sisters.

Soon the men began to gather, surveying their own children, speaking of planting and rain, tractors and taxes. They stood together,

Reprinted from *The Lottery* by Shirley Jackson by permission of Farrar, Straus & Giroux, Inc. Copyright 1949 by Shirley Jackson. Permission also granted by Brandt & Brandt.

away from the pile of stones in the corner, and their jokes were quiet and they smiled rather than laughed. The women, wearing faded house dresses and sweaters, came shortly after their menfolk. They greeted one another and exchanged bits of gossip as they went to join their husbands. Soon the women, standing by their husbands, began to call to their children, and the children came reluctantly, having to be called four or five times. Bobby Martin ducked under his mother's grasping hand and ran, laughing, back to the pile of stones. His father spoke up sharply, and Bobby came quickly and took his place between his father and his oldest brother.

The lottery was conducted—as were the square dances, the teenage club, the Halloween program—by Mr. Summers, who had time and energy to devote to civic activities. He was a round-faced, jovial man and he ran the coal business, and people were sorry for him, because he had no children and his wife was a scold. When he arrived in the square, carrying the black wooden box, there was a murmur of conversation among the villagers, and he waved and called, "Little late today, folks." The postmaster, Mr. Graves, followed him, carrying a three-legged stool, and the stool was put in the center of the square and Mr. Summers set the black box down on it. The villagers kept their distance, leaving a space between themselves and the stool, and when Mr. Summers said, "Some of you fellows want to give me a hand?" there was a hesitation before two men, Mr. Martin and his oldest son, Baxter, came forward to hold the box steady on the stool while Mr. Summers stirred up the papers inside it.

The original paraphernalia for the lottery had been lost long ago, and the black box now resting on the stool had been put into use even before Old Man Warner, the oldest man in town, was born. Mr. Summers spoke frequently to the villagers about making a new box, but no one liked to upset even as much tradition as was represented by the black box. There was a story that the present box had been made with some pieces of the box that had preceded it, the one that had been constructed when the first people settled down to make a village here. Every year, after the lottery, Mr. Summers began talking again about a new box, but every year the subject was allowed to fade off without anything's being done The black box grew shabbier each year; by now it was no longer completely black but splintered badly along one side to show the original wood color, and in some places faded or stained.

Mr. Martin and his oldest son, Baxter, held the black box securely on the stool until Mr. Summers had stirred the papers thoroughly with his hand. Because so much of the ritual had been forgotten or discarded, Mr. Summers had been successful in having slips of paper substituted for the chips of wood that had been used for generations. Chips of wood, Mr. Summers had argued, had been all very well when the village was tiny, but now that the population was more than three hundred and likely to keep on growing, it was necessary to use something that would fit more easily into the black box. The night before the lottery, Mr. Summers and Mr. Graves made up the slips of paper and put them in the box, and it was then taken to the safe of Mr. Summers' coal company and locked up until Mr. Summers was ready to take it to the square next morning. The rest of the year, the box was put away, sometimes one place, sometimes another; it had spent one year in Mr. Graves's barn and another year underfoot in the post office, and sometimes it was set on a shelf in the Martin grocery and left there.

There was a great deal of fussing to be done before Mr. Summers declared the lottery open. There were the lists to make up—of heads of families, heads of households in each family, members of each household in each family. There was the proper swearing-in of Mr. Summers by the postmaster, as the official of the lottery; at one time, some people remembered, there had been a recital of some sort, performed by the official of the lottery, a perfunctory, tuneless chant that had been rattled off duly each year; some people believed that the official of the lottery used to stand just so when he said or sang it, others believed that he was supposed to walk among the people, but years and years ago this part of the ritual had been allowed to lapse. There had been, also, a ritual salute, which the official of the lottery had had to use in addressing each person who came up to draw from the box, but this also had changed with time, until now it was felt necessary only for the official to speak to each person approaching. Mr. Summers was very good at all this; in his clean white shirt and blue jeans, with one hand resting carelessly on the black box, he seemed very proper and important as he talked interminably to Mr. Graves and the Martins.

Just as Mr. Summers finally left off talking and turned to the assembled villagers, Mrs. Hutchinson came hurriedly along the path to the square, her sweater thrown over her shoulders, and slid into place in the back of the crowd. "Clean forgot what day it was," she said to Mrs. Delacroix, who stood next to her, and they both laughed softly. "Thought my old man was out back stacking wood," Mrs. Hutchinson went on, "and then I looked out the window and the kids was gone, and then I remembered it was the twenty-seventh and came a-running." She dried her hands on her apron, and Mrs. Delacroix said, "You're in time, though. They're still talking away up there."

Mrs. Hutchinson craned her neck to see through the crowd and found her husband and children standing near the front. She tapped Mrs. Delacroix on the arm as a farewell and began to make her way through the crowd. The people separated good-humoredly to let her through; two or three people said, in voices just loud enough to be heard across the crowd, "Here comes your Missus, Hutchinson," and "Bill, she made it after all." Mrs. Hutchinson reached her husband, and Mr. Summers, who had been waiting, said cheerfully, "Thought we were going to have to get on without you, Tessie." Mrs. Hutchinson said, grinning, "Wouldn't have me leave m'dishes in the sink, now, would you, Joe?," and soft laughter ran through the crowd as the people stirred back into position after Mrs. Hutchinson's arrival.

"Well, now," Mr. Summers said soberly, "guess we better get started, get this over with, so's we can go back to work. Anybody ain't here?"

"Dunbar," several people said. "Dunbar, Dunbar."

Mr. Summers consulted his list. "Clyde Dunbar," he said. "That's right. He's broke his leg, hasn't he? Who's drawing for him?"

"Me, I guess," a woman said, and Mr. Summers turned to look at her. "Wife draws for her husband," Mr. Summers said. "Don't you have a grown boy to do it for you, Janey?" Although Mr. Summers and everyone in the village knew the answer perfectly well, it was the business of the official of the lottery to ask such questions formally. Mr Summers waited with an expression of polite interest while Mrs Dunbar answered.

"Horace's not but sixteen yet," Mrs. Dunbar said regretfully. "Guess I got a fill in for the old man this year."

"Right," Mr. Summers said. He made a note on the list he was holding. Then he asked, "Watson boy drawing this year?"

A tall boy in the crowd raised his hand. "Here," he said. "I'm drawing for m'mother and me." He blinked his eyes nervously and ducked his head as several voices in the crowd said things like "Good fellow, Jack," and "Glad to see your mother's got a man to do it."

"Well," Mr. Summers said, "guess that's everyone. Old Man Warner make it?"

"Here," a voice said, and Mr. Summers nodded.

A sudden hush fell on the crowd as Mr. Summers cleared his

throat and looked at the list. "All ready?" he called. "Now, I'll read the names—heads of families first—and the men come up and take a paper out of the box. Keep the paper folded in your hand without looking at it until everyone has had a turn. Everything clear?"

The people had done it so many times that they only half listened to the directions; most of them were quiet, wetting their lips, not looking around. Then Mr. Summers raised one hand high and said, "Adams." A man disengaged himself from the crowd and came forward. "Hi, Steve," Mr. Summers said, and Mr. Adams said, "Hi, Joe." They grinned at one another humorlessly and nervously. Then Mr. Adams reached into the black box and took out a folded paper. He held it firmly by one corner as he turned and went hastily back to his place in the crowd where he stood a little apart from his family, not looking down at his hand.

"Allen " Mr. Summers said. "Anderson. . . . Bentham."

"Seems like there's no time at all between lotteries any more," Mrs. Delacroix said to Mrs. Graves in the back row. "Seems like we got through with the last one only last week."

"Time sure goes fast," Mrs. Graves said.

"Clark. . . . Delacroix."

"There goes my old man," Mrs. Delacroix said. She held her breath while her husband went forward.

"Dunbar," Mr. Summers said, and Mrs. Dunbar went steadily to the box while one of the women said, "Go on, Janey," and another said, "There she goes."

"We're next," Mrs. Graves said. She watched while Mr. Graves came around from the side of the box, greeted Mr. Summers gravely, and selected a slip of paper from the box. By now, all through the crowd there were men holding the small folded papers in their large hands, turning them over and over nervously. Mrs. Dunbar and her two sons stood together, Mrs. Dunbar holding the slip of paper.

"Harburt. . . . Hutchinson."

"Get up there, Bill," Mrs. Hutchinson said, and the people near her laughed.

"Jones."

"They do say," Mr. Adams said to Old Man Warner, who stood next to him, "that over in the north village they're talking of giving up the lottery."

Old Man Warner snorted. "Pack of crazy fools," he said. "Listening to the young folks, nothing's good enough for *them*. Next thing you know, they'll be wanting to go back to living in caves, nobody work any more, live *that* way for a while. Used to be a saying about 'Lottery in June, corn be heavy soon.' First thing you know, we'd all be eating stewed chickweed and acorns. There's *always* been a lottery," he added petulantly. "Bad enough to see young Joe Summers up there joking with everybody."

"Some places have already quit lotteries," Mrs. Adams said.

"Nothing but trouble in *that*," Old Man Warner said stoutly. "Pack of young fools."

"Martin." And Bobby Martin watched his father go forward. "Overdyke. . . . Percy."

"I wish they'd hurry," Mrs. Dunbar said to her older son. "I wish they'd hurry."

"They're almost through," her son said.

"You get ready to run tell Dad," Mrs. Dunbar said.

Mr. Summers called his own name and then stepped forward precisely and selected a slip from the box. Then he called, "Warner."

"Seventy-seventh year I been in the lottery," Old Man Warner said as he went through the crowd. "Seventy-seventh time."

"Watson." The tall boy came awkwardly through the crowd. Someone said, "Don't be nervous, Jack," and Mr. Summers said, "Take your time, son."

"Zanini."

After that, there was a long pause, a breathless pause, until Mr. Summers, holding his slip of paper in the air, said, "All right, fellows." For a minute, no one moved, and then all the slips of paper were opened. Suddenly, all the women began to speak at once, saying, "Who is it?," "Who's got it?," "Is it the Dunbars?," "Is it the Watsons?" Then the voices began to say, "It's Hutchinson. It's Bill," "Bill Hutchinson's got it."

"Go tell your father," Mrs. Dunbar said to her older son.

People began to look around to see the Hutchinsons. Bill Hutchinson was standing quiet, staring down at the paper in his hand. Suddenly, Tessie Hutchinson shouted to Mr. Summers, "You didn't give him time enough to take any paper he wanted. I saw you. It wasn't fair."

"Be a good sport, Tessie," Mrs. Delacroix called, and Mrs. Graves said, "All of us took the same chance."

"Shut up, Tessie," Bill Hutchinson said.

"Well, everyone," Mr. Summers said, "that was done pretty fast,

and now we've got to be hurrying a little more to get done in time."
He consulted his next list. "Bill," he said, "you draw for the Hutchinson
family. You got any other households in the Hutchinsons?"

"There's Don and Eva," Mrs. Hutchinson yelled. "Make *them*
take their chance!"

"Daughters draw with their husbands' families, Tessie," Mr.
Summers said gently. "You know that as well as anyone else."

"It wasn't *fair*," Tessie said.

"I guess not, Joe," Bill Hutchinson said regretfully. "My daughter
draws with her husband's family, that's only fair. And I've got no
other family except the kids."

"Then, as far as drawing for families is concerned, it's you," Mr.
Summers said in explanation, "and as far as drawing for households is
concerned, that's you, too. Right?"

"Right," Bill Hutchinson said.

"How many kids, Bill?" Mr. Summers asked formally.

"Three," Bill Hutchinson said. "There's Bill, Jr., and Nancy, and
little Dave. And Tessie and me."

"All right, then," Mr. Summers said. "Harry, you got their
tickets back?"

Mr. Graves nodded and held up the slips of paper. "Put them in
the box, then," Mr. Summers directed. "Take Bill's and put
it in."

"I think we ought to start over," Mrs. Hutchinson said, as quietly
as she could. "I tell you it wasn't *fair*. You didn't give him time enough
to choose. *Every*body saw that."

Mr. Graves had selected the five slips and put them in the box,
and he dropped all the papers but those onto the ground, where the
breeze caught them and lifted them off.

"Listen, everybody," Mrs. Hutchinson was saying to the people
around her.

"Ready, Bill?" Mr. Summers asked, and Bill Hutchinson, with
one quick glance around at his wife and children, nodded.

"Remember," Mr. Summers said, "take the slips and keep them
folded until each person has taken one. Harry, you help little Dave."
Mr. Graves took the hand of the little boy, who came willingly with
him up to the box. "Take a paper out of the box, Davy," Mr. Summers
said. Davy put his hand into the box and laughed. "Take just *one* paper,"
Mr. Summers said. "Harry, you hold it for him." Mr. Graves took
the child's hand and removed the folded paper from the tight fist and

held it while little Dave stood next to him and looked up at him wonderingly.

"Nancy next," Mr. Summers said. Nancy was twelve, and her school friends breathed heavily as she went forward, switching her skirt, and took a slip daintily from the box. "Bill, Jr.," Mr. Summers said, and Billy, his face red and his feet over-large, nearly knocked the box over as he got a paper out. "Tessie," Mr. Summers said. She hesitated for a minute, looking around defiantly, and then set her lips and went up to the box. She snatched a paper out and held it behind her.

"Bill," Mr. Summers said, and Bill Hutchinson reached into the box and felt around, bringing his hand out at last with the slip of paper in it.

The crowd was quiet. A girl whispered, "I hope it's not Nancy," and the sound of the whisper reached the edges of the crowd.

"It's not the way it used to be," Old Man Warner said clearly. "People ain't the way they used to be."

"All right," Mr. Summers said. "Open the papers. Harry, you open little Dave's."

Mr. Graves opened the slip of paper and there was a general sigh through the crowd as he held it up and everyone could see that it was blank. Nancy and Bill, Jr., opened theirs at the same time, and both beamed and laughed, turning around to the crowd and holding their slips of paper above their heads.

"Tessie," Mr. Summers said. There was a pause, and then Mr. Summers looked at Bill Hutchinson, and Bill unfolded his paper and showed it. It was blank.

"It's Tessie," Mr. Summers said, and his voice was hushed. "Show us her paper, Bill."

Bill Hutchinson went over to his wife and forced the slip of paper out of her hand. It had a black spot on it, the black spot Mr. Summers had made the night before with the heavy pencil in the coal-company office. Bill Hutchinson held it up, and there was a stir in the crowd.

"All right, folks," Mr. Summers said. "Let's finish quickly."

Although the villagers had forgotton the ritual and lost the original black box, they still remembered to use stones. The pile of stones the boys had made earlier was ready; there were stones on the ground with the blowing scraps of paper that had come out of the box. Mrs. Delacroix selected a stone so large she had to pick it up with both hands and turned to Mrs. Dunbar. "Come on," she said. "Hurry up."

Mrs. Dunbar had small stones in both hands, and she said, gasping for breath, "I can't run at all. You'll have to go ahead and I'll catch up with you."

The children had stones already, and someone gave little Davy Hutchinson a few pebbles.

Tessie Hutchinson was in the center of a cleared space by now and she held her hands out desperately as the villagers moved in on her. "It isn't fair," she said. A stone hit her on the side of the head.

Old Man Warner was saying, "Come on, come on, everyone." Steve Adams was in the front of the crowd of villagers, with Mrs. Graves beside him.

"It isn't fair, it isn't right," Mrs. Hutchinson screamed, and then they were upon her.

The Span of Life

ROBERT FROST

The humor and edge of this two-line poem derive from its symbolic nature. Write a paragraph explaining the symbolism.

The old dog barks backward without getting up.
I can remember when he was a pup.

From *Complete Poems of Robert Frost*. Copyright 1936 by Robert Frost. Copyright © 1964 by Lesley Frost Ballantine. Reprinted by permission of Holt, Rinehart and Winston, Inc., and Jonathan Cape, Ltd.

Figurative Language

MONROE C. BEARDSLEY

It is both strange and ironic that figurative language, one of the most important and fascinating aspects of language, should be so misunderstood. Many people associate figurative language solely with poetry; moreover, they regard it as a kind of poetic decoration, the frosting on the cake merely, sweet and pleasant tasting but not really necessary. Such a view of figurative language is wrong on both counts. Figures of speech, it is true, do play a prominent part in poetry, but they also play an important role in prose, not only in imaginative works such as novels and short stories but also in expository and persuasive works. Indeed, though you may not be highly conscious of it, figures of speech occur frequently in your everyday conversation. And in whatever form figurative language appears—in poetry, prose writing, or ordinary speech—it is an integral and vital part; it is not decorative but functional.

Professor Monroe Beardsley, of Swarthmore College, opens the discussion of figurative language with an examination of the simile and the metaphor.

Take up a book, or article, on education—or start yourself thinking about that subject by asking yourself some questions. What good is it? Should everyone go on to school to the limit of his capacities? Should private and parochial schools be given financial help by the Government? . . . . The chances are that you won't read far, or think long, without comparing education, consciously or half-consciously, with something else. Is an education like other things that you believe everyone has a right to? Are the skills and talents of American citizens like natural resources, which ought to be conserved? Is knowledge like tools, or like money, or like a hobby?

This tendency to make comparisons is a fact worth noting about the way we think. Education, for example, is a complicated process, of which we know much less than we should like to know. And when

Monroe Beardsley, *Thinking Straight*. © 1950. Prentice-Hall, Inc., Englewood Cliffs, N. J.

we study a complicated process, we are apt to begin by setting aside some of its complexities. We try to see what light we can throw on it by comparing it with another process we think we understand better. We simplify. If we did not, it is hard to see how we could come to understand anything.

Moreover, such comparisons often fix themselves in the very language we use. Many of the words and phrases that come to mind when we think about education embody comparisons that were made long ago. We speak of education in a number of different ways: (1) eating and drinking: "the omnivorous reader," "undigested facts," "crumbs of information," "ruminating," "swallowing the story whole," "drinking of the Pierian spring"; (2) writing on blank paper or a tablet: "inscribed on the memory," "impressed on the mind," Locke's "*tabula rasa*"; (3) piling up goods in a warehouse or store: "his mind was well stocked," "taking inventory of his knowledge," "loads of learned lumber in his head"; (4) mining: "digging out information," "delving into philosophy"; (5) going on a journey: "adventures of ideas," "traveling in the realms of gold." And there are many others.

These terms are borrowed from simpler activities of human beings and applied to education. At first such a borrowed term may help us to focus upon an important aspect of the process. Thus we may say that one's personality is "molded" by his schooling, because we see that it makes him more of a definite person than he was: it "shapes" his personality, for good or ill. But once we use the term "molded," our thinking will be partly guided by the comparison of teacher with sculptor. And this can easily lead to a serious mistake, if it makes us think that the student is or should be as passive as the clay.

. . . therefore, we must reckon with an important characteristic of language: its power to evoke in our minds the vivid recollection of our sensory experience, the pictures, smells, tastes, sounds, and touch sensations of our waking life. Language does this when it is *concrete*, that is, when it is rich in images.

An *image* is a term that designates characteristics that we can experience by our senses. "Red," "dark cloud," and "pretty girl" are images, because some of the characteristics of these things we can know by direct perception. But "atom", "government," and "civil rights" are not images: these things are conceived, but they are not sensed.

Of course, we can think, and we can understand words, *abstractly* —that is, without imagining concrete things and happenings. And the actual memories that appear to the mind when a word is spoken or heard vary greatly from person to person. When you hear the word "horse," perhaps you imagine a white horse whereas the speaker imagines a brown one; but you won't get into trouble as long as the two horses both satisfy the designation of the term (in having four legs, for example), and as long as you both get the same connotations from the term in its context.[1] The difference in imagination will not hurt your thinking or hinder your communication, if you keep your thinking from being dominated and controlled by these private little pictures. But images can trip the unwary thinker, whether writer or reader, by leading him to wander into interesting but irrelevant thoughts. And so in this chapter we shall look over the principles that will help you manage them, in your ordinary reading and writing.

Simile and metaphor

Images become involved in our thinking (for better or for worse) when they enter into what are commonly called "*figures of speech.*" A figure of speech consists in a comparison between two things, which we may label "X" and "Y". Generally one of the things, say X, is the one we are saying something about, and the X-term (or **primary term**) denotes the thing *to which* some other thing is compared. In figure of speech we say something about X by comparing Y *to* it; the Y-term (or **secondary term**) denotes the thing which is compared to X.[2] In "love is blind," "love" is the primary term and "blind (person)" is the secondary term. Or when H. G. Wells says that the brain of man is a "food-getting instrument, like the snout of a pig," "brain" is the primary term and "snout of a pig" is the secondary term. When the figurative statement is elliptical, we have to supply part of the terms ourselves.

All figures of speech are comparisons, but not all comparisons are figures of speech. To begin with a simple example, we may say that "James was as angry as a hornet" is figurative, but that "James was angry as John" is *not*. It is not hard to see that there is a difference

---

[1] *Designation*, as Beardsley uses the term, means the defining characteristics of a thing. For example, the term *widow* designates the characteristics of being human, being female, having been married, and being one whose husband is dead. *Connotation* means those characteristics which are not strictly a part of the *designation* of a word. [eds.]

[2] The primary term is also referred to as the *tenor*, the secondary term as the *vehicle*, as in I. A. Richards' essay, p. 228. [eds.]

here, but it is impossible to state the difference exactly without using highly technical language. James and John are evidently much more alike than James and the hornet, for James and John both belong to the same biological species. Thus James and John can *both* be angry, in the same sense of the word. But James and the hornet *cannot* both be angry in the same sense of the word: the hornet doesn't feel the same way, and he doesn't behave the same way. He can't get red in the face or stamp his feet with rage: he can only zoom, buzz, and sting.

Thus there is a distinction between a comparison that is figurative and one that is not figurative, but the distinction is one of degree. Suppose you compare the human heart with a goat's heart, a pump, and a television relay. There is a greater difference between a human heart and a pump than there is between a human heart and a goat's heart. And there is a greater difference between a human heart and a television relay than there is between a human heart and a pump. If the difference is great enough, in a particular case, we say that the comparison is figurative. But "The heart is a pump" is a borderline case: it is figurative in some contexts, but not in others.

It is not possible, or necessary for ordinary purposes, to be very precise about this distinction. The important thing is the degree of difference between the two things compared. When you want to understand a comparison clearly, there are three things to do. First, identify clearly the two terms of the comparison. Second, consider the chief points of likeness and of unlikeness between the two things. And third, examine the context in which the characteristics of the things are stressed. If the two things are *unlike* in some important way that is indicated by the context, then it is reasonable to say that the comparison is figurative.

The teacher of literature, who is skilled in dealing with highly figurative language, must make a number of distinctions. There are, for example, similes, metaphors, analogies, parables, tropes, myths. And besides these there are various technical terms of rhetoric for more special kinds of figure: as when we speak of a thing as a person ("personification"), a part as a whole ("synecdoche"), or one thing as another that is associated with it ("metonymy"). These distinctions are useful for analyzing certain kinds of discourse, but . . . [here] we are concerned with more general features of discourse. Yet there is one fundamental distinction that any critical reader must make: that is the distinction between a *simile* and a *metaphor*.

A **simile** is an explicit figurative comparison: that is, it is a statement that one thing is like another. Thus it contains a comparative word: "like," "as," "similar," or "same." And we may distinguish further between two kinds of similes: *closed similes* and *open similes.* Compare these two excerpts from a description of international political developments in the summer of 1949:

(1) "The international situation was *as tense as* a ball-game tied up in the ninth inning." (*Closed simile.*)

(2) "The international situation was *like* a ball-game tied up in the ninth inning." (*Open simile.*)

In both of these figures we have a primary term ("the international situation") and a secondary term ("a ball-game tied up in the ninth inning"). But the first figure not only compares the two things; it specifies the *respect* in which they are compared (the one was "as tense as" the other). Similes that do this we shall call "**closed similes.**"

An **open simile** is one that makes no mention of the respect, or respects, in which the two things are to be compared. Thus an open simile, by itself, doesn't give any definite information. It puts us in a frame of mind to note the points of likeness, but it leaves us in suspension. We have to search the context of the simile for an indication of the points of likeness that are relevant to the subject under discussion. *Any* two things are alike in *some* respects: the question is, what are the important, and relevant, respects? Perhaps the writer means that in the international situation the watchers were divided into two hostile groups, or perhaps he means that most people were fearful of the outcome, or perhaps he means that the suspense was likely to continue for some time. The simile, *by itself*, is noncommittal; its specific reference must be supplied by the context.

Thus an open simile is likely to be vague if it is not carefully handled. It might mean a good deal, or it might mean very little. When a poet says that "the evening is spread out against the sky/ Like a patient etherized upon a table," we must hold the terms of this comparison in mind until the rest of his poem tells us *how* the two things are alike. The same principle applies to similes when they occur in ordinary discourse.

When the words "like" and "as" are dropped out of a figure, and the primary and secondary terms are jammed together, the figure becomes a *metaphor*. A metaphor does not *state* a comparison, but it *suggests* a comparison. The reporter quoted previously went on to say:

The diplomats made errors, and a few hits, but neither side scored. Everybody muffed the ball, and the peoples of the world breathlessly watched their chosen leaders swinging at wild curves as the international struggle dragged on.

Here is a whole string of metaphors, but take just one: "their chosen leaders swinging at wild curves." Y (a batter vainly trying to hit a badly pitched curve) is compared to X (a national leader dealing with an international crisis). But when we put this situation in the form of a statement, "Their chosen leaders swung at wild curves," we see that the metaphor is elliptical, for part of the comparison is left out. . . .

The simplest sort of metaphor has the form "X is Y": "He is a wolf." The secondary term doesn't have to be a predicate, however. It may be an adjective ("He has a wolfish appetite"), or a verb ("He wolfs his food"). To get the terms of the metaphor straightened out, we can always restate the metaphor in the simple form. We can write: "His appetite is wolfish," "His manner of eating is that of a wolf." This restatement will do violence to the metaphor, and it is not an exact substitute for it; it is merely a device for being clear about the structure of the metaphor. The same device can be applied to those richer metaphors that have added so much to the clarity, and confusion, of recent history: "New Deal," "pump-priming," "maginot-line mentality," "brass hats," "bottlenecks," "fox holes," "underground," "reconversion," "the Iron Curtain," and "Fair Deal."

In figurative language of the richest sort, similes and metaphors are interwoven in a complicated way, and it may take considerable analysis to understand exactly what is being said.

> Life, like a dome of many-coloured glass,
> Stains the white radiance of Eternity,
> Until Death tramples it to fragments.

This remarkable figure has several parts, which can be artificially separated for examination. Ordinary discourse seldom poses such complicated problems. Still, figurative language, even outside poetry, can be quite puzzling. A figure of speech can confuse your thinking, if you are not clear about its primary term and its secondary term, and if you do not recognize what kind of figure it is. . . .

Interpreting a metaphor

Metaphor is a handy linguistic tool, because it crams so many meanings into a few words. But metaphor is difficult to use skillfully, and, in the hands of a careless or malicious workman, it often gives the reader or listener a good deal of trouble. Metaphor can be a very subtle aid to slanting. And the more meaning that is packed into a metaphor, the harder it is for the critical reader to think *through* it. Therefore, in this section we shall take up the question of finding out just what a metaphor means.

We may begin by noting the common distinction between a "literal" sense and a "metaphorical" sense of a term. The *literal* meaning of "pig" is just its designation: that is, the characteristics of having four legs, having a snout, and so forth. If you say, "The animal in that pen is a pig," this statement *can* be literally true; an animal can have four legs. In this context, the connotations of "pig" are not stressed. But if you say, "That man over there is a pig," it is clear that this sentence *cannot* be literally true. For, if he is a man, he has *not* four legs. So, if this statement is to be true at all, it is not the designation, but only the *connotation*, of "pig" that is being ascribed to the man. In this case "pig" is used *metaphorically*. And this metaphorical statement is (or may be, depending on the context) equal to a number of literal statements: he is greedy, he is gross, he is dirty, he is lazy, he is fat.

We can now give a fairly clear definition of "metaphor." This term covers both statements ("The fire is dying") and noun-phrases ("a dying fire"). Let us consider statements first. We shall say that a statement is "metaphorical" if it has both of the following character-istics: First, it must be *literally* false. That is, the subject cannot possibly have the characteristics designated by the secondary term. Take, for example, the architectural slogan of an earlier decade: "A house is a machine for living." In the ordinary sense of the term, a machine is something that does work; we apply some form of energy (muscular effort, coal, gasoline, falling water) to it, and by the motions of its parts it changes the energy into a different form. This capacity is one of the characteristics designated by the term "machine." But a house is *not* a machine in this sense. Second, a metaphorical sentence *may* be (it does not have to be) true on the level of connotation. That is, the sub-ject *can* have the characteristics connotated by the secondary term. "Machine" connotes the characteristics of being useful, of being de-signed to fulfill certain specific functions, of not having parts it doesn't need to serve its ends. And (whether or not it ought to be) a house *can* be a machine in this sense.

A noun-phrase may be called a "metaphor" if it can be transformed into a metaphorical statement. In this way we speak of "pork-barrel legislation," "the voice of doom," "a living death" as metaphors.

It is important to keep "literal meaning" (that is, designation) distinct from *etymological* meaning. It is misleading to say, for example, that "budget" (from the French *bougette*) literally means *wallet*. The word "budget" literally means just what the dictionary gives as its *two* standard senses: (*a*) an accumulation, as a "budget of paradoxes" (this meaning seems to be on the way out), and (*b*) a financial statement for the ensuing period. There *is* on record the *obsolete* English sense (*c*) a bag with its contents; that once was one of the designations of "budget," but is not its "literal meaning" today.

This example reminds us of the constantly shifting character of the distinction between the literal and metaphorical senses of words (or between their designations and connotations). When we speak of "dead metaphor" we mean something that *was* a metaphor but is not any longer. "Spinster" is a "dead metaphor." Once it designated *a person who spins* (man or woman). Then, because most such people were unmarried women, it came to connote that characteristic. But when it began to be used very widely in contexts that emphasized this connotation, the connotation came to be so closely linked with the word that *unmarried woman* became the standard meaning, or designation. Today, in the proper context, it can *connote* the characteristic of being one who spins, but it does not now *designate* that characteristic.

When we speak of the "eye of a needle," we do not feel that we are comparing an eye to the aperture of the needle (even though there is more than one respect in which they are similar). This use of "eye" is just one of its designations; the metaphor has "died." But when we read of the "eyes of Night," the context and the personification of Night present a situation in which we *do* feel a comparison of the star to the eye. This is a genuine metaphor. Of course, in between, there will be "half-dead" metaphors, borderlines cases, such as, perhaps, "seeing eye-to-eye," in which the comparative element is almost lost and the phrase has practically hardened into an idiom.

It follows that the term "metaphor" is vague; there is no sharp line to divide living metaphors from dead ones. But for a full grasp of any discourse, you must make a good estimate of the amount of life left in its metaphors, especially when you are dealing with material from the social studies or psychology, where the borderline cases are frequent. In these fields, the technical vocabulary is often created by putting a metaphor to death. This is legal, but metaphors sometimes die hard. Hence the vocabulary of Freudian psychiatry has many terms, such as "repression," "censor," "projection," which are not yet fully under control. They are not quite dead enough so that their connotations can be ignored, and they can confuse the writer and reader.

We cannot tell whether a metaphorical statement is true or false until we know its meaning. To *interpret*, or *expand*, a metaphorical statement is to give a list of literal statements which, taken in combination, are equal in meaning to the original statement. In the case of "He is a pig," it may be possible to give a *complete interpretation*, but it would be an almost endless task to list *all* the characteristics wound up together in the meaning of a very rich metaphor. For most purposes this need not trouble us: usually we don't have to know *all* the characteristics connoted—but we do want to know whether a certain *particular* characteristic is connoted or not. Thus we must be able to give at least a *partial interpretation* of the metaphor, to bring out its special bearing upon the point of an argument.

As an example of a partial interpretation, let's consider the sentence "Russia has drawn an iron curtain across Europe," as it turns up in a discussion of American foreign policy. The first thing to do is to get the *terms* of the metaphor straight. We see that this metaphor is a double one. In the *main* me aphor, drawing an iron curtain is compared to Russian diplomatic and military behavior toward Eastern and Western Europe. But within the secondary term of the main metaphor, the "curtain" is stated to be an "iron" one.

The second step is to consider the connotations of the terms, beginning with the smallest units. You think of the characteristics of curtains (the kind you draw): their tendency to shut out air and light, to billow in a wind, to get dusty. Next you think of the characteristics of iron: its hardness, its brittleness, its uses for war. When you put these two groups of connotations together, they cancel each other out, in part, and in part they coalesce into the image of something that is strong, guarded, hard to penetrate. When you add the characteristics of drawing a curtain (the secrecy and suspense), you have a complicated skein of characteristics that are all wound up together in the meaning of the metaphor. The sentence *says* (whether it is true or false) that Eastern and Western Europe are being prevented from communicating with each other; that this is keeping information from getting into and out of Eastern Europe; that the lack of communication is entirely the fault of the Russians; that the boundary line is manned by armed troops—and there are many other meanings.

Clearly, when you ask whether the metaphorical sentence is *true* or not, you find that it is, in fact, a bundle of different statements, some of which may be true and some false. When metaphors turn up in the course of an argument, it is not safe to take them as they appear and leave it at that. You must interpret them; that is, you must break them down a bit, in order to make explicit exactly what is, and what is not, being stated.

SUGGESTED ASSIGNMENTS

1. Here are some simple metaphors from Melanesian Pidgin English, a language of the southwest Pacific:

rope he-got blut	vein, artery
he-got bone all-same water	cowardly
grass belong head (belong = of)	hair
eye belong musket	gun mouth
smoke belong bush	mist
smoke belong ground	dust

   Identify the primary and secondary terms in these metaphors and indicate the points of likeness and unlikeness.

2. Robert Burns begins a well-known poem with two open similes:

   > My love is like a red, red rose
   >   That's newly sprung in June:
   > My love is like the melodie
   >   That's sweetly played in tune.

   Does *love* refer to his beloved or to the feeling in his heart? Jot down all the points of likeness for each simile and bring them to class for discussion. What do these many points of likeness suggest to you about the role of the reader in interpreting figurative language?

3. A metaphor can say a great deal in little space. Let us suppose that you hear a student say as he comes out of class, "Well, Professor X certainly spun his wheels today." Write a literal statement of all that is suggested by this metaphor.

4. The area of animal life is a rich source of metaphor. Write ten sentences, each containing a metaphor or simile relating to one of these animals: chicken, duck, goose, horse, mule, weasel, ferret, wolf, fox, ox, cat, dog, monkey, hawk, sheep, cattle, lion, gopher, bear, deer, antelope, shark, butterfly, rooster, pigeon.

5. Students make considerable use of metaphors drawn from sports: I didn't get to first base with him; I got thrown for a loss in that exam. Choose one sport with which you are familiar and in ten minutes write as many metaphors as you can which are derived from it.

6. Many proverbs and folk sayings are metaphors: Don't put all your eggs in one basket; Too many cooks spoil the broth. Find a good metaphorical proverb from a book of proverbs in the library. Then write a paragraph in which you give a complete interpretation of all the metaphor implies.

7. Language, it has been said, is a graveyard of dead metaphors. Using an unabridged or an etymological dictionary, look up the etymology of ten of the following words and report the live metaphors that they once embodied: *examine, stimulate, ponder, calculate, deliberate* (verb), *daisy, easel, stagnate, caper* (verb), *pavilion, dandelion, grenade, cocoanut, thrilling, cocky, window.*

8. A "mixed metaphor" occurs when two or more metaphors are used together, the secondary terms of which are incongruent. The effect is often ludicrous to the alert reader. Point out the mixed metaphors in the following examples:

   a. The British Lion will never pull in its horns or crawl back into its shell.

   b. His was the task—with his staff—to go over the state's school system with a fine-tooth comb, ferreting out the facts that will apply a yardstick to the system.

   c. Crisis, complications, and a whole series of vicious cycles are the fare upon which he and his revolutionary regime thrive. Unfortunately for him and for the whole Arab world, it is upon these same elements that the tentacles of the Soviet Union are feeding, blossoming and bearing fruit in the Middle East.

   d. The Indians had a chance in mid-May to put open water between themselves and the Yanks, who still were trying to find themselves. Instead, Cleveland went into a tailspin of its own, stalling badly and giving the Yanks a chance to catch their breath. And now the shoe is on the other foot. The Yanks are in front again, with the throttle open and the gas pedal on the floor.

9. Skillful speakers often employ metaphors that are drawn from the occupations of their listeners. For example, a political speaker might want to say that the promises of the other party sound fair but are not to be trusted. Here is the way he might express this idea metaphorically to different audiences:

   a. (To bankers) The Republicratic promises are nothing but watered stock.

   b. (To airplane pilots) The Republicratic promises are nothing but bent beams that will lead you to a crash on a mountain side.

c.   (To Texas ranchers) The Republicratic promises are nothing but loco weeds. They look edible and nourishing, but if your stock eats them, you will lose your herd.

d.   (To housewives) The Republicratic promises are the good berries on top of the basket.

Imagine yourself as an educational speaker touring the country. One idea you wish to express forcefully is this: The higher one advances in his education, the more difficult the work becomes. If you were speaking in a mountain area you might use this metaphor: The higher one climbs up the peak of education, the rockier the way becomes. Now, describe three other groups whom you might address and write metaphors fitting the background of each to express your idea.

10.   One of the differences between dull, pedestrian prose and lively, pungent writing is the presence or absence of effective metaphors. Read an article or two in a quality magazine such as the *Atlantic, Harper's, Reporter, Saturday Review, New Yorker* (note especially its "Talk of the Town."). Collect a few of the effective metaphors and be prepared to discuss their effectiveness in class.

11.   The metaphors that we accept, consciously or unconsciously, can become a strong influence in our thinking and on our actions. If, for instance, a college president or dean or professor accepts the metaphor that a college is a brain *factory*, the implications can be something like these:

a.   Every student, like an object on the assembly line, should receive exactly the same educational treatment: take the same standardized courses taught in the same way. And when a given number of operations have been performed on a student (as shown by his credit hours earned), he is a finished product, identical with the others.

b.   Every instructor, like an assembly-line worker, has one special job to do, and does it the same on every student.

c.   In time of haste, as in war, or of overcrowding, the assembly-line can be moved faster. Thus we can get more of the same products in less time, e.g., doctors in six years instead of eight years.

Assume that the dean of instruction in your college accepts this metaphor: A college is a nursery which grows many kinds of trees, shrubs, flowers, and plants. Write out the implications that this metaphor might have on your educational life.

12.   Perhaps the most commonly used metaphors in the world are those based on the parts of the body, for the human body is a universal in the societies of men. We speak, for example, of the *face* of a clock or a cliff and the *mouth* of a river or a pitcher. Write one metaphor for each of the following body parts: *head, hair, brow, ear, nose, lip, tongue, eye, neck, shoulder, elbow, hand, finger, bosom, waist, leg, knee, foot, toe, heel.*

The Command of Metaphor

I. A. RICHARDS

For more than forty years I. A. Richards' seminal mind has been a stimulative force in the field of language study. His pioneer work, *The Meaning of Meaning*, written in collaboration with C. K. Ogden and published in 1923, has influenced a whole generation of scholars in their thinking about language. Richards is especially interested in the psychological aspects of language and in literary theory. His book *The Philosophy of Rhetoric*, a series of lectures given at Bryn Mawr College in 1936, contains a penetrating analysis of metaphor which goes far beyond the rather elementary treatment by Beardsley. In profundity and importance, Richards' discussion ranks with that of Aristotle and of Coleridge as a major contribution to our understanding of the nature of metaphor.

Last time[1] I generalized, or stretched, the sense of the term metaphor—almost, you may think, to breaking point. I used it to cover all cases where a word, in Johnson's phrase, "gives us two ideas for one," where we compound different uses of the word into one, and speak of something as though it were another.[2] And I took it further still to include, as metaphoric, those processes in which we perceive or think of or feel about one thing in terms of another—as when looking at a building it seems to have a face and to confront us with a peculiar expression. I want to insist that this sort of thing is normal in full perception and that study of the growth of our perceptions (the animistic world of the child and so on) shows that it must be so.

Let me begin now with the simplest, most familiar case of verbal metaphor—the *leg of a table* for example. We call it dead but it comes

From *The Philosophy of Rhetoric* by I. A. Richards. Reprinted by permission of the publisher, Oxford University Press, Inc., copyright 1936.

[1] This essay, the last in the series, was preceded by a résumé of previous ideas about metaphor and an introduction to Richards' theory of the interaction of tenor and vehicle, terms equivalent to Beardsley's "primary term" and "secondary term" (see p. 218). [eds.]

[2] Dr. Samuel Johnson, the eighteenth-century lexicographer and literary critic, had written: "As to metaphorical expression, that is a great excellence in style, when it is used with propriety, for it gives you two ideas for one." Richards had commented in the previous lecture that Johnson's statement represented "the limited traditional view of metaphor." [eds.]

to life very readily. Now how does it differ from a plain or literal use of the word, in *the leg of a horse*, say? The obvious difference is that the leg of a table has only some of the characteristics of the leg of the horse. A table does not walk with its legs; they only hold it up and so on. In such a case we call the common characteristics the ground of the metaphor. Here we can easily find the ground, but very often we cannot. A metaphor may work admirably without our being able with any confidence to say how it works or what is the ground of the shift. Consider some of the metaphors of abuse and endearment. If we call some one a pig or a duck, for example, it is little use looking for some actual resemblance to a pig or a duck as the ground. We do not call someone a duck to imply that she has a bill and paddles or is good to eat. The ground of the shift is much more recondite. The *Oxford Dictionary* hints at it by defining a "duck" in this use as "a charming or delightful object." An extremely simplified account of the ground here would make it something like this: that some feeling, of "tender and amused regard," say, that it is possible to have towards ducks is being felt towards a person.

A very broad division can thus be made between metaphors which work through some direct resemblance between the two things, the tenor and vehicle, and those which work through some common attitude which we may (often through accidental and extraneous reasons) take up towards them both. The division is not final or irreducible, of course. *That we like them both* is, in one sense, a common property that two things share, though we may, at the same time, be willing to admit that they are utterly different. When I like tobacco and logic, that is no very obvious character that they have in common. But this division, though it does not go very deep, may at a certain level help us sometimes to avoid one of the worst snares of the study— the assumption that if we cannot see how a metaphor works, it does not work.

Let us go back to *leg* for a moment. We notice that even there the boundary between literal and metaphoric uses is not quite fixed or constant. To what do we apply it literally? A horse has legs literally, so has a spider, but how about a chimpanzee? Has it two legs or four? And how about a star-fish? Has it arms or legs or neither? And, when a man has a wooden leg, is it a metaphoric or a literal leg? The answer to this last is that it is both. It is literal in one set of respects, metaphoric in another. A word may be *simultaneously* both literal and metaphoric, just as it may simultaneously support many different metaphors, may serve to focus into one meaning many different meanings. This point is of some importance, since so much misinterpretation comes from supposing that if a word works one way it cannot simultaneously work in another and have simultaneously another meaning.

Whether, therefore, a word is being used literally or metaphorically is not always, or indeed as a rule, an easy matter to settle. We may provisionally settle it by deciding whether, in the given instance, the word gives us two ideas or one; whether, in the terms I suggested last time, it presents both a tenor and a vehicle which cooperate in an inclusive meaning. If we cannot distinguish tenor from vehicle then we may provisionally take the word to be literal; if we can distinguish at least two co-operating uses, then we have metaphor.

For example, when Hamlet says:

"What should such fellows as I do crawling between earth and heaven?" Or when Swift makes the Brobdingnagian King say to Gulliver: "The bulk of your natives appear to me to be the most pernicious race of little odious vermin that nature ever suffered to crawl upon the face of the earth," are *crawling* and *crawl* to be regarded as literal or metaphoric?

My answer is that they are metaphoric. Hamlet or man may crawl literally—as babies and big-game hunters undoubtedly do at times— but in both passages there is an unmistakable reference to other things that crawl, to the motions of foul insects, to vermin, and this reference is the vehicle as Hamlet, or man and his ways, are the tenor. By this test, of course, most sentences in free or fluid discourse turn out to be metaphoric. Literal language is rare outside the central parts of the sciences. We think it more frequent than it is through the influence of that form of the usage doctrine which ascribes single fixed meanings to words and that is why I have spent so much time in these lectures inveighing against that doctrine.

Let us consider, now, some of the varying relations between tenor and vehicle. It is convenient to begin with the remark, which you will meet with everywhere, that a metaphor involves a comparison. What is a comparison? It may be several different things: it may be just a putting together of two things to let them work together; it may be a study of them both to see how they are like and how unlike one another; or it may be a process of calling attention to their likenesses or a method of drawing attention to certain aspects of the one through the co-presence of the other. As we mean by comparison these different things we get different conceptions of metaphor. If we mean calling

attention to likenesses, we get a main 18th Century doctrine of metaphor. Dr. Johnson, for example, praises Denham's[3] lines on the Thames
because "the particulars of resemblance are so perspicaciously collected." These are the lines,

> O could I flow like thee, and make thy stream
> My great exemplar as it is my theme!
> Though deep, yet clear; though gentle, yet not dull;
> Strong without rage; without o'erflowing, full.

Here the flow of the poet's mind, we may say, is the tenor, and the
river the vehicle; and it is worth noting, as an exercise in anlaysis,
that in the last two lines there is a repeated alternation of the relative
positions of tenor and vehicle and of the direction of the shift between
them. "Though deep, yet clear": the words are literally descriptive of
the vehicle, the river; derivatively or metaphorically descriptive of
the mind. "Though gentle yet not dull": "gentle" certainly is literally
descriptive of the mind, the tenor, derivatively of the river, the other
way about; but "dull," I suppose, goes from the river to the mind
again. "Strong without rage" goes, for me, unquestionably from mind
to river, and "without o'erflowing, full" goes back again from river,
does it not? to mind. All through, of course, it is not etymology but
how *we* take the words which settles these questions.

These details of order are not important to notice in themselves—
though to do so gives practice in the peculiar sort of attention which
is the method of the whole study. Still, this alternating movement in
the shifts may have not a little to do with the rather mysterious power
of the couplet, the way it exemplifies what it is describing:

> Though deep yet clear; though gentle, yet not dull;
> Strong without rage; without o'erflowing, full.

And also it may have something to do with what Johnson is rightly
remarking when he says that "the flow of the last couplet is so smooth
and sweet that the lines have not been overpraised." [*sic*]

"The particulars of resemblance (between tenor and vehicle) are
so perspicaciously collected," that is a typical 18th Century conception
of the kind of comparison that metaphor should supply, the process
of pointing out likenesses—perspicuously collecting particulars of resemblance. But it does not really apply as an account of how these lines
work. The more carefully and attentively we go over the senses and

[3] Sir John Denham (1615–1669), the author of the famous poem "Cooper's
Hill," which contains the lines on the Thames. [eds.]

implications of *deep, clear, gentle, strong* and *full* as they apply to a stream and to a mind, the less shall we find the resemblances between vehicle and tenor counting and the more will the vehicle, the river, come to seem an excuse for saying about the mind something which could not be said about the river. Take *deep*. Its main implications as regards a river are, "not easily crossed, dangerous, navigable, and suitable for swimming, perhaps." As applied to a mind, it suggests "mysterious, a lot going on, rich in knowledge and power, not easily accounted for, acting from serious and important reasons." What the lines say of the mind is something that does not come from the river. But the river is not a mere excuse, or a decoration only, a gilding of the moral pill. The vehicle is still controlling the mode in which the tenor forms. That appears at once if we try replacing the river with, say, a cup of tea!

> Though deep, yet clear; though gentle, yet not dull;
> Strong without rage; without o'erflowing, full.

Comparison, as a stressing of likenesses, is not the whole mode of this metaphor though it commonly is in 18th Century writing—where, too, the tenor is usually the most important partner in the metaphor. The opposed conception of comparison—as a mere putting together of two things to see what will happen—is a contemporary fashionable aberration, which takes an extreme case as norm. Here it is, in a summary and exaggerated form. This is André Breton, the leader of the French Super-Realists, stating the doctrine very plainly:

"To compare two objects, as remote from one another in character as possible, or by any other method put them together in a sudden and striking fashion, this remains the highest task to which poetry can aspire." (*Les vases communicants.*)

" 'To put them together in a sudden and striking fashion' "—"*les mettre en présence d'une manière brusque et saisissante.*" That, as "the highest task to which poetry can aspire"! It is a doctrine well worth some examination. Like Mr. Max Eastman, with his insistence (in *The Literary Mind*) that metaphor works by attempting "impracticable identifications," M. Breton sees no need to consider what should be put with what—provided they are sufficiently remote from one another —nor does he distinguish between the very different effects of such collocations. This is the opposite position from Johnson's for whereas Johnson objected to comparisons being, like Cowley's,[4] "far fetched,"

[4] Abraham Cowley (1618–1667), one of the "metaphysical poets," was condemned by Johnson for his penchant for "the unexpected and surprising." [eds.]

it is the distance of the fetching here which is the merit. Mr. Eastman shares this indifference as to the precise effect of the encounter of disparates. For him the poet "communicates a kind of experience not elsewhere accessible" and, to do so, Mr. Eastman says, he "must arouse a reaction and yet impede it, creating a tension in our nervous system sufficient and rightly calculated to make us completely aware that we are living something—and no matter what." (*The Literary Mind*, p. 205.) "No matter what?" These last words are heroic certainly. Tie a man down and approach him with a red-hot poker; you will arouse a reaction and sufficiently impede it to make him completely aware, I believe, that he is living something. This same heroism haunts a good deal of current literary theory and practice—not only in the Super-Realists' cult of artificial paranoias. It comes, I think, from a crude conception of the mode of action of metaphors. . . .

Let us consider more closely what happens in the mind when we put together—in a sudden and striking fashion—two things belonging to very different orders of experience. The most important happenings —in addition to a general confused reverberation and strain—are the mind's efforts to connect them. The mind is a connecting organ, it works only by connecting and it can connect any two things in an indefinitely large number of different ways. Which of these it chooses is settled by reference to some larger whole or aim, and, though we may not discover its aim, the mind is never aimless. In all interpretation we are filling in connections, and for poetry, of course, our freedom to fill in—the absence of explicitly stated intermediate steps— is a main source of its powers. As Mr. Empson well says (in his *Seven Types of Ambiguity*, p. 32), "Statements are made as if they were connected, and the reader is forced to consider their relations for himself. The reason why these statements should have been selected is left for him to invent; he will invent a variety of reasons and order them in his own mind. This is the essential fact about the poetical use of language." The reader, I would say, will try out various connections, and this experimentation—with the simplest and the most complex, the most obvious and the most recondite collocations alike—is the movement which gives its meaning to all fluid language.

As the two things put together are more remote, the tension created is, of course, greater. That tension is the spring of the bow, the source of the energy of the shot, but we ought not to mistake the strength of the bow for the excellence of the shooting; or the strain for the aim. And bafflement is an experience of which we soon tire, and rightly. But, as we know, what seems an impossible connection, an "impracticable identification," can at once turn into an easy and powerful adjustment if the right hint comes from the rest of the discourse. Here is an instance.

An incautious recent writer on the general theory of language says: "In England the symbol *house* may symbolise a reference to many different kinds of houses; metaphorically its reference may be so generalised as to refer to many more other things; but it can hardly ever have the same reference as, let us say, *bread*."

That sets us a problem; find an occasion in which *bread* may be metaphorical for house, or *house* for bread. It would not be hard, I think, to find several—but here is a fairly obvious one, from Gerard Manley Hopkins. From that rather distressing and unhappy poem, *The Drummer Boy's Communion*,[5] when Hopkins is speaking of the wafer as the dwelling of the Divine Presence. This is the line:

> Low-latched in leaf-light housel his too huge godhead.

There is no strain, surely, in speaking of the bread here as the little house, housel.

But it is the rest of the poem that makes the connection easy and obvious, which witnesses to a general truth. The mind will always try to find connections and will be guided in its search by the rest of the utterance and its occasion.

I conclude then that these contemporary exploiters of the crude "clash them together—no matter what" view of metaphor are beguiling themselves with by-products of the process of interpretation and neglecting the more important cares of critical theory. But still one point of importance emerges clearly from examining these exaggerations. We must not, with the 18th Century, suppose that the interactions of tenor and vehicle are to be confined to their resemblances. There is disparity action too. When Hamlet uses the word *crawling* its force comes not only from whatever resemblances to vermin it brings in but at least equally from the differences that resist and control influences of their resemblances. The implication there is that man should not so crawl. Thus, talk about the identification or fusion that a metaphor effects is nearly always misleading and pernicious. In general, there are very few metaphors in which disparities between tenor and vehicle are not as much operative as the similarities. Some

---

[5] Author is referring to "The Bugler's First Communion" from *Poems of* Gerard Manley Hopkins (New York: Oxford University Press, 1931). [eds.]

similarity will commonly be the ostensive ground of the shift, but the peculiar modification of the tenor which the vehicle brings about is even more the work of their unlikenesses than of their likenesses.

This has, I believe, very important consequences for literary practice and theory at innumerable points. Insufficient analysis here has led not only to false doctrine and crude reading but to attempts in writing to make words behave in fashions which conflict with the nature of language as a medium. To take the danger of false doctrine first. One of the most influential of modern critics has been T. E. Hulme. His death in the War was a very heavy loss for many reasons—not least, perhaps because his doctrine of metaphor was left at a half-way stage from which, I believe, he would certainly have developed it. As it stands, in the interpretation in which it has been vigorously infective for the last nineteen years—and especially since his papers on "Modern Art" and on "Romanticism and Classicism" were published in 1924 in the volume called *Speculations*—it seems to me most deceiving.

It says (p. 137) "Plain speech is essentially inaccurate. It is only by new metaphors . . . that it can be made precise." This you will see is only Shelley's point again,[6] and we can accept it, with a demurrer as to some of the implications of "new" here—a demurrer that Hulme himself hints on an earlier page when he says, "Works of art aren't eggs," and so need not be fresh or new laid. But he added various points about the precision that he supposed metaphor to aim at, and it is these that give occasion for mistakes. "The great aim," he says, "is accurate, precise and definite description." Poetry, fluid discourse, as opposed to prose, "is not a language of counters, but," he holds, "a visual concrete one. It is a compromise for a language of intuition which would hand over sensations bodily. It always endeavours to arrest you, and make you continuously see a physical thing, to prevent you gliding through an abstract process."

I have three quarrels with this account. First with that *always*. Only remember Shakespeare and you will not say that the language of poetry *always* does anything of this sort. My second quarrel is with the words *visual* and *see:* "make you continuously see a physical thing and prevent you gliding through an abstract process." That is patently false.

---

[6] Shelley's point was that "Language is vitally metaphorical; that is, it marks the before unapprehended relations of things and perpetuates their apprehension, until words, which represent them, become, through time, signs for portions or classes of thought instead of pictures of integral thoughts: and then, if no new poets should arise to create afresh the associations which have been thus disorganized, language will be dead to all the nobler purposes of human intercourse." [eds.]

> If thou didst ever hold me in thy heart
> Absent thee from felicity awhile
> And in this harsh world draw thy breath in pain
> To tell my story.

You need *see* nothing while reading that, and the words certainly do not work by making you see anything. Besides, you already have the actors to look at. My third quarrel is with this fear of the abstract. The language of the greatest poetry is frequently abstract in the extreme and its aim is precisely to send us "gliding through an abstract process."

> This she? No, this is Diomed's Cressida.
> If beauty have a soul, this is not she,
> If souls guide vows, if vows be sanctimony,
> If sanctimony be the gods' delight,
> If there be rule in unity itself,   5
> This is not she.

We are not asked by Shakespeare here to perceive beauty, but to understand it through a metaphoric argument as the "rule in unity itself" and to understand its place in the soul's growth.

What can have happened to make so shrewd and acute a writer as Hulme blunder in this gross fashion? I have two explanations, which combine. The first is that he is tricking himself with the word *see* into supposing that he means it literally when his doctrine would only be sanctioned if he were using it metaphorically. Obviously if, in an argument, we say "I see your point!" we are using *see* metaphorically. So when Hulme wrote *see* and *visual* here, the words are to be taken metaphorically too or the doctrine must be condemned at once. What discourse "always endeavours" to do is to make us apprehend, understand, gain a realizing sense of, take in, whatever it is that is being meant—which is not necessarily any physical thing. But if we say "a realizing sense," we must remember that this is not any "sense" necessarily, such as sense-perception gives, but may be a feeling or a thought. What is essential is that we should really take in and become fully aware of—whatever it is.

This blunder with the word *see* may seem too crude to be likely. But the patient toil of scores of teachers is going every day, in courses about the appreciation of poetry, into the effort to make children (and adults) visualize where visualization is a mere distraction and of no service. And little books appear every few months encouraging just this gross misconception of language. For words cannot, and should not attempt to "hand over sensations bodily"; they have very much more important work to do. So far from verbal language being a "compromise for a language of intuition"—a thin, but better-than-nothing, substitute for real experience,—language, well used, is a *completion* and does what the intuitions of sensation by themselves cannot do. Words are the meeting points at which regions of experience which can never combine in sensation or intuition, come together. They are the occasion and the means of that growth which is the mind's endless endeavour to order itself. That is why we have language. It is no mere signalling system. It is the instrument of all our distinctively human development, of everything in which we go beyond the other animals.

Thus, to present language as working only through the sensations it reinstates, is to turn the whole process upside down. It overlooks what is important in Mallarmé's[7] *dictum* that the poet does not write with thoughts (or with ideas or sensations or beliefs or desires or feelings, we may add) but with words. "Are not words," so Coleridge asked, "parts and germinations of the plant? And what is the law of their growth? In something of this sort," he wrote, "I would endeavour to destroy the old antithesis of Words and Things: elevating, as it were, Words into Things and living things too." We must do so if we are to study metaphor profitably. Hulme and the school teachers are forgetting everything that matters most about language in treating it as just a stimulus to visualization. They think the image fills in the meaning of the word; it is rather the other way about and it is the word which brings in the meaning which the image and its original perception lack.

That is one part, I think, of the explanation of these disorders of thought — the mistaking of *see* and *perceive* in the literal sense instead of a wide and open metaphoric sense. But the other part of the explanation goes deeper: it is the mistaking of what I have been calling the tenor-vehicle antithesis for that between the metaphor (the double unit including tenor and vehicle) and its meaning. These two antitheses are easy to confuse, indeed, it is hard to keep them steadily distinct — especially when *metaphor* (and its synonyms), . . . sometimes means "vehicle," sometimes means "vehicle and tenor together." Nothing but habituation makes this shift manageable and keeps it from deceiving

[7] Etienne Stéphane Mallarmé (1842–1898), French Symbolist poet. [eds.]

us. I think it deceived Hulme here — and I know it deceives others. When he says, "The great aim is accurate, precise and definite description" we can agree, if that is saying no more than "the words somehow must make us fully and rightly aware of whatever it is, the language must really utter its meaning." That is, the metaphor (the whole thing, tenor and vehicle together) should mean what it should. But Hulme turns his remark into something about a supposedly needful accuracy of correspondence between vehicle and tenor, and so into something which is false. "Plain speech is essentially inaccurate. It is only by . . . metaphors . . . that it can be made precise. When the analogy has not enough connections with the thing described to be quite parallel with it, when it overlays the thing it describes and there is a certain excess" it is inferior. "But where the analogy is every bit of it necessary for accurate description . . . If it is sincere, in the accurate sense, when the whole of the analogy is necessary to get out the exact curve of the feeling or thing you want to express—there you seem to me (he says) to have the highest verse." In part of this, Hulme is thinking of the whole metaphor and its meaning; in other parts he is thinking of the vehicle and tenor. Something which is obvious and true of the whole metaphor and its meaning thus lends an illusory plausibility to a false view of the correspondence of vehicle to tenor. Hulme seems not to be distinguishing these two couples and it is as fatal to confuse them as it would be in chemistry to mistake the order of complexity of a molecule and an electron, or in algebra, to ignore the brackets. His confidence in a truism — that speech should mean what it should mean—makes him (as I read his pages) certain that vehicle must correspond to tenor — the whole of the analogy be necessary to get out the exact curve — and that, in the sense in which I read him, is not a truism, but an easily demonstrable error, a misdescription of all our current practice.

For one thing, there is no whole to any analogy, we use as much of it as we need; and, if we tactlessly take any analogy too far, we break it down. There are no such limits to the relations of tenor and vehicle as this account puts. The result of the doctrine may be seen in those anxious, over-careful attempts to *copy* perceptions and feelings *in words*, to "hand over sensations bodily," of which modern prose at its most distinguished too often consists. Words are not a medium in which to copy life. Their true work is to restore life itself to order.

The error of mistaking the tenor-vehicle relation for the relation between tenor plus vehicle together and what they mean, has consequences which go far beyond what we are apt to regard (on a limited view) as literary matters. They enter into the ways we envisage all our most important problems. For example, into the question of belief. Must we believe what an utterance says if we are to understand it fully? Does the Divine Comedy, or the Bible tell us something which we must accept as true if we are to read it aright? These are questions that we cannot possibly answer satisfactorily unless we are clear as to the ways in which metaphoric utterances may say or tell us something. Mr. Eliot remarks somewhere of the Divine Comedy that the whole poem is one vast metaphor.[8] It is. And, if so, what is it that we might believe in it? Is it the tenor or the vehicle or their joint presentation; or is it "that tenor and vehicle are thus and thus related there"? Or is the belief required no more than a readiness to feel and will and live, in certain respects, in accordance with the resultant meaning in so far as we apprehend that meaning—or rather in so far as that meaning apprehends, grasps, takes control of, us? We are accustomed to distinguish between taking an utterance literally and taking it metaphorically or anagogically, but, at the simplest, there are at least four possible modes of interpretation to be considered, not two. And the kinds of believing that will be appropriate will as a rule be different. We can extract the tenor and believe that as a statement; or extract the vehicle; or, taking tenor and vehicle together, contemplate for acceptance or rejection some statement about their relations, or we can accept or refuse the direction which together they would give to our living. We need not go to the Alexandrian schools of early Christian interpretation, or to the similar exegetical developments of other religions, to find instances to show how immense the consequences for belief of those choices may be. The varying possibilities of understanding of any metaphoric utterance will show them.

A "command of metaphor" — a command of the interpretation of metaphors — can go deeper still into the control of the world that we make for ourselves to live in. The psycho-analysts have shown us with their discussions of "transference" — another name for metaphor — how constantly modes of regarding, of loving, of acting, that have developed with one set of things or people, are shifted to another. They have shown us chiefly the pathology of these transferences, cases where the vehicle — the borrowed attitude, the parental fixation, say — tyrannizes over the new situation, the tenor, and behavior is

<hr/>

[8] T. S. Eliot. The reference is to Eliot's essay "Dante," included in *Selected Essays 1917-1932* (New York, Harcourt, Brace & World, Inc., 1932), p. 206. [eds.]

inappropriate. The victim is unable to see the new person except in terms of the old passion and its accidents. He reads the situation only in terms of the figure, the archetypal image, the vehicle. But in healthy growth, tenor and vehicle — the new human relationship and the family constellation — co-operate freely; and the resultant behavior derives in due measure from both. Thus in happy living the same patterns are exemplified and the same risks of error are avoided as in tactful and discerning reading. The general form of the interpretative process is the same, with a small-scale instance — the right understanding of a figure of speech — or with a large scale instance — the conduct of a friendship.

But the literary instance is easier to discuss and more accessible to investigation. It is an old dream that in time psychology might be able to tell us so much about our minds that we would at last become able to discover with some certainty what we mean by our words and how we mean it. An opposite or complementary dream is that with enough improvement in Rhetoric we may in time learn so much about words that they will tell us how our minds work. It seems modest and reasonable to combine these dreams and hope that a patient persistence with the problems of Rhetoric may, while exposing the causes and modes of the misinterpretation of words, also throw light upon and suggest a remedial discipline for deeper and more grievous disorders; that, as the small and local errors in our everyday misunderstandings with language are models in miniature of the greater errors which disturb the development of our personalities, their study may also show us more about how these large scale disasters may be avoided. That at least was Plato's hope, as it was Spinoza's belief that there is but one end for the sciences. "Above all things, a method must be thought out of healing the understanding and purifying it at the beginning, that it may with the greatest success understand things correctly."

Interpretational Hypothesis of Matthew Arnold's "To Marguerite"

SEYMOUR CHATMAN
and MORSE PECKHAM

In the essay, "The Command of Metaphor," I. A. Richards discussed the complex interrelationships that may exist between tenor and vehicle, and the resultant richness of thought and emotion embodied in metaphorical language. It is the poet, more than anyone else, who knows and uses metaphor in this way. Oftentimes a metaphor is not limited to a line or stanza but informs a whole poem. Matthew Arnold's "To Marguerite," built on an extended tenor-vehicle relationship, is such a poem. The functional nature of this relationship is clearly revealed in the analysis following the poem. Morse Peckham is Professor of English at the University of Pennsylvania; Seymour Chatman is Assistant Professor of Speech at the University of California at Berkeley.

SWITZERLAND

5: TO MARGUERITE — CONTINUED

Yes! in the sea of life enisled,
With echoing straits between us thrown.
Dotting the shoreless watery wild,
We mortal millions live *alone*.
The islands feel the enclasping flow,   5
And then their endless bounds they know.

But when the moon their hollows lights,
And they are swept by balms of spring,
And in their glens, on starry nights,
The nightingales divinely sing;   10
And lovely notes, from shore to shore,
Across the sounds and channels pour —

From *Word, Meaning, Poem* by Seymour Chatman and Morse Peckham. Reprinted by permission of the authors and Thomas Y. Crowell Company.

Oh! then a longing like despair
Is to their farthest caverns sent;
For surely once, they feel, we were   *15*
Parts of a single continent!
Now round us spreads the watery plain —
Oh might our marges meet again!

Who order'd, that their longing's fire
Should be, as soon as kindled, cool'd?   *20*
Who renders vain their deep desire? —
A God, a God their severance ruled!
And bade betwixt their shores to be
The unplumb'd, salt, estranging sea.

Matthew Arnold
(1822-1888)

Arnold published this poem under various titles: "To Marguerite, in Returning a Volume of the Letters of Ortis" (1852), next as number V in the sequence of poems called "Switzerland" with the title as simply "To Marguerite" (1853), next as number VI in that series and with the same title (1854), then as number VII but with the new title "Isolation" (1857), again as number 7 of "Switzerland" with the title as given above (1869), and finally as number 5 (1888). Since these titles were used at various times for other poems in the same series, this poem is best identified and remembered by its first line.

Of these various titles only that of 1857, "Isolation," is the kind of title that gives some information about the poem itself. "Insula" in Latin and "isola" in Italian, "île" in French, and "isle" or "island" in English all have the same meaning. The land of an island is separated by the surrounding sea from other land. Hence an "isolated" person is separated from other persons. What physically isolates a prisoner from society is concrete: stone walls and bars. What emotionally isolates an individual from society is a sense of separation from others because he does not share with them feelings which emotional communication makes possible. All these uses are metaphorical developments of "to be an island." In the first line the poem states that it is true, emphatically true ("Yes!"), that we are islands in the sea of life. The separating medium, then, is life itself, or the conditions of existence in which we find ourselves. Between us are echoing straits. Two questions arise here. Why "echoing" and why "thrown"? An echo is the return of one's voice to oneself by other than a human agency. The word brings out the failure of communication between the islands, or individuals. Although isolated individuals may attempt to establish emotional communication with others, they "hear only their own voices," i.e. they experience no answering emotional response. "Thrown" implies that some power external to the conditions of life is responsible for the existence of the straits. But that power is not identified. It raises the expectation that it will be. Whether that expectation will be fulfilled or disappointed remains to be seen. The "wild" or wilderness of the water is appropriate because it is consistent that there is no communication, as we have seen, between the islands; and thus the wild is shoreless. But this word raises a question. Do not islands have shores? Yes, but so do continents. The sea of life, then, is different from the actual seas of the earth which are bordered by the shores of continents. In the sea of life, the conditions of existence in which we find ourselves, there are no continents, continuous bodies of lands; there is no such thing as human solidarity. Thus "we mortal millions live alone," each separate on his own little island. The italicization of *alone* is a typographical device to indicate emphasis.

At first glance, lines 5–6 seem to add nothing to what has been said, until we consider "feel" and "know." The metaphor is now extended. Not only are human beings isolated; they are also aware of being isolated. They are clasped or firmly caught in the "flow" or continuously changing medium of isolation. When the individual feels that he is inescapably separated from other human beings by the continuously shifting conditions of experiences, then he is aware, consciously, of his "endless bounds." This last phrase is a paradox, since a "bound" or frontier *is* an "end" or limit. Thus the phrase means "boundless bounds," or "no bounds at all." The phrase is a way of saying, "There are no bounds, no frontiers, to the personality; that is, one personality never genuinely impinges on, confronts, meets, and contacts another personality." The two lines, then, are concerned with the raising of an emotional response to the level of an intellectual conception.

This explains the force of the "But" in the first line of the next stanza (l. 7): "In spite of their knowledge, in spite of their intellectual certainty that this isolation is the condition of life and always will be —." The implication is that a longing for communication and a sense of solidarity and communication with other human beings will appear and will be felt. The rest of this stanza, then, is concerned with the conditions under which such a longing will occur. Having established that the metaphor of "island" equals "individual human personality" and "sea" equals "conditions of existence," the poet now speaks for a time entirely in terms derived from the vehicle. When the moonlight shines into the dark and hidden places of the islands, when the sweet winds of spring blow across them, when the nightingales, the birds of spring and love, sing on perfect nights, and their notes are heard across the straits, the sounds, and the channels, then the islands feel in their deepest caverns a desire which is like despair, that is, a desire which involves an awareness that the desire cannot be gratified. With "feel" the language of the tenor is reintroduced. If the whole preceding passage is expressed in the language of the tenor, we have something like this: When the individual finds himself experiencing a great sensuous gratification (the moonlit spring nights) and a great emotional gratification (the song of the nightingales from island to island), that is, considering the traditional significance of the nightingale, when he is in love (the poem, after all, is addressed to a woman) and finds himself experiencing the feeling of communication, then, the very depths of his personality (the farthest caverns), he experiences a longing which he knows cannot be gratified. The "for" in line 15 connects the ensuing statement with the preceding one. It implies, "We are justified in feeling this longing. Surely, all men at one time were part of a single, continuous human solidarity ('Single continent'). Although the conditions of life separate us from each other, we have a terrible longing to experience that continuity" (that is, in the language of the vehicle, that the islands' edges or marges ["bounds," l. 6] meet and the islands join together to form a single continent).

In the next stanza the voice of the islands has ceased and the poet speaks. In "order'd" is picked up and developed the implication of "thrown" in line 2. The conditions of life do not merely exist; they were made that way. A new metaphor is now introduced. The vehicle is the kindling and then cooling or extinguishing of a fire. The tenor is the arousing and then suppression of emotional desire, or longing, among human beings. The longing is suppressed as soon as felt, because it is futile ("vain"); and it is futile because he has already raised the feeling of isolation to intellectual certainty (ll. 5–6), and because he has further concluded that longing is hopeless. Again the question is asked (l. 21): "What force makes it impossible that the deep desire of the islands for communion be satisfied?" The poet again shifts into the language of the basic vehicle of the poem. "A God decreed that islands should be separate and that between their shores should always exist the unfathomable, salty, and separating sea." In the language of the tenor: "Some force which we cannot control or understand" (i.e. it is "a God," not the Christian God or some particular non-Christian God; the God involved is not identified) "is responsible for the fact that some barrier always prevents the emotional communication of human beings with one another and that that barrier is at once incomprehensible ('unplumb'd'), sterile or destructive of emotional gratification ('salty'), and capable of making us feel like strangers to one another, people with nothing in common ('estranging')."

The poem, then, is concerned with the emotional isolation of human beings from each other, with the desire that that isolation should be transcended or destroyed, and with the knowledge that that desire can never be gratified, even in love under the most sensuously and aesthetically perfect conditions.

SUGGESTED ASSIGNMENTS

Printed below is Shakespeare's "Sonnet LXXIII." A magnificent example of metaphor in action, it is built on a series of figures (one basic figure in each quatrain) revolving about the same central idea. Study the poem carefully until you think you understand it as fully as you can. Then write a detailed explanation of the basic metaphor in either quatrain two or three, making clear the points of comparison between tenor and vehicle. William Empson's famous discussion of the last line of the first quatrain is an example of how you might proceed: "... the comparison holds for many reasons; because ruined monastery choirs are places in which to sing, because they involve sitting in a row, because they are made of wood, are carved into knots and so forth, because they used to be surrounded by a sheltering building crystallised out of the likeness of a forest, and coloured with stained glass and painting like flowers and leaves, because they are now abandoned by all but the grey walls coloured like the skies of winter, because the cold and Narcissistic charm suggested by choir-boys suits well with Shakespeare's feeling for the object of the Sonnets, and for various sociological and historical reasons (the protestant destruction of monasteries; fear of puritanism), which it would be hard now to trace out in their proportions; these reasons, and many more relating the simile to its place in the Sonnet, must all combine to give the line its beauty, and there is a sort of ambiguity in not knowing which of them to hold most clearly in mind. Clearly this is involved in all such richness and heightening of effect, and the machinations of ambiguity are among the very roots of poetry."[1]

[1] William Empson, *Seven Types of Ambiguity*, rev. ed. (London, Chatto and Windus, 1949), pp. 2–3.

SONNET LXXIII

That time of year thou mayst in me behold
When yellow leaves, or none, or few, do hang
Upon those boughs which shake against the cold,
Bare ruin'd choirs, where late the sweet birds sang.
In me thou see'st the twilight of such day   5
As after sunset fadeth in the west,
Which by and by black night doth take away,
Death's second self, that seals up all in rest.
In me thou see'st the glowing of such fire,
That on the ashes of his youth doth lie,   10
As the death-bed whereon it must expire
Consum'd with that which it was nourish'd by.
  This thou perceiv'st, which makes thy love more strong,
  To love that well which thou must leave ere long.

William Shakespeare
(1564–1616)

Sound Symbolism in Poetry

NORMAN C. STAGEBERG
and WALLACE L. ANDERSON

In "An Essay on Criticism," Alexander Pope states as a
principle that in the language of poetry "The sound must
seem an Echo to the sense." Yet many of the essays in this
book have stressed the conventional and arbitrary nature of
language symbols. Was Pope just a benighted product of
the unenlightened eighteenth century or is there a glimmer
of truth in his remark? The possibility that there might be
has interested scholars for many years. Recent psycho-
linguistic experiments by such people as F. W. Householder,
Roger Brown, Morton Bloomfield, M. S. Miron, Norman
Markel, and Eric Hamp support the view that there is some
correspondence between sound and sense. The next essay
is a discussion of how sound symbolism operates in poetry.
Two short poems, illustrative of sound symbolism in poetry,
follow the essay.

From *Poetry as Experience* by Norman C. Stageberg and Wallace L. Anderson.
Reprinted by permission of the publisher, the American Book Company, copyright
1952.

Sound symbolism is a natural correspondence between sound and sense. There are words, writes Otto Jespersen, eminent Danish linguist, "which we feel instinctively to be adequate to express the ideas they stand for, and others the sound of which are felt to be more or less incongruous with their signification . . . everybody must feel that the word *roll* . . . is more adequate than the Russian word *katat'*."[1] This is to say, the very sounds of the word *roll* make it more expressive of its sense than the sounds of its Russian synonym *katat'*. Psychological experiments and the study of primitive languages both affirm correspondences of sound and sense.[2] As a simple example of psychological evidence, try the following experiment on your friends. Show the two drawings reproduced below and ask your friends to match these with the meaningless words *taketa* and *naluma*. If most of them agree about which word goes with which drawing, then it appears likely that some correspondence does exist between the sounds and the visual impressions.[3]

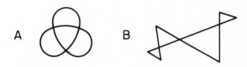

Sound symbolism in poetry is of three kinds: (1) speech sounds which imitate actual sounds; (2) speech sounds which have been so arranged as to make them difficult or easy to articulate; (3) speech

---

[1] *Language, Its Nature, Development, and Origin* (London, George Allen and Unwin, 1922), p. 398.

[2] See, for example:
Edward Sapir, "A Study in Phonetic Symbolism," *Selected Writings of Edward Sapir* (Berkeley, University of California Press, 1949), pp. 61–72.
Wolfgang Köhler, *Gestalt Psychology* (New York, Liveright Publishing Corp., 1929), p. 242.

[3] Adapted from Wolfgang Köhler, *Gestalt Psychology* (New York, Liveright Publishing Corp., 1929), pp. 242–243. See also G. W. Hartmann, *Gestalt Psychology* (New York, The Ronald Press Company, 1935), pp. 147–148.
Also: "There is no doubt that synaesthetic combinations and associations permeate all languages and that these correspondences have been, quite rightly, exploited and elaborated by the poets." René Wellek and Austin Warren, *Theory of Literature* (New York, Harcourt, Brace, & World, Inc., 1949), p. 164.

sounds which in themselves suggest meaning; these are called phonetic intensives.

ONOMATOPOEIA.   The simplest kind of sound symbolism consists of speech sounds which imitate actual sounds, such as we hear in the words *sizz* and *roar*. Such imitation is called onomatopoeia. Onomato-poetic words are found in many languages. For example, the meaning of the English onomatopoetic word *murmur* is expressed by *omumu* in Tahitian, by *murmuru* in Tamil, and by *marmara-* in Sanskrit. In Zulu the word *bomboloza* means to rumble in the bowels.

The human speech organs, however, are incapable of articulating with exactness many of the sounds of nature; hence the speech sounds used to represent natural sounds are often only approximate. For instance the English *whisper*, the French *chucoter*, the German *flüstern* — the English *bow-wow* and the French *gnaf-gnaf* — are all attempts, inexact but suggestive, to represent natural sounds. The reason for the success of such inexactly imitative sounds has been explained by the English philologist Henry Bradley, who has pointed out that the resemblance of an onomatopoetic word to the sound it names

. . . consists not so much in similarity of impression on the ear as in similarity of mental suggestion. For instance, it is not at all literally true that a gun, or a heavy body impinging on a door, "says bang." But the sequence of the three sounds of which the word consists is of such a nature that it can easily be uttered with force, so as to suggest the startling effect of a sudden violent noise, while the final consonant admits of being prolonged to express the notion of a con-tinued resonance. In this instance and in many others, the so-called "imitative" word represents an inarticulate noise not so much by way of an echo as sym-bolically. That is to say, the elements composing the sound of the word combine to produce a mental effect which we recognize as analogous to that produced by the noise.[4]

As examples of onomatopoeia in poetry we may cite Pope's *the torrent roars;* Nashe's bird calls, *cuckoo, jug-jug, pu-we, to-witta woo;* and Poe's description of the susurrus of silk, *the silken sad uncertain rustling*.

An onomatopoetic word may express, not only a sound, but the being which produces the sound, as in the English *peeweet*, in the Australian *twonk*, which means frog, and in the Annamese *cupcup*, which means a tiger, the sounds resembling those made by the tiger when

---

[4] *The Making of English* (New York, The Macmillan Company, and London, Collier-Macmillan, Ltd., 1904), p. 156.

stalking his prey. An onomatopoetic word may also express the sound plus the movement that causes it, as in *tap* and *bubble*, *e.g.*, Tennyson's

Bubbled the nightingale and heeded not.[5]

Words sometimes lose their onomatopoetic quality as in the course of time they undergo changes of sound. For example, the Latin *pipio*, a peeping bird, is now English *pigeon*, its original imitative force having been lost through a series of sound changes. But language also takes on new onomatopoetic words as human beings invent new combinations of sounds that seem expressive of meaning. If, for instance, we should be told that a car *whooshed* by or that a *yakity-yak* issued from a room in the women's dormitory, we should have no difficulty in understanding these imitative words, even though we had never heard them before.

EXERCISE

Point out the onomatopoetic words in the following passages.

1. [DESCRIPTION OF THE SOUNDS OF SERPENTS]
                A dismal universal hiss
                                        John Milton

2.   . . . the sea, playing on the yellow sand,
                Sends forth a rattling murmur to the land.
                                        Christopher Marlowe

3. [DESCRIPTION OF THE SOUND OF ICE-LADEN BRANCHES]
                . . . they click upon themselves.
                                        Robert Frost

4.   The myriad shriek of wheeling ocean-fowl,
            The league-long roller thundering on the reef,
            The moving whisper of huge trees that branched
            And blossomed in the zenith, or the sweep
            Of some precipitous rivulet to the wave.   5
                                        Alfred, Lord Tennyson

5.   When the hounds of spring are on winter's traces,
                The mother of months in meadow or plain
            Fills the shadows and windy places
                With lisp of leaves and ripple of rain.
                                        Algernon C. Swinburne

[5] Of this line from *The Princess*, Tennyson remarked:
"When I was in a friend's garden, I heard a nightingale singing with such a frenzy of passion that it was unconscious of everything else, and not frightened though I came and stood quite close beside it. I saw its eye flashing and felt the air bubble in my ear through the vibration." *The Works of Tennyson*, with notes by the author, ed. by Hallam, Lord Tennyson (New York, The Macmillan Company, 1923 edition), p. 916.

6.   I hear lake water lapping with low sounds by the shore.[6]

William Butler Yeats

7.   And the plashing of waterdrops
            In the marble fountain
            Comes down the garden paths.[7]

Amy Lowell

8.   The moan of doves in immemorial elms
            And murmuring of innumerable bees.[8]

Alfred, Lord Tennyson

9.   How often, these hours, have I heard the monotonous
        crool of a dove.[9]

Walter de la Mare

EASE OF ARTICULATION.   The second kind of sound symbolism consists of speech sounds which have been so arranged as to make them difficult or easy to articulate. Clusters of consonant sounds which require difficult or labored muscular effort seem appropriate for the description of difficult or violent movement, or for harsh effects, *e.g.*, Pope's

When Ajax strives some rock's vast weight to throw.

On the other hand, words that move easily in utterance, unimpeded by difficulty of articulation, seem fitting for the description of smooth and easy movement, *e.g.*, Milton's description of the road from the universe to Hell,

Smooth, easy, inoffensive down to Hell.

Here the effortless transitions between *smooth* and *easy* and *inoffensive* suggest the easiness of the descent.

[6] From William Butler Yeats, *Collected Poems* (New York, The Macmillan Company, 1928; renewed 1956 by Georgie Yeats).
[7] From Amy Lowell, *Complete Poetical Works* (Boston, Houghton Mifflin Company, 1955).
[8] If the sounds in these lines are reproduced in a line of different meaning, *e.g.*,

More ordure never will renew out midden's pure manure,

the suggestiveness of the original is lost. The lesson is clear: onomatopoeia cannot by itself convey meaning; it can only fortify the sound impressions described by meaningful words. This example is taken from Laura Riding and Robert Graves, *A Survey of Modernist Poetry* (Garden City, New York, Doubleday & Company, Inc., 1928), p. 37.
[9] From Walter de la Mare, *Rhymes and Verses* (London, The Society of Authors, 1923).

EXERCISE

1. Of the two passages below by Milton the first describes the opening of the gates of Hell; the second, the opening of the gates of Heaven. Point out how the sounds help to indicate the manner of the opening of each.

   a.   Then in the key-hole turns
       Th' intricate wards, and every bolt and bar
       Of massy iron or solid rock with ease
       Unfast'ns. On a sudden op'n fly,
       With impetuous recoil and jarring sound,   5
       Th' infernal doors, and on their hinges grate
       Harsh thunder.

   b.   Heaven op'n'd wide
       Her ever-during gates, harmonious sound
       On golden hinges moving.

2. The two following passages by Milton deal with movement. The first describes Satan's struggle as he makes his difficult way through a turbulent chaos. The second describes a dance of nature. In what parts of these lines do the sounds themselves seem to reinforce the sense?

   a.   So he with difficulty and labour hard,
        Moved on, with difficulty and labour he.

   b.   The sounds and seas with all their finny drove,
        Now to the moon in wavering morrice move,
        And on the tawny sands and shelves
        Trip the pert fairies and the dapper elves;

3. In the following poem by Thomas Hardy there are many consonant combinations that are hard to say. These consist of the end group in a word plus the beginning consonants of the following word. Read the poem aloud to find out these consonant clusters and see what purpose they serve in the poem as a whole.

   IN TENEBRIS, I

   Wintertime nighs;
   But my bereavement-pain
   It cannot bring again:
       Twice no one dies.

   Flower-petals flee;   5
   But, since it once hath been,
   No more that severing scene
       Can harrow me.

> Birds faint in dread:
> I shall not lose old strength   *10*
> In the lone frost's black length:
> Strength long since fled!
>
> Leaves freeze to dun;
> But friends cannot turn cold
> This season as of old   *15*
> For him with none.
>
> Tempests may scath;
> But love cannot make smart
> Again this year his heart
> .   Who no heart hath.   *20*
>
> Black is night's cope;
> But death will not appal
> One who, past doubtings all,
> Waits in unhope.

Thomas Hardy

PHONETIC INTENSIVES.[10]   The third kind of sound symbolism consists of speech sounds which in themselves suggest meaning; these are
called phonetic intensives.[11] An example occurs in the word *flare*,
whose initial sounds, [fl], carry a suggested meaning of moving light.
The origin of the association between phonetic intensives and their
meanings is unclear. For instance, we do not know whether the initial
[fl] in some words suggests moving light because of some inherent fitness
between the sounds [fl] and their meaning, or because the accidents
of linguistic history have produced words like *flash, flare, flame, flicker*,
whose initial [fl]s and similar meanings have caused [fl] to become
associated with moving light. Nevertheless, words containing such
phonetic intensives may have a special intensity because the denotation
of the word as a whole is strengthened by the suggested meanings of
some of the sounds it contains. Let us examine the word *glimmer* as an
example. Its [gl] has behind it a meaning of light, borne out by such
words as *glow, glare, glint, gleam, glisten;* its [ɪ] suggests smallness, as in
dim, bit, sip, pin, chip, slim; its [ɚ] indicates repetition, as in *twitter,
flicker, flutter, sputter, chatter.* Thus these three sounds in *glimmer* suggest
the meaning of a small, repeatedly moving light, and in so doing
intensify the denotative sense of the word as a whole.

[10] Known also as "phonesthemes."
[11] For the pronunciation of the symbols given in brackets, see Table of Sound
Symbols on page 308.

Of the many phonetic intensives found in poetry, we shall discuss only a few here.

Three pairs of sounds are employed with great frequency. The vowels [u], as in *doom*, and [o], as in *woe*, are used to suggest a state of feeling that may be loosely described by terms like *melancholy, unhappiness*, and *mournfulness;* thus words like *gloom, forlorn, moan, sorrow* are in frequent use, and the [u] or [o] sounds may dominate a passage concerned with unhappiness. The vowels [i], as in *peep*, and [ɪ], as in *drip*, suggest smallness, exemplified in *wee, teeny, thin, wink, flicker, trickle.* At the ends of words the sounds [l], spelt -*le*, and [ɚ], spelt -*er*, suggest the frequent repetition of an action. Of these our language has countless examples, such as *clatter, jingle, glitter, sparkle, twinkle, ripple, mutter, shatter, trickle.* In some words, a closing [l] suggests the repetition not of an action but of some visual detail, as in *dapple, stipple, freckle, bramble, bristle.*[12]

Of the consonants used as phonetic intensives we have already mentioned [fl] for moving light and [gl] for light. Among others at the beginnings of words, [b] gives the impression of impact, as in *bang, bump, bounce, bat;* [bl] carries the idea of impetus and use of breath or air, as in *blow, blast, bluster, blizzard;* [gr] suggests roughness and coarseness, as in *grind, grit, gravel, gride, grate;* [skr] indicates a grating impact or sound, as in *scratch, scrape, scrabble, scrannel;* [sp] indicates a point, as in *spire, spark, spot, spout, spike, spade;* [str] has the sense of thinness and narrowness, as in *strait, strip, stream, strap, street.*

Of the consonants at the end of words [p], [t], and [k] give the sense of an abrupt stoppage of movement, whereas [ʃ], spelt -*sh*, indicates an unabrupt stoppage of movement. These contrasting effects become evident when we compare *clap* with *clash*, *bat* with *bash*, and *smack* with *smash*. In the end position an [n] or [ŋ], spelt -*ng*, after a vowel suggests resonance, as in *clang*.

Knowledge of the meanings of phonetic intensives is sometimes helpful in understanding why particular words in poems seem to be especially appropriate and even inevitable. A double caution, however, is needed. First, we must bear in mind that this kind of sound symbolism is operative only when the sense of the word as a whole is related to the sense of the phonetic intensive which it contains. The [fl] in *flea*, for

[12] In a study of over 600 English monosyllables, Professor F. W. Householder found that the vowel [ʌ], as in *mud*, has, in the large majority of cases, a general meaning of "undesirable." "On the Problem of Sound Meaning, an English Phonestheme," *Word*, 2:83–84 (1946).

example, and the [ɪ] in *big* have no suggestive power because the potential meanings of these sounds, respectively moving light and smallness, are outside the areas of meaning of the words themselves. Second, we must understand that an automatic stimulus-response relationship does not exist between the phonetic intensives and their imputed meanings. Rather, the meanings are latent, and rise to the surface of consciousness only when the enclosing context — its sense, feeling, and general import — offers conditions favorable to their emergence. Such conditions may be brought about by a poet's delicate and sensitive handling of language, and it is then that these intensives flash into life and help create that vividness and intensity of experience that is sometimes attributed to "word magic." For example, the atmosphere of the next poem, with its slow rhythm and low-keyed imagery, builds up a feeling of sadness. In this context the [o] sounds release their latent suggestiveness to reinforce the total impression.

> ALL DAY I HEAR
> All day I hear the noise of waters
>   Making moan,
> Sad as the sea-bird is, when going
>   Forth alone,
> He hears the winds cry to the waters'   5
>   Monotone.
>
> The grey winds, the cold winds are blowing
>   Where I go.
> I hear the noise of many waters
>   Far below.   10
> All day, all night, I hear them flowing
>   To and fro.[13]
>
> *James Joyce*

On the contrary, the [o] sounds have no suggestion of melancholy in

> More hope arose within his joyous heart
> As, note by note, the bugles nearer blew.

because the context is not sympathetic to such a meaning.

The phonetic intensive in a word may be given special emphasis by the repetition of the sound in other words in the passage. A. E. Housman, for example, uses this means of strengthening the effect of *snap:* "And sharp the link of life will *snap.*"

---

[13] From *Collected Poems* by James Joyce. Copyright 1918 by B. W. Huebsch, Inc., 1946 by Nora Joyce. Reprinted by permission of The Viking Press, Inc., the executors of the James Joyce Estate, and Jonathan Cape, Ltd.

EXERCISE

In the italicized words of the following quotations point out each phonetic intensive and its suggested meaning.

1.   She is a winsome *wee* thing.

Robert Burns

2.   Now fades the *glimmering* landscape on the sight.

Thomas Gray

3.   A late lark *twitters* from the quiet skies.

William E. Henley

4.   . . . crickets *jingle* there.

Wilfred Owen

5.   *Blow, blow*, thou winter wind.

William Shakespeare

6.   The *moan* of multitudes in *woe*.

John Masefield

7.   The birds sit *chittering* in the thorn.

Robert Burns

8.   The naked stars . . . *glinting* on the puddles.

Siegfried Sassoon

9.   Down the road someone is practicing scales
        The notes like little fishes vanish with a *wink*
        of tails.[14]

Louis Macneice

10. [A FOLK PRAYER]
        From ghoulies and ghosties and long-legged beasties
        And things that go *bump* in the night,
        Good Lord, deliver us.

Anonymous

11.   . . . the *flickering* gunnery rumbles.

Wilfred Owen

12. [DESCRIPTION OF THE SONG OF A WOODLARK]
        Teevo, cheevo cheevio chee:
        O where, what can that be?
        Weedio-weedio: there again!
        So tiny a *trickle* of song-strain.[15]

Gerard Manley Hopkins

[14] From Louis Macneice, *Collected Poems*, 1925–1948. New York: Oxford University Press © 1963.
[15] From Gerard Manley Hopkins, *Poems of Gerard Manley Hopkins*. New York: Oxford University Press, copyright 1918.

13.   This is the way the world ends
                   Not with a *bang* but a *whimper*.[16]

                                           T. S. Eliot

14.   I turned about and looked where branches break
           The *glittering* reaches of the flooded lake.[17]

William Butler Yeats

15.   Three jolly gentlemen
                       At break of day
                   Came *clitter-clatter* down the stairs
                   And galloped away.[18]

Walter de la Mare

16.   The mugger *cracked* his whip and sang.

W. W. Gibson

17.   The moon, *dwindled* and *thinned* to a fringe of
           a fingernail held to the candle.[19]

Gerard Manley Hopkins

18.   When will return the glory of your prime?
           No more—Oh, never *more*!

Percy Bysshe Shelley

19.   [DESCRIPTION OF A SALOON BAR]
                            . . . the *glush* of
           squirting taps plus *slush* of foam knocked off.[20]

E. E. Cummings

20.   Water *ruffled* and *speckled* by galloping wind.

F. S. Flint

21.   What sound was dearest in his native dells?
           The mellow *lin-lan-lone* of evening bells.

Alfred, Lord Tennyson

22.   A full sea *glazed* with muffled moonlight.

Alfred, Lord Tennyson

23.   The street-lamp *sputtered*,
                   The street-lamp *muttered*.[21]

T. S. Eliot

[16] From T. S. Eliot, *Collected Poems of T. S. Eliot, 1909–1935*. New York: Harcourt, Brace and World, Inc.
[17] From W. B. Yeats, *Collected Poems of William Butler Yeats*. New York: The Macmillan Company, copyright 1928, 1952.
[18] From Walter de la Mare, *Rhymes and Verses*. London: Society of Authors.
[19] *Op. cit.*
[20] From E. E. Cummings, *Fifty Poems*. New York: Duell, Sloan and Pearce, copyright 1939. Copyright 1940 by E. E. Cummings.
[21] *Op. cit.*

24. [DESCRIPTION OF THE STRIDENT PIPES OF SHEPHERDS]
    And when they list, their lean and flashy songs
    Grate on their *scrannel* pipes of wretched straw.

                                                John Milton

25. [DESCRIPTION OF A SNAKE AT A WATER TROUGH]
    He sipped with his *straight* mouth . . .
    And *flickered* his two-forked tongue . . .[22]

                                                D. H. Lawrence

26. [DESCRIPTION OF A KNIGHT, ENTERING A DARK CAVE]
    His *glist'ring* armour made
    A little *glooming* light, much like a shade.

                                                Edmund Spenser

27. [DESCRIPTION OF THE CHARIOT OF THE SON OF GOD]
    And from about him fierce Effusion roll'd
    Of smoke and *bickering* fire, and *sparkles* dire.

                                                John Milton

Bredon Hill

A. E. HOUSMAN

The following poem presents a life-death opposition with a
corresponding contrast of mood. The change of mood from
joy to gloom is accompanied by, and strengthened by, a
change in imagery that moves from a summer scene to a
winter one. Sound symbolism also plays a supporting role.
At what points and by what specific means does sound
function symbolically in "Bredon Hill"? The name of the
hill, by the way, is pronounced as if it were spelled Breedon.

[22] From D. H. Lawrence, *Collected Poems*. Copyright 1929 by Jonathan Cape
and Harrison Smith, Inc., 1957 by Frieda L. Rangli.

From "A Shropshire Lad"—Authorised Edition—from *The Collected Poems of A. E.
Housman*. Copyright 1939, 1940, © 1959 by Holt, Rinehart and Winston, Inc.
Reprinted by permission of Holt, Rinehart and Winston, Inc., The Society of
Authors, and Jonathan Cape, Ltd.

In summertime on Bredon
  The bells they sound so clear;
Round both the shires they ring them
  In steeples far and near,
  A happy noise to hear.   *5*

Here of a Sunday morning,
  My love and I would lie,
And see the coloured counties,
  And hear the larks so high
  About us in the sky.   *10*

The bells would ring to call her
  In valleys miles away:
'Come all to church, good people;
  Good people, come and pray.'
  But here my love would stay.   *15*

And I would turn and answer
  Among the springing thyme,
'Oh, peal upon our wedding,
  And we will hear the chime,
  And come to church in time.'   *20*

But when the snows at Christmas
  On Bredon top were strown,
My love rose up so early
  And stole out unbeknown
  And went to church alone.   *25*

They tolled the one bell only,
  Groom there was none to see,
The mourners followed after,
  And so to church went she,
  And would not wait for me.   *30*

The bells they sound on Bredon,
  And still the steeples hum.
'Come all to church, good people,' —
  Oh, noisy bells, be dumb;
  I hear you, I will come.   *35*

The Harbor

CARL SANDBURG

The basic structure of "The Harbor" is relatively simple. It consists of two contrastive images. But though the structure is simple, the poem has a rich complexity because there are so many points of contrast—in imagery, movement, feeling, idea, and sound. Read the poem aloud slowly and carefully. Note the patterns of sound in both vowels and consonants. Study the use of sound in relation to the imagery and ideas in the poem. Then write a paper entitled "Sound Symbolism in 'The Harbor.' "

Passing through huddled and ugly walls
By doorways where women haggard
Looked from their hunger-deep eyes,
Haunted with shadows of hunger-hands,
Out from the huddled and ugly walls,   *5*
I came sudden, at the city's edge,
On a blue burst of lake,
Long lake waves breaking under the sun
On a spray-flung curve of shore;
And a fluttering storm of gulls,   *10*
Masses of great gray wings
And flying white bellies
Veering and wheeling free in the open.

From *Chicago Poems* by Carl Sandburg. Copyright 1916 by Holt, Rinehart and Winston, Inc. Copyright 1944 by Carl Sandburg. Reprinted by permission of Holt, Rinehart and Winston, Inc., and Jonathan Cape, Ltd.

Grammatical Analysis and Literary Criticism

SUMNER IVES

In poetry, grammatical structures tend to deviate from the normal because of restraints like rhyme, meter, and compression which the poet accepts and within which he writes. Thus a first step in approaching a poem is to make certain of the grammatical relationships. For example, what is the subject of the verb, what modifies what, and which structures are parallel with which others? Only when we are clear about these relationships, and of course know the meanings of the words, are we ready to read a poem as a work of art. Sumner Ives, who examines here the grammatical relationships of a particular poem, is a linguist and Professor of English at Syracuse University and the author of A New Handbook for Writers.

One of the chief concerns of both modern linguists and of modern literary criticism is structure. Both assume that a structure is more than an accumulation of primary items. Both look on the object which they study — in one case, say, a sentence, in the other, say, a poem — as essentially a kind of gestalt, in which there are physical items and there are stable relations between these items, so that any unsystematic rearrangement of the items is destructive to the whole. Both regard the object which they study as an instance of social interaction and as an instance of purposive activity. And both accept non-uniqueness of solutions. That is, a linguist assumes that more than one analysis is possible, although he may prefer one of these to the others. And a large number of literary critics accept the notion that more than one poem may derive from a particular arrangement of words on paper, although a critic may personally find one more acceptable than others. (I do not say that a particular arrangement necessarily represents more than one poem; I merely provide for the possibility.)

If we assume that a poem is an utterance, something said in a language, and that literature implies both writing and reading, the activities of linguists and literary critics are related. These assumptions

Revised by the author from *Monograph Series on Languages and Linguistics, No. 13*. Reprinted by permission of the publisher, the Georgetown University Press, copyright 1962.

imply a third: that a critic must first discover a physical poem; he must first read it as a linguistic utterance before he can assess it as a critic. He must settle on what poem is, for him, represented by the physical symbols of language, spoken or written, within which the poetic idea is embedded. It is in this initial effort, this attempt to find a poem to examine critically, that grammatical analysis is not merely useful but inevitable. If linguistics does its work well, it provides the literary critic with a sharper and more comprehensive perception into the workings of the linguistic medium, with a better methodology for applying this perception, and with a better terminology for transmitting the results of his perception to others. Until he finds a particular gestalt of tangible linguistic elements, the problem of the literary critic is within the area of the linguist. (Of course, there is some indeterminacy here, some allowance for variant solutions, but the linguist can provide a list of possibilities and some guide to probabilities.)

To illustrate this pre-critical step, I have prepared a limited presentation of the grammatical structure in Archibald MacLeish's "You, Andrew Marvel." Although somewhat unconventional, this structure can be described well enough for this purpose with even the limited resources of traditional terminology. I do not claim that this presentation is a complete linguistic analysis of the poem, but it does reveal some aspects of the physical poem on which critical analysis can be performed. When I have carried this kind of analysis to its ultimate limits, making all the probabilistic decisions which are required, when I have considered the items lexically and pointed out the indicated semantic relationships, and when I have added phonological patterns which run concurrent with these results, my work as a linguist is complete. Further consideration of the poem is an operation of literary criticism. I consider what critics call sensibility to be necessary to useful critical analysis, and I think that sensibility becomes more valuable with experience. I also grant that the real worth of this poem, as distinct from the display of linguistic virtuosity which this analysis reveals, must await that further consideration which is the province of literary criticism. However, I feel reasonably sure that some such analysis as I have provided, done intuitively or systematically, mentally or on paper, is a necessary prelude to its consideration as literature.

I shall not discuss this diagrammatic representation in detail, or discuss all the syntactic decisions made within it, some of which are certainly probable rather than certain. One instance of double syntax is indicated by the broken line in the eighth stanza. In fact, the poem is full of the kind of syntactic ambiguity which Empson speaks of. For example, one can argue that the final word in the fourth stanza is a noun and not, as I have indicated, a verb. My interpretation is based on the presence, in the preceding line, of the adverbial phrase "through the twilight," and it requires that "westward" be regarded as having a nominal function. The solid lines connect subjects with verbs and verbs with objects or complements. Note also that I have supplied a few words not in the original, those written with capital letters. These are not random insertions, nor are they based on semantic considerations. I think that all can be justified solely on syntactic grounds.

First, note that stanzas two, three, and four constitute one grouping matched by a grouping consisting of stanzas five, six, and seven. As I have interpreted the syntax, the first two stanzas in each group begin with the same infinitive and express movement of a sort by means of other infinitives. The final stanza in each group begins with a descriptive statement about a scene and ends with a statement that something is moving in this scene. In stanza four, "travelers pass" and in stanza seven, "sails loom and disappear." The eighth stanza and line 9a, which is spaced like a separate stanza in the original, recapitulates this pattern on a smaller scale. The phrase "that land," in line 8d, recalls stanza four, and the phrase "on the sea," in line 9a, recalls the seventh stanza. The final three lines constitute a summary of the pattern. Line 9b repeats the pattern of the first two lines. Line 9c has two parts in parallel structure. The choice of words is, it seems, significant. "Swift" is active and fits the verbs of stanzas two and three: "creep," "grow," "take," and "change." And "secretly" fits verbs of stanzas five and six: "darken," "steal on," "deepen," and "fade out." Then the syntax of the final line recalls the syntax of stanzas four and seven, each the concluding stanza of a section, in that this line and these stanzas contain finite verb forms.

The poem as a whole gives an effect of very slow, almost glacial movement. It contains only four finite verb forms — one at the end of the first set of stanzas, two in parallel structure near the end of the second set, and one in the final line of the poem, a line that, grammatically echoes these stanzas at the ends of internal sections. The poem has three marked infinitives, all instances of "to feel," a verb that is relatively static in meaning. It has fourteen unmarked infinitives, two gerunds, and three participles. All the gerunds and participles are in the first three stanzas. It has several words ending in -ward, an element that implies action but does not denote it. These are placed in strategic spots: line 1b, line 4d (end of one internal set), and line 7b, in the stanza that ends the second internal set. None of these words is an adverb, although *-ward* is often an adverbial ending. Thus, the movement of the poem is carried primarily by nonfinite rather than by finite verb forms and by non-adverbial elements with adverbial endings.

Whatever else may be said about this poem, and a great deal more can be said about it, it has design. It illustrates the thesis that the poetic idea and the poetic form should be welded together — that structure and meaning should be congruent, that pattern and content should be integrated, that the two parts of the symbolic experience should be mutually supporting.

You, Andrew Marvell[1]

Archibald MacLeish

(Modifications have been made to indicate grammatical ingredients. The original poem is printed in quatrains, but the first line of the final quatrain is spaced like a separate stanza. All lines are set even to the left margin. In this version, some grammatical parallels are indicated by indentation, and a few words have been added in capital letters. Slash marks indicate major structural divisions within lines, hyphens indicate compounds, and some grammatical elements are indicated thus: FINITE VERBS, *infinitives*, **subjects, objects of verbs.**)

1a   And here face down beneath the sun

 b   And here upon earth's noonward height

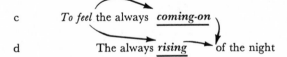

 c   *To feel* the always *coming-on*

 d   The always *rising* of the night

2a   *To feel creep* up the curving east

 b   The earthy **chill** of dusk / and slow

 c   Upon those under-lands the vast

 d   And ever-climbing **shadow** *grow*

<hr />

[1] Archibald MacLeish, *Poems: 1924–1933* (Boston, Houghton Mifflin Company, 1933), p. 58. Reprinted by permission of the publisher.

3a   And *TO FEEL* strange at Ectaban the **trees**

b   *Take* leaf by leaf the *evening* / strange

c   The flooding dark about their knees

d   The **mountains** over Persia *change*

4a   And now at Kermanshah the **gate** IS

b   Dark-empty and the withered **grass**

c   And through the twilight now the late

d   Few **travelers** in the westward PASS

5a   And *TO FEEL* **Baghdad** *darken* and the **bridge**

b   Across the silent river *TO BE* gone

c   And through Arabia the **edge**

d   Of evening *widen* and *steal-on*

6a   And *TO FEEL* *deepen* on Palmyra's street

b   The **wheel-rut** in the ruined stone

c   And **Lebanon** *fade-out* and **Crete**

d   High through the clouds and overblown

7a   And over Sicily the **air** IS

b   Still FLASHING with the landward gulls

c   And LOOM and slowly DISAPPEAR

d   The **sails** above the shadowy hulls

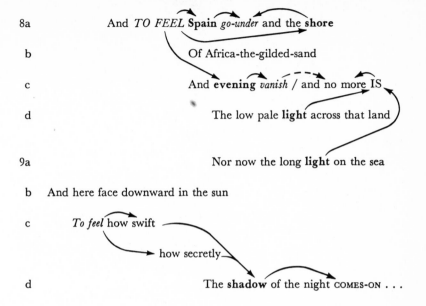

8a   And *TO FEEL* Spain *go-under* and the shore

b   Of Africa-the-gilded-sand

c   And **evening** *vanish* / and no more IS

d   The low pale **light** across that land

9a   Nor now the long **light** on the sea

b   And here face downward in the sun

c   *To feel* how swift

how secretly

d   The **shadow** of the night COMES-ON . . .

SUGGESTED ASSIGNMENTS

The poem below was written by Thomas Gray. It is a satire upon Cambridge University as a seat of ignorance. The poem was probably written upon Gray's return to Cambridge after an absence of three years.

HYMN TO IGNORANCE

A FRAGMENT

Hail, horrors, hail! ye ever gloomy bowers,
Ye gothic fanes, and antiquated towers,
Where rushy Camus'[1] slowly-winding flood
Perpetual draws his humid train of mud:
Glad I revisit thy neglected reign,   5
Oh take me to thy peaceful shade again.

But chiefly thee, whose influence breathed from high
Augments the native darkness of the sky;
Oh, Ignorance! soft salutary power!
Prostrate with filial reverence I adore.   10
Thrice hath Hyperion[2] roll'd his annual race,
Since weeping I forsook thy fond embrace.

[1] The river Cam. [eds.]
[2] A sun god of the Greeks. [eds.]

> Oh say, successful dost thou still oppose
> Thy leaden aegis 'gainst our ancient foes?
> Still stretch, tenacious of thy right divine,   15
> The massy sceptre o'er thy slumb'ring line?
> And dews Lethean through the land dispense
> To steep in slumbers each benighted sense?
>
> If any spark of wit's delusive ray
> Break out, and flash a momentary day,   20
> With damp, cold touch forbid it to aspire
> And huddle up in fogs the dangerous fire. . . .

As you read this poem, did you keep the grammatical relationships clear? Let's see. In line seven, what is the grammatical function of *thee* in the sentence? Remember here that the eighteenth century forms of the personal pronoun in the second person singular were: nominative, *thou;* possessive, *thy;* objective, *thee.* In line seventeen what other verbs is *dispense* parallel with, and what is *dews Lethean* the object of?

Pippa's Song: Two Attempts at Structural Criticism

ARCHIBALD A. HILL

An eminent linguist here takes issue with an eminent literary critic over the interpretation of a simple lyric by Browning. His key principle—that form gives meaning—is one that is basic to descriptive linguistics but also invests a good deal of literary criticism. Professor Hill is the executive secretary of the Linguistic Society of America and author of *Introduction to Linguistic Structures.*

> The year's at the spring
> And day's at the morn;
> Morning's at seven;
> The hill-side's dew-pearled;

From The University of Texas *Studies in English,* 35:51–56 (1956). Reprinted by permission of the publisher, University of Texas Press.

The lark's on the wing;   5
The snail's on the thorn:
God's in his heaven —
All's right with the world!

John Crowe Ransom, in an able and important critical study, recently remarked of "Pippa's Song" that its last two lines were "a tag of identification so pointed as to be embarrassing." Thereafter he went on to justify the statement:

She spends three lines dating the occasion very precisely. . . . Then come three details which constitute the concrete: the hillside, the lark, the snail. . . . And that would be the poem; except that she must conclude by putting in her theological Universal. . . .[1]

Ransom's approach is structural. He sees in the poem a pattern of two three-line groups followed by a two-line conclusion. He condemns the conclusion because it does not seem to be properly related to the preceding material. It would appear that the units with which he has operated are essentially semantic: units of time, units of concrete experience, and a unit of abstract theological universality. If the operating units are valid, his statement of the structure and the resultant evaluation follow almost inevitably.

His units are not, however, the only ones that might be chosen. In metrical structure the poem is remarkably rigid, each line being ended by a terminal juncture, with no terminal junctures within the lines.[2] Each juncture-group has the grammatical form of a sentence, with subject, verb, and complement. The lines of the poem therefore invite the interpretation that they are the normal first segments, since they are defined as units by their formal and grammatical structure. Even at this stage, divergence from Ransom's segmentation results. Ransom has taken the last two lines as one unit, not two, because both are concerned with the "theological Universal." To group them thus, he must disregard the linguistic characteristics which mark line eight as separate from line seven.

Yet the eight separate lines cannot be presumed to be unrelated. A second task is therefore, to search for and describe this relationship, since if the poem has a general pattern it must reside in its parts and

[1] "The Concrete Universal, II," *Kenyon Review*, XVII (1955), 395.
[2] A terminal juncture is, roughly speaking, a sense of pause or break. There are three terminal junctures, which are described by Paul Roberts on page 447 as single bar, double bar, and double cross junctures. [eds.]

their relationship to each other and to the whole. Because the parts are sentences, the relationships between them belong to the study of stylistics (which deals with relationships between sentences) rather than linguistics (which deals with relationships within sentences). Typical stylistic relationships show themselves in the repetition of formal patterns from one sentence to the next.

The first three lines have the grammatical structure of noun, copula, and prepositional phrase headed by a noun. Line four, on the other hand, has the structure of noun, copula, and phrasal modifier. Lines five, six, and seven repeat the structure of the first three lines. Line eight has the structure found in line four: noun, copula, and modifying phrase. There is therefore a formal similarity between lines one, two, and three and lines five, six, and seven, and further similarity between line four and line eight. In form, then, line eight is related to line four, rather than primarily to line seven as Ransom stated. The formal similarity between lines four and eight is backed by their linkage in rhyme.

The relationships so far stated have been arrived at by study of formal characteristics. Such a procedure is similar to that of linguistic analysis. It is true that the subject of analysis is here a printed text, in contrast to the oral material with which linguistics habitually operates. The difference is more apparent than real. Browning's punctuation, like that of English written composition generally, does not give a clear picture of the phonological structure. In analysis of any printed text it is necessary to read it aloud, so that thereafter it can be treated as a spoken utterance. The reading given to the poem is not to be defended as the necessarily right interpretation. It has been checked with several other speakers of English, and can therefore be described as a natural and possible rendering, however it may differ in detail from others.

If formal characteristics have been exhausted, the next step is consideration of lexical meanings. The content of line one, "The year's at the spring," can be stated in general terms. *Year* is a large unit of time, and *spring* is a unit contained within it. Many readers would agree that, in human terms, *spring* is the best of the contained units. The statement that *spring* is the best unit within the year is not forced by the structure of this line. It is a hypothesis to be tested by its results in analysis of the rest of the poem.

Line two, "And day's at the morn," also contains a larger unit of time and a contained unit, though the larger unit of this line is smaller than the larger unit of the first line. When sentences are stylistically linked by structure, it is to be expected that there will be analogies in meaning as well. If the hypothesis about line one is correct, it is reasonable to suppose that *morn* is also the best of the contained entities.

In line three, "Morning's at seven," there is once more a larger unit of time, and a contained unit. By stylistic implication, the contained unit is again the best of its group. There is, moreover, an additional fact which emerges from line three. *Morning* is a form exchangeable with *morn*, so that the contained unit of line two is the containing unit of line three. In stylistic relations, particularly those in the relatively permanent form of literature, spans of interpretation can spread backward as well as forward, and it is therefore possible to reinterpret the relationships in the earlier lines. The entities in the first three lines descend in a general order from larger to smaller. Yet it is possible that the pattern is even more precisely parallel and that *spring* and *day* are in the same relationship to each other as *morn* and *morning*. The point cannot be settled, since it is obvious that *spring* and *day* are not exchangeable, but the suggestion is certainly there. A reasonable reading might therefore assume that the structure of the poem has equated the two words. The first three lines can now be given in a schematic statement of the stylistic structure which emerges from lexical examination:

> Large A is at contained B (its best)
> Smaller B is at contained C (its best)
> Still smaller C is at contained D (its best).

In the grammatically different line four, "The hill-side's dew-pearled," *hill-side* can be defined as a part of the physical scene. In contrast to a unit like *world*, in line eight, it is a small and immediate part. The phrasal modifier, *dew-pearled*, indicates a state in which the hillside is certainly attractive. A generalized statement is "Little X is good Y." Line four, though related to line eight, is also related to the lines which precede. Carrying forward the hypothesis that the contained units are the best of the several groups, it is possible to see in the attractive state of the hillside a similar excellence: being dew-pearled is its best state. The formulaic statement should therefore be revised to "little X is good Y (its best)." Further relationships between the first three lines and line four are not explicitly indicated, but as stated earlier there is a change in grammatical form and content with line four. The tightly knit sequence of the first three lines is broken by a statement of a different sort, though one which is related to the preceding. In linguistic analysis, as in the everyday interpretation of speech, it is a sensible procedure to settle on the interpretation of highest probability and disregard all others. There is no reason why this technique should not be used here. The most probable interpretation of the meaning of such an incremental change is that the relationship is one of cause and result. *Post hoc ergo propter hoc* may not be good logic, but it is a good probabilistic interpretation of stylistic sequences. A final statement of line four is then: "Therefore small X is Y (its best)."

Now that the lexical and stylistic pattern has been tentatively established, the rest of the poem can be more quickly described. Lines five, six, and seven move in general from small objects to large. The objects are living beings, and the prepositional phrases which follow the copulas are, by analogy from the content of the first four lines, the proper and best place for each of these beings. It is true that *wing* is not strictly a place in the same sense as *thorn* or *heaven*, but the minor difference is overridden by stylistic similarity to the surrounding sentences. The order from small to large is a reversal of the order in the first group of lines. Yet this ascending order is itself reversed by lines five and six, where *snail* is smaller than *lark*. The break has a startling result in that it brings the extremes of the scale, *snail* and *God*, into immediate juxtaposition. We can therefore represent lines five, six, and seven thus:

> Small E is on F (its best place)
> Smaller G is on H (its best place)
> Large I is in J (its best place).

Line eight is also readily describable. It is, like line four, a result — "therefore the large scene is at its best." The statement that the poem deals with best entities and states has up to this time been a hypothesis — not contradicted at any point, but without confirmation. The last line furnishes explicit confirmation in the words "all's right." A final statement of the pattern of the poem is now: three analogically related descending statements and their results on a small scale, then three analogically related ascending statements and their results on a large scale. The surprise in structure is the departure from order which brings the smallest entities of the second part into contiguity. . . .

Ransom has called the last two lines a well-schooled theological tag. Pippa breaks her strict analogical pattern to bring *snail* and *God* together. The juxtaposition does not correlate with the way we expect theologians to talk about God. It correlates, instead, with the way we expect children to talk of Him, in concrete and simple terms. Pippa's statement also correlates with our belief that simplicity like hers often contains insights somehow better than those found in the words of the most philosophically sophisticated. One is tempted to find, in the breaking of the pattern Browning has established for her, a sort of model of the cultural contradiction in our attitudes toward children. We treat them as not yet perfected human beings, yet we remember the Biblical "out of the mouths of babes and sucklings."

It remains only to state the differences between Ransom's method and that used here. Ransom is structural in his approach, but uses semantically defined units without having worked through the formal linguistic differentia. His method is therefore similar to that of traditional grammar, where a formal word-class, such as nouns, is defined in terms of the semantic count of the class. In contrast, the analysis given here rests on one of the most basic assumptions in linguistics, that it is form which gives meaning and not meaning which gives form. Ransom's assumptions are commonly used by critics, those used here by linguists. Since the two sets of assumptions are correlated with differing kinds of activity, it is impractical to measure which set is the more reasonable. Fortunately the two analyses can be measured otherwise. They must be assumed to be significantly different, since one cannot be mechanically translated into the other. If different, both cannot be true; one must be more complete, more consistent, and more simple than the other. Evaluation may be left to the reader.

A Linguistic Analogy in Literary Criticism

ALAN B. HOWES

Professor Kenneth Pike of the University of Michigan, a leading exponent of tagmemic analysis in linguistics, has developed a theory of particle-wave-field that Alan B. Howes here puts to use in the analysis of three poems. The result will

perhaps remind psychologically minded students of Gestalt
theory. Professor Howes is a member of the English Department at the University of Michigan and is the author of
Yorick and the Critics and *An Outline of English Composition.*

The use of analogy in literary criticism has a respectable tradition
going back at least as far as Aristotle, who took an analogy from
biology when he said that the plot of an epic "should have for its
subject a single action, whole and complete, with a beginning, a
middle, and an end" and thus "resemble a living organism in all its
unity." He used the same analogy in speaking of the necessary "magnitude" of the action imitated in a tragedy, since "a beautiful object,
whether it be a living organism or any whole composed of parts,
must not only have an orderly arrangement of parts, but must also be
of a certain magnitude."[1]

As literary critics, amateur or professional, all writers use this
analogy and others. Whether his audience is an English instructor or
the readers of the *Saturday Review*, the writer often points out the
"organic" unity of works of literature and likewise aims at the same
kind of unity in his own writing: but he often finds it difficult to grasp
a work in its totality, or at least to demonstrate such a grasp in a critical
essay. If he is to write more intelligently about literature, to become a
more competent literary critic, the writer should be constantly looking
for new analogies, new approaches.

Traditionally, the perspectives for arriving at literary insights
have tended to fall into two broad categories: first, the conventional
breakdown into parts — plot, setting, character, and theme for fiction;
or image, idea or theme, metrics, and so on for poetry; and second,
some rather specialized approaches ranging from the Freudian
interpretation to the historical or biographical approach, all reductive
to one degree or another because they insist upon a single perspective
which often tends to limit rather than to enlighten.

Even the more sophisticated and more fruitful specialized approaches such as those described in Reuben Arthur Brower's "The

Revised by the author from *College Composition and Communication* 15:141–144 (1964).
Reprinted with the permission of the National Council of Teachers of English and
Professor Alan B. Howes.

[1] S. H. Butcher, *Aristotle's Theory of Poetry and Fine Art*, 4th ed. (Dover Publications, Inc., 1951), pp. 89, 31.

Speaking Voice" or Cleanth Brooks' "The Language of Paradox," though they provide fresh and stimulating insights, sometimes tempt a writer to apply the theory too rigidly to a literary work where it may not be altogether appropriate. There has been no ideal approach that forced the reader and writer to pay attention in a systematic way to all the parts of a literary work, the interrelationships of those parts, and the whole work as made up of different kinds of parts in interaction. It is hard to resist the temptation either to catalogue separate elements or to apply a specialized approach where it may not work: that is, either to talk about imagery, rhyme scheme, and theme as if they bore no relationship to each other, or to see irony, personas, or Freudian symbols behind every tree.

Thus, when Professor Kenneth Pike suggested to me that perhaps his "model" (as he called it) or "analogy" (as I would call it) of particle, wave, and field, which he had been developing for the study of language, might also be a useful tool in the study of literature, I thought it would be worthwhile to see whether it might help in solving some of the problems I have mentioned. In general terms, the theory behind the model affirms that insights can be complete only when one views things from three separate points of view: first, as segments, collections of details, or smaller units — that is, particles; second, as interrelationships in which boundaries between segments are "smeared" (to use his term) and the individual particles take on new meaning as one perceives a wave-like overlapping among them; and finally, as total contexts or "fields" in which the individual parts become fused into a whole which derives its character from the intersection and inter-relationship of all its parts.

The analogy may be applied to literature at different levels. A word, a rhyme, a line, a stanza, or a major division of a poem, for example, may be seen as particle, viewed along with other particles of like size. (Two separate sonnets might even be viewed as particles within a sonnet sequence.) A wave can involve the overlapping rela-tionship between words, lines, or major divisions of a work. Likewise, though the concept of field would most often be applied to total works, any sizable subdivision — a stanza, an image, a section, even a line — might well be viewed as a field within the larger field of the whole poem. The theory promotes flexibility of perspective, and it may be applied to widely differing works of literature.

Let me illustrate its application to one kind of poem by showing

how it might be used as a tool of literary criticism in discussing Ezra
Pound's two line poem, "In a Station of the Metro":

> The apparition of these faces in the crowd;
> Petals on a wet black bough.[2]

I choose this poem because it represents in little a good many of the
problems of analysis that one has in dealing with longer poems. The
reader's first impression of this poem — in other words, his first vague
perception of field — includes the setting in the Paris subway, as indicated in the title, and the sharp image in which the faces in the crowd
are compared to petals on a wet-black bough. Various connotations
are also a part of the initial impression — especially those associated
with the usual drabness of the subway crowd and those associated
with the freshness of the rain drenched branch of the tree, laden with
petals. The task of analysis is in part to show the relationship of the
two parts of the metaphor and further to see whether this relationship
suggests a thematic statement. At this point, let us see whether the
analogy of particle, wave, and field is of help.

The poem may be seen as consisting of two major particles, represented by the division into two lines, a division which also reflects the
two parts of the metaphor. But there are also other ways of looking
at its "parts." One may take the key words — "apparition," "faces,"
"crowd," "petals," "wet," "black," and "bough." Within the two
major particles, the two parts of the metaphor, there are correspondences: "faces" to "petals" and "crowd" to "bough." Thus each of
these words achieves full meaning only when viewed with the other
and hence there is a wave-like relationship between them. There is
also a correspondence between "apparition" and "petals" — grammatically, the two are equated. And here a further interrelationship is
suggested, with the two meanings of "apparition" (both "appearance"
and "ghostly appearance") serving to join the two parts of the metaphor
with a wave-like motion, since the dual connotations of "apparition"
affect the connotations in the rest of the poem.

Let us return to the "field" or total context of the poem. This context can obviously be viewed in various ways. First of all, there is the
situation in which the poet speaks, the setting, the character of the
speaker, the audience to which he speaks. Second, there is the context

[2] From *Personae* by Ezra Pound. Copyright 1926, 1954 by Ezra Pound. Reprinted by permission of the publishers, New Directions.

of the words, their denotative and connotative dimensions, and of the image with all its details. Finally, there is the context of the traditions of the form — the short, unrhymed poem of irregular rhythm, in this case derived, as Pound tells us, from Japanese haiku. The intersection of these various contexts makes up the field. From the context of the traditions of form we are prepared to have the poem present an insight sharply, using a metaphor from nature. From the context of the situation, we are prepared by the juxtaposition of the scene in the subway and the scene from nature for an insight which will bring seemingly discordant things together. Finally, from the context of the language itself and its connotations we take the final step in seeing beauty in an unlikely place and arriving at an understanding of the theme of the poem. We arrive at this "field" view of the poem, however, only by putting all of these contexts together. We share the wonder of the poet at finding beauty in the unlikely setting of the subway crowd only if we sense the unpromising nature of the scene, follow him in the metaphor he develops with connotations of individual words by which he suggests a new way to view the scene, and accept the validity of the overall aesthetic method he takes of presenting a kind of epiphany, a concisely stated insight drawing upon an image from nature.

Let me give a further illustration of the application of this approach to a rather different kind of poem, though again one consisting of two lines, Robert Frost's "The Secret Sits":

> We dance round in a ring and suppose,
> But the Secret sits in the middle and knows.[3]

Here, to be briefer, one may again take each line as a major particle, and also consider the key words. The parts of the metaphor are somewhat more elusive, because the fusion of the two parts is more complete and only a few details are given, mainly those which create the contrast between "We," "dance," "ring," and "suppose," on the one hand, and "Secret," "sits," "middle," and "knows" on the other. The full meaning of the first line is apparent only when the wave-like overlapping of the contrast, introduced by "But," is complete. In the field, various contexts converge. There are the suggestion of the child's game and all its associations, the religious overtones from the capitalization of "Secret," the somewhat comic effect of the rhyme — all these contribute to the partially comic and amused tone of the whole, which

[3] From *Complete Poems of Robert Frost*. Copyright 1942 by Robert Frost. Reprinted by permission of Holt, Rinehart and Winston.

in turn contributes to the thematic statement: an amused and detached description of the human condition.

One final example with a somewhat different application of the analogy should provide a further test of the theory. William Blake wrote two versions of his poem, "London," versions which appear to say very similar things yet contain rather significant differences.[4] Let us see whether the anaolgy of particle, wave, and field will help to bring out the differences between the two versions:

I wander thro' each dirty street,	I wander thro' each charter'd street,
Near where the dirty Thames does flow,	Near where the charter'd Thames does flow,
And mark in every face I meet	And mark in every face I meet
Marks of weakness, marks of woe.	Marks of weakness, marks of woe.
In every cry of every man,	In every cry of every Man,
In every infant's cry of fear,	In every Infant's cry of fear,
In every voice, in every ban,	In every voice, in every ban,
The mind forg'd manacles I hear.	The mind-forg'd manacles I hear.
How the chimney sweeper's cry	How the Chimney-sweeper's cry
Blackens o'er the churches' walls,	Every black'ning Church appalls;
And the hapless soldier's sigh	And the hapless Soldier's sigh
Runs in blood down palace walls.	Runs in blood down Palace walls.
But most the midnight harlot's curse	But most thro' midnight streets I hear
From every dismal street I hear,	How the youthful Harlot's curse
Weaves around the marriage hearse	Blasts the new born Infant's tear,
And blasts the new born infant's tear.	And blights with plagues the Marriage hearse.

Perhaps the best place to begin is to note the particles in the two versions that are different. There are the changes from "dirty" to "charter'd," "midnight harlot" to "youthful Harlot," and "every dismal street" to "midnight streets," as well as the changes in capitalization. There are also the more drastic changes in line 10 and the rearrangement of the last stanza with the changes especially in the last two lines. Before these differences can be assessed, however, one should try to isolate the significant particles common to both versions. These may be seen as falling into three groups: those concerned with the

---

[4] Actually, Blake's manuscript shows that he went through a series of changes before arriving at a final form for the poem. The version which is printed on the left and which I have called the first version is a kind of composite of early drafts and is printed in this form in the Modern Library edition of *The Complete Poetry and Selected Prose of John Donne and the Complete Poetry of William Blake* (New York, Random House, Inc., 1941), p. 572.

setting (the streets, the river, the churches, the palace), those concerned with the human activity within the scene (the people and their various cries), and those concerned with the social forces which control human activity (the "bans," the "mind-forg'd manacles," the Church and the monarchy as institutions, and the "Marriage hearse"). Looking at the differences between the particles of the two versions, we can note at this point the hint of greater universality through the capitalizations in the second version, the greater dramatic force of "appalls" and of "*youthful* Harlot," and the substitution of "blights with plagues" for "weaves around," with the consequently more powerful indictment of the institution of marriage as not only stifling to freedom but also as indirectly responsible for the spreading of venereal disease.

Though these changes in general add dramatic force to the second version, they do not in themselves explain the difference in effect between the two. This may be seen more clearly through the anaolgy with wave. In both versions there is a dramatic progression from part to part as our perception of the setting and the people in it changes in intensity. In the first version the initial picture of the "dirty" streets and the "dirty Thames" is intensified by the ironic "blackening" of the churches' walls and the midnight scene in the "dismal" streets. Parallel with this is the progressive revelation of human "weakness" and human "woe." The "cry of every man," relatively neutral, takes on more intensity when we come to "every infant's cry of *fear*," and gains further force when we see it in the same context with the "chimney sweeper's cry" and the "hapless soldier's sigh." A climax is reached with the "harlot's curse" which "blasts the new born infant's tear." A third parallel is provided by the development of the social context of the poem. The "bans" and the "mind forg'd manacles," acting through the social institutions of church, monarchy, and marriage, are perceived first to be responsible for the miserable plight of the chimney sweeper, then for the spilling of the soldier's blood, and finally for the "marriage hearse" and the existence of the harlot. The word "most" signals the climactic meeting of the three strands or waves in the last stanza. The "dismal" midnight scene, the curse of the harlot and the tear of the new born infant, and the marriage *hearse* (testimony to the failure of social institutions to allow man fulfillment even in his most basic relationships) all come together in a crescendo of horror at seemingly inescapable human weakness and woe.

The second version has the same three strands or waves, but the wave-like overlapping among the three is more complex. The key here is the substitution of "charter'd" for "dirty." "Dirty" mainly suggests the squalor of the setting (although the "*marks* of weakness, *marks* of woe" pick up a faint echo from "dirty" with the vague suggestion that the dirt of the setting is also found in the faces of its inhabitants). "Dirty" does not have any direct connection with the social strand. "Charter'd," on the other hand, a word with a much richer range of connotation and denotation, unites all three strands. The etymological echo from "chart" (the root word is the same) suggests the pattern of rigidity of streets and river, a pattern which is paralleled by the rigidity of human institutions (the "mind-forg'd manacles") and is also seen as responsible for the "marks" of human weakness and human woe. "Charter'd" in the sense of "hired out" is picked up in the activities of the chimney sweeper and the soldier, and especially of the harlot in the last stanza. The primary meaning of the word, a "written contract between man and man" indicts the society in which such an agreement should bring guarantees of freedom (cf. the Magna Charta), but ironically brings its exact opposite: bans and mind-forged manacles which take away freedom and produce weakness and woe. Thus the chimney sweeper's cry, the soldier's sigh, and the harlot's curse are traced more directly to the nature of society itself. Chartering of human activity through the institutions of church, monarchy, and marriage leads to weakness, woe, fear, poverty, the spilling of blood, disease, and the blighting of relationships between man and woman.

The fields of the two versions show similar differences in complexity. In the first version the physical and social setting is mainly a backdrop against which the plight of human individuals is seen. The chimney sweeper is placed in ironic juxtaposition with the church in the first version, while in the second his cry "appalls" the church. Here again a word with rich connotations creates a more complex pattern of associations, since "appalls" can mean both "cause to grow pale," "overcome with fear," and "cause to fail." Thus the church is seen as bearing responsibility for the chimney sweeper's cry: it has been a part of the chartering and consequent social corruption that has caused chimney sweepers to exist, at the same time that it is indicted by the fact of their existence. Just as the government is responsible for the soldier's plight, the church bears responsibility for the plight of the chimney sweeper. The whole third stanza of the second version has thus sacrificed the neat grammatical parallelism of the first version in order to gain a closer parallel in situation.

A comparison of the last stanzas of the two versions likewise points up the differences in field, since in each case the stanza serves as a climax to the rest of the poem. While the first version places the new born infant's tear in the final emphatic position (thus suggesting an emphasis on the plight of the human being), the second version places the marriage hearse in the final position and emphasizes the cause of the individual's plight in the corruption of the whole society. The indictment of society is strengthened by the ironic fact of the harlot's youthfulness and the insistence on disease in the phrase "blights with plagues." Thus the first version puts the "weakness" and "woe" of the individual against a backdrop of squalor and corruption, while the second version sees the plight of the individual and the plight of society as one, parts of a closely interlocking chain of cause and effect. While the first version presents a succession of images and ideas about man and society, often juxtaposed for ironic effect with the suggestion of connections, the second version fuses images and ideas into a more complex picture of human misery and a more telling indictment of society's "mind-forg'd manacles." The final horror of the second version is that the very streets should reflect not just man's own misery and squalor, but the rigidity which has stifled his natural impulses, robbed him of his freedom, and trapped him in a "chartered" world of weakness and woe.

There are several potential advantages in approaching a work of literature through the analogy of particle, wave, and field. Above all, the analogy encourages flexibility of perspective. It also demands that the critic consider a number of details before choosing the important ones for discussion, it emphasizes transitions and interrelationships more firmly than many approaches, and it stresses the dynamic or organic nature of the whole. Further, it promotes analysis and synthesis at the same time, since it encourages the reader or writer to be aware of whole and parts simultaneously. Finally, it has the advantage of having limits and hence avoiding the reductionism of most critical formulas: it helps the critic to see all the significant elements, but it doesn't tell him which elements are more crucial than others. It is a tool for arriving at the raw material of critical insights, but it doesn't force that raw material into a preconceived mould. It is too early to tell whether the analogy of particle, wave, and field is the best tool of this sort; but it appears promising because it promotes the flexibility necessary to true insight and at the same time promotes within that flexibility a completeness of view.

At the Fringe
of Language

C. S. LEWIS

In this essay C. S. Lewis distinguishes between *emotional* language and *emotive* language. Emotional language is found at the fringe of language, "the frontier between language and inarticulate vocal sounds." Emotive language, on the other hand, is the language of imaginative writing, especially of poetry. The distinction the author draws is a subtle and significant one. A careful, thoughtful reading will, among other things, extend your knowledge of one source of poetic power. C. S. Lewis, who died in 1963, was Professor of Medieval and Renaissance English at the University of Cambridge and Fellow of Magdalene College.

Language exists to communicate whatever it can communicate. Some things it communicates so badly that we never attempt to communicate them by words if any other medium is available. Those who think they are testing a boy's "elementary" command of English by asking him to describe in words how one ties one's tie or what a pair of scissors is like, are far astray. For precisely what language can hardly do at all, and never does well, is to inform us about complex physical shapes and movements. Hence descriptions of such things in the ancient writers are nearly always unintelligible. Hence we never in real life voluntarily use language for this purpose; we draw a diagram or go through pantomimic gestures. The exercises which such examiners set are no more a test of "elementary" linguistic competence than the most difficult bit of trick-riding from the circus ring is a test of elementary horsemanship.

Another grave limitation of language is that it cannot, like music or gesture, do more than one thing at once. However the words in a great poet's phrase interinanimate one another and strike the mind as a quasi-instantaneous chord, yet, strictly speaking, each word must be read or heard before the next. That way, language is as unilinear as

From *Studies in Words* by C. S. Lewis. Reprinted by permission of the Cambridge University Press.

time. Hence, in narrative, the great difficulty of presenting a very complicated change which happens suddenly. If we do justice to the complexity, the time the reader must take over the passage will destroy the feeling of suddenness. If we get in the suddenness we shall not be able to get in the complexity. I am not saying that genius will not find its own ways of palliating this defect in the instrument; only that the instrument is in this way defective.

One of the most important and effective uses of language is the emotional. It is also, of course, wholly legitimate. We do not talk only in order to reason or to inform. We have to make love and quarrel, to propitiate and pardon, to rebuke, console, intercede, and arouse. "He that complains," said Johnson, "acts like a man, like a social being." The real objection lies not against the language of emotion as such, but against language which, being in reality emotional, masquerades —whether by plain hypocrisy or subtler self-deceit—as being something else.

All my generation are much indebted to Dr. I. A. Richards for having fully called our attention to the emotional functions of language.[1] But I am hardly less indebted to Professor Empson for having pointed out that the conception of emotional language can be very easily extended too far.[2] It was time to call a halt.

We must obviously not call any utterance "emotional" language because it in fact arouses, even because it must arouse, emotion. "It is not cancer after all," "The Germans have surrendered," "I love you"—may all be true statements about matter of fact. And of course it is the facts, not the language, that arouse the emotion. In the last the fact communicated is itself the existence of an emotion but that makes no difference. Statements about crime are not criminal language; nor are statements about emotions necessarily emotional language. Nor, in my opinion, are value-judgements ("this is good," "this is bad") emotional language. Approval and disapproval do not seem to me to be emotions. If we felt at all times about the things we judge good the emotion which is appropriate, our lives would be easier. It would also be an error to treat "I am washed in the blood of the Lamb" as emotional language. It is of course metaphorical language. But by his metaphor the speaker is trying to communicate what he believes to be a fact. You

[1] See especially I. A. Richards, *Practical Criticism* (New York, Harcourt, Brace & World, Inc., 1929). [eds.]

[2] William Empson, *The Structure of Complex Words* (New York, New Directions Pub. Corp., 1951), Chap. 1.

may of course think the belief false in his particular case. You may think the real universe is such that no fact which corresponded to such a statement could possibly occur. You may say that the real cause which prompts a man to say things like that is a state of emotion. But if so, an emotion has produced erroneous belief about an impossible fact, and it is the fact erroneously believed in which the man is stating. A man's hasty belief that the Germans had surrendered (before they did) might well be caused by his emotions. That would not make "The Germans have surrendered" a specimen of emotional language. If you could find a man nowadays capable of believing, and saying, "The Russians have all been annihilated by magic," even this would not be emotional language, though his belief in magic might be a belief engendered by emotion.

All this is fairly plain sailing. We reach something harder in the things said by poets. For there the purpose of the utterance would be frustrated if no emotion were aroused. They do not merely, like the sentences cited above, arouse emotion in fact; it is their purpose — at any rate, part of their purpose — to do so. But we must be very careful here. Having observed that a poetical utterance in fact arouses emotion, and is intended to arouse emotion, and that if taken as a statement about reality — or even about the make-believe "realities" of a ficti-tious narrative — it would be nonsensical or at least false, can we conclude that it communicates nothing but emotion? I think not.

Nothing will convince me that "My soul is an enchanted boat"[3] is simply a better way — however much better — of doing what might be done by some exclamation like "Gee!" Asia has risen from the dark cave of Demogorgon. She is floating upwards. She is saluted as "Life of Life!" The reversed temporal process in ll. 97–103 ("We have passed

---

[3] *Prometheus Unbound*, II, v, 72. The line referred to comes toward the end of Act II of Shelley's reinterpretation of the ancient myth. The full stanza is printed below. [eds.]

> My soul is an enchanted boat,
>   Which, like a sleeping swan, doth float
> Upon the silver waves of thy sweet singing;
>   And thine doth like an angel sit
>   Beside a helm conducting it,   5
> Whilst all the winds with melody are ringing.
>   It seems to float ever, for ever,
>   Upon that many-winding river,
>   Between mountains, woods, abysses,
> A paradise of wildernesses!   10
> Till, like one in slumber bound,
> Borne to the ocean, I float down, around,
> Into a sea profound, of ever-spreading sound:

Age's icy caves" etc.),[4] borrowed from Plato's *Politicus* (269ᶜ *sq.*), marks the fact that at this moment the whole cycle is reversed and cosmos begins anew. She is undergoing apotheosis. What did it feel like? The poet says to us in effect "Think of going in a boat. But quite effortless" ("Like a sleeping swan" gliding with the current, he adds in the next line), "Like a boat without sail or oar; the motive power undiscoverable. Like a magic boat — you must have read or dreamed of such things — a boat drawn on, drawn swiftly on, irresistible, smoothly, by enchantment." Exactly. I know now how it felt for Asia. The phrase has communicated emotion. But notice how. By addressing in the first instance my imagination. He makes me imagine a boat rushing over waves, which are also identified with sounds. After that he need do no more; my emotion will follow of itself. Poetry most often communicates emotions, not directly, but by creating imaginatively the grounds for those emotions. It therefore communicates something more than emotion; only by means of that something more does it communicate the emotion at all.

Burns compares his mistress to "a red, red rose"; Wordsworth his to "a violet by a mossy stone Half hidden from the eye." These expressions do communicate to me the emotion each poet felt. But it seems to me that they do so solely by forcing me to imagine two (very different) women. I see the rose-like, overpowering, midsummer sweetness of the one; the reticent, elusive freshness, the beauty easily overlooked in the other. After that my emotions may be left to themselves. The poets have done their part.

This, which is eminently true of poetry, is true of all imaginative writing. One of the first things we have to say to a beginner who has brought us his MS. is, "Avoid all epithets which are merely emotional. It is no use *telling* us that something was 'mysterious' or 'loathsome' or 'awe-inspiring' or 'voluptuous.' Do you think your readers will believe you just because you say so? You must go quite a different way to work. By direct description, by metaphor and simile, by secretly evoking powerful associations, by offering the right stimuli to our nerves (in the right degree and the right order), and by the very beat and vowel-

---

[4] The lines are as follows: [eds.]

> We have passed Age's icy caves,
> And Manhood's dark and tossing waves,
> And Youth's smooth ocean smiling to betray:
> Beyond the glassy gulfs we flee
> Of shadow-peopled Infancy,   5
> Through Death and Birth, to a diviner day;

melody and length and brevity of your sentences, you must bring it about that we, we readers, not you, exclaim 'how mysterious!' or 'loathsome' or whatever it is. Let me taste for myself, and you'll have no need to *tell* me how I should react to the flavour."

In Donne's couplet

> Your gown going off, such beautious state reveals
> As when from flowry meads th'hills shadow steales[5]

beautious is the only word of the whole seventeen which is doing no work.

There are exceptions to this principle. By very successful placing, a great author may sometimes raise such words to poetic life. Wordsworth's lines are a specimen:

> Which, to the boundaries of space and time,
> Of melancholy space and doleful time,
> Superior—[6]

Here we have almost the reverse of the process I have been describing. The object (space and time) is in one way so familiar to our imaginations and in another so unimaginable — we have read so many tedious attempts to exalt or over-awe us with mere superlatives or even with simple arithmetic — that nothing can be made of it. This time, therefore, the poet withdraws the object (the ground for emotion) altogether and appeals directly to our emotions; and not to the quite obvious ones. Another exception is naturally to be found in drama or very dramatic lyric, where the poet — with discretion and a proper use of illusion — imitates the speech of people in some highly emotional situation — even, at need, their inarticulate cries. This in its purity, which purity a good poet never sustains for long, belongs to poetry not in so far as poetry is a special use of language but in so far as poetry is *mimesis*.[7] In themselves the "Ah! Ah!" or "Otototoi" or "Iou! Iou!" of characters in a Greek tragedy are not specimens of poetry any more than the "Bé, bé" of the lamb or the "Au! Au!" of the dog in Aristophanes.

In general, however, the poet's route to our emotions lies through our imaginations.

We must also exclude from the category "emotional language" words such as I have taken *supernatural* to be. The class of things which they refer to may be bound together chiefly by a common emotion;

[5] *Elegy* xix, 13.
[6] *Prelude* vi, 134.
[7] *Mimesis.* A term derived from Plato and Aristotle, who defined poetry as a mimetic art, an art of imitation or representation. [eds.]

but the purpose of using the words is to assign something to that class, not merely to communicate the emotion which led to the classification.

Having thus narrowed the field, we can now make a new start. It will be noticed that I have throughout used the word *emotional* rather than *emotive*. This is because I think the latter word applicable to only one aspect of emotional language. For an "emotive word" ought to mean one whose function is to arouse emotion. But surely we ought to distinguish utterances which arouse, from those which express, emotion? The first is directed towards producing some effect on a (real or imagined) hearer; the second discharges our own emotion, cleanses our stuffed bosom of some perilous stuff.

The distinction will seem straw-splitting if we have in mind the language of love. For, as Samson says, "love seeks to have love," and it would be hard to say whether endearments serve more as expressions of love in the speaker or incitements to it in the beloved. But that tells us more about the nature of love than about the nature of language. One of my old headmasters once wisely said it was a pity that *amare* was the first Latin verb we all learn. He thought this led to an imperfect grasp of the difference between the active and the passive voice. It might be better to begin with *flagellare*. The difference between flogging and being flogged would come home to the business and bosoms of schoolboys far more effectively than that of loving and being loved. On the same principle, we can best see the distinction between the stimulant and the expressive functions of emotional language in a quarrel; and best of all where the same word performs both. The man who calls me a low hound both expresses and (actually or intentionally) stimulates emotion. But not the same emotion. He expresses contempt; he stimulates, or hopes to stimulate, the almost opposite emotion of humiliation.

Again, in the language of complaint we often find the expressive without the stimulant. When two people who have missed the last train stand on the silent platform saying "Damn" or "Bloody" or "Sickening," they neither intend nor need to stimulate each other's disappointment. They are just "getting it off their chests."

The vocabulary of endearment, complaint, and abuse, provides, I think, almost the only specimens of words that are purely emotional, words from which all imaginative or conceptual content has vanished, so that they have no function at all but to express or stimulate emotion, or both. And an examination of them soon convinces us that in them we see language at its least linguistic. We have come to the frontier

286 LANGUAGE AND LITERATURE

between language and inarticulate vocal sounds. And at that frontier we find a two-way traffic going on.

On the one hand we find inarticulate sounds becoming words with a fixed spelling and a niche in the dictionary. Thus English *heigh-ho* and Latin *eheu* are clearly formalized imitations of the sigh; *ah*, of the gasp; *tut-tut*, of the tongue clicked against the hard palate. These are general. In particular situations the "verbification" of the inarticulate may occur *ad hoc*. A voluntary scream may become a cry for mercy. A voluntary groan, from a wounded man, uttered to attract the attention of the stretcher-bearers, may be the equivalent of a sentence ("There is a wounded man in this ditch").

But we also see the frontier being crossed in the opposite direction. In the vocabulary of abuse and complaint we see things that once were words passing out of the realm of language (properly so called) and becoming the equivalents of inarticulate sounds or even of actions; of sighs, moans, whimperings, growls, or blows.

The "swear-words" — *damn* for complaint and *damn you* for abuse — are a good example. Historically the whole Christian eschatology lies behind them. If no one had ever consigned his enemy to the eternal fires and believed that there were eternal fires to receive him, these ejaculations would never have existed. But inflation, the spontaneous hyperboles of ill temper, and the decay of religion, have long since emptied them of that lurid content. Those who have no belief in damnation — and some who have — now damn inanimate objects which would on any view be ineligible for it. The word is no longer an imprecation. It is hardly, in the full sense, a word at all when so used. Its popularity probably owes as much to its resounding phonetic virtues as to any, even fanciful, association with hell. It has ceased to be profane. It has also become very much less forceful. You may say the same of *sickening* in its popular, ejaculatory, use. There are alarms and disappointments which can actually produce nausea, or, at least, emotions which we feel to be somehow similar to it. But the man who says *sickening!* when he has missed the train is not thinking about that. The word is simply an alternative to *damn* or *bloody*. And of course far weaker than it would be if it still carried any suggestion of vomiting.

So with abusive terms. No one would now call his schoolfellow or next door neighbor a *swine* unless someone had once used this word to make a real comparison between his enemy and a pig. It is now a mere alternative to *beast* or *brute* or various popular unprintable words. They are all interchangeable. *Villain*, as we know, once really compared your enemy to a *villein*. Once, to call a man *cad* or *knave* assigned to him the status of a servant.[8] And it did so because, earlier still, these words meant "boy" or "junior" (you address a slave as "boy" in Greek and a waiter as *garçon* in French).

Thus all these words have come down in the world. None of them started by being *merely* abusive, few of them by being abusive at all. They once stimulated emotion by suggesting an image. They made the enemy odious or contemptible by asserting he was like somebody or something we already disliked or looked down on. Their use was a sort of passionate parody of the syllogism: pigs (or servants or my juniors) are contemptible — John is like a pig (or servant or adolescent) — therefore John is contemptible. That was why they really hurt; because hurting was not the whole of what they did. They stimulated emotion because they also stimulated something else; imagination. They stimulated emotion in the particular case because they exploited emotions which already existed towards whole classes of things or persons. Now that they are nothing whatever but emotional stimulants, they are weak emotional stimulants. They make no particular accusation. They tell us nothing except that the speaker has lost his temper.

And even this they do not tell us linguistically, but symptomatically; as a red face, a loud voice, or a clenched fist, might do equally well. The fact of the other person's anger may hurt or frighten us; hurt us if we love him, or frighten us if he is larger and younger than ourselves and threatens violence. But his language as such has very little power to do the only thing it is intended to do. It would have been far more wounding to be called *swine* when the word still carried some whiff of the sty and some echo of a grunt; far more wounding to be called a *villain* when this still conjured up an image of the unwashed, malodorous, ineducable, gross, belching, closefisted, and surly boor. Now, who cares? Language meant solely to hurt hurts strangely little.

This can be seen clearly when we catch a word "just on the turn." *Bitch* is one. Till recently — and still in the proper contexts — this accused a woman of one particular fault and appealed, with some success, to our contempt by calling up an image of the she-dog's comical and indecorous behaviour when she is on heat. But it is now increasingly used of any woman whom the speaker, for whatever reason, is annoyed with — the female driver who is in front of him, or a female magistrate whom he thinks unjust. Clearly, the word is far more wounding in its narrower usage. If that usage is ever totally lost — as I think it will be — the word will sink to the level of *damn her*.

[8] These are examples of semantic change known as deterioration, or catachresis. See Simeon Potter's essay, pp. 120–122. [eds.]

Notice, too, how *cat* (of a woman) is still strong and useful because the image is still alive in it.

An important principle thus emerges. In general, emotional words, to be effective, must not be solely emotional. What expresses or stimulates emotion directly, without the intervention of an image or concept, expresses or stimulates it feebly. And in particular, when words of abuse have hurting the enemy as their direct and only object, they do not hurt him much. In the field of language, however it may be in that of action, hatred cuts its own throat, and those who are too "willing to wound" become thereby impotent to strike. And all this is only another way of saying that as words become exclusively emotional they cease to be words and therefore of course cease to perform any strictly linguistic function. They operate as growls or barks or tears.

"Exclusively" is an important adverb here. They die as words not because there is too much emotion in them but because there is too little — and finally nothing at all — of anything else. . . .

SUGGESTED ASSIGNMENTS

Below, you will find one of the famous Lucy poems by Wordsworth. Read the poem carefully, noting especially the use of figurative language and the choice of words for emotive effect. Next, study the second version, which includes the stanzas and lines that the poet rejected in the process of composition. Finally, write an analytical theme explaining why you think the poet made these rejections.

SHE DWELT AMONG THE UNTRODDEN WAYS

She dwelt among the untrodden ways
  Beside the springs of Dove,
A Maid whom there were none to praise
  And very few to love:

A violet by a mossy stone   5
  Half hidden from the eye!
Fair as a star, when only one
  Is shining in the sky.

She lived unknown, and few could know
  When Lucy ceased to be;   10
But she is in her grave, and oh,
  The difference to me!

William Wordsworth
(1770–1850)

SHE DWELT AMONG THE UNTRODDEN WAYS

[First stanza rejected:]
[My hope was one, from cities far,
Nursed on a lonesome heath;
Her lips were red as roses are,
Her hair a woodbine wreath.]

She dwelt among the untrodden ways   *1*
  Beside the springs of Dove,   *2*
A Maid whom there were none to praise   *3*
  And very few to love: *4*
A violet by a mossy stone   *5*
  Half hidden from the eye!   *6*
—Fair as a star, when only one   *7*
  Is shining in the sky.   *8*

[Fourth stanza rejected:]
[And she was graceful as the broom
That flowers by Carron's side;
But slow distemper checked her bloom,
And on the Heath she died.]

She lived unknown, and few could know   *9*
  When Lucy ceased to be;   *10*
But she is in her grave, and oh,   *11*
[Long time before her head lay low   9R
Dead to the world was she: 10R
But now she's etc.]   11R
  The difference to me!   *12*

FURTHER READINGS

Brown, Roger, Abraham Black, and Arnold E. Horowitz. "Phonetic Symbolism in Natural Languages." *Journal of Abnormal and Social Psychology* 62:623–630 (May 1961).

Brown, Roger. *Words and Things.* New York: The Free Press of Glencoe, Inc. 1958. For a summary of research on sound symbolism and metaphor, see pp. 110–154.

Chatman, Seymour. "Linguistics and Teaching Introductory Literature." *Language Learning* 7:3–10 (1956–1957).

Harris, Robert T. and James L. Jarrett. *Language and Informal Logic.* London: Longmans, Green & Co., Ltd., 1956. On signs and symbols, see pp. 18–38.

Hill, Archibald A. "An Analysis of 'The Windhover,' an Experiment in Structural Method." *Publications of the Modern Language Association* 70:968–978 (December 1955).

Jespersen, Otto. "Symbolic Value of the Vowel I (1922)." *Linguistica.* Copenhagen: Levin and Munksgaard, 1933.

Levin, Harry. "Symbolism and Fiction." *Contexts of Criticism.* Cambridge: Harvard University Press, 1957. (Paperbound by Atheneum, 1963).

Lewis, C. S. "Bluspels and Flalansferes." *Rehabilitations and Other Essays.* London: Oxford University Press, 1939. On metaphor.

Miron, M. S. "A Cross-Linguistic Investigation of Phonetic Symbolism." *Journal of Abnormal and Social Psychology* 62:623–630 (May 1961).

Marchand, Hans. *The Categories and Types of Present-Day English Word-Formations.* Wiesbaden: Otto Harrassowitz, 1960. On phonetic symbolism, see pp. 313–343.

Rosenthal, M. L. and A. J. M. Smith. *Exploring Poetry.* New York: The Macmillan Company, 1955. On poetic symbolism, see pp. 497–511.

Wellek, René and Austin Warren. *Theory of Literature.* New York: Harcourt, Brace & World, Inc., 1942, 1947, 1949. On image, metaphor, symbol, and myth, see pp. 190–218.

6

THE SOUNDS
OF LANGUAGE

The Sound System of English

NORMAN C. STAGEBERG

In defining language, Edward Sapir, you will remember, stressed the primacy of speech, and made the point that writing is a derived form composed of symbols once removed from the original speech sounds. Important as the written symbols are in fastening down and making more or less permanent what otherwise would be gone with the wind, they nonetheless limit our perception of the nature of language. Such basic matters as vowels and consonants, for example, are misunderstood by those who think of them in terms of the letters of the alphabet rather than in terms of the sounds themselves.

This essay deals with matters of fundamental importance in understanding language as a system of sounds, especially with the production and classification of speech sounds. The material is technical but not difficult, and it is fundamental to the three succeeding essays. In fact, you really cannot discuss pronunciation intelligently unless you know how speech sounds are made and what their system is. Since not all linguists use exactly the same set of symbols to represent the sounds of language, the essay is followed by a table of all the symbols that you will meet in the four essays of this section.

Adapted from *An Introductory English Grammar*. Reprinted by permission of the publisher, Holt, Rinehart & Winston, Inc., copyright 1965.

1. The speech-producing mechanism

Speech sounds are sound waves created in a moving stream of air. They are disturbances of the medium such as you would observe if you were to drop a stone on the quiet surface of a pool. The air is expelled from the lungs, passes between the two vocal cords in the larynx (Adam's apple), and proceeds upward. As you will note on diagram 1, this moving stream of air has two possible outlets. It can pass through the nasal cavity and emerge through the nose, or it can pass through the oral cavity and come out through the mouth. But why doesn't it go through both passages, which are shown to be open on the diagram? Because in speech one of them is ordinarily closed. And how does this happen? Let us consider the oral sounds first. On diagram 1 you will notice the velum, marked *V*. This is a movable curtain of flesh. If you will run your finger back along the roof of your mouth, you will feel at first the bony structure of the hard palate, marked *P*. Just behind this hard palate you will feel the soft flesh of the velum. It ends in a pear-shaped pendant, called the uvula, which you can see hanging in your throat if you look in the mirror. Now, when you produce any oral sound, one that goes out through the mouth, for example a-a-a-a-a-a-a, you at the same time raise the velum until it touches the back of the throat, cutting off the nasal cavity. You can actually see this raising of the velum if you will open your mouth wide, look in the mirror, and say a-a-a-a-a-a several times in succession. The process is illustrated in diagram 2.

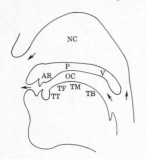

[1] Meaning of abbreviations:

AR = alveolar ridge
NC = nasal cavity
OC = oral cavity
P = soft palate
TT = tongue tip
TF = tongue front
TM = tongue middle
TB = tongue back
V = velum

DIAGRAM 1.   Speech-producing mechanism.[1]

Now let us turn from the oral sounds to the nasals, those that pass through the nasal cavity. To make the three nasal sounds of English, you leave the velum in the position shown on diagram 1 and block off the oral cavity in one of three ways: with the lips (diagram 3), with the tongue tip (diagram 4), or with the tongue back (diagram 5).

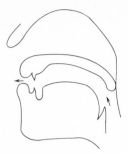

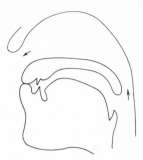

DIAGRAM 2.
Air passing through oral cavity.
Tongue position for /ɑ/

DIAGRAM 3.
Air passing through nasal cavity.
Lip position for /m/

Thus, with the oral cavity blocked off, the sound can emerge only through the nasal cavity. It is evident now that every speech sound we utter is either an oral or a nasal sound. For illustration of oral and nasal sounds, try pronouncing the list of words below and hold the final sound for some time. As you hold each final sound, stop your nose with your fingers. If this action stops the sound, the sound is obviously a nasal. But if the sound continues, then close your lips. The sound will thereupon be cut off, demonstrating that it is an oral sound. The words are: *rim, saw, bin, see, sing, tall, trim, pain, wrong.* You may wonder about the "nasal twang" that you occasionally hear. This is caused by the habit of slightly lowering the velum for sounds that are normally oral, thus permitting some of the air to go out through the nasal cavity. You have now learned the three nasals of English,

DIAGRAM 4.
Air passing through nasal cavity.
Tongue position for /n/

DIAGRAM 5.
Air passing through nasal cavity.
Tongue position for /ŋ/

which we symbolize in a special notation as /m/, /n/, and /ŋ/. The /m/ is a bilabial nasal, made by closing the two lips. The /n/ is an alveolar nasal, made by stopping the flow of air with the tongue tip against the alveolar ridge. The /ŋ/ is a velar nasal, made by stopping the flow of air with the back of the tongue against the velum. In all three the air moves through the nasal cavity. They are illustrated on diagrams 3, 4, and 5. But one element is missing from our description of the three nasals. Where does the sound come from? To answer this question we must examine the vocal cords. Inside the larynx (Adam's apple) are two short bands of flesh and muscle stretching from front to rear. In breathing and during the production of some speech sounds, like *f* and *s*, these are held open, allowing free ingress and egress of air, as shown in diagram 6. But with many sounds they are pressed tightly together, and the air passing between them causes them to vibrate, as shown in diagram 7.

DIAGRAM 6.   *DIAGRAM 7.*
Position of vocal cords   Position of vocal cords
during exhalation   when vibrating

Reprinted by permission of the copyright owners, the Regents of the University of Wisconsin, from R.-M.S. Heffner, *General Phonetics*, 1950, the University of Wisconsin Press.

These vibrations are given resonance by the cavities of the mouth and nose and the result is the phenomenon called voicing. In the making of every speech sound, then, these vocal cords are either vibrating or not vibrating. If they are vibrating, the sound is called voiced. If they are not vibrating, the sound is called voiceless. In order to hear for yourself the voicing and voicelessness of speech sounds, hold your hands tightly over your ears and pronounce the last sound in each of the following words. You will hear clearly the hum of the vibration of your vocal cords for the voiced sounds, and this hum will be absent for the voiceless sounds. The words are: *less, hum, if, pin, sheath, among, mush, fin, song.* Now try the same thing with the first sound of these words: *fine, vine, thin, then, seal, zeal, shock, late, rate.*

2. The phoneme

Before continuing with an inventory of English speech sounds and the ways of producing them, we must clearly understand one basic concept—the phoneme.

The phoneme is easily understood: it is a speech sound that makes a difference in meaning. Consider, for example, the words *dime* and *dine*. They sound exactly alike except for the /m/ and the /n/, yet their meanings are different. Therefore it must be the /m/ and /n/ which make the difference in meaning, and these two nasals are thereby established as English phonemes. Likewise, if we compare the sounds of *sin* and *sing*, we find only one difference between them: *sin* ends in the alveolar nasal /n/ and *sing* in the velar nasal /ŋ/. (Don't be deceived by the spelling of *sing;* the letters *ng* represent a single sound /ŋ/, one which you can prolong as long as your breath holds out.) This contrast is evidence that /n/ and /ŋ/ are both phonemes. Pairs of words like those above which demonstrate a phonemic contrast are called minimal pairs. A phoneme may be pronounced in different ways, depending on its position in the utterance, and still remain the same phoneme. As an example, let us take /l/. If you pronounce *lit* and *well* slowly and distinctly, you will hear two different [l]s. The second one seems to be preceded by an "uh" sound. With a little practice you can place your tongue tip on the alveolar ridge and change from the first to the second [l] without moving the tongue tip. Now, if you pronounce *well* with the [l] of *lit*, the word will sound different, a little un-English, but the meaning will not be changed. The use of one or the other of these two [l]s never makes a difference in meaning; hence they are not two phonemes but merely variants of the /l/ phoneme. You will sometimes hear still another [l] in words like *play* and *sled*. Here there may be a voiceless [l̥], whereas the [l]s of both *well* and *lit* were voiced. But whether you pronounce *play* and certain other words with a voiced or a voiceless [l], the meaning remains unchanged; so this third [l̥] is another variant of the /l/ phoneme. Such variants of a phoneme are called allophones. Allophones are enclosed in brackets with the occasional addition of diacritical marks to indicate the exact pronunciation. Phonemes are enclosed in slants. Thus we may say that the /l/ phoneme has three allophones: [l] as in *lit*, [ɫ] as in *well*, and [l̥] as in *play*. A phoneme then is not an individual sound but a small family of similar sounds.

With this introduction to the concept of the phoneme, we are now ready to continue the inventory of English phonemes.

3. The English phonemic system: vowels

The classification of English vowels is a complex and controversial matter; it is even difficult to define a vowel with precision. But we can make four statements about vowels that will help to show their nature.

(1) All vowels are oral sounds. In some dialects and in certain contexts, vowels may become partially nasal, but normally they are orals, not nasals.

(2) All vowels are voiced.

(3) Vowels are characterized by a free flow of air through the oral cavity.

(4) The distinguishing features of the different vowels are determined largely by tongue position.

English may be said to have 13 vowels—five front, four back, and four central vowels—which we shall now take up systematically.

FRONT VOWELS. If you pronounce the final sound of *be*, symbolized by /i/, and hold the /i/, you will find that the tongue front and middle is humped high in the mouth, leaving a narrow passage for the flow of air between the hard palate and the surface of the tongue. The tongue position of /i/ is the top one on diagram 8. Next, say the same vowel /i/, holding your jaw in your hand, and then say the first sound of *add*, symbolized by /æ/. You will observe a considerable drop of the jaw and some flattening of the tongue. The tongue position of the vowel /æ/ is the bottom one on diagram 8. To fix these differences of position in your mind, hold your jaw and say /i/, /æ/ rapidly a number of times in succession.

Between these two extremes, /i/ and /æ/, are three other vowels. To hear them in order from the top tongue position to the bottom one, pronounce the following words, noting the middle sound: *beat, bit, bait, bet, bat*. Now say just the vowels in the same order, holding your jaw, and observe how the jaw drops a little as each one is uttered. These five vowels are called the FRONT VOWELS, because they are formed in the front of the mouth by the position of the tongue front. For each front vowel the lips are spread, or unrounded. The tongue positions are shown on diagram 8; the symbols are given above. English spelling cannot be used to represent accurately the speech sounds of English because of its inconsistencies. How,

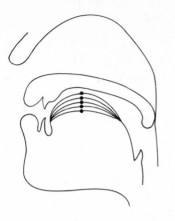 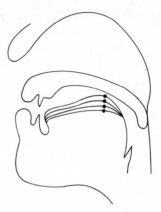

DIAGRAM 8. Front vowels   *DIAGRAM 9.* Back vowels

for example, would you symbolize the vowel of *bait* in English spelling? By *ai* as in *wait*, *eig* as in *reign*, *ey* as in *they*, *ay* as in *say*, *a* as in *late*, *ei* as in *vein*, *au* as in *gauge*, *ea* as in *steak*? So to represent the sounds of words, we shall use a special alphabet in which one symbol always represents one and the same speech sound, and each sound is always represented by only one symbol. In this alphabet the five illustrative words in the preceding paragraph are written as follows:

beat = /bit/   bit = /bɪt/   bait = /bet/   bet = /bɛt/   bat = /bæt/

The phonemic symbols and words written in these symbols are enclosed in slants, like /bɛt/.

BACK VOWELS.   Pronounce the final sound of *too*, symbolized by /u/. For this vowel /u/ the lips are rounded and the back of the tongue is raised to a position near the velum, leaving a little space for the air to flow. The tongue position is the top one on diagram 9. Now pronounce the sound you make when you say "aw," as in "Aw, come on." For most Americans this is the vowel of *saw*, *raw*, and *jaw*. It is symbolized by /ɔ/. The tongue position is the bottom one on diagram 9. Next, utter the vowels /u/ and /ɔ/ in rapid succession, with your hand on your jaw. This will show you the upper and lower extremes of the range of the four vowels that are called back vowels. If you will also look in the mirror while uttering the successive /u/s and /ɔ/s, you will see the close rounding of the lips for /u/ and the open rounding for /ɔ/.

As the back of the tongue is lowered from the /u/ position,

it reaches in turn the positions for the three other back vowels: /ʊ/ as in *pull*, /o/ as in *note*, and /ɔ/ as in *ought*, *law*, and *ball*. And at each of these three positions the rounding of the lips is successively opened, as you can observe in the mirror. The four back vowels, from top to bottom, are illustrated by this series:

fool = /ful/   full = /fʊl/   foal = /fol/   fall = /fɔl/

CENTRAL VOWELS.   English has four central vowels. The first one is a high central vowel symbolized by /ɨ/. It is often heard in unstressed positions, as in the unstressed *just* of "Just a minute." In uttering this phrase you probably have a /ɨ/ in *just* unless you stress it or unless you have schooled yourself to use the vowel of *us* in the word. This unstressed *just* contrasts in pronunciation with *gist*, which is usually pronounced with the lower high front vowel /ɪ/. You can easily hear this contrast if you are able to pronounce *just* the same way in isolation that you pronounce it in the key phrase above. This high central vowel /ɨ/ is also heard in the unstressed *can* of "I can do more." This *can* /kɨn/ contrasts with *kin* /kɪn/ and with stressed *can* /kæn/. The /ɨ/ is made by raising the tongue rather high in the central part of the mouth and spreading the lips, though not as widely as for /ɪ/. One way to find the /ɨ/ position is to pronounce the vowel of *up* and then to raise the tongue toward the roof of the mouth. In the speech of many persons, the /ɨ/ is heard in the parts of the following words printed in regular type: *started*, *folded*, *thesis*, *habit*, *because*, *degree*, *children*, *roses*. Its position is the top one in diagram 10, and it is often called the barred *i*.

The second central vowel requires special consideration. If you pronounce *fur*, *sir*, *her*, you are uttering, as the final sound, a central r-colored vowel, that is, if you belong to the majority of Americans who do not "drop their r's." But there are other Americans who pronounce words like these with a /ə/ plus an r sound, as in hurry /həri/, instead of with the single r-colored vowel. Thus we shall use the pair of symbols /ər/ to represent both pronunciations—the single, central, r-colored vowel and also the schwa plus an r sound.

The third central vowel may be illustrated by the first sound of *up* and *upon*. It is written /ə/, like an upside-down *e*, and its position is shown in diagram 10. It is heard as the pronunciation of the underlined vowels in the following words:

Stressed: s*u*n, d*o*ne, fl*oo*d
Unstressed: sof*a*, *a*lone, princi*p*al, speci*m*en, sci*e*nce,
kingd*o*m, c*o*nnect, diffic*u*lt, s*u*ppose

The /ə/ is a vowel of high frequency in English, especially in unstressed syllables, and is technically called "schwa." You will find it a good practice exercise to pronounce repeatedly the word *hunted*, using for the *-ed* the three vowels /ɪ/, /ɨ/, and /ə/. Which do you find is your normal pronunciation?

The fourth central vowel is the sound you make when the doctor says, "Open your mouth wide and say a-a-a-a." For most Americans this is the vowel of *not* and the first vowel of *father*. It is symbolized by /a/. In sounding this vowel you will note that the mouth is widely opened and that the tongue is nearly flat. The tongue position is the bottom one in diagram 10. The central vowels from, top to bottom, are illustrated in this series:

potted = /patɨd/   purr = /pər/   pup = /pəp/   pot = /pat/

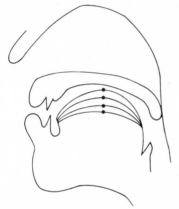

DIAGRAM 10.   Central vowels

The thirteen vowel phonemes of English can be seen in relation to one another on the vowel chart on page 300.
This is a two-dimensional grid of tongue positions, the mouth being at the left and the throat at the right. Using this chart we can easily give to the 13 vowels descriptive names which will be useful in discussing them. The names are these:

/i/ High front

/u/ High back rounded

/ɪ/ Lower high front   /ɨ/ High central

/ʊ/ Lower high back rounded

/e/ Higher mid front   /ər/ Higher mid-central

/o/ Mid back rounded

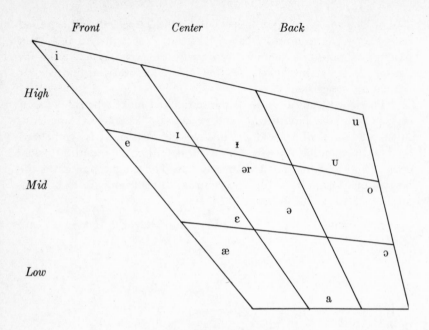

Chart of English vowel phonemes

/ɛ/ Lower mid front   /ə/ Lower mid-
                             central   /ɔ/ Low back rounded
/æ/ Low front   /a/ Low central

It must be realized that the classification of vowels by tongue position is imprecise and generalized. Also, there are further classifications—tense, lax; close, open; narrow, wide; long, short—that we are bypassing in the interest of a stringent simplicity. But by and large the above description and classification of vowel phonemes will serve for the fleeting glance to which we are limited.

THE SYLLABLE. Before moving ahead to the next group of phonemes, the diphthongs, it is necessary for us to examine the nature of the syllable.

When we speak we can observe that certain sounds have a greater sonority or carrying power than others. For example, in *soap* /sop/, the /o/ has greater sonority than the /s/ or the /p/, even though all are spoken with equal force. If /sop/ is spoken at some distance from the listener, he may hear distinctly only the /o/. In *potato* /pəteto/, the /ə/, /e/, and /o/ are more sonorous, more audible, than the /p/ and the /t/s. The sounds which have this greater inherent sonority or carrying power are mostly the vowels. Thus, as we utter connected discourse, we become aware of a peak-and-valley effect of sonority or audibility. The peaks of sonority are the vowels and the valleys of less distinctness are the consonants, as in *echo* /ɛko/, or the slight diminution of loudness, as in *create* /kri-et/. This brings us to the syllable. A syllable is a sound or a short sequence of sounds which contains one peak of sonority. This peak is usually a vowel, and the vowel is said to be the center of the syllable. A segment of speech, then, contains as many syllables as there are peaks. Here are some examples of words with the peaks, or syllabic centers, underlined.

One syllable	be	/bi̱/
	string	/strɪ̱ŋ/
Two syllables	believe	/bɪli̱v/
	being	/bi̱ɪŋ/
	stirring	/stə̱rɪŋ/
Three syllables	believing	/bɪli̱vɪŋ/
Four syllables	unbelieving	/ənbɪli̱vɪŋ/
Five syllables	unbelievingly	/ənbɪli̱vɪŋli/

We have seen that vowels are peaks of sonority and are therefore syllabic centers. But there are four consonants—/m/, /n/, /ŋ/, and /l/ —which also have considerable sonority and which can constitute syllables.

As our first example, let us take the two-syllable expression *stop 'em*. This can be uttered in two ways. The first is /stapəm/. After the lips are closed to make the /p/, they are opened for the /ə/, and closed again for the /m/. The second way is /stapm/. Here the lips are closed for the /p/ and remain closed for the /m/. Try it and see for yourself. While you are making the /p/, no air can escape from the mouth. The closed lips shut off the mouth exit and the raised velum shuts off the nasal exit. Now, holding the lips closed, you open the velum by lowering it, and what happens? The air escapes with a slight explosion through the nasal cavity. This is what happens in /stapm/. Here the /m/ is a peak of sonority and by itself constitutes a syllable. This /m/ is called a syllabic /m/. For illustration, pronounce the following, leaving your lips closed at the /p/: *leap 'em, rob 'em, open.* The last will sound like /opm/.

The syllabic /n/ is formed similarly. Consider for example *button*.

You may pronounce it /bətən/ by dropping the tongue from the /t/ position on the alveolar ridge, uttering the /ə/, and then replacing the tongue for the /n/. But you can also pronounce *button* without removing the tongue, as in /bətn/. At the /t/ position the air is prevented from escaping by the tongue against the alveolar ridge and by the closed velum, which shuts off the nasal cavity. If you hold the tongue in the /t/ position and open the velum, you will get an /n/ as the air escapes through the nasal cavity. For illustration, pronounce the following words without removing the tongue after it is touching the /t/ position: *beaten, cotton, sudden*. The syllabic /ŋ/, which is less frequent, is heard in expressions like *Jack and Jill*, /ǰækŋ ǰɪl/. At the /k/ position the air is held in by the back of the tongue against the velum and by the velum, which has been raised to cut off the nasal cavity. With a lowering of the velum, the nasal cavity is opened and the syllabic /ŋ/ is heard. For illustration, pronounce the following expressions without removing the tongue after it has reached the /ŋ/ position: *back and forth, bag and baggage, rack and ruin*. The syllabic /l/ is somewhat differently articulated. To make the common /l/, you place the tongue on the alveolar ridge, vibrate the vocal cords, and let the air flow over and off the tongue on one or both sides and escape through the mouth. Now, to make the syllabic /l/, as in *rattle*, you first have the air completely closed off by the tongue in the /t/ position on the alveolar ridge and by a raised velum cutting off the nasal cavity. Then you open one or both sides of the tongue, without removing the tip from the alveolar ridge, letting the air go around the tongue and out the mouth. As illustration, pronounce the following words by keeping your tongue at the /t/ or /d/ position while pronouncing the syllabic /l/: *cattle, saddle, beetle*.

Although it is easy to locate the peaks of sonority that indicate syllable centers, the vowels and syllabic consonants, it is sometimes impossible to find the boundary between syllables, that is, the point of minimum sonority. In the two-syllable *hushing* /həšŋ/, for example, where is the syllable boundary? After the /ə/? Before the /ɪ/? Or in the middle of /š/? It is like trying to establish in a valley the exact line separating the two hills on either side. For our purpose here we need not be much concerned with syllable division, and where the boundary is not audible, we can resort to an arbitrarily selected break.

DIPHTHONGS.   A diphthong consists of two vowels which occur in the same syllable, the tongue moving smoothly from one position to the other without hiatus, as in *sigh*, /sai/, *sow* (female pig), /sau/, and *soy*, /sɔi/. The two vowels together represent the peak of sonority, though one always has greater prominence than the other. Many of our vowels are diphthongized in various subareas of English, and four of them are normally diphthongized in Standard English: /i/, /e/, /u/, and /o/. For these, however, we shall use the symbols just given, since there is no phonemic difference between the pure vowels and the diphthongized vowels.[1] According to the system we are using, the diphthong PHONEMES are only three: /ai/ as in *by*, /au/ as in *bough*, and /ɔi/ as in *boy*. Under the heading of "diphthongs" we shall consider the "r" sounds. You have already met the /r/ consonant as in *race* /res/ and the central r-colored vowel as in *cur* /kər/. This leaves us to consider the "r" sound that occurs after vowels in the same syllable. Our practice here will be to consider these "r"s as consonantal

	Bilabial	Labio-dental	Inter-dental	Alveolar	Alveo-palatal	Velar	Glottal
Stops							
vl	p			t		k	
vd	b			d		g	
Fricatives							
vl		f	ɵ	s	š		h
vd		v	ð	z	ž		
Affricates							
vl					č		
vd					ǰ		
Nasals							
	m			n		ŋ	
Lateral							
				l			
Glides							
				r	y	w	

Chart of English consonant phonemes

[1] You may think that you are uttering single vowels in words like *cease* /sis/, *maim* /mem/, *noon* /nun/, and *moan* /mon/. But the vowel sounds you are actually making are diphthongized vowels something like these: 1. [ɪi], 2. [ei], 3. [ʊu], and 4. [ou]. If you can find a tape recorder which plays backward, you can easily hear them for yourself: simply record these four words and then play them backward.

and to transcribe them with the /r/ symbol, thus: *farm* /farm/; *pore* /por/; *poor* /pur/; *fair* /fer/; *fear* /fɪr/. The symbols /ər/ will be reserved for occasions when this sound is the center of a syllable, as in the two-syllable *stirring* /stərɪŋ/ contrasted with the one-syllable *string* /strɪŋ/.

Vowels, you have learned, are characterized by a free flow of air. Consonants, on the other hand, are produced by stopping or obstructing this flow of air, except for the three nasals. The first six consonants presented here are those produced by a stoppage of air: /p b t d k g/.

STOPS. /p/, /b/. If you hold your velum and lips closed and exert outward air pressure, nothing will happen except that your cheeks may puff out. Now if you suddenly open your lips the air explodes outward and you have made a /p/. This consonant is called a voiceless bilabial stop because (1) the vocal cords do not vibrate, (2) two lips are used, and (3) a complete stop of the air flow is made. If during the same process you vibrate your vocal cords, you will produce a /b/, a voiced bilabial stop.

/t/, /d/ Instead of using the lips, you can stop the air flow by holding the tongue against the alveolar ridge, with the velum closed. A sudden removal of the tongue will then produce a /t/, a voiceless alveolar stop. But if the vocal cords vibrate during the process, you will produce a /d/, a voiced alveolar stop.

/k/, /g/. The third pair of stops is produced by raising the tongue back against the velum, which is also raised to cut off the nasal cavity. When the tongue back is released, the outrushing air results in a /k/, a voiceless velar stop, or a /g/, a voiced velar stop, depending on whether or not the vocal cords are vibrating.

To increase your awareness of the three stop positions, pronounce slowly and in succession /p/, /t/, and /k/, and try to feel, tactually and kinesthetically, what is going on inside your mouth. Do this six times and then repeat the sounds in reverse.

FRICATIVES. English contains nine consonants which are produced by an obstruction of the air stream causing audible friction. These nine fricatives are:

/f v ɵ ð s z š ž h/

We shall discuss the first eight in pairs, beginning with those in the front of the mouth and moving to the back.

The first pair, /f/ and /v/, are heard in *fail* and *vale*. They are produced when the outgoing air is obstructed by the lower lip touching the upper teeth. The /f/ is called a voiceless labiodental fricative, and /v/ a voiced labiodental fricative. They differ only in the fact that /v/ is voiced. You can feel the vibration of the vocal cords for /v/ if you press your fingers around the top of the larynx, sound a continuous /f/, and then change without stopping to a /v/. The next three pairs of fricatives can be tested in the same way for voicelessness and voicing.

The second pair, /ɵ/ and /ð/, are heard in *ether* and *either*. They are made with the tongue obstructing the air stream between the upper and lower teeth, or at the bottom of the upper teeth. The /ɵ/ is a voiceless interdental fricative, and /ð/ a voiced interdental fricative.

The third pair is /s/ and /z/, as in *face* and *faze*. These are pronounced by the tongue permitting a small stream of air to hiss over its surface at the alveolar ridge. The /s/ is a voiceless alveolar fricative, and /z/ a voiced alveolar fricative.

The fourth pair of fricatives are /š/, the third consonant in *dilution*, and /ž/, the third consonant in *delusion*. These are made by the friction of moving air between the tongue front and the palatal region just behind the alveolar ridge. The /š/ is a voiceless alveopalatal fricative, and /ž/ a voiced alveopalatal fricative. To get the feel of the voiceless alveolar and alveopalatal fricatives, take a deep breath and on a continuous stream of air repeat /s/ and /š/ in alternation, noting the movements of the tongue and the lips.

The last fricative is /h/, as in *hat* contrasted with *at*. This is produced by the breath rushing through the open vocal cords. The fricative's tongue and lip position is that of the following vowel. You can see this easily by preparing your mouth to say *ha, he, who*. It is called the voiceless glottal fricative, the glottis being the space between the vocal cords.

AFFRICATES. English has two affricates—the voiceless /č/ as in *chill*, and the voiced /ǰ/ as in *Jill*. The /č/ begins with the voiceless stop /t/, which is exploded as a voiceless fricative /š/. Thus it is sometimes written /tš/. It is known as the voiceless alveopalatal affricate. The /ǰ/ consists of a voiced stop /d/, which is exploded as a voiced fricative /ž/, and is sometimes written /dž/. It is called the voiced alveopalatal affricate.

NASALS. The three nasals—/m/, /n/, and /ŋ/—have already been described above.

LATERAL. The lateral, /l/ as in *louse*, is made by placing the tongue tip on the alveolar ridge and vibrating the vocal cords as the air passes out on one or both sides of the tongue. To feel the tongue position, hold the tongue firmly at the alveolar ridge and make a series of /l/s and /n/s, noting how the sides of the tongue open and close as you alternate sounds.

GLIDES. The three glides—/y/, /r/, and /w/—are signalized by a moving, not a stationary, tongue position. They are all voiced.

With /y/, as in *yoke* contrasted with *oak*, the tongue begins in the /i/ region and moves toward the position for the following vowel. It is called the high front glide. In the case of /r/, as in *rate* contrasted with *ate*, the tongue begins in the position of the r-colored vowel of *purr*, /ər/, and moves toward the following vowel. It is known as the retroflex alveolar glide, though this name is not descriptive of some /r/s. The third glide is /w/, as in *will* versus *ill*. Here the tongue takes a /u/ position and then moves into the following vowel. It is called the high back glide.

We have now covered briefly the 13 vowels, 3 diphthongs, and 24 consonants of English. The vowels and consonants are charted on the diagrams on pages 300 and 303.

SUGGESTED ASSIGNMENTS

(The first three exercises will give you practice in reading phonemic script, which will help you with the next three selections in the book. At the same time they will reveal the systematic aspect of four English inflectional endings.)

1. If asked to tell how the past tense of our regular verbs is formed, most people would say by the addition of *d* or *ed* to the stem form; e.g., *love* plus *d* is *loved*, *walk* plus *ed* is *walked*. Such a description is based on spelling and does not accurately describe the different sounds involved. Actually, this past-tense ending takes three phonetic forms. To find out what these three forms are, first read the following transcriptions and write after each its spelled form.

pæst _____	rabd _____	ratɪd _____
læft _____	simd _____	lodɪd _____
mapt _____	lond _____	sitɪd _____
bækt _____	rɔŋd _____	sadɪd _____

rəšt _____	həgd _____	nidɨd _____
rɛnčt_____	revd _____	ripitɨd _____
	mɪld _____	
	stərd _____	

Now, in the spoken language, what are the three endings that signal the past tense? These endings are not distributed randomly but according to a system. You can easily discover this system if you will compare the voicing or voicelessness of the last sound of each verb stem with that of the ending.

2. In English spelling we have two "s" plurals, -s and -es. But in spoken language there are three "s" plurals with a systematic distribution. To discover these three plurals and the system of their distribution, first read the following transcriptions and write after each its spelled form.

staps _____	mabz _____	glæsɨz _____
raits _____	raidz _____	rozɨz _____
keks _____	frɔgz _____	dɪšɨz _____
mufs _____	wevz _____	gərajɨz _____
brɛəs _____	səmz _____	dɪčɨz _____
	sənz _____	ɛjɨz _____
	sɔŋz _____	
	dalz _____	
	fɪrz _____	

3. Is the same system as in exercise 2 operative for the noun possessive? Compare, for example, /jæks/ (= Jack's), /janz/ (= John's), and /jɔrjɨz/ (= George's). And is this also true of the third person present singular of the verb, as in /lɪfts/ (He *lifts*), /ridz/ (He *reads*), and /mɪsɨz/ (He *misses*)? (The next three exercises will give you transcription practice and at the same time illustrate some of the irregularities of English spelling.)

4. Transcribe the following words with phonemic symbols and notice all the ways in which the phoneme /i/ is spelled.

feet _____	beat _____	ravine _____
me _____	deceive _____	key _____
Caesar _____	amoeba _____	quay _____
people _____	relieve _____	

5. Transcribe the following words with phonemic symbols and notice the various phonemes which the letter *a* represents.

dame _____	father _____	lunar _____
fare _____	ball _____	opera _____
pan _____	pillage _____	

6. Transcribe the following words with phonemic symbols and notice the silent letters.

corps _____	debt _____	pneumatic _____
island _____	reign _____	colonel _____

7. By transcribing the following words, you will meet all the vowels, diphthongs, and consonants of the preceding essay.

palm	_____	ether	_____	rang	_____
taste	_____	sister	_____	root	_____
keen	_____	song	_____	wade	_____
coon	_____	wash	_____	your	_____
bought	_____	voted	_____	have	_____
dull	_____	breathe	_____	boy	_____
gadding	_____	lazy	_____	house	_____
chicken	_____	measure	_____	few	_____
dredge	_____	lamb	_____	mine	_____
fig	_____	gnawed	_____	physics	_____

8. Since there are more phonemes in English than letters in the alphabet,
some letters must represent more than one sound. Yet, surprisingly, our
alphabet has three unnecessary letters. If you will transcribe the four words
that follow, you will see which these letters are.

    queen _____   cede _____

    six _____   cut _____

9. It has often been proposed that we abandon our inefficient alphabet and
substitute a phonemic system of writing in which each symbol represents
one sound only and in which each sound is represented by only one symbol. Thus, it is asserted, anyone who can talk can learn to read and write
in a few weeks. Write a theme in this area of thought on a subject like one
of these:

a. The Advantages of a Phonemic Writing System
b. Why a Phonemic Writing System Won't Work
c. Don't Abandon the Alphabet
d. Practical Ways to Simplify English Spelling.

Table of Sound Symbols Used in This Section

	Symbol	Example
Consonants		
Stops	p	_p_are, s_p_are, sto_p_
	b	_b_are
	t	_t_are
	d	_d_are
	k	_c_are
	g	_g_et
Fricatives	f	_f_ish
	v	_v_ase
	θ	_th_ink
	ð	_th_en
	s	_s_ink

	Symbol	*Example*
	z	*z*ink
	š, ʃ	*s*ure
	ž, ʒ	plea*s*ure
	h	*h*ow
	ç	*h*uge (with friction between tongue front and palate)
Affricates	č, tʃ, tš	*ch*ur*ch*
	ǰ, dʒ, dž	*j*u*dg*e
Nasals	m	*m*y
	n	*n*ose
	ŋ	si*ng*
Lateral	l	*l*ike
Glides	r	*r*ye
	y, j	*y*es
	w	*w*ait
	ʍ, hw	s*w*eet (voiceless *w*), *wh*y
Vowels		
Front	i	m*ee*t
	ɪ	s*i*t
	e	r*a*te
	ɛ	p*e*t
	æ	p*a*t
Central	ɨ	start*e*d
	ər, r, ɝ, ɚ	f*ur*
	ə, ʌ	sof*a*, *u*p
	a, ɑ	f*a*ther
Back	u	f*oo*l
	ʊ	f*u*ll
	o	n*o*te
	ɔ	s*aw*
	ɒ	n*o*t British (slightly rounded)
Diphthongs	aɪ, ai, ɑɪ, ɑi	m*i*ne
	ɔɪ, ɔi, oɪ, oi	b*oy*
	aʊ, au, ɑʊ, ɑu	h*ow*
	iu	f*ew*
	ju	*u*se

Primary and secondary stresses are shown by vertical lines. A high vertical line indicates that the following syllable has primary stress. A low vertical line indicates that the following syllable has secondary stress. Example: ˈsɛkrəˌtɛri. Primary stress is also shown by a ′ after the syllable. Examples: bihev′, ɪmpɔr′tənt

Phonetic Change: Assimilation

CHARLES KENNETH THOMAS

You probably have wondered why it is that the word *cupboard*, which is obviously a compound of *cup* plus *board*, is not pronounced in accordance with its spelling. If you were to write *cubberd* for *cupboard*, you would be branded as an illiterate, even though *cubberd* represents the pronunciation, certainly as old as "Old Mother Hubbard," more accurately than the standard spelling. As a matter of fact, *cubberd*, along with *cubbourd*, *cubboorde*, *cubbord* and others, was a common spelling during the sixteenth and seventeenth centuries. It was not until the eighteenth century that the spelling became standardized as *cupboard*, but people went right on saying *cubberd*. Clearly something interesting is at work in the spoken language that is not adequately reflected in writing.

When we speak we do not utter a series of individuated units of sound. Rather, we speak in a continuous flow of sounds; vowels and consonants are constantly jostling each other, often blurring or wearing away the edges of adjoining sounds especially. In other words, under certain conditions phonetic changes take place. One type of phonetic change is assimilation, which Charles Thomas, Professor of Speech at the University of Florida, discusses in the following essay. An understanding of assimilation will let you in on the secret of some of the mysteries of English pronunciation.

Variations in pronunciation . . . should convince us that language is not static and uniform, but that it develops and changes. We notice this development even more if we read the literature of earlier periods. Shakespeare's English is noticeably different from our own, even though our present-day archaic spelling masks some of the differences. To understand Chaucer we must frequently refer to a glossary; to appreciate his rhythms and rhymes we must also know something about the language spoken in fourteenth-century London. To read Old English,

From Charles Kenneth Thomas, *An Introduction to the Phonetics of American English*, Second Edition. Copyright 1958 The Ronald Press Company.

of the time of King Alfred for instance, we must study it as we would a foreign language.

Changes in the language are usually imperceptible till afterward, and often seemingly capricious. Analysis of the historical changes shows, however, that the patterns of development are usually clear in retrospect, and that definite causes can be assigned to some of them. . . . we are going to examine one type of historical change, in order to throw light on the changeable nature of present-day speech.

Assimilation

The usual pronunciation of *income* is [ˈɪnˌkʌm],[1] with primary stress on the first syllable, secondary stress on the second syllable, and a distinct syllabic division between [n] and [k]. When we use the word as an adjective, however, in the phrase *income tax*, the pronunciation may be [ˈɪnˌkʌm ˈtæks], but often it changes to [ˈɪŋkəm ˌtæks]. The reduced vowel represents reduced stress. The change from [n] to [ŋ] illustrates what is known as *assimilation*, a type of phonetic change which occurs frequently enough to warrant detailed examination.

When *income* becomes part of the larger unit, *income tax*, we scan the details more rapidly. The succession of three stressed syllables conflicts with our normal rhythmic patterns, and we weaken the second syllable from [ʌ] to [ə]. The phrase as a whole telescopes within itself, and the amount of time available for the shift from one syllable to the next is shortened. The tongue, however, requires an appreciable amount of time to shift from the alveolar contact of [n] to the velar contact of [k]. If the time is too short, the tongue anticipates the velar contact by shifting from [n] to [ŋ], since the sequence [ŋk] can be made with a single contact of the tongue, instead of the sequence of contacts required for [nk]. Furthermore, as Kent has pointed out,[2] thought constantly outstrips utterance, and this mental anticipation is closely associated with the mechanical adjustment just described.

Assimilation may therefore be defined as the process whereby one sound is changed to a second under the influence of a third;[3] in *income tax* the alveolar [n] changes to the velar [ŋ] under the influence of the

---

[1] For a table of phonetic symbols, see pp. 308–309. [eds.]

[2] Roland G. Kent, "Assimilation and Dissimilation," *Language*, XII (1936), pp. 245–258.

[3] Compare Daniel Jones, *An Outline of English Phonetics*, 8th ed. (New York, E. P. Dutton & Co., Inc., 1956), pp. 217–218.

velar [k]. Another useful definition is that of Bloomfield,[4] who points out that the position of the speech agents for the production of one sound is altered to a position more like that of a neighboring sound.

All assimilations start in a manner similar to that of *income tax*. The change may take place as soon as the two original sounds come close together: we have every reason to suppose that the sequence [ŋk] formed as soon as the word *sank* was formed. On the other hand, the change may take place more slowly if, as in *income tax*, the sequence is brought gradually together in the act of compounding. That is, many assimilations start as accidental mispronunciations of an accepted sequence of sounds. Some never progress beyond this stage, for they may be noticeable enough to cause adverse criticism, and to induce speakers to avoid the assimilation.

A substandard pronunciation of *length* illustrates this accidental type of assimilation. The shift from the velar [ŋ] to the linguadental [θ] is apparently too great for some speakers' muscular control. Consequently the tongue anticipates the dental position, [ŋ] changes to [n] in anticipation of the following [θ], and we hear the new pronunciation [lɛnθ], rhyming with *tenth* [tɛnθ]. The pronunciation [lɛnθ] has never, however, risen to the standard level, because it has always been noticeable enough to provoke adverse criticism. Most people pronounce *length* as [lɛŋθ] or [lɛŋkθ], the added [k] serving as a kind of insulation against assimilation.

On the other hand, some assimilations are adopted so promptly and generally that adverse criticism is futile. For example, derivatives of the Latin preposition *cum* occur in English with all three nasal consonants. The original [m] of *cum* survives in such words as *combine* [kəm'baɪn], *compare* [kəm'pɛr], and *comfort* ['kʌmfɚt]; but it has become [n] in such words as *contact* ['kɑn,tækt], *condemn* [kən'dɛm], and *constant* ['kɑnstənt]; and has become [ŋ] in such words as *congress* ['kɑŋgrəs] and *conquer* ['kɑŋkɚ]. A glance at the consonant which follows the nasal shows that in every word the nasal has approximated the position of the following consonant; [m] has assimilated to [n] before alveolar consonants, and to [ŋ] before velars. Many of these assimilations took place in the Latin period.

The assimilative process is essentially the same, whether in *length*, *income tax*, *condemn*, or *congress*, but the effect of adverse criticism has been

[4] Leonard Bloomfield, *Language* (New York, Holt, Rinehart and Winston, Inc., 1933), p. 372.

selective. There was probably no appreciable criticism of the assimilations based on Latin *cum;* most of them were completely established and accepted before English adopted the words from Latin or French.

Between the extremes of accidental, substandard assimilations of the type of [lɛnθ] and established, standard assimilations of the type of ['kɑŋgrəs] lie a few instances on which a final verdict has not yet been made. Some people object to ['ɪŋkəm ˌtæks]; others accept it, not only without objection, but often without even being aware that any change in pronunciation has taken place. Some people object to the assimilated ['hɔrʃˌʃu] for *horseshoe;* others accept it without noticing that they have lost the [s] of *horse* [hɔrs]. The fate of these and similar assimilations will be decided only in the future. In and of themselves, assimilations are neither good nor bad. General acceptance or rejection of a particular assimilation is completely irrelevant to the assimilative process.

When we consider the inherent nature of the assimilative process, we notice that in all the illustrations used thus far the preceding sound has been influenced in anticipation of the sound that follows. Though this is the most common type,[5] the direction of influence may be otherwise.

Americans who pronounce *tune* [tun] and *duty* ['duti] often wonder why British and Canadian speakers sometimes insert a seemingly gratuitous [ʃ] in *tune* [tʃun] and *duty* ['dʒuti]. Far from being gratuitous these sounds represent the assimilations that sometimes develop from [tjun] and ['djuti]. The sequences [tj] and [dj] are unstable, not because of the distance through which the tongue must move, but because of the delicacy of adjustment required. In [tʃun], the tongue has moved forward from the position of [j] to that of [ʃ], which blends more readily with [t]. In ['dʒuti], the tongue has moved forward from the position of [j] to that of [ʒ]. Thus [t] has assimilated [j] to [ʃ]; [d] has assimilated [j] to [ʒ]. The articulation of [t] and [d] is vigorous enough to move the place of articulation forward for the following sound, and the voiceless quality of [t] also carries over to the following sound. A more subtle illustration can be shown in the comparison of *rip, drip,* and *trip.* In *rip,* most Americans use the ordinary frictionless [r]. In *drip,* the tip of the tongue is so close to the gum ridge after [d], that a frictional allo-

    [5] See Roland G. Kent, "Assimilation and Dissimilation," *Language,* XII (1936), 246; Leonard Bloomfield, *Language* (New York, Holt, Rinehart and Winston, Inc., 1933), p. 372; E. H. Sturtevant, *Linguistic Change* (Chicago, University of Chicago Press, 1917), p. 49.

phone of [r] often results.⁶ In *trip*, the allophone of [r] may be both frictional and voiceless. In all these instances in which the preceding sound influences the sound that follows, classify the assimilation as *progressive*. When the second sound influences the first, as in *length* and *congress*, we call it *regressive*.

Finally, there is a third assimilative classification known as *reciprocal*, in which the two sounds influence each other and combine to produce a single sound which is a compromise between the two. The word *sure*, for instance, was formerly pronounced [sjʊr]; but the sequence [sj] required a more delicate adjustment than most speakers gave it. Consequently, the tongue slipped further back for [s] and further forward for [j], perhaps through some intermediate stage like [ʃj] or [sç], until the two sounds came together at the position for [ʃ] and gave us our present pronunciation [ʃʊr].

A similar reciprocal assimilation has taken place in *vision* ['vɪʒən], from earlier ['vɪzjən]. In *issue* and a few similar words, Americans habitually use the assimilated ['ɪʃu]; the most frequent British pronunciation seems to be the unassimilated ['ɪsju].⁷ Similarly, the change from [hw] to [ʍ] in such a word as *when* is a reciprocal assimilation in which [ʍ] takes its adjustment of tongue and lips from [w] and its voiceless quality from [h].

Assimilation and voicing

From the direction of influence in the assimilative process we now turn to the nature and varieties of the physical changes. First, assimilation may produce a change in the voicing of consonants. In *north* [nɔrθ] and *worth* [wɝθ], the final consonant is voiceless, but in *northern* ['nɔrðɚn] and *worthy* ['wɝði], the voiceless [θ] has been assimilated to the voiced [ð] by the voiced quality of the following vowels. In *thieves* [θivz], in comparison with *thief* [θif], [v] results from an earlier assimilation to a vowel which is now no longer pronounced.

⁶ The term *allophone* can be easily explained. The first consonant sound in *goose* is not exactly the same as the first consonant sound in *geese*. You can test this easily by whispering these sounds. Yet, though both are a *g* sound, the difference between the two never makes a difference in meaning in English. We call each of these *g* sounds an allophone of the *g*, which is called a phoneme. A phoneme is a speech sound, which may have allophonic variations, that makes a difference in meaning. Our *g* is a phoneme because it distinguishes the meaning of *goose* from *loose, moose, noose*, and so on. A phoneme is usually written between slants, e.g., /g/, and an allophone is written between brackets, e.g., [g]. [eds.]

⁷ See the 1956 edition of Daniel Jones, *An English Pronouncing Dictionary*.

Instances of the change from a voiced to a voiceless consonant are more numerous. The inflectional ending *-ed* . . . ends in [d] so long as the ending remains a separate syllable and [d] follows either of the voiced sounds [ɪ] or [ə], as in *heated* [ˈhitɪd] or *heeded* [ˈhidɪd].[8] But when inflectional *-ed* becomes nonsyllabic, it remains [d] after voiced sounds, as in *begged* [bɛgd], but assimilates to the voiceless [t] after voiceless consonants, as in *baked* [bekt].

Similarly, inflectional *-es* continues to end in [z] when the ending is syllabic, as in *guesses* [gɛsɪz]. When reduced to nonsyllabic status, inflectional *-es* and *-s* remain [z] after voiced sounds, as in *begs* [bɛgz], but assimilate to the voiceless [s] after voiceless consonants, as in *bakes* [beks].

A double assimilation takes place in the phrase *used to*. The verb *used* [juzd] has been assimilated to [just] by the following [t], and has acquired the meaning "formerly accustomed." The unassimilated pronunciation, with looser juncture, has been kept for the meaning "utilized." Thus, *the pen he used to* [ˈjustə] *write with* means the pen he was accustomed to write with; *the pen he used to* [juzd tə] *write with* means the pen he utilized for writing.

Something similar occurs in the phrases *have to* and *has to* when they denote compulsion. *That is all I have to* [ˈhæftə] *do* means that that is all I am compelled to do. *That is all I have to* [hæv tə] *do* means that that is all I have on hand at the moment to do. In the sentence, *That is all he has to do*, [ˈhæstə] and [ˈhæz tə] indicate the same distinction in meaning. The form [ˈjustə] is fully established in standard speech; the assimilated [ˈhæftə] and [ˈhæstə], despite their usefulness, still impress some conservatives as substandard.

A few minor instances, such as the occasional assimilation of *width* [wɪdθ] to [wɪtθ] and *breadth* [brɛdθ] to [brɛtθ], complete the list of changes from voiced to voiceless consonants. There is an element of unvoicing in the assimilation of [sj] to [ʃ] in *sure* and of [tj] to [tʃ] in *tune*, but these assimilations are primarily positional. . . .

Assimilation of nasal consonants

Another class consists of those assimilations which involve a change in the place of articulation of nasal consonants. We have already seen this class illustrated in such derivatives of Latin *cum* as *compound* [ˈkɑmˌpɑund], *combine* [kəmˈbaɪn], and *comfort* [ˈkʌmfɚt], which retain

---

[8] The inflectional ending *-ed* is syllabic when it follows a base which ends in *t* or *d*. *Heated* and *heeded* are also pronounced [hitɪd] and [hidɪd]. [eds.]

the unassimilated [m] before labials and labiodentals; and *content* [kənˈtɛnt], *condemn* [kənˈdɛm], *constant* [ˈkɑnstənt], *conquer* [ˈkɑŋkɚ], and *congress* [ˈkɑŋgrəs], which illustrate assimilation of the nasal to the place of articulation of the following consonant.

Other illustrations in this class usually depend on the loss of an "insulating" sound. After the loss, an instable sequence results, and assimilation is likely to take place. Thus if *open* [ˈopən] loses [ə] and becomes [ˈopn], it is likely to assimilate to [ˈopm], the alveolar [n] giving way to the labial [m] under the influence of the labial [p]. Similar assimilations may take place in *ribbon*, which may change from [ˈrɪbən] to [ˈrɪbn], and then assimilate to [ˈrɪbm]; in *bacon*, which may change from [ˈbekən] to [ˈbekn], and then assimilate to [ˈbekŋ]; in *wagon*, which may change from [ˈwægən] to [ˈwægn], and then assimilate to [ˈwægŋ]; *grandpa*, which may change from [ˈgrændpɑ], to [ˈgrænpɑ], and then assimilate to [ˈgræmpɑ]; and in *pumpkin*, which may change from [ˈpʌmpkɪn] to [ˈpʌmkɪn], and then assimilate to [ˈpʌŋkɪn].

Partial assimilations

Most of the assimilations discussed thus far are readily audible, even to speakers with little or no phonetic training. Most of them involve shifts from one phoneme to another. There remain some minor assimilations in which the change is slight enough not always to be audible to the untrained listener. Most of these changes involve only a shift from one allophone to another. Thus the [g] of *goose* has the normal contact of the back of the tongue with the soft palate. The [g] of *geese*, however, is a different allophone, partially assimilated to the front vowel [i] which follows it, and articulated farther forward in the mouth, sometimes as far forward as the back part of the hard palate. In *sing*, [ŋ] is similarly assimilated to a more forward allophone by the preceding front vowel [ɪ]; in *song*, a more backward allophone of [ŋ] follows the back vowel [ɔ]. The [t] of *eighth* [etθ], the [d] of *width* [wɪdθ], the [n] of *tenth* [tɛnθ], and the [l] of *health* [hɛlθ] are not ordinarily the usual alveolar allophones, but are usually assimilated to the dental position in anticipation of the dental [θ].

In initial sequences of voiceless consonants followed by voiced semivowels, the voicing of the semivowel may be slightly delayed by assimilation to the preceding voiceless consonant. This assimilation is most noticeable after voiceless fricatives. *Sweet* [swit] may become [sʍit] or [sʍit]; *thwart* [θwɔrt] may become [θʍwɔrt] or [θʍɔrt]. *Sled, frame, flame, throw,* and *shred* may have voiceless or partly voiceless [l] and [r] instead of the usual voiced allophones.

After voiceless stops, the assimilative unvoicing is a little less noticeable, but *twice* [twaɪs] may become [tᴍwaɪs] or [tᴍaɪs]; *quart* [kwɔrt] may become [kᴍwɔrt] or [kᴍɔrt]; and *play, pray, tray, clay,* and *crane* may have partly or completely unvoiced allophones of [l] or [r]. *Smell* and *snail* may have partly unvoiced [m] or [n].

Except for the idiomatic phrases *used to, have to,* and *has to,* single words have been used to illustrate the assimilative process. But assimilation may also take place at the junction of words, whenever the words are spoken without a pause. Thus we may hear such assimilations as *Miss Shaw* [mɪʃ ˈʃɔ], *Miss Young* [mɪʃ ˈjʌŋ] or [mɪʃ ʃʌŋ], *did you?* [ˈdɪdʒə], *was sure* [wəʒ ˈʃʊr] or [wəʃ ˈʃʊr], and *in court* [ɪŋ ˈkɔrt]. Though the social status of some of these illustrations is not secure, it must be realized that they look stranger than they sound.

The question of standard speech is, as we have seen, quite distinct from that of assimilation. The latter is a phonetic process, continually taking place, and restricted at times by conservative opinions. Many of the results of the assimilative process have been accepted on the standard level, immediately or eventually. Some of the assimilated forms characterized in this chapter as substandard may come to be accepted as standard in the future. Others may continue indefinitely to carry the stigma of substandard usage. The classification of particular assimilations as standard or substandard is therefore but one aspect of the question of standard or substandard speech in general. Questions of standards involve the judgments of speakers and critics of the language; they must not be confused with the "natural history" of the language itself.

SUGGESTED ASSIGNMENTS

1. A device that writers use to characterize illiterate persons is to represent the way they talk, e.g., "I da wanna go!" or "I betcha can't." Often the result in print produces a humorous effect, as writers of humorous stories and comic strips well know. Examine a comic book that contains dialogue of this sort and see to what extent the distorted spelling represents assimilations that are normal in colloquial language. Write a theme on your findings, identifying and explaining the assimilations you come across.
2. Many people have difficulty spelling words like *aggravate* and *alleviate.* If you find such words troublesome, here is where you can make your

investment in the study of assimilation pay dividends. Examine carefully the following list: *accept, addict, admonish, affix, aggravate, alleviate, announce, appear, arrive, assimilate.* (a) How do you account for the double letters in all the words except *admonish?* (If you can't figure it out for yourself, consult a good college desk dictionary.) (b) What causes the spelling difficulty? (c) Arrange in columns as many words as you can that are patterned after each of the words in the list except *admonish.*

3. If you were to make a list of words patterned after *admonish,* you would probably include such words as *adapt, adhere, adjacent, adjective, adjourn, adjudicate, adjust, admire, adorn, adverb, advocate.* These words appear to be identical in structure, *ad* plus a base, yet five of them are often misspelled. Which ones are they, and what causes the difficulty?

4. In English the prefix *in-* has a double set of meanings; sometimes it means in or into, as in *inhale,* to breathe in, and at other times it has the negative sense of no, not, without, as in *incomplete,* not complete. As a result of assimilation *in-* appears in a number of other forms, e.g., *il-,* as in *illegal.* What are the other assimilated forms of *in-?* Make four lists of words, one for each of the prefix forms, and then formulate a statement that explains the conditions under which assimilation takes place.

5. One of the things we all had to learn as children was to say *feet* instead of *foots, geese* instead of *gooses.* Words like *feet* and *geese* are often referred to as irregular plurals. In comparison with words like *boys, cats, books,* and *stones,* they are irregular. But these "irregular" forms did not come about in a haphazard fashion; they are the result of a regular sound change that occurred centuries ago. With your knowledge of assimilation, and with a bit more information, you should be able to explain the presence of these peculiar plurals in English. The pattern *foot-feet, goose-geese,* you will note, reveals a contrast of back to front vowels. The problem is how to account for the fronting. In Old English the forms of *foot* looked like this:

	Singular	*Plural*
Nominative	fōt	fēt
Genitive	fōtes	fōta
Dative	fēt	fōtum
Accusative	fōt	fēt

Notice that in Old English the dative singular as well as the nominative and accusative plural contained a front vowel. If we go farther back in time to the Germanic ancestor of English, we find that the Primitive Germanic dative singular was **fōti* and that the nominative and accusative plural was **fōtiz.* Somewhere along the line **fōti* and **fōtiz* became *fēt.* Philologists speak of the change that occurred as "i-umlaut," which is just another instance of assimilation. Can you explain what assimilation took place? The same sort of thing happened with *man, tooth, mouse,* and *louse.*

Spelling Pronunciation

JOHN SAMUEL KENYON

If you pronounce the word *victuals* as *vittles* and spell it as you pronounce it, your writing would be regarded as non-standard. If you spell *victuals* and pronounce it in ac- cordance with its spelling, your pronunciation would be non-standard. Only if you spell it *victuals* but pronounce it *vittles* would you be using standard forms in both writing and speech. We are back once more, you see, to that knotty problem of the relationship between speech and writing. Why is it that with a word like *cupboard* you would never think of pronouncing it the way it is spelled but with *victuals*, for many people, there would be a strong tendency to do so? You can find the answer to this question in the following essay by John S. Kenyon. Professor of the English Language for many years at Hiram College, he made important con- tributions to the study of language, especially in the areas of speech and phonetics. He was co-editor, with Thomas A. Knott, of *A Pronouncing Dictionary of American English*.

. . . Phonetic change is concerned primarily with the spoken language, and not with the written or printed representation of it. Most phonetic change is unconscious, and some of it has begun with the illiterate and afterwards found its way into cultivated usage. As a rule the changes that have occurred have either never found their way permanently into the spelling—as seen in the word *use*, which has gained an initial j that has not appeared in the spelling; or if the spelling has been changed to express the new sound, as it was in the word *you* (formerly without *y* or j sound), this has always happened long after the new pronunciation has become firmly fixed in speech. Thus it was two or three hundred years after the final syllable ceased to be sounded on words like *sunne*, *runne*, *houre*, *seeme*, *heare*, and hundreds of others, before the spelling was changed to *sun*, *run*, *hour*, *seem*, *hear*, to correspond with the sound; and in numerous cases the spelling has not even yet conformed to changes in sound made hundreds of years ago, as in such words as *have*, *love*, *make*,

From *American Pronunciation*, Tenth Edition, by John Samuel Kenyon. Reprinted by permission of the publisher, George Wahr Publishing Company, copyright 1950.

cause, tell, said, etc. Reflection on this aspect of the development of English shows how entirely without foundation is the reasoning frequently heard when a question is raised about the pronunciation of a word: "It is spelt so and so; therefore it should be pronounced so and so." E.g., it is argued that *clerk* and *sergeant* cannot properly be pronounced kla(r)k and sa(r)dӡənt because they are spelt with *er*. Yet *clerk* is regularly so pronounced in England, and *sergeant* so generally. Such reasoning puts the cart before the horse. The logical reasoning would be, since *clerk* and *sergeant* are pronounced kla(r)k and sa(r)dӡənt, they should be spelt with *a* instead of *e*.

It happens that the spelling of most words like *star, carve, smart, hart, far, farm,* has, in fact, conformed to the pronunciation. These words, like *clerk* and *sergeant*, formerly were all spelt with *er*, and continued to be so written long after the sound had changed from ɛr to ɑr. . . .

Those who reason that words should be pronounced as they are spelt scarcely realize what a revolution would be wrought in present English if they carried out their rule to any extent. Transcribe the following words in a spelling-pronunciation; that is, with the pronunciation they would have if all the letters were sounded in what would seem to you their most usual way:

Among, slough, brought, anxious, said, nothing, worst, people, pretty, brief, fiend, friend, money, could, bargain, road, abroad, scarce, farce, mouse, rouse, famous, where, here, hear, heard, beard, treat, great, leak, break, steak, ever, fever, done, gone, tone, none, whose, those, whole, whale, poor, moor, door, floor, seven, even, early, nearly, pearly, pear, fear, goer, doer, swear, answer, swore, sword, word, ford, form, worm, though, thought, tough, bough, through, home, some, mere, there, pays, says, gown, grown, down, mown, eight, height, caught, laughed, draught, evil, devil, double, doubtless, beeches, breeches, been, cloven, oven, bother, other, honor, honest, host, heir, weir, shelf, self, half, Ralph, revived, lived, power, mower, finger, singer, longer, anger, hanger, sorehead. forehead, hew, sew, county, country, grove, above, move, prove, over, cover, mover, all, shall, believe, sieve, wholly, jolly, surmise, promise, dully, gully, fully, pullet, mullet, goes, toes, does, shoes, frowned, owned, cross, gross, toward, coward, hearing, bearing, pouch, touch. . . .

The influence of spelling on standard pronunciation has been especially important since the middle of the 18th c., and especially owing to the influence of Dr. Johnson, who, though he recognized both a colloquial and a formal style of pronunciation, stated this principle: "For pronunciation, the best general rule is to consider those as the most elegant speakers who deviate least from the written words." This

statement was made in apparent disregard of the utter impossibility of
carrying it out in the state of English spelling then and since. His
influence was strengthened by the prevailing idea of the time that the
written form of the language was the language itself. This appears
clearly in the dictionaries of John Walker (1791 and on), in which
letters are treated as the elements of language, with "powers" of sound,
as if they were a kind of seed from which the spoken language sprouted
and grew, and therefore the original source to which all questions of
correct pronunciation were to be referred back.

This point of view is still current and influential. Its adherents cry
in triumph, "Isn't there a *t* in *often?* Why should we neglect to pronounce it?" As Dr. Fuhrken has aptly expressed it, they are willing to
mispronounce words in order to show that they know how they are
spelt. In addition to being fundamentally in error about the nature,
origin, and growth of all language, they strangely ignore the fact that
they neither do nor can carry out their own rule, as the exercise above
is sufficient to show.

A spelling-pronunciation that departs from the traditional pronunciation (the one that is transmitted by word of mouth and learned by
ear) is a blunder, of the same kind that it would be to pronounce *many*
as mænɪ or menɪ instead of mɛnɪ. But when such a blunder is adopted
into general good use, as was swun, formerly by regular sound-law
pronounced sun (cf. *sword* sord), or 'æsɪg‚neʃən (cf, *sign* saɪn), and a
large number of others, it is accepted and supersedes the correct traditional form. So a very considerable number of words—though a very
small proportion of all—have conformed in some respect to the spelling
which happened to be current when the change was made. Such changes
are, however, apt to be isolated ones, leaving unchanged many other
words spelt in the same way. Thus the pronunciation kɑnstəbl, a spelling-
pronunciation for the traditional kʌnstəbl, or kɑmræd for traditional
kʌmræd, have become isolated in pronunciation from the many other
words in which ʌ is spelt with *o*, as *honey, love, above, some, come,* etc. In
two groups, however, (1) words like *host, human, hospital,* etc., which
all came into English from OF without a h sound . . ., and (2) words
like *theater, author, apothecary,* etc., which came into English with *t* spelt
th—spelling-pronunciation has changed nearly all the words to pronunciations with the *h* sound and the θ sound. . . .

On comparing *host, human, hospital,* with *hour, honest, honor,* and
theater, author, apothecary with *Thomas, Thames, Esther,* an underlying
principle of spelling-pronunciation is revealed. The words that have

resisted spelling-pronunciation (*hour*, *Thomas*) are more common words, and therefore more likely to be thoroughly learned by children before they learn to read and write. On the other hand, if we first learn words from books, or if we see them in print oftener than we use them, we are more apt to guess at the pronunciation from the spelling. As a great many people are apt to do this, and many even cultivated and influential people unconsciously reason that words should be pronounced as they are spelt, many such spelling-pronunciations get into good use, and older traditional and phonetically natural pronunciations are gradually abandoned.

Spelling-pronunciation is especially apt to affect proper names—particularly names of places pronounced from the spelling by people who do not live in them and hence do not know the traditional pronunciation. So *Greenwich*, *Woolwich*, and *Norwich* in England are pronounced by the inhabitants of those towns grɪnɪdʒ, wʊlɪdʒ, nɛrɪdʒ (the latter riming with "cold pease porridge"). But people not personally familiar with the places themselves and seeing the names in print are likely to call them grinwɪtʃ, wʊlwɪtʃ, nɔrwɪtʃ. So *Cirencester* sɪsɪtɚ is apt to be called elsewhere saɪrənsɛstɚ. *Concord* kɛŋkəd and *Chelmsford* tʃɛmzfəd are usually called kɑnkɔrd and tʃɛlmzford outside of New England. The student can easily find other examples of the same sort.

Evidence that the influence of spelling on pronunciation is increasing with the advance of popular education is seen in that in recent times in some of the places themselves the traditional pronunciation is giving way to the spelling-pronunciation. Thus the inhabitants of Cirencester and others in England are beginning to call the place saɪrənsɛstə,-tɚ. *Ravenna* (Ohio) is called by its old residents rɪ'væne, but it is now commonly rə'vɛnə. *Mantua* (Ohio) is locally 'mæntə,we, but sometimes called 'mæntʊə or 'mæntʃʊə by those who depend on the spelling.[1]

The comparatively recent increase in the influence of spelling on pronunciation has resulted in the fact that certain places in England have the traditional name, often widely separated from the fixed spell-

[1] Regarding the correctness of the different pronunciations, it should be remembered that a different law governs in personal and place names from that of speech in general. In the latter, general usage of the cultivated determines correctness. But in personal and place names, it is personal and local usage that determines the pronunciation. For example, all the rest of the country cannot properly change the name of Concord, Massachusetts, to |kanˌkɔrd so long as the local inhabitants regularly call it |kaŋkəd. The same principle holds in family names. See Allen W. Read, *Amer. Speech*, Feb. 1933, pp. 42–46. [The ɐ represents a sound between ɑ and ɔ.]

ing, while places in America with the same names have the more theoretical pronunciation according to the spelling. Thus we have grınıdʒ in England, but grinwıtʃ in Connecticut; the river tɛmz in England, but ɵemz in Connecticut, except as the English name is imitated; *Waltham* wɒltəm in England, but wɒleəm, wɔleæm in Massachusetts; *Edinburgh* ɛdnbʌrə in Scotland, and ɛd(ɪ)nbɝg, various American towns; *Marlborough* mɔlbərə, England, and *Marlboro* 'mɑ(r)l‚bɝo Massachusetts.

In some cases, compounding of names brings together certain letters so as to suggest sounds not found originally in the name. Thus the name *Waltham* is composed of *Walt* + *ham* ('home,' 'dwelling'), in the same way as *Windham* wındəm, *Durham* dɝəm; so we should expect wɒltəm, as we find in England. But the spelling *th* has suggested the sound ɵ, which is used in the American name wɔleæm. *Chatham*, however, remains tʃætəm, and is often ˈtʃætˌhæm in the Ohio town and on Cape Cod, being also a spelling-pronunciation, but with a different result. *Windham*, Vermont, is locally often ˈwındˈhæm. Similar to *Waltham* are *Eltham* in England ɛltəm, ɛlɵəm, *Bentham* bɛntəm, bɛnɵəm, *Walsham* wɒlsəm, wɒlʃəm, *Lewisham* luɪsəm, luɪʃəm, *Feversham* fɛvəzəm, fɛvəʃəm.

In personal names spelling-pronunciation is seen in *Leópold*, formerly lɛpḷd (cf. *leopard*), now, from the spelling, liəpold; *Ralph*, formerly, and still in England ref, now rælf; *Theobald*, formerly tɪbḷd, now ɵiəbold; *Walter*, formerly wɒtɚ, now wɔltɚ. Personal names, being applied to many individuals and families, often split up into several different forms. Thus the name *Theobald* is represented by the various forms of the older pronunciation tɪbḷd in the names *Tibbits*, *Tibalt* (*Tybalt* in *Romeo & Juliet*), *Tibbals*, and the spelling-pronunciation ɵiəbɔld. *Walter* shows relics of its earlier pronunciation in the derivatives *Watt*, *Waters*, *Watson*, *Watkins*. . . .

Sometimes the spelling of a name has conformed to the earlier traditional pronunciation. So in the name *Ker*, *Kerr* kɑr, changed in spelling to *Carr* to correspond to the sound; and vice versa, the pronunciation of other instances of the same name has conformed to the spelling *Kerr*, becoming kɝ. So with *Berkeley* and *Barclay*. *Berkeley* was formerly pronounced bɑ(r)klɪ, as still in England, and accordingly sometimes spelt *Barkley*, *Barclay*, while in other cases the pronunciation conformed by spelling-pronunciation to the form *Berkeley* and became bɝklɪ.

Of words other than names, spelling-pronunciation has changed some that have become less familiar than formerly. Often both pronunciations are used—the older traditional one, and the newer spelling-pronunciation. So it is, frequently, with a class of words having the sound ʌ spelt with *o*, such as *love, dove, above, come, shove,* etc. The commoner words have retained the ʌ sound. But the word *wont* wʌnt, "custom," "accustomed," is now often pronounced wont from the spelling. Words which formerly had ʌ but now have ɐ, ɑ from the spelling are *dromedary* 'drʌmə₁dɛrɪ, *comrade, constable, bomb, groveling.* The old pronunciation with ʌ is still heard in these, and commonly in some of them.

A group of words like *fault, vault, falcon,* borrowed from French, in which the spelling with *l* is due to imitation of their Latin originals, had no l sound when they became English, and for long afterwards. But most of them have now conformed to the spelling; *fault* was fɔt in the 18th century. This accounts for the pronunciation of *Walter* mentioned above, . . .

Miscellaneous examples of spelling-pronunciation are: *steelyards,* formerly stɪljɚdz, now sometimes |stil⌐jɑrdz; *registrar,* formerly r ɛdʒɪstrɚ, now 'rɛdʒɪs₁trɑr; *nephew* nɛvju, now mostly nɛfju; *apothecary,* formerly ə'pɛtɪ|kɛrɪ, now ə'pɑθə₁kɛrɪ; *author,* formerly ɔtɚ, now ɔθɚ; *soldier,* formerly sodʒɚ, now soldʒɚ; *Wandsworth,* formerly wɛndzə, now wɛndzwəθ; *Southwark* sʌðək, sometimes now sauθwək.

SUGGESTED ASSIGNMENTS

1. The names of which states of the United States are likely to be mispronounced by foreigners because of the spelling?
2. Pronounce the following words: *blackguard, clapboard, breeches, calm, comptroller, provost marshal.* Now look up the pronunciations given in the dictionary. Which ones did you pronounce with a spelling-pronunciation?
3. Make a list of place names in your state that you think outsiders would be likely to mispronounce because of the spelling. Ask one of your college friends from a different state to pronounce the names on your list. Then tell him the correct pronunciation and note his reaction.

Standards of Acceptable English: Pronunciation

CHARLES CARPENTER FRIES

How often have you heard people criticize the pronunciation of others? "He said *ab'domen* when he should have said 'abdomen." "Did you hear that? Ac'climate! Everybody knows it should be '*acclimate.*" Or again, "He said *toozdi* instead of *tiuzday.*" Such self-appointed arbiters of the language are more often in error than those whom they criticize. Not because their pronunciation is wrong, but because they are under the false assumption that the pronunciation of Standard English is uniform, and there is only one acceptable pronunciation of a word. Actually the pronunciation of many words varies considerably among educated people; it varies from place to place, from group to group, and from individual to individual. A New Yorker does not speak like a Georgian, nor does a Texan speak like a Vermonter. Nor do all New Yorkers speak like each other. As a matter of fact, each individual has his own unique way of speaking. No one speaks like anyone else in every respect.

Diversity of pronunciation is not, as was formerly thought, something to be deplored. Although linguists have long recognized diversity of pronunciation as natural and inevitable, it is only recently that their views have gained acceptance. This change in attitude is due in part to the work of Charles C. Fries, Professor of English, Emeritus, and former Director of the English Language Institute at the University of Michigan. The achievement of Professor Fries in helping to bring about a more realistic attitude toward our language as well as a more accurate description of it can not be overestimated. He is the author of numerous articles and books. Especially noteworthy are his *American English Grammar* (1940) and *The Structure of English* (1952).

From *The Teaching of English* by Charles C. Fries. Reprinted by permission of the publisher, George Wahr Publishing Company, copyright 1949.

> "Somwhat he lipsed, for his wantonesse,
> To make his English swete up-on his tonge;"

Although lisping in "wantonesse" may have gone out of fashion, the effort of Chaucer's Friar "to make his English swete up-on his tonge" still lives. Some find this sweetness in imitating a few sounds of the British pronunciation of southern England; some in struggling to conquer the vowel sounds of an older New England; some in reproducing the intonations peculiar to our southern "quality." Our schools, however, seem less concerned with cultivating a charming speech than with trying to develop "correct pronunciation." And just as the rules of the common school grammars have been looked upon as the infallible guide to correct constructions so our purists in pronunciation have usually found measures of a similar character which furnished the objects of their idolatry.

The most common of these idols to be worshipped as the infallible guide to correct pronunciation is the pronouncing dictionary and those books of lesser dignity, the little handbooks of "correct speech."[1] Of course the attitude upon which this practice rests is simply another manifestation and survival of the eighteenth century views of language. The dictionaries, like the grammars, have fulfilled the function of an "academy" in setting up standards by which to judge good speech from bad. Thus whenever a question arises concerning any pronunciation the first impulse of most of us is to ask, "What does the dictionary say?" It is practically always *the* dictionary that is called for, as if there were but one; we never specify a particular one. And despite the date of publication, the pronunciation recorded in any dictionary, elementary or unabridged, or in any speech manual which happens to be at hand, is accepted as the *correct* one. Fortunately for our faith we seldom consult more than one book for the same word and thus raise no questions concerning the disagreements of the various "authorities."

To be convinced that such disagreements exist one needs only to consult the lists given in the unabridged editions of both Webster's *New International Dictionary* and the *Standard Dictionary*. In the latter the "Disputed Pronunciations" occupy pages 2763 to 2779 inclusive, a list of more than 2200 words. A similar list of something over 1600 words is given in the former dictionary, pages LIX to LXXVIII. Both lists

---

[1] Typical handbooks are Vizetelly's *A Desk-Book of 25,000 Words Frequently Mispronounced*, Pfyfe's *18,000 Words often Mispronounced*, and J. W. Abernethy's *Correct Pronunciation, a Manual of 2000 Common Words Frequently Mispronounced*.

contain only those words in respect to which the important dictionaries record and prefer essentially different pronunciations. An interesting as well as an enlightening exercise for one who has never tried it is to record first his own pronunciation of some words like those in the following list, and then to note and compare the pronunciations given in at least four different dictionaries:[2] *Asiatic, adult, Christian, glacial, nausea, suggest, codify, isthmus, gaseous, apron.*

Of course it would be a perfectly reasonable attitude to insist that any pronunciation appearing in any dictionary is to be approved; that where dictionaries differ the variant sounds are equally acceptable. Too frequently in practice, however, the pronunciation recorded in the particular book consulted is not only accepted as *a* correct one but as *the* correct one and all others condemned as wrong. Thus to use a dictionary as a final authority of correct pronunciation and to condemn all variations from the one or two renderings there recorded is entirely contrary to the views of the editors of our recent dictionaries,[3] if their statements as given in the prefaces fairly represent their attitude toward the marking of pronunciation.

The function of a pronouncing dictionary is to record as far as possible the pronunciations prevailing in the best present usage, rather than to attempt to dictate what that usage should be. In so far as a dictionary may be known and acknowledged as a faithful recorder and interpreter of such usage, so far and no farther may it be appealed to as an authority. . . .

In the case of diverse usages of extensive prevalence, the dictionary must recognize each of them, preferring that pronunciation which is used by the majority of the well-educated; . . .

Even when the actual usage to be adopted as a standard is determined upon, only approximation to exactness can be attained in its indication. The sounds which must be indicated by the same symbol are often subject to a considerable variation as spoken, not only by members of different communities, but also, frequently by members of the same community. . . .

There exist . . . especially in some of the vowel sounds, actual variations in pronunciation (all equally good, or allowable) that are so wide as to require special mention. Such, for example, are the sounds of *o* in *glory*, and the *a* in *vary*. The vowel sounds indicated in marking pronunciations are rarely in-

[2] The four outstanding dictionaries of today seem to be *The New English Dictionary* (also frequently called the *Oxford English Dictionary*), *The Century Dictionary*, *Webster's New International Dictionary* (1934), and *the Standard Dictionary*.

[3] The editors of the older dictionaries, those of the latter part of the eighteenth century and the early nineteenth century, did attempt to legislate on the matter of pronunciations. . . .

variable; what is marked in any case is the average or typical sound, around which the one actually spoken may vary according to conditions.[4]

Correctness in pronunciation, like correctness in diction, depends upon the consensus of usage among educated people. There are many words in the language regarding the correct pronunciation of which expert orthoepists and scholars as well as dictionaries do not agree. The correctness of English pronunciation should obviously be determined by the best and widest usage among the English speaking people.[5]

Still greater than the variation in the orthography, even the accepted orthography, of English words, is the variation in the pronunciation. . . . No attempt is made to record all the varieties of popular, or even of educated, utterance, or to report the determinations made by different recognized authorities. It has been necessary, rather, to make a selection of words to which alternative pronunciations should be accorded, and to give preference among these according to the circumstances of each particular case, in view of the general analogies and tendencies of English utterance.[6]

From the composite character of the English Vocabulary, the pronunciation, also, of many words is in a very unsettled state. This is the fact not merely with words from other modern languages, the pronunciation of which depends largely upon the linguistic knowledge and taste of the person who uses them, but also with derivatives from Latin or Greek, for which there exist two or more analogies. . . . The conflict of analogies, or the absence of any analogy, appears still more in purely scientific words, in which there may be said to be no general standard of pronunciation. The Editor was once present at a meeting of a learned society, where, in the course of discussion, he heard the word *gaseous* systematically pronounced in six different ways by as many eminent physicists.[7]

Two more considerations must be kept in mind in our attempt to judge the dictionaries as measures of correct pronunciation. It is to be noted, first, that although all these editors insist that correctness of pronunciation must rest fundamentally upon usage there has never been a comprehensive and scientific survey of English pronunciation and thus the records offered in any book are necessarily limited to the observations of the particular staff who worked on it. Our trust in the validity of the markings must depend solely upon our faith in the *opinions* of those individuals who edited the dictionary. More than that, all agree that usage in the matter of pronunciation is continually

[4] *Webster's New International Dictionary* (1925), pp. xxxviii.
[5] *The Standard Dictionary*, p. xii.
[6] *The Century Dictionary*, p. xiii.
[7] *The New English Dictionary*, p. xxiv.

changing. As a record of usage, therefore, any dictionary, by the time the material has been collected and printed, and the books offered for sale, is already behind the times. In some respects, at least, usage will have changed and the printed record be inaccurate.

Second, most of us need to be reminded that all our dictionaries (with the exception of the great *Oxford English Dictionary*) have been the product of private business enterprises. Quite frankly the purposes of these firms have been neither philanthropic nor scientific; they have invested capital in the making of books that would sell and return a profit. In line with good business policy they have sought the best editors and staff they could secure for the salaries they could afford to pay but have seldom attracted to the actual work of dictionary making the very best scholars in the field of English language.[8] The particular materials to be included in the dictionaries have been dictated primarily by the practical considerations of selling values. As a policy, no such dictionaries, even for the sake of scientific truth and language accuracy, could afford to oppose the prejudices and the common beliefs of the school public which buys the dictionaries. That public has demanded an authoritative standard of pronunciation and the dictionaries have in practice provided it[9] despite the careful statements of some editors to the contrary. Our blind faith in *the dictionary* as the authoritative measure of right and wrong in pronunciation has called forth from our scholars in the English language such statements as the following from the late Professor T. R. Lounsbury of Yale University:

It seems never to have occurred to any of the compilers of dictionaries, and to but few of those who consult them, that the simple solution of the whole difficulty is that in the matter of pronunciation there is no standard of authority at all. Nor, as things now are, can there be. Pronunciation must and will vary widely among persons of equal intelligence and cultivation. A dictionary which sets out to establish on a solid base an authoritative standard is bound to take into account the practice of the whole body of educated men the world over who are entitled to consideration. How is that to be ascertained? The mere statement of the fact shows its physical impossibility. It is a task beyond the power of any one person or any number of persons to accomplish.

Even this is not the worst. If everybody worth consulting could be consulted, we should still be left in precisely the same state of uncertainty in which

---

[8] This situation has improved considerably in the past few years. There are now a number of good dictionaries that have been prepared with the help of competent linguistic scientists. [eds.]

[9] G. & C. Merriam Company advertise *Webster's New International Dictionary* as "The 'Supreme Authority.' "

we were before. . . . Still this belief in the existence of a standard authority is one that will die hard even with the educated class. With the semi-educated class it will never die at all.[10]

A second idol reverenced by many as a sound guide to correct pronunciation is the spelling, Mr. Vizetelly says, for example,

Unfortunately, we have with us a large class of persons who speak without thinking how our words are spelled, and who, therefore, squeeze all the juice out of our speech by refusing to enunciate carefully all the niceties of sound that the words contain.[11]

It seems also to be a regard for the spelling which lies at the basis of such rules as the following:

Pronounce clearly and distinctly the first syllables of words beginning with *be* or *de:*

de cide	*not*	di *or* duhcide
de note	*not*	di *or* dunote
de test	*not*	di *or* duhtest
be lieve	*not*	bi *or* buhlieve

Pronounce carefully the final syllables in the following words:

fountain	*not*	fountun
mountain	*not*	mountun
certain	*not*	certun
Boston	*not*	Bostun
pupil	*not*	pupul
angel	*not*	angul
hovel	*not*	hovul [12]

From this point of view it is insisted that the *spelling* demands four syllables in the pronunciation of *usually* and three in *every*, that there must be no "p" in *warmth*, or in *something*, or in *comfort*, that *Arctic* has a *c* in the first syllable and must therefore be pronounced [arktɪk];[13] that *recognize* is spelled with a *g* and is therefore correctly pronounced [rɛkagnaɪz]; that in the words *hundred* and *children* the *r* precedes the *e* in the final syllable and therefore these words must be pronounced [həndrɛd] and [čɪldrɛn] not [həndərd] and [čɪldərn]; and finally that the vowels in the unstressed syllables of words, to be pronounced correctly, must be given the sounds of the letters with which they are spelled and not reduced to the obscure and colorless [ə] sound.

[10] T. R. Lounsbury, *The Standard of Pronunciation in English*, pp. 213–216.
[11] F. H. Vizetelly, *A Desk-Book of 25,000 Words Frequently Mispronounced*, p. VIII.
[12] Annie E. Polk, *Better Speech*, p. 13.
[13] For a table of phonetic symbols, see pp. 308–309. [eds.]

This view underlies the arguments offered in many discussions of correct pronunciation although it is not often expressly stated as a general principle. In attempting to test its validity three considerations demand attention.

First, the editors of at least three of our most important dictionaries have, in the prefaces to those works, made vigorous statements condemning the approach to modern English pronunciation through the spelling.

The pronunciation is the actual living form or forms of a word, that is, *the word itself*, of which the current spelling is only a symbolization—generally, indeed, only the traditionally-preserved symbolization of an earlier form, sometimes imperfect to begin with, still oftener corrupted in its passage to our time. . . .

In modern English speech, vowels are regularly obscured in syllables that have neither primary nor secondary stress, especially in those that follow the main stress; they then approach, or fall into, the sound of the mid-mixed vowel or [ə].[14]

One of the most peculiar characteristics of English pronunciation is the way in which it slights the vowels of most unaccented syllables, not merely lightening them in point of quantity and stress, but changing their quality of sound. To write (as systems of re-spelling for pronunciation, and even systems of phonetic spelling generally do) the vowels of unaccented syllables as if they were accented, is a distortion, and to pronounce them as so written would be a caricature of English speech.[15]

The spoken form of language is always more changeable than the written form, and changes in pronunciation are only slowly reflected in the spelling. Moreover since the invention of printing, English spelling has tended to become more and more conventional and fixed, while changes in pronunciation have continued. One has only to call to mind such common words as *busy, bosom, colonel, women, bough, enough, tough, night,* to realize how unphonetic their spelling is with reference to their present pronunciation. Again the written forms of some words, as *mountain, fountain, evil, devil, often, soften, Christmas, chestnut, handsome, handkerchief,* more nearly phonetic, mislead many persons, who feel that they should speak as they write, into pronunciations that depart from the best usage by making *-tain* rime with *rain*, *-il* rime with *hill*, by sounding the *t* in *often, Christmas,* etc.[16]

Second, the general principle of "pronouncing all the letters of our words as they are now spelled" is not only incapable of any wide application because of the acknowledged unphonetic character of the spelling

[14] *The New English Dictionary*, Preface, p. xxiv.
[15] *The Century Dictionary*, Preface, p. xiv, xv.
[16] *Webster's New International Dictionary* (1925), p. xxxviii.

of many words but it is also incapable of consistent application even in any narrow group of words. Not even the strongest advocate of spelling as the guide to pronunciation would dare sound the following words as they are spelled: *deign, sovereign, foreign, doubt, debt, island, aisle, know, knight, knee, knave, mortgage, any, many, English, two, whole, fatigue, tongue, ghost, does, calm, limb, lamb, sepulchre, choir, answer, sword, write*. Nor can one pronounce in any single way the same groups of letters. What, for instance should be the single sound given to the combination *ing* in the following words: *singer, finger, ginger?* What sound for the *eo* spelling in *Leopold, leopard, pigeon* and *people?* If *hoof, roof, root*, because of the *oo* spelling, must be pronounced as [huf], [ruf], [rut], and never [hʊf],[rʊf], [rʊt], should we consistently demand the same pronunciation of the following words which historically had the same vowel sound and retain a similar spelling, *book, good, stood, hood, hook?* I did find one teacher, and that in a large city school system, who with the courage of strong conviction was bound to be consistent. She insisted that the word *laughter* since it was spelled like *daughter* and *slaughter* must be pronounced in similar fashion, thus [lɔtər], and was drilling her pupils to pronounce it that way.

Even in the matter of following in pronunciation the order of the letters as they stand in the spelling one can hardly be consistent. He may say [həndrɛd] and [čɪldrɛn]; he may even school himself to say[eprən] rather than [epərn] for the word *apron*. He will hardly, however, say [airən] for the word *iron* rather than [aiərn]. If he does he invents a pronunciation, one not recorded in any of our dictionaries nor heard in the usage of people.

As a third consideration respecting the validity of spelling as a guide to correct pronunciation one must view a few of the important facts in the history of English spelling.[17] "How came we to spell as we do, and how is it that the written symbol so frequently gives a totally false impression of the true sound of the spoken word?" Although the writing of French shows probably a greater "divergence between sound and symbol," "English shows the maximum of irregularity and arbitrariness."[18] During the Old English period (*i.e.*, before 1100 A.D.) and even during a large part of the Middle English period (1100–1500)

---

[17] The history of English spelling is treated at some length by W. W. Skeat in *Principles of English Etymology*, First Series, Chapter XVI, pp. 294–333, and is touched upon by A. J. Ellis in *Early English Pronunciation*, Chapter VI, pp. 565–632, and by Henry Sweet in *A History of English Sounds*, pp. 59–73.

[18] Encyclopædia Britannica, article *Phonetics*, 11th edition, Vol. 21, p. 459.

the spelling of English was fairly phonetic and changed with the changing pronunciation. Consistency of spelling was not then a virtue.
Chaucer, for instance, spells the word *high* in three different ways
within a space of fifty lines, thus:

and hye on horse he sat	A-271[19]
and ful of hy sentence	A-301
and for his heigh renoun	A-316

Differences in spelling usually furnished some evidence of differences in
sound. Even at this time, however, the spelling not only lagged behind
changes in pronunciation, but it had been subjected to such treatment
as further to spoil its phonetic accuracy. The practice of doubling
vowel letters to indicate vowel length (hōf—hoof, hrōf—roof, bōk—
book, cwēn—queen) was only partly carried out as was also that other
practice of doubling the consonant after a short vowel (biter—bitter,
soper—supper, somer—summer). Many long vowels still remained
single in spelling and many short vowels were still followed by single
consonants (meddle, medal; mettle, metal; copper, proper). The
respelling of the language by Anglo-French scribes in the thirteenth
and fourteenth centuries accounts for many changes from the particular
letters in use during the Old English period. Thus, for example, *cw*
was replaced by *qu*, þ and ð were replaced by *th*, and *c* was used at
times to represent the sound [s].

The two most important facts in the development of English
spelling for our view here, however, are matters of the fifteenth and
sixteenth centuries. First, the introduction of printing and the increase
of books worked to crystallize or conventionalize the spelling and
prevent it from further adapting itself to the pronunciation. From the
printers' point of view the ideal spelling is one that is absolutely uniform
and unchangeable. It has been this influence that has led to the setting
up of "correct" spelling and adherence to this *uniformity* as a skill to be
cultivated.

At the time that the influence of the printers was making for a
hard and fast system of spelling, the so-called "etymological" idea was
introduced. The sixteenth-century pedants, who were enthusiastic for
the classics, attempted to find traces of Latin in English words. Some,
indeed, insisted that all the English language came from Latin. In order
then to render this connection between English and Latin words more

---

[19] This instance should probably not be included, for *hye* is here an adverb,
not an adjective as it is in the other instances.

evident to the eye they changed the spellings of many words. Of course this kind of etymologizing could be applied to but a part of the language. It was the learned words rather than the very common words which were thus treated to "etymological" spelling. Unfortunately the scholarship of these pedants was unequal even to the task of dealing with the learned words of the vocabulary, and they introduced many errors. Thus an *s* was inserted in the word *island* to show a connection with the Latin word *insula*, although *island* (spelled by Chaucer *iland*) is not in any way related to *insula* but is in fact a good old Anglo-Saxon word, *ig-land*, meaning *waterland*. Many of these errors still exist and account for some of the worst of our present spellings; witness, for instance, the *g* in *sovereign* and in *foreign*.

English spelling since the sixteenth century has been dominated by two principles. The phonetic principle has applied to popular words and the so-called "etymological" principle has applied to the more learned words. But neither principle has been carried out consistently even in its own province. More than that, pronunciation changes since the sixteenth century have been very great while spelling changes have been comparatively few. We have thus today a petrified system of spelling which very imperfectly represented the pronunciation of English during the time of Shakespeare but is now used to represent a twentieth century pronunciation. With such a situation, despite the fact that there is enough phonetic connection between the written symbols and the word sounds to enable us to guess approximately the pronunciation of many words we cannot ever be sure as to any particular word and we cannot by any means accept the view of Dr. Johnson "to consider those as the most elegant speakers who deviate least from the written words."[20]

In addition to dependence upon the spelling as the basis for determining the proper sounds of words and the reverence for the pronouncing dictionaries as the authority, there is a third idol very generally worshipped as a guide to *correct* pronunciation. It is the principle that borrowed words must continue their sounds from the language from which they come. From this point of view it is asserted that the only correct pronunciation for a borrowed French word is the sound which that word has in French; that the "analogies" of the Latin language should determine the pronunciation of Latin words in English. Thus in application of this view, it is demanded that *inquiry* should be pro-

[20] Samuel Johnson, Preface to *Dictionary* (1755).

nounced [ɪ'nkwaɪ rɪ] never [ɪ'nkwɪrɪ]; that *acclimate* must be [æklaɪ'mɪt] never [æ'klɪmet]; that *arbutus* must be stressed on the first syllable and *abdomen* on the second. By similar reasoning it is insisted that *prestige* must be pronounced [prɛsti'ž] never [prɛsti'ǰ], and *garage* always [gəra'ž] never [gəra'ǰ] and certainly not [gæ'rɪǰ].

As a matter of fact it is the borrowed words in our language which cause many of the problems of pronunciation. English has an immense number of these foreign words from many sources. Nearly half of our vocabulary is made up of words from the Latin language, if we include as Latin element both direct borrowings from Latin itself and also those words that have come through French. Some of these borrowed words remain learned words, restricted in their use to those people who are likely to have some familiarity with the language from which they come. These words cling to their foreign sounds and accent even after centuries of use. Thus *caprice*, a seventeenth-century borrowing, shows in usage no signs of shifting from its present pronunciation, [kəpri's]. It is not a word used by the ordinary man of the street. On the other hand, words which become popular and are used by many who are unfamiliar with the sounds of the foreign language tend to a pronunciation adjusted to English sounds and English stress. Thus the word *garage*, although of comparatively recent importation, is used by people of all stations in life for almost every family has one. The Englishing of the pronunciation of this word has come rather quickly. In many communities it has become [gæ'rɪǰ]; certainly [gəra'ǰ] is more general than [gəraž].

As a principle to guide pronunciation the attempt to continue the foreign sound of a borrowed word is impossible of consistent application.[21] Even those who are most careful to observe the foreign sounds of the comparatively few words to which their attention happens to be directed would not, in accord with that principle, insist upon stressing the following words on the next to the last syllable, *audi'tor*, *ora'tor*, *sena'tor*, *victo'ry*. If this principle is sufficient ground for condemning

---

[21] It is really impossible for most of us to jump suddenly into the speech pattern of a foreign language in the midst of an English sentence. Our rendering of the pronunciation of a foreign word is, therefore, only approximately correct, rarely accurate. See, for instance, the comment of Jespersen in *How to Teach a Foreign Language*, p. 92.

"Let me remark in passing that I have always given my pupils French names [in classes in French] immediately in one of the first lessons; . . . the teacher has the advantage of being able to use their names in the middle of a French sentence without marring the run of the language."

the pronunciation [gæ'rɪ]] as incorrect, then to pronounce *courage* and *carriage* as most of us do is equally incorrect. Even in the matter of foreign proper names the principle of preserving the foreign pronunciations cannot be maintained in the cases of names that become very generally used. The word *Paris* is a case in point, or the name *Beatrice.*

In passing, we need but call attention to the fact that most of those who cling to the belief that a word borrowed from another language is correctly pronounced only when it maintains the foreign sounds apply the principle only to words from those languages with which they happen to be familiar. Words from Arabic or Hebrew or the American Indian languages are Englished with no apologies. In the pronunciation of the many foreign words in our language, therefore, we cannot accept this principle as the standard of acceptable pronunciation.

If, then, we must repudiate all three of the measures of correct pronunciation so commonly used what can we offer as the standards of acceptable English speech? First of all, the actual sound of the word as it is heard in the present usage of English speakers, not the spelling, not the etymology, must be the basis of all the "correctness" there can be in pronunciation. The *practical* standard of pronunciation must thus be the speech of those we actually *hear.* With the development in means of communication, increasing travel and moving from place to place, and especially the rapidly spreading use of the radio, these personal contacts are likely to have a much wider range than formerly, and as a result, there ought to be an increasing number of people with speech characteristics of approximate similarity. Certainly those who carry on the affairs of English-speaking people are now more frequently and more widely heard by voice than could have been possible in preceding times. I should insist, then, that the pronunciations common in the usage of those in positions of influence and respect must furnish the starting point for determining what is acceptable English in respect to pronunciation.

When one examines this usage, even superficially, he discovers very soon that the same word is frequently pronounced differently *by the same person* when used in differing circumstances. We must conclude, then, that there is no *one* pronunciation of a word that is the true pronunciation for that word under all circumstances. The amount of stress given the word in a sentence and the character of the surrounding sounds must organically affect the pronunciation. The word *him,* for instance, stressed in such a sentence as "Give it to hím, not to Máry," has a very distinct initial [h]. But in the following sentence, with a heavy stress on the words *to* and *from*, "Give it tó him—don't take it fróm him," the initial aspirate disappears and the word becomes [ɪm]. Again, no one actually speaking *English* would give the same sounds to both the conjunction *that* and the demonstrative *that* in such a combination as "in order *that that* nation might endure." This difference between the sounds of words when pronounced alone or under stress and when sounded in an unemphasized part of a sentence the dictionaries generally recognize. Such recognition, however, is usually expressed only in the preface and most of us miss it.

The difference between the pronunciation of a word when taken alone and as it occurs in a sentence should also be kept carefully in mind; thus *and* considered alone is *and*, but in such a combination as *bread and butter* it is usually weakened to *'nd*, or even to *'n; a* in the phrase *for a day* becomes *ȧ* (sof' *ȧ*), etc.[22]

Again, even a superficial examination of the pronunciation of those speakers of English in positions of respect and influence reveals also the fact that there are many differences in these pronunciations from speaker to speaker. The lists of the so-called "disputed pronunciations" in our dictionaries (see above page 326) offer some evidence for this assertion. As in the case of grammar, the problems arise out of these differences of usage. It is because many people who rightfully claim our respect pronounce the word *suggest* [səǰest] and many others meriting equal respect insist on the pronunciation [səgǰest] that we raise the question as to which is the *correct* sound. When these differences amount to more than mere individual peculiarities and become really significant divisions of usage, one can maintain the following point of view:

(1) Where this general spoken usage differs in respect to the sound of any word, no *one* pronunciation is the *sole* correct one. The several pronunciations in actual usage are thereby acceptable.[23]

(2) In such cases of divided usage, however, a reasonable choice may be made in accord with the following considerations:

(a) In the matter of borrowed words, for that pronunciation which is in harmony with English sounds and English accent.

[22] *Webster's New International Dictionary* (1925), p. xxxviii.
[23] The very definite use of ambiguous symbols in the dictionaries would substantiate this view. In the Preface of the *New English Dictionary* (p. xxiv) we have the following, "The vowel in *pass*, command, variously identified by different speakers with *a* in man, and *a* in father, is symbolized by the avowedly ambiguous *a̤*. Similarly, the doubtful length of the *o* in *off*, soft, lost (by some made *short* as in got, by some long as in Corfe, by others medial) is indicated by *ǫ̇*." In this connection I must again call attention to the fact that I am in these chapters discussing standards of *acceptable* English, not the problem of *beautiful* or *artistic* language.

(b) For that pronunciation which is in harmony with the tendencies of English speech in the matters of unstressed vowels, and organically phonetic assimilations of consonants.

Concerning the unstressed vowels the quotations from *The New English Dictionary* and *The Century Dictionary*, given above on page 331, indicate the practice in English.

Phonetic assimilation in the case of consonants is illustrated in part by the following quotation from *The Century Dictionary*.

On the side of consonant utterance, there is a very large class of cases where it can be made a question whether a pure *t* or *d* or *s* or *z* is pronounced with an *i*- or *y*-sound after it before another vowel or whether the consonant is fused together with the *i* or *y* into the sounds *ch*, *j*, *sh*, *zh* respectively—for example, whether we say *natūre* or *nachur*, *gradūal* or *grajöal*, *sūre* or *shör*, *vizūal* or *vizhöal*. There are many such words in which accepted usage has fully ranged itself on the side of the fused pronunciation: for example, *vizhon*, not *vizion*, for vision; *azhur*, not *azūre* for azure; but with regard to the great majority usage is less decided, or else the one pronunciation is given in ordinary easy utterance and the other when speaking with deliberation or labored plainness, or else the fused pronunciation is used without the fact being acknowledged.[24]

Other examples of such assimilations are the following pronunciations: *chestnut* as [čɛsnət], *friends* as [frɛnz], *something* as [sʌmpɵɪŋ], *length* as [lɛŋkɵ], *ink* as [ɪŋk], *handkerchief* as [hæŋkərčɪf], *pumpkin* as [pʌŋkɪn].

(c) For that pronunciation which maintains a careful discrimination of those sounds that the English speech pattern uses to distinguish many meanings. Two quotations may aid to clarify this point although it is by no means simple.

The latitude of correctness is very far from being the same in different languages. Some sounds in each language move within narrow boundaries, while others have a much larger field assigned to them; each language is punctilious in some, but not in all points. Deviations which in one language would be considered trifling, in another would be intolerable perversions.[25]

The voiced or voiceless character of the consonants and the quality of the vowel sounds in stressed syllables are examples of such important points in the English speech pattern. Thus, for instance we distinguish many words simply by a differentiation of a single vowel sound: heat [hit], hit [hɪt], hate [het], hat [hæt], hut [hət], hot [hat], hoot [hut], height [haɪt]. Examples of differentiation by means of voicing only are the following: pin–bin, tin–din, cold–gold, fine–vine.

[24] *The Century Dictionary*, Preface, p. XIV.
[25] Otto Jespersen, *Language*, p. 283.

The second quotation touches my point from another angle:

I found that it was difficult or impossible to teach an Indian to make phonetic distinctions that did not correspond to 'points in the pattern of his language,' however these differences might strike our objective ear, but that subtle, barely audible, phonetic differences, if only they hit the 'points in the pattern,' were easily and voluntarily expressed in writing. In watching my Nootka interpreter write his language, I often had the curious feeling that he was transcribing an ideal flow of phonetic elements which he heard inadequately from a purely objective standpoint, as the intention of the actual rumble of speech.[26]

If the view of English pronunciation given in this chapter has any validity it must be evident that in dealing with matters of pronunciation, especially in attempting to determine what is acceptable English speech, it is well to cultivate the virtue of tolerance. There is comparatively little difficulty in settling upon some one pronunciation for any word that must be acknowledged acceptable. Justly to render a negative judgment, however, to condemn any pronunciation that one hears generally used, demands much greater caution as well as knowledge. The suggestions here given as considerations to guide one's choice in matters of divided usage are to be taken as standards of acceptable pronunciation only from the positive point of view. It must not be assumed that all other pronunciations are necessarily unacceptable.

SUGGESTED ASSIGNMENTS

1. The following passage is taken from the Preface to *A Critical Pronouncing Dictionary and Expositor of the English Language* by John Walker (1732-1807), a lexicographer whose work was highly regarded during the first half of the nineteenth century:

   . . . If the analogies of the language had been better understood, it is scarcely conceivable, that so many words in polite usage would have a diversity of pronunciation which is at once so ridiculous and embarrasing: nay, perhaps it may be with confidence asserted, that if the analogies of the language were sufficiently known, and so near at hand as to be applicable on inspection to every word, that not only many words which are wavering between contrary usages would be settled in their true sound, but that many words, which are fixed by custom to an improper pronunciation, would by degrees grow regular and analogical; and those which are so already would be secured in their purity, by a knowledge of their regularity and analogy.

[26] Edward Sapir, *Language*, p. 58 (footnote).

Write a theme in which you discuss (1) the assumptions held by Walker, and (2) the fallacies involved in his solution to the "ridiculous and embarrassing" problem.

2. In each of the following pairs of sentences the "same" word is used, but the pronunciation is not the same. Read each sentence aloud in a natural, conversational tone and rhythm.

   a. Yes, they *are*!
   b. They *are* at the station.

   c. She is good to look *at*.
   d. Look *at* him go!

   e. You should do everything you *can*.
   f. I *can* see it in the distance.

   g. He gets better from *day* to *day*.
   h. Sun*day* is the best time.

   i. Who is it *for*?
   j. Look *for* the answer in the book.

   k. Look at *him*, not her.
   l. I saw *him* at the station.

   m. He is a *just* man.
   n. *Just* a minute, I'm coming.

   o. *There* he is.
   p. *There* were three of them in the room.

How, specifically, does the underlined word in the second sentence of each pair differ in pronunciation from its counterpart in the first sentence? What causes the difference?

3. Pronounce each of the following expressions in a natural, conversational way:
   a. snow and ice
   b. cup and saucer
   c. bread and butter
   d. up and down
   e. jack and queen
   f. this and that, not this or that

How many different pronunciations did you have for *and*? How many of these different pronunciations of *and* are listed in your dictionary? Who is right, you or the dictionary?

4. Examine one of the How-to-Improve-Your-Speech books written for the popular market and available in most drugstores and supermarkets. Write a theme on the discussion of pronunciation which you find in it. You might

consider some of the following points: a. Is pronunciation discussed in terms of isolated words or of actual running speech? b. What attitude, if any, is expressed toward assimilation? c. Is any mention made of the desirability of adapting one's speech to various situations?

5. Force yourself to listen for fifteen minutes to a radio announcer or commentator who you think has speech mannerisms that cause you to react negatively to him or her. Prepare a talk in which you analyze the reasons for your reactions, citing specific evidence from the program. If you could tape-record the program, it would be helpful in illustrating your points.

6. In *College English*, October 1951, there is an article entitled "The Eye, the Ear, and the Misspelled Word." The main idea of the essay is that misspelling is often the result of mispronunciation. Read the essay, examine the evidence presented, and then write a theme in which you evaluate the author's position.

7. Write a theme in which you discuss tendencies leading toward greater uniformity of pronunciation in the United States.

FURTHER READINGS

Bronstein, Arthur J. *The Pronunciation of American English*. New York: Appleton-Century-Crofts, 1960. On standards of pronunciation, see pp. 3-18; on assimilation, pp. 207-215.

Hall, Robert A., Jr. *Linguistics and Your Language*. New York: Doubleday & Company, Inc. (Anchor Books), 1960. On the sound system, see Chapter 6.

Kenyon, John Samuel. *American Pronunciation*, 10th ed. Ann Arbor, Michigan: George Wahr Publishing Company, 1961. On the sound system, see especially pp. 33-73; on assimilation, pp. 76-80.

——— "Cultural Levels and Functional Varieties of English," *College English*, Vol. 10 (October 1948), pp. 31-36.

Robertson, Stuart and Frederic G. Cassidy. *The Development of Modern English*. Englewood Cliffs, New Jersey: Prentice-Hall, Inc., 1954. On the sound system, see pp. 52-76; on assimilation, pp. 79-80; on spelling and spelling reform, pp. 353-374 (there is a useful bibliography on p. 374); on pronunciation, Chapter 12.

Thomas, Charles Kenneth. *Phonetics of American English*, 2d ed. New York: The Ronald Press Company, 1958. On standards of pronunciation, see pp. 253-260.

Sapir, Edward. *Language*. New York: Harcourt, Brace & World, Inc., 1921. On the sound system, see Chapter III.

7

USAGE

Bargain Basement English

WILSON FOLLETT

Our relationship to knowledge is paradoxical. We have, on
the one hand, an insatiable desire for knowledge, a questing
spirit that will not be denied. Yet when new knowledge is
discovered it is not always welcomed. Indeed, at times it is
strongly resisted and comes to be accepted only gradually
and reluctantly. One of the hardest things to do is to accept
new knowledge that runs counter to what we have been
taught. It means giving up old knowledge, relinquishing
what we have regarded as established fact. One would think
that a "fact," of all things, would remain constant. Yet the
history of knowledge is built, in part, on the shattered facts
of the past. Astrology and alchemy long ago gave way to
astronomy and chemistry. And even today Newtonian
physics, long accepted and firmly established, has given
way to the more modern theories of Einstein and his successors. So too in language. Until fairly recently, most
people accepted unquestioningly principles and rules of
usage and grammar laid down by eighteenth-century grammarians. Contemporary linguists, however, have not only
challenged but have actually repudiated many of the
eighteenth-century views. They assert that just as the "laws"
of Newtonian physics can no longer be accepted as an
adequate description of the natural universe, so too the
"rules" of the eighteenth-century grammarians constitute
an outmoded and inaccurate description of our language,
both in usage and in grammar.

It should come as no surprise to learn that these new

From *The Atlantic Monthly* (February 1960). Originally published as "Grammar Is
Obsolete." Title changed by request of the author; reprinted by his permission.

views have not been welcomed with open arms by all. Indeed, instead of embracing the new knowledge, adherents of the older tradition have taken up arms of a different sort to engage in intellectual combat. Nor have proponents of the new been unmilitant in advancing their cause. This running battle has been going on for more than thirty years. During this period the ground has shifted a number of times, positions have not always been clear, and misunderstanding, on both sides, has been ever present. Although it is clear that the forces of the new hold the field, the battle is not entirely over. One skirmish occurred in the pages of the *Atlantic,* from which the next two readings were taken. In the first one, Wilson Follett, author and editor, deplores what he regards to be the consequences of modern linguistic scholarship.

Linguistic scholarship, once an encouragement to the most exacting definitions and standards of workmanship, has for some time been dedicating itself to the abolition of standards; and the new rhetoric evolved under its auspices is an organized assumption that language good enough for anybody is good enough for everybody. We have come into a time when the ideals preached and, sometimes, practiced by exalted authority can only take shape in uses of English that are at best tolerable and at worst revolting. Such official pressure as is now put on the young learner is no longer in the direction of forcing him to ask himself whether his way of saying something could have been made better at a bearable cost — as, in a language so rich and various as ours, it generally could have. Everything now taught him concentrates on the lowly question, Will it do at a pinch?

For the handiest possible conspectus of what the new ideal is, one can do no better than to glance at a recent comprehensive manual of rhetorical practice. *A Dictionary of Contemporary American Usage,* by Bergen Evans and Cornelia Evans, comes from authors of prestige and influence, one of them a university professor of English and conductor of a radio and television program devoted to questions of spoken and written usage, the other a writing consultant in the Department of Health, Education, and Welfare and a prize-winning novelist. The reason for turning to this 570-page, 600,000-word volume is not that its publisher proclaims it to be "up-to-date, complete, authoritative" — an assertion of three attributes inherently unattainable by any such work compiled by mortals — but rather that it is declared with strict accuracy to be "based on modern linguistic scholarship." It is essentially a popularization of findings about modern English arrived at and promulgated by contemporary philologists, semanticists, virtuosos of historical and descriptive (as opposed to prescriptive) grammar and morphophonetics, and learnedly implacable assailants of the discarded idea that to speak or write well means hard work, the taking of sometimes painful thought, the constant rejection of labor- and thought-saving alternatives, and the practice of canons that are mastered only by arduous self-cultivation and discipline.

The Evanses manage to convey, along with many shrewd discriminations and salutory warnings often very engagingly phrased, an overall impression that acceptable usages are arrived at by a process about as automatic as breathing; that to torment oneself with questions of better and not so good is to be a seeker after gratuitous trouble and, what is worse, a purist; and that the way to attain effective expression is to keep our ears open, bank on our natural and inescapable linguistic inheritance, and cultivate an English that will make us indistinguishable from the ostensibly educated surrounding majority. Let us see where anyone will come out if he accepts and applies the combination of what these authors recommend, what they defend or condone, and what they do themselves. He will come out speaking and writing an American English faithfully represented by the scattering that follows:

"Ask whoever you see." "He had as much or more trouble than I did." "He works faster than me"; "he is taller than me." "More unique." "Different than." "The reason is because. . . ." "I can't imagine it being him." "Let's you and I"; "let's you and me." "Bob as well as Frank were there." "Neither D. nor A. are at home"; "neither he nor I are timid"; "either of them are enough to drive a man to distraction"; "neither of them had their tickets"; "I do not think either of them are at home"; "each carried their own pack"; "each of the men were willing to contribute." "Every member brings their own lunch"; "either the boy or the girl left their book." "I cannot help but think." "Nobody was killed, were they?" "Less than three." "If one loses his temper." "We did not find a one." "The sheriff with all his men were at the door." "Not one of them were listening." "Some grammarians claim that this is not permissible." "He allowed that we were right." "Refer back to." "Back of" (behind). "Between each house"; "between every pause." "He blamed it on me." "I haven't

but a minute to spare." "I don't doubt but that you are surprised."
"Who did you see?" "Who are you looking for?" "Children whom we
know are hungry." "Everyplace"; "anyplace"; "someplace"; "someway"; "noplace"; "I have looked everyplace." "It is not I who is
angry." "These kind of men are dangerous." "You don't know Nellie
like I do." "It is you who will be blamed for it, not them." "That's her
at the door now." "A minimum of sufficiency." "We most always go
shopping on Saturday." "Very amused." "Overly cautious." "Datas";
"phenomenas"; "much data"; "very little data"; "the data is now in."
"I asked him what was he doing." "The rationale for his attack on the
President." "As regards." "Somebody left their umbrella." "I will
get one someway." "There will only be him left." "Subsequent to his
release from the Air Force he got a job with a commercial air line."
"A continuous use [of a word in a specified way] is vulgar." "He went
no further than Philadelphia." "Neither of these reasons justify the
use of the present tense." "He failed, due to carelessness."

This little anthology could be several times multiplied from the
same source; thus much will do to imply a general pattern. Some of
the specimens are patently better, or less bad, than others. Say of the
whole, if you wish: "Some of it might be worse." There is no point
in using a microscope on the gradations or on the merits of the arguments used to defend this locution or that. It is enough if we perceive—
as we cannot very well escape doing—that collectively they define a
stratum of diction that invites defense and seems to require it, one that
it is now fashionable to defend with all the resources of specialized
learning. No one could possibly contemplate any such handful and
then declare its components above challenge and in no need of con-
doning; no one could associate them with an unremitting effort to
discover and to utilize the best that our common language is capable of.
A collection of the same size could hardly vary much from this one
if it deliberately set out to specialize in the marginal, the dubious, the
suspect. What it seems to represent is the pattern of habits deliberately
adopted by the educated when they set out to show that they are no
better than anyone else, if as good. It goes to show the lengths to which
we can carry conformism and the terror of being noticeable in a society
that is (as Bierce said of the republic long before H. L. Mencken was
heard of) daft with democracy and sick with sin.

If anyone wanted to execute a piece of writing that would be from
beginning to end the densest possible concentration of what the elder
rhetoricians classified as solecisms, he could hardly do better than to

attune his prose to the dicta laid down in *A Dictionary of Contemporary American Usage*. The book is an astute, artful, and tireless harvesting of whatever in American speech is barely tolerable to those who do not make a virtue of pushing either tolerance or intolerance to pathological extremes. And it is a translation into practical advice of what the most erudite philologists and lexicographers have for some time been telling us about the sources of health and vitality in our language. The great nuclear principle seems to be that we should speak and write not as well as we can learn how, but ignobly enough to escape notice.

Now, a resort to this kind of first aid may result in some tactical advantage to the purveyor of insurance or real estate, the chairman of a fund-raising campaign, the soapbox orator, the candidate for minor office. Even that advantage can be doubted: there seems to be a fairly powerful undertow of envious popular respect for the man who uses language with easy distinction, provided that he does it in quiet assurance with no air of showing off or of spitting on his hearers to see if they can swim, as the rude old Yankee folk saying has it. An instance is the standing that ex-Governor Adlai Stevenson seems to have with all classes of his fellow countrymen, whether they applaud his political opinions or not. But whatever the practical momentary advantages of slovenly diction, what is its long-range bearing on education, on the language itself, on its literature? Will, say, two or three consecutive generations of calculated effort to speak and write without excellence enhance the prospect of our producing an Irving, a Hawthorne, a Melville, a Henry James, a Howells, a Sarah Orne Jewett, a Willa Cather? Or will it tend to blight that prospect? Did the virtue of English prose, from Sir Thomas Browne and the King James translators to Bernard Shaw, come out of the acceptance of langauge on the permissive or lowest-common-denominator basis—out of a pre-occupation with what was tolerable, what could barely be endured in default of better?

Is it not one of the shames of modern scholarship that it has so little to say for what is really good, what is best, and so much to say for what is merely allowable or defensible? Scholarship is trying, of course, to discount the factor of taste as nonscientific: but is it scientific to discount it? Taste is the faculty of criticism, the faculty of intelligent choice; and to it belongs the last word about any given use of language. After all, the argument from usage carries only a permissive force, not a mandatory one. Even if it were possible to prove an overwhelming preponderance for "He failed, due to carelessness" and "You don't know Nellie like I do," the proof could mean only that one may use these expressions without being condemned. There would be nothing to say that anyone has to use them, and all of us would still have the freedom of "His failure was due to carelessness" or "Carelessness caused him to fail" and "You don't know Nellie as I do" or "the way I do," which will never raise any problems or any eyebrows.

Nobody is under compulsion to like a construction just because it exists or to use it if he does not like it. This is a principle that applies equally to present and to past usages. We have the whole range of linguistic resources at our disposal; and there is no virtue in flirting with ways of expression that we think dubious or inferior when there are alternative ways—as there always are—to which no exception can be taken. The formation of any style, even a bad one, is an affair of constant acceptances and rejections; and everyone has to lean on his own taste for acceptance of the better and rejection of the worse.

The discussion of usage was probably never shrouded in more fog than it is now. Those who want to fling wide the gates to all manner of laxity maintain firmly that change is the great inescapable law, that the only criterion is what people are doing with language *now*, and they can find no words severe enough for resistance to change, especially when resistance takes the form of quoting classic sources; but if they can unearth in Chaucer or Wycliffe or Donne or Hazlitt some parallel to whatever change is being resisted, they cite it as if it settled the matter forever. Whether the use cited was typical or exceptional in that author is a question not raised; it is enough that the passage exists. The Evanses give us a list of twenty authors, Shakespeare to Maugham—a list as easily extended back to Chaucer—who use *like* as a conjunction, but there is no attempt to show that any one of them regularly or even frequently used it so. A dictionary that illustrates a secondary meaning with a quotation may, for all we can tell, be using the only known occurrence of the word in that sense.

The radical, the innovator, the grammatical iconoclast and libertine is ready to beat down all opposition as tradition-bound and ridiculously conservative, but he is equally ready to demonstrate that whatever is objected to has been English for four or five hundred years. Both forms of argument are supposed to be unanswerably crushing. If some locution now current defies a past consensus, so much the worse for the past; but at the same time any locution ever written by a good writer is *ipso facto* attack-proof, and if a precedent can be adduced for anything, however shabby, the case is closed.

Actually not everything ever written by a good writer, or even by quite a number of good writers, is good, any more than everything ever written by a bad writer is bad. Every good writer has committed himself at one time or another to practices without which he would have been a better writer. It is our privilege to pick and choose, alike from the superior and the inferior, alike from the past and the present. For the winnowing of the past we have the guidance of perspective in addition to taste; for the present, taste alone has to suffice. For taste there is no substitute, nor is there any excuse for not using as much of it as we have. The unexpressed excuse that underlies most refusals to use it is the delusive feeling that every demolition of a barrier, old or new, is a freeing of the language from needless restraints and a further emancipation of its users.

What is overlooked is that language and its users grow by restraints, too. Especially in a time when looseness of many kinds is a dominant fashion, it may be salutary to cultivate a tightness and exactitude not cutomarily demanded. Linguistic resources are expanded not only by the seizing of new liberties as fast as they become available but also by the rejection of liberties that may be only license. A writer is not alone what he writes; he is likewise everything that he will not write because he finds it not good enough, and his power may be as much a function of his renunciations as of self-indulgences. The libertarians will pity him as self-deprived and call his austerity a crotchet, but he and we are the gainers by his discriminations, and the language may be the loser by the indiscrimination of the loose constructionist.

In no domain is there a clearer illustration of the power of negative choice than in the domain of diction. Good writing has always been marked, and is marked today, by selection of words for their central and not their peripheral meanings. A word, particularly an abstract word, has a core of meaning from which it gradually spreads over associated meanings, perhaps in several directions, until it overlaps words that have likewise spread out from entirely different, possibly remote centers.

The liberalistic view now regnant ranks all such extensions as improvements of language, all as equally good. But the fine writer or speaker is habitually aiming at bull's-eyes, not at general target areas, and he does not care for the idea of shelling the woods with language.

His dictionary gives *apparent* as one synonym of *evident*, and vice versa, but he still finds an important kind of integrity in applying *apparent* to the thing that seems to be so whether it or is not and in saving *evident* for that which both seems to be and is so. *Infer* once meant exactly what *imply* means now—it is generally, perhaps always, so used in the seventeenth-century plays of John Ford—but the two words have developed a clear differentiation whereby *imply* goes with the transmitting end and *infer* with the receiving end of the same process of deduction; smoke *implies* fire, but when you smell smoke you *infer* fire. It is a clear loss, not a gain, when we ignore the differentiation in such sentences as these from the best-selling murder story of the decade: "The defense is trying to infer that the prosecution is trying to conceal something." "And surely you do not mean to infer that it would be an unjust verdict if X. were acquitted on the ground of temporary insanity?" *Infer* is being so chronically abused by many who should know better that lexicography no longer quite sees what to do with it, but a decent writer sees, and he is well aware that the widespread confusion makes the English vocabulary not richer, but poorer. True, "language grows," as Greenough and Kitteridge said in 1901, "by the felicitous misapplication of words"; but there is no profit to be had out of misapplication per se, without the felicity—a reservation that brings us straight back to the necessity of taste.

The obvious and growing indifferences of many publishing houses to hundreds or thousands of such distinctions as those illustrated cannot be called one of the more gladdening signs of the times. No practicing editor of any great competence ever sees a book manuscript for which he could not do appreciable favors if he had a free hand and time, and ninety-nine of any hundred published books could have profited by good offices that they never received. But these phenomena, depressing as they are, seem not quite so shocking as the latter-day hospitality of the very learned to every popular usage that volunteers to make the language more fuzzy, inarticulated, and fumbling.

What steadily preoccupies everyone fit to be called a writer is the possibility of improving everything in his work that is improvable. In no other way can he contribute his much or his little to the effectiveness of language as an instrument of precision combined with power. The linguistic scholarship that impedes and discourages where it might help him is operating beneath its privilege, not to say beneath its obligation. Let those who choose define usage as what a swarm of folk say or write by reason of laziness, shiftlessness, or ignorance; the tenable definition is still what the judicious do as a result of all that they can muster of conscious discrimination. It is time we had a philosophy of usage grounded in the steadfast conviction that the best, whether or not we have it in us to attain it, is not too good to be aspired to.

Grammar for Today

BERGEN EVANS

It would hardly do to call this essay a companion piece to Wilson Follett's "Bargain Basement English," since, figuratively at least, the two authors could not break bread comfortably together. Bergen Evans, Professor of English at Northwestern University, has made a name for himself as a writer and speaker on American English. Though frequently criticized by upholders of the eighteenth-century tradition, Professor Evans has done much to bring before the public the views of our twentieth-century linguists. "Grammar for Today" was published as a reply to Mr. Follett's charges against modern linguistic scholarship. You will notice that the differences in attitude expressed in these two essays toward contemporary usage stem from fundamentally different beliefs about the nature of language.

In 1747 Samuel Johnson issued a plan for a new dictionary of the English language. It was supported by the most distinguished printers of the day and was dedicated to the model of all correctness, Philip Dormer Stanhope, Fourth Earl of Chesterfield. Such a book, it was felt, was urgently needed to "fix" the language, to arrest its "corruption" and "decay," a degenerative process which, then as now, was attributed to the influence of "the vulgar" and which, then as now, it was a mark of superiority and elegance to decry. And Mr. Johnson seemed the man to write it. He had an enormous knowledge of Latin,

From *The Atlantic Monthly* (March 1960). Reprinted by permission of the author.

deep piety, and dogmatic convictions. He was also honest and intelligent, but the effect of these lesser qualifications was not to show until later.

Oblig'd by hunger and request of friends, Mr. Johnson was willing to assume the role of linguistic dictator. He was prepared to "fix" the pronunciation of the language, "preserve the purity" of its idiom, brand "impure" words with a "note of infamy," and secure the whole "from being overrun by . . . low terms."

There were, however, a few reservations. Mr. Johnson felt it necessary to warn the oversanguine that "Language is the work of man, a being from whom permanence and stability cannot be derived." English "was not formed from heaven . . . but was produced by necessity and enlarged by accident." It had, indeed, been merely "thrown together by negligence" and was in such a state of confusion that its very syntax could no longer "be taught by general rules, but [only] by special precedents."

In 1755 the *Dictionary* appeared. The noble patron had been given a great deal more immortality than he had bargained for by the vigor of the kick Johnson had applied to his backside as he booted him overboard. And the *Plan* had been replaced by the *Preface*, a sadder but very much wiser document.

Eight years of "sluggishly treading the track of the alphabet" had taught Johnson that the hopes of "fixing" the language and preserving its "purity" were but "the dreams of a poet doomed at last to wake a lexicographer." In "the boundless chaos of living speech," so copious and energetic in its disorder, he had found no guides except "experience and analogy," Irregularities were "inherent in the tongue" and could not be "dismissed or reformed" but must be permitted "to remain untouched." "Uniformity must be sacrificed to custom . . . in compliance with a numberless majority" and "general agreement." One of the pet projects of the age had been the establishment of an academy to regulate and improve style. "I hope," Johnson wrote in the *Preface*, that if "it should be established . . . the spirit of English liberty will hinder or destroy (it)."

At the outset of the work he had flattered himself, he confessed, that he would reform abuses and put a stop to alterations. But he had soon discovered that "sounds are too volatile and subtle for legal restraints" and that "to enchain syllables and to lash the wind are equally undertakings of pride unwilling to measure its desires by its strength." For "the causes of change in language are as much superior to human resistance as the revolutions of the sky or the intumescence of the tide."

There had been an even more profound discovery: that grammarians and lexicographers "do not form, but register the language; do not teach men how they should think, but relate how they have hitherto expressed their thoughts." And with this statement Johnson ushered in the rational study of linguistics. He had entered on his task a medieval pedant. He emerged from it a modern scientist.

Of course his discoveries were not strikingly original. Horace had observed that use was the sole arbiter and norm of speech and Montaigne had said that he who would fight custom with grammar was a fool. Doubtless thousands of other people had at one time or another perceived and said the same thing. But Johnson introduced a new principle. Finding that he could not lay down rules, he gave actual examples to show meaning and form. He offered as authority illustrative quotations, and in so doing established that language is what usage makes it and that custom, in the long run, is the ultimate and only court of appeal in linguistic matters.

This principle, axiomatic today in grammar and lexicography, seems to exasperate a great many laymen who, apparently, find two hundred and five years too short a period in which to grasp a basic idea. They insist that there are absolute standards of correctness in speech and that these standards may be set forth in a few simple rules. To a man, they believe, of course, that they speak and write "correctly" and they are loud in their insistence that others imitate them.

It is useless to argue with such people because they are not, really, interested in language at all. They are interested solely in demonstrating their own superiority. Point out to them—as has been done hundreds of times—that forms which they regard as "corrupt," "incorrect," and "vulgar" have been used by Shakespeare, Milton, and the Bible and are used daily by 180 million Americans and accepted by the best linguists and lexicographers, and they will coolly say, "Well, if they differ from me, they're wrong."

But if usage is not the final determinant of speech, what is? Do the inhabitants of Italy, for example, speak corrupt Latin or good Italian? Is Spanish superior to French? Would the Breton fisherman speak better if he spoke Parisian French? Can one be more fluent in Outer Mongolian than in Inner Mongolian? One has only to ask such questions in relation to languages other than one's own, language within which our particular snobberies and struggles for prestige have no stake, to see the absurdity of them.

The language that we do speak, if we are to accept the idea of "corruption" and "decay" in language, is a horribly decayed Anglo-Saxon, grotesquely corrupted by Norman French. Furthermore, since Standard English is a development of the London dialect of the fourteenth century, our speech, by true aristocratic standards, is woefully middle-class, commercial, and vulgar. And American speech is lower middle-class, reeking of counter and till. Where else on earth, for instance, would one find crime condemned because it didn't *pay!*

In more innocent days a great deal of time was spent in wondering what was the "original" language of mankind, the one spoken in Eden, the language of which all modern tongues were merely degenerate remnants. Hector Boethius tells us that James I of Scotland was so interested in this problem that he had two children reared with a deaf and dumb nurse on an island in order to see what language they would "naturally" speak. James thought it would be Hebrew, and in time, to his great satisfaction, it was reported that the children were speaking Hebrew!

Despite this experiment, however, few people today regard English as a corruption of Hebrew. But many seem to think it is a corruption of Latin and labor mightily to make it conform to this illusion. It is they and their confused followers who tell us that we can't say "I am mistaken" because translated into Latin this would mean "I am misunderstood," and we can't say "I have enjoyed myself" unless we are egotistical or worse.

It is largely to this group—most of whom couldn't read a line of Latin at sight if their lives depended on it—that we owe our widespread bewilderment concerning *who* and *whom*. In Latin the accusative or dative form would always be used, regardless of the words' position in the sentence, when the pronoun was the object of a verb or a preposition, But in English, for at least four hundred years, this simply hasn't been so. When the pronoun occurs at the beginning of a question, people who speak natural, fluent, literary English use the nominative, regardless. They say "Who did you give it to?" not "Whom did you give it to?" But the semiliterate, intimidated and bewildered, are mouthing such ghastly utterances as a recent headline in a Chicago newspaper: WHOM'S HE KIDDING?

Another group seems to think that in its pure state English was a

Laputan tongue, with logic as its guiding principle. Early members of this sect insisted that *unloose* could only mean "to tie up," and present members have compelled the gasoline industry to label its trucks *Flammable* under the disastrous insistence, apparently, that the old *Inflammable* could only mean "not burnable."

It is to them, in league with the Latinists, that we owe the bogy of the double negative. In all Teutonic languages a doubling of the negative merely emphasizes the negation. But we have been told for a century now that two negatives make a positive, though if they do and it's merely a matter of logic, then three negatives should make a negative again. So that if "It doesn't make no difference" is wrong merely because it includes two negatives, then "It doesn't never make no difference" ought to be right again.

Both of these groups, in their theories at least, ignore our idiom. Yet idiom—those expressions which defy all logic but are the very essence of a tongue—plays a large part in English. We go to school and college, but we go to *the* university. We buy two dozen eggs but a couple *of* dozen. *Good and* can mean *very* ("I am good and mad!") and "a hot cup of coffee" means that the coffee, not the cup, is to be hot. It makes a world of difference to a condemned man whether his reprieve is *upheld* or *held up*.

There are thousands of such expressions in English. They are the "irregularities" which Johnson found "inherent in the tongue" and which his wisdom perceived could not and should not be removed. Indeed, it is in the recognition and use of these idioms that skillful use of English lies.

Many words in the form that is now mandatory were originally just mistakes, and many of these mistakes were forced into the language by eager ignoramuses determined to make it conform to some notion of their own. The *s* was put in *island*, for instance, in sheer pedantic ignorance. The second *r* doesn't belong in *trousers*, nor the *g* in *arraign*, nor the *t* in *deviltry*, nor the *n* in *passenger* and *messenger*. Nor, so far as English is concerned, does that first *c* in *arctic* which so many people twist their mouths so strenuously to pronounce.

And grammar is as "corrupted" as spelling or pronunciation. "You are" is as gross a solecism as "me am." It's recent, too; you won't find it in the Authorized Version of the Bible. *Lesser, nearer,* and *more* are grammatically on a par with *gooder. Crowed* is the equivalent of *knowed* or *growed*, and *caught* and *dug* (for *catched* and *digged*) are as "corrupt" as *squoze* or *snoze* for *sneezed*.

Fortunately for our peace of mind most people are quite content to let English conform to English, and they are supported in their sanity by modern grammarians and linguists.

Scholars agree with Puttenham (1589) that a language is simply speech "fashioned to the common uderstanding and accepted by consent." They believe that the only "rules" that can be stated for a language are codified observations. They hold, that is, that language is the basis of grammar, not the other way round. They do not believe that any language can become "corrupted" by the linguistic habits of those who speak it. They do not believe that anyone who is a native speaker of a standard language will get into any linguistic trouble unless he is misled by snobbishness or timidity or vanity.

He may, of course, if his native language is English, speak a form of English that marks him as coming from a rural or an unread group. But if he doesn't mind being so marked, there's no reason why he should change. Johnson retained a Staffordshire burr in his speech all his life. And surely no one will deny that Robert Burn's rustic dialect was just as good a form of speech as, and in his mouth infinitely better as a means of expression than, the "correct" English spoken by ten million of his southern contemporaries.

The trouble is that people are no longer willing to be rustic or provincial. They all want to speak like educated people, though they don't want to go the trouble of becoming truly educated. They want to believe that a special form of socially acceptable and financially valuable speech can be mastered by following a few simple rules. And there is no lack of little books that offer to supply the rules and promise "correctness" if the rules are adhered to. But, of course, these offers are specious because you don't speak like an educated person unless you are an educated person, and the little books, if taken seriously, will not only leave the lack of education showing but will expose the pitiful yearning and the basic vulgarity as well, in such sentences as "Whom are you talking about?"

As a matter of fact, the educated man uses at least three languages. With his family and his close friends, on the ordinary, unimportant occasions of daily life, he speaks, much of the time, a monosyllabic sort of shorthand. On more important occasions and when dealing with strangers in his official or business relations, he has a more formal speech, more complete, less allusive, politely qualified, wisely reserved. In addition he has some acquaintance with the literary speech of his language. He understands this when he reads it, and often enjoys it, but he hesitates to use it. In times of emotional stress hot fragments of it may come out of him like lava, and in times of feigned emotion, as when giving a commencement address, cold, greasy gobbets of it will ooze forth.

The linguist differs from the amateur grammarian in recognizing all of these variations and gradations in the language. And he differs from the snob in doubting that the speech of any one small group among the languages' more than 300 million daily users constitutes a model for all the rest to imitate.

The methods of the modern linguist can be illustrated by the question of the grammatical number of *none*. Is it singular or plural? Should one say "None of them is ready" or "None of them are ready"?

The prescriptive grammarians are emphatic that it should be singular. The Latinists point out that *nemo*, the Latin equivalent, is singular. The logicians triumphantly point out that *none* can't be more than one and hence can't be plural.

The linguist knows that he hears "None of them are ready" every day, from people of all social positions, geographical areas, and degrees of education. He also hears "None is." Furthermore, literature informs him that both forms were used in the past. From Malory (1450) to Milton (1650) he finds that *none* was treated as a singular three times for every once that it was treated as a plural. That is, up to three hundred years ago men usually said *None is*. From Milton to 1917, *none* was used as a plural seven times for every four times it was used as a singular. That is, in the past three hundred years men often said *None is*, but they said *None are* almost twice as often. Since 1917, however, there has been a noticeable increase in the use of the plural, so much so that today *None are* is the preferred form.

The descriptive grammarian, therefore, says that while *None is* may still be used, it is becoming increasingly peculiar. This, of course, will not be as useful to one who wants to be cultured in a hurry as a short, emphatic permission or prohibition. But it has the advantage of describing English as it is spoken and written here and now and not as it ought to be spoken in some Cloud-Cuckoo-Land.

The descriptive grammarian believes that a child should be taught English, but he would like to see the child taught the English actually used by his educated contemporaries, not some pedantic, theoretical English designed chiefly to mark the imagined superiority of the designer.

He believes that a child should be taught the parts of speech, for example. But the child should be told the truth—that these are functions of use, not some quality immutably inherent in this or that word. Anyone, for instance, who tells a child—or anyone else—that *like* is used in English only as a preposition has grossly misinformed him. And anyone who complains that its use as a conjunction is a corruption introduced by Winston cigarettes ought, in all fairness, to explain how Shakespeare, Keats, and the translators of the Authorized Version of the Bible came to be in the employ of the R. J. Reynolds Tobacco Company.

Whether formal grammar can be taught to advantage before the senior year of high school is doubtful; most studies—and many have been made—indicate that it can't. But when it is taught, it should be the grammar of today's English, not the obsolete grammar of yesterday's prescriptive grammarians. By that grammar, for instance, *please* in the sentence "Please reply" is the verb and *reply* its object. But by modern meaning *reply* is the verb, in the imperative, and *please* is merely a qualifying word meaning "no discourtesy intended," a mollifying or de-imperatival adverb, or whatever you will, but not the verb.

This is a long way from saying "Anything goes," which is the charge that, with all the idiot repetition of a needle stuck in a groove, the uninformed ceaselessly chant against modern grammarians. But to assert that usage is the sole determinant in grammar, pronunciation, and meaning is *not* to say that anything goes. Custom is illogical and unreasonable, but it is also tyrannical. The latest deviation from its dictates is usually punished with severity. And because this is so, children should be taught what the current and local customs in English are. They should not be taught that we speak a bastard Latin or a vocalized logic. And they should certainly be disabused of the stultifying illusion that after God had given Moses the Commandments He called him back and pressed on him a copy of Woolley's *Handbook of English Grammar*.

The grammarian does not see it as his function to "raise the standards" set by Franklin, Lincoln, Melville, Mark Twain, and hundreds of millions of other Americans. He is content to record what they said and say.

Insofar as he serves as a teacher, it is his business to point out the limits of the permissible, to indicate the confines within which the writer may exercise his choice, to report that which custom and practice have made acceptable. It is certainly not the business of the grammarian to impose his personal taste as the only norm of good English, to set forth his prejudices as the ideal standard which everyone should copy. That would be fatal. No one person's standards are broad enough for that.

Differences in Language Practices

CHARLES CARPENTER FRIES

That there are sharply conflicting attitudes toward contemporary usage should be evident from your reading of the two preceding essays. That these attitudes derive from differing basic assumptions about the nature of language should be equally clear. In the following essay, Professor Fries explains more fully the cleavage that separates the two points of view. At the same time, he presents the rationale of the scientific point of view in the study of language, arrives at a sound definition of Standard American English, and discusses the obligation of the schools with respect to differences in language practices. The essay is the introductory chapter of his *American English Grammar*, a revolutionary book in the teaching of English. Professor Fries has already been identified on p. 325.

"English" maintains its place as the most frequently *required subject* of our school and college curriculums because of the unanimous support given it both by the general public and by education authorities. This support rests upon the general belief that the mastery of *good English* is not only the most important asset of the ambitious but also an obligation of every good citizen. There is, however, in many quarters a very hazy idea of the specific elements which make *good English*. A great deal of vigorous controversy ignores all the larger problems of

From *American English Grammar* by Charles Carpenter Fries. Reprinted by permission of the author and the National Council of Teachers of English, copyright 1940. Published by Appleton-Century-Crofts.

effective communication and centers attention upon the criteria to be applied in judging the acceptability of particular words and language forms. All of this controversy is direct evidence that there do exist many differences in the language practice of English speaking people; for no controversy could arise and no choice be offered unless differing language forms presented themselves in the actual practice of English speech. It is the purpose of this chapter to set forth the general character of these differences and to analyze their significance in relation to the obligations resting upon our schools. The chapter as a whole will therefore present the principles underlying this whole investigation and the point of view which has determined its material and method.

I

Underlying many of the controversies concerning words and language forms is a very common attitude which I shall call here the "conventional point of view." Frequently stated explicitly, sometimes only implied, it appears in most handbooks and manuals of correct English, in grammars and rhetorics, in educational tests and measures, and in many editorials of the press. This conventional point of view assumes not only that there is a correctness in English language as absolute as that in elementary mathematics but also that the measures of this correctness are very definite rules. The following quotations are typical:

A college professor rises to defend 'ain't' and 'it is me' as good English. The reed upon which he leans is majority usage. . . . 'Ain't,' as a legitimate contraction of 'am not,' would not require defense or apology if it were not for widespread misuse. Unfortunately the same cannot be said of 'it is me.' This solecism could not be given the odor of good English by a plurality as great as Warren G. Harding rolled up in 1920. . . . A vast amount of wretched English is heard in this country. The remedy does not lie in the repeal of the rules of grammar; but rather in a stricter and more intelligent enforcement of those rules in our schools. . . . This protest against traditional usage and the rules of grammar is merely another manifestation of the unfortunate trend of the times to lawlessness in every direction. . . . Quite as important as keeping undesirables out of the vocabulary is the maintaining of respect for the rules of grammar, which govern the formation of words into phrases and sentences. . . . Students should be taught that correct speaking is evidence of culture; and that in order to speak correctly they must master the rules that govern the use of the language.[1]

[1] From an editorial in *The Detroit Free Press* (December 9, 1928).

Grammar consists of a series of rules and definitions. . . . Since . . . ninety-five per cent of all children and teachers come from homes or communities where incorrect English is used, nearly everyone has before him the long, hard task of overcoming habits set up early in life before he studied language and grammar in school. . . . Such people are exposed to the ridicule of those who notice the error, and the only way in which they can cure themselves is by eternal vigilance and the study of grammar.[2]

This is a test to see how well you know correct English usage and how well you can select the *rule or principle in accordance with which a usage is correct.* In the left hand column a list of sentences is given. In each sentence there are two forms in parentheses, one correct, and the other incorrect. In the right hand column a list of rules or principles is given, some one of which applies to each sentence. . . .

	Sentences	*Principles*
( ) 1.	(Whom) (Who) did you meet?	a. The indirect object is in the objective case.
( ) 2.	He told John and (I) (me) an interesting story.	b. The subject of the verb is in the nominative case.
		c. The object of a verb is in the objective case.

. . . Read the first sentence in Section I; then mark out the incorrect form. Read the rules in Section I, until you find one that applies to this first sentence. Place the letter of this rule in the square preceding the first sentence.[3]

One purpose of this report is to describe and illustrate a method of constructing a grammar curriculum upon the basis of the errors of school children. . . . it is apparent that the first step is *to ascertain* the rules which are broken and to determine their relative importance.[4]

The point of view expressed in these quotations, assuming as it does that certain definite rules[5] are the necessary standards by which to measure language correctness, also repudiates *general usage* as a valid guide to acceptability, even the usage of the so-called "educated." The following quotation represents dozens of similar statements:

[2] W. W. Charters, *Teaching the Common Branches,* rev. ed. (New York, The Macmillan Co., 1924), pp. 96, 98, 115.

[3] T. J. Kirby, *Grammar Test,* University of Iowa Standard Tests and Scales.

[4] "Minimal Essentials in Language and Grammar," in *Sixteenth Yearbook* of the National Society for the Study of Education (Bloomington, Ind., Public School Publishing Co., 1917), pp. 86, 87.

[5] For a statement of the development of this point of view see C. C. Fries, *Teaching of the English Language* (New York, Thomas Nelson & Sons, 1927), Chap. I, "The Rules of Grammar as the Measure of Language Errors."

The truth is, however, that authority of general usage, or even of the usage of great writers, is not absolute in language. There is a misuse of words which can be justified by no authority, however great, and *by no usage however general.*[6]

From this, the "conventional point of view," the problem of the differences in our language practice is a very simple one. Only two kinds of forms or usages exist—correct forms and mistakes, In general, the mistakes are thought to be corrupt forms or illegitimate meanings derived by carelessness from the correct ones. In some cases a grudging acquiescence accepts some forms which are contrary to the rules when these forms are sanctioned by an overwhelming usage, but here the view remains that these forms, although established by usage, are still *incorrect* and must always be incorrect. To this point of view these incorrect forms sanctioned by usage are the "idioms" of the language. In all the matters of differing language practices, therefore, those who hold this point of view regard the obligation of the schools as perfectly clear and comparatively simple—the schools must root out the *mistakes* or *errors* and cultivate the language uses that are *correct according to the rules.*[7]

Opposed to this "conventional point of view" is that held by the outstanding scholars in English language during the last hundred years. I shall call it here "the scientific point of view." Typical expressions of it abound.

In considering the use of grammar as a corrective of what are called 'ungrammatical' expressions, it must be borne in mind that the rules of grammar have no value except as statements of facts: whatever is in general use in a language is for that very reason grammatically correct.[8]

The grammar of a language is not a list of rules imposed upon its speakers by scholastic authorities, but is a scientific record of the actual phenomena of that language, written and spoken. If any community habitually uses certain forms of speech, these forms are part of the grammar of the speech of that community.[9]

[6] R. G. White, *Words and Their Uses*, rev. ed. (Boston, Houghton Mifflin Company, 1899), p. 14.

[7] "Some better reason than a custom arising from ignorance . . . is needed for changing the English language. It would seem to be still the part of the schools to teach the language *strictly according to rule*, and to place emphasis on such teaching, rather than to encourage questionable liberties of usage." From an editorial in *The Christian Science Monitor*, Boston (February 23, 1923).

[8] Henry Sweet, *New English Grammar*, Vol. I (Oxford, Clarendon Press, 1891), p. 5.

[9] Grattan and Gurrey, *Our Living Language* (London, Thomas Nelson & Sons, 1925), p. 25.

It has been my endeavor in this work to represent English Grammar not as a set of stiff dogmatic precepts, according to which some things are correct and others absolutely wrong, but as something living and developing under continual fluctuations and undulations, something that is founded on the past and prepares the way for the future, something that is not always consistent or perfect, but progressing and perfectible—in one word, human.[10]

A Grammar book does not attempt to teach people how they ought to speak, but on the contrary, unless it is a very bad or a very old work, it merely states how, as a matter of fact, certain people do speak at the time at which it is written.[11]

In these typical expressions of "the scientific point of view" there is, first of all, a definitely stated opposition to the fundamental principle of the "conventional attitude." All of them insist that it is unsound to take the rules of grammar as the necessary norms of correct English and to set out to make all usage conform to those rules. In these expressions of the scientific view there is, also, a clear affirmation of the fundamental principle of the attitude that usage or practice is the basis of all *correctness* there can be in language.[12] From this, the scientific point of view, the problem presented by the differences in our language is by no means a simple one. Instead of having to deal with a mass of diverse forms which can be easily separated into the two groups of *mistakes* and *correct language* according to perfectly definite measures, the language scholar finds himself confronted by a complex range of differing practices which must be sorted into an indefinite number of groups according to a set of somewhat indistinct criteria called "general usage."[13] Those who hold this scientific point of view insist, therefore, that the first step in fulfilling the obligation of the schools in the matter

---

[10] Otto Jespersen, *A Modern English Grammar* (Heidelberg, 1909), I, Preface.

[11] H. C. Wyld, *Elementary Lessons in English Grammar* (Oxford, Clarendon Press, 1925), p. 12.

[12] This statement must not be taken to imply that *mere correctness* is to be considered the ultimate ideal of language. The scientific point of view does not in any way conflict with the artistic view of *good English*. See the discussion of "The Scientific and the Artistic Points of View in Language," in C. C. Fries, *The Teaching of the English Language*, pp. 102–121.

[13] One should, perhaps, call attention at this point to the fact that the great *Oxford English Dictionary* is the outstanding document in this "scientific view of language." The principle underlying the production of the *Oxford Dictionary*, the very foundation of its method, was the insistence upon use or practice as the sole criterion of the legitimate meaning of words. Compare, for example, the treatment of the word *nice* (especially sense 15) in this dictionary with the usual statements concerning it as given in the conventional handbooks.

of dealing with the English language is to record, realistically and as completely as possible, the facts of this usage.

This investigation and report assumes as its first principle this scientific point of view with its repudiation of the conventional attitude toward language errors. We shall, therefore, ignore the conventional classification of *mistakes* and *correct forms*, and attempt to outline the types of differences that appear in our American language practices.

II

All of us upon occasion note and use for the purpose of identification the many differences in the speech of those about us. By differences in pitch of voice, for instance, we can usually tell whether the person talking to us over the telephone is a man, or a woman, or a child. By certain characteristic differences of pronunciation and of grammar, the speech of "Amos and Andy" as it comes over the radio makes us visualize two uneducated negroes. Through the speech of "Clara, Lou, and Em," we see three women of little education who have had a very limited range of social contacts. In similar fashion we should with little difficulty recognize the speech of a Scot like Harry Lauder as differing from that of a native of Georgia or Alabama. If one could conjure up Shakspere or Spenser or Milton, he would find their English strange to his ears not only in pronunciation but in vocabulary and in grammar as well. The speech of Chaucer and of Wycliffe would sound even less like English. In other words, even if one ignores such details as separate the speech of every single person from that of any other, there are at least four large types of differences to be noted in our discussion here.

First, there are historical differences. Chaucer used, as we do, *they* as the nominative plural of the pronoun of the third person, but he did not use *their* as the genitive and *them* as the dative-accusative form. Instead, he used the forms *her* or *hir*, for the genitive plural, and *hem* for the dative-accusative or objective forms. In Chaucers' language it was still the practice to distinguish carefully between the singular and plural forms of the past tense of many verbs. He would say *I rood* (rode) but we *ride (n)*, *he sang* but they *sunge (n)*. In the late sixteenth century it was no longer the practice to distinguish between the singular and plural in the past tense, and Shakspere therefore used *we rode* as well as *I rode*. For him, however, *learn* was often used with the meaning we give to *teach*, and *thou* was frequently used to address those of inferior rank or intimate friends. Thus the language forms of each age have differed in some respect from those of any other time. Constant change is the outstanding characteristic of a live language used by an intellectually active people. The historical changes do not come suddenly, nor do they affect all the users of a language equally. Thus at any time there will be found those who cling to the older methods and those who use the newer fashion. Many of the differences we note in the language of today find their explanation in this process of historical change. These older forms constitute a fairly large proportion of the materials usually called errors by those who maintain the conventional point of view. The so-called double negative, as in "They didn't take no oil with them," is thus a perpetuation of an old practice exceedingly common in the English language for centuries. It was formerly the normal way of stressing a negative. The form *foot*, in such expressions as "He is six foot tall," "The height of the bar is now six foot and two inches," is again the perpetuation of an old practice in the English language which the modern fashion has abandoned. It is an old genitive plural following the numeral. A few other examples out of dozens of such historical differences are *clomb*, usually spelled *clum*, as the past tense of the verb *climb*, instead of *climbed*; *wrought*[14] as the past tense of the verb *work*, instead of *worked; stang* as the past tense of the verb *sting*, instead of *stung*. Such differences belong not only in this group called "historical differences" but often also to some of the other three groups to be explained below. In fact, the four types of differences are not by any means mutually exclusive classifications but merely loose divisions with convenient labels.

Second, there are regional differences. In the south of England, in early Modern English, the inflectional ending of the verb in the third person singular present indicative was -*eth*, as in "God *loveth* a cheerful giver." In the north of England this inflectional ending was -*es*, as "God *loves* a cheerful giver." Late Modern English has adopted the form that was used only in the northern region. In the language practice of the United States, *gotten* as a past participle form of *get* is fairly general; in England it seldom appears. *You all* as a plural of *you* is especially characteristic of southern United States. In some colleges one takes a course *under* a professor; in others it is *from* one or *with* one; in still others it is *to* one. Some of the differences we note in the language

---

[14] One should note that in the case of *wrought* the old form has not the flavor of "vulgar" English as have the other examples here given but suggests super-refinement.

practices of those about us find their explanation in the fact that the fashions in one community or section of the country do not necessarily develop in others. Regional or geographical differences show themselves more clearly in matters of vocabulary. That part of an automobile that is called a *hood* in the United States is called a *bonnet* in England. That which they call the *hood* in England we call the *top*. *Lumber*, to most of us in the United States means *timber;* in England it still means *rubbish*. In some sections of the United States a *paper bag* is usually called a *sack*, in others a poke. Such regional differences become especially noticeable when a person from one section of the country moves into another bringing with him the peculiar fashions of the district from which he comes. In the new community these language differences challenge attention and give rise to questions of correctness and preference.

Third, there are literary and colloquial differences. The language practices of conversation differ in many subtle ways from those used in formal writing. Most apparent is the abundance of contractions in the language of conversation. Thoroughly unnatural would sound the speech of those who in conversation did not constantly use *I'm, you'll, isn't, don't, aren't, they'd better, we've*, instead of the fully expanded *I am, you will, is not, do not, are not, they had better, we have*. And in similar fashion the formal writing that habitually employed such contractions would seem equally unnatural because of the impression of very informal familiarity which they would create. Apparent, too, although less obvious are the differences between conversation and formal writing in the matter of sentence completeness. Conversation abounds in groups of words that do not form conventionally complete and logical sentences. Many verbs are omitted; clauses are uttered which are to be attached to the whole context of the conversation rather than to any particular word in a parsable sentence; single words stand for complete ideas. In formal writing the situation demands much more logical completeness of expression, and most of the sentences appear to satisfy the demands of a conventional grammatical analysis. Less apparent but not less real are the differences which arise out of the fact that many perfectly familiar expressions occur practically only in conversational situations and are found very seldom in literary English unless they appear in attempts to report conversation in writing. Occasions seldom arise in anything except conversational situations to use *Who* (or *whom*) *did you call?* or *It is me* (or *I*).

Many assume that the language practices of formal writing are the best or at least that they are of a higher level than those of colloquial or conversational English. When, therefore, they find an expression marked "colloquial" in a dictionary, as is the phrase *"to get on one's nerves"* in Webster's *New International Dictionary*, they frown upon its use. As a matter of fact, thus to label an expression "colloquial" is simply to say that it occurs in good conversation but not in formal writing.[15] Unless one can assume that formal writing is in itself more desirable than good conversation, the language practices peculiar to conversation cannot be rated in comparison with those of formal writing. Each set of language practices is best in its own special sphere of use; one will necessarily differ from the other.

Fourth, there are social or class differences. Despite the fact that America in its national life has struggled to express its belief in the essential equality of human beings and to free the paths of opportunity from arbitrary and artificial restraints, there still do exist some clear differences between the habits and practices of various social groups. It is, of course, practically impossible to mark the limits of any social class in this country. It is even extremely difficult to describe the special characteristics of any such class because of the comparative ease with which one passes from one social group to another, especially in youth, and the consequent mixture of group habits among those so moving. Our public schools, our churches, our community welfare work, our political life, all furnish rather frequent occasions for social class mixture. All that can be done in respect to such a description is to indicate certain facts which seem generally true for the *core* of any social group, realizing that these same facts may also be true separately of many who have connections with other groups. There are, for example, those who habitually wear formal dress clothes in the evening and those

[15] The word *colloquial* as applied to English words and structures is frequently misunderstood, even by teachers of English. Some confuse it with *localism*, and think of the words and constructions marked "colloquial" as peculiarities of speaking which are characteristic of a particular locality. Others feel that some stigma attaches to the label "colloquial" and would strive to avoid as *incorrect* (or as of a *low level*) all words and phrases so marked. The word *colloquial*, however, as used to label words and phrases in a dictionary like Webster's *New International Dictionary* has no such meaning. It is used to mark those words and constructions whose range of use is primarily that of the polite conversation of cultivated people, of their familiar letters and informal speeches, as distinct from those words and constructions which are common also in formal writing. As a matter of fact, even the language, of our better magazines and of public addresses has, during the last generation, moved away from the formal toward the informal.

who never wear them. Many of the former frequent the opera and concerts of the best music; many of the latter find their entertainment solely in the movies. The families of the wealthy, especially those whose wealth has continued for several generations, ordinarily mix but little with the families of unskilled laborers; and the families of college professors even in a small city have usually very little social life in common with the families of policemen and firemen.

Just as the general social habits of such separated social groups naturally show marked differences, so their language practices inevitably vary. Pronunciations such as "*ketch*" for *catch* and "git" for *get;* and grammatical forms such as "He *seen* his mistakes as soon as he *done* it" or "*You was*" are not the characteristic modes of speech of university professors, or of the clergymen who preach from the pulpits in our large city churches, or of the judges of the supreme court, or of the presidents of our most important banks, or even of those who habitually patronize the opera. Such language practices, therefore, if used in these particular social groups attract as much attention as a pair of overalls might at an evening gathering where custom demands formal dress clothes. In fact, part of the significance of the social differences in language habits can well be illustrated by a comparison with clothes. Fundamentally the clothes one wears fulfill the elementary practical functions of comfort by keeping one warm and of modesty by avoiding indecent exposure of one's person. These two practical purposes could just as well be accomplished by rather shapeless simple garments produced over a standard pattern for everyone and worn upon all occasions. Such clothes could be made to fulfill their primary functions very efficiently with a minimum of cost. In such a situation, however, aside from the significance of differing degrees of cleanliness, the clothes would show us very little concerning the individuals who wore them. With our present habits of dress the clothes connote or suggest, in a broad general way, certain information concerning the wearers. Among other things they suggest the *circumstances in which we usually see them worn.* A dress suit suggests an evening party (or in some places a hotel waiter); overalls suggest a piece of dirty work or possibly a summer camp. In like manner language forms and constructions not only fulfill a primary function of communicating meaning; they also suggest the circumstances in which those particular forms and constructions are usually employed. If, then, one uses the pronunciations and grammatical forms given earlier in this paragraph, they may serve to communicate his meaning unmistakably, but they will also suggest that he habitually associates with those social groups for whom these language forms are the customary usage and not with those for whom they are not characteristic. We must, therefore, recognize the fact that there are separate social or class groups even in American communities and that these groups differ from one another in many social practices including their language habits.

As indicated earlier the four kinds of differences in language practice here outlined are by no means mutually exclusive. Many historical differences and some sectional differences have become also social differences. For our purpose here the social or class differences are of most concern; other types of differences will be treated only as they bear upon these social or class dialects.

III

In order to grasp the significance of these social differences in language practice for the obligation of the schools one must understand clearly what is meant by "standard" English, and that can perhaps best be accomplished by tracing the course by which a particular kind of English became "standard." As one examines the material written in England during the twelfth and thirteenth centuries—a period from one hundred to two hundred years after the Norman Conquest—he finds a situation in which three things are of especial note:

(1) Most of the legal documents, the instruments which controlled the carrying on of the political and the business affairs of the English people, were not written in the English language but in French or in Latin. This fact was also true of much of the literature and books of learning familiar to the upper classes.

(2) Although some books, especially historical records and religious and moral stories and tracts, were written in English, there was no single type of the English language common to all English writings. The greatest number used what is called the Southern dialect. This particular kind of English had been centered in Winchester, which was the chief city of King Alfred and his successors until the time of the Norman Conquest.

(3) There was, therefore, no "standard" English in twelfth and thirteenth century England, for no single type of the English language furnished the medium by which the major affairs of English people were carried on. Instead, English people used for these purposes

French, Latin, and at least four distinct varieties of English. The particular kind of English spoken in southern England came nearest to fulfilling the function of a "standard" English because more writings and more significant writings were produced in this type of English than in any other.

In the fourteenth and early fifteenth centuries, however, this situation changed. London had become the political and in some respects the social head of English life in a much more unified England. Many of the major affairs of the realm had to be handled in London. More and more the English language, the English of London, was used in the legal documents of politics and business. Solely because of the fact that more of the important affairs of English life were conducted in this London English rather than in Winchester English, London English became "standard" English. Naturally, then, the growing use of this particular type of English for the important affairs of English life gathered such momentum that even writers to whom other types of English were more natural felt constrained to learn and to use the fashionable London English. Gower, for example, a Kentishman, did not write his native kind of English but practically the same forms, constructions and spellings as Chaucer, a Londoner born. Naturally, too, this London English gained a social prestige because of the fact that its use connoted or suggested relations with the center of affairs in English life, wheareas the inability to use London English suggested that one did not have such social contacts. "Standard" English, therefore, is, historically, a local dialect, which was used to carry on the major affairs of English life and which gained thereby a social prestige.[16]

Many changes occurred in this dialect of English and these changes especially affected the usage of the younger rather than of the older generations in the centers of fashionable social life. Thus the continued use of the older forms rather than the newer changes always suggested a lack of direct contacts with those who were active in the conduct of important matters. In this connotation lay the power of "standard" English to compel the ambitious to conform to its practices.

In America, however, we have had no one recognized center for our political, business, social, and intellectual affairs. More than that, the great distances between various parts of the United States made very difficult frequent actual social contacts in the earlier days. Our

[16] "Standard" French, "Standard" Italian, "Standard" Dutch, etc., have similar histories.

coast cities, Boston and New York, maintained direct relations with London long after the earlier settlers had moved west, but the middle western settlements had practically no relations with Boston and New York. This fact can probably explain the differences between our middle-western speech and that of nineteenth century Boston and New York. Because of the fact that New England so long dominated our intellectual life there has been a good deal of feeling in many parts of the United States that the language usages of New England connoted a connection with a higher culture than did the language of the Middle West. Hence the rather widespread attempt to imitate certain New England speech characteristics. On the whole, however, if we ignore the special differences that separate the speech of New England, the South, and the Middle West, we do have in the United States a set of language habits, broadly conceived in which the major matters of the political, social, economic, educational, religious life of this country are carried on. To these language habits is attached a certain social prestige, for the use of them suggests that one has constant relations with those who are responsible for the important affairs of our communities. It is this set of language habits, derived originally from an older London English, but differentiated from it somewhat by its independent development in this country, which is the "standard" English of the United States. Enough has been said to enforce the point that it is "standard" not because it is any more correct or more beautiful or more capable than other varieties of English; it is "standard" solely because it is the particular type of English which is used in the conduct of the important affairs of our people. It is also the type of English used by the *socially acceptable* of most of our communities and insofar as that is true it has become a social or class dialect in the United States.

IV

With this analysis it is not difficult to understand the nature of the obligation assumed by our schools in respect to the teaching of the English language. Long have we in our national life adhered to the principle that no individual in his attempts to rise to the highest positions should be disqualified by artificial restraints. Our people have been devoted to education because education has furnished the most important tool of social advancement. Our public schools have therefore held to the ideal that every boy and girl should be so equipped that he shall not be handicapped in his struggle for social progress and recognition, and that he may rise to the highest positions. In the matter of the English language it is clear that any one who cannot use the language habits in which the major affairs of the country are conducted, the language habits of the socially acceptable of most of our communities, would have a serious handicap. The schools, therefore, have assumed the burden of training every boy and girl, no matter what his original social background and native speech, to use this "standard" English, this particular social or class dialect. To some pupils it is almost a foreign language; to others it is their accustomed speech. Many believe that the schools have thus assumed an impossible task. Certainly the widespread and almost unanimous condemnation of the results of their efforts convinces us that either the schools have not conceived their task adequately or they have chosen the wrong materials and methods to accomplish it. We shall find, I think, that seldom have school authorities understood the precise nature of the language task they have assumed and very frequently have directed their energies to teaching not "standard" English realistically described, but a "make-believe" correctness which contained some true forms of real "standard" English and many forms that had and have practically no currency outside the classroom.[17]

A few brief statements will serve both to summarize the preceding discussion and to bring into a single view the principles which underlie this investigation and report.

(1) All considerations of an *absolute* "correctness" in accord with the conventional rules of grammar or the dicta of handbooks must be set aside, because these rules or these dicta very frequently do not represent the actual practice of "standard" English but describe forms which have little currency outside the English classroom. We assume, therefore, that there can be no "correctness" apart from usage and that the *true* forms of "standard" English are those that are actually used in that particular dialect. Deviations from these usages are "incorrect" only when used in the dialect to which they do not belong. These deviations suggest not only the particular social dialect or set of language habits in which they usually occur, but also the general social and cultural characteristics most often accompanying the use of these forms.

[17] See, for example, H. B. Allen's article "The Standard of Usage in Freshman Textbooks," in *English Journal*, college ed., Vol. 24 (1935), pp. 564–571; and R. C. Pooley, *Grammar and Usage in Textbooks on English*, Bulletin 14, Bureau of Educational Research, University of Wisconsin (1933).

(2) It is the assumed obligation of the schools to attempt to develop in each child the knowledge of and the ability to use the "standard" English of the United States—that set of language habits in which the most important affairs of our country are carried on, the dialect of the socially acceptable in most of our communities.

(3) The first step in fulfilling that obligation is the making of an accurate and realistic survey and description of the actual language practices in the various social or class dialects. Only after we have such information in hand can we know what social connotations are likely to attach to particular usages.

Language, Individual and Society

ROBERT A. HALL, JR.

This essay looks at the range and diversity of language from two points of view. The first part views language as a series of related and expanding circles, moving out from the speech of a single individual to the larger units of linguistic familial relationships. The second part places in sharp perspective the range and diversity of expression within a single language in terms of dialectal divisions and functional levels of usage. Robert A. Hall, Jr., Professor of Linguistics at Cornell University, is himself a wide ranger in language. A specialist in Italian and Romance philology, he is also an authority on pidgin and creole languages. He is perhaps most well known to the general reader for his book *Leave Your Language Alone!*, later revised as *Linguistics and Your Language*.

Language is . . . both an individual and a social phenomenon. It is individual because it manifests itself only in the habits—potential or actualized—of each individual speaker. Since these habits are controlled in the brain—though it is not yet known for certain in which part of the brain, or even if there is a specific part of the brain which controls language habits—we may speak of linguistic activity as having its

From *Introductory Linguistics* by Robert A. Hall, Jr. Reprinted by permission of Chilton Books.

locus existendi in the individual brain. At the same time, language is intimately connected with society through its function, which is primarily that of communicating messages from any given individual to one or more others; nor could human society exist without language. These two aspects of language, the individual and the social, are therefore extremely closely interconnected. Language forms the major link between the individual and society, and makes it possible for him to live at the same time as an individual personality complete in himself, and as a fully functioning member of his social group.

By the age of twelve or thirteen, the normal individual has a fully developed and functioning linguistic system, and may be referred to as a linguistic adult. (We are referring here to the *structure*, not to the *vocabulary*, involved in the linguistic system; one's stock of vocabulary items can of course undergo even considerable expansion after the age of twelve or thirteen.) Each person's total set of language habits is termed his *idiolect*, and is peculiar to him as an individual. This does not mean that the individual invents his idiolect out of thin air. On the contrary, the individual "creates" nothing in his idiolect, except in the sense that he has been building it up, in his behavior patterns, since his earliest childhood; but every idiolect is developed through imitation of other idiolects. The individual normally imitates very closely those models with whom he has been in continual and intensive contact, especially in his early years (parents, playmates, teachers), and less closely those with whom his contacts have been less intimate. Yet, since each individual has different experiences from those of every other individual, in language as in other matters, each idiolect is different, at least in slight details, from every other. No two idiolects are absolutely identical in every respect, any more than any two sets of fingerprints.

Yet of course, humans are able to communicate with each other, by virtue of the similarity of idiolects. Whenever two or more individuals are able to talk together and understand each other, the resultant group is termed a *speech-community*. The degree of closeness of similarity between two or more idiolects—and hence the degree of mutual comprehension, and of cohesiveness of the speech-community— is relative. In small, closely-knit groups, all of whose members are in continual contact with each other, the cohesiveness of the speech-community is correspondingly great, and the differences between idiolects are minor. This is the case in small families, tribes, or communities which live isolated from other groups while having intense contacts within their own group (e.g., the Amish in eastern Pennsylvania, or many mountain tribes in Central and South America). At the opposite extreme is the type of large, even immense modern speech-community like those of English, French, or Chinese, with hundreds of millions of speakers and numerous sub-divisions. In such large groups, the speakers within each major sub-division (say, North America, Great Britain, Australia, etc., within the English-speaking world) have little difficulty in understanding each other, and even speakers from neighboring sub-divisions (e.g., Australia and New Zealand). At the extremes of linguistic divergence, however, even those who belong to the same over-all speech-community (say, a Georgia "cracker" and a Scottish Highlander, or a North Chinese and a Cantonese) have considerable difficulty in achieving mutual comprehension.

It follows that all the terms which refer to linguistic groupings (*language, dialect, sub-dialect*) larger than the individual idiolect are likewise all relative. (Here we must avoid a widespread confusion of terms: linguistic analysts use the term *dialect*, not in its popular pejorative sense of "vulgar, uneducated, foreign, or rustic speech," but to refer to any sub-division of a language, even the most prestigious literary variety.) Usually, the term *language* is reserved for the largest linguistic grouping within any speech-community (e.g., English, French, German, Italian, Spanish). The term *dialect* refers to any sub-division thereof, such as Tuscan, Lombard, Piedmontese, etc., in Italian; and *sub-dialect* refers to a lesser division within a dialect, such as Milanese, Bergamasque, and so on among the varieties of Lombard. At the other extreme of size, larger groups of related languages which have developed by differentiation out of a common source are called *families*, and a group of related families is a *stock*. Thus, Spanish, Italian, French, and the other Romance languages, which are developed out of Latin, form the Romance family; and the Latin, Celtic, Germanic, Balto-Slavic, Indo-Iranian, and several other families make up the Indo-European stock. However, since these terms too are relative, considerable variation exists in their use, and some scholars will even refer to the language families which make up the Indo-European stock as "the Indo-European dialects" because, at one time, they undoubtedly were simply varieties of one language.

Within any given speech-community, there are lines of greater or lesser *density of communication*—in other words, any given individual talks more to some people than to others. In theory, those individuals who talk most to each other—between whom the density of communication is greatest—should influence each other most and should therefore show the greatest similarity in their speech. Actually, however, other factors enter into play as well, especially that of prestige, so that any given speaker may be influenced more (say, in following a given pronunciation, grammatical feature, or item of vocabulary) by one or more prestige-bearing persons who are relatively removed from him socially, than by a much larger number of close everyday associates. The interplay of social contact and prestige groups, in influencing any given idiolect, is often very complicated, especially in modern times, when prestige figures are beginning to exert considerable influence through newspapers, radio, and television.

In analyzing the reflection of social structure in the differentiation of a speech-community, we must distinguish two planes: that of dialectal divisions, and that of functional levels of usage. Leonard Bloomfield's statement of the relation between dialects is classical (*Language*, p. 52):

The main types of speech in a complex speech community can be roughly classified as follows:

(1) *Literary standard*, used in the most formal discussion and writing (example: *I have none*);

(2) *Colloquial standard*, the speech of the privileged class (example: *I haven't any* or *I haven't got any*—in England only if spoken with the southern "public school" sounds and intonation);

(3) *Provincial standard*, in the United States probably not to be differentiated from 2, spoken by the "middle class," very close to 2, but differing slightly from province to province (example: *I haven't any* or *I haven't got any*, spoken, in England, with sounds or intonations that deviate from the "public school" standard);

(4) *Substandard*, clearly different from 1, 2, and 3, spoken in European countries by the "lower middle" class, in the United States by almost all but the speakers of types 2 and 3, and differing topographically, without intense local difference (example: *I ain't got none*);

(5) *Local dialect*, spoken by the least privileged class; only slightly developed in the United States; in Switzerland used also, as a domestic language, by the other classes; differs almost from village to village; the varieties so great as often to be incomprehensible to each other and to speakers of 2, 3, and 4 (example: *a hae nane*).

Intersecting with these lines of dialectal division, and especially with that between standard and nonstandard, is the difference in functional level, between formal and informal, first formulated by the late John S. Kenyon, one of the ablest observers of American English speech. Kenyon established a four-way distinction, between:

(a) *Formal standard:* Normally used only in very "correct" situations and elegant writing, oratory, and what used to be termed "elocution" (e.g., *it is I*).

(b) *Informal standard:* Used by socially acceptable people in their ordinary everyday contacts (e.g., *it's me; he went away; that's yours*).

(c) *Informal nonstandard:* Essentially equivalent to Bloomfield's "substandard" (e.g., *he beat it; he took it on the lam; that's yourn; you and me better go home*).

(d) *Formal nonstandard:* A variety which arises when those whose native speech is informal nonstandard try to achieve the formal level, and often create forms or combinations which no standard speaker would ever use on any level (e.g. *between you and I*).

The boundaries between dialectal divisions and between functional levels are, of course, subject to many gradations and are constantly shifting in space, time, and social level. Features of usage are constantly passing from one status to another, either rising or falling in prestige. Thus, *leisure* used to be pronounced with the vowel of *beat* in the first syllable throughout the English-speaking world, as it still is in the United States; in British standard usage, this pronunciation has been replaced by one rhyming with *measure*, and the earlier pronunciation has been relegated to the status of a rather archaic provincialism. To pronounce the names of the days of the week (*Sunday, Monday,* etc.) with the full vowel of the word *day* in the second part of the compound (e.g., *Sún-dày* instead of *Súndy*) used to be an outstanding example of formal nonstandard usage; Kenyon cites the instance of a broadcaster who announced "Sún-dày will be Móther's Dày," which many of his hearers interpreted as "Some day will be Mother's Day." Similarly, the use of *presently* in the sense of "at present" instead of "soon" used to be formal nonstandard, with a connotation of rather vulgar, pretentious journalese. Both of these usages, however, and many others like them, have by now become so widespread that they have passed from the status of formal nonstandard to that of informal standard, even though many members of the speech-community (the present writer included!) still dislike them.

In a geographical sense, too, the boundaries of speech-communities or of their subdivisions are almost never absolutely sharp or fixed. Even in the case of different languages (e.g., French and Flemish in

Belgium, French and German in France and Switzerland, or French and English in Canada), there are often tiny islands or enclaves of one language within the territory along the frontier. In a city like Brussels, which lies athwart the boundary between French and Flemish, the interpenetration of the different speech-communities becomes extremely complicated. Furthermore, there are continual shifts taking place from day to day and from hour to hour, not only with the casual movements of individuals along the frontier and beyond it, but also with changes of residence on a more or less permanent basis. Many individuals, both in and out of border zones, are bilingual or multilingual, and hence can be said to have two or more idiolects and to belong to more than one speech-community. The same considerations hold true, with even greater force, for the boundaries between dialects within a single speech-community; here, social mobility is a further factor tending to blur the divisions even more. Consequently, any lines which we may draw between one dialect and another, or even one language and another, can never be more than an approximation. However, in this as in many other aspects of mass phenomena, we must use approximations, *faute de mieux*, simply because a complete and detailed description would be beyond any possibility of achievement.

Linguistic features serve both centripetal and centrifugal purposes in social structure. Without the cement of communication through language, humans could never have achieved anything like the complicated methods of cooperation on which even the simplest society depends. On the other hand, most social divisions, although not caused by language, are accentuated by the existence of linguistic differences and the use which many persons make of these latter for enhancing their social position, a process of linguistic snobbery. Both positively and negatively, our use of language is inextricably interwoven with our existence both as individuals and as members of human society.

SUGGESTED ASSIGNMENTS

1. Most good dictionaries identify by means of usage labels the level or variety of a particular word or of different senses of a word, e.g., *Colloq.*, *Dial.* In order to discuss usage intelligently you should know what these usage labels mean. Look up the definitions of the following: *archaic, colloquial, dialect, localism, slang, obsolete.* Note especially the meaning of *colloquial;* many people confuse it with *localism* or identify it with *slang.*

2.   Are high school and college freshman composition textbooks reliable guides to current usage? This question was investigated by Dr. Jean Malmstrom, who spent five years making a study of 57 items of American usage. Some of her findings have been published in an article entitled "Linguistic Atlas Findings versus Textbook Pronouncements on Current American Usage," *The English Journal*, April, 1959. Read the article and prepare an oral summary of it for your class.

3.   Some textbooks still cite elaborate rules for the use of *shall* and *will*. Read Fries' discussion of this topic in his *American English Grammar*, p. 151 ff., and make a report to the class on the origin of the rules and their validity.

4.   Many composition textbooks and handbooks contain a section on items of usage, often entitled "Glossary of Usage" or "Glossary of Diction" (sometimes "Faulty Diction"), with comments about the acceptability or nonacceptability of these items as Standard American English and their appropriateness to various language situations. Compare the judgments of any three textbooks about each of the following: *aggravate, different from-different than, due to, enthuse, farther-further, like, who-whom* (interrogative). Then look up each of the items in three dictionaries, compare the dictionary statements with each other and with your original findings, and present your data to the class for discussion.

5.   The whole of the English language can be partitioned into various groupings. In the readings of this section, we have seen it divided into two social dialects, standard and nonstandard English. Still another grouping consists of those words which are used in limited areas of discourse, like the special vocabularies of skiers, carpenters, astronauts, skin divers, and so on. Such specialized groups of words are called shoptalk.

Make a list of shoptalk expressions in a particular area of life with which you are familiar, e.g., jazz, trout fishing, hi-fi, boxing, amateur radio work, dog raising, woodworking, painting, stamp collecting, theater, hot rods. Include only those expressions that you believe are not understood by the general public. Bring them to class, where a discussion of the lists will probably reveal how much of our own language many of us do not know.

6.   Running through all varieties of English is a special vein called slang. Slang is a roguish kind of language. At its best it is piquant and picturesque, and holds for us the black-sheep attraction of forbidden pleasures. But when the novelty of a new slang expression wears thin, its sparkle dwindles away and it becomes dull as an old penny. Although slang cannot be defined with precision, most students of language will probably agree that the following statements can be made about it:

a.   It occurs more frequently in speech than in writing.

b.   It is found in both standard and nonstandard English.

c.   It seems to originate from a desire for novelty and freshness of expression.

d. It tends to change more rapidly than the rest of the language.
e. It consists largely of these kinds of words:
   (1) Old words with new meanings.
   (2) Newly invented words.
   (3) Standard words used in a figurative sense.
   (4) Words borrowed from shoptalk.
   (5) Clipped words.[1]

Meet with a friend and see how many slang expressions you can jot down in fifteen minutes. Classify them according to the divisions under *e*. How would you classify those that you have left over?

7. The youth of each generation seems to have its special slang terms to express such meanings as these: an attractive girl, a handsome young man, an objectionable person, a girl of questionable virtue, a girl of impregnable virtue, a dance, a party, drunk, very good, very bad. What are your slang terms, if any, for these meanings? Interview a person of middle age whom you suspect of having had a lively youth and write a theme comparing his or her slang with yours.

8. Write a theme on one of these subjects:
   a. Slang, Sparkling and Stale
   b. Slang That Has Endured
   c. Some Slang of the 19th Century
   d. Slang of the Sports Page
   e. The Slang My Father Used

9. Write a paragraph describing a person or relating an event in nonstandard English. Then write a second paragraph doing the same in standard English. In class, when students' paragraphs are compared, be prepared to comment on such matters as liveliness, breadth of vocabulary, complexity of sentence structure, and grammatical forms.

10. Imagine that you are interested in getting a job at a summer camp as a counselor. Write a close friend about it, explaining why you think you are qualified for the job. Then write a letter of application to the camp director setting forth your qualifications. Try to write naturally in each case, adapting your language to the recipient.

FURTHER READINGS

Allen, Harold B., ed. *Readings in Applied English Linguistics*, 2d ed. New York: Appleton-Century-Crofts, 1964. See the section "Linguistics and Usage," pp. 271–341.

[1] A clipped word is a word that has been reduced to one of its parts. Examples: *lab, exam, plane, phone, flu, still, co-ed, prom.* [eds.]

Baugh, Albert C. *A History of the English Language,* 2d ed. New York: Appleton-Century-Crofts, 1957. For discussion of the eighteenth-century grammarians and their attitude toward matters of usage, see Chapter 9.

Bryant, Margaret M. *Current American Usage.* New York: Funk and Wagnalls Co., Inc., 1962. Summary of research on many problems of usage.

Evans, Bergen and Cornelia Evans. *A Dictionary of Contemporary American Usage.* New York: Random House, Inc., 1957.

Fries, Charles C. *The Teaching of English.* Ann Arbor, Michigan: George Wahr Publishing Company, 1949. See especially Chapter I, "The Rules of Grammar as the Measure of Language Errors"; Chapter II, "Standards of Acceptable English: Grammar"; Chapter III, "Standards of Acceptable English: Vocabulary."

Hall, Robert A., Jr. *Introductory Linguistics.* Philadelphia: Chilton Books, 1964. On usage, see pp. 444–448.

——. *Linguistics and Your Language.* New York: Doubleday & Company, Inc., 1960. See Chapter I, "Which Should I Say?" and Chapter II, "Right vs. Wrong."

Jespersen, Otto. *Mankind, Nation, and Individual.* London: George Allen & Unwin, Ltd., 1946.

Quirk, Randolph. *The Use of English.* New York: St. Martin's Press, Inc., 1962. On usage see especially pp. 64–68 and 199–215.

Robertson, Stuart and Frederic G. Cassidy. *The Development of Modern English.* Englewood Cliffs, New Jersey: Prentice-Hall, Inc., 1954. See pp. 291–325.

Several periodicals frequently publish articles on usage: *American Speech, College English,* and *The English Journal.* Up to 1962, the latter two had a section devoted specifically to usage: "Current English Forum" in *College English* and "Current English" in *The English Journal.*

8

LINGUISTIC GEOGRAPHY

Some Words Stop
at Marietta, Ohio

GLEDHILL CAMERON

Linguistic geography, also called dialect geography, is the systematic study of language differences within a specified area, usually a country or a part of a country. The differences are those of pronunciation, vocabulary, and grammar. To get accurate information, trained linguists hold long interviews with native informants, who have been carefully selected so as to offer a representative sampling of the speech of the area.

When all the information has been collected and edited, it is made public by a series of maps (See pages 393, 413, 414) or by books and articles. As a result, we get a detailed account of both regional and social dialects.[1] One caution must be urged here. As you study the data in the readings

From *Collier's* (June 25, 1954). Reprinted by permission of the author. Copyright 1954.

[1] The 416 informants for the *Linguistic Atlas of New England* were classified into these types:

"Type I: Little formal education, little reading and restricted social contacts.
Type II: Better formal education (usually high school) and/or wider reading and social contacts.
Type III: Superior education (usually college), cultured background, wide reading and/or extensive social contacts.
Type A: Aged, and/or regarded by the field worker as old-fashioned.
Type B: Middle-aged or younger, and/or regarded by the field worker as more modern."
From Hans Kurath, *Handbook of the Linguistic Geography of New England* (Washington, D. C., American Council of Learned Societies, 1939), p. 44.

With this information we can generalize on the social class using any given pronunciation, word, or grammatical form. In other words, we can decide which forms are standard English and which are nonstandard English, also called "substandard English" and "vulgate." [eds.]

381

of this section, you must remember that this information pertains to the SPOKEN language, and may or may not be true of the written language.

The first reading below, by Gledhill Cameron, is an entertaining but sound report on the field work of the linguistic geographer.

What language do you speak? Would you call it "plain American"? If so, you may be surprised to learn that despite the vast influence of radio, TV, the movies, magazines, books and national advertising, many of the words and expressions you use every day might not even be understood by people elsewhere in the United States—who also speak "plain American."

If you're a housewife, do you make bacon and eggs in a frying pan—or, as many other American women do, in a *spider, creeper,* or *drip-drop?* When you clean house, do you *straighten up* or *tidy up, rid up* or *redd up* (as women do in some parts of New England, Ohio and Indiana); *make ménage* (as in New Orleans), or *muck out* (as in some Colorado mining communities)?

If Junior sneaks away from school, do your neighbors say he *skips, bags* or *lays out of* school, or that he *plays hooky* or *hooks Jack?* When he reports on how he spent his time, does he tell you he climbed trees, or that he *clim, clum, clome, cloom, clam* or *clammed* them? If he ate too many green apples, does he get sick *to, at, in, with* or *about* his stomach?

To chart the differences in vocabulary, grammar and pronunciation from one American community to another, a small band of language experts—professors and graduate students representing a number of universities—has been traveling around the country for the last 20 years, asking people what words they use for all sorts of simple, everyday objects and actions. They have compiled long lists of variants for everything from the words for the clavicles of a chicken (*wishbone, witch bone, pull bone, pully bone, lucky bone, merry-thought*) to our expressions for the woman who's going to have a baby (she might be *in health, in the family way, in preggety, on the road to Boston, fragrant* or *footbroke*—the last a local Southern expression derived from an African word).

Sometimes the linguistic geographers use tape or disc recordings, but most of their minutely detailed data are collected in thousands of bulky notebooks, in a special phonetic script which can reproduce about 400 differences in vowel sounds alone. Using this script, the interviewers write down the casual conversations of men and women all over America exactly as they talk on their own front porches (*stoops, piazzas, galleries*).

The linguistic fieldworker must be part historian and part sociologist; he must also have in him the spirit of the bloodhound and more than a trace of the gossip. He will go wherever he can find an informant willing to give the six to 20 hours it takes to answer his questions, which cover from 500 to 800 items of everyday speech. The language experts have carried their notebooks into saloons, cotton fields, race tracks, mines, hospitals, schools, courthouses, shops and factories. One linguist obtained a fruitful interview while riding around in a patrol car with the chief of police of a small Southern town, then got another by sitting for hours on a sidewalk curb, chatting with his subject.

A second researcher spent one whole day quizzing a hard-working barber; another day talking to a railroad-crossing watchman who kept a nervous lookout for the road detective (visitors, inquiring professors included, were contrary to regulations); another day perched on a tractor interviewing a farmer; and another in a hospital, where the subject was recovering from an unexpected operation which had interrupted their first interview.

The information so exhaustively collected is going into a colossal work titled *Linguistic Atlas of the United States and Canada* (Canada is included to cover colloquial expressions which ignore the international boundary). When the atlas is finished, an estimated 10 years from now, it will contain thousands of maps showing local and regional speech differences and the geographical boundaries, called isoglosses, that limit the areas in which the words and expressions are used. The work is being done under the direction of the University of Michigan's Dr. Hans Kurath—an internationally known linguist who has been a leader of the atlas project since its origin in 1929.

At work on many linguistic atlases

The atlas actually will consist of a series of regional sets, the first of which, *Linguistic Atlas of New England*, already has been published. Its six volumes (price for the set: $185) were brought out by Brown University and the American Council of Learned Societies from 1939 to 1943, at a cost of about $250,000. Additional atlases are in various stages of completion, two at the University of Michigan, and others at the Universities of Minnesota, Colorado, New Mexico and California, the University of Washington at Seattle and Louisiana State University.

Preliminary studies have been made for still another at the University of Texas.

Three kinds of maps are used by the researchers to plot variations. First there's the lexical map, which shows the different words Americans use to indicate the same object or action. For example, "something extra" is *lagniappe* in New Orleans, something *to boot* in Kentucky, a *brawtus* in Charleston, South Carolina, a *pillon* in New Mexico —all good American words.

The linguists use a second, phonetic map to show differences in the pronunciation of the same words. The classic example is provided by the old lady in North Carolina who said about her crop of tomatoes, "Oh, we'll eat what we *kin*, and what we *cain't* we'll *can*."

The morphological map, the third type, indicates differences in grammar. Widespread education is rapidly wiping out grammatical variations, the linguists have found. One Georgia man summed up the changes that are occurring: "I used to say, 'I drink water' and 'I have drinked,'" he proudly told an atlas fieldworker. "Now I say, 'I drink,' 'I drank' and 'I have drank.'"

Most of the regional departures from the common language of Americans (technically, we all speak what linguists call American English) involve the homey aspects of life: family relationships, kitchens and cookery, farm work, daily chores, children's play and other activities which are relatively immune from outside influences. Some of these localisms are confined to very small geographic areas, says Dr. Kurath. If you say *hook Jack*, meaning to be absent from school without leave, you are most probably from Cape Cod. If you call cows by hollering *chay!*, you're from Williamsburg County, South Carolina. If you're an old-timer from eastern Long Island, you might call a barnyard or cowpen a *pightle* (it rhymes with "title").

New England, which had many isolated settlements in colonial times, still carries the traces of that isolation in its current colloquialisms. A deep-dish apple pie is *apple Jonathan* in Rhode Island, *apple grunt* around Plymouth and on Cape Cod, in Massachusetts, and *apple slump* in the Narragansett-Bay region. A garbage pail is an *orts pail* in Essex County, Massachusetts, and (as far as the researchers can tell) nowhere else. A spring onion is a *rareripe* only in certain sections of eastern New England.

According to some people in the great valley of Pennsylvania, a horse doesn't whinny, it *laughs*, and a setting hen may be known in the same region as a *clook*.

Judging from research to date, it's only in Indiana that a child coasting down a hill on a sled or wagon goes *bellity-bump*; and only around New London that he goes *belly-kuhchunk!* In the upper Midwest he may go downhill *boy fashion* and in Louisiana he'll go *scooting* or *head fo'most*. In other parts of the country he may go *belly flop, gut, bunt, bump, bumpus, button, bust, booster, wop, whack, womp, slide, slam, kuhchug* or *grinder*.

A quaint tale of courtship

The rural areas retain some of the most colorful speech localisms. In some sparsely settled parts of Maine, for example, you might still hear of a *gorming* (stupid) man who gets *all of a biver* (excited) about a *ding-clicker* (a pretty young woman) and invites her to a *hog-wrestle* (a dance). But he wouldn't propose until he was sure she wasn't *pizen neat* (too neat) or a *drozzel tail* (slovenly person).

It's also in the more remote sections that linguistic geographers report the greatest resistance to interviews. One of the most successful of the atlas fieldworkers is Dr. Raven Ioor McDavid, Jr., of Western Reserve University, Cleveland,[2] a South Carolinian who has conducted chatty sessions with 470 housewives, farmers, lumbermen, miners, businessmen, politicians, Civil War veterans, literary ladies and stenographers all over the country. Dr. McDavid recalls an occasion in Georgia where he couldn't get *anyone* to talk to him. He finally discovered that the small town he was visiting had recently been described by a metropolitan newspaper as a "typical hick town." The citizens were now so sensitive that almost no one was willing to talk to any stranger, whatever his apparent purpose. (The local grocer eventually consented to see McDavid—after insisting that the interview be conducted in the back of his store, at night.)

In his home state of South Carolina, McDavid—who customarily carries 15 or 16 colored pencils, mechanical pencils and fountain pens in his pocket for marking symbols—was accused of being an FBI agent by a man who shut the door on him.

Dr. Harold B. Allen of the University of Minnesota, who has conducted almost 200 interviews for the Atlas of the Upper Midwest, says he was accused of being a Communist spy once, by a hardware merchant in Bemidji, Minnesota. ("Who else," said the hardwareman reasonably, "would ask all those questions?")

[2] Now at the University of Chicago. [eds.]

The late Dr. Guy S. Lowman, Jr., who did most of the field interviews for the New England, Middle and South Atlantic regions, once came out of a house in West Virginia to find the air let out of his automobile tires. (He had been mistaken for a revenuer.) Another time he was chased out of a house by the irate son of a genteel Southern lady, who felt that the linguist had put an indelicate question to his mother: "Madam, what do you call the male kind of cow?" (Cityfolk may not realize it, but the word "bull" is never used in mixed company in some parts of the country. Among the more polite substitutes linguistic geographers have recorded are the *masculine*, rhyming with "vine" and heard only on Nantucket Island, Massachusetts, and in West Virginia, the *surley*, in eastern New Mexico and some parts of Texas, and, more generally, the *old man*, the *roarer*, the *mister*, the *master*, *male critter*, *toro*, *gentleman cow*, *preacher cow*, *beast*, *brute*, *jock*, *major*, *top cow*, *tuppin' ox*, *ranger* and the *he*.)

But fieldworkers get only too hospitable a welcome in most places. That is one of the joys, as well as one of the burdens, of a linguistic geographer's life. In the good cause of recording our American speech, they have eaten veritable mountains of home-made cakes, pies, cookies, breads and biscuits of varying degrees of specific gravity, as well as countless doughnuts (*crullers*, *olicooks*, *fat-cakes*, *fried cakes*, *riz doughnuts*, *fossnocks*).

McDavid recalls with satisfaction the day he shared a lunch of mule ears or meat pastys (it rhymes with "nasty") with miners in northern Michigan, and heard a classic argument as to whether the pastys, which provide the miners with a substantial midday meal, keep better carried in the shirt or in the boot.

But a home-cooked meal in Georgia in "lay-by-time," when the cotton is opening up and before it's ready to pick, is best remembered as the occasion for what McDavid, who prides himself on "blending in with the foliage," describes as his greatest tribute.

"The lunch was a mess of something pretty greasy and full of red pepper," he says, "but I fell to. I noticed my informants' elderly sister, who had cooked the meal, watching me with great satisfaction. Then she said: 'I could have gone and kilt a chicken, Mr. McDavid. But I figured *you* didn't want to be treated like no preacher.' "

The fieldworkers admit that it is surprising that people are willing to be interviewed and to talk long, readily and freely. Except in the most general way, they aren't told exactly what the interview is about; if they knew, they might become self-conscious—and it's the unguarded response of natural, everyday conversation that the linguist hopes to capture.

Armed with lists of the kinds of words he wants the subject to use, the researcher conducts the interview in as close an approximation to casual conversation as he can. He must also be keenly alert to pronunciation and grammar. McDavid usually starts out with what he calls shotgun questions: "What do you call this room that we're in?" "What are those utensils on the stove?" "What do you call other rooms in the house?" The fieldworker never asks a subject to repeat, and answers are never directly suggested.

"For example," explains Dr. Allen, "I'll say to the person, 'I suppose you fry your eggs in a . . .' then he'll take it from there and fill in 'skillet' or 'frying pan' or whichever word comes most naturally. Often he'll look surprised that I don't know. Each person requires a different approach. We ask about familiar things—expressions of time, weather, farm crops, and utensils, vehicles, animals, food, the family and its relations, the human body, social life and institutions, religion and so on.

"I usually start out by explaining we're making a study of the changing names for things. That pleases the old folks, who have thought all along that kids nowadays are pretty dumb not to know the difference between a 'hame' and a 'chokestrap' (parts of a harness)."

A community is selected for interviews only after a careful study of its history, population shifts and the influence of foreign groups who may have settled there. McDavid wouldn't be surprised, for example, to hear a native of Hudson, New York, say he *ran afoul of* something, instead of *ran across* or *ran onto*. The seafaring expression comes naturally in Hudson because it was settled by whalers from Nantucket, Massachusetts.

Around Marietta, Ohio, he'd be prepared to hear people use such New England terms as *pail* instead of bucket, *chipmunk* instead of ground squirrel, and *boss!* instead of *sook* when they call a cow—although the second expressions are the more common elswhere in Ohio. A New England commercial company once sent an entire community to Marietta early in its settlement days, so that linguists today call Marrietta and its environs a Yankee "speech island."

The linguistic geographer tries to talk to two distinct types of people in each community studied. The first type is an older person with family roots deep in the community, someone with limited education, and with few outside social contacts which might tend to blur or even erase certain localisms from his speech. The second type is younger, usually middle-aged, with more education and broader social contacts or travel experience. In some communities, a third type of informant—representing the "cultivated" speech of the community—is also interviewed. By sampling the speech of these three groups, the linguist can determine which local expressions are used by everyone in the community, which tend to disappear, and, if so, what replaces them as the community grows more educated or "cultured." An interesting discovery: one town's speech vulgarity may be a perfectly acceptable regionalism in another community, even among the "cultivated" inhabitants.

Linguists believe that recording the living language of America for the first time should lead to a more realistic approach to the teaching of English in schools and colleges. For, they ask, isn't it a waste of time for English teachers to try to stop New Englanders from saying "hadn't ought to" when linguistic studies show that this grammatically "wrong" expression is used by nearly everyone in New England, educated or not? Or to try to remove "ain't" from the speech of Southerners, when it is generally accepted in the colloquial speech of cultivated persons in the South?

Thus far, a major fact established by atlas investigations is that although there's a popular idea of Northern and Southern speech, divided by the Mason and Dixon's line in the Eastern part of the country, there are, in fact, three distinct speech areas in the East. The third is a clear Midland dialect area between North and South, corresponding to the Pennsylvania settlement area of early days. The North-Midland speech boundary runs in a westerly direction from below Sandy Hook in New Jersey through northern Pennsylvania; the line separating Midland from South runs in a southwesterly direction from Dover, Delaware, through Baltimore and along the Blue Ridge in Virginia. And in the Eastern states from Maine to South Carolina, linguistic geographers can plot 18 dialect divisions largely created by the original colonial settlements and the subsequent routes of migrations.

This Eastern coastal area, oldest in point of settlement, still retains the nation's greatest diversity of speech from one community to another. But then, as the dialect divisions flow westward on the map—the way our population did—they begin to unravel, and strands of the three begin to overlap.

"Man takes his speech ways with him wherever he goes," Dr.

Kurath explains. "The three main types of English were carried west-ward and blended into new regional varieties; new words were coined, old words came to be used in new senses, and words were borrowed from Indian languages, from the German and Scandinavian languages spoken in the Midwest, and from the Spanish of the Southwest. But the main stock of English vocabulary in this country is nevertheless clearly derived from the earlier settlements on the Atlantic slope."

While the trend today is away from regional words and expres-sions, linguistic geographers don't anticipate complete uniformity in the speech of democratic America—where the way we talk, as well as the way we live, is based on the belief that men can be different, and still be equal.

"While some vocabulary and grammatical differences may disap-pear," says Dr. McDavid, "the differences in word pronunciations are likely to persist. I don't think anyone can impose a single set of patterns on Americans—for speech or for anything else."

Regional
and Social Variations

ALBERT H. MARCKWARDT

In this selection Albert H. Marckwardt, Professor of English at Princeton University, discusses the origins of American regional dialects, explains the making of a linguistic atlas, and presents information on class or social dialects. Pro-fessor Marckwardt is director of the *Linguistic Atlas of the North-Central States* project, which includes the territory of Wisconsin, Michigan, Illinois, Kentucky, Ohio, Indiana, and part of Ontario.

The English language is spoken natively in America by no less than 145 million persons over an area of some three million square miles. Various parts of the United States differ considerably from each

From *American English* by Albert H. Marckwardt. Reprinted by permission of the publisher, Oxford University Press, Inc., copyright 1958.

The assignments for all the essays in this section have been placed on page 421.

other with respect to climate, topography, plant and animal life, economic conditions, and social structure. Sociologists and historians recognize at least six regional cultures within the continental borders of the country. The assumption that differences in culture and environmental background bring about differences in language will[1] justify the inference that the language is likely not to be uniform throughout the country. The American novelist John Steinbeck in his *Grapes of Wrath* offers convincing evidence of the plausibility of this assumption:

"I knowed you wasn't Oklahomy folks. You talk queer kinda—That ain't no blame, you understan'."

"Everbody says words different," said Ivy. "Arkansas folks says 'em different, and Oklahomy folks says 'em different. And we seen a lady from Massachusetts, an' she said 'em differentest of all. Couldn' hardly make out what she was sayin'."

Early travelers to America and native commentators on the language agree on the existence of regional differences at an early period in our national history. Mrs. Anne Royal called attention to various Southernisms in the works which she wrote during the second quarter of the nineteenth century, and as early as 1829, Dr. Robley Dunglison had identified many of the Americanisms, in the glossary he compiled, with particular portions of the country. Charles Dickens recognized regional differences in the English he encountered in his first tour of the United States, and William Howard Russell, reporting on Abraham Lincoln's first state banquet, at which he was a guest, mentions his astonishment at finding "a diversity of accent almost as great as if a number of foreigners had been speaking English."

A number of other observers, however, were sufficiently impressed by the uniformity of the language throughout the country to make this a matter of comment. De Tocqueville, in a rather extended treatment of the language of the young republic, flatly declared, "There is no patois in the New World," and John Pickering, along with Noah Webster easily the most distinguished of our early philologists, also remarked on the great uniformity of dialect through the United States, "in consequence," as he said, "of the frequent removals of people from one part of our country to another."

There is truth in both types of comment. People in various parts of the United States do not all speak alike, but there is greater uni-

---

[1] Text slightly but not materially altered by permission of the author. [eds.]

formity here than in England or in the countries of Western Europe, and this makes the collection of a trustworthy body of information upon the regional variations in American English a somewhat difficult and delicate matter.

The gathering of authentic data on the dialects of many of the countries of Western Europe began in the latter decades of the nineteenth centruy. The *Atlas linguistique de la France* followed closely upon the heels of the *Sprachatlas des deutschen Reichs*, and the activities of the English Dialect Society were initiated about the same time. In 1889 a group of American scholars organized the American Dialect Society, hoping that the activities of this organization might result in a body of material from which either a dialect dictionary or a series of linguistic maps, or both, might be compiled. The society remained relatively small, however, and although some valuable information appeared in its journal *Dialect Notes*, a systematic survey of the regional varieties of American English has not yet resulted from its activities.

The past quarter of a century, however, has seen the development of such a survey. Beginning in 1928, a group of researchers under the direction of Professor Hans Kurath, now of the University of Michigan, undertook the compilation of a *Linguistic Atlas of New England* as the first unit of a projected *Linguistic Atlas of the United States and Canada*. The New England atlas, comprising a collection of some 600 maps, each showing the distribution of a single language feature throughout the area, was published over the period from 1939 to 1943. Since that time, field work for comparable atlases of the Middle Atlantic and of the South Atlantic states has been completed, and the materials are awaiting editing and publication. Field records for atlases of the North Central states and the Upper Middle West are virtually complete, and significant beginnings have been made in the Rocky Mountain and the Pacific Coast areas. Surveys in Louisiana, in Texas, and in Ontario are also under way. It is perhaps not too optimistic to predict that within the next twenty-five years all of the United States and Canada as well will have been covered in at least an initial survey.

For a number of reasons it is not easy to collect a body of valid and reliable information on American dialects. The wide spread of education, the virtual extinction of illiteracy, the extreme mobility of the population—both geographically and from one social class to another —and the tremendous development of a number of media of mass communication have all contributed to the recession of local speech forms. Moreover, the cultural insecurity of a large portion of the

American people has caused them to feel apologetic about their language. Consequently, they seldom display the same degree of pride or affection that many an English or a European speaker has for his particular patois. Since all dialect research is essentially a sampling process, this means that the invesitgator must take particular pains to secure representative and comparable samples from the areas which are studied. Happily, the very care which this demands has had the result of developing the methodology of linguistic geography in this country to a very high level.

In general, the material for a linguistic atlas is based upon the natural responses of a number of carefully selected individuals representing certain carefully chosen communities, which in themselves reflect the principal strains of settlement and facets of cultural development in the area as a whole. Since the spread of education generally results in the disappearance of local or regional speech forms, and since the extension of schooliing to virtually all of the population has been an achievement of the past seventy-five years, it became necessary for the American investigator to differentiate between the oldest generation, for whom schooling beyond the elementary level is not usual, and a middle-aged group who is likely to have had some experience with secondary schools. In addition, it is highly desirable to include some representatives of the standard or cultivated speech in each region, that their language may serve as a basis of comparison with the folk speech. Accordingly, in the American atlases, from each community represented, the field worker will choose at least two, and sometimes three representatives, in contrast to the usual practice of European researchers, who may safely content themselves with one. Moreover, it is equally necessary to make certain that the persons chosen in any community have not been subject to alien linguistic influences; consequently, only those who have lived there all of their lives, and preferably those who represent families who have long been identified with the area in question, are interviewed, although as one moves westward into the more recently settled areas this is not always possible.

Since complete materials are available only for the eastern seaboard and for the area north of the Ohio River as far west as the Mississippi, tentative conclusions relative to the regional variations in American English can be presented only for the eastern half of the country. The principal dialect areas presented in Kurath's *Word Geography of the Eastern United States* are indicated on the accompanying map.

The three major dialect boundaries, it will be noted, cut the country into lateral strips and are labeled by Professor Kurath *Northern, Midland,* and *Southern* respectively. The line which separates the Northern and Midland areas begins in New Jersey a little below Sandy Hook, proceeds northwest to the east branch of the Susquehanna near Scranton, Pennsylvania, then goes westward through Pennsylvania

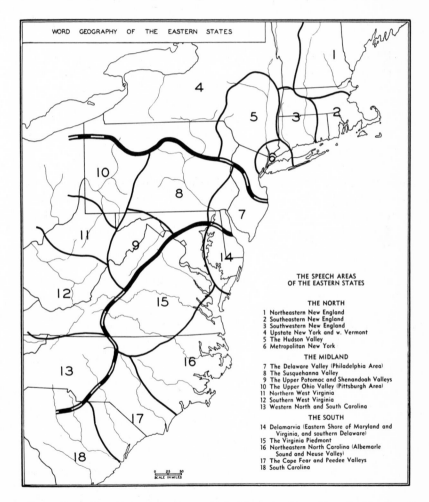

WORD   GEOGRAPHY   OF   THE   EASTERN   STATES

THE SPEECH AREAS
OF THE EASTERN STATES

THE NORTH
1 Northeastern New England
2 Southeastern New England
3 Southwestern New England
4 Upstate New York and w. Vermont
5 The Hudson Valley
6 Metropolitan New York

THE MIDLAND
7 The Delaware Valley (Philadelphia Area)
8 The Susquehanna Valley
9 The Upper Potomac and Shenandoah Valleys
10 The Upper Ohio Valley (Pittsburgh Area)
11 Northern West Virginia
12 Southern West Virginia
13 Western North and South Carolina

THE SOUTH
14 Delmarvia (Eastern Shore of Maryland and
    Virginia, and southern Delaware)
15 The Virginia Piedmont
16 Northeastern North Carolina (Albemarle
    Sound and Neuse Valley)
17 The Cape Fear and Peedee Valleys
18 South Carolina

SCALE IN MILES

From *A Word Geography of the Eastern United States* by Hans Kurath. Reprinted by permission of the publisher, The University of Michigan Press, copyright 1949.

just below the northern tier of counties. In Ohio the boundary dips below the Western Reserve, then turns northwest again, passing above Fort Wayne, Indiana. When it approaches South Bend it dips slightly to the southwest and cuts through Illinois, reaching the Mississippi at a point slightly above Quincy. The other principal boundary, that separating the Southern and Midland areas, begins at a point somewhat below Dover in Delaware, sweeps through Baltimore in something of an arc, turns sharply southwest north of the Potomac, follows the crest of the Blue Ridge in Virginia, and south of the James River swerves out into the North Carolina Piedmont. As we approach the lower part of South Carolina and Georgia the boundary is as yet unknown,

Even these necessarily incomplete results of the survey carried on under Professor Kurath and his associates have modified considerably our previous conceptions of the regional distribution of American speech forms. This modification is brought about principally by adding one concept and eliminating another. The concept thus eliminated has been variously known as Middle Western, Western, or General American. The older view of American dialects, reduced to its simplest terms, recognized the existence of a New England type of speech, a Southern type, and the remainder was generally blanketed by some such term as General American.

It seems clear now that what is neither New England nor Southern —which includes, of course, something between three-quarters and nine-tenths of the continental United States—is far too diverse and lacking in homogeneity to be considered a single major dialect. We know, for example, that there are a significant number of differences, both in vocabulary and in verb inflections, between the folk speech of most of Pennsylvania and that of New York state, and between Michigan and Wisconsin on the one hand, and most of Indiana and large portions of Illinois and Ohio on the other. As our information for the rest of the country becomes available, there can be little doubt that this conclusion will be strengthened.

The concept which has been added is the recognition of a Midland type of speech as distinct from both North and South. An examination of the evidence which Professor Kurath presents in his *Word Geography* leaves no doubt that the speech of this area, though it is by no means uniform, is sufficiently differentiated from both North and South to justify its classification as a major dialect area. This conclusion is supported not only by Atwood's study of the verb forms in the eastern portion of the country but by the available materials from the North Central States.

The map shown on page 393 includes also a few, but not all, of the sub-dialect areas which merit recognition. In the North the principal area is that which separates coastal New England from western New England, New York state, and the territory to the west. In general, this boundary follows the line of the Green Mountains, the Berkshire Hills, and the Connecticut River. The Metropolitan New York area consists of a broad circle with the city itself at the center; the Hudson Valley area encompasses the original Dutch settlements in New York and northern New Jersey, spreading into northeastern Pennsylvania. The Midland area is divided into northern and southern sub-areas, the line of demarcation being just a little south of the Old National Road in Ohio, Indiana, and Illinois. Within the Southern dialect region, the Virginia Piedmont and the Delmarva peninsula constitute distinct sub-areas.

Thus far it is the lexical materials gathered in connection with the various atlas projects which have been analyzed most extensively, and as the title of Professor Kurath's work indicates, his plotting of the major dialect areas is based upon vocabulary evidence. For example, characteristic Northen expressions that are current throughout the area include *pail, swill, whiffletree* or *whippletree, comforter* or *comfortable* for a thick quilt, *brook, co-boss* or *come-boss* as a cow call, *johnnycake, salt pork,* and *darning needle* for a dragonfly. In the Midland area we find *blinds* for roller shades, *skillet, spouting* or *spouts* for eaves, a *piece* for food taken between meals, *snake feeder* for a dragonfly, *sook* as the call to calves, *armload* for an armful of wood; and one *hulls* beans when he takes off the shells, A quarter *till* the hour is a typical Midland expression, as is the elliptical *to want off,* or *out,* or *in.* The South has *lightwood* as the term for kindling, a *turn* of wood for an armful; stringbeans are generally *snap beans; hasslet* is the term for the edible inner organs of a pig, *chittlins* for the small intestine; and in this area cows are said to *low* at feeding time.

The sub-dialect areas also have their characteristic forms. In coastal New England, for instance, *pigsty* is the normal term for pigpen, *bonny clapper* for curdled sour milk, *buttonwood* for a sycamore, and *pandowdy* for a cobbler type of dessert. Eastern Virginia has *cuppin* for a cowpen, *corn house* for a crib. *Lumber room* survives as the term for a storeroom. A grasshopper is known as a *hopper grass,* and *batter bread* is used for a soft cornbread containing egg.

As far as the sectors of the American lexicon which reflect regional differences are concerned, the matter is trenchantly summarized in Kurath's *Word Geography*, where the author points out first of all that the vocabularies of the arts and sciences, of industries, commercial enterprises, social and political institutions, and even many of the crafts, are national in scope because the activities they reflect are organized on a national basis. He then goes on to say:

Enterprises and activities that are regionally restricted have, on the other hand, a considerable body of regional vocabulary which, to be sure, may be known in other parts of the country, even if it is not in active use. The cotton planter of the South, the tobacco grower, the dairy farmer, the wheat grower, the miner, the lumberman, and the rancher of the West have many words and expressions that are strictly regional and sometimes local in their currency.

Regional and local expressions are most common in the vocabulary of the intimate everyday life of the home and the farm—not only among the simple folk and the middle class but also among the cultured . . . Food, clothing, shelter, health, the day's work, play, mating, social gatherings, the land, the farm buildings, implements, the farm stocks and crops, the weather, the fauna and flora—these are the intimate concern of the common folk in the countryside, and for these things expressions are handed down in the family and the neighborhood that schooling and reading and a familiarity with regional or national usage do not blot out.

It is not only in the vocabulary that one finds regional differences in American speech. There are pronunciation features as well. Throughout the Northern area, for example, the distinction between [o] and [ɔ] in such word pairs as *hoarse* and *horse*, *mourning* and *morning* is generally maintained; [s] regularly occurs in *grease* (verb) and *greasy*, and *root* is pronounced by many with the vowel of *wood*.[2] Within the Northern area such sub-dialects as coastal New England and Metropolitan New York also show many characteristic forms; the treatment of the vowel of *bird* is only one of these, and words of the *calf*, *pass*, *path*, *dance* group constitute another. In the Midland area speakers fail to distinguish between *hoarse and horse*. Rounding is characteristic of the vowels of *hog*, *frog*, *log*, *wasp* and *wash*, and in the last of these words an *r* often intrudes in the speech of the not too highly educated. The vowels of *due* and *new* will resemble that of *food* rather than *feud*. In the South, *r* is 'lost' except before vowels, as it is in eastern New England and New

[2] See page 308 for the sounds represented by the phonetic symbols in brackets here. [eds.]

York City but not in the Northern area generally. Words like *Tuesday*, *due*, and *new* have a y-like glide preceding the vowel, and final [z] in Mrs. is the normal form.

Among the older, relatively uneducated group and even to some extent among the middle-aged informants who have had some secondary schooling there are also regional differences in inflectional forms and syntax. For example, *hadn't ought* for "oughtn't," *see* as a past tense form, *clim* for "climbed" among the oldest sector of the population, *wan't* for "wasn't," *be* in such expressions as *How be you?*, and the choice of the preposition *to* in *sick to his stomach* are all characteristic of the Northern area. *Clum* for "climbed," *seen* for "saw," *all the further* and *I'll wait on you* are to be found in the Midlands, whereas *belongs to be*, *heern* for "heard," *seed* as the past tense of "to see," *holp* for "helped," *might could* and *mought have* are characteristic of the South.

All of this raises the question as to how the regional forms of American English developed in our three and one-half centuries of linguistic history. The first factor which must be taken into account is settlement history. Where did our earliest settlers come from, and what dialects did they speak? . . . at the time of the earliest settlements, English local and regional dialects were in a stronger position than they are today in that they constituted the natural speech of a greater portion of the English-speaking population and were in customary use farther up the social scale.

Moreover, it is quite unlikely that any single local settlement, even at the outset, ever consisted entirely of speakers of the same dialect. Of ten families of settlers gathered in any one place, two might well have spoken London English, three or four others one of the southern or southeastern county dialects. There would be in addition a couple of families speaking northern English and another two or three employing a western dialect. In the course of their being in constant contact with each other, compromises for the everyday terms in which their dialects differed would normally have developed, and one could reasonably expect to find a southern English term for a water receptacle, a northern word for earthworm, and a western designation for sour milk. Matters of pronunciation would eventually, perhaps after a slightly longer time, be compromised in much the same manner. Moreover, the resultant compromises for various localities would be different. In the first place, no two localities would have had exactly the same proportions of speakers of the various English dialects, and even if they had, the two localities would not have arrived at precisely the same set of compromises. Thus, early in our history we developed, at various points on the Atlantic seaboard, a number of local cultures, each with distinctive social characteristics of its own—including a dialect which was basically a unique blend of British types of speech, supplemented in its vocabulary by borrowings from the Indians and from Dutch and German neighbors.[3]

With the beginning of the nineteenth century, three changes occurred which were to have a profound effect upon the language situation in America. First, the industrial revolution resulted in the growth of a number of industrial centers, uprooting a considerable proportion of the farm population and concentrating it in the cities. The development of the railroad and other mechanical means of travel increased greatly the mobility of the average person. The large-scale migrations westward also resulted in some resettlement and shifting, even among those who did not set out on the long trek. All of this resulted in a general abandonment of narrowly local speech forms in favor of fewer, more or less general, regional types. Some local speech forms have remained even to the present day. These are usually known as relics, particularly when they are distributed in isolated spots over an area rather than in concentration. *Open stone peach*, for example, is a relic for freestone peach, occurring in Maryland. *Smurring up*, "getting foggy," survives as a relic in eastern Maine and more rarely on Cape Cod and Martha's Vineyard.

Even prior to the shifts in population and changes in the culture pattern, certain colonial cities such as Boston, Philadelphia, and Charleston had acquired prestige by developing as centers of trade and foci of immigration. They became socially and culturally outstanding, as well as economically powerful, thus dominating the areas surrounding them. As a consequence, local expressions and pronunciations peculiar to the countryside came to be replaced by new forms of speech emanating from these centers. A fairly recent instance of this is to be found in the New England term *tonic* for soda water, practically co-extensive with the area served by Boston wholesalers. Professor Kurath considers the influence of these centers as second only to the influence of the original settlement in shaping the regional types of speech on the Atlantic seaboard and in determining their geographic boundaries.

Nor was the general process of dialect formation by any means

[3] See selection by Thomas Pyles on page 78. [eds.]

completed with the settlement of the Atlantic seaboard. As the land to the west came to be taken up in successive stages (for example, western New York, Michigan, Wisconsin in the North; southern Ohio, Indiana, and southern Illinois in the Midland area) the same mixtures of speech forms among the settlers were present at first, and the same linguistic compromises had to be worked out. The same processes occurred in the interior South, in Texas, and later on in the Far West. Consequently, the complete linguistic history, particularly with respect to regional forms, of the United States will not be known until all of the facts concerning the present regional distribution of speech forms have been collected, and until these facts have been collated with the settlement history of the various areas and the speech types employed by the settlers at the time they moved in. In its entirety this would necessitate a greater knowledge of the local dialects of seventeenth-century England than we have at present.

Moreover, such environmental factors as topography, climate, and plant and animal life also play their parts in influencing the dialect of an area, just as they did in the general tranplanting of the English language to America. The complexity and size of the network of fresh-water streams will affect the distribution and meaning of such terms as *brook, creek, branch,* and *river.* In parts of Ohio and Pennsylvania, for example, the term *creek* is applied to a much larger body of water than in Michigan. It is even more obvious that in those parts of the country where snow is a rarity or does not fall at all, there will be no necessity for a battery of terms to indicate coasting face down on a sled. It is not surprising that those areas of the country where cows can be milked outside, for at least part of the year, will develop a specific term for the place where this is done: witness *milk gap* or *milking gap* current in the Appalachians south of the James River. The wealth of terms for various types of fences throughout the country is again dependent, in part at least, on the material which is available for building them, be it stones, stumps, or wooden rails.

Different types of institutions and practices which developed in various parts of the country also had their effect upon regional vocabulary. Those settlements which did not follow the practice of setting aside a parcel of land for common grazing purposes had little use for such terms as *green* or *common.* The meaning of *town* will vary according to the place and importance of township and county respectively in the organization of local government. The same principle applies equally well to foods of various kinds, which reflect not only materials which are readily available but folk practices as well. The German custom of preparing raised doughnuts as Lenten fare survives in the Pennsylvania term *fossnocks*, shortened from *Fastnachtskuchen*.

Finally, a new invention or development introduced into several parts of the country at the same time will acquire different names in various places. The baby carriage, for example, seems to have been a development of the 1830's and 40's, and this is the term which developed in New England. Within the Philadelphia trade area, however, the article became known as a *baby coach*, whereas *baby buggy* was adopted west of the Alleghenies and *baby cab* in other regions throughout the country. Nor have we necessarily seen an end to this process. Within the last two decades the building of large, double-lane, limited-access automobile highways has been undertaken in various parts of the country, yet the terminology for them differs considerably. In eastern New York, Connecticut, and Rhode Island these are *parkways*, but *turnpikes* in Pennsylvania, New Jersey, New Hampshire, Maine, Massachusetts, Ohio, and Indiana. In New York *thruway* is used, and they are *expressways* in Michigan and *freeways* in California. These would seem to be regionalisms in the making.

It is of interest also to look at the dialect situation from the point of view of various words which are employed in various parts of the country for the same concept. One of the most interesting and instructive distributions is to be found in connection with the terms used for *earthworm*. This word is used by cultivated speakers in the metropolitan centers. *Angleworm* is the regional term in the North, *fishworm* in the Midland area, and *fishing worm* in the coastal South. *Fish bait* and *bait worm* occupy smaller areas within the extensive *fishworm* region, but are also distributed over a wide territory.

In addition, there is a large number of local terms, many of which are used principally by the older and less-educated inhabitants. The Merrimack Valley, in New Hampshire, and Essex County, Massachusetts, have *mud worm*. *Eace worm* is used in Rhode Island. *Angle dog* appears in upper Connecticut, and *ground worm* on the Eastern Shore of Virginia. *Red worm* is used in the mountains of North Carolina, and an area around Toledo, Ohio, uses *dew worm*. Scattered instances of *rainworm* appear on Buzzards Bay in Massachusetts, throughout the Pennsylvania German area, and in German settlements in North Carolina, Maine, and Wisconsin. We have, thus, a wealth of older local terms, three distinct regional words, and the cultivated *earthworm* appearing in addition as a folk word in South Carolina and along the

North Carolina and Virginia coast. Where and how did the various terms originate, and what can be determined about their subsequent history?

Earthworm itself is not an old word; it appears to have been compounded only shortly before the earliest English migrations to America. The earliest *Oxford English Dictionary* citation of the word in its present form is 1591; it appears also as *yearth worm* some thirty years earlier. The various regional terms all seem to have been coined in America; the dictionaries either record no British citations or fail to include the words at all.

The local terms have a varied and interesting history. *Mud worm* seems to occur in standard British English from the beginning of the nineteenth century on. *Eace worm*, as a combined form, goes back at least to Middle English; the first element was a term for "bait" as early as Aelfric; it is used today in a number of southern counties in England from Kent to Gloucester. *Angle dog* is used currently in Devonshire. *Ground worm*, though coined in England, was transferred to North Carolina and Maryland in the eighteenth century. *Red worm* appears first in England in 1450 and continues through to the mid-nineteenth century, though chiefly in books on fishing, as does *dew worm*, which goes back even farther, to the late Old English period. *Rainworm*, though it appears in Aelfric as *renwyrm*, may be a reformation, even in British English, on the pattern of *Regenwurm* in German, for there is a gap of seven centuries in the citations in the *Oxford English Dictionary* and there is reason to believe that its revival in 1731 was influenced by the German form. Moreover, with but one exception, it has been cited for the United States only in areas settled by Germans.

Thus we have in the standard cultivated term one of relatively recent British formation. Apparently the regional terms were compounded in America, whereas the local terms represent survivals either of dialect usage or anglers' jargon and one loan translation.[4] It is worth noting that the common Old English term, *angle twicce*, surviving as *angle twitch* in Cornwall and Devon, seems not to have found its way to America, and there are, furthermore, such other English formations as *tag worm*, *marsh worm*, and *garden worm* which have not been recorded in America.

[4] A loan translation is a composite form made up of a literal translation of the component parts from the foreign tongue into the new tongue. Examples: English *skyscraper* becomes French *gratte-ciel;* French *ça va sans dire* becomes English *that goes without saying*. [eds.]

At times, too, changes in meaning seem to have entered into the dialect situation, as is illustrated by the development of the regional terms *skillet* and *spider*, the former current in the Midland and the Virginia Piedmont, the latter in the North and in the Southern tidewater area. *Frying pan* is the urban term and is slowly supplanting the others *Spider* was originally applied to the cast-iron pan with short legs, from which the name was presumably derived, but it was ultimately transferred to the flat-bottomed pan as well. This would seem also to explain the local term *creeper*, used in Marblehead, Massachusetts. *Skillet*, a term of doubtful etymology, first appears in English in 1403, when it was applied to a long-handled brass or copper vessel for boiling liquids or stewing meat. It is still so used in dialects throughout England. The shift in meaning to a frying pan took place only in America, but an advertisement of 1790, offering for sale "bakepans, spiders, skillets," would suggest that even as late as this a distinction between the two was recognized. The examples above have been offered only as a suggestion of the various language processes which have played a part in the distribution and meaning of some of our dialect terms, It is quite obvious that no definitive conclusions about these matters can be reached until the actual facts of dialect distribution are better known than they are at present.

Thus far our concern has been only with regional dialects or speech differences, although we have recognized these as occurring particularly on certain social levels. This raises the question of the extent to which social dialects occur in American English. Is there a so-called vulgate which has reasonably uniform characteristics throughout the country, and if so, what is it?

For the most part, the language of the uncultivated will be recognized in terms of its inflectional characteristics, or at any rate it is this aspect of the language for which the most authentic information is available. Before these matters are taken up in detail, therefore, one or two points about the operation of inflections should be clearly understood.

First, we must recognize that our inflectional endings are in reality a series of patterns which are applied quite automatically whenever a situation demanding their use occurs. Even in highly inflected languages, such as Modern Finnish or Ciceronian Latin, the speaker does or did not find it necessary to recite a paradigm to determine the proper case ending. Second, throughout the history of the language, there are two forces constantly at work upon the inflectional system:

sound change, which often introduces irregularities or disturbances in the system, and analogy,[5] which tends to simplify or to straighten these out by extending the scope of the already existing pattern. As we look at some of the features of present-day substandard English, we shall see how these forces operate.

Possibly the one inflectional form most characteristic of the nouns in substandard American English is the unchanged plural after numbers: *six mile down the road, five foot tall*, and similarly applied to *month, year*, and *gallon*. Actually this is the preservation of an old partitive genitive plural after numbers,[6] which resisted the analogical extension of the -*s* inflection to cases other than the nominative and accusative. The lesson to be learned from this is that the substandard language frequently preserves linguistically older forms than Standard English, a fact not too surprising when it is recalled that sub-standard English depends entirely on oral transmission from one generation to another.

Certain of the pronoun inflections, however, demonstrate precisely the contrary tendency: the development of innovations or new forms and patterns in substandard English. This is true, for example, of the possessive pronoun in its so-called absolute form,[7] which in the standard language represents a strange and inconsistent mixture of patterns indeed. *Mine* and the archaic *thine* are formed from the adjectival form by adding -*n*. *Hers, ours, yours*, and *theirs*, on the other hand, add -*s* to the adjectival form, probably on the pattern of the noun genitive. *His* and *its* are indistinguishable so far as their secondary and absolute forms are concerned. In contrast, the substandard *mine, yourn, hisn, hern, ourn, theirn* present a perfectly regular pattern formed by an analogical extension of *mine* and *thine* to the third person singular and to the plural forms. At one time or another, several of these forms appeared in Standard English, but they seem never to have caught on and were, as we have seen, replaced in part by the -*s* forms. But the substandard language carried out the innovations completely and consistently except for *its*, which is virtually never used in the absolute form anyway.

A further point worth mentioning is that although speakers of the substandard language are rarely trained in school grammar, their

---

[5] See selection by Eugene Nida on page 107. [eds.]

[6] E.g., the Old English genitive plural *siex fōta* (six of feet) before an adjective developed into the modern English *six foot*. [eds.]

[7] The form used when the possessive pronoun does not precede a noun: *mine, thine, his, hers, its, ours, yours, theirs*. [eds.]

language observes its own laws—not those of Standard English—in a thoroughly rigorous manner, *Hisn*, for example, is the absolute, not the secondary or adjectival form, and the two are never confused. Most speakers of the substandard language might be expected to say *the book is hisn;* no speaker of substandard English would ever say *hisn book.*

The reflexive pronouns give us another instance of a more regular operation of analogy on the substandard level than on the standard. In Standard English, *myself, yourself, ourselves,* and *yourselves* are combinations of the genitive pronoun plus the singular or plural of the -*self* form; *himself* and *themselves* employ the object form of the pronoun, whereas *herself* and *itself* could be either. Substandard English, in substituting *hisself* and *theirself* in the third person and adhering to the singular of *self* in *ourself* and *yourself* (plural), is not only more consistent but more economical in that the latter combinations signal the plural only once and avoid the tautology of the plural -*selves.* The only ambiguity is in the second person, but the second personal pronoun has lost its distinctions between singular and plural anyway, except for the Southern form *you all.*

One curious feature of the substandard pronoun is the substitution of the object for the subjective form in such sentences as *Us girls went home, John and her was married, Me and him was late.* This seems to occur principally when the subject is compound or when one or more words intervene between the pronominal subject and verb, as in *us girls.* Postverbally the reverse type of substitution (subject for object form) is often found, as in *She gave it to mother and I, She took all of we children.* Since these locutions are found considerably higher up the social and educational scale than those previously mentioned, it is possible, at least, that they are the result of overcorrection.

Space does not permit an exhaustive treatment of all the inflectional forms of substandard English, but a few that are typical deserve brief mention. *Them* as a demonstrative adjective (*them books*) probably harks back to the days when the English article and the demonstrative *that* (dative ðæm) were one and the same form. The multiple negative[8] was also a regular and accepted feature of older English, as was the so-called flat adverb[9] without the -*ly* derivative suffix. However, since the standard and substandard languages are undoubtedly farthest apart with respect to verb forms, some features of the verbs of the

[8] E.g., Shakespeare's "I will not budge for no man's pleasure, I." [eds.]
[9] E.g., *Go slow;* come *quick.* [eds.]

vulgate, as they were once called by the late Robert Menner, should be described.

First of all, with respect to the present tense, there is some tendency to dispose of the distinctive inflection for the third person singular, either by eliminating it in such forms as *he want, she write,* etc., or by extending the peculiar form of the third person to the first and second— *I has some good friends, You is in lots of trouble.*

It is in the preterit[10] and past participle forms, chiefly of those verbs which are somewhat irregular in Standard English, that the widest deviations occur. Again one may recognize here the two opposing tendencies: the retention of older forms and the simplification of irregularities through analogical processes.

The older forms retained in the substandard language owe their origin chiefly to the fact that the so-called strong verb[11] in earlier stages of the language had four principal parts, a past tense singular as well as a past tense plural, in addition to the infinitive and present participle. Thus *writ* as a past tense of *write* represents an older preterit plural form, as do *begun* and *swum.*

On the other hand, the overwhelming tendency in English verb development throughout the last seven or eight centuries has been toward an aggrandizement of the regular or weak inflection[12] at the expense of the older minor conjugations. This is in effect a tendency toward a two-part verb, the infinitive or present stem opposed to an identical past tense and past participle. In general, this has been brought about through analogical processes. Deviant substandard forms are usually the result of analogies which have not operated in Standard English and which take one of two directions: either the extension of the weak past inflections to such irregular verbs as *know* and *see* (*knowed, seed*) or the amalgamation of the strong preterit or past participle with the complementary form (*I taken, he done* as preterits; *have gave, have wrote, has went* as past participial forms).

In one sense, therefore, the differences between the grammatical systems of standard and substandard English represent a difference in the direction and rapidity of inflectional changes. Unquestionably

[10] The preterit means the simple past tense, e.g., He *swam* across. [eds.]

[11] A "strong verb" is one that forms its past tense by an internal vowel change, e.g., *drink, drank; write, wrote; steal, stole.* (This is an oversimplified statement of a complex situation.) [eds.]

[12] A "weak verb" is one that forms its past tense by the addition of a *-t, -d,* or *-ed,* e.g., *dreamt, told, started.* For the phonetic aspect of these endings, see page 306, assignment 1. [eds.]

the easy transition from one social class to another in the United States has resulted in a very hazy line of demarcation between what is acceptable and what is considered illiterate. According to the most rigorous schoolbook standard some of the language employed in American legislative councils and in business life would not pass muster. The awareness of this, combined with an unrealistic treatment of language in our schools, has resulted at times in a defiance of these questionable standards. More often it has given people a guilt complex about the language they use. James West, in his community study entitled *Plainville, U.S.A.* makes a pertinent comment upon this very point:

"Inferior" English has been selected as a primary and almost universal trait for apology because the school teacher, the press, and the radio have all co-operated to arouse self-consciousness concerning dialect forms, phrases, and phonetics. All but the "most backwoodsy" speakers frequently ridicule and parody the stratum or strata of speech beneath or older than their own, and at the same time feel uncertain about their own usages.

Consequently, few Americans, even among the well-educated, are confident and assured of the essential aptness and correctness of their speech. It will take at least a half-century of a more enlightened attitude toward language in the public schools to bring about any perceptible change in this state of affairs. In the meantime, what is sadly needed is an entertaining, yet scientific, treatment of vulgate speech to demonstrate how interesting a phenomenon it really is.

On Accepting
Participial *Drank*

HAROLD B. ALLEN

The use of *drank* as a past participle, as in "He has *drank* his morning coffee," is generally condemned by textbooks as nonstandard English. Harold B. Allen, Professor of English at the University of Minnesota, here brings together evidence from the collected data from three linguistic atlases to show that *drank* is a standard English past participle in spoken

English of the East and Midwest. Professor Allen is director of the *Linguistic Atlas of the Upper Midwest* project, cover-ing the Dakotas, Minnesota, Iowa, and Nebraska.

As additional fieldwork is completed for the regional atlases associated in *The Linguistic Atlas of the United States,* additional evidence accumu-lates about numerous grammatical forms long adjudged controversial. A case in point is provided by the new data for the past participle *drank*.

The verb *drink* has come down to us from that interesting third class of Old English strong verbs with two stem vowels in the past tense forms: one (*a*) peculiar to the past and found in the first and third persons singular; the other (*u*) used in the second person singular and in the plural but also indentical with the stem vowel of the past participle.[1] In this class the subtle power of analogy,[2] operating with increasing strength in Middle English as inflectional changes lost their phonetic distinctiveness, also inevitably favored the more fre-quently occurring *u* in the process of simplifying the verb patterns.

By the eighteenth century this process had gone so far that the *u* vowel was comfortably and exclusively established in the preterit[3] of the following third class strong verbs: *bind, cling, fight, fling, grind, slink, spin, sting, string, swing, win, wind,* and *wring*.[4] In the other sur-viving members of this class the process was now to be retarded, though not blocked, by the prestigious pronouncement of Dr. Johnson in the Grammar prefaced to his *Dictionary* in 1755. Reflecting the philosophy of the ancient Greek Analogists, Johnson believed that every grammatical function should have its own overt grammatical form, and accordingly declared: "He shall seldom err who remembers, that when a verb has a participle distinct from its preterite, as *write, wrote, written,* that distinct participle is more proper and elegant, as *The book is written,* is better than *The book is wrote,* though *wrote* may be used in poetry."

From *College English* (February, 1957). Reprinted by permission of the author and the National Council of Teachers of English.

[1] The Old English conjugation of the past tense of *drincan,* to drink, is as fol-lows: *ic dranc, þu drunce, he dranc, we druncon, ge druncon, hie druncon.* The Old English past participle is *druncen.* [eds.]

[2] For analogy, see the selection from Eugene Nida, page 107. [eds.]

[3] Preterit means the simple past tense, as *rode, clung, spun, swung, drank.* [eds.]

[4] Because the original Old English *u* underwent phonetic change through the influence of certain neighboring sounds, some of the past tense forms now in use, such as *fought* and *ground,* do not immediately betray their historical membership in the class.

Although even the prestige of Johnson's *Dictionary* and the authoritative copying of his dictum in scores of school grammars were unable to stop the trend toward the simple *u* in the preterit, a great many cultivated speakers were undoubtedly influenced by the bald injunction that nothing but *a* can be the proper preterit vowel. As a result, for the past one hundred and fifty years there actually has been divided usage among cultivated speakers.

We may look at *shrink* as typical of the larger group of those strong verbs which in moving toward a single form for past and participle have popularly used the vowel common to both. Although the textbooks list the contrast between *shrank* as preterit and *shrunk* as participle, actually the findings of the fieldwork for *The Linguistic Atlas of the Upper Midwest* indicate that 86.5% of all informants responding to this item use *shrunk* as the preterit. Nor do the findings reveal the existence of a small educated minority clinging to a favored *shrank*, for the relative frequency of *u* is nearly the same in all three groups: 89% of the uneducated, 89% of the high school graduates, and 86% of the college graduates.

Some regional variation, hardly enough to be significant, may be suggested by the slightly lower frequency in Midland than in Northern speech areas: Minnesota, 96%; North Dakota, 92%; Iowa, 86%; South Dakota, 81% and Nebraska, 72%. But within the divided usage the general dominance of *shrunk* is certain, despite the contrary statements of the textbooks.

The inaccuracy of the textbooks with respect to the past of *shrink* and of other verbs exhibiting the tendency toward the *u* vowel in the preterit is matched by their inaccuracy with respect to the one verb which stands out in exception to the trend. The verb *drink* is the only verb in this group that in moving toward simplicity has tended not only to retain the original *a* vowel in the preterit, but also to entrench it in the past participle. Indeed, Professor Walter S. Avis has recently suggested that "we cannot refuse to accept the participle *drank* as Standard American English, at least in the regions where the evidence argues for its acceptance."[5]

It is true that even without Avis's evidence some grammarians have not been as dogmatic as the textbook writers in their attitude toward participial *drank*. Even Goold Brown, back in the mid-nineteenth century, said in his many-editioned and voluminous *Grammar of English*

[5] Walter S. Avis, *American Speech*, XXVIII (May, 1953), 106–111.

Grammars that *"drank* seems to be a word of greater delicacy, and perhaps it is sufficiently authorized." Among recent linguistic grammarians, Curme in his *Parts of Speech and Accidence* (1935) said of *drank* as a participle, "sometimes used in older English in the literary language. It survives in popular speech." And Jespersen, in the sixth volume of his *Modern English Grammar* (1942), wrote, ". . . a participle *drank* has been in frequent use for centuries, possibly to avoid misunderstanding with *drunk* 'intoxicated.' It is now getting rare, but instances occur in all the best-known authors from Bunyan down to our time." He cited Scott, Shelley, Keats, Trollope, and Kingsley, and referred to Mencken as listing *drank* as a participle.

Nor are current dictionaries more accurate in describing contemporary usage. The Merriam-Webster *NID* (2nd ed.) offers *drunk*. Similarly with the Thorndike-Barnhart dictionaries, although the Barnhart-edited *ACD*, less pressed for space, takes room to admit cagily, "sometimes *drank*." The *WNW* does give *drank* as participle but labels it "archaic."

Yet such recognition as that by Curme and the *ACD* is nothing like Avis's bold statement based upon Atlas evidence. This evidence is that even in New England, "the citadel of the prestige dialect," 38% of the cultivated informants regularly use *drank* as the participle and an additional 11.9% use it along with *drunk*, while in New York 27.7% of such speakers use it, in West Virginia 83.3%, and in Pennsylvania 43.7%. For the North Central states (except Kentucky, where fieldwork is still in process) revised figures later than Avis's are now provided by Virginia McDavid (Mrs. Raven I. McDavid, Jr.) in her recent unpublished Minnesota dissertation. In the North Central area, 54% of the interrogated high school graduates and 33% of the college graduates use the participle *drank*.

To all this evidence there now can be added a whole new set of data from the recently completed field records of *The Linguistic Atlas of the Upper Midwest*.[6] In this large five-state area Avis's conclusion finds even stronger corroboration. Here 80.5% of the interviewed high school graduates use *drank* as the past participle, and nearly half (47%) of the cultivated speakers. There is no significant regional variation within the Upper Midwest, almost the same relative frequencies being found in Minnesota, Iowa, the Dakotas, and Nebraska. Certainly it would appear that in this area, as well as in New England

[6] For significance of such records in the field of usage see H. B. Allen, *English Journal*, XLV (April, 1956), 188–194.

and the North Central states, *drank* is an accepted standard form of the past participle.

Explanation of the exceptional development with *drink* usually coincides with that offered by Jespersen, namely, that there is an aversion to the historical *drunk* because of the link with intoxication. On the supposition that women might feel greater hesitation on this score than men would, a further breakdown of the Upper Midwest figures was made. The complete picture, including the data for uneducated speakers, is of some interest. Of the 9.7% of uneducated informants who use *drunk* as the participle not one is a woman. Of the male high school graduates 12% use *drunk;* of the female high school graduates, 28.3%. Of the male college graduates 60% use *drunk;* of the female college graduates, 40%. Certainly there is aversion by women to the use of *drunk*, but chiefly among the uneducated. Among cultivated speakers the distinction by sex is hardly significant. But since linguistic taboos of this type seem to be stronger among uneducated people, it may well be that the association with intoxication is the ultimate cause for the preference for participial *drank*.

Whatever the cause of the large-scale rejection of *drunk*, however, the general acceptance of competing *drank* by from one-third to one-half of the cultivated speakers in New England, the North Central states, the Midland area, and the Upper Midwest supports the conclusion that we have here a condition of divided usage, with no sound basis for present objection to either *drank* or *drunk* as the single exclusive form in standard spoken English.

Linguistic Atlas Findings

Work on the regional linguistic atlases for different parts of the United States is in various states of progress. For New England all of the data have been gathered, and the atlas is in print. For three regions—the Middle and South Atlantic States, the North Central States, and the Upper Midwest—the collecting of data has been completed. These collections are a rich mine of primary source material about contemporary American English, and researchers are making use of them for books and articles. To date, several books have been published, from two of which the excerpts below have been chosen. Hans Kurath's *A Word Geography of the Eastern United States* describes the distribution of vocabulary items and sets forth the dialect and subdialect areas of the Eastern States. Professor Kurath was the editor of the *Linguistic Atlas of New England* and is now editor of the *Middle English Dictionary* at the University of Michigan. The second book is E. Bagby Atwood's *A Survey of Verb Forms in the Eastern United States.* Here Professor Atwood confines his attention to variant verb forms. To get his information, he examined the *Linguistic Atlas* field records of more than 1400 informants, about 400 from New England and about 500 each from the Middle Atlantic States and the South Atlantic States. Mr. Atwood, recently deceased, was Professor of English at the University of Texas, which in recent years has become an important linguistic center.

Creek

Creek is the most common word for a small fresh-water stream in the Eastern States. It is current everywhere except in the greater part of New England, where *brook* or *river* are the usual terms.

Outside New England, Long Island, and Metropolitan New York *brook* is rare as a common noun, but it appears in the proper names of many streams in the New England settlement area as far west as Erie, Pennsylvania.

The Midland term for a smaller stream is *run*, but in Pennsylvania and the northern half of West Virginia *creek* is now the common noun. However, *run* occurs in the names of many streams in this area. As a common noun, *run* is now characteristic of an area extending from Delaware Bay to the James River (except Lower Delamarvia) and westward to the Shenandoah and the upper reaches of the Potomac in West Virginia. It is also fairly common along the Neuse in North Carolina.

In the South and in the South Midland as far north as the Kana-

The first three items—*creek, bull, you-all*—are from *A Word Geography of the Eastern United States* by Hans Kurath. Reprinted by permission of the publisher, The University of Michigan Press, copyright 1949. The following four items—*dive, lie, he doesn't, ought not*—are from *A Survey of Verb Forms in the Eastern United States* by E. Bagby Atwood. Reprinted by permission of the publisher, The University of Michigan Press, copyright 1953.

wha Valley *branch* is the usual designation of the tributary of a *creek* or a *river*. *Branch* is also current on Delaware Bay beside *run*.

The Dutch word *kill* for a small watercourse survives only in the names of certain creeks or rivers in the Dutch settlement area, such as the *Batten Kill* in Vermont, the *Catskill Creek* in New York, and the *Schuylkill River* in Pennsylvania.

Bull

The plain term *bull* is current everywhere, and in the North Midland and New York State other expressions are rare. In New England, the South, and the South Midland, however, the plain term is not used by older folk of one sex in the presence of the other. Even many of the younger generation prefer the veiled expressions of the Victorian era.

New England expressions for the bull are: *sire, animal* or *male animal, critter, toro* (New Hampshire and Vermont), *seed ox* (rare), *gentleman cow, gentleman ox* (found also on Chesapeake Bay), and *masculine* (riming with *fine*, on Nantucket).

Southernisms are equally varied: *male* and *male cow* in Virginia, adjoining parts of North Carolina, and on Delamarvia (occasionally also in New England); *beast, stock beast, male beast* in the coastal section of the Carolinas; *stock brute, male brute* in westernmost North Carolina; *steer* from southern Maryland to Albemarle Sound; *ox* in the Virginia Tidewater, central West Virginia, and sporadically elsewhere; *gentleman cow* on Chesapeake Bay (also in New England); and *masculine* (riming with *fine*) in southern West Virginia (also on Nantucket). West Virginia further contributes *Durham, jock,* and *major*.

Some of these expressions are now rare or used only jestingly, but in the Southern area such expressions as the *male,* the *beast,* and the *brute* are common, and if one used the plain word *bull* to a lady, one might be in trouble.

You-all

The form *you* is used as a plural in all parts of the Eastern States. By the side of *you*, the greater part of the Midland and all of the South have the specific, emphatic, or "generous" plural forms *you'ns, you-all,* and *mongst-ye*. All these forms have a possessive case: *you'ns's, you-all's, mongst-ye's.* [See page 413]

You-all is current throughout the South and the South Midland (in all of West Virginia, except the northwestern section around Wheeling and Parkersburg).

You'ns is the Midland form and occurs in the folk speech of Pennsylvania west of the Susquehanna, in large parts of West Virginia, and in the westernmost parts of Virginia and North Carolina.

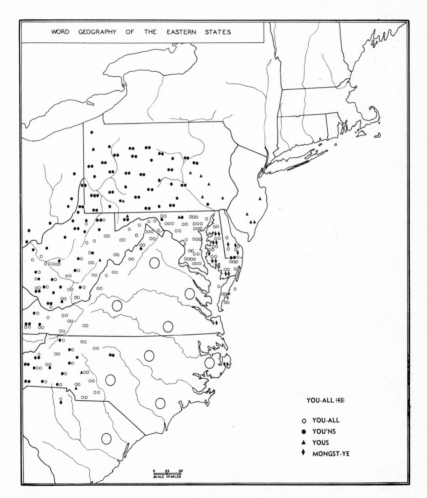

From *A Word Geography of the Eastern United States* by Hans Kurath. Reprinted by permission of the publisher, The University of Michigan Press, copyright 1949.

The form *mongst-ye* is common in the folk speech of the central part of Delamarvia, and rare instances are found from the mouth of Chesapeake Bay to Albermarle Sound.

Dive

The preterite is recorded in the context "He (dived) in."
The geographical distribution of the forms is indicated below.

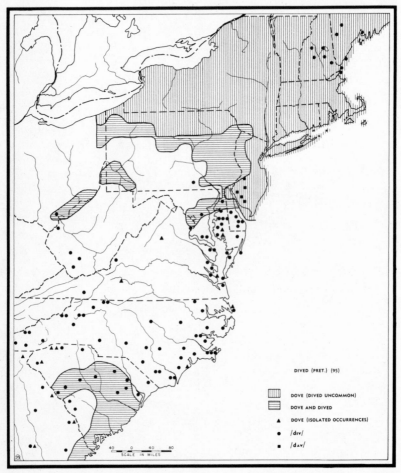

From *A Survey of Verb Forms in the Eastern United States* by E. Bagby Atwood. Reprinted by permission of the publisher, The University of Michigan Press, copyright 1953.

Dived/daivd/ is uncommon throughout N. Eng., N.Y., n. Pa., and e. N.J.; in this whole territory it is used by less than one out of 15 of the informants, without distinction as to type (about one eighth of the cultured informants in N. Eng. use it). In a belt in n. c. and e. Pa. and along the upper Ohio, *dived* and *dove*/dov/ occur about equally, the former being more common among older informants. Elsewhere in the M. A. S. and the S. A. S.[1] to and including N. C., *dived* heavily predominates on all levels, being limited only by *div* (see below).

In the northeastern area indicated on the map *dove* is almost universal. Within the areas of divided usage the more modern informant uses *dove* in more than three fourths of the communities, and at least that proportion of cultured informants choose this form in these areas. There is not the slightest doubt that the area of *dove* is extending itself to the south and west.[2]

South of the Peedee in S. C. *dove* is also fairly common, and it has some currency in coastal Ga. In these areas it is quite frequent in urban and cultured speech, somewhat less so in rustic speech.

The form *div*/dɪv/ shows the typical distribution of an archaism, being most common in n.e. N. Eng. and the coastal and mountain areas of the South and the South Midland. About six out of seven of the informants who use it fall in Type I (or Types IA and IIA in N. Eng.), and three N. C. Negro informants use it.

There are five occurrences of *duv*/dʌv/, concentrated in s. N. J. near the mouth of the Delaware.

A few Negro informants use the uninflected *dive*.

Lie

The present infinitive the preterite are recorded in the contexts "I'm going to (lie) down" and "He (lay) in bed all day."

In general, the present form *lie*/lai/ predominates in all major areas, being used by from three fifths to two thirds of all informants, without any significant geographical distribution. The alternate form

[1] The Middle Atlantic States (M.A.S.) include New York, New Jersey, Pennsylvania, eastern Ohio, and West Virginia. The South Atlantic States (S.A.S.) include Delaware, Maryland, Virginia, North Carolina, South Carolina, and approximately the eastern half of Georgia. [eds.]

[2] Another characteristic of an advancing form is its appearance in the more populous centers ahead of the main line of advance (in this instance, the Pittsburgh, Baltimore, and Washington areas). Professor Robert Hall has applied the metaphor "parachuting" to this phenomenon.

lay/le/ is slightly more common among Type I informants (about half of whom use it) than among Type II. On the whole, however, *lay* seems characteristic of certain communities, rather than of certain more old-fashioned informants within those communities. Only a scattering of cultured informants give the present form *lay*, and then usually alongside *lie*.

The preterite forms can best be surveyed in terms of their corresponding present forms. The combination *lie : lay* is of very limited occurrence. In n. N. Eng. and in e. N. Eng. (except for a few points in R. I. and e. Conn.) this combination is quite rare outside of cultured speech, and only about half the cultured informants in these areas use it. In s.w. N. Eng. *lie : lay* is universal in cultured usage and occurs among a fair number of noncultured informants as well.

In the entire M. A. S. *lie : lay* is uncommon among noncultured informants (being used by less than one twelfth of the group), and is confined to about one third of the cultured group.

In the S. A. S. *lie : lay* is rare in Del., Md., and the Piedmont area of Va., but becomes much more common (and might even be called the dominant popular usage) on the Eastern Shore of Va. and throughout most of N. C. and part of S. C. A little less than half the cultured informants in the S. A. S. use the *lie : lay* combination.

A much more common practice is the combination of the present *lie* with the *laid*/led/ ("going to lie down" : "laid in bed"). Of those who use the present *lie*, a considerable majority (two thirds in N. Eng. four fifths in the M. A. S.) combine it with the preterite *laid*. Only in N. C. and on the Eastern Shore of Va. is this combination somewhat uncommon. In e. N. Eng. about half the cultured informants give *lie : laid;* in the M. A. S. and the S. A. S. something more than half do so.

Some eight informants in N. Eng. and five in other areas use the combination *lie : lied*/laid/. This feature shows no concentration and may represent a groping for a "correct" form rather than habitual usage.

Of those who use the present *lay*, a heavy majority in most areas form the preterite as *laid*. An exception may be found in N. C., where a considerable number use the leveled present and preterite *lay : lay*. This leveling also occurs in a very scattered way in N. Eng. and parts of Pa.

Nearly all Negro informants use the forms *lay : laid;* one (S. C.), however, uses the leveled forms *lie : lie*.

In summary, we may say that as a present form *lie* is predominant in all areas, and that as the preterite of both *lie* and *lay*, *laid* is very heavily predominant everywhere except in the areas of the S. A. S. mentioned above where *lay* predominates as preterite.

He doesn't

The third person singular of the negative form is recorded in the context "He (doesn't) care."

In contrast to the positive form (*does*), the negative form lacks the inflectional -*s*/z/ among a large majority of informants in all areas.

In N. Eng. *he don't*/dont/ is used by about two fifths of the cultured informants (mostly in the older group) and by more than five sixths of the other types. It is most common in Type IA (nearly nine tenths use it) and decreases in frequency in proportion to the youth and better education of the informants, occurring among only $\frac{6}{17}$ of Type IIIB.

In the M. A. S. *he don't* is all but unanimous in Types I and II, there being but 15 or 20 occurrences of *doesn't* in these groups. Of the cultured informants, nearly three fourths use *he don't* (in a few instances alongside *doesn't*). Cultured informants who use only *doesn't* are mostly to be found in or near New York City or Philadelphia.

In the S. A. S., also, *don't* is universal in Types I and II. About half of the cultured informants use *don't*, occasionally alongside *doesn't*.

Ought not

The negative form of *ought* is recorded in the context "He (oughtn't) to."

In the southern two thirds of Pa. and nearly everywhere to the southward oughtn't/ɔtənt/ is in universal use in all types. In the South Midland and throughout N. C. phonetic, and probably phonemic, /r/ very generally appears in this form: /ɔrtənt/.

In N. Eng., N. Y., n. Pa., and most of N. J. the usual form is *hadn't ought*. . . . Throughout most of this area nearly all the non-cultured informants use this form; however, in s. N. Eng. only about half the informants use it, often alongside *oughtn't* or *ought not*. One third of the cultured informants in N. Eng. (nearly all of those who were interviewed in the northeast) use *hadn't ought*. There are only three instances of *didn't ought* in N. Eng.

In a small area of s. Ohio extending northeast from Marietta, and in part of n. e. N. C. *hadn't ought* is also current, though not universal.

Real and Like

MARGARET M. BRYANT

Interest in the dialect of English spoken in the United States, and the various subdialects within the country, goes back to the time of our independence, when the United States separated politically from England. From the time of John Pickering's *Vocabulary or Collection of Words and Phrases Which Have been Supposed to be Peculiar to the United States of America* (1816), word lists of Americanisms and of regional differences have been published. The early lists were gathered haphazardly, and judgments of the status of individual items were for the most part subjective and debatable. Until recently, the contemporary systematic and objective studies of American English have appeared largely in professional journals and other specialized publications. Now Margaret M. Bryant, Professor of English at Brooklyn College of the City University of New York, has brought together in a single handy compendium "the most recent information about frequently debated points of usage in English speech and writing." Entitled *Current American Usage*, it incorporates data not only from linguistic findings already published "but also from some 900 fresh investigations undertaken specially for use in this book." The two items that follow are excerpted from Miss Bryant's work.

REAL, REALLY

Summary: In formal English, real *precedes a noun, as in "real courage"; in colloquial English,* real *serves as an intensifier, meaning "very"; really, an adverb meaning "truly" or "genuinely," is employed in both formal and informal English.*

Data: *Real* as an adverbial intensifier of adjectives or adverbs is common in informal, cultivated speech, as illustrated by "I had a real good time"; "Will everyone be *real* quiet so that I can hear the sound of a pin when it drops?"; "Run *real* fast"; "I thought it was a *real* good time to invite over someone . . ." (Margaret Arlen, *WCBS*, Jan. 12, 1952, 8:50 A.M.). It sometimes finds its way into informal writing, as in "I've needed to remember that lesson a few times since, and it's been *real* helpful"

Reprinted from *Current American Usage* by Margaret M. Bryant. By permission of the publishers, Funk & Wagnalls Co., Inc., N. Y.

(*Reader's Digest*, Nov., 1960, 47). Though frequently employed in this way by speakers of standard English, adverbial *real*, according to three studies[1] . . . does not occur in formal written prose. One extensive study . . . of current periodicals and fiction showed *really* used 85% of the time and *real* 15%. When *real* occurred, it was in either conversation or conversational writing.

Nevertheless, a sentence like "The boy is *really* bad" is not the exact equivalent of "The boy is *real* bad," nor would anyone use "I will write *really* soon" for "I will write soon." *Really*, an adverb meaning "genuinely" or "truly," as in "a *really* extraordinary person," is not always an adequate substitute for *real*.

LIKE, conj.

Summary: Like *as a conjunction rarely appears in formal written English, but occurs in spoken English and in conversational written English. As is the preferred conjunction in formal English, with as if and as though fairly common variants.*

Like has had a long history as a conjunction. It was used so by Shakespeare and Keats, and in the Bible we find: "*Like as* a father pitieth his children, so the Lord pitieth them that fear him" (*Psalms*, 103:13), where *like* and *as* appear together. Since then, the *as* has been dropped; the *like* remains.

Data: In modern usage, professors, lawyers, clergymen, radio and television commentators, and journalists employ *like* as a subordinating conjunction to introduce clauses in standard English situations. From two of the fifty-two studies undertaken for this entry . . ., one finds these examples: "We don't take abuse *like* our mother would have" (F. Scott Fitzgerald, *The Last Tycoon*, 1941, p. 68); " 'All clear?' he asked, *like* he was getting ready to roll up the maps again" (Walter Van Tilburg Clark, *The Ox Bow Incident*, 1940, p. 125); and "The situation here is beginning to look more *like* it did in the days immediately following Pearl Harbor" (David Lawrence, *Detroit Free Press*, July 4, 1950, 4) Advertisers use it widely, as in the slogan "Winston tastes good/*Like* a cigarette should." The expressions "*like* I say (said)" and "*like* I told you" are common in speech: "*Like* I said, they won't find a clue"; "*Like* I told you, it is difficult to do."

In one study . . ., *like* as a substitute for *as* was found in spoken English two and one-half times as often as in written. Investigators . . . found it in advertisements, quotations from speakers, dialogue, or in-

---

[1] The names of the investigators here and later in this selection have been omitted. They are readily available in the original source. [eds.]

formal English of a folksy nature. In fifty-two studies of contemporary fiction, newspapers, and periodicals, investigators . . . found 109 examples, 50 of which were substitutes for *as*, which occurred 571 times. Comparing these two figures, one sees that *like* occurred only 8% of the time for *as* and *as* occurred 92%, mostly in newspapers and magazines. The evidence of seventeen studies . . . supports the traditional contention that *like* is rarely used for *as* in formal written English.

In informal English, however, *like* substitutes not only for *as*, but for *as if* and *as though*, as in "He stood there *like* he didn't know what to do" (Nathaniel Lamar, "Creole Love Song," *The Best American Short Stories*—1956, p. 238) and "It sounded *like* the whole fort was groaning" (Niel H. Swanson, *Unconquered*, 1947, p. 331). One investigator . . . found, in reading 9 . . . short stories, 6 examples of *like* as a conjunction, 5 of which were variants of *as if* or as *though*. In the 109 examples mentioned above, 59 were substitutes for as *if* and *as though*, which occured 242 times, *as if* 164 and *as though* 78. *Like* was used 19.6% of the time and *as if* and *as though* 80.4%. Most of these examples of *like* were in dialogue or in quoted speech, not in formal English.

According to two studies . . . of the Linguistic Atlas records, in the context of "It seems *as if* he'll never get well," New England informants use *as if* and *as though* without distinction. *Like* is of rare and scattered occurrence. In the Upper Midwest, *like* and *as though* are used with almost equal frequency, *as if* being relatively rare. In the North Central States, *like* predominates heavily over *as though* and *as if* combined; the two latter forms occur about equally. In the North Central and Upper Midwest States, *like* is used by almost half of the Type III informants (cultivated), and from half to almost three-fourths of the Type II informants (with some secondary school education). Though no investigation was carried out in the Middle Atlantic or South Atlantic States, the evidence available suggests that *like* is standard usage in the speech of all areas except New England and is expanding vigorously to the South and West.

Studies . . . show that *as if* or *as though* is usual in formal English, one interchangeable with the other. In certain constructions, like "The dress looks *like* new" and "He ran *like* mad," *like* has been acceptably substituted for *as if*.

Hypercorrectness accounts for the substitution of *as* for *like* as in "She sings *as* a bird," or "The freeways, *as* pipes which carry water, were designed to and can only carry as much traffic . . ." where the preposition *like* is correct in standard English.

SUGGESTED ASSIGNMENTS

1. Here are fifteen groups of words in which dialect differences in pronuncia-
    tion exist: 1. *barn, dark, far, far away;* 2. *curl, first, bird;* 3. *orange, foreign;*
    4. *greasy, Miss, Mrs.;* 5. *dog, frog, lot, pot;* 6. *ask, aunt, calf, afternoon;* 7. *ice,
    mine, time;* 8. *Tuesday, new, tune, duty;* 9. *Mary, merry, marry;* 10. *morning,
    mourning, horse, hoarse;* 11. *wash, water;* 12. *caller, collar;* 13. *house, out, town,
    down;* 14. *poor, sure;* 15. *on, from* (in stressed positions, as "Is it *on?*" and
    "Where are you *from?*") Select five groups and put the words into simple,
    natural sentences. Then find a student from a part of the country different
    from yours and ask him to read them. Make a note of the pronunciations
    that differ from yours and be prepared to contribute these to a class discus-
    sion of dialect differences.

2. One can often ascertain the vocabulary items of a dialect by direct ques-
    tions such as these
    a. What do you call the yellow part of an egg? (*yolk* or *yelk*)
    b. When does *evening* begin? (After midday in the South)
    c. What time does my watch show? (The setting is fifteen minutes before
        the hour to elicit "a quarter *to, till,* or *of* . . .")
    Write five questions designed to elicit vocabulary items from the following
    groups. Most of these words are taken from Hans Kurath's *A Word Geog-
    raphy of the Eastern United States.*
    a. *bag, poke, sack*
    b. sick (*at, to, till, on*) the stomach
    c. *porch, piazza, stoop*
    d. *creek, brook, run, branch, kill*
    e. *frying pan, spider, skillet*
    f. *you, you-all* (plurals)
    g. *doughnut, raised doughnut, cruller, fried cake, nut cake, fat cake, olicook,
        cookies.* (Use an informant east of the Alleghenies for these, and
        distinguish between the raised and the unraised, sweetened variety.)
    h. *pancake, griddle cake, fritter, hot-cake, flannel cake, batter-cake, flapjack*
    i. *earthworm, night crawler, fish worm, angle worm, mud worm, angle dog,
        ground worm, red-worm, rain worm*
    j. *pop, soda, tonic, soda pop, soda water*
    Choose a speaker from a region other than yours and ask him your ques-
    tions. Note his responses for class discussion. Although Kurath's material
    is taken from the eastern seaboard and New England, you can use a speaker
    from elsewhere because many of these terms have spread.

3. Assume that you are a linguistic field-worker planning an interview with
    an informant. You want to find out which grammatical forms he uses in
    sentence situations like those listed below. If you ask him point-blank, he
    may report the one he thinks to be "correct" instead of what he normally

uses. Devise the means whereby you can get him to use the forms in parentheses below, or whatever he naturally uses instead of them, and then go ahead with an interview.

a. He (*dived   dove*) from the high board.
b. She (*had drank   had drunk*) all her medicine.
c. You (*hadn't ought   ought not*) to drive so fast.
d. Yesterday he (*lay   laid*) in bed all day.
e. My shirt (*shrank   shrunk*) in the laundry.
f. It (*don't   doesn't*) matter.
g. He (*waked up   woke up*) early.
h. She lives (*on   in*) Broad Street.
i. This is (*all the further   as far as   all the farther*) I go.
j. Who (*rang   rung*) the bell?

4. We have seen that, within the boundaries of our country, there are dialects and subdialects. But we can go further. Any small, closely knit group, such as a family or a group of close friends, is likely to have language peculiarities of its own. It may even be truly said that the speech of every person is unique. This individual speech of a single person we call an *ideolect*. Observe carefully for a week the speech of a person of whom you see a good deal every day. Make a list of the specific ways in which his speech differs from yours—in his pronunciation of words, in his choice of grammatical forms, and in his choice of words and word-combinations. Bring this list to class for discussion.

5. To convey some meanings there is no nationally used word. Instead, there are only various regional words. What, for example, does one call the strip of ground between the sidewalk and the street? Ask as many students as you know from different parts of the country and list the words they use. Similarly, find out the different words used to name a new superhighway.

6. When you have completed the readings, exercises, and class discussions on linguistic geography, write a theme on "Dialect Differences I Have Observed."

FURTHER READINGS

Allen, Harold B. "Aspects of the Linguistic Geography of the Upper Midwest." *Studies in Languages and Linguistics*, Albert Marckwardt, ed. Ann Arbor: The English Language Institute, University of Michigan, 1964.

——. "The Linguistic Atlases: Our New Resource." *The English Journal* 45: 188–194 (April 1956).

American Speech, a Quarterly of Linguistic Usage. This periodical contains many articles on regional speech and linguistic geography, as well as a current bibliography of matters of linguistic interest.

Atwood, E. Bagby. *A Survey of Verb Forms in the Eastern United States.* Ann Arbor: University of Michigan Press, 1953.

——. *The Regional Vocabulary of Texas*. Austin: University of Texas Press, 1962.
Bloomfield, Leonard. *Language*. New York: Holt, Rinehart and Winston, Inc., 1933. See chapter on dialect geography, pp. 321–345.
Francis, W. Nelson. *The Structure of American English*. New York: The Ronald Press Company, 1958. For a short, up-to-date (1958) description of linguistic geography and its accomplishment, see pp. 485–499. Emphasis is on American work.
Hall, Robert A. Jr. *Introductory Linguistics*. Philadelphia: Chilton Books, 1964. See pp. 239–252.
——. *Linguistics and Your Language*. New York: Doubleday & Company, Inc., 1960. See pp. 135–166.
Hockett, Charles F. *A Course in Modern Linguistics*. New York: The Macmillan Company, 1958. See pp. 471–484.
Kurath, Hans. "Area Linguistics and the Teacher of English." *Language Learning*, Special Issue No. 2, March 1961. Also in Harold B. Allen, *Readings in Applied English Linguistics*, 2d ed. New York: Appleton-Century-Crofts, 1964.
——. *A Word Geography of the Eastern United States*. Ann Arbor: University of Michigan Press, 1949.
Malmstrom, Jean and Annabel Ashley. *Dialects—U.S.A.* Champaign, Ill.: National Council of Teachers of English, 1963. A simple but sound presentation.
Potter, Simeon. *Modern Linguistics*. London: Andre Deutsch, 1957. See pp. 123–140. Emphasis is on the European and British scene.
Publications of the American Dialect Society. This periodical specializes in articles on dialects and linguistic geography.

9

STRUCTURAL AND TRANSFORMATIONAL GRAMMAR

Revolution in Grammar

W. NELSON FRANCIS

For two centuries we have been using in English a grammar based on Latin, constructed by British grammarians of the eighteenth century. This grammar is entrenched in our dictionaries and is widely taught in the schools. It is serviceable in certain ways; for example, it gives us a technical vocabulary with which to discuss problems of writing and speaking, and it enables us to analyze English sentences in a rough-and-ready way. But with the advance of linguistic science in recent decades, the structural grammarians find this Latinized grammar too crude an instrument for the thorough linguistic analyses they wish to make. Beginning with new premises, they have been forging new grammars that are highly refined and that enable us to see with greater clarity the marvelously complex structure of our language. W. Nelson Francis discusses these two types of grammars, the Latinized and the scientific, in the important article below. Professor Francis, of Brown University, is the author of *The Structure of American English*, a college textbook that offers an excellent insight into the structural point of view toward grammar.

From *Quarterly Journal of Speech* (October 1954). Reprinted by permission of the Speech Association of America.

424

I

A long overdue revolution is at present taking place in the study of English grammar—a revolution as sweeping in its consequences as the Darwinian revolution in biology. It is the result of the application to English of methods of descriptive analysis originally developed for use with languages of primitive people. To anyone at all interested in language, it is challenging; to those concerned with the teaching of English (including parents), it presents the necessity of radically revising both the substance and the methods of their teaching.

A curious paradox exists in regard to grammar. On the one hand it is felt to be the dullest and driest of academic subjects, fit only for those in whose veins the red blood of life has long since turned to ink. On the other, it is a subject upon which people who would scorn to be professional grammarians hold very dogmatic opinions, which they will defend with considerable emotion. Much of this prejudice stems from the usual sources of prejudice—ignorance and confusion. Even highly educated people seldom have a clear idea of what grammarians do, and there is an unfortunate confusion about the meaning of the term "grammar" itself.

Hence it would be well to begin with definitions. What do people mean when they use the word "grammar"? Actually the word is used to refer to three different things, and much of the emotional thinking about matters grammatical arises from confusion among these different meanings.

The first thing we mean by "grammar" is "the set of formal patterns in which the words of a language are arranged in order to convey larger meanings." It is not necessary that we be able to discuss these patterns self-consciously in order to be able to use them. In fact, all speakers of a language above the age of five or six know how to use its complex forms of organization with considerable skill; in this sense of the word—call it "Grammar 1"—they are thoroughly familiar with its grammar.

The second meaning of "grammar"—call it "Grammar 2"—is "the branch of linguistic science which is concerned with the description, analysis, and formulization of formal language patterns." Just as gravity was in full operation before Newton's apple fell, so grammar in the first sense was in full operation before anyone formulated the first rule that began the history of grammar as a study.

The third sense in which people use the word "grammar" is "linguistic etiquette." This we may call "Grammar 3." The word in this sense is often coupled with a derogatory adjective: we say that the expression "he ain't here" is "bad grammar." What we mean is that such an expression is bad linguistic manners in certain circles. From the point of view of "Grammar 1" it is faultless; it conforms just as completely to the structural patterns of English as does "he isn't here." The trouble with it is like the trouble with Prince Hal in Shakespeare's play—it is "bad," not in itself, but in the company it keeps.

As has already been suggested, much confusion arises from mixing these meanings. One hears a good deal of criticism of teachers of English couched in such terms as "they don't teach grammar any more." Criticism of this sort is based on the wholly unproved assumption that teaching Grammar 2 will increase the student's proficiency in Grammar 1 or improve his manners in Grammar 3. Actually, the form of Grammar 2 which is usually taught is a very inaccurate and misleading analysis of the facts of Grammar 1; and it therefore is of highly questionable value in improving a person's ability to handle the structural patterns of his language. It is hardly reasonable to expect that teaching a person some inaccurate grammatical analysis will either improve effectiveness of his assertions or teach him what expressions are acceptable to use in a given social context.

These, then are the three meanings of "grammar": Grammar 1, a form of behavior; Grammar 2, a field of study, a science; and Grammar 3, a branch of etiquette.

II

Grammarians have arrived at some basic principles of their science, three of which are fundamental to this discussion. The first is that a language constitutes a set of behavior patterns common to the members of a given community. It is a part of what the anthropologists call the culture of the community. Actually it has complex and intimate relationships with other phases of culture such as myth and ritual. But for purposes of study it may be dealt with as a separate set of phenomena that can be objectively described and analyzed like any other universe of facts. Specifically, its phenomena can be observed, recorded, classified, and compared; and general laws of their behavior can be made by the same inductive process that is used to produce the "laws" of physics, chemistry, and the other sciences.

A second important principle of linguistic science is that each language or dialect has its own unique system of behavior patterns. Parts of this system may show similarities to parts of the systems of other languages, particularly if those languages are genetically related. But different languages solve the problems of expression and communication in different ways, just as the problems of movement through water are solved in different ways by lobsters, fish, seals, and penguins. A couple of corollaries of this principle are important. The first is that there is no such thing as "universal grammar," or at least if there is, it is so general and abstract as to be of little use. The second corollary is that the grammar of each language must be made up on the basis of a study of that particular language—a study that is free from preconceived notions of what a language should contain and how it should operate. The marine biologist does not criticize the octopus for using jet-propulsion to get him through the water instead of the methods of a self-respecting fish. Neither does the linguistic scientist express alarm or distress when he finds a language that seems to get along quite well without any words that correspond to what in English we call verbs.

A third principle on which linguistic science is based is that the analysis and description of a given language must conform to the requirements laid down for any satisfactory scientific theory. These are (1) simplicity, (2) consistency, (3) completeness, and (4) usefulness for predicting the behavior of phenomena not brought under immediate observation when the theory was formed. Linguistic scientists who have recently turned their attention to English have found that, judged by these criteria, the traditional grammar of English is unsatisfactory. It falls down badly on the first two requirements, being unduly complex and glaringly inconsistent within itself. It can be made to work, just as the Ptolemaic earth-centered astronomy can be, but at the cost of great elaboration and complication. The new grammar, like the Copernican sun-centered astronomy, solves the same problems with greater elegance, which is the scientist's word for the simplicity, compactness, and tidiness that characterize a satisfactory theory.

III

A brief look at the history of the traditional grammar of English will make apparent the reasons for its inadequacy. The study of English grammar is actually an outgrowth of the linguistic interest of the Renaissance. It was during the later Middle Ages and early Renaissance that the various vernacular languages of Europe came into their own. They began to be used for many kinds of writing which had previously always been done in Latin. As the vernaculars, in the hands of great writers like Dante and Chaucer, came of age as members of the linguistic family, a concomitant interest in their grammars arose. The earliest important English grammar was written by Shakespeare's contemporary, Ben Jonson.

It is important to observe that not only Ben Jonson himself but also those who followed him in the study of English grammar were men deeply learned in Latin and sometimes in Greek. For all their interest in English, they were conditioned from earliest school days to conceive of the classical languages as superior to the vernaculars. We still sometimes call the elementary school the "grammar school"; historically the term means the school where Latin grammar was taught. By the time the Renaissance or eighteenth-century scholar took his university degree, he was accustomed to use Latin as the normal means of communication with his fellow scholars. Dr. Samuel Johnson, for instance, who had only three years at the university and did not take a degree, wrote poetry in both Latin and Greek. Hence it was natural for these men to take Latin grammar as the norm, and to analyze English in terms of Latin. The grammarians of the seventeenth and eighteenth centuries who formulated the traditional grammar of English looked for the devices and distinctions of Latin grammar in English, and where they did not actually find them they imagined or created them. Of course, since English is a member of the Indo-European family of languages, to which Latin and Greek also belong, it did have many grammatical elements in common with them. But many of these had been obscured or wholly lost as a result of the extensive changes that had taken place in English—changes that the early grammarians inevitably conceived of as degeneration. They felt that it was their function to resist further change, if not to repair the damage already done. So preoccupied were they with the grammar of Latin as the ideal that they overlooked in large part the exceedingly complex and delicate system that English had substituted for the Indo-European grammar it had abandoned. Instead they stretched unhappy English on the Procrustean bed of Latin. It is no wonder that we commonly hear people say, "I didn't really understand grammar until I began to study Latin." This is eloquent testimony to the fact that the grammar "rules" of our present-day textbooks are largely an inheritance from the Latin-based grammar of the eighteenth century.

Meanwhile the extension of linguistic study beyond the Indo-European and Semitic families began to reveal that there are many different ways in which linguistic phenomena are organized—in other words, many different kinds of grammar. The tone-languages of the Orient and of North America, and the complex agglutinative languages of Africa, among others, forced grammarians to abandon the idea of a universal or ideal grammar and to direct their attention more closely to the individual systems employed by the multifarious languages of mankind. With the growth and refinement of the scientific method and its application to the field of anthropology, language came under more rigorous scientific scrutiny. As with anthropology in general, linguistic science at first concerned itself with the primitive. Finally, again following the lead of anthropology, linguistics began to apply its techniques to the old familiar tongues, among them English. Accelerated by the practical need during World War II of teaching languages, including English, to large numbers in a short time, research into the nature of English grammar has moved rapidly in the last fifteen years. The definitive grammar of English is yet to be written, but the results so far achieved are spectacular. It is now as unrealistic to teach "traditional" grammar of English as it is to teach "traditional" (i.e. pre-Darwinian) biology or "traditional" (i.e. four-element) chemistry. Yet nearly all certified teachers of English on all levels are doing so. Here is a cultural lag of major proportions.

IV

Before we can proceed to a sketch of what the new grammar of English looks like, we must take account of a few more of the premises of linguistic science. They must be understood and accepted by anyone who wishes to understand the new grammar.

First, the spoken language is primary, at least for the original study of a language. In many of the primitive languages,[1] of course, where writing is unknown, the spoken language is the *only* form. This is in many ways an advantage to the linguist, because the written language may use conventions that obscure its basic structure. The reason for the primary importance of the spoken language is that language

---

[1] "Primitive languages" here is really an abbreviated statement for "languages used by peoples of relatively primitive culture"; it is not to be taken as implying anything simple or rudimentary about the languages themselves. Many languages included under the term, such as native languages of Africa and Mexico, exhibit grammatical complexities unknown to more "civilized" languages.

originates as speech, and most of the changes and innovations that occur in the history of a given language begin in the spoken tongue.

Secondly, we must take account of the concept of dialect. I suppose most laymen would define a dialect as "a corrupt form of a language spoken in a given region by people who don't know any better." This introduces moral judgments which are repulsive to the linguistic scholar. Let us approach the definition of a dialect from the more objective end, through the notion of a speech community. A speech community is merely a group of people who are in pretty constant intercommunication. There are various types of speech communities: local ones, like "the people who live in Tidewater Virginia"; class ones, like "the white-collar class"; occupational ones, like "doctors, nurses, and other people who work in hospitals"; social ones, like "clubwomen." In a sense, each of these has its own dialect. Each family may be said to have its own dialect; in fact, in so far as each of us has his own vocabulary and particular quirks of speech, each individual has his own dialect. Also, of course, in so far as he is a member of many speech communities, each individual is more or less master of many dialects and shifts easily and almost unconsciously from one to another as he shifts from one social environment to another.

In the light of this concept of dialects, a language can be defined as a group of dialects which have enough of their sound-system, vocabulary and grammar (Grammar 1, that is) in common to permit their speakers to be mutually intelligible in the ordinary affairs of life. It usually happens that one of the many dialects that make up a language comes to have more prestige than the others; in modern times it has usually been the dialect of the middle-class residents of the capital, like Parisian French and London English, which is so distinguished. This comes to be thought of as the standard dialect; in fact, its speakers become snobbish and succeed in establishing the belief that it is not a dialect at all, but the only proper form of the language. This causes the speakers of other dialects to become self-conscious and ashamed of their speech, or else aggressive and jingoistic about it—either of which is an acknowledgment of their feelings of inferiority. Thus one of the duties of the educational system comes to be that of teaching the standard dialect to all so as to relieve them of feelings of inferiority, and thus relieve society of linguistic neurotics. This is where Grammar 3, linguistic etiquette, comes into the picture.

A third premise arising from the two just discussed is that the difference between the way educated people talk and the way they write is a dialectal difference. The spread between these two dialects may be very narrow, as in present-day America, or very wide, as in Norway, where people often speak local Norwegian dialects but write in the Dano-Norwegian *Riksmaal*. The extreme is the use by writers of an entirely different language, or at least an ancient and no longer spoken form of the language—like Sanskrit in northern India or Latin in western Europe during the Middle Ages. A corollary of this premise is that anyone setting out to write a grammar must know and make clear whether he is dealing with the spoken or the written dialect. Virtually all current English grammars deal with the written language only; evidence for this is that their rules for the plurals of nouns, for instance, are really spelling rules, which say nothing about pronunciation.

This is not the place to go into any sort of detail about the methods of analysis the linguistic scientist uses. Suffice it to say that he begins by breaking up the flow of speech into minimum sound-units, or phones, which he then groups into families called phonemes, the minimum significant sound-units.[2] Most languages have from twenty to sixty of these. American English has forty-one: nine vowels,[3] twenty-four consonants, four degrees of stress, and four levels of pitch. These phonemes group themselves into minimum meaningful units, called morphemes. These fall into two groups: free morphemes, those that can enter freely into many combinations with other free morphemes to make phrases and sentences; and bound morphemes, which are always found tied in a close and often indissoluble relationship with other bound or free morphemes. An example of a free morpheme is "dog"; an example of a bound morpheme is "un-" or "ex-." The linguist usually avoids talking about "words" because the term is very inexact. Is "instead of," for instance, to be considered one, two, or three words? This is purely a matter of opinion; but it is a matter of fact that it is made up of three morphemes.

In any case, our analysis has now brought the linguist to the point where he has some notion of the word-stock (he would call it the

---

[2] E.g., /l/ is a phoneme because it is significant, that is, because it can be used to signify differences in meaning. It is the /l/, for instance, that distinguishes *light* from such words as *night, might, sight, tight, right, bite, height*. But there is more than one *l* sound: the last sound in *well* differs from the *l* in *light* in that it is preceded by an *uh* sound. However, the difference between these two *l*'s does not distinguish meaning. Thus these two *l*'s are not two different phonemes but simply two members of the family known as the /l/ phoneme. [eds.]

[3] According to the Trager-Smith system. [eds.]

"lexicon") of his language. He must then go into the question of how the morphemes are grouped into meaningful utterances, which is the field of grammar proper. At this point in the analysis of English, as of many other languages, it becomes apparent that there are three bases upon which classification and analysis may be built: form, function, and meaning. For illustration let us take the word "boys" in the utterance "the boys are here." From the point of view of form, "boys" is a noun with the plural ending "s" (pronounced like "z"), preceded by the noun-determiner "the," and tied by concord to the verb "are," which it precedes. From the point of view of function, "boys" is the subject of the verb "are" and of the sentence. From the point of view of meaning, "boys" points out or names more than one of the male young of the human species, about whom an assertion is being made.

Of these three bases of classification, the one most amenable to objective description and analysis of a rigorously scientific sort is form. In fact, many conclusions about form can be drawn by a person unable to understand or speak the language. Next comes function. But except as it is revealed by form, function is dependent on knowing the meaning. In a telegraphic sentence like "ship sails today"[4] no one can say whether "ship" is the subject of "sails" or an imperative verb with "sails" as its object until he knows what the sentence means. Most shaky of all bases for grammatical analysis is meaning. Attempts have been made to reduce the phenomena of meaning to objective description, but so far they have not succeeded very well. Meaning is such a subjective quality that it is usually omitted entirely from scientific description. The botanist can describe the forms of plants and the functions of their various parts, but he refuses to concern himself with their meaning. It is left to the poet to find symbolic meaning in roses, violets, and lilies.

At this point it is interesting to note that the traditional grammar of English bases some of its key concepts and definitions on this very subjective and shaky foundation of meaning. A recent English grammar defines a sentence as "a group of words which expresses a complete thought through the use of a verb, called its predicate, and a subject, consisting of a noun or pronoun about which the verb has something to say."[5] But what is a complete thought? Actually we do

[4] This example is taken from C. C. Fries, *The Structure of English* (New York, 1952), p. 62. This important book will be discussed below.
[5] Ralph B. Allen, *English Grammar* (New York, 1950), p. 187.

not identify sentences this way at all. If someone says, "I don't know what to do," dropping his voice at the end, and pauses, the hearer will know that it is quite safe for him to make a comment without running the risk of interrupting an unfinished sentence. But if the speaker says the same words and maintains a level pitch at the end, the polite listener will wait for him to finish his sentence. The words are the same, the meaning is the same; the only difference is a slight one in the pitch of the final syllable—a purely formal distinction, which signals that the first utterance is complete, a sentence, while the second is incomplete. In writing we would translate these signals into punctuation: a period or exclamation point at the end of the first, a comma or dash at the end of the second. It is the form of the utterance, not the completeness of the thought, that tells us whether it is a whole sentence or only part of one.

Another favorite definition of the traditional grammar, also based on meaning, is that of "noun" as "the name of a person, place, or thing"; or, as the grammar just quoted has it, "the name of anybody or anything, with or without life, and with or without substance or form."[6] Yet we identify nouns, not by asking if they name something, but by their positions in expressions and by the formal marks they carry. In the sentence, "The slithy toves did gyre and gimble in the wabe," any speaker of English knows that "toves" and "wabe" are nouns, though he cannot tell what they name, if indeed they name anything. How does he know? Actually because they have certain formal marks, like their position in relation to "the" as well as the whole arrangement of the sentence. We know from our practical knowledge of English grammar (Grammar 1), which we have had since before we went to school, that if we were to put meaningful words into this sentence, we would have to put nouns in place of "toves" and "wabe," giving something like "The slithy snakes did gyre and gimble in the wood." The pattern of the sentence simply will not allow us to say "The slithy arounds did gyre and gimble in the wooden."

One trouble with the traditional grammar, then, is that it relies heavily on the most subjective element in language, meaning. Another is that it shifts the ground of its classification and produces the elementary logical error of cross-division. A zoologist who divided animals into invertebrates, mammals, and beasts of burden would not get very far before running into trouble. Yet the traditional grammar

[6] *Ibid.*, p. 1.

is guilty of the same error when it defines three parts of speech on the basis of meaning (noun, verb, and interjection), four more on the basis of function (adjective, adverb, pronoun, conjunction), and one partly on function and partly on form (preposition). The result is that in such an expression as "a dog's life" there can be endless futile argument about whether "dog's" is a noun or an adjective. It is, of course, a noun from the point of view of form and an adjective from the point of view of function, and hence falls into both classes, just as a horse is both a mammal and a beast of burden. No wonder students are bewildered in their attempts to master the traditional grammar. Their natural clearness of mind tells them that it is crazy patchwork violating the elementary principles of logical thought.

V

If the traditional grammar is so bad, what does the new grammar offer in its place?

It offers a description, analysis, and set of definitions and formulas —rules, if you will—based firmly and consistently on the easiest, or at least the most objective, aspect of language, form. Experts can quibble over whether "dog's" in "a dog's life" is a noun or an adjective, but anyone can see that it is spelled with " 's" and hear that it ends with a "z" sound; likewise anyone can tell that it comes in the middle between "a" and "life." Furthermore he can tell that something important has happened if the expression is changed to "the dog's alive," "the live dogs," or "the dogs lived," even if he doesn't know what the words mean and has never heard of such functions as modifier, subject, or attributive genitive. He cannot, of course, get very far into his analysis without either a knowledge of the language or access to someone with such knowledge. He will also need a minimum technical vocabulary describing grammatical functions. Just so the anatomist is better off for knowing physiology. But the grammarian, like the anatomist, must beware of allowing his preconceived notions to lead him into the error of interpreting before he describes—an error which often results in his finding only what he is looking for.

When the grammarian looks at English objectively, he finds that it conveys its meanings by two broad devices: the denotations and connotations of words separately considered, which the linguist calls "lexical meaning," and the significance of word-forms, word-groups, and arrangements apart from the lexical meanings of the words, which the linguist calls "structural meaning." The first of these is the domain of the lexicographer and the semanticist, and hence is not our present concern. The second, the structural meaning, is the business of the structural linguist, or grammarian. The importance of this second kind of meaning must be emphasized because it is often overlooked. The man in the street tends to think of the meaning of a sentence as being the aggregate of the dictionary meanings of the words that make it up; hence the widespread fallacy of literal translation—the feeling that if you take a French sentence and a French-English dictionary and write down the English equivalent of each French word you will come out with an intelligible English sentence. How ludicrous the results can be, anyone knows who is familiar with Mark Twain's retranslation from the French of his jumping frog story. One sentence reads, "Eh bien! I no saw not that that frog has nothing of better than each frog." Upon which Mark's comment is, "if that isn't grammar gone to seed, then I count myself no judge."[7]

The second point brought out by a formal analysis of English is that it uses four principal devices of form to signal structural meanings:

(1) Word order—the sequence in which words and word-groups are arranged.

(2) Function-words—words devoid of lexical meaning which indicate relationships among the meaningful words with which they appear.

(3) Inflections—alterations in the forms of words themselves to signal changes in meaning and relationship.

(4) Formal contrasts—contrasts in the forms of words signaling greater differences in function and meaning. These could also be considered inflections, but it is more convenient for both the lexicographer and the grammarian to consider them separately.

Usually several of these are present in any utterance, but they can be separately illustrated by means of contrasting expressions involving minimum variation—the kind of controlled experiment used in the scientific laboratory.

To illustrate the structural meaning of word order, let us compare the two sentences "man bites dog" and "dog bites man."—The words are identical in lexical meaning and in form; the only difference is in

---

[7] Mark Twain, "The Jumping Frog; the Original Story in English; the Retranslation Clawed Back from the French, into a Civilized Language Once More, by Patient and Unremunerated Toil," *1601 . . . and Sketches Old and New* (n.p., 1933), p. 50.

sequence. It is interesting to note that Latin expresses the difference between these two by changes in the form of the words, without necessarily altering the order: "homo canem mordet" or "hominem canis mordet." Latin grammar is worse than useless in understanding this point of English grammar.

Next, compare the sentences "the dog is the friend of man" and "any dog is a friend of that man." Here the words having lexical meaning are "dog," "is," "friend," and "man," which appear in the same form and the same order in both sentences. The formal differences between them are in the substitution of "any" and "a" for "the," and in the insertion of "that." These little words are function-words; they make quite a difference in the meanings of the two sentences, though it is virtually impossible to say what they mean in isolation.

Third, compare the sentences "the dog loves the man" and "the dogs loved the men." Here the words are the same, in the same order, with the same function-words in the same positions. But the forms of the three words having lexical meanings have been changed: "dog" to "dogs," "loves" to "loved," and "man" to "men." These changes are inflections. English has very few of them as compared with Greek, Latin, Russian, or even German. But it still uses them; about one word in four in an ordinary English sentence is inflected.

Fourth, consider the difference between "the dog's friend arrived" and "the dog's friendly arrival." Here the difference lies in the change of "friend" to "friendly," a formal alteration signaling a change of function from subject to modifier, and the change of "arrived" to "arrival," signaling a change of function from predicate to head-word in a noun-modifier group. These changes are of the same formal nature as inflections, but because they produce words of different lexical meaning, classifiable as different parts of speech, it is better to call them formal contrasts than inflections. In other words, it is logically quite defensible to consider "love," "loving," and "loved" as the same word in differing aspects and to consider "friend," "friendly," "friendliness," "friendship," and "befriend" as different words related by formal and semantic similarities. But this is only a matter of convenience of analysis, which permits a more accurate description of English structure. In another language we might find that this kind of distinction is unnecessary but that some other distinction, unnecessary in English, is required. The categories of grammatical description are not sacrosanct; they are as much a part of man's organization of his observations as they are of the nature of things.

If we are considering the spoken variety of English, we must add a fifth device for indicating structural meaning—the various musical and rhythmic patterns which the linguist classifies under juncture, stress, and intonation. Consider the following pair of sentences:

> Alfred, the alligator is sick.
> Alfred the alligator is sick.

These are identical in the four respects discussed above—word order, function-words, inflections, and word-form. Yet they have markedly different meanings, as would be revealed by the intonation if they were spoken aloud. These differences in intonation are to a certain extent indicated in the written language by punctuation— that is, in fact, the primary function of punctuation.

VI

The examples so far given were chosen to illustrate in isolation the various kinds of structural devices in English grammar. Much more commonly the structural meaning of a given sentence is indicated by a combination of two or more of these devices: a sort of margin of safety which permits some of the devices to be missed or done away with without obscuring the structural meaning of the sentence, as indeed anyone knows who has ever written a telegram or a newspaper headline. On the other hand, sentences which do not have enough of these formal devices are inevitably ambiguous. Take the example already given, Fries's "ship sails today." This is ambiguous because there is nothing to indicate which of the first two words is performing a noun function and which a verb function. If we mark the noun by putting the noun-determining function-word "the" in front of it, the ambiguity disappears; we have either "the ship sails today" or "ship the sails today." The ambiguity could just as well be resolved by using other devices: consider "ship sailed today," "ship to sail today," "ship sail today," "shipping sails today," "shipment of sails today," and so on. It is simply a question of having enough formal devices in the sentence to indicate its structural meaning clearly.

How powerful the structural meanings of English are is illustrated by so-called "nonsense." In English, nonsense as a literary form often consists of utterances that have a clear structural meaning but use words that either have no lexical meanings, or whose lexical meanings are inconsistent with one another. This will become apparent if we subject a rather famous bit of English nonsense to formal grammatical analysis:

> All mimsy were the borogoves
> And the mome raths outgrabe.

This passage consists of ten words, five of them words that should have lexical meaning but don't, one standard verb, and four function-words. In so far as it is possible to indicate its abstract structure, it would be this:

> All . . . .y were the . . . . .s
> And the . . . . . .s . . . . . .

Although this is a relatively simple formal organization, it signals some rather complicated meanings. The first thing we observe is that the first line presents a conflict: word order seems to signal one thing, and inflections and function-words something else. Specifically, "mimsy" is in the position normally occupied by the subject, but we know that it is not the subject and that "borogoves" is. We know this because there is an inflectional tie between the form "were" and the "s" ending of "borogoves," because there is the noun-determiner "the" before it, and because the alternative candidate for subject "mimsy," lacks both of these. It is true that "mimsy" does have the function-word "all" before it, which may indicate a noun; but when it does, the noun is either plural (in which case "mimsy" would most likely end in "s"), or else the noun is what grammarians call a mass-word (like "sugar," "coal," "snow"), in which case the verb would have to be "was," not "were." All these formal considerations are efficient to counteract the effect of word order and show that the sentence is of the type that may be represented thus:

> All gloomy were the Democrats.

Actually there is one other possibility. If "mimsy" belongs to the small group of nouns which don't use "s" to make the plural, and if "borogoves" has been so implied (but not specifically mentioned) in the context as to justify its appearing with the determiner "the," the sentence would then belong to the following type:

> (In the campaign for funds) all alumni were the canvassers.
> (In the drought last summer) all cattle were the sufferers.

But the odds are so much against this that most of us would be prepared to fight for our belief that "borogoves" are things that can be named, and that at the time referred to they were in a complete state of "mimsyness."

Moving on to the second line, "and the mome raths outgrabe," the first we note is that the "And" signals another parallel assertion to follow. We are thus prepared to recognize from the noun-determiner "the," the plural inflection "s," and the particular positions of "mome" and "outgrabe," as well as the continuing influence of the "were" of the preceding line, that we are dealing with a sentence of this pattern:

And the lone rats agreed.

The influence of the "were" is particularly important here; it guides us in selecting among several interpretations of the sentence. Specifically, it requires us to identify "outgrabe" as a verb in the past tense, and thus a "strong" or "irregular" verb, since it lacks the characteristic past-tense ending "d" or "ed." We do this in spite of the fact that there is another strong candidate for the position of verb: that is, "raths," which bears a regular verb inflection and could be tied with "mome" as its subject in the normal noun-verb relationship. In such a case we should have to recognize "outgrabe" as either an adverb of the kind not marked by the form-contrast "ly," an adjective, or the past participle of a strong verb. The sentence would then belong to one of the following types:

And the moon shines above.
And the man stays aloof.
And the fool seems outdone.

But we reject all of these—probably they don't even occur to us—because they all have verbs in the present tense, whereas the "were" of the first line combines with the "And" at the beginning of the second to set the whole in the past.

We might recognize one further possibility for the structural meaning of this second line, particularly in the verse context, since we are used to certain patterns in verse that do not often appear in speech of prose. The "were" of the first line could be understood as doing double duty, its ghost or echo appearing between "raths" and "outgrabe." Then we would have something like this:

All gloomy were the Democrats
And the home folks outraged.

But again the odds are pretty heavy against this. I for one am so sure that "outgrabe" is the past tense of a strong verb that I can give its present. In my dialect, at least, it is "outgribe."

The reader may not realize it, but in the last four paragraphs I have been discussing grammar from a purely formal point of view. I have not once called a word a noun because it names something (that is, I have not once resorted to meaning), nor have I called any word an adjective because it modifies a noun (that is, resorted to function). Instead I have been working in the opposite direction, from form toward function and meaning. I have used only criteria which are objectively observable, and I have assumed only a working knowledge of certain structural patterns and devices known to all speakers of English over the age of six. I did use some technical terms like "noun," "verb," and "tense," but only to save time; I could have got along without them.

If one clears his mind of the inconsistencies of the traditional grammar (not so easy a process as it might be), he can proceed with a similarly rigorous formal analysis of a sufficient number of representative utterances in English and come out with a descriptive grammar. This is just what Professor Fries did in gathering and studying the material for the analysis he presents in the remarkable book to which I have already referred, *The Structure of English*. What he actually did was to put a tape recorder into action and record about fifty hours of telephone conversation among the good citizens of Ann Arbor, Michigan. When this material was transcribed, it constituted about a quarter of a million words of perfectly natural speech by educated middle-class Americans. The details of his conclusions cannot be presented here, but they are sufficiently different from the usual grammar to be revolutionary. For instance, he recognizes only four parts of speech among the words with lexical meaning, roughly corresponding to what the traditional grammar calls substantives, verbs, adjectives and adverbs, though to avoid pre-conceived notions from the traditional grammar Fries calls them Class 1, Class 2, Class 3, and Class 4 words. To these he adds a relatively small group of function-words, 154 in his material, which he divides into fifteen groups. These must be memorized by anyone learning the language; they are not subject to the same kind of general rules that govern the four parts of speech. Undoubtedly his conclusions will be developed and modified by himself and by other linguistic scholars, but for the present his book remains the most complete treatment extant of English grammar from the point of view of linguistic science.

VII

Two vital questions are raised by this revolution in grammar. The first is, "What is the value of this new system?" In the minds of many who ask it, the implication of this question is, "We have been getting along all these years with traditional grammar, so it can't be so very bad. Why should we go through the painful process of unlearning and relearning grammar just because linguistic scientists have concocted some new theories?"

The first answer to this question is the bravest and most honest. It is that the superseding of vague and sloppy thinking by clear and precise thinking is an exciting experience in and for itself. To acquire insight into the working of a language, and to recognize the infinitely delicate system of relationship, balance, and interplay that constitutes its grammar, is to become closely acquainted with one of man's most miraculous creations, not unworthy to be set beside the equally beautiful organization of the physical universe. And to find that its most complex effects are produced by the multi-layered organization of relatively simple materials is to bring our thinking about language into accord with modern thought in other fields, which is more and more coming to emphasize the importance of organization—the fact that an organized whole is truly greater than the sum of all its parts.

There are other answers, more practical if less philosophically valid. It is too early to tell, but it seems probable that a realistic, scientific grammar should vastly facilitate the teaching of English, especially as a foreign language. Already results are showing here; it has been found that if intonation contours and other structural patterns are taught quite early, the student has a confidence that allows him to attempt to speak the language much sooner than he otherwise would.

The new grammar can also be of use in improving the native speaker's proficiency in handling the structural devices of his own language. In other words, Grammar 2, if it is accurate and consistent, *can* be of use in improving skill in Grammar 1. An illustration is that famous bugaboo, the dangling participle. Consider a specific instance of it, which once appeared on a college freshman's theme, to the mingled delight and despair of the instructor:

Having eaten our lunch, the steamboat departed.

What is the trouble with this sentence? Clearly there must be something wrong with it, because it makes people laugh, although it was not the intent of the writer to make them laugh. In other words, it produces a completely wrong response, resulting in total breakdown of communication. It is, in fact, "bad grammar" in a much more serious way than are mere dialectal divergences like "he ain't here" or "he never seen none," which produce social reactions but communicate effectively. In the light of the new grammar, the trouble with our dangling participle is that the form, instead of leading to the meaning, is in conflict with it. Into the position which, in this pattern, is reserved for the word naming the eater of the lunch, the writer has inserted the word "steamboat." The resulting tug-of-war between form and meaning is only momentary; meaning quickly wins out, simply because our common sense tells us that steamboats don't eat lunches. But if the pull of the lexical meaning is not given a good deal of help from common sense, the form will conquer the meaning, or the two will remain in ambiguous equilibrium—as, for instance, in "Having eaten our lunch, the passengers boarded the steamboat." Writers will find it easier to avoid such troubles if they know about the forms of English and are taught to use the form to convey the meaning, instead of setting up tensions between form and meaning. This, of course, is what English teachers are already trying to do. The new grammar should be a better weapon in their arsenal than the traditional grammar since it is based on a clear understanding of the realities.

The second and more difficult question is, "How can the change from one grammar to the other be effected?" Here we face obstacles of a formidable nature. When we remember the controversies attending on revolutionary changes in biology and astronomy, we realize what a tenacious hold the race can maintain on anything it has once learned, and the resistance it can offer to new ideas. And remember that neither astronomy nor biology was taught in elementary schools. They were, in fact, rather specialized subjects in advanced education. How then change grammar, which is taught to everybody, from the fifth grade up through college? The vested interest represented by thousands upon thousands of English and Speech teachers who have learned the traditional grammar and taught it for many years is a conservative force comparable to those which keep us still using the chaotic system of English spelling and the unwieldy measuring system of inches and feet, pounds and ounces, quarts, bushels, and acres. Moreover, this army is constantly receiving new recruits. It is possible in my state to become certified to teach English in high school if one has had eighteen credit hours of college English—let us say two semesters of freshman composition (almost all of which is taught by people unfamiliar with the new grammar), two semesters of a survey course in English literature, one semester of Shakespeare, and one semester of the contemporary novel. And since hard-pressed school administrators feel that anyone who can speak English can in a pinch teach it, the result is that many people are called upon to teach grammar whose knowledge of the subject is totally inadequate.

There is, in other words, a battle ahead of the new grammar. It will have to fight not only the apathy of the general public but the ignorance and inertia of those who count themselves competent in the field of grammar. The battle is already on, in fact. Those who try to get the concepts of the new grammar introduced into the curriculum are tagged as "liberal" grammarians—the implication being, I suppose, that one has a free choice between "liberal" and "conservative" grammar, and that the liberals are a bit dangerous, perhaps even a touch subversive. They are accused of undermining standards. of holding that "any way of saying something is just as good as any other," of not teaching the fundamentals of good English. I trust that the readers of this article will see how unfounded these charges are. But the smear campaign is on. So far as I know, neither religion nor patriotism has yet been brought into it. When they are, Professor Fries will have to say to Socrates, Galileo, Darwin, Freud, and the other members of the honorable farternity of the misunderstood, "Move over, gentlemen, and make room for me."

Transformational Grammar

PAUL ROBERTS

In the preceding essay, Professor Francis described the revolution against traditional grammar by the proponents of a new, structurally based grammar called structural grammar or immediate-constituent grammar. After this essay had been written, a new and different kind of grammar came into being as a revolution against immediate-constituent grammar. This is known by various names, such as trans-

The assignments for all the essays in this section have been placed on page 476.

formational grammar, generative grammar, or generative-
transformational grammar. The new grammar is described
by Paul Roberts in the essay below. Mr. Roberts is Professor
of Linguistics at Cornell University. He is well qualified to
evaluate contending schools of grammar, for he himself is
the author of four textbooks on grammar—one traditional,
one structural, and two transformational. His latest one,
English Syntax, is a lucid programed introduction to transformational grammar.

. . . Immediate-constituent grammar was a product of linguistics—
largely American linguistics—of the 1930's and 40's. It was most available to the general reader in a book called *The Structure of English* by
Charles Carpenter Fries of the University of Michigan, published in
1952. The grammar was characterized by certain fundamental tenets
which still characterize work in linguistics and presumably always will:

(1) *That language is primarily speech and only secondarily writing.* This
is not to degrade writing or to say that it is not properly the central
concern of the school system. It is only to indicate the actual relationship
of writing and speech. Writing is a symbolization of speech and not
vice versa. We approach writing and its problems more easily if we
understand what it is.

(2) *That word classes (parts of speech and their subgroups) can be identified only by their distribution, their formal characteristics, and the like that they
share.* Efforts to define them on the basis of meaning are doomed to
failure. Such definitions turn out always to be either false or circular.

(3) *That correctness in language is a relative matter, not an absolute one.*
There are no *linguistic* considerations for preferring one variety of
English to another, but only sociological ones. In the sight of both God
and logic, "He brung it" is no better and no worse than "He flung it."
But to say that correctness is a sociological matter is not to say that
it is unimportant. Obviously children being educated must learn that
"He brung it" is not what educated people say. . . .

Immediate-constituent grammar

Immediate-constituent analysis makes the basic assumption that
sentences can be viewed as being made up of two-part constructions
on a series of levels. A sentence consists of two main parts (two immedi-

From *Teacher's Manual, English Sentences* by Paul M. Roberts. Reprinted by permission of Harcourt, Brace & World, Inc., Copyright 1962.

ate constituents); each of those parts consists of two parts; each of those of two parts, until one gets down to the ultimate constituents, the smallest meaningful units in the sentence—i.e., words or morphemes. For many sentences this structure can be shown very easily:

The little girls walked to the store.
The little girls / walked to the store.
The / little girls   walked / to the store.
The   little / girls   walk / ed   to / the store.
The   little   girl / s   walk   ed   to   the / store.

Not only did this analysis provide interesting insights into the nature of the sentence, but it proved to have various useful practical applications in solving problems of modification and the like.

However, there were certain types of constructions to which immediate-constituent analysis proved difficult to apply. What are the immediate constituents, for example, of "Did the little girls walk to the store?" If it consists of two parts, what are they? The further one tried to push the concept of immediate constituents, the more one confronted problems to which only uncertain or arbitrary answers could be given.

This difficulty, along with many others that had troubled linguistics, was surmounted by the development of transformational analysis, which was certainly the most interesting advance of linguistic science in the 1950's. . . .

Transformational grammar

Transformational analysis begins with the assumption that the sentences of English or of any language are of two basic types: *kernel sentences* and *transformed sentences*. The heart of the grammar is a relatively small set of kernel or basic-sentence types. These are basic in the sense that they cannot be derived from any sentences or sentence types underlying them. They are the foundation on which all else is built. All the rest of the language can be most economically described as a series of changes rung on the kernel sentences, as transformations of them.

Thus, for example, the sentence "John saw Bill" is a kernel sentence. The following are all transformations of it:

Did John see Bill?   Who saw Bill?
John didn't see Bill.   Whom did John see?
John did see Bill.   Where did John see Bill?

John saw Bill, didn't he?	John's seeing Bill
Bill was seen by John.	that John saw Bill
Bill wasn't seen by John.	for John to see Bill

And so on.

. . . What we might try to do in this place is to see some of the more general consequences of transformational analysis and some of its relationship both to immediate-constituent grammar and to prescientific grammar.

One thing that transformational analysis demonstrates is that immediate-constituent analysis applies wholly and simply *only to kernel sentences*. Indeed, transformational analysis provides, for the kernel, a much more powerful proof of immediate-constituent theory than was ever possible before. It is quite easy to show that any kernel sentence can be evolved by a simple forking process, each higher or more general unit splitting into two lower or more particular units until actual words are reached:

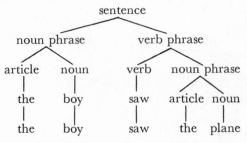

This process, refined to take into account the various types of predicates possible in English and to indicate the grammatical agreements necessary and the compatibility of various word groups, can display the whole kernel of English in a relatively small space. The entire kernel is produced by simple forking into immediate constituents.

But this system will not work to produce all of English sentences. One cannot produce "Did the boy see the plane?" for example, in this fashion. The easiest way to arrive at "Did the boy see the plane?" is to describe the changes made in the statement to produce the question. "Did the boy see the plane?" is a transformation of "The boy saw the plane." Like all transformations, it involves additions, the switching around of things, and the like. Its production requires rules or directions of a fundamentally different sort than the rules and directions which produce kernel sentences. Because it cannot be reached by a simple forking process, immediate-constituent analysis does not apply to it, or at least does not apply in the same simple way that it applies to the kernel.

It must be emphasized that transformational analysis is much more than simply a neater or more defensible way of describing language. It goes a long way to describe how languages are learned in the first place. It explains something of how virtually all human beings, even the dullest, manage to grasp and use at least one language. Language appears as a finite and comprehensible system. We somehow, as children, learn the kernel plus the rules for transforming the kernel into the various structures permitted by the language. This makes the possibilities infinite, and makes it possible for us to produce sentences which are completely grammatical but which we have never specifically learned. Given the kernel sentence "The boy saw the plane" and knowledge of how to make that kind of statement into a yes/no question, we can produce "Did the boy see the plane?" without ever having heard the question previously. Thus grasp of a finite system permits us to produce infinitely many grammatical sentences.

We are led from here to a much better understanding of the complex question of grammaticality. What do we mean when we say a sentence is or is not grammatical? We obviously can't mean that it makes sense. The sentence "Chicago is a dish of fried sofas" makes no sense, but we accept it as wholly grammatical. Neither do we mean that a grammatical sentence is one that occurs frequently in a language. "Chicago is a dish of fried sofas" has a zero frequency in English. It has, presumably, never occurred before. Yet it is quite as grammatical as, say, "Chicago is the hog butcher of the world."

Immediate-constituent grammar tends to make and describe an inventory. In theory, at least, it simply records the sentences—more precisely, a sample of the sentences—that have occurred in a language and then describes their features. Transformational analysis goes much further than this. It seeks to figure out the grammatical system of a language and then project it. Thus it not only recognizes sentences as grammatical because they have occurred but also undertakes to predict what sentences will be grammatical when and if they occur in the future.

Word classes

The problem of grammaticality is closely connected with the problem of definition of word classes, something that has plagued students and teachers of grammar since at least the time of Aristotle. Grammars previous to transformational analysis have tended to begin with the smallest units and work up to the sentence unit. One begins by describing the sounds, then shows how these go together to make morphemes, how these make words, how the words are arranged in word classes, and how the word classes go together to form sentences. In this process, definition is crucial. One had to find some way of identifying each class and fencing it off from its neighbors. Both scientific and prescientific grammars spent much time in this pursuit with no really satisfactory conclusion. Thus we find in grammars of one sort or another the following definitions of *adjective:*

(1) A word that modifies a noun. (Absurd. This would put *bad* and *bank* in the same class: "a bad robber," "a bank robber.")

(2) A word that indicates a quality. (Absurd. This puts *courageous* and *courage* in the same class: "He's courageous," "He has courage.")

(3) A word that patterns with *very*. (Absurd. This puts *old* and *much* in the same class: "very old," "very much.")

(4) A word that takes the endings /ər/ and /əst/ (*-er, -est*). (Absurd. This puts *fine* and *tear* in the same class: *fine, finer, finest*— /fayn/, /faynər/, /faynəst/; *tear, terror, terraced*— /ter/, /terər/, /terəst/.)*

Thus, though some of the definitions proposed work pretty well in a general sort of way, all of them encounter absurdity when pushed to conclusion. Transformational analysis does not solve the problem by providing better definitions in the same sense of *definition*. Rather it avoids the problem altogether by beginning with the largest, most abstract level—sentence—and working down to the concrete items. Every higher-level concept is automatically defined by indicating what it consists of on the next level down. There is never any need to frame a definition of *sentence*, because the whole grammar is a definition of sentence. The whole grammar is a level-to-level description of the make-up of sentences in some particular language. . . .

We start with some such rule as this:

$$S \rightarrow NP + VP$$

S stands for *sentence*. The arrow means "rewrite as." Formulas of this type define the term to the left of the arrow by the terms given to the

---

* Chomsky's example.

right of the arrow. The formula $S \rightarrow NP + VP$ means that any sentence consists of an NP and a VP, whatever they are. (NP stands for *noun phrase*, and VP for *verb phrase*, but the terms and symbols are arbitrary; we could just as well write $S \rightarrow X + Y$; the meaning of NP and VP, or X and Y, will be indicated in successive rules below.)

$$NP \rightarrow T + N$$
$$T \rightarrow \text{the, a}$$
$$N \rightarrow \text{man, boy, table} \ldots$$

Thus an NP is shown to consist of a T and an N, and T and N are defined, as we arrive at the concrete level, by showing the words, or examples of the words, that occur in these classes—articles and nouns. We would come at adjective in the VP:

$$VP \rightarrow Aux + V$$
$$V \rightarrow \begin{Bmatrix} Vi \\ Vt + NP \\ Vs + Adj \end{Bmatrix}$$
$$Vi \rightarrow \text{occur, arrive} \ldots$$
$$Vt \rightarrow \text{see, find} \ldots$$
$$Vs \rightarrow \text{seem, appear} \ldots$$
$$Adj \rightarrow \text{old, fine} \ldots$$

The class *adjective*, when it appears, appears as a set of words. But it is a set of words in a complex, a piece in the pattern that goes to make up grammatical English sentences. Classroom experience shows that when word classes are approached in this direction, the problem of definition largely vanishes. It just isn't there any more. Teacher and student are relieved of the burden and enabled to proceed to examination of the actual characteristics of the sentences of English. *

A transformational grammar is intended to produce all grammatical sentences of a language and only those. That is, if you follow out all the possibilities given in the rules, you eventually can construct all the grammatical sentence types, but you will not produce any sentences that are not grammatical. This clearly necessitates the subdivision of word classes. If, for example, we have a sentence type "noun-verb-noun"

---

* These examples are not intended to display the actual content of a transformational grammar, either a scholarly or a textbook one. A full grammar would have to be considerably more elaborate in the area shown and would proceed differently in respect to some particulars. . . .

and if the verb class contains all verbs with no differentiation, we would be able to derive not only the grammatical "The boy saw the table" but also "The boy occurred the table," which is not grammatical. So we must subdivide verb into transitive, intransitive, and various other subclasses, as traditional grammar has done, too.

We come eventually, however, to a point at which grammatical subclassification stops. This is the point where grammar leaves off and semantics begins. For example, there is no *grammatical* way to rule out the sentence "Chicago is a dish of fried sofas." There is no grammatical way to classify the words *Chicago, dish, fried,* and *sofa* to keep them from coming together in this order, though semantic groupings might be possible. This is why we say that the sentence, though semantically absurd, is perfectly grammatical. . . .

It would be a mistake to make too much of the newness of transformational analysis or to suggest that it is a rejection of the work in linguistics of the past or is unrelated to that work. Much of transformational analysis is implicit in immediate-constituent grammars—in such books as Fries's *The Structure of English* or Francis's *Structure of American English* or Lloyd and Warfel's *American English in Its Cultural Setting.* In all these works we find descriptions of basic-sentence types (something that looks very much like the kernel) and descriptions of the mechanism for expanding the basic sentences (something that looks very much like transformation). All these books share with transformational analysis the same kind of interest in speech, in form and function, in language as a signaling system. All look at the same language in the same objective way, working from the same data to very similar conclusions. . . .

Transformational analysis is more truly conceived as a going-on, as a building on earlier work. Penetrating more profoundly into very general questions concerning the nature of language, of grammar, of linguistics, it gains a vantage point from which to discern more promising new routes to the solution of old problems. It explains conclusions which before were only intuited. Often, in working with immediate-constituent grammar, one felt that beyond certain points progress became steeply difficult. The description was right as far as it went, but one couldn't take it farther. In transformational analysis one doesn't have this sense of a blocking-off. One feels that the way is open from a rough and general sketch to a complete and satisfying description of English. If this also is illusory, the illusion is at least not easily dispelled. . . .

Sentence Analysis
and Parts of Speech

CHARLES CARPENTER FRIES

In 1952 a highly important contribution to American grammar appeared. It was C. C. Fries's *The Structure of English*.
In this analytical work Fries used as his basic data some
fifty hours of conversations, recorded mechanically, of about
three hundred speakers of Standard English. With these
data Fries produced an original descriptive study of such
grammatical matters as kinds of sentences, parts of speech,
and functions of sentence elements. Though the book was
a center of linguistic controversy, its findings have been
incorporated into a number of textbooks of grammar. In
the following two selections from this book, Professor Fries
explains his major basic assumption—that structural signals
are matters of form—and discusses parts of speech in the
light of this assumption.

In the analysis of sentences to be carried out here, just as in our establishing of a practically useful definition of the sentence and in our
classifying of the various kinds of sentences, the procedure differs
markedly from that usually employed in the schools. Perhaps it will
help clarify our discussion to bring into sharp contrast the characteristic features of the conventional approach to the analysis of sentences
and those of the approach to be used here.

In the usual approach to the grammatical analysis of sentences one
must know the total meaning of the utterance before beginning any
analysis. The process of analysis consists almost wholly of giving
technical names to portions of this total meaning. For example, given
the sentence *the man gave the boy the money*, the conventional grammatical
analysis would consist in attaching the name "subject" to the word *man*,
the name "predicate" to the word *gave*, the name "indirect object" to
the word *boy*, the name "direct object" to the word *money*, and the
name "declarative sentence" to the whole utterance. If pressed for the
basis upon which these names are given to these words, one would,

From *The Structure of English* by Charles Carpenter Fries, copyright, 1952, by
Harcourt, Brace & World, Inc., and Longmans, Green & Co., Ltd.

in accord with the traditional method, say that the word *man* is called "subject" because it "designates the person about whom an assertion is made"; that the word *gave* is called "predicate" because it is "the word that asserts something about the subject"; that the word *boy* is called "indirect object" because it "indicates the person to or for whom the action is done"; and that the word *money* is called "direct object" because it "indicates the thing that receives the action of the verb."[1] The sentence is called a "declarative sentence" because it "makes a statement." The whole procedure begins with the total meaning of the sentence and consists solely in ascribing the technical terms "subject," "predicate," "indirect object," "direct object," and "declarative sentence" to certain parts of that meaning, "Knowing grammar" has thus meant primarily the ability to apply and react to a technical terminology consisting of approximately seventy items.[2] It is this kind of "grammatical knowledge" that is assumed in the usual discussions of the value of "grammar" for an effective practical command of English, or for English composition, or for mastery of foreign language. It is this kind of grammatical analysis, this starting with the total meaning, *and the using of this meaning as the basis for analysis*—an analysis that makes no advance beyond the ascribing of certain technical terms to parts of the meaning already known—it is this kind of grammatical analysis that modern linguistic science discards as belonging to a prescientific era.

What, then, have we, in contrast, to substitute for this type of grammatical analysis? Let us begin again with the sentence given above, *the man gave the boy the money.* First of all, we need to distinguish sharply at least two kinds of meaning in the total meaning of this utterance. There are, for example, the meanings of the separate words as the dictionary would record them—the lexical meanings. The dictionary would tell us something of the kinds of creatures referred to by the words *man* and *boy;* it would tell us the sort of thing the word *money* represents; and it would tell us the kind of action indicated by the word *gave.* Beyond these meanings the dictionary does not go. And yet we get from this sentence a whole range of meanings not expressed in the

---

[1] These definitions appear in nearly all the school textbooks that contain any "grammar."

[2] See *Report of the Joint Committee on Grammatical Terminology*, reprinted 1918, adopted by the Modern Language Association of America, the National Education Association, and the American Philological Association. See also the thirty items in C. D. Thorpe, *Preparation for College English* (Ann Arbor, 1945), p. 13. Also *English Grammar for Language Students*, by Frank X. Braun (Ann Arbor, 1947).

lexical records of the words themselves. We are told, for example, that the "man" performed the action, not the "boy"; we are told that only one man and only one boy are involved; we are told that the action has already taken place, it is not something in process, not something planned for the future; the information is given to us as a statement of fact, not something that is questioned, nor something that is requested. Such meanings constitute what we shall call the *structural meanings* of the sentence.[3] The total linguistic meaning of any utterance consists of the lexical meanings of the separate words plus such structural meanings. No utterance is intelligible without both lexical meanings and structural meanings. How, then, are these structural meanings conveyed in English from the speaker to a hearer? Structural meanings are not just vague matters of the context, so called; they are fundamental and necessary meanings in every utterance and are signalled by specific and definite devices. It is the devices that signal structural meanings which constitute the grammar of a language. *The grammar of a language consists of the devices that signal structural meanings.*

The contrast between the older traditional procedure of grammatical analysis and the approach used here lies in the fact that the conventional analysis starts from the undifferentiated total meaning of an utterance and raises the question, "What names apply to various parts of this meaning?" whereas our analysis[4] starts from a description of the formal devices that are present and the patterns that make them significant *and arrives at the structural meanings as a result of the analysis.* From a practical point of view we are concerned, too, with the utterances in which clear grammatical signals are not present, and thus *when* and *why* the structural meanings of any utterance become ambiguous.

Does a child of four who has learned to talk English as his native language know the grammar of that language? The answer to this question will depend upon the particular meaning one attaches to the word *know*. If *know* means the ability to make generalizing statements about the devices that signal structural meanings in English, then certainly he does not know the grammar of his language; nor, for that matter, do most adult speakers of English. But how will he react

---

[3] The borderline between lexical meanings and structural meanings in a language like English that uses "function" words is not always sharp and clear. . . . More important, perhaps, is the fact that meanings which in one language are signalled by patterns of form and arrangement, in another language may depend upon the choice of vocabulary items.

[4] The word *analysis* here does not mean our procedure for the investigator.

if he hears directed to him such an utterance as *is your mother home?* Will he recognize it as a question and reply with an answer? In other words, has he learned to respond to the particular devices by which English signals the fact that a particular utterance is a question? Or, again, when he hears, in the story that is being read to him, that *the hunters killed the wolf*, will he know that it was the hunters that survived and not the wolf? In so far as he has learned to respond to the signals of such structural meanings as these, he "knows" the grammar of his language. One cannot speak or understand a language without "knowing" its grammar—not consciously, of course, but in the sense of making the proper responses to the devices that signal structural meanings and also of producing the proper signals of his own structural meanings.

One of the earliest steps in learning to talk is this learning to use automatically the patterns of form and arrangement that consitute the devices to signal structural meaning. So thoroughly have they become unconscious habits in very early childhood that the ordinary adult speaker of English finds it extremely difficult not only to describe what he does in these matters but even to realize that there is anything there to be described.[5] One of the basic assumptions of our approach here to the grammatical analysis of sentences is that all the structural signals in English are strictly formal matters that can be described in physical terms of forms, correlations of these forms, and arrangements of order. An example of part of what this basic assumption covers is furnished by a comparison of an Old English sentence with a parallel word-for-word arrangement of the Modern English lexical equivalents.

O. E.	Glædne	giefend	lufað	God
Mdn. E.	Cheerful	giver	loves	God

But the Modern English word for word equivalents of the Old English words do not represent the meaning of the Old English sentence. The lexical meanings are the same but the structural meanings differ. In the Old English sentence the *-ne* on the end of the word *glædne* signals the fact that the *glædne giefend* (the cheerful giver) is the object of God's love. The inflectional ending of the word, not the word order within the sentence, constitutes the structural signal in the Old English sentence. To render this structural meaning in Modern English

---

[5] Several months ago even a college professor confronted with the demand to explain how he knew that the utterance *is the teacher here* is a question, could offer no better answer than, "Because it asks for information."

the positions of the words must be changed to *God loves cheerful giver*. In the sentences

| *O. E.* | Glædne | giefend | lufað | God |
| *Mdn. E.* | God | loves | cheerful | giver |

the structural meanings are the same, but the formal devices that signal these similar meanings differ.

The following comparison will furnish another example.

| *O. E.* | In | ænium | oþerum | mynstres | þingum |
| *Mdn. E.* | In | any | other | monastery's | things |

As these expressions stand, the structural meaning of the Modern English rendering does not represent the structural meaning of the Old English phrase. In the Modern English expression the word-order arrangement signals the fact that *any* and *other* go with the word *monastery*. In the Old English sentence, however, the *-um* endings on the words *ænium* (*any*) and *oþerum* (*other*) signal the fact that these belong to *þingum* (*things*) which has the same *-um* ending. The Modern English equivalent of the structural meaning of the Old English expression cannot be rendered with the words in the same order as they stand in Old English. To represent the Old English meaning the Modern English words would have to be *in any other things of the monastery*, with *any* and *other* preceding the word *things*, and the word-group *of the monastery* following it. In the Old English example, the endings or the forms of the words are the determining signals indicating the word to which *any* and *other* are to be attached; in the Modern English rendering, the word-order arrangement is the important feature of the structural signal. In each, however, there is a definite formal device to signal this particular structural meaning. The lexical meanings of the words themselves give no clue concerning such a meaning. Some type of formal grammatical device, the endings or forms of the words, the order of the words, or both, must signal the direction of modification. We have thus assumed that the signals of all structural meanings in English are similarly formal matters that can be described in terms of forms, correlations of these forms, and arrangements of order.

Another of the basic assumptions of our approach here to the grammatical analysis of sentences is that the formal signals of structural meanings operate in a system—that is, that the items of form and arrangement have signalling significance only as they are parts of patterns in a structural whole. An illustration may help to explain the significance of this second assumption.

A man stands sixty feet away from a flat object lying on the ground. He throws a ball of a certain size so that it passes directly over the flat object at a height of three feet, and two inches inside the right edge. This act is of practically no significance in itself, but if this throwing occurs within the structural frame of a baseball game, by virtue of the patterns of that game, it gets a special significance—it is a "strike." Again, the man may throw the ball so that it passes over the flat object (the "plate") at a height of only two and a half feet, but three inches inside the left edge. In spite of all the specific differences, because of the patterns of the game, this also has the same significance; it too is a "strike." Again, the thrown ball may pass directly over the center of the plate but at a height of four and a half feet. According to the pattern this may or may not be a "strike." It will depend upon a different kind of contrast, upon whether the "batter" is a tall or a short man. The height of the ball over the plate must be above the knees but not above the shoulders of the batter. Or again, the ball may not pass over the plate at all, but six inches outside the right edge. This, according to the pattern, may be a "ball"; but, by a still different significant contrast, that is, if the batter attempts to hit the ball with his bat and misses, it can also be a "strike." Or again, the batter may strike at the ball and hit it so that it drops to the ground outside the playing "diamond." This, is of course, a "foul"; but if the batter has not already had two "strikes" against him, it is also a "strike." In spite of the very great specific differences from all the others, this "strike" is structurally the "same" as the others. Every one of these throwings by the "pitcher" differs from all the others, and yet, as far as the patterns of the game are concerned they are the "same." They are all significant as "strikes." The number of specifically different throwings that can fit into the pattern of the "strike" is almost infinite, as is the number of differing actions that can fit into the pattern of an "out." But the number of the patterns themselves in the structural whole of the game of baseball is very limited. The game itself is a system of contrastive patterns that give significance to an infinite variety of specific actions.[6] In similar fashion, a language as a whole

---

[6] Animals other than man can be taught to throw a ball, to catch it, to hit it, and to perform various other specific acts that occur in the game of baseball; but, so far as I can discover, they cannot be taught to "play the game" of baseball—they cannot grasp the system of contrastive patterns that give significance to the specific acts of one who is "playing the game."

consists of a system of contrastive patterns that give significance to an infinite variety of specific acts of speech. It is only these patterns that can give significance to the features of form and arrangement that operate as the devices of structural meaning. It is our task, therefore, not only to describe the items of form and arrangement which constitute the devices that signal structural meanings, but also, and especially, to set forth the contrastive patterns of the system through which these items acquire signaling significance.

What then are the basic items of the patterns of grammatical structure in present-day English?

Sometimes, at street intersections, signs which alternately show the single words *Go* and *Stop* control the traffic. When the word *Go* appears, the traffic facing that sign moves forward. When the word *Stop* appears, that traffic ceases its forward movement. We recognize these single-word utterances as "commands" or "requests." To other single-word utterances such as $\overline{Wai}\,\rfloor\,ter$, $\overline{Mo}\,\rfloor\,ther$, $\overline{Boy}$ we respond differently; we recognize these as "calls." Would an utterance of the single word $\overline{Skip}$ be a "call" like $\overline{Wai}\,\rfloor\,ter$, $\overline{Mo}\,\rfloor\,ther$, $\overline{Boy}$ or a "command" like $\overline{Go}\,\overline{Stop}$, $\overline{Walk}$?[7] It could be either; as it stands, with no other clues to the situation in which it is uttered, it is ambiguous. As the nickname for a boy, it would be a call. If no such boy is present, it would be a command. The linguistic difference between single-word utterances such as *Waiter, Mother, Boy, Dad, John* on the one hand and those of *Go, Stop, Walk, Run, Smile* on the other is a matter of the "form-class," the "part of speech," to which the words belong. The ambiguity of single-word utterances like *Skip* (or *Hope* or *Rush*) without further clues arises from the uncertainty concerning the form-class or part of speech to which this word, in this particular utterance, belongs. Some type of structural ambiguity always results in English whenever the form-classes of the words are not clearly marked.

The utterance *ship sails today* (which might appear in a telegram) is ambiguous as it stands because of the absence of clear part-of-speech markers. If a clear part-of-speech marker, *the*, is put before the first word as in "*The* ship sails today" there is no ambiguity; we have a statement. If, however, the same marker is put before the second word as in "Ship *the* sails today" there is also no ambiguity, but the utterance is different; we then have a request. Other clear part-of-speech markers

---

[7] The lines indicate a drop from a voice pitch above normal to the low pitch below normal. This is discussed in the following reading by Paul Roberts. [eds.]

would also resolve the ambiguity, as with the addition of such a marker as the ending *-ed*.

Ship*ped* sail today
Ship sail*ed* today

Newspaper headlines very frequently are structurally ambiguous because of the lack of definite part-of-speech or form-class markers. Some typical examples out of many are the following:

1. "Vandenberg Reports Open Forum."

The ambiguity of this heading could be cleared by the use of such markers as *the* or *an*, as:

Vandenberg Reports Open *the* Forum
Vandenberg Reports *an* Open Forum

2. "Unfavorable Surveyor Reports Delayed Michigan Settlement."

The ambiguity of this heading would be cleared by the use of such markers as *have* or *a:*

Unfavorable Surveyor Reports *Have* Delayed Michigan Settlement
Unfavorable Surveyor Reports *a* Delayed Michigan Settlement

3. "Briton to Be Tried for Missing Jewish Youth's Murder."
Such a marker as *a* would clear the ambiguity here:

Briton to Be Tried for *a* Missing Jewish Youth's Murder
Briton to Be Tried for Missing *a* Jewish Youth's Murder

4. "Marshall Calls on Congress to Help Prostrate Europe."
Here again the markers *a* or *-ed* would clear the ambiguity:

Marshall Calls on Congress to Help Prostrat*ed* Europe
Marshall Calls on Congress to Help *a* Prostrate Europe

Or the marker *to* would make unmistakable the other meaning.

Marshall Calls on Congress to Help *to* Prostrate Europe

As we examine the utterances of English, we shall find that unless certain large form-classes or parts of speech have their characteristic markers the structural meanings of the utterance will be ambiguous.

We have assumed in our approach here that the signals of all structural meanings are formal matters that can be described in terms of form and arrangement. We have assumed, too, that these items operate in a system, that they have signalling significance only as they are parts of patterns in a structural whole. In our attempt to describe the contrastive patterns of the system through which the structural meanings of English are signalled we find that the basic items to be distinguished are certain large form-classes of the words, the lexical units. *An English sentence then is not a group of words as words but rather a structure made up of form-classes or parts of speech.* In order to know the structural meanings signalled by the formal arrangements of our sentences *one need not know the lexical meanings of the words but he must know*[8] *the form-classes to which the words belong.* Our description of the patterns of devices to signal structural meanings will, therefore, be in terms of the selection of these large form-classes or parts of speech and the formal arrangements in which they occur.

Parts of speech

A number of examples given in the preceding pages were used to demonstrate the fact that, in English, some type of structural ambiguity results whenever an utterance consists of certain important form-classes or parts of speech without clear markers. The markers that distinguish these important parts of speech in English are therefore of primary importance in our description of the patterns of the devices that signal structural meanings—a description which will be made in terms of the selection of these parts of speech and the formal arrangements in which they occur. What parts of speech, then, can we—or, rather, must we—recognize in English for a basic description of our utterances, and what are the special markers of these parts of speech?

All the conventional school grammars deal extensively with the "parts of speech," usually given as eight in number, and explained in definitions that have become traditional. It has often been assumed that these eight parts of speech—noun, pronoun, adjective, verb, adverb, preposition, conjunction, interjection—are basic classifications that can be applied to the "words" of all languages[9] and that the traditional definitions furnish an adequate set of criteria by which to make the classifications.

---

[8] "Know" in the sense of "respond to."

[9] "The distinctions between the various parts of speech . . . are distinctions in thought, not merely in words." John Stuart Mill, *Rectorial Address at St. Andrews* (1867).

As a matter of fact our common school grammars of English have not always used eight parts of speech. Some have named ten, making the "article" and the "participle" separate classes.[10] Some have included the "adjective" under the name "noun" and have given as subclasses of "nouns" the "noun substantive" and the "noun adjective."[11] Others have insisted that "interjections" are not "parts of speech" but "sentence words." Some of the early Greek grammarians recognized only three parts of speech, ὄνομα (names), ῥῆμα (sayings), and συνδέσμοι (joinings or linkings). The Latin grammarian, Varro, distinguished four parts of speech: (1) words with cases (nouns), (2) words with tenses (verbs), (3) words with both cases and tenses (participles), (4) words with neither cases nor tenses (particles). The current conventional classification for words into the particular eight parts of speech now common seems to have begun with Joseph Priestley and to have been generally accepted in the grammars since 1850.[12] We cannot assume without question that the eight parts of speech thus inherited from the past will be the most satisfactory or the essential classification of the form-classes of present-day English, but will instead examine anew the functioning units in our collection of utterances, with a view to establishing the minimum number of different groups needed for a basic description of the signals of the most important structural meanings.

Unfortunately we cannot use as the starting point of our examination the traditional definitions of the parts of speech. What is a "noun," for example? The usual definition is that "a noun is the name of a person, place, or thing." But *blue* is the "name" of a color, as is *yellow* or *red*, and yet, in the expressions *a blue tie, a yellow rose, a red dress* we

[10] See Goold Brown, *The Grammar of English Grammars*, 10th ed. (New York, 1868), pp. 220–223.

[11] "How mony partyse of speche ben þer? Viii. Wych viii? Nowne, pronowne, verbe, aduerbe, partycypull', coniunccion, preposicion, and interieccion. . . . How mony maner of nownys ben' there? Ii. Wyche ii? Nowne substantyfe & nowne adiectyfe." From Douce Ms. 103 (fifteenth century). Text printed in *PMLA*, 50 (1935), 1012–1032.

"Nouns are distinguished into two sorts, called noun substantives and noun adjectives." William Ward, *A Practical Grammar of the English Language* (London, 1765), p. 324.

[12] "I shall adopt the usual distribution of words into eight classes. . . . All the innovations I have made hath been to throw out the *Participle*, and substitute the *Adjective*, as more evidently a part of speech." Joseph Priestley, *Rudiments of English Grammar* (London, 1769; 1st ed., 1761), p. 3.

do not call *blue* and *yellow* and *red* "nouns." We do call *red* a noun in the sentence *this red is the shade I want. Run* is the "name" of an action, as is *jump* or *arrive. Up* is the "name" of a direction, as is *down* or *across.* In spite of the fact that these words are all "names" and thus fit the definition given for a noun they are not called nouns in such expressions as "We *ran* home," "They were looking *up* into the sky," "The acid made the fiber *red*." The definition as it stands—that "A noun is a name"—does not furnish all the criteria necessary to exclude from this group many words which our grammars in actual practice classify in other parts of speech.

In the expressions *a blue tie, a yellow rose, a red dress,* the words *blue, yellow,* and *red,* in spite of the fact that according to their meanings they are "names" of colors, are called "adjectives," because the adjective is defined as "A word that modifies a noun or a pronoun." A large part of the difficulty here lies in the fact that the two definitions —the definition of the noun and the definition of the adjective—are not parallel. The one for the noun, that "a noun is a name," attempts to classify these words according to their *lexical meanings;* the one for the adjective, that "an adjective is a word that modifies a noun or a pronoun," attempts to classify the words according to their *function in a particular sentence.* The basis of definition slides from meaning to function. For the purposes of adequate classification, the definitions of the various classes must consider the same kind of criteria.

Even with the usual definition of an adjective the criteria are not always consistently applied. Many grammars will not classify *boy's* as an adjective in *the boy's hat,* nor *his* as an adjective in *his hat,* in spite of the fact that both words, *boy's* and *his,* "modify" the word *hat,* and thus fit the definition. *Boy's* is usually called "noun in the possessive case," and *his,* a "possessive pronoun" or a "pronoun in the possessive case." Here again, criteria that are not included in the definition— in this case certain formal characteristics—are used in practice to exclude the classification items that fit the definition.

The common definition for a pronoun presents even more difficulty. "A pronoun is a word used instead of a noun." But just what kind of substitution is to be called "pronoun" in the following examples? In the sentence *John and James brought their letters of recommendation* there should be no question that *John* and *James,* as the names for two perons, are nouns. In the following series of words "substituted for these two nouns" just which are to be called pronouns and why?

John and James ⎫
The two boys   ⎪
The undersigned ⎪
A few   ⎪
The two   ⎪
Two   ⎬ brought their letters of recommendation
A couple   ⎪
Several   ⎪
Some   ⎪
Both   ⎪
These   ⎪
They   ⎭

A slightly different kind of series, substituted for the noun *Wednesday* in the sentence *Wednesday is the time to see him*, presents the same problem. Which of the following substitutes are "pronouns"?

Wednesday ⎫
Tomorrow ⎪
Today   ⎪
Next week ⎪
Later   ⎬ is the time to see him
Now   ⎪
When   ⎪
This   ⎪
That   ⎪
It   ⎭

Obviously even in the usual procedure of classifying words into "parts of speech"—noun, adjective, pronoun—the criteria indicated in the definitions, that "names" are nouns, that "modifiers of nouns" are adjectives, and that "substitutes for nouns" are pronouns, do not include all that is actually used, and these definitions, therefore, cannot provide the basis for our approach here. We cannot use "lexical" meaning as the basis for the definition of some classes, "function in the sentence" for others, and "formal characteristics" for still others. We must find, as the basis for our grouping into parts of speech, a set of criteria that can be consistently applied.

Two problems then confront us:

(1) We have concluded above that the structural signals of English consist of arrangements, not of words as words, but of words as parts

of speech. We should be able, then, to express our descriptions of the patterns that signal structural meanings in terms of formulas with the various parts of speech as the units. Our first problem, then, is to discover just how many different kinds of these functioning units the formulas for English require, and precisely what they are.

(2) We have insisted that unless these functioning units, these parts of speech, are clearly marked, are identifiable in an utterance, some type of structural ambiguity will result. The ambiguity of the following utterances, for example, arises because of the uncertainty of the kind of functioning unit of each of the italic words:

> *Ship sails* today
> *Time flies*
> The dogs looked *longer* than the cat
> Avoid infection by *killing* germs

The conventional definitions do not provide the necessary criteria. Our second problem is to discover just what the criteria are that the users of the language actually employ to identify the necessary various form-class units when they give and receive the signals of structural meaning.

You will remember Alice's experience with the poem of the Jabberwocky:[13]

> Twas brillig, and the slithy toves
>   Did gyre and gimble in the wabe;
> All mimsy were the borogoves,
>   And the mome raths outgrabe. . . .
>
> "Somehow [she said], it seems to fill my head
> with ideas—only I don't exactly know what they are!"

What are the "ideas" she gets and how are they stimulated? All the words that one expects to have clearly definable meaning content are nonsense, but any speaker of English will recognize at once the frames in which these words appear.

> Twas ———, and the ———y ———s
> Did ——— and ——— in the ———;
> All ———y were the ———s,
> And the ——— ———s ———'—.

---

[13] For the suggestion of this type of use of nonsense words I am indebted to Prof. Aileen Traver Kitchin. I had used algebraic symbols for words but not with the success she has attained with "Jabberwocky" material.

The "ideas" which the verse stimulates are without doubt the structural meanings for which the framework contains the signals. Most of these nonsense words have clearly marked functions in frames that constitute familiar structural patterns. These "ideas" seem vague to the ordinary speaker because in the practical use of language he is accustomed to dealing only with total meanings to which lexical content contributes the elements of which he is conscious.

For the Jabberwocky verse certain familiar words of the frame in which the nonsense appeared furnished important clues to the structures; but such clues are often unnecessary. One need not know the lexical meaning of any word in the following:

     1. Woggles ugged diggles
     2. Uggs woggled diggs
     3. Woggs diggled uggles

If we assume that these utterances are using the structural signals of English, then at once we know a great deal about these sequences. We would know that *woggles* and *uggs* and *woggs* are "thing" words of some kind; that in each case there is more than one of these "things," and that they at some time in the past performed certain "actions"; and that these actions were directed toward other "things," *diggles*, *diggs*, and *uggles*.

As speakers of English, given the three utterances above, we should not hesitate to make such new utterances as the following:

     4. A woggle ugged a diggle
     5. An ugg woggles diggs
     6. A diggled woggle ugged a woggled diggle

We would know that *woggles* and *uggs* and *woggs* are "thing" words, in sentences 1, 2, 3, because they are treated as English treats "thing" words—by the "positions" they occupy in the utterances and forms they have, in contrast with other positions and forms. We would know that *ugged* and *woggled* and *diggled* are "action" words in these same sentences because they are treated as English treats "action" words— by the "positions" they occupy and the forms they have, in contrast with the positions and forms of the other "words."

We would make the new utterances 4, 5, 6, with confidence because in these we simply proceed to continue to treat the various units of the utterances in accord with the formal devices which constitute the grammar of English. For all of this it has not been necessary to know the meaning of a single word. As native speakers of English

we have learned to use certain formal clues by which we identify
the various kinds of units in our structures. The process is wholly
unconscious unless some failure attracts attention;—just as unconscious
as our responses to sight clues with the muscular adjustments of
balancing when we walk. . . .

Intonation

PAUL ROBERTS

In the preceding selection, C. C. Fries defined grammar in
this way: "The grammar of a language consists of the devices that signal structural meanings." By structural meanings he meant all the meaning that remains in a sentence
after the dictionary meanings have been subtracted. Now,
since some of these structural meanings are signaled by
three voice features—stress, pitch, and juncture—these
features must be considered a part of grammar, A few examples may be appropriate. In the sentence "I think that
man is honest" the word *that* is either a conjunction or a
demonstrative, depending on the stress you give it. Next,
consider *who* in this example: "The boss is going to ·get a
new secretary." "Who?" The answer you will get to "Who?"
depends on whether you pronounce it with a rising or a
falling pitch. The third voice feature, juncture, refers to the
divisions we sense in the flow of speech. For instance, it is
one of the four kinds of juncture that enables us to distinguish between such pairs as "see Mabel" and "seem
able," "cease taking" and "ceased aching." In the selection
following, Paul Roberts explains in a simple way these three
grammatical features. Professor Roberts is the author of
four textbooks of grammar that are notable for their lucidity
and good sense.

Besides the thirty-three vowels and consonants, English has a series of
phonemes of an entirely different kind — or rather of three different
kinds. These are the features called stress, pitch, and juncture. Taken

From *Patterns of English* by Paul M. Roberts, copyright, © 1956, by Harcourt,
Brace & World, Inc.

together, stress, pitch, and juncture make up what we call intonation. Every time we utter a sentence, we use some kind of intonation, and the meaning of our sentences changes according to the intonation we use.

The whole story of English intonation is a very complicated matter, and we won't try to explain all the details here. But it is easy to see some of the contrasts of intonation and to realize that we react accurately to them whenever we hear English.

Stress

Probably the simplest feature of intonation to understand is stress. Stress is simply the loudness or softness with which we utter the different syllables in the speech stream. We make use of stress all the time in forming our sentence patterns. For instance, if we use the word *subject* as a noun, we pronounce the *sub* louder than the *ject:*

What's the súbject?

But if we use it as a verb, we pronounce the *ject* part louder:

We'll subjéct him to an examination.

We have the same contrast in *íncrease* and *incréase*, *prótest* and *protést*, *réfuse* and *refúse*, and many other pairs.

But that's by no means all there is to stress in English. Each speaker of English makes use of four different stresses — four degrees of loudness — when he speaks his sentences. The names and symbols for them are these:

Primary, the loudest degree /´/
Secondary, the next to loudest /^/
Tertiary, the third from loudest /`/
Weak, the softest /ˇ/

Here's a sentence that has all of them:

The Whíte Hòuse is a whĭte house.

If you'll pronounce the sentence naturally, you'll see that you don't say "White House" quite as you say "white house." The difference is mainly in the stress.

Stress usually distinguishes adjectives modifying nouns from nouns modifying nouns. You may remember our ambiguous sentence "He's a sweet salesman," where you can't tell whether the salesman is sweet or sells candy. But this is ambiguous in writing only. In speech, *sweet* will have secondary stress if it's an adjective but primary stress if it's a noun.

> He's a sweet salesman. (The salesman is sweet.)
> He's a sweet salesman. (He sells candy.)

Stress is so important that if the speaker gets the stresses mixed up the result is likely to be nonsense. You might not be surprised to get a "writing desk" for Christmas. But you would probably be very much surprised if you got a "writing desk."

Pitch

The second feature of intonation is pitch. Pitch is caused by the vibration of the sounds as they come from our mouths. If they vibrate fast — say 800 times a second — we get what we call high pitch. If they vibrate slowly — say 200 times a second — we get low pitch.

We are all familiar with pitch, because we know, for example, that women's voices are generally higher than men's and that adults' voices are lower than children's. What most people don't realize, however, is that each of us — whether his voice is generally high or generally low — makes use of four contrasting pitch points or pitch phonemes. We give these numbers, not names. The highest pitch phoneme is /4/; the next to highest is /3/; the next to lowest is /2/; the lowest is /1/.

We can also indicate them by drawing lines above and below the letters. A line just over the letters means pitch /3/; a line well above the letters means pitch /4/; a line just under the letters means pitch /2/; and a line well below the letters means pitch /1/.

For instance, suppose we want to mark the pitch on the sentence "What are you doing?" This could be said in several ways, but the most common way would be to begin on pitch /2/, to stay on that until the stressed syllable is reached, to rise to /3/ on the stressed syllable, and then to fall to /1/. Like this:

What are you | do | ing?

We use pitch for many purposes in our sentences. It is closely bound up with the structural patterns of our sentences. But we also use it to express such meanings as surprise, indignation, insistence, panic, boredom, and many others. For example, one could put a note of panic into the question "What are you doing?" by rising to the fourth pitch instead of the third:

What are you | do|ing?

Or if one is just sort of exasperated with the other person and what he's doing, he might say:

What | are | you |do|ing?

Often we make jokes by deliberately using the wrong pitch. Here's one:

What did you put in the | sa|lad? Alice?

In place of:

What did you put in the | sa|lad, Alice?

Juncture

The third part of intonation is juncture. Juncture is a way of breaking or stopping the speech flow. English intonation seems to go in fours, and there are four junctures just as there are four stresses and four pitches; the first one, however, is quite different from the other three. Junctures are named after the symbols used to indicate them.

The first juncture is called plus juncture because it is marked with a plus sign: $/+/$.

The second juncture is called single bar juncture. It is marked with one upright line or bar: $/|/$.

The third juncture is called double bar juncture. It is marked with two upright lines: $/\|/$.

The last juncture is called double cross juncture. It is marked with two crossing lines: $/\#/$.

Plus juncture is a special kind of break between phonemes. It is the difference between *I scream* and *ice cream*. In *I scream* we have plus juncture before the /s/ phoneme: /ay+skriym/. In *ice cream* the plus juncture comes after the /s/ phoneme: /ays+kriym/. The reason that the two sounds are different is that in *I scream* we have the kind of /s/ that comes at the beginning of a word and the kind of /k/ that comes after /s/; but in *ice cream* we have the kind of /s/ that comes at the end of a word and the kind of /k/ that comes at the beginning. This is what plus juncture does; it breaks up the phonemic flow and makes words, although the phonemic words are not always identical with the ones we commonly write.

The other junctures come at the end of groups of words. These junctures are closely tied up with stress and pitch. If a sentence has only one primary (loudest) stress, then we won't have any junctures inside the sentence. But if we have two primary stresses, then we will have a single bar or double bar juncture between them.

For instance, we can say the sentence "The man on your right is her brother" with just one primary stress; then there is no juncture inside the sentence:

The man on your right is her bró́ther.

Or we can say it with two primary stresses; then there will be a single bar juncture after the first primary stress:

The man on your rí́ght | is her bró́ther.

If there are three primary stresses, there will be two single bar junctures:

The má́n | on your rí́ght | is her bró́ther.

This would be a very slow and emphatic way of saying the sentence.

The difference between single bar, double bar, and double cross juncture is a matter of what happens to the pitch. If the pitch stays the same, we have single bar; if it goes up a little (but not to the next pitch level) we have double bar; if it goes down a little, we have double cross.

The sentence "The man digging in the garden is Mr. Jones" might have one or two single bar junctures, depending on the number of primary stresses; or it might have none at all:

The má́n | digging in the gá́rden | is Mr. Jó́nes.

The man digging in the gá́rden | is Mr. Jó́nes.

The man digging in the garden is Mr. Jó́nes.

But the sentence "Mr. Jones, digging in his garden, found a worm" would be pronounced quite differently. There would be three primary stresses with double bar junctures separating them:

Mr. Jónes ‖ digging in his gárden ‖ found a wórm.

That is, the pitch would rise slightly after *Jones* and after *garden*. The pitch would be something like this:

| Mr. | Jon | es, digging in his | gar | den, found a | wo | rm |

Double bar juncture corresponds more or less to a comma in writing.

Double cross juncture is a slight drop in pitch. Notice in the last example that a slight drop is shown at the very end, after *worm*. This is a double cross juncture, in its usual place at the end of a sentence:

Mr. Jones ‖ digging in his garden ‖ found a worm #

By and large, double cross junctures in speech correspond to semicolons and periods in writing.

Here are a few more examples showing primary stresses and the different junctures. There would be other ways of saying some of these of course:

Where are you góing #

Where áre | you góing #

Running into the hóuse ‖ Agnes told us the néws #

We invited Ál ‖ who had a cár #

Ál ‖ who had a cár ‖ offered to take ús #

Al had a cár # therefore we had to invíte him #

Al had a cár # he wouldn't ‖ howéver ‖ let us úse it #

People who own cars are pretty lúcky #

People who own cárs | are pretty lúcky #

A Quick Look at English

WALDO B. SWEET

In the selection entitled "Sentence Analysis and Parts of Speech" on pages 451–465, C. C. Fries asserts that the classification of English words into eight parts of speech is based on a logical fallacy, namely that the basis of classification is not the same for all. To this assertion, the natural rejoinder is, "Well, then, how should we set up these word classes that we call parts of speech?" A cogent answer is offered by Waldo B. Sweet in the meaty and highly condensed essay below. This was written for university students as a grammatical preface to a beginning course in Latin utilizing a structural approach. Mr. Sweet is Professor of Latin at the University of Michigan.

Oddly enough, in the past languages were taught on the assumption that they were fundamentally alike. It was believed that there was a universal grammar which applied to all languages, although it was often noted that language X was deficient in a certain respect or that language Y seemed to have an extra item or two in its inventory.

Now one important thing that languages do share in common is that they contain meaning. It is possible to take this meaning, analyze it, and give names to the divisions that result. You *can* make a classification of persons, places, and things, and if you wish to call these nouns, that is your privilege. The only trouble with it is that it isn't very consistent and it doesn't seem to describe the facts of language as well as the newer approach.

What is a noun in English? Does it have the marker -*tli*, like Nahuatl? What is an English verb? Does it end in -*t*, like Latin verbs?

In English, just as in every other language, there are formal markers for such distinctions. If no such markers can be found, then the language lacks this particular feature. Much of the difficulty which students have had with English grammar has arisen from the fact that they were asked to identify things which exist in Latin but are

From *Latin: a Structural Approach* by Waldo B. Sweet. Reprinted by permission of the publisher, The University of Michigan Press, copyright 1957.

not present in English, since the "universal grammar" to which we referred above was based on Latin. Here then is a description of English, condensed into a single lesson.

Parts of speech

In English we distinguish five major parts of speech: nouns, verbs, adjectives, adverbs, and a class with many subdivisions called function words. Sometimes morphology[1] clearly indicates the part of speech to which a word belongs, as in *breadth, broaden, broad,* and *broadly.* In many cases, however, it is necessary to see the morphology and *distribution*[2] of an English word before we can determine the form class. *Gardens* is a noun in *The gardens are beautiful this spring* but a verb in *He gardens with great pleasure.* The distribution tells us whether it is noun or verb.

A *noun* in English has the following characteristics:

(1) Morphologically[3] it has a distinction between singular and plural (*man/men*) and between the common form and the possessive (*man/man's* and *men/men's*). In most nouns, if we disregard the apostrophe (which corresponds to nothing in the spoken language), the contrast is the same in both instances (*boy/boys*).

(2) Distributionally it fits into the frame *The* _____ *is good* or _____*is good.*

There is a small but important subclass of nouns called *pronouns.* In addition to the contrast which nouns have between singular and plural and common case and possessive case, pronouns have a further contrast between subjective and objective case: *I/me, she/her,* etc. Although in general they have the same distribution as nouns they do not take the noun-markers *the* or *a.*

A *verb* in English has the following characteristics:

(1) Morphologically it has a distinction between singular and plural of the present tense in the third person (*write/writes*) and between present and past (*write/wrote*).

(2) Distributionally it fits into one or more of the following frames:

      a. *The man*_____*s the house.*
      b. *The man*_____*s there.*
      c. *The man*_____*s wise.*

[1] The form. [eds.]
[2] The positions in which a form occurs. [eds.]
[3] In form. [eds.]

Verbs that fit into the first frame (*see*, *build*, etc.) are *transitive;* those that fit into the second (*sit*, *swim*, etc.) are *intransitive;* those that fit into the third (*look*, *is*, *seem*, etc.) are *connecting*. Some verbs fit into more than one frame (*run*, *sink*, etc).

An *adjective* in English has the following characteristics:

(1) Morphologically it has a distinction between the positive form, the comparative form, and the superlative form (*big*, *bigger*, *biggest*).

(2) Distributionally it fits into both of these frames:

    a. *The_____man arrived.*

    b. *The man is_____.*

An *adverb* in English has the following characteristics:

(1) Morphologically it has the morpheme *-ly*.

(2) Distributionally it fits into the frame *The man fell_____.*

Words which do not qualify morphologically but have the same distribution as one of these four parts of speech are called by names which have the suffix *-al* or *-ial*, as *adjectival, adverbial*.[4] The word *slow* in *Drive slow* (leaving aside the question of whether it is correct) is an adverbial; it does not have the morpheme marker *-ly*, but it fits into the frame *The man fell slow*. *Slowly*, in *Drive slowly*, is an adverb: it is morphologically marked by the *-ly* and fits into the frame *The man fell slowly*.

The real complexity of English grammar lies in the residue of words, called *function words:*

    the, a, every, no (noun markers)

    may, can, must, should (auxiliaries)

    not (negator)

    very, more, pretty, rather (qualifiers)

    and, or, not, but, rather than (connectives)

    for, by, in, from, of (prepositions)

    when, why, where, how (interrogators)

    because, after, when, although (subordinators)

    well, oh, now, why (responders)

[4] The other two are *verbal* (for verb) and *nominal* (for noun). These apply to grammatical units which can occupy the same positions as verbs and nouns respectively. For example, in the sentence "The poor are always with us," the word *poor* is morphologically an adjective because one can add to the form the ending *-er*, a characteristic of adjectives, but one cannot add the plural ending *-s*, a characteristic of nouns. Distributionally, however, it is a nominal because it is in a position normally occupied by nouns, e.g., "The *girl* is my sister," "The *girls* are my sisters." [eds.]

The criteria for establishing these classes is distribution. In *The dog is barking* we could substitute the other noun markers (*A dog, every dog, no dog*) but not the qualifiers or any other group.

Bear in mind that every language has its own criteria for setting up such classes, whether by form or distribution or by both.

Syntax

Syntax (the formal signals that indicate meaning) is shown in English primarily by *word order* and *function words*, only secondarily by morphological change. Subject and object, for example, are indicated by word order:

> The *man* sees the bear. (*man* is subject)
> The bear sees the *man*. (*man* is object)

Latin does not signal subject and object in this way.

When pronouns replace nouns in the subject or object position, they generally take the subjective or objective forms:

> *He* sees the bear.
> The bear sees *him*.

It should be noted that word order is the primary signal, and the change in the pronoun is secondary. If you were to hear *John saw Mary and I downtown today*, the word order would tell you that *I* was object of the sentence in spite of the subjective case.

The situation is different in Latin, where, although there is a favorite order (subject, object, verb), about half the time we find one of the other five permutations (object, verb, subject; verb, subject, object, etc.) without any change in syntactical meaning.

In English there are a few variations of subject, verb, object:

> "Stop!" cried the cop: object, verb, subject.
> Came the dawn: verb, subject.
> Did he see the bear? auxiliary, subject, verb, object.

Modification of nouns is shown in English by word order:

> The *big* man sees the bear.
> The man sees the *big* bear.

Modification is not signalled in Latin in this way.

In English most adjectives and adjectivals precede the noun they

modify. A few petrified phrases, most long phrases, and all prepositional phrases follow:

> God Almighty, house beautiful, courts-martial
> The man, shaking all over, saw a bear.
> The man who was here yesterday saw a bear.
> The man with a gun saw a bear.

Verbs in English are modified by adverbs, adverbials, prepositional
phrases, and certain function words. There is some freedom in the
position of some of them:

> We go to the lake in the summer.
> We go in the summer to the lake.
> In the summer we go to the lake.

Notice that although there is the same general meaning conveyed,
there is a different emphasis. This shift in emphasis is meaning on a
quite different level from the contrast between *The man saw the bear* and
The bear saw the man.

The importance of word order in English may be seen in the pair
an awful pretty hat/a pretty awful hat. Word order tells us that *awful* is a
qualifier in the first and an adjective in the second. Notice too that the
order of adjectives in series is fixed. In *all those fat little old American
tourists over there* we cannot change the order of any of the modifiers.
Such facts as these, traditionally ignored in grammars, are part of the
English language. To teach a foreigner English it is necessary to set up
special drills that will teach him to respond *automatically* to these signals.

Nouns may modify nouns in English; the signal is the placing of a
noun immediately before the noun it modifies. Notice the difference
in the following pairs:

> chair arm/arm chair   station bus/bus station
> race horse/horse race   leather shoe/shoe leather

The following questions will test your comprehension of this chapter. Forget the old criteria of meaning and try to apply the new ones
of form and distribution. For example, the word *home* in *d* of the first
set is not a noun but an adverbial; in *e*, however, it is a noun.

(1) Identify the parts of speech of the italicized words:

    a. John has an *inclination* to be lazy.

    b. The girl has a *pretty* dress.

    c. The dog was *pretty* ugly.

    d. The man ran *home.*

    e. The woman ran her *home* well.
    f. The catcher hit a *home* run.
    g. The batter knocked the runner *home*.
    h. The player hits *well*
    i. The driller hit a *well*.

(2) If you saw on the menu the item "chicken lobster" what would you get if you ordered it, chicken or lobster? What is the signal?

(3) Some English grammars have stated that in English we signal questions by raising the voice at the end. Observation shows, however, that whereas the voices is raised at the end of some questions, it must be lowered at the end of others, and it may be either raised or lowered at the end of still others. Test this by reading aloud the following sentences:

"Where do you work?" "I work in New Jersey."
"Where?" "In New Jersey, I said; didn't you hear me?"

"Where do you work?" "I work in New Jersey."
"Where?" "In Passaic." "Where?" "On Main Street."
"Where?" "1905 Main."

(4) How do we signal commands in English?

SUGGESTED ASSIGNMENTS

1. Review what C. C. Fries has to say about lexical and structural meanings. Then point out all the structural meanings in the following sentences and tell whether they are signaled by form or by word order.
   a. The swaggles faculated my gluddest neap.
   b. Her fillydoop, a swalish threet, was spooving his rambent dirm.
   c. That subful slig tiligates my spoom loubously.
2. Write three sentences like the foregoing to show as many structural meanings as you can. Note that you can use nonsense words only for those parts of speech that are traditionally called nouns, verbs, adjectives, and adverbs. Nearly all other kinds of words convey mostly structural meaning, though the line between lexical and structural meanings is sometimes hard to draw.
3. Fries points out that if a sentence contains words whose form-class (part of speech) classification is unclear, the sentence will contain a structural ambiguity, that is, it will have two possible meanings. In the following newspaper headlines, point out the structural ambiguities caused by form-class uncertainty:

   a. SUSPECT SHOT AFTER HOLDUP
   b. EUROPE CROOKS
      BECKONING FINGER
      AT LOCAL RESIDENTS
   c. OPEN HOUSE
      FOR NEW SCHOOL
   d. RULE BOOK NOT OBSCENE

4. In writing, the structural signals of stress, pitch, and juncture are absent. Thus there is always the possibility that the reader, by "hearing" these signals in a way different from that intended by the writer, may misinterpret. Read the following items aloud so as to bring out more than one meaning:
   a. I have a son, David, who is a doctor.
   b. The soldiers were issued twenty four hour passes.
   c. What did you do then?
   d. Mammoth tooth found in creek near Vinton.
   e. A girl watcher.
   f. Do you want tea or coffee?
   g. I am an outdoor lover.
   h. Roger slipped on his shoe.
   i. A clever boy's story.

5. Read these sentences aloud with a double-cross juncture just before the second clause:
   a. It was light enough to play *although the sun was already down.*
   b. Jack invited Helen to the prom, *which was what she had expected.*
Many college freshmen write such clauses as complete sentences, preceded by a period and beginning with a capital letter. Explain why they do so.

6. Why do most people find talking so easy and writing so difficult? Write a theme on this question, choosing your own title.

7. Here is an exercise in descriptive grammar on which to try your wings. Collect about fifty sentences containing *some, something, any, anything.* You can get them from your reading, from spoken discourse, and by asking friends to devise a few for you. Then, using your collected data, write an accurate descriptive statement about how the four words are used that will show a foreigner how to use them as Americans do. Next, test your statement by trying to find exceptions. If you find exceptions, modify the statement to include them. See if your statement will help the Dutch high school students who uttered the following sentences:
   a. I want to ask you any questions about America.
   b. Did you ever hear something about Leonardo da Vinci?
   c. I want to tell you anything about the South Seas.
   d. It is not the use to eat or drink something after that.
   e. I want to tell you anything about dancing.

    f.   I do not have some paper today.

    g. Any students think that Greek is easy.

    h. I did not have some money left.

8. As a native speaker of English you have a working knowledge of English grammar; that is, you can construct sentences using the same forms and patterns as other Americans, with the result that you are understood and your language sounds natural. But you are perhaps not conscious of all the complexities of the intricate system that you use so easily. Here is a pertinent exercise. Study the sentences below, all of which were spoken by foreign students. Each group represents one kind of abnormality that makes it non-English. Choose one group and write an explanation of what is wrong in such a way that the speaker will be able to avoid the same kind of mistake in the future. It will not be very helpful merely to show the normal way to express the sentence. You will have to find a principle or general pattern that can be followed.

    a. (1) We have very often clouds.

          (2) I like very much sport.

          (3) You learn quickly English.

          (4) We could take each morning a bath.

          (5) He has been for three weeks minister.

    b. (1) . . . another big house where is a tennis court.

          (2) Before the window is an ivy where lived many birds.

    c. (1) I will be tomorrow there.

          (2) We go at nine o'clock to bed.

          (3) I went at ten o'clock to the office.

    d. (1) What you like with your pancakes?

          (2) Why you never come to our class?

          (3) To which factory you wrote?

          (4) How you like my speech?

    e. (1) I have born in The Hague.

          (2) Where did you born?

          (3) Where have you born?

          (4) Where are you born?

    f. (1) He made the mistake to show his picture.

          (2) We had no hope to see our cat back.

9. For the ambitious student here are some harder sentences to explain to the foreign student:

    a. Yesterday I must go shopping.

    b. It is not pleasant too.

    c. The eggs were been packed in a box.

    d. The game is during forty-five minutes.

    e. It is much comfortable.

10. There has been a long-standing controversy as to whether the study of grammar improves one's ability to use his native language. Using your

own experience as material, write a theme on "What Grammar Did to/for Me."

11. "Revolution" occurs in all fields of knowledge as new facts are discovered, new ways of looking at facts are developed, and new theories emerge. If you have cultivated a special area of knowledge—whether it is concerned with mathematics or art or fishing tackle or raising calves or techniques of cooking—you are probably aware of a new direction or "revolution" that is currently accepted as the latest and the best. Thus you have material at your hand for writing an illuminating expository theme on a subject like "The Current Revolution in ——" or "A New Direction in ——."

12. Here is an exercise that will give you an idea of how a linguistic scientist works with a corpus (collected words, phrases, and sentences) to formulate a grammar. You will find below thirty-eight sentences in Melanesian Pidgin, a language spoken in New Guinea and neighboring islands. These utterances were elicited from speakers of MP by Robert A. Hall, Jr., a linguist at Cornell University. Your assignment is to answer the questions given at intervals, using as your source of information any sentences in the preceding part of the total corpus.

(1) You savvy disfela man?   (1) Do you know this man?

(2) Long disfela place i-got twofela man i-fight.   (2) At this place there are two men (who are) fighting.

(3) Disfela saucepan i-no-good.   (3) This utensil is no good.

(4) Who's 'at i-kaikai-im taro belong me?   (4) Who has eaten my taros?

(5) Rouse-im alltogether disfela box.   (5) Take away all these boxes.

(6) Fireup belong musket i-bigfela.   (6) The explosion of the gun is loud.

(7) Alltogether master i-make-im bigfela Christmas.   (7) All the white men are having a big celebration.

Q. 1. What form do MP nouns have in the plural? (Don't worry about the verbal prefix *i*-. This merely signals that a verb or predicate is about to follow.)

Q. 2. How does MP signal the genitive or possessive, that is, the *of* or *'s* idea?

(8) Police-sergeant i-line-im alla policeboy.   (8) The police sergeant lines up all the native policemen.

(9) Police-sergeant i-cart-im pass along number-two kee-ap.   (9) The police sergeant carries a letter for the subordinate official.

(10) Behind i-got place i-got water.   (10) Then there is a swamp.

Q. 3. How does MP handle the definite article? (i.e., *the*)

Q. 4. How does MP handle the indefinite article? (i.e., *a/an*)

(11)	Me no make-im.	(11) I couldn't do it.
(12)	All-time all-time em i-fight-im me.	(12) He is always hitting me.
(13)	Me no can loose-im you.	(13) I wouldn't desert *you*. (sg.)
(14)	Bimeby me go one-time youfela.	(14) I will go with *you*. (pl.)
(15)	Mefela like kitch-im showman.	(15) We want to get a guide.
(16)	You-me no got talk.	(16) We (you and I) have nothing to say (in this matter).
(17)	Em i-fight-im youfela.	(17) He hits *you*. (pl.)
(18)	Em i-fight-im mefela.	(18) He is hitting us.
(19)	Em i-got threefela picka-ninny finish.	(19) She already has three children.
(20)	All i-wind-im deewai.	(20) They blow the flutes.
(21)	All-right-im bed.	(21) Make the bed.
(22)	Em i-all-right finish.	(22) It is already made.
(23)	You go help-im man be-long steer.	(23) Go and help the steersman.
(24)	Youfela mus' go long bush.	(24) You (pl.) must go to the back-woods.
(25)	All i-go finish.	(25) They have gone.

Q. 5. Below are the nominative and objective forms of our English pronominal system. In the blank after each term, place its equivalent in Melanesian Pidgin. If there is no equivalent in the corpus, use a zero.

Q. 6. When you have finished Question 5, study the pattern of the MP pronouns. In the light of this pattern, what forms would you predict that the zero slots might contain? A prediction like this, based on symmetry of pattern, is often made by the linguistic scientist. It is an hypothesis, which the examination of further data may confirm or invalidate.

	Singular				*Plural*	
	Nom.	*Obj.*			*Nom.*	*Obj.*
1.	I ____	me ____			we ____	us ____
2.	you ____	you ____			you ____	you ____
3.	he ____	him ____			they ____	them ____
	she ____	her ____				
	it ____	it ____				

Q. 7. What is the distinction between *mefela* and *you-me*, both of which have the same translation in English?

(26)	Me razor-im grass belong face.	(26)	I am shaving my beard.
(27)	Lapun man i-lookout-im pickaninny.	(27)	The old man looked after the child.
(28)	Bimeby me come.	(28)	I will come.
(29)	Sun i-burn-im ground.	(29)	The sun burns the ground.
(30)	I-got dry water.	(30)	There is an ebb tide.
(31)	Long disfela tin, i-got bull-ma-cow.	(31)	In this tin there is beef.
(32)	I-got sheepy-sheep?	(32)	Is there any mutton?
(33)	Me stop here.	(33)	I am here.
(34)	Me stop policeboy.	(34)	I am a native policeman.
(35)	Dis-kind man i-no-stop goodfela alltime.	(35)	This kind of man is not always good.
(36)	Papa i-go finish.	(36)	The father is gone.
(37)	Man belong long-way place i-kaikai finish.	(37)	The foreigners have eaten.
(38)	Behind, me cut-im bush.	(38)	I shall cut the bush.

Q. 8. Do MP verbs change in form to show past, present, or future time? (For example, English verbs change in form to show past time, as in *beam, beamed,* but do not change in form to show future time, as in *beam, will beam.* Instead, a word must be added to show the future.)

Q. 9. What does the verbal suffix *-im* indicate?

Q. 10. How is the meaning "there is" expressed?

Q. 11. How is the verb *to be* (*am, is, are, was, were*) expressed?

Q. 12. What is the signal for completed action?

Q. 13. How does Melanesian Pidgin show that a happening will occur in the future?

FURTHER READINGS

Davies, Hugh Sykes. *Grammar Without Tears.* New York: The John Day Company, Inc., 1953

Francis, W. Nelson. *The English Language.* New York: W. W. Norton & Company, Inc., 1963, 1965. See pp. 13–68.

Gleason, H. A., Jr. *Linguistics and English Grammar.* New York: Holt, Rinehart and Winston, Inc. 1965.

Hall, Robert A. Jr. *Linguistics and Your Language*. New York: Doubleday & Company, Inc., 1960. See pp. 97–120.

Laird, Charlton. *The Miracle of Language*. New York: The World Publishing Company, 1953. See pp. 141–210.

Ornstein, Jacob and William W. Gage. *The ABC's of Languages and Linguistics*. Philadelphia: Chilton Books, 1964. See pp. 80–86.

Postal, Paul M. "Underlying and Superficial Linguistic Structure." *Harvard Educational Review* 34:246–266. (Special issue, Spring 1964). On transformational grammar.

Potter, Simeon. *Modern Linguistics*. London: Andre Deutsch, 1957. See pp. 104–122.

Roberts, Paul. *Understanding Grammar*. New York: Harper & Row, Publishers, 1954. See pp. 1–24.

———. *English Sentences*. New York: Harcourt, Brace & World, Inc., 1962. A simple introduction to transformational grammar.

Sapir, Edward. *Language*. New York: Harcourt, Brace & World, Inc., 1921. See pp. 59–126.

Sledd, James. *A Short Introduction to English Grammar*. Chicago: Scott, Foresman and Company, 1959. For a good explanation of intonation and stress, see pp. 20–36.

Smith, Henry Lee, Jr. *Linguistic Science and the Teaching of English*. Cambridge: Harvard University Press, 1956.

Stageberg, Norman C. *An Introductory English Grammar*. New York: Holt, Rinehart and Winston, Inc., 1965. For material on stress and intonation, see pp. 45–73.

Thomas, Owen. *Transformational Grammar and the Teacher of English*. New York: Holt, Rinehart and Winston, Inc., 1965. A short introduction to transformational grammar.

10

CLEAR THINKING

Are All Generalizations False?

LIONEL RUBY

Occasionally one hears a person praised as a "smooth talker" or as having "the gift of gab." More often than not such expressions are disparaging, for they suggest mere verbalization, clever manipulation of words. We have spent a good deal of time in these readings trying to understand language as a structural system of meaningful signals. We must not forget that this marvelous system is after all symbolic, that it is, in Sapir's words, a "method of communicating ideas, emotions, and desires." We have an obligation to use verbal symbols, our language, responsibly—to speak and write with clarity and precision. And this involves clear thinking. In the readings that follow we shall be concerned with matters of clear thinking and with some of the traps that lie in wait for the unwary.

We constantly make inferences and judgments based on past knowledge and experience and on our observations of the world around us. We constantly make assumptions that what was true in one particular instance is true in another. In other words, we constantly generalize. Moreover, we act on the basis of these generalizations as if they were in fact true. Sometimes we are right, and sometimes we are wrong. Which generalizations are reliable guides? Can we ever be sure? Are all generalizations false? These are some of the questions Lionel Ruby deals with in the next selection. Professor Ruby is Chairman of the Philosophy Department at Roosevelt University in Chicago.

From *The Art of Making Sense*, by Lionel Ruby. Copyright 1954 by Lionel Ruby. Published by J. B. Lippincott Co.

We begin with a generalization: human beings are great generalizers. Every race has its proverbs, and proverbs are generalizations. "It never rains but it pours." "Faint heart never won fair lady." "Familiarity breeds contempt." Sometimes, of course, these proverbs are incompatible with each other, as in "Absence makes the heart grow fonder," and "Out of sight, out of mind."[1]

Listen attentively to those around you, and note the generalizations that float into every conversation: Europeans are lazy and shiftless. European girls make good wives. American girls are selfish. Politicians are crooks. Gentlemen prefer blondes. On a somewhat more "intellectual" level, we find: Liberals never think a matter through. Intellectuals always show a lack of practical judgment. Americans are idealists. Americans are materialists. All American men suffer from "momism." Economics is bunk. Modern art is trash. Psychiatrists never bring up their own children properly. In the middle ages everyone was religious. And so on. After more of the same we may be tempted to agree with Justice Holmes that "the chief end of man is to frame general propositions, and no general proposition is worth a damn."

Our awareness of the inadequacy of "sweeping generalizations" may lead us to say that all generalizations are false. But this is truly a sweeping generalization! And worse: if it is true, then the witticism that "all generalizations are false, *including this one*" would appear to be justified. But this will not do either, for this generalization asserts that it itself is false, from which it follows that it is not the case that all generalizations are false. Or perhaps we should say that "all generalizations are half-truths—including this one"? But this is not much better. The fact of the matter is that some generalizations are true, others are false, and still others are uncertain or doubtful. The deadliness of this platitude may be forgiven because of its truth.

By a "generalization" is meant a general law or principle which is inferred from particular facts. As a sample of the way in which we arrive at such generalizations consider the following: Some years ago I visited France, and ate at a number of Parisian restaurants that had been recommended to me. The food was excellent in each. Then one day I was unable to get to any of my customary eating places. I ate in a small restaurant in an outlying district of Paris. The food was excellent. I then tried other restaurants always with the same results.

[1] Once translated by a foreign student as "invisible idiot."

I ate in large restaurants, small restaurants, on ships and trains, and in railway station restaurants. I generalized: All French restaurants serve excellent meals.

A generalization is a statement that *goes beyond* what is actually observed, to a rule or law covering both the observed cases and those that have not as yet been observed. This going-beyond is called the "inductive leap." An inductive leap is a "leap in the dark," for the *generalization may not be true*, even though the *observations* on which it is based *are* true. Thus, somewhere in France there may be a poor French restaurant—happily I am ignorant of its location—but if so, then I should not say that *all* are good.

A generalization involves an "inductive leap." The word *induction*, from Latin roots meaning "to lead in," means that we examine particular cases (French restaurants), and "lead in" to a generalization. Induction is the method we use when we learn lessons from our experience: we generalize from particular cases. *Deduction*, on the other hand, refers to the process of "drawing out" the logical consequences of what we already know (or assume) to be true. By induction we learn that French cooking is delectable. If a friend tells us that he had tasteless meals while in Europe, then by deduction we know that he did not eat in French restaurants. Both induction and deduction are essential characteristics of rational thinking.

A generalization is a statement of the form: "All A's are B's." "All" means exactly what it says: *all* without exception. A single exception overthrows a generalization of this kind. Before we proceed further we must first dispose of a popular confusion concerning the expression: "The exception proves the rule." This is a sensible statement when properly interpreted, but it is sometimes understood in a manner that makes it nonsense. If I say that "all A's are B's," a single exception will make my statement false. Now, suppose that someone says: "The fact that there is a poor French restaurant proves that *all* are good because *it* is an exception, and the exception proves the rule!" Does a wicked woman prove that all women are saints? The sensible interpretation of the expression, "The exception proves the rule" is this: When we *say* that a certain case *is* an "exception," we imply that there is a rule which is generally true. When a mother tells her daughter, "Have a good time at the prom, and, for tonight, you have my permission to stay out until 3 A.M.," she implies that this is an exception to the rule which requires earlier reporting. A statement that *creates* an exception implies a rule for all non-exceptional cases; but a generalization that is stated as a rule without exceptions (all A's are B's) would be overthrown by a single exception.

All too often "general propositions are not worth a damn," as Holmes remarked. This is because we generalize too hastily on the basis of insufficient evidence. The fallacy called the "hasty generalization" simply refers to the fact that we jump too quickly to conclusions concerning "all." For example, we see a woman driving carelessly, and generalize: "All women are poor drivers." We see a car weaving in and out of traffic, and note that it has a California license: "Wouldn't you know," we say. "A California driver. That's the way they all drive out there." Anita Loos' gay heroine thought that gentlemen preferred blondes because she was a blonde and men were attracted to her.

We learn that Napoleon got along on five hours of sleep. From this we may conclude that "five hours of sleep is all that anybody really needs." Our assumption is that what Napoleon could do, anybody can do, until we learn that we are not Napoleons. (If we don't learn this eventually, we aren't permitted to circulate freely.) The next example is undoubtedly the worst example of generalizing ever committed: A man declared that all Indians walk single file. When challenged for his evidence, he replied, "How do I know that? I once saw an Indian walk that way."

Hasty generalizing is perhaps the most important of popular vices in thinking. It is interesting to speculate on some of the reasons for this kind of bad thinking. One important factor is prejudice. If we are already prejudiced against unions, or businessmen, or lawyers, or doctors, or Jews, or Negroes, then one or two instances of bad conduct by members of these groups will give us the unshakeable conviction that "they're all like that." It is very difficult for a prejudiced person to say, "Some are, and some aren't." A prejudice is a judgment formed *before* examining the evidence.

A psychological reason for asserting "wild" generalizations is exhibitionism: The exhibitionist desires to attract attention to himself. No one pays much attention to such undramatic statements as "Some women are fickle," or that some are liars, or "Some politicians are no better than they ought to be." But when one says that "all women are liars" this immediately attracts notice. Goethe once said that is it easy to appear brilliant if one respects nothing, not even the truth.

Let us avoid careless and hasty generalizing. The proverb warns us that one swallow does not make a summer. Unfortunately, we usually forget proverbs on the occasions when we ought to remember them. We ought to emulate "the Reverend" in Faulkner's novel, *The Hamlet*. He was discussing the efficacy of a rural remedy. "Do you know it will work, Reverend?" his friend asked. "I know it worked once," the Reverend answered. "Oh, then you have knowed it to fail?" "I never knowed it to be tried but once." The fault of bad generalizing, however, need not make us take refuge in the opposite error: the refusal to generalize. This error is illustrated in the anecdote concerning the student who wrote an essay on labor relations, in which he argued for equal pay for women. Women, he wrote, work hard, they need the money, they are the foundation of the family, and, most important, they are the mothers of most of the human race! There is another old anecdote about the cautious man whose friend pointed to a flock of sheep with the remark, "Those sheep seem to have been sheared recently." "Yes," said the cautious man, "at least on this side."

Generalizations are dangerous, but we must generalize. To quote Justice Holmes once more: he said that he welcomed "anything that will discourage men from believing general propositions." But, he added, he welcomed that "only less than he welcomed anything that would encourage men to make such propositions"! For generalizations are indispensable guides. One of the values of knowledge lies in its predictive power—its power to predict the future. Such knowledge is stated in generalizations. It is of little help to me to know that water froze at 32° F. yesterday unless this information serves as a warning to put anti-freeze in my car radiator before winter comes. History, in the "pure" sense of this term, merely tells us what has happened in the past, but science furnishes us with general laws, and general laws tell us what *always* happens under certain specified conditions.

Science is interested in the general, rather than in the particular or individual. When Newton saw an apple fall from a tree in his orchard—even if this story is a fable, and therefore false in a literal sense, it is true in its insight—he was not interested in the size and shape of the apple. Its fall suggested an abstract law to him, the law of gravity. He framed this law in general terms: Every particle of matter attracts every other particle of matter with a force directly proportional to the product of their masses and inversely proportional to the square of their distances. Chemists seek general laws concerning the behavior of matter. The physician wants to know the general characteristics of the disease called myxedema, so that when he has a case he will recognize it and know exactly how to treat it. The finding of general laws, then, is the aim of all science—including history insofar as it is a science.

The problem of the scientist is one of achieving sound generaliza-tions. The scientist is careful not to make assertions which outrun his evidence, and he refuses to outtalk his information. He generalizes, but recognizes that no generalization can be more than probable, for we can never be certain that *all* the evidence is in, nor can the future be guaranteed absolutely—not even future eclipses of the sun and moon. But the scientist knows that certain laws have a very high degree of probability.

Let us look at the logic involved in forming sound generalizations. The number of cases investigated in the course of formulating a scien-tific law is a factor in establishing the truth of the law, but it is by no means the most important one. Obviously, if we observed one hundred swans, all of which are white, our generalization that "all swans are white" does not have the same probabliity it would have if we observed one thousand swans. But no matter how great the number of specimens involved in this type of observation, no more than a high degree of probability is ever established. Countless numbers of white swans were observed throughout the ages (without any exceptions) and then in the nineteenth century black swans were observed in Australia.

The weakness of the method of "induction by simple enumeration of cases" is amusingly illustrated by Bertrand Russell's parable in his *A History of Western Philosophy:*

There was once upon a time a census officer who had to record the names of all householders in a certain Welsh village. The first that he questioned was called William Williams; so were the second, third, fourth. . . . At last he said to himself: "This is tedious; evidently they are all called William Williams. I shall put them down so and take a holiday." But he was wrong; there was just one whose name was John Jones.

Scientific generalizations based on other types of evidence than simple enumeration often acquire a much higher degree of probability after only a few observations. When a chemist finds that pure sulphur melts at 125° C., in an experiment in which every factor is accurately analyzed and controlled, the law concerning the melting point of sulphur achieves as great a degree of certainty as is humanly attainable. Accurate control of every element of one case, then is more important in establishing probabilities than is *mere enumeration* of many cases.

A single carefully controlled experiment, such as the sulphur ex-periment, can give us a much higher degree of probability than the mere observation of thousands of swans. The reason is that we also know that no chemical element thus far observed has a variable melting point under conditions of constant pressure. The chemical law is thus consistent with and is borne out by the rest of chemical knowledge, whereas the "law" holding that all swans are white was based on an "accidental" factor. Or consider the generalization concerning the mortality of mankind. This law is based not merely on the fact that countless numbers of human beings have died in the past, but also on the fact that all living beings must, by reason of physiological limitations, die; and that all matter wears out in time. So the harmony of a particular generalization with the rest of our knowledge is also a factor in giving it a high degree of probability.

So much for the logical analysis of generalizations. Thus far, we have been concerned with "uniform" generalizations, which take the form: "all A's are B's." A generalization, we have seen, is a statement that says something about "all" of a group, the evidence consisting of observations of items in which we always find a single characteristic. The observed cases are taken as a *sample* of the whole group or population with which we are concerned. We observe a number of swans, and take these as a sample of all swans, past, present, and future. We find that all are white, and make the inductive leap: Swans are always white, everywhere.

We shall now examine "statistical" statements. Statistical statements give us information not about characteristics possessed by *all* of a group or population, but by a definite proportion (or most) of the group or population, as when we say, "Most A's are B's" or "Sixty-five per cent of all A's are B's" The first thing to note here is that statistical statements may in fact be *generalizations*, and thus involve the notions of "all." This point involves very important (and common) misunderstandings.

In order to make this point clear, let us re-interpret our "uniform" generalizations. We say: "The sample is so-and-so (all observed swans are uniformly white)—*therefore*, the whole population of swans are uniformly white." Now, we do the same sort of thing in statistical generalizations. We say: "In the sample of red-heads we examined, fifty-three per cent were hot-tempered—therefore, fifty-three per cent of *all* redheads are hot-tempered." (Or: fifty-three per cent of the whole population of red-heads is hot-tempered.) Logically, both examples, uniform and statistical, are of the same type, for in each we make the inductive leap from the sample to the whole population. The only difference between them is that in the one case we assert a *uniform*

character in the whole population; in the other we assert that a characteristic holds in a certain *proportion* in the whole population.

This fundamental point will help us to evaluate the degree of
probability of a statistical generalization. We saw earlier that uniform
generalizations can never be absolutely certain—though for practical
purposes we often consider them so, especially in the physical sciences.
The probability of a generalization depends especially on the *quality*
and also on the *quantity* of the cases that constitute the sample. The
same holds for statistical generalizations, which may have a high
probability, depending on the character of the evidence. Though the
inductive leap is involved in all generalizations, in some cases the leap
is justified. Let us examine the criteria of justification for the leap.

Before we proceed we shall discuss an important distinction: that
between the sample and the inference we draw from it. It is one thing
to describe a sample accurately; quite another to draw an accurate
inference. If I say, "I have observed ten swans [the sample] and all
were white," we may assume that the sample is accurately described.
But if I now go on to generalize (that is, draw the inference) concerning
all swans, my inference may not be a good one. A generalization always
involves a "leap in the dark," sometimes justified and sometimes not.
Similarly, if I say, "I have talked to ten friends concerning their
income, and six [sixty per cent] told me that they earned more than
$10,000 a year," the description of the sample may be accepted as true.
But suppose I now go on to make the following inference: "Therefore,
sixty per cent of all Americans earn more than $10,000 a year." This
would be a hasty generalization indeed.

We distinguish, then, between the sample and the inference. A
statistical statement concerning the sample is purely descriptive. The
book *They Went to College* is a statistical study as of 1947, of 9,064 college
graduates. Averages are given. Fifty-three per cent were in business,
sixteen per cent were doctors, lawyers or dentists, sixteen per cent were
teachers. The doctors earned the most: over half making more than
$7,500 a year. Teachers and preachers earned the least: median income
$3,584. Now, these averages involve no inferences. They simply describe
the actual facts *in the sample*. We draw an inference, on the other hand,
when we assume that the whole population of six million college
graduates will show the same kinds of averages as the sample. In our
discussion, henceforth, we shall be concerned only with the logical
problems in statistical inferences.

Suppose that a public opinion poll was recently taken. The polling organization tells us that fifty-eight per cent of the American people approve of the record of the present administration in Washington. How do they know this? Let us examine the evidence on which this finding is based. Obviously not everyone was consulted. A sample was taken. There were three thousand interviews. Since there are seventy-five million adults in the United States, each individual in this sample is taken as representative of twenty-five thousand adults. Further, in the sample, one thousand persons said that they had "no opinion." Eleven hundred and sixty said that they "approved," and eight hundred and forty said they did not. Thus fifty-eight per cent of those with opinions approved, and this means, we are told, that forty-three and one-half million Americans approve. The pollsters assume that the undecided individuals will probably divide in the same proportion as the others when they make up their minds.

Now, we are not raising any questions concerning the truth of the report made of the sample. But is the inductive leap from the sample to the generalization concerning seventy-five million people justified? It may be. It all depends upon the reliability of the sample. What makes a sample reliable? It must be *fair, unbiased,* and *representative* of the whole. But what determines whether it has these characteristics? This is the crucial question.

The size of the sample is obviously important. A sample of one hundred would not be so reliable as one of one thousand, and one thousand would not be so reliable as one of a million. But numbers in themselves are not the most important factor in establishing the reliability of generalizations or inferences.

The unimportance of large numbers as such is best illustrated by the ill-fated *Literary Digest* presidential election poll in 1936. The magazine sent pre-election ballots to ten million persons, and received over two million responses. The responses showed Landon running ahead of Roosevelt. In the election in November, however, Roosevelt got about twenty-eight million votes; Landon around eighteen million.

The reason for this colossal failure was the unrepresentative character of the sample. The *Digest* took names "at random" from telephone directories and lists of registered owners of automobiles. These were relatively well-to-do folk. The lower income groups, however, were completely, or almost completely, unrepresented.

An ideal sample is one taken "at random" from the entire population, and not from a selected portion of the population being studied. The Gallup, Roper, and Crossley polls have proved more successful—

barring a spectacular failure in 1948—than the *Literary Digest* poll. Let us see how the Gallup poll operates. A sample of three thousand individuals is taken, but with great care to make the sample representative. The population is classified into sub-groups by geographic regions, by rural or urban residence, economic status, age, education, and declared politics. In 1948, for example, Gallup estimated that twenty-eight per cent of the American people live in the Middle Atlantic states, ten percent on the West Coast; that thirty-four per cent live in cities of over 100,000 population; that twenty-three per cent are of an "average" economic station; that forty-three per cent are between the ages of thirty and forty-nine; that forty-two per cent have gone to high schools; and that thirty-eight per cent call themselves Democrats, thirty-six per cent Republicans, and twenty-six per cent independents or members of smaller parties. The three thousand interviews in the sample are distributed so that each geographic area, each economic group, etc., will be represented in its appropriate numerical strength.

Individuals are then chosen "at random," rather than by selection, from within each sub-group, and the resulting sample is highly representative of the whole population. The Gallup poll enjoys a successful record, on the whole, except for 1948. In other words, the method works, and one must respect its findings. But no poll can ever eliminate the possibility of error, or guarantee accuracy except within a margin of error of several percentage points. And in a presidential election forecast the pollster is either completely right or completely wrong in predicting who will win. Odds of 10 to 1 against a candidate of one of the major parties are probably not justified even if all the polls are unanimous as to the final results. These were the odds against Harry Truman in 1948!

An election prediction can be judged by the election results, and a long series of successful predictions gives us confidence in the methods of the pollsters. This check cannot be made on polls which tabulate public opinion on issues of the day, for the whole population is never counted. Similarly for polls which rate television shows, for the whole audience is not counted. Such polls, of course, also generalize on the basis of samples. To illustrate the logical problems in assessing the reliability of a statistical study of the "public opinion poll" type we shall comment on *Sexual Behavior in the Human Female* by Alfred C. Kinsey and his staff.

Kinsey's study tabulates and classifies data concerning 5,940 white American females, ages two to ninety. He does not claim that his averages necessarily apply to all human females, despite the title of his book, nor even to all American women, of whom there are approximately seventy millions. It is inevitable, however, that such inferences will be drawn, and our question is: Are such inferences justified? This depends entirely on the representativeness of Kinsey's sample.

Critics of Kinsey's report have emphasized the unrepresentativeness of his sample. His subjects are not distributed proportionately in geographic areas: most are from Illinois, Florida, and California. They are more highly educated than a representative cross-section of the population: seventy-five per cent of his subjects went to college, as compared with a national average of thirteen per cent. Three per cent of his women did not go beyond grade school as compared with the national average of thirty-seven per cent. A larger than average proportion are from middle and upper economic groups. Very few of the women were Roman Catholics or orthodox Jews.

Critics have also argued that the very nature of the study involves a kind of bias, for many women will refuse to discuss matters of such "delicate privacy" with interviewers, so that his volunteers must be unrepresentative of women in general. And there is also the problem of credibility. Critics have said that people who like to talk about such things tend to understate or overstate, and even to fabricate a little.

Kinsey, of course, recognizes the limitations and incompleteness of his sample, and, as noted, does not claim that it is representative of the whole population. But it will be interpreted in this way, and if Kinsey wished to avoid such interpretations, he should have called his study "Sexual Behavior of 5,940 Women." Inferences would probably be drawn however, even if he had so titled his study.

The elements of distortion in Kinsey's sample detract from its reliability as a basis for generalizing. On the other hand, as a review of the book in *Life* put it, though the statistics are not perfect they are at any rate "the only statistics in town." His study is by no means worthless as an index of sexual behavior. We must not use an "all or nothing" approach here. The reliability of his sample with respect to university women as a single group, for example, is certainly much higher than that for the female population as a whole. But we cannot conclude that the whole female population resembles the sample since the sample is not a representative one.

Generalizations in statistics, then, are judged by the same logical criteria we use in judging any generalizations. Fallacies, however, are more common in statistical than they are in uniform generalizations.

For it is easier to check on the reliability of a uniform generalization: one exception overthrows the general rule or "law." In statistics, however, since nothing is said about any specific individual, an exception" is a meaningless term. An exceptional individual does not disprove an "average." But there is, as we have already noted, a method for checking the reliability of a statistical generalization concerning a population, and that is to count the whole "voting" population. But even a test of this kind is not conclusive, for many of the voters do not vote on election day, because of laziness, overconfidence, or some other reason.

Errors of inference in statistics are frequently overlooked because of the mathematical language in which statistics are presented. The spell which numbers weave often prevents us from seeing errors in arguments—errors which would be obvious were they not clothed in mathematical garb. And many dishonest reasoners take advantage of this fact and present highly selected data for purposes of propaganda rather than information. Misuses of the science of statistics have resulted in such jibes as, "Figures don't lie, but liars figure," and "There are three kinds of lies: ordinary lies, damnable lies, and statistics." But these cynical remarks should not be taken as criticisms of statistics. The fault never lies with the figures, or with the science, but with their careless use. It is simply not the case that "you can prove anything with figures" (or statistics), just as it is never the case that "you can prove anything by logic." To the uninitiated, it just *seems* that you can.

SUGGESTED ASSIGNMENTS

1. Study the following sample assignment: Stand near a soda fountain for exactly one hour during a rush period. Make a count of the male and female customers who order (1) coffee, cokes or other cola drinks, (2) sundaes, ice cream sodas, malted milks, milk shakes, pie, cake, and cookies, (3) sandwiches. From your assembled data, make any generalizations that seem justifiable. You might come up with generalizations like these:
   a. Women (or men) eat more fattening food than men (or women).
   b. At soda fountains, men prefer sandwiches while women prefer sweets.
   c. Men drink more stimulants than women do.
   d. At such and such a soda fountain between the hours of . . . and . . . , more men than women order sandwiches.
   e. Women get more hungry than men between the hours of . . . and . . .

Bring to class any generalizations that seem valid to you, together with one or two that you think questionable, for class discussion.

Now, try to devise a simple statistical study like the one above and write up your data, making one or more sound generalizations, if possible.

2. An AP feature story begins by pointing out that the four sons of a famous popular singer have given their father trouble. Then the story continues by telling of the children of other celebrities: "His brother Bob's son, Chris, 15, was once arrested when police said he tried to steal a car.

"Edward G. Robinson, Jr., has been in the news repeatedly with drunk arrests.

"John Barrymore, Jr., made the papers recently with a felony hit and run, drunk driving charge. His half-sister, Diana, wrote a teary book about her long battle with alcoholism.

"Charles Chaplin, Jr., has a police record for drunkenness.

"Barbara Ann Burns, daughter of the late comedian Bob Burns, was sentenced to 90 days for drug addiction.

"Chris Crawford, adopted son of Joan Crawford, was arrested on a delinquency charge . . . after a shooting spree with an air rifle. And then there was Cheryl Crane, daughter of Lana Turner, who killed her mother's lover—but was later absolved of blame."

On the basis of this evidence, what generalization could you safely make about the character of the children of movie actors and actresses?

3. The following case is based on fact, but the details are hypothetical. A university professor recently found some spelling tests that had been given to high school students 25 years ago in the area of Indiana and Illinois, and he found the scores made by these students. He gave the same tests to 100 students each in 10 high schools in the same states. Then he compared the results. He found that the students he tested did appreciably better than those students who had taken the same tests 25 years ago. And from these cases he drew this conclusion, or generalization: "Our high schools today are teaching students to spell better than did the schools of 25 years ago." Write a paragraph discussing the soundness of his generalization.

4. The following events are both true:

    a. A news story carried by *Time* magazine for April 21, 1947 reported that a well-behaved high school sophomore, Stuart Allen, murdered a church sexton in cold blood by striking him over the head with a hammer as hard as he could. When arrested, he confessed readily and made it clear that he had never disliked the sexton. "He was a nice fellow," Stuart said. But he had to admit that he didn't feel a bit sorry. With an apologetic chuckle he confided, "I have no remorse at all." Stuart's father was the rector of the Christ Episcopal Church. Stuart had been adopted when he was three months old.

b. Another news story given out by the Associated Press two days later reported that a 23-year-old youth had shot two policemen to death in a street corner battle. This youth was the son of a Northwestern University professor. He had also been adopted. From these cases what generalizations would you make about the following:
    (1) The character of adopted children
    (2) The kind of upbringing that professional men give their children.
    (3) The effect of heredity upon character

5. Specify two situations in which a single case is satisfactory for a generalization (e.g., the temperature of the water in a bath tub).

6. Comment on the following generalization: "Poets are crazy. Look at Blake and Cowper and Smart—they were all wacky and I can prove it."

7. Many of our folk proverbs are generalizations which are said to represent the accumulated wisdom of the people through many generations. How can we account for the presence of contradictory proverbs like these:
    a. Two heads are better than one.
        Too many cooks spoil the broth.
    b. He who hesitates is lost.
        Look before you leap.

8. A university professor who examined the letters of about 500 college graduates found 45 "if" clauses containing either a *was* or a *were*. Of these clauses, 12 contained the construction type "If I were" and 33 contained an "If I was." From this evidence, what generalization could he safely make about the use of *was* or *were* in an "if" clause among college graduates?

9. Write a theme on "The Values and Hazards of Generalizing."

Evaluation of Evidence

W. W. LITTLE, W. H. WILSON, and W. E. MOORE

Much of what is studied in college is presented in the form of theories, propositions, and conclusions. All of these involve not only facts but also inferences—somebody's interpretation of the facts. For example, inferences are involved in the study of sociology and that of economics, as well as in the study of history and of law. Whenever we read material of this kind, we engage, consciously or unconsciously, in a continuous process of acceptance, rejection, or suspended judgment. When the evidence is con-vincing, we accept what we read; when the evidence is unconvincing, we reject it; when no evidence is presented, or when we have no basis for evaluating the evidence, we mark the place with a mental question mark and withhold judgment. The interesting question in this process is how do we know when evidence is convincing? Not all evidence is of the same sort, nor is it all equally reliable. If you were to make an assertion that seemed to you to be true, and were asked to give evidence to support your statement, you might reply that you arrived at your belief on the basis of personal observation, or the observation of others, or that you had it on good authority. In some instances, your con-clusions might involve all three. These three different sorts of evidence and the problems involved in evaluating each kind are discussed in the next essay by Messrs. Little, Wil-son, and Moore, all professors of logic at the University of Florida.

Personal observation

The raw material of inference, we have noted, is *fact*, which we defined as "a thing which has been demonstrated to be true by direct observa-tion, without inference or interpretation." When the witness testifies in court that he saw the defendant leaving the scene of the crime, carrying a smoking revolver, he is *claiming* to be stating a fact, for the thing he says happened could have been verified by direct observation without benefit of inference or interpretation. Even so, the jury must decide whether to accept his statement as fact or to take it with reservations. For the witness could be lying or mistaken about what he saw. The jury must, in effect, judge the reliability of the testimony as evidence. Henceforth, to keep our meaning clear, let us label any statement which claims to be a description of what happened and to be free of inference or interpretation an *allegation of fact;* let us reserve the single word *fact* for statements which we have tested and found to be reliable. For example, let us label the testimony of our witness an allegation of fact until we have ample reason to believe that what he claimed happened actually did happen. In judging the reliability of allegations

The selection from Winston W. Little, W. Harold Wilson, and W. Edgar Moore, *Applied Logic*, copyright 1955, is reprinted by permission of and arrangement with Houghton Mifflin Company, the authorized publishers.

of fact we shall rely mainly on the correspondence theory, for what we want to know is whether or not the allegation coincides with reality. The criterion we shall apply, then, is observation through our sensory equipment.

If you have been in the habit of assuming that your personal observations are always reliable, the time has come to disillusion yourself. Observation is not so simple and accurate as we might like to think, for it involves a mental process called *perception*. Perception is interpretation of physical sensations. I see and hear an object coming down the road; I *perceive* that it is an automobile. The visual and auditory sensations are merely clues which I interpret to be coming from an automobile.

One need reflect only a moment to realize that we make innumerable errors of perception. We interpret the sparkle of dew in the grass for the dime we are looking for, we are frightened in the night when we interpret garments hanging on a chair to be a burglar, we interpret the backfire of an automobile to be a gunshot. In recent years deer hunting has become a dangerous sport because eager hunters sometimes interpret a movement in the underbrush to be a deer and fire away. They perceive the movement to be a deer without waiting for sufficient clues to make an accurate interpretation.

The degree of reliability of personal observations will depend on a number of factors, six of which are discussed here.[1]

(1) The first of these factors is the *physical equipment* of the observer. Sensory acuity varies greatly among individuals. What one individual sees sharply at one hundred feet another will see only as a blur. What one individual hears distinctly another will not hear at all. Even the sharpest eye can be fooled by an optical illusion.[2] In scientific procedure, where accurate measurement is essential, elaborate instruments and techniques for measurement have been designed to reduce reliance on the senses as much as possible. The laboratory technician who estimated temperature and weight by feel, or length by sight, would not last long in his job.

(2) The second factor is the *physical conditions* surrounding the observation. When one is sitting in the grandstand well to one side of home plate, his physical situation is not as favorable for calling balls

---

[1] For a more complete discussion of observation, see Harold L. Larrabee, *Reliable Knowledge* (Boston, Houghton Mifflin Company, 1945), pp. 127–164.

[2] A number of these illusions appear on p. 146 of Larrabee, *op. cit.*

and strikes as is that of the umpire. The coach at a football game is not in a good position to observe some aspects of the action on the field, and for that reason stations an observer in the press box high above the field. The further away you are from the scene of an accident the less reliable your perceptions of it will be. One should not expect his perceptions to be entirely reliable when the light is poor or when other conditions make accurate perception difficult.

(3) Some types of observation require a high degree of *skill*. The observer stationed in the press box by the coach will be useless unless he is a skilled observer of football. The average spectator at the game would be quite unable to determine such matters as whether the linemen are charging properly or whether the blockers are carrying out their assignments.

(4) The accuracy of observations is affected adversely by *prejudice*. What we see in a situation is determined to a considerable measure by what we are looking for. In a fight between two students, the fraternity brother of one of the participants may *see* that the other student provoked the fight and landed all the underhanded blows. The boxing coach, on the other hand, may *see* only the skill or the lack of it displayed by the two antagonists. A little experimentation will quickly show that observation is selective. We rarely perceive all the elements in a situation. Instead, we tend to perceive those elements in which we are interested or those which call themselves to our attention. All of us, walking into a dormitory room, would probably perceive a blazing wastebasket, but once the fire is extinguished the occupant of the room and a housing official would probably not perceive the same elements in the situation. We tend to perceive the things in which we are most interested.

(5) Our accuracy as observers is affected adversely by *emotion*. To a person who is afraid, the snake looks bigger than it is; the rowboat in rough, open water seems smaller than it is; an approaching car seems to be moving faster than it is; and an innocent gesture by an antagonist becomes the motion of reaching for a gun. Under emotional stress a person is more susceptible to suggestion. If the emotional stress is strong enough, a person may become subject to hallucinations and delusions.

(6) When we must depend upon *memory* to recall our observations, they are hardly ever exact. The more time that elapses between the observation itself and the moment we try to recall it, the more opportunity there is for our imaginations to help us re-create the situation

to conform to what we wanted to happen. We seldom remember that which we feel no need to remember. Witness how quickly we forget the telephone number we do not expect to use again. If we are later called upon to recall something we did not expect to have to remember, we may unconsciously call upon our imaginations to supply the forgotten perceptions.

The careful thinker would do well to learn his own limitations as an observer and to be suspicious of his own observations whenever the situation demands skill or sensory acuity close to his limits, whenever prejudice or emotion are present, and whenever he must depend upon memory to recall what happened. Certainty is rarely obtainable in observation, and few observations should be accepted as facts unless they have been confirmed by more than one observer.

Reported observations

When the evidence consists of observations made by persons other than ourselves, all the considerations affecting personal observations apply. In determining the reliability of the observation we should ask ourselves how good the observer's sensory equipment is, how favorable the physical conditions were for making such an observation, whether the observer has sufficient skill for making such an observation, what the observer's bias is, whether emotion was present in the observer, and how much the observer had to depend upon memory. And there is an additional question we should ask: is the observer telling the truth as he knows it?

Some of the problems of evaluating this type of evidence can be seen in a trial at law, where the testimony of witnesses may constitute most or even all of the evidence.[3] Over the years our courts have evolved an elaborate code to protect themselves against testimony which is false or undesirable from a judicial point of view. The code governs such matters as what kind of testimony may be admitted in evidence, who may give the testimony and under what circumstances and at what stage in the proceedings, and how the testimony of a witness may be attacked or questioned. One of the principal functions of the judge is to act as umpire in enforcing these rules of evidence. Should he make a questionable decision on whether a given bit of

[3] The student interested in a non-technical description of legal proof should read *You Be the Judge,* by Ernest Mortenson (London, Longmans, Green & Co., Ltd., 1940), pp. 343–399.

evidence may be admitted for consideration, the decision may be made the basis of an appeal for a new trial. So elaborate have these rules become and so encrusted with qualifications and exceptions that ten heavy volumes are required to cover them.

Any lengthy examination of the code of evidence would be out of place in this text, but a brief discussion of a few points will serve to illustrate some of the ways in which the flaws in reported observations may be revealed in everyday life as well as in the courtroom. A considerable part of the code of evidence is designed to determine the relevancy of evidence. The problem is a difficult one. If attorneys were permitted to introduce all evidence that might possibly be relevant, the trial might drag on interminably and result in intolerable expense to the state and to the litigants. On the other hand, no evidence that is vital to the case should ever be excluded. Ruling on this point has furrowed the brow of many a judge.

Even a superficial study of the rules of evidence will show that the courts have been concerned with the same problems of evaluation which were discussed under the first topic of this chapter. When one side has presented a witness, the rules permit the other side to show if possible, either through cross-examination or through the introduction of other witnesses, that the witness did not have the physical equipment to observe accurately what he claimed to have observed, or that the physical conditions were not such as to make such observations accurate or that he lacked the skill to make such an observation, or that he was motivated by prejudice or emotion, or that his memory was faulty. There are rules, of course, complete with exceptions, to govern how this may be done. For example, a person may not be disqualified as a witness because of any mental defect unless this defect renders his testimony substantially untrustworthy on the specific point at issue.

Any attempt to discredit the testimony of a witness by an attack on his character may, of course, involve the fallacy of argumentum ad hominem. The judge must decide whether a given attack is relevant, and the jury must decide the value of any such evidence after it has been admitted. As might be expected, many entries in the code cover this point. For example, the prosecution is not permitted to introduce testimony attacking the character of the defendent except in rebuttal where the defense has offered testimony to show the good character of the defendant. This seemingly innocent little rule may pose a critical question for the defense. If the defense introduces any testimony at all to show the good character of the defendant, the prosecution may, by rebuttal, introduce testimony devastating to the character of the defendant.

As a general rule, the courts will not admit hearsay evidence, that is, testimony based on what the witness has heard others say, because experience has shown this kind of evidence to be generally unreliable. The person making the statement may have been mistaken in the first place, and he is not available for cross-examination. In the second place, the witness may be lying, and his observations as to what the other person said are subject to the usual errors of perception and understanding of language.

The principal weapon used in court against the unreliable witness, and particularly against the witness who is lying, is cross-examination. Any inconsistency in testimony, even on a minor point, which the cross-examiner can bring out helps to discredit the remainder of the testimony. Only a very clever witness is able to fabricate testimony without being caught by a skillful cross-examiner. The use of cross-examination is illustrated by a famous story about Abraham Lincoln's first defense at a murder trial. The prosecution's case rested mainly on testimony of a witness who swore that he saw the defendant fire the fatal shot and run away. In cross-examining this witness, Lincoln led him into testifying to a number of details: that he was standing twenty feet or more from the defendant at the time of the shooting, that the shooting occurred in heavy timber, that he could see how the pistol was pointed, that the shooting occurred at night and the nearest lights were candles three quarters of a mile away, that he saw the shooting by moonlight. Then Lincoln dramatically produced an almanac, offered it in evidence, and read from it that the moon did not rise until several hours after the shooting. Under the strain of the excitement, the witness broke down and confessed that he had fired the fatal shot himself.[4]

Evidence from authority

Frequently in everyday life we must depend on the opinions of authorities and use their opinions instead of factual evidence. When we go to a physician for diagnosis of an ailment, we must depend on his analysis and interpretation of facts in the form of symptoms. We must either accept his opinion or keep trying new doctors until we find

[4] For an account of this and other cases in which cross-examination played a vital part, see Francis L. Wellman, *The Art of Cross-Examination* (New York, The Macmillan Company, 1911).

one whose opinion we are willing to accept. Courts of law are coming to depend increasingly on expert witnesses as crime detection becomes more and more scientific. Physicians, psychiatrists, ballistics experts, fingerprint experts, and handwriting experts are frequently called to give testimony. Without the assistance of these experts, the average layman sitting on the jury would be helpless in trying to determine whether the defendant is insane, or whether the bullet that caused the death of the decedent came from the gun belonging to the defendant, or whether the ransom note was written by the defendant, or whether the prints left at the scene of the crime are those of the defendant or of his brother-in-law.

As citizens we cannot ourselves go to Washington to conduct a personal investigation of the affairs of our government; we must depend on reports and commentaries in the newspapers and on the radio. In more complicated affairs we must frequently rely on interpretations by commentators. Elmer Davis, a well-known radio commentator, has pointed out that newspapers, in their effort to be objective, do not tell the whole truth.[5] When one political personage falsely accuses another of being a Communist, the newspaper, trying to be objective, reports merely that so-and-so says so-and-so is a Communist. It does not point out to its readers that the speaker has no great reputation for veracity and has no way of knowing whether the accused person is or is not a Communist. Yet, without this background information, the newspaper reader has little chance to evaluate the statement correctly. This is one explanation, Mr. Davis thinks, for the increasing popularity of newspaper columnists and radio commentators. They supply the interpretation for which the public feels a need.

We are especially dependent on authorities in the field of value judgments. If I paint a picture which I think is good and you think is terrible, we can argue at length, and I can point out why I think it is good and you can point out why you think it is not. If the argument progresses far enough we may consult an expert, and if his opinion is contrary to mine, I can go hunt another expert. In matters of taste and value in any of the arts, about the best sources of evidence we have are the experts who have devoted much of their lives to a study of the subject. In ethical judgments our authorities are the philosophers. In religion the authorities we commonly turn to are the ministers of our own denomination.

[5] For an interesting discussion of this problem see Mr. Davis' article in the *Atlantic* (August, 1952).

How can we evaluate these authorities on whom we are forced to depend in making some of our most important decisions? There is no certain way, but there are certain earmarks which reliable authorities usually have and which unreliable ones frequently do not have.

In the first place, reliable authorities safeguard the accuracy of their conclusions by practicing the same techniques described in this book, together with some additional ones peculiar to their fields. They do not make snap judgments about important matters; they do carefully consider all the available evidence before making a decision. They do not search only for evidence to support the conclusions they wish to reach or have already reached; they do search for evidence contrary to the conclusions they would like to reach, and they weigh this evidence fully. They rarely commit such fallacies as undistributed middle.[6]

In the second place, reliable authorities do not resort to propaganda devices in presenting their findings. They do not merely present their opinions and depend on prestige, and perhaps confident manner, to gain acceptance for them; they do present the reasons for their conclusions, and they frequently express doubt about their conclusions, especially if the matter is difficult or complex. They do not present one-sided arguments; they do present both sides of the question fairly.

When an important issue is at stake, we need concern ourselves not only with the general reliability of the authority but with his reliability concerning the specific issue at stake. The student will be well advised to cultivate the habit of asking himself three questions about an authority before accepting his opinion.

(1) *How much does he know about the specific question at issue?* We are likely to assume that, because a man has achieved renown as an authority in one field, he must be a person of superior intelligence and therefore a competent authority in other fields as well. But we may be mistaken, for the world's greatest authority on ballistics may be the world's poorest authority on politics. Granted that he had to be a person of superior intellect to become a great authority in any field, he probably had to concentrate his effort on ballistics, to the neglect

---

[6] A common logical fallacy which may be illustrated by this syllogism:
Communists favor disarmament without international inspection.
Joe Blavatsky favors disarmament without international inspection.
Therefore
Joe Blavatsky is a Communist. [eds.]

of other matters. When we consult an authority, it is his competence in the field in question that matters. While there is no completely reliable rule for determining competence, there are a number of clues which will be helpful. In the learned professions membership in learned societies may be a clue. It is not necessarily true that a surgeon who is a Fellow in the American College of Surgeons is a better sugeon than one who is not, but the fact that he has been recognized by such an organization makes it probable that he is. Another clue is the degrees held and the institutions granting them. Possession of a Ph.D. degree from a reputable institution is not an absolute guarantee of competence in the field of the degree, but it is strong evidence in that direction. But remember that a Ph.D. in zymology does not qualify its holder as an authority in English literature. Your librarian can usually assist you in looking up clues to an authority's competence.

(2) *What is his personal interest in the matter in question?* Courts of law long ago recognized that the testimony of a witness is less reliable if he has a pecuniary or emotional interest in the matter on which he is testifying. If personal interest may make factual testimony unreliable, it may have an even more adverse effect on the reliability of opinions, and authorities are not exempt from this influence. In important matters it is well to try to ascertain what the authority's own peculiar interest is, if any, and discount his opinion accordingly. Civilian and military authorities may differ, for example, on how much money is needed for national defense. One should not infer that either of these authorities deliberately gives a false opinion in order to promote his own interests. Rather, the point is that as human beings they tend to see what they want to see. When the salesman tells you that the car he sells is the best in its field, he is not necessarily lying; he may merely blinded by his enthusiasm, and he could be right. We should be careful not to overlook emotional interests, which may frequently be more powerful than pecuniary ones. For example, an authority who gains renown for an opinion or a conclusion tends to develop an emotional attachment for it which will not allow him to give it up easily.

(3) *What do other authorities say about the matter?* When the issue is important, one should never depend on a single authority. No matter how reliable he seems, he may still be mistaken. This question is particularly applicable to radio commentators. By hearing several of them, preferably from different networks, discuss the same issue, one may not only come nearer to the whole truth but also gain some evidence as to which is the most reliable—provided, of course, he

listens critically and does not merely search for the commentator whose views most nearly coincide with his own.

SUGGESTED ASSIGNMENTS

1. In the present context, an observation is a statement of what one observes with his senses. An inference is a conclusion that one draws from his observations. Clip a large picture from a magazine. (Try to get one that is clear and has sharp contrasts so that it will be easy to see if your instructor projects it on the screen for discussion.) Write a series of observations about the picture, making sure to exclude all inferences. The class discussion will reveal whether you have been able to separate observations from inferences.

2. Clip a picture that is filled with detail. Ask two friends whom you know well, a man and a woman, to write a list of observations about the picture. Study the two lists to see whether they illustrate the old dictum: "We see things not as they are, but as we are."

3. Write a short, simple narrative or description of a situation, a place, or a person. Use only factual details and exclude inferences. Then show it to two friends and ask each to make as many inferences as he can from your observations. What do the two lists suggest about the reliability of hearsay?

4. Clip an advertisement that quotes a so-called authority to sell its product. Write a paragraph in which you apply the tests of authority given in the selection above and reach a conclusion about the validity of the testimonial.

5. Human knowledge is so vast today that one must rely on authority in many situations of daily life. And countless specialists are available for our consultation. Who, for example, would you consult if you
   Had an aching tooth?
   Were sued for an auto accident?
   Needed a stout pair of walking shoes?
   Wanted facts on Eisenhower's or Johnson's life for a biographical sketch?
   Wanted to know the best material for a drip-dry summer dress?
   Wanted help in choosing your major, or your career?
   Were planning a bicycle tour of Europe next summer?
   Had to organize a collection of material into a coherent speech?
   Wanted to find a good picnic spot for your club?
   Wanted to know the name and habits of a strange bird you have seen?
   Wanted to learn to understand the paintings of abstract expressionism?

6. Find for yourself a theme subject relating to authority, compose a thesis sentence, and write a short theme developing your thesis. You might use a thesis sentence like one of these:

a. An important part of college education is learning about reliable sources of information.
b. Modern man is often victimized by his ignorance.
c. It is difficult to choose a doctor in a strange community.
d. A blind trust in the opinion of an obliging friend once taught me a valuable lesson.
e. Long ago I learned not to ask everyone's advice.

Post Hoc Rides Again

DARRELL HUFF

One of the most engaging characters in American fiction is Huckleberry Finn. Huck, you will remember, is generally pragmatic in his approach to things; he is particularly good at sizing up a situation, coming to his own conclusions, and then acting in accordance with the facts as he sees them. That he is also superstitious, putting his faith in charms and omens, does not make him an inconsistent character, as the following anecdote makes clear. Huck is speaking: ". . . I've always reckoned that looking at the new moon over your left shoulder is one of the carelessest and foolishest things a body can do. Old Hank Bunker done it once, and bragged about it; and in less than two years he got drunk and fell off of the shot-tower, and spread himself out so that he was just a kind of a layer, as you may say; and they slid him edgeways between two barn doors for a coffin, and buried him so, so they say, but I didn't see it. Pap told me. But anyway it all come of looking at the moon that way, like a fool." This miniature tall-tale illustrates in a humorous fashion the fallacy of *post hoc, ergo propter hoc* (after this, therefore because of this), the topic of the next essay. Darrell Huff is primarily concerned with the occurrence of this fallacy in statistics. He writes in a style that is refreshingly breezy, but he is nonetheless serious. His warning is clear: Look for the facts behind the figures.

Reprinted from *How to Lie with Statistics* by Darrell Huff and Irving Geis, Copyright 1954, by Darrell Huff and Irving Geis, W. W. Norton & Company, Inc., New York. Selection reprinted by permission of the publisher and A. Watkins, Inc.

Somebody once went to a good deal of trouble to find out if cigarette smokers make lower college grades than nonsmokers. It turned out that they did. This pleased a good many people and they have been making much of it ever since. The road to good grades, it would appear, lies in giving up smoking; and, to carry the conclusion one reasonable step further, smoking makes dull minds.

This particular study was, I believe, properly done: sample big enough and honestly and carefully chosen, correlation having a high significance, and so on.

The fallacy is an ancient one which, however, has a powerful tendency to crop up in statistical material, where it is disguised by a welter of impressive figures. It is the one that says that if B follows A, then A has caused B. An unwarranted assumption is being made that since smoking and low grades go together, smoking causes low grades. Couldn't it just as well be the other way around? Perhaps low marks drive students not to drink but to tobacco. When it comes right down to it, this conclusion is about as likely as the other and just as well supported by the evidence. But it is not nearly so satisfactory to propagandists.

It seems a good deal more probable, however, that neither of these things has produced the other, but both are a product of some third factor. Can it be that the sociable sort of fellow who takes his books less than seriously is also likely to smoke more? Or is there a clue in the fact that somebody once established a correlation between extroversion and low grades—a closer relationship apparently than the one between grades and intelligence? Maybe extroverts smoke more than introverts. The point is that when there are many reasonable explanations you are hardly entitled to pick one that suits your taste and insist on it. But many people do.

To avoid falling for the *post hoc* fallacy and thus wind up believing many things that are not so, you need to put any statement of relationship through a sharp inspection. The correlation, that convincingly precise figure that seems to prove that something is because of something, can actually be any of several types.

One is the correlation produced by chance. You may be able to get together a set of figures to prove some unlikely thing in this way, but if you try again, your next set may not prove it at all. As with the manufacturer of the tooth paste that appeared to reduce decay, you simply throw away the results you don't want and publish widely those you do. Given a small sample, you are likely to find some substantial correlation between any pair of characteristics or events that you can think of.

A common kind of co-variation is one in which the relationship is real but it is not possible to be sure which of the variables is the cause and which the effect. In some of these instances cause and effect may change places from time to time or indeed both may be cause and effect at the same time. A correlation between income and ownership of stocks might be of that kind. The more money you make, the more stock you buy, and the more stock you buy, the more income you get; it is not accurate to say simply that one has produced the other.

Perhaps the trickiest of them all is the very common instance in which neither of the variables has any effect at all on the other, yet there is a real correlation. A good deal of dirty work has been done with this one. The poor grades among cigarette smokers is in this category, as are all too many medical statistics that are quoted without the qualification that although the relationship has been shown to be real, the cause-and-effect nature of it is only a matter of speculation. As an instance of the nonsense or spurious correlation that is a real statistical fact, someone has gleefully pointed to this: There is a close relationship between the salaries of Presbyterian ministers in Massachusetts and the price of rum in Havana.

Which is the cause and which the effect? In other words, are the ministers benefiting from the rum trade or supporting it? All right. That's so farfetched that it is ridiculous at a glance. But watch out for other applications of *post hoc* logic that differ from this one only in being more subtle. In the case of the ministers and the rum it is easy to see that both figures are growing because of the influence of a third factor: the historic and world-wide rise in the price level of practically everything.

And take the figures that show the suicide rate to be at its maximum in June. Do suicides produce June brides—or do June weddings precipitate suicides of the jilted? A somewhat more convincing (though equally unproved) explanation is that the fellow who licks his depression all through the winter with the thought that things will look rosier in the spring gives up when June comes and he still feels terrible.

Another thing to watch out for is a conclusion in which a correlation has been inferred to continue beyond the data with which it has been demonstrated. It is easy to show that the more it rains in an area, the taller the corn grows or even the greater the crop. Rain, it seems,

seems, is a blessing. But a season of very heavy rainfall may damage or even ruin the crop. The positive correlation holds up to a point and then quickly becomes a negative one. Above so-many inches, the more it rains the less corn you get.

We're going to pay a little attention to the evidence on the money value of education in a minute. But for now let's assume it has been proved that high-school graduates make more money than those who drop out, that each year of undergraduate work in college adds some more income. Watch out for the general conclusion that the more you go to school the more money you'll make. Note that this has not been shown to be true for the years beyond an undergraduate degree, and it may very well not apply to them either. People with Ph.D.'s quite often become college teachers and so do not become members of the highest income groups.

A correlation of course shows a tendency which is not often the ideal relationship described as one-to-one. Tall boys weigh more than short boys on the average, so this is a positive correlation. But you can easily find a six-footer who weighs less than some five-footers, so the correlation is less than 1. A negative correlation is simply a statement that as one variable increases the other tends to decrease. In physics this becomes an inverse ratio: The further you get from a light bulb the less light there is on your book; as distance increases light intensity decreases. These physical relationships often have the kindness to produce perfect correlations, but figures from business or sociology or medicine seldom work out so neatly. Even if education generally increases incomes it may easily turn out to be the financial ruination of Joe over there. Keep in mind that a correlation may be real and based on real cause and effect—and still be almost worthless in determining action in any single case.

Reams of pages of figures have been collected to show the value in dollars of a college education, and stacks of pamphlets have been published to bring these figures—and conclusions more or less based on them—to the attention of potential students. I am not quarreling with the intention. I am in favor of education myself, particularly if it includes a course in elementary statistics. Now these figures have pretty conclusively demonstrated that people who have gone to college make more money than people who have not. The exceptions are numerous, of course, but the tendency is strong and clear.

The only thing wrong is that along with the figures and facts goes a totally unwarranted conclusion. This is the *post hoc* fallacy at its best.

It says that these figures show that if *you* (your son, your daughter) attend college you will probably earn more money than if you decide to spend the next four years in some other manner. This unwarranted conclusion has for its basis the equally unwarranted assumption that since college-trained folks make more money, they make it because they went to college. Actually we don't know but these are the people who would have made more money even if they had not gone to college. There are a couple of things that indicate rather strongly that this is so. Colleges get a disproportionate number of two groups of kids: the bright and the rich. The bright might show good earning power without college knowledge. And as for the rich ones . . . well, money breeds money in several obvious ways. Few sons of rich men are found in low-income brackets whether they go to college or not.

The following passage is taken from an article in question-and-answer form that appeared in *This Week* magazine, a Sunday supplement of enormous circulation. Maybe you will find it amusing, as I do, that the same writer once produced a piece called "Popular Notions: True or False?"

Q: What effect does going to college have on your chances of remaining unmarried?

A: If you're a woman, it skyrockets your chances of becoming an old maid. But if you're a man, it has the opposite effect—it minimizes your chances of staying a bachelor.

Cornell University made a study of 1,500 typical middle-aged college graduates. Of the men, 93 per cent were married (compared to 83 per cent for the general population).

But of the middle-aged women graduates only 65 per cent were married. Spinsters were relatively three times as numerous among college graduates as among women of the general population.

When Susie Brown, age seventeen, reads this she learns that if she goes to college she will be less likely to get a man than if she doesn't. That is what the article says, and there are statistics from a reputable source to go with it. They go with it, but they don't back it up; and note also that while the statistics are Cornell's the conclusions are not, although a hasty reader may come away with the idea that they are.

Here again a real correlation has been used to bolster up an unproved cause-and-effect relationship. Perhaps it all works the other way around and those women would have remained unmarried even if they had not gone to college. Possibly even more would have failed to marry. If these possibilities are no better than the one the writer insists upon, they are perhaps just as valid conclusions: that is, guesses.

Indeed there is one piece of evidence suggesting that a propensity for old-maidhood may lead to going to college. Dr. Kinsey seems to have found some correlation between sexuality and education, with traits perhaps being fixed at pre-college age. That makes it all the more questionable to say going to college gets in the way of marrying.

Note to Susie Brown: It ain't necessarily so.

A medical article once pointed with great alarm to an increase in cancer among milk drinkers. Cancer, it seems, was becoming increasingly frequent in New England, Minnesota, Wisconsin, and Switzerland, where a lot of milk is produced and consumed, while remaining rare in Ceylon, where milk is scarce. For further evidence it was pointed out that cancer was less frequent in some Southern states where less milk was consumed. Also, it was pointed out, milk-drinking English women get some kinds of cancer eighteen times as frequently as Japanese women who seldom drink milk.

A little digging might uncover quite a number of ways to account for these figures, but one factor is enough by itself to show them up. Cancer is predominantly a disease that strikes in middle life or after. Switzerland and the states mentioned first are alike in having populations with relatively long spans of life. English women at the time the study was made were living an average of twelve years longer than Japanese women.

Professor Helen M. Walker has worked out an amusing illustration of the folly in assuming there must be cause and effect whenever two things vary together. In investigating the relationship between age and some physical characteristics of women, begin by measuring the angle of the feet in walking. You will find that the angle tends to be greater among older women. You might first consider whether this indicates that women grow older because they toe out, and you can see immediately that this is ridiculous. So it appears that age increases the angle between the feet, and most women must come to toe out more as they grow older.

Any such conclusion is probably false and certainly unwarranted. You could only reach it legitimately by studying the same women— or possibly equivalent groups—over a period of time. That would eliminate the factor responsible here. Which is that the older women grew up at a time when a young lady was taught to toe out in walking, while the members of the younger group were learning posture in a day when that was discouraged.

When you find somebody—usually an interested party—making a fuss about a correlation, look first of all to see if it is not one of this type, produced by the stream of events, the trend of the times. In our time it is easy to show a positive correlation between any pair of things like these: number of students in college, number of inmates in mental institutions, consumption of cigarettes, incidence of heart disease, use of X-ray machines, production of false teeth, salaries of California school teachers, profits of Nevada gambling halls. To call some one of these the cause of some other is manifestly silly. But it is done every day.

Permitting statistical treatment and the hypnotic presence of numbers and decimal points to befog causal relationships is little better than superstition. And it is often more seriously misleading. It is rather like the conviction among the people of the New Hebrides that body lice produce good health. Observation over the centuries had taught them that people in good health usually had lice and sick people very often did not. The observation itself was accurate and sound, as observations made informally over the years surprisingly often are. Not so much can be said for the conclusion to which these primitive people came from their evidence: Lice make a man healthy. Everybody should have them.

As we have already noted, scantier evidence than this—treated in the statistical mill until common sense could no longer penetrate to it—has made many a medical fortune and many a medical article in magazines, including professional ones. More sophisticated observers finally got things straightened out in the New Hebrides. As it turned out, almost everybody in those circles had lice most of the time. It was, you might say, the normal condition of man. When, however, anyone took a fever (quite possibly carried to him by those same lice) and his body became too hot for comfortable habitation, the lice left. There you have cause and effect altogether confusingly distorted, reversed, and intermingled.

SUGGESTED ASSIGNMENTS

1. Write a paragraph discussion of cause in relation to one of the following:
   a. From an advertisement: "Deanie Cates, Miss Florida, in the 19— Miss Universe Contest, was once a blimpish, unhappy teen-ager. Then she went to the Stauffer System. Stauffer remolded her figure and

Deanie went on to become a beauty queen. Come in and learn what we can do for you."

b. Several years ago in Florida a spry Confederate Veteran of 104 gave an interview to the press. He spoke cheerfully of his good health and attributed his long span of years to "living right, drinking plenty of good homemade moonshine liquor, and staying away from doctors."

c. A former Commissioner of the Office of Education in Washington said in a newspaper interview that Americans are "among the most fortunate people in the world and this position is due in a substantial part to our schools."

d. It has been shown by careful statistical studies that students who have cars get lower grades than those who don't.

e. Students who major in mathematics generally rank high scholastically. Therefore, it is evident that the study of math sharpens the mind.

f. In 1953, after the testing of several atomic bombs in Nevada, there were many tornadoes in the United States. Many people agitated against further testing on the grounds that it was the cause of dangerous tornadoes.

2. a. In one year figures showed that juvenile delinquency rose strikingly and that images of violence on TV increased markedly. What does this correlation show?

b. In one year the salaries of Iowa school teachers were raised generally, and, at the same time, the sale of whiskey in the state liquor stores rose. What does this show?

3. Publishers who advertise books purporting to increase the reader's vocabulary often use an argument like this one: "Out of a test group of 100 young men whose vocabularies were scientifically measured, all who passed in the upper 10 per cent had attained executive positions 5 years later—but not a single young man of the lower 25 per cent had become an executive!" The moral is obvious: buy our vocabulary-builder and become an executive. Write a brief analys s of this argument.

4. The official report of the Department of Public Safety of Iowa contains these facts about motor vehicle traffic deaths in 1955:

Occurred on straight road	409
″ on other roads	102
″ on dry road	428
″ on icy road	35
″ between four and five a.m.	3
″ ″ five and six p.m.	44

Therefore, for safest driving one should drive on an icy, curved highway between four and five in the morning. Criticize this conclusion.

Analogies

MONROE C. BEARDSLEY

The following quotation from the *New Yorker* affords an illustration of analogy: "The living language is like a cow-path: it is the creation of the cows themselves, who, having created it, follow it or depart from it according to their whims and needs. From daily use, the path undergoes change. A cow is under no obligation to stay in the narrow path she helped to make, following the contour of the land, but she often profits by staying with it and she would be handicapped if she didn't know where it was and where it led to. . . ." Let us note three things here: this is a comparison, dissimilar things are compared, and they are compared in a number of respects. Such, roughly stated, is what constitutes an analogy. In the selection below, Monroe Beardsley defines analogy more precisely and shows both its desirable uses and the traps it holds for the unwary thinker. Professor Beardsley teaches logic at Swarthmore College.

Analogies: their use and misuse

In a closed simile two things are compared in certain respects, which are specified by the simile.[1] Now, there are two different kinds of characteristics, or respects, in which things may be compared. They may be compared in terms of *qualities:* for example, they may both be hot, noisy, or angry. Or, they may be compared in terms of *relationships.* Any thing, considered as a *whole,* consists of parts that are arranged in certain ways, and this arrangement, or organization, of the parts is a web of relationships that each part has to the other parts. Now, if we compare, say, a brick building with a *papier-mâché* model of it, we can't make the comparison in terms of the qualities of the parts. For the parts are made of different material. But we can make the comparison in terms of the relationships *between* the parts. For if the model is a good one, the positions of the floors and windows and doors, for example,

Monroe Beardsley, *Practical Logic.* © 1950. Prentice-Hall, Inc., Englewood Cliffs, N.J.

[1] E.g. "The international situation is *as tense as* a ball-game tied up in the ninth inning." [eds.]

will be related to each other in exactly the same way as in the building itself.

This notion of relationship is what marks an analogy. An analogy is simply a rather extensive closed simile in which the comparison is in terms of relationships.

Consider, for example, a map. The dots on the map (say, a map of the United States) are not very much like actual cities, and the lines on the map are not tall like mountains or wet like rivers, and the colors of the map are not at all like the colors of the earth in various states. But the structure of the map, if it is a good one, *corresponds to* the structure of the country it represents. That is, the shapes of the states are like the shapes on the map; the relative sizes of the states are like the relative sizes of the shapes; and the relative distances between actual cities are like the relative distances between the dots on the map. So the analogy between the map and the country is very close. When we can find such *strong* analogies as this, we can use one thing to represent the other.

The analogies we ordinarily use are not nearly so strong as in this example. But they can nevertheless be very useful. In particular, there are *two* ways in which analogies are a help to effective thinking, and there is a *third* way in which they are harmful to effective thinking.

First, we often use analogies to illustrate and clarify general principles. If you are trying to explain the way a steam engine or a gasoline motor works, it may be helpful to find something simpler that works on a similar principle. Popular science is full of ingenious, and often extremely illuminating, analogies of this sort. They act as small-scale models of the real thing, and they make an easy first step toward complete understanding.

But, of course, all such analogies break down at some point. Comparison with ocean waves will take the beginner a little way in a study of sound waves, and comparison with sound waves will take him a little way in a study of radio waves. But the comparison can be pushed to a point where the two things are so unlike that the analogy becomes misleading. The "ether" is not an ocean.

Second, analogies are fruitful for suggesting ideas that may lead to important discoveries—*working hypotheses* that can be put to experimental test. Suppose you are studying one thing—say, lightning—for the first time. And suppose you notice that it has many characteristics in common with electric sparks. You know that electricity can produce a current, and you wonder whether lightning may be like electricity in this way, too. Of course *you* know it is. But Benjamin Franklin did not know the answer until he tried his famous experiment. The analogy between the growth of the embryo and the course of evolution, between electro-magnetic fields and gravitational fields, between the solar system and the structure of the atom—all these, and many others, have been very useful in the history of science.

But, again, these are only analogies. An analogy doesn't *prove* anything; it merely calls to mind a *possibility* that might not have been thought of without the analogy. It's the experiment that counts in the end. Bohr's classic model of the atom is *only* a picture. It has clarified some points about the atom, it has hinted at some good hypotheses; but if you take it as *proving* anything about the atom, you are misusing the analogy. You can be fooled just as much by it as were those early inventors who tried to construct airplanes that flapped their wings, on the analogy with birds. Analogies *illustrate*, and they lead to *hypotheses*, but thinking in terms of analogy becomes fallacious when the analogy is used as a *reason for* a principle. This fallacy is called the "argument from analogy."

The makers of a patented drug to relieve headaches used to advertise their product over the radio with this patter: "It is like a doctor's prescription, since it contains not one, but many, proven ingredients." One interesting thing about this argument—apart from its imbecility—is that the conclusion is merely *suggested* by the context, and not very definitely at that. You gather that the advertiser is suggesting that the drug is safe to take, is designed for your specific illness, is scientifically prepared by a pharmacist. You think: This must be all right for me, if the doctors say so. Of course, the advertisers were careful not to come out and *state* these claims, since there is a Federal Bureau which keeps a watchful eye on false advertising claims.

Probably this argument has actually convinced many people that the drug is better than aspirin for a headache. In any case, the form of the argument from analogy is pretty clear from this simple example:

> X has certain characteristics a, b, c . . . . .
> Y has the characteristics a, b, c . . . . .
> But Y also has other characteristics x, y, z.

Therefore:

> X has the characteristics x, y, z.

The argument begins with two things, X (the drug) and Y (a doctor's prescription). It proceeds from certain *assumed resemblances* (they both contain many "proven ingredients") to certain *inferred resemblances* (they are both recommended by doctors, for example). The underlying principle is: If X and Y have a number of characteristics in common, then it is likely that any *further* characteristics found in Y will *also* be found in X.

We have said that if two things have a good deal in common, we may guess that they may have even more in common. The likeness may justify a further investigation to see whether they actually *do* have more in common. But it does *not* justify our believing that they have more in common *without* the further investigation. It remains a guess. This is so because, no matter how many characteristics a pair of things have in common, there may be any number of other ways in which they are different. You can't even say that the more known resemblances there are between X and Y, the more likely it is that X will have any further characteristic found in Y.

The above argument is not a good one, but it could be the *beginning* of a good one. When we see what it would take to make a good argument, it will be easier to see why the argument from analogy is unsound. Suppose you analyzed a number of things, each of which contains several "proven" ingredients (*a*) but which is very different from the rest in other ways (a sponge cake, a plastic toy, blood, an Old Fashioned). And suppose that in every case you found that these things were recommended by doctors (*z*). Then you might make a generalization: "Everything that has *a* also has *z*." You might say: "Here is this drug. It has many proven ingredients. If my generalization is true, this drug will also be recommended by doctors." This is the way you would ordinarily extend a generalization to a new case where it can applied. But, of course, in this case the generalization would obviously be untrue.

. . . The important point here is that it takes at least a *fairly large number of different kinds* of cases to make a good generalization. The argument from analogy is an attempt to short-circuit this rule without appearing too implausible. If the relevant generalization about the drug is already proved, then the argument is *not* an argument from analogy any more: it is a legitimate extension of a known generalization to a new case. If the relevant generalization has *not* been proved, there is no basis whatever for the argument.

Answering an analogy

The argument from analogy turns up constantly in ordinary discourse; it is one of the commonest fallacies. When you find such an argument trying to impose upon your thinking, the first thing to do is get the argument straight by analyzing the assumed resemblances and the inferred resemblances. Then you know exactly what the argument is, and you are ready to answer it. There are *three* different ways of showing what is wrong with an argument from analogy.

(1) To begin with, the assumed resemblances may *not* be actual resemblances at all. If this is so, the simplest answer to the argument is to point out succinctly the weakness of the analogy. Suppose someone argues for a world federal government by analogy with the American colonies. There will be *some* resemblances, but there may be also important differences that have been overlooked. Of course, if the arguer stacks up a number of historical examples—the unification of Germany, Italy, Switzerland, Greek city-states—then he may be trying to establish a generalization. But if he merely gives *one* example, he is arguing by analogy, and the first question is: how *strong* is the analogy?

If the analogy is weak, then, you can answer it by *attacking the assumed resemblances:*

> A: "We shouldn't blame the movie-makers for   *Statement*
> the cultural level of their pictures. Movies are   *of Analogy*
> simply manufactured goods. They are just like
> washing machines; therefore, producers are
> justified in selling whatever pictures the public
> will buy."
>
> B: "I admit movies are manufactured, but they   *Attack on*
> are not much like washing machines. A poor   *Assumed*
> washing machine is merely a waste of money;   *Resemblances*
> a poor movie is bad for the mind."

(2) The assumed resemblances may really *be* resemblances, as far as they go. Nevertheless, even if X and Y are both red, and Y is round, it doesn't follow that X is round—unless there is some reason for believing that probably everything that is red is also round. In short, only the generalization would justify the inference. To answer the argument from analogy it is enough to show that the generalization is untrue. To do this, give examples that tell against it.

The second answer, then, consists in *attacking the underlying generalization:*

> A: "Fellow temperance-workers, we know   *Statement*
> that the delicate membranes of the stomach are   *of Analogy*

like the delicate membranes of the eye, and if
you want to see what alcohol does to the stomach,
just pour some gin in your eye."

B: "This is no argument at all, unless the   *Attack on*
speaker is suggesting that anything that hurts   *Underlying*
the eye will also hurt the stomach, which is   *Generalization*
absurd. If it were true, lemonade would not be
good to drink."

(3) But even if the required generalization is true, a person who
argues from analogy lays himself open, frequently, to a simple but
effective retort. If he says, "We should not change horses in mid-
stream," it's easy to reply, "Oh, but when the horse has bogged down,
and the flood-waters are rising, you have to change horses or drown."

This answer consists in *extending the analogy* to the point where it
boomerangs. Of most of the loose and confused analogies that figure in
political argument, especially the old one comparing the state with a
ship, it may be said that, if they proved anything (which they don't),
they would prove *too much*. Almost any such analogy can be extended
to include points that the original user would find embarrassing. This
third way of answering the analogy is, of course, *not* an argument
against the truth of the other person's conclusion. It merely uses the
analogy to show that the original argument was fallacious, which is a
legitimate refutation.

Sometimes it is also the most convincing refutation. Notice how
B, in the passage below, turns A's analogy against him. B uses the
analogy as an *illustration* to show that the principle of the argument
from analogy cannot be defended.

A: "If we want to find out who is the best   *Statement*
100-yard sprinter, we have to have a race and   *of Analogy*
let everyone compete in it; and we must not
interfere with the race by holding up some
runners and helping others. Now, economic
competition is just like a race, and if we want
the most efficient industries to come out on
top, we must leave them alone."

B: "Your analogy is an excellent one, only   *Extension*
you don't carry if far enough. For we can't   *of Analogy*
run a fair race without *rules*, to keep the runners

from jumping the gun and tripping each other up. That's the only way you can be sure that the winner really is the best runner, not merely the best tripper. Thus your analogy implies that we must have strong rules to keep down monopoly, and price-fixing conspiracies, to make the economic race a fair one. Moreover, your analogy implies that, to ensure fairness, we should start everyone off at the same place, with an equal amount of money."

SUGGESTED ASSIGNMENTS

1. Put yourself in this situation. You have a three-record album of Verdi's *Aïda* and you accidentally break one of the records. You therefore write to the record manufacturer ordering a replacement. The company replies, expressing regret that they do not sell single records of this album and that you must buy the entire album to get the record you want. This gets your dander up, and you answer hotly that they are in the same position as an automobile manufacturer, who feels himself obligated to furnish parts for the cars he sells. But the company has a neat riposte for you. "No," they say, "we are really like a book publisher" and defend themselves with a counter-analogy. See if you can finish their analogy. Which one of you is right?

2. At a poorly marked railroad crossing, a loaded passenger car is demolished by a passenger train. As a result, the newspapers are filled with agitation for gates and an automatic signal. But the company objects. "Why," they ask, "should we put up a signal and gates now? That's just like locking the barn door after the horse is stolen." Point out the fallacy in this analogy.

3. In the American Association of University Professors *Bulletin* for Autumn, 1951, page 514, Edwin H. Reeder points out that the average professor and the average layman accept what John Dewey once called the "cold storage" idea of learning, which he explains in this way: "They visualize the mind as a sort of cold storage warehouse, which is empty at birth. The process of learning consists in hanging on the walls of the warehouse chunks of fact and information. Teaching consists in superintending this process, in assuring that the correct chunks are carried into the warehouse and hung on its walls. The chunks hang there in the same condition in which they were first stored until some day the student needs one or more of them; then he can go to the warehouse, unhook the right chunk, and use it for some mature purpose which he could not have conceived in the immature

condition of his mind when he first acquired the material." Write a theme in which you explode this analogy by (1) attacking the assumed resemblances and (2) extending the analogy to the point where it boomerangs.

4. Analogy is often used not to convince or persuade but to clarify a description or illustrate an explanation. You will find analogies frequently in your college reading. Here is an example from Mortimer Adler's *How to Read a Book*. Professor Adler is clarifying the point that the reader should set forth the major parts of the book and see how these are organized into a whole by being related to one another and to the whole. His analogy is as follows:

> You know the difference between a heap of bricks, on the one hand, and the single house they constitute, on the other. You know the difference between one house and a collection of houses. A book is like a single house. It is a mansion of many rooms, rooms on different levels, of different sizes and shapes, with different outlooks, rooms with different functions to perform. These rooms are independent, in part. Each has its own structure and interior decoration. But they are not absolutely independent and separate. They are connected by doors and arches, by corridors and stairways. Because they are connected, the partial function which each performs contributes its share to the usefulness of the whole house. Otherwise the house would not be genuinely livable.
>
> The architectural analogy is almost perfect. A good book, like a good house, is an orderly arrangement of parts. Each major part has a certain amount of independence. As we shall see, it may have an interior structure of its own. But it must also be connected with the other parts—that is, related to them functionally—for otherwise it could not contribute its share to the intelligibility of the whole.
>
> As houses are more or less livable, so books are more or less readable. The most readable book is an architectural achievement on the part of the author. The best books are those that have the most intelligible structure and, I might add, the most apparent. Pages 163–164.

Write an analogy to clarify or illustrate, carrying it as far as it can legitimately go. You might use such subjects as these:
a. My roommate's study habits remind me of a fisherman.
b. Going on a blind date is like reading an unfamiliar book.
c. Human life is like a highway (a game of chess or poker, a bridge, a river).
d. College life resembles a trackmeet.

5. Analogies are frequently used to convince or persuade and can be very successful among the unthoughtful. They tend to appear when controversy or self-interest is strong, as in political campaigns and in labor-management disputes. Here is the complete advertisement of a chiropractor. Analyze it for its soundness.

> The nervous system is very much the same as a telephone system. The central office is the brain, the nerves are the wires, and each cell in the body is a

telephone user. If all the wires from the central office came out at one point as a cable, it would be as the spinal cord which is made up of billions of nerves which serve the same purpose as wires carrying messages to and from the brain.

The brain controls all the activities of the cells through this network of wires. Irritation of these nerves by pressure from vertebrae slipping out of place would produce somewhat the same results in the body as a short or 'crossed wires' in a telephone system.

A person with such a condition would be known as a highly nervous wreck with symptoms far and many, such as tired feeling, sleeplessness, loss of appetite, highly irritable [sic], fidgety [sic], hallucinations, digestive disturbances etc., and might lead to a nervous breakdown.

Chiropractors are as highly specialized linemen who ferret out these 'shorts' and adjust them with the result that normal service is resumed.

6. Write an analogy to convince your readers of a proposition you wish to uphold. Here is the kind of analogy you might try:

   a. A writer should understand grammar for the same reasons that a doctor should know his anatomy.

   b. One grading system for all students is unfair. Instead, students should be graded in relation to their aptitude and ability as shown by reliable tests. The student body can fairly be compared to a large garden with a wide variety of growth.

   c. In a liberal arts curriculum all students should take the same courses if we are to produce liberally educated graduates. Do engineering schools offer electives in the training of engineers?

Ambiguity

LIONEL RUBY

A college freshman once wrote, "During my twelve years in school I have had about thirty odd teachers." This remark is an example of ambiguity, an expression that has more than one meaning in the context in which it appears. The writer faces an ever-constant struggle as he chooses and arranges words so that his message will be free from ambiguity. The difficulty may be gauged by the fact that it is easier for the perceptive reader to find examples of

From *Logic: An Introduction*, Second Edition, by Lionel Ruby. Reprinted by permission of the publisher, J. B. Lippincott Co., copyright 1960.

ambiguity than of almost any other writing blunder. Yet in a world deluged with both spoken and written communications, what can be more important than precision and clearness of statement? Lionel Ruby, Professor of Philosophy at Roosevelt University, here offers a survey of the pitfalls of ambiguity.

The meaning of ambiguity

There are many obstacles in the path of successful communication, but ambiguity is undoubtedly the worst offender. An ambiguous word is one that may be understood in more than one sense. Thus a symbol may be interpreted differently by speaker and hearer; communicators and communicatees are at cross-purposes and there is no meeting of minds.

Most of the words in any language have more than one referent. This is in many ways a boon rather than an evil, for the range of possible meanings in any limited number of words is greatly increased. Our vocabularies are enlarged when one word has different meanings in different contexts; the single word then becomes the equivalent of many different words. In many cases the differences in referents may be on a "large" scale, as when the word "secretary" refers in turn to "a person who attends to correspondence," "an executive officer in the government," "a writing desk," and "a South African bird with long legs." There are many other words in which the differences in the referents are of a more subtle nature, the shifts in meaning being less obvious, as in the different ways in which the word "man" is used in the following contexts:

All *men* are mortal.
The child is father to the *man*.
Those were the days when *men* were *men*.
What a piece of work is *man!* How infinite in capacity!
The football team is under*manned*.

Successful communication occurs only when the reader correctly interprets the symbols used by the writer . . . . When the communication is successful then the communicator and the communicatee have their minds referred to the same referents; they have the same terms in mind. They have "come to terms." But ambiguous words are obstacles to such happy consummations; communication is frustrated.

. . . When such failures of communication occur, the speaker and the hearer have different referents in mind.

But note that ambiguity is an evil only when it results in these frustrations of communication. In scientific discourse, where the aim is to achieve clear and precise reference, ambiguity is an unmitigated evil. But there are other fields of thought in which ambiguity may have certain desirable effects. This is the case in poetry, where ambiguity may sometimes contribute to the poetic effect by suggesting a rich aura of implied meanings: "Life is a tale told by an idiot, full of sound and fury, signifying nothing"; "Faith is the substance of things hoped for; the evidence of things not seen." In this manner poetry approximates the effects produced by music, which, among all of the arts, is certainly the most expressively ambiguous. One of the great charms of music lies in the ambiguity with which it expresses moods, so that each hearer may interpret the musical score in his own way. Ambiguity also has more mundane uses. Diplomatic language has developed the art of saying things ambiguously so that failure to agree will be masked by "face-saving" language. Finally, the ambiguous aspects of words are exploited as a rich source of humor. Gagsters and punsters thrive on the double-meanings of words. Our primary interest, of course, is to learn how to avoid ambiguity in scientific discourse.

Ambiguity is the direct opposite of synonymity (the use of synonymous words). An ambiguous word refers to several referents; in synonymity a single referent is referred to by several different words. "Spade" refers to at least two referents: a playing card and a garden implement. Fool, lout, simpleton, oaf, dunderhead, ninny, nincompoop, addle-pate, and dope, all refer to the same referent, or to substantially the same referent, since few synonymous words are absolutely identical in meaning. . . .

The analysis of ambiguity

Though many words have more than one meaning, the context of surrounding circumstances will usually clarify the sense in which the word is used. The initial ambiguity is often completely eliminated by the context. We shall be primarily concerned with examples in which the ambiguity is not eliminated by the context, with a resulting blockage of communication. . . .

When two or more interpretations of an author's language are possible, the reader does not know what is in the author's mind. We should be clear as to the task of the logician in analyzing instances of ambiguity. The logician cannot eliminate ambiguity; his primary task is to call attention to the fact that ambiguity occurs and to show the different ways in which it occurs. The logician can also help to make the reader sensitive to ambiguities in places where ambiguity might be unsuspected. The logician can also advise the reader to find out what was in the author's mind before the reader interprets ambiguous language. The reader's task here may be likened to that of a judge whose task is to decide what the legislature meant by the ambiguous language in a law. The court will investigate the circumstances in which the law was passed, the remarks of legislators concerning the intent of the law, and so on. In other words, the context will be studied for light on the probable meaning of the words.

We shall examine the manner in which ambiguity occurs in the use of words, phrases, and sentences. Ambiguity, as we know, is a fruitful source of humor, and we shall note some of the entertaining aspects of its various forms. Humorists deliberately use the ambiguities of language in various kinds of jokes and "gags." Finally, we shall examine some of the "fallacies" of ambiguity. This aspect of ambiguity is of greatest interest to the logician. The failure to recognize ambiguity often results in misinterpretations of meanings and in erroneous inferences.

The types of ambiguity

1. SIMPLE AMBIGUITY

By *simple* ambiguity we shall mean the fact that single words or phrases may refer to more than one referent, even after we have examined their contexts. Verbal disagreements are based upon this type of ambiguity. Any statement containing a word which is ambiguous in its context exemplifies this vice: "The early Christians were communists." Since the word "communist" has more than one referent in this context, ambiguity exists. "Communist$_1$" means one who favors a system of social organization in which goods are held in common; "communist$_2$" means an advocate of "the dictatorship of the proletariat." Before we affirm or deny the truth of a statement we should find out what the writer means. Questions may also involve simple ambiguity, as in "Do you believe in God?" "God" means different things to different persons, and a yes-or-no answer is inappropriate until we learn what referent the questioner has in mind. Spinoza, for example, defined God as "everything which exists." Spinoza was a deeply religious man whose pantheistic philosophy was permeated with devotion to God. The Catholic Church, however, has condemned his pantheism as equivalent to atheism.

Simple ambiguity is closely related to "vagueness," but should be distinguished from it. An ambiguous word has several distinct referents; a vague word lacks precision and definiteness in its reference. Thus, the question, "Has there been any progress during the past 2,000 years?" involves the use of the vague word "progress." The reader spontaneously responds to such a question with his own questions: "Progress in what sense? In spiritual growth? In the advancement of the common man? In a material sense?" The word "progress" is vague rather than ambiguous, for in each case it means "advancement toward a definite goal," but the question does not specify the goal involved.

Vagueness, rather than ambiguity, will also be found in the following incident. In the summer of 1947 General Eisenhower was reported to have said that "the United States Army is a 'poor second' to that of Russia." Congressman Short asked, "In what sense?" In quantity? In quality? The United States Army has never been equal to the Russian army in size either in war or peace. Here too, "poor second" is not ambiguous, since it means "far behind the first," but its meaning is not precise.

Questions containing vague words cannot be answered without further clarification of their meaning. We should also note how careful thinking may result in the discovery that "clear" words are actually vague. Thus, the question "Is this building moving?" may appear to be clear. But we must ask: "In relation to which frame of reference?" In relation to the sun, this building is moving at a speed of eighteen miles per second. In relation to the earth, however, it is stationary.

Simple ambiguity has two forms, written and oral. The phonetic sound "teers" may stand for two different words: "tiers" and "tears." An amusing example of oral ambiguity based on this sound is found in the following:

A reporter was describing a scene at the House of Commons to another reporter. "There, on the floor of the House, stood the Prime Minister speaking," he said, "back of him were the members of the Cabinet, in front of him sat the members of the Opposition, and in tiers around him sat the other members of the House."

The second reporter was very young and very earnest. "Not really *tears*," he exclaimed. "Poor chaps!" (Albert Levi and Albert Frye, *Rational Belief*, Harcourt, Brace, 1941, p. 108.)

Simple ambiguity lies at the basis of much humor, especially in puns, as in Wordsworth's remark, "If I had a mind to, I could write like Shakespeare."

2. AMPHIBOLY

"I shall lose no time in reading your manuscript," the noted critic wrote to the aspiring young author. Should the author have been pleased with this message? Would the critic read his manuscript soon or never?

The critic's remark is an example of an amphibolous sentence. Its meaning is ambiguous though no *word* in the sentence is ambiguous. The ambiguity results from the way in which the words are put together in the sentence.

Amphiboly refers to the fact that the meaning of a sentence may be ambiguous, not because any of its words are ambiguous, but because the grammatical construction of the sentence permits several interpretations as to its meaning. The amphibolous sentence is capable of being understood in more than one sense. This may result in a failure in communication. A sentence combines words in order to express a thought. The referents have a certain relationship in the mind of the speaker. The grammatical construction of the sentence may fail to direct the hearer's mind to the relationship referred to by the speaker. The logician calls the reader's attention to these factors. The grammarian seeks to teach writers how to make themselves clear.

Vivid examples of amphiboly are found in humorous exaggerations of this fault. Thus, the following account was reportedly given by a newspaper reporter, with reference to the departure of the famous prewar dirigible from the Lakehurst airport: "The Graf Zeppelin was leaving the Lakehurst airport. Among the last to enter was Mrs. Smith, lone woman passenger. Slowly her huge nose was turned into the wind. Then, like some huge beast, she crawled along the grass . . ."

Grammarians have noted a type of error similar to amiphiboly in the error called "the dangling participle," as in "Zooming along under her own power, Jane was fascinated by the spectacle of the glider before her." The participle "zooming" seems to refer to Jane. The words are unambiguous, but ambiguity results from the manner in which they are put together.

A famous historical source of amphiboly is found in the Delphic oracle, in ancient Greece. The oracle was certainly the most astute diplomat who ever lived and also the Nostradamus of its time, except that, unlike Nostradamus, the oracular pronouncements were right 100 per cent of the time. This success was due to the use of amphiboly. The oracle was consulted on the eve of great undertakings, in order to obtain its "inspired" predictions as to success or failure. The oracle always retained its reputation for infallibility because of the manner in which it made its pronouncements: "Apollo says that the Greeks the Persians shall subdue." Cyrus, the Persian King, sent messengers to the oracle for a prophecy concerning a projected war. The messengers were informed that "the King yet lives that Cyrus shall depose." The variant interpretations of these statements are obvious.

Amphibolous sentences of the type just noted may be called *completely* amphibolous in that the reader does not know how to interpret them correctly. In most cases, though two or more interpretations are possible, it will generally appear that one interpretation is more reasonable than the others, either from the context or the customs of speech. Thus, when a law court is presented with an amphibolous document, the "reasonable" interpretation will be applied. For example, a licensing agreement between the holder of a patent and the manufacturer provided that the manufacturer would pay the patentee "50¢ a unit for producing 5,000 units or less, and 30¢ a unit for all units of an output of over 5,000 units." The manufacturer claimed that when the output exceeded 5,000 units he was obligated to pay 30¢ per unit for *all* units produced. The court ruled that the agreement meant "50¢ for the first 5,000 units and 30¢ for all units in excess of 5,000." Otherwise the patentee would receive less royalties for a production of 6,000 units than he would receive for 4,000.

It is impossible to state whether a sentence is true or false until we understand its meaning. An amphibolous sentence must be given a definite interpretation before we can judge it as true or false. For example, a man says, "All women are not fickle." By this he may mean either that "some women are not fickle" or that "no women are fickle." If the speaker is available we should question him to determine what he meant. If he is not available, how shall we interpret the statement?

Note that the sentence takes the "All . . . are not . . ." formation. The logician adopts a rule of interpretation here, stating that all such statements shall be read as if they meant "*Not all* women are fickle" or "Some women are not fickle," unless he has clear evidence from the context or elsewhere that the speaker meant "No women are fickle." In the sentence "All human beings are not perfect" the speaker probably means "No human beings are perfect," but in "All Russians are not communists" he probably means "Some Russians are not communists."

Other types of amphiboly that require interpretation are such sentences as "All agree with me who are not ignorant of the facts." This may mean either "All who agree with me are persons who are not ignorant of the facts" or it may mean "All who are not ignorant of the facts agree with me." The speaker may mean either one, but in the absence of further evidence, the grammarian will adopt the latter interpretation as the more likely one.

3. AMBIGUITY IN EMPHASIS

A unit of discourse may make different kinds of sense depending upon which of its parts we accent or emphasize. We should always seek to give writings the emphasis which the author intended them to have, but when the writing is ambiguous in this respect, the reader may be unable to determine where the proper emphasis lies. The full and complete meaning of a sentence may even require that we hear it spoken. Thus the invitation "I hope that you will come to dinner" may accent "I," "you," or "dinner" when it is spoken. When you leave, you say, "The dinner was very good." You may accent "dinner." It is for this reason that classroom instruction is superior to mere reading for most students, since the instructor gives oral emphasis to the most important words.

Ambiguity of emphasis occurs when a reader does not know which parts of a writing deserve chief emphasis. Troublesome cases of this sort occur when a writer presents somewhat conflicting points of view, as in Book V of Plato's *Republic*, concerning the nature and status of women in his ideal state. The reader will find "equalitarian" remarks such as, "The only difference between men and women consists in the fact that women bear and that men beget children," and "The differences between men and women do not justify different types of education for the two sexes. Women as well as men, should be trained to qualify as rulers of the state." But elsewhere Plato says that "women are inferior to men in all pursuits followed by each." Again, that "men and women possess the same qualities and differ only in their comparative strength and weakness." Does Plato believe that women are essentially the same as men, or does he hold that the weaker sex is the inferior sex? No one can answer this question with certainty.

When summaries are made of writings, ambiguity of emphasis may create similar difficulties. The summarizer should emphasize the most important elements. When excerpts and quotes are given they should be truly representative of the author's meaning. Summaries, however, open the door to many errors of carelessness or deliberate misinterpretation, to be discussed further under the "fallacies of ambiguity." Book reviewers are often accused of "not having read the whole book" when the author thinks that his position has been misinterpreted. The reviewer's misinterpretation, however, may be due in whole or in part to the author's failure to make his points clear. Or the author may state somewhat conflicting positions, as in the selections from Plato's *Republic*.

A different type of problem concerning emphasis or "accent" occurs in problems of punctuation. Literary scholars seek to interpret Shakespeare's meanings accurately, but there are variant readings of many of the plays. The Folio and the Second Quarto editions, the oldest sources, differ in many important respects. Consider the different possible readings of Hamlet's speech to Guildenstern (II, 2, 315). The Neilson and Hill version of the speech, based upon the Quarto version, is stated as follows:

What a piece of work is a man! How noble in reason! How infinite in faculty! in form and moving! How express and admirable in action! How like an angel in apprehension! How like a god!

The Everyman's edition, following the Folio version, prints the lines as follows:

What a piece of work is man! How noble in reason! how infinite in faculty! In form and moving how express and admirable! in action how like an angel! in apprehension how like a god!

4. THE AMBIGUITY OF SIGNIFICANCE

By this type we refer to statements whose semantical meaning may be clear, but whose factual significance is not. A statement may contain no ambiguous words, its sentence structure may convey an unambiguous meaning, and it may contain no ambiguities of emphasis. But its significance may be "ambiguous." As an illustration, consider the statement that there were 454 deaths due to traffic accidents in the United States during the Thanksgiving holiday weekend last year. The significance of such a statement is ambiguous in many respects. An isolated fact means something, of course. We all deplore the large number of deaths reported. But its full significance would require knowing whether the number was higher or lower than the number killed during the previous year's holiday weekend, and whether the figures for a non-holiday weekend are higher or lower.

It should be apparent that alertness to this kind of "ambiguity" is almost synonymous with the scientific attitude. Every statement whatsoever will have different kinds of significance depending upon its context or surrounding circumstances. It should also be obvious that this kind of "ambiguity" is not a genuinely semantical problem. We deal with it here only because it concerns a kind of uncertainty to which readers should be alerted, and because ambiguity in its broadest sense refers to doubtfulness or uncertainty.

Many other examples of such ambiguous isolated statements come to mind. "There are 3 million unemployed in the United States." Up or down since last month? In comparison with last year? What is the normal number of unemployed even in periods of "full employment?" Many statements are ambiguous to the uninitiated though not to well-informed. "You have 5 billion germs in your mouth." What is the significance of that fact to a non-physiologist? In all the examples cited we find statements whose referential meaning is unambiguous, but whose significance is subject to varying interpretations.

The significance of many statements is ambiguous until we answer the questions: "Who said it?" and "under what circumstances?" In the fall of 1947 a United States Congressman said, "We will be at war with Russia in one month." Who was the speaker? A responsible or an irresponsible talker? When we listen to criticism of the foreign or domestic policies of the federal administration, we should of course judge these criticisms on their own merits, but we should also be concerned with the background of the critic. Is he a member of the opposition party? Is he blindly partisan? In the absence of coercive evidence we will give greater or lesser weight to criticism depending upon the stature of the critic. If the speaker is thought to be impartial, greater weight will be given to his criticism. In a law court great weight is given to statements which are called "admissions against one's own interest."

Another important distinction concerns the question as to whether a statement is being made in jest or in earnest. "Smile when you call me that" is a type of comment which emphasizes the ambiguity of significance. Persons whose humor is "dry" often make ironical or sarcastical statements that should not be interpreted literally.

An amusing example of the ambiguity of significance occurred when the late Heywood Broun, a wit among drama critics, once wrote that a certain actor, *J*, was "the world's worst 'actor,' " Broun was sued for libel and acquitted. Sometime later, *J* appeared in another play, and Broun, reporting the performance, wrote: "Mr. *J* was not up to his usual standard last night."

The fallacies of ambiguity

Thus far we have noted four different types of ambiguity. When confronted with ambiguities we are not certain as to how we should interpret (1) single words or phrases, (2) the sense of a sentence, (3) the emphases or accents desired by the writer or speaker, or (4) the significance of a statement. The careful reader will be alert to the presence of these uncertainties. He will ask the appropriate questions in order to get information that will help to interpret the statements correctly.

A *fallacy* of ambiguity is a distortion of meaning or an error of reasoning based upon an incorrect interpretation of an ambiguous word or phrase. These errors of reasoning usually occur in *use* (by the writer). Distortions of meaning, on the other hand, occur in *interpretation* (by the reader).

Note that the presence of ambiguity is not, in itself, an "error." If a friend tells us that he shot a secretary (meaning a bird) on his last safari to Africa, we may or may not be aware of the ambiguity of the word "secretary." If we jump to the conclusion that he shot a beautiful female of the human species, this would be an error resulting from our faulty interpretation of the ambiguous word. We shall now examine two major fallacies arising from the various types of ambiguity: equivocation and accent.

1. EQUIVOCATION

The fallacy of equivocation is an error of use, rather than of interpretation, i.e., it is committed by writers and speakers rather than readers and listeners. It occurs when a writer (or speaker) uses an ambiguous word (or root or phrase) in more than one sense in a given unit of discourse, such equivocal use resulting in an unjustified inference. Some examples: A speaker says: "I am sure that communists really believe in God. It is generally agreed that for its followers communism is a religion, and religious people believe in God." The term "religion" is used in two different senses. Communism is a religion in the sense that its followers show an ardent devotion and fidelity to its tenets, but it is not a religion in the traditional sense of "conviction of the existence of a Supreme Being." The failure to distinguish these meanings resulted in an unjustified inference.

Our second example involves the ambiguous term "law." In its legal sense law means a rule regulating human conduct established by an appropriate governing body. In science, a law refers to the uniform behavior of natural events, i.e., to an order or pattern in nature that is regarded as unvarying under the given conditions. An example is the law of gravitation. It is impossible to "violate" such a law, nor can it have exceptions, for if there is an exception the behavior is not uniform and there is no law. A convenient way of distinguishing the two senses of law is to say that a law of nature is a *description* (of nature); a legal or civil law is a *prescription*, a command. Now suppose one were to argue as follows:

Science has discovered many laws of nature. This is proof that there is a God, for a law implies the existence of a lawgiver, and God is the great Lawgiver of the universe.

The term "law" is used equivocally in this argument. Law in the sense of an order or command implies the existence of a lawgiver or commander, but law in the sense of a description does not.

Equivocation may of course be used deliberately for the purposes of wit and humor. "Your argument is sound, nothing but sound." Thus Benjamin Franklin's pun, "If we don't hang together, we'll hang separately." Or the absurd syllogism, "Some dogs have shaggy ears. My dog has shaggy ears. Therefore, my dog is *some* dog."

Note that equivocation can occur only if the ambiguous term is used at least twice in the same unit of discourse. When an ambiguous word is used only once, this is simple ambiguity. It goes without saying that equivocation should be avoided in our discussions. A word should be used in the same sense throughout a unit of discourse. If we do not use our words consistently there can be no communication or reasoning.

2. ACCENT

The fallacy of "accent" is an error which results from giving an obviously improper accent or emphasis to the words in a sentence or to the ideas in a unit of discourse.

Such improper accenting or distortion of meaning may be done deliberately, in order to deceive, but usually occurs where there is ambiguity of emphasis. Misinterpretations may then occur because of careless writing or careless interpretation. We shall note three typical ways in which the fallacy occurs:

a. The incorrect emphasis of the words in a sentence

The commandment says, "Thou shalt not bear false witness against thy neighbor."

If one were to stress the word "neighbor," implying that it is permissible to bear false witness against those who are not our neighbors, this would be an obvious minsiterpretation.

b. The incorrect interpretation of amphibolous sentences

If one were to interpret the example given earlier (p. 528) as meaning that *Jane* was zooming along under her own power, the amphibolous sentence would be misinterpreted.

c. Incorrect summaries

When a summary is made of an author's statements, it should represent his most important thoughts. When a unit of discourse is improperly summarized, the fault may lie, of course, with the author, whose meaning was not clear. On the other hand, the summarizer may distort the author's meaning either carelessly or with the intent to deceive. We shall now examine some of the forms in which this type of accent occurs.

The reader should always be on the alert when excerpts from a writing are presented. Dishonest examples of "excerpt-lifting" abound. A dramatic critic writes that he "liked all of the play except the lines, the acting, and the scenery." He is quoted as having said that "he liked all of it." Ironical remarks are open to this kind of misinterpretation. A schoolteacher tells her civics class that "communism is the best type of government if you care nothing for your liberty or your material welfare." She is quoted as having said that "communism is the best type of government." Unwitting errors of the same sort occur when a student fails to distinguish between a lecturer's own views and those which he quotes, or even between a speaker's own views and those which he attacks.

The careful thinker will always be on his guard against quotations taken out of their context and he will ask, "Let's have the whole of that quotation." This does not mean that quotations are improper, but only that quotations should be fair and accurate representations of the meaning of the author.

Newspaper headlines purportedly summarize the news, but may distort the meaning by improper emphasis. The "headline reader" is thereby misled. "Let me write the headlines," an editor once said, "and I care not who writes the news." Advertisements may achieve similar results by the use of large case type in bold letters. The "come-on" elements will be presented in large letters, and the less attractive ones will be minimized by the use of small type. A famous example is one that was used by Barnum to advertise the first Canadian concert of the Belgian violinist, Ysaye. It read,

THEIR EXCELLENCIES,
THE PRINCE AND PRINCESS OF BELGIUM
have been asked whether they
WILL ATTEND THE CONCERT OF YSAYE,
WORLD'S GREATEST VIOLINIST

A form of summary called "special pleading" or "stacking the cards" is perhaps of greatest importance in this connection. Speakers emphasize only those elements in a report which suit their purposes and omit the rest. This may be permissible practice for debaters and lawyers who seek to win a case, but it is not in the spirit of the seeker after truth. Thus, in the days when India was struggling for its inde-dence, rioting was frequent. A pro-Indian spokesman on a radio panel was denouncing the British for their callous disregard of elementary decency and reported an incident in the House of Commons in which the Conservative members of parliament "stood up and cheered" when informed that the British Army in India had killed 500 Indians. His audience was profoundly shocked by this report. But another speaker on the same program then read from the full Parliamentary report of the incident. This report stated that many British soldiers had been killed during the rioting, that about 500 Indians had been killed, and the report ended with the Prime Minister's declaration that the government intended to preserve law and order at all costs. (Cheers from Conservative benches.)

Accent, of course, is sometimes a fruitful source of humor when the incorrect interpretation of accent or emphasis is deliberate. Thus, Humpty-Dumpty says to Alice: "They gave it me—for an unbirthday present." "I beg your pardon?" Alice said with a puzzled air. "I'm not offended," said Humpty-Dumpty.

Another: "Would you—be good enough"—Alice panted out after running a little farther, "to stop a minute—just to get one's breath again?" "I'm *good* enough," the King said, "only I'm not strong enough. You see, a minute goes by so fearfully quick. You might as well try to catch a bandersnatch!"

SUGGESTED ASSIGNMENTS

1. The following items are examples of simple ambiguity or amphiboly, although the line between these is sometimes hard to distinguish. Revise each one so that it will be clear in writing.
   a. Paul beat the man around the corner.
   b. How will he find his dog when he returns?
   c. Davidson ordered another drink and sat tight.
   d. At 10 a.m. today, the anchor will be carried out into Lake Ontario aboard a naval craft and consigned to the waters. The three chaplains will accompany it.
   e. I don't know what kind of car you have to sell.
   f. Here is the box you used to pack your books in years ago.
   g. In their old age they lived in a poor house.
   h. Rev. Keith Hammond was congratulated on being able to get his parish plastered. Soon it will be the finest social center in Tujunga-Sunland.
   i. Our business is growing (nursery advertisement).
   j. Persons who find that they cannot use their seats at any performance are requested to notify the committee.
   k. Your answers to the questions were all right.
   l. Mary didn't care for the pigeons.
   m. Use more realistic details.
   n. Nothing is too good for you.
   o. He rented the house for $80.00 a month.
   p. The local weather bureaus are not permitted to dispute the predictions of the central bureau, regardless of whether they are right or not.
2. The *New Yorker* magazine often prints short news items which contain amusing ambiguities. Here are a few. Point out how the ambiguities could have been avoided.

   a. In the evening he will speak on "How to Keep Sane in the First Methodist Church under the direction of Rev. David Young."
   b. Headline: FRENCH DAM SITE BETTER OFF WITH U. S. AID FUNDS
   c.   Peanut-Butter Grilled Corn
   Husk fresh corn; spread ears lightly with peanut butter. Wrap each ear

with bacon slice; fasten with toothpick. Place on grill; grill over glowing coals, turning, until done—about ten minutes. Or, let everyone grill his own ears, using long skewers to do so.

   d. Whatever her thoughts, they were interrupted as the hotel lobby door swung open and a young woman carrying her baby and her husband entered.

3. Revise the following examples of amphiboly:
   a. Newspapers always print the bad things that teenagers do on the front page.
   b. Everything $.50 (Sign on table with articles for sale).
   c. . . . Win Bruner, wife of the doctor, who grew up in Rochester.
   d. I like Joe as well as George.
   e. Zola was able to describe the characters, the places they went, and the things they did very well.
   f. I spent most of the afternoon talking about the books I had read with the librarian.
   g. This easy, longer waist line . . . lets you step into the fashion light looking and feeling elegantly relaxed.
   h. What we believe profoundly influences our ability to listen fairly to any subject.
   i. There is a theater located in the business district which is crowded every night.
   j. All the conditions were not bad.
   k. The club will be open to members only from Monday to Thursday.
   l. Jigger was taken to a small animal hospital.
   m. Give me a piece of fresh apple pie.

4. An informative and interesting book on the difficulties of framing unambiguous and serviceable questions is Stanley L. Payne's *The Art of Asking Questions*. Mr. Stanley writes from the point of view of one who prepares public-opinion polls. Read Chapter 10, pages 158–176, and report to the class on simple words that produce ambiguity.

5. Such words as prepositions, conjunctions, and articles can be ambiguous. Margaret Bryant has written a book on the part that these words play in legal decisions. It is called *English in the Law Courts*. Look up the cases on pages 101–105 involving the preposition *between* and report how the ambiguity of this word has been legally resolved.

6. A list of twenty grammatical situations that are open to amphiboly is given in an article entitled *Some Structural Ambiguities* in the *English Journal*, November, 1958, pages 479–486. Write one example for each situation listed and bring the examples to class for discussion and revision.

7. Go to the library, choose a newspaper at random, read all the headlines, copy down any ambiguous headlines that you find, and bring them to class for discussion.

FURTHER READINGS

Black, Max. *Critical Thinking*. Englewood Cliffs, New Jersey: Prentice-Hall, Inc., 1952. On ambiguity, see pp. 183–202.

Castell, Alburey. *A College Logic*. New York: The Macmillan Company, 1935. On analogy, see pp. 58–66.

Frye, Albert M. and Albert W. Levi. *Rational Belief*. New York: Harcourt, Brace & World, Inc., 1941. On ambiguity, see pp. 103–129.

Mander, A. E. *Logic for the Millions*. New York: Philosophical Library, Inc., 1947. On generalization, see Chapter 5; on evidence, see Chapters 3 and 4; on *post hoc*, see pp. 130–133.

Reichmann, W. J. *Use and Abuse of Statistics*. New York: Oxford University Press, Inc., 1961. On cause and effect, see pp. 118–131.

Stebbing, L. Susan. *Thinking to Some Purpose*. Baltimore: Penguin Books, Inc., 1939. On generalization, see pp. 205–236; on analogy, see pp. 106–126.

Thouless, Robert H. *How to Think Straight*. New York: Simon and Schuster, Inc., 1950. On generalization, see pp. 20–30; on analogy, see pp. 100–118; on ambiguity and vagueness, see pp. 132–146.

INDEX

TO

AUTHORS

INDEX TO AUTHORS

**INDEX
TO
TITLES**

INDEX TO TITLES